# e-business
# With Net.Commerce

ISBN 0-13-083808-X

90000

# e-business
# With Net.Commerce

SAMANTHA SHURETY

PRENTICE HALL PTR, UPPER SADDLE RIVER, NEW JERSEY 07458
http://www.phptr.com

© **Copyright International Business Machines Corporation 1999. All rights reserved.**

Note to U.S. Government Users — Documentation related to restricted rights — Use, duplication or disclosure is subject to restrictions set forth in GSA ADP Schedule Contract with IBM Corp.

Editorial/production supervision: *Joan L. McNamara*
Cover design director: *Jayne Conte*
Cover designer: *Bruce Kenselaar*
Composition/formatting: *Samantha Shurety*
Manufacturing manager: *Pat Brown*
Marketing manager: *Kaylie Smith*
Acquisitions editor: *Michael Meehan*
Editorial assistant: *Bart Blanken*

Published by Prentice Hall PTR
Prentice-Hall, Inc.
A Simon & Schuster Company
Upper Saddle River, NJ 07458

Prentice Hall books are widely used by corporations and government agencies for training, marketing, and resale.
The publisher offers discounts on this book when ordered in bulk quantities.
For more information, contact

Corporate Sales Department,
Phone 800-382-3419; FAX: 201-236-7141
E-mail (Internet): corpsales@prenhall.com

Or Write:  Prentice Hall PTR
Corporate Sales Department
One Lake Street
Upper Saddle River, NJ 07458

This book includes illustrations of how customers use IBM products. Many factors contribute to results and benefits achieved. IBM does not guarantee comparable results.

IBM is a registered trademark of IBM Corp.

All other products or services mentioned in this book are the trademarks or service marks of their respective companies or organizations.

All rights reserved. No part of this book may be
reproduced, in any form or by any means,
without permission in writing from the publisher.

Printed in the United States of America
10  9  8  7  6  5  4  3  2  1

ISBN   0-13-083808-X

Prentice-Hall International (UK) Limited, *London*
Prentice-Hall of Australia Pty. Limited, *Sydney*
Prentice-Hall Canada Inc., *Toronto*
Prentice-Hall Hispanoamericana, S.A., *Mexico*
Prentice-Hall of India Private Limited, *New Delhi*
Prentice-Hall of Japan, Inc., *Tokyo*
Simon & Schuster Asia Pte. Ltd., *Singapore*
Editora Prentice-Hall do Brasil, Ltda., *Rio de Janeiro*

*To Alex, for his loving support.*

# Table of Contents

# Chapter 12, Planning Overridable Functions ................... 349

# Chapter 13, Writing Overridable Functions ................... 377

# Executive Foreword

How many people will be connected to the Internet in five years? In ten years? In twenty years? A hundred million, five hundred million, a billion? Projections vary, and no one can say for sure. But what we do know for sure is that the trajectory is up, and for the first time since the birth of the Information Age, we have the potential to connect virtually everyone in the world. A sleepless, global, "intelligent" information infrastructure is in the making.

What will people and businesses ultimately do with this vast new resource? At this stage, no one can tell. After all, the phenomenon is still at a formative stage, and when people and devices begin interacting on such an incredible scale, who can tell what their networked creativity will generate?

For now, people are using the Internet to do what they have always done, only faster and more conveniently. They are getting news when they want it, in the depth that they require. They are getting all sorts of information that makes their lives simpler. They are communicating more freely and frequently with family, friends, and colleagues.

Likewise, companies are using the Web to carry on business as usual, but with extraordinary speed, reach, and efficiency. By integrating Internet standards and technologies into their existing IT, businesses are opening up their critical information systems to existing customers and to whole new populations of customers. Redesigning their core business processes around the new model of e-business is letting them focus all their activities—internal and external, from start to finish—on the customer.

Most are starting at a simple level, perhaps with e-mail and an Internet Web site on which they publish company information for the public, or an intranet site where their employees can find information about benefits or human resource issues. Before long, the site begins to grow and become more interactive, perhaps first adding simple transactions that are fulfilled off-line, and then adding more sophisticated transactions in which pre-sale, sale, fulfillment, and customer service activities are all completed online.

Numerous firms, small and large, have already reached the latter stage. The Lehigh Valley Safety Supply Company in Pennsylvania, for example, placed 50 different models of safety shoe on the Web for sale, began getting orders from all over the world, and realized a substantial increase in revenue. Charles Schwab started a revolution when it introduced its Internet trading system, and now its customers manage tens of billions of dollars in assets online. AMP, the world's largest producer of specialized electrical and electronic connectors, now offers 92,000 items online to a worldwide clientele, and is even marketing its electronic commerce expertise to other companies who wish to do business online. 1-800-Batteries, the United States' leading supplier of batteries and accessories for camcorders, laptops and cell phones, launched its Web site in December 1997; in just over a year its Web sales increased 220 percent and overall traffic increased 111 percent.

For e-business in general, and particularly for electronic commerce, security is paramount. Customers, whether businesses or consumers, must have confidence that their transactions are at least as safe in this environment as they are in traditional environments. The technology must be open, so that all of the firm's processes can be integrated. And, to be credible to customers, the technology must have 24-hour, year-round reliability and be scalable so that it can be adjusted to meet demand.

As e-business evolves, each of these issues is being resolved. A credit card purchase that is transacted online is already more secure than one transacted in a store or over the telephone, and the security blanket is being extended to other forms of payment as well. More and more, the marketplace is imposing standards such as Java, so back-end systems can be integrated with the Web more easily and applications can be run on all systems without wholesale rewriting. And reliability and scalability reached new heights with the official Web site of the 1998 Nagano Winter Olympic Games, powered by IBM technology, which sustained 650 million hits over the 16 days of the Games—at one point experiencing 103,429 hits per minute! Given the heady progress of technology from day to day, it is understandable that cautious business owners may decide to hold off investing in the new technology "until it gets better." But the technology will always get better. The key to succeeding in e-business and electronic commerce is to start. Start at a simple level if you will, or start at a sophisticated level right off the bat. This book describes a platform that permits you to do both.

*Karl Salnoske,*
*General Manager,*
*Electronic Commerce,*
*IBM Software Solutions Division*

# Preface

The movement of society to the Web seems inexorable. It took radio almost 40 years to reach 50 million listeners in the United States. Television took about 13 years and cable TV approximately 10 years to reach that many viewers. Once the Web came to the attention of the world at large, it took only five years to enter that league. With emerging networking standards, the Internet is now a medium for audio, video and interactive, person-to-person and computer-to-computer communication that surpasses its electronic forebears in flexibility and dynamism.

There are between 15 million and 60 million Internet users today, depending on who's counting. That's somewhere between the number of people in the greater metropolitan area of New York City and the population of England! It's a big market. It's getting bigger by leaps and bounds, and the Internet covers the globe. The Internet can really change the way businesses operate.

## About This Book

This book describes how to set up and maintain an e-commerce Web site for selling products or services globally over the World Wide Web using Net.Commerce 3.1.1 on the Windows NT or AIX operating system. It provides all the essential information needed, covering everything from a crash course in e-business to how to implement a customized storefront.

Most companies recognize the value of becoming e-businesses; however, many—especially small- to medium-sized ones—don't have the necessary technical expertise in-house, and the pace of change can make it hard for them to keep up to date or to make informed decisions about which solution to implement. This book is designed to take away these challenges. It shows how to quickly and easily implement an effective e-business solution, and hand-holds readers through the entire process of building and customizing an e-commerce Web site that meets their business and customer needs.

## Workshops

At the end of each task-oriented chapter is a hands-on workshop that gives readers an opportunity to apply the concepts described by stepping them through a specific task. A reader who completes all the workshops will have created a fully functioning store using a variety of creation and customization techniques.

## Accompanying CD

The CD that accompanies this book contains a 60-day evaluation copy of Net.Commerce PRO version 3.1.1 for Windows NT, including all the sample code presented in the examples and the material for the workshops.

# Who Should Use This Book

More and more businesses are turning to the Web to expand their market reach, uncover new markets, and reduce labor and costs. Implementing a successful e-business solution is critical for anyone who wants to compete in this fast-growing and extremely competitive new marketplace. Currently, almost two-thirds of the estimated 30 million Internet users around the world use the Internet for business. Experts predict that within five years, e-business will reach $30 billion in the United States alone. By the year 2000, revenue from electronic payments will account for two-thirds of all non-cash transactions in the United States.

This book is for anyone who wants to become a player in this e-business era and who will be using Net.Commerce version 3.1.1 as the implementation solution. It is a must for businesses who want to venture into the e-business arena but do not know where to begin, and for the millions of small and large businesses actively looking for and evaluating e-business solutions.

The book is designed to both help users who are new to e-business become experts in this field, and to provide the information required for more technical users, such as programmers who are interested in the customization aspects, to deliver unique customer solutions.

Other audiences for this book include the thousands of Internet Service Providers and Web Affiliates committed to hosting or implementing e-commerce sites, and those looking for a professional solution for e-commerce.

# What You Should Know

Before using this book, you should have already installed and configured Net.Commerce 3.1.1. For instructions, refer to the *Installing and Getting Started* guide located in the \Docs directory on the accompanying CD.

To use this book productively, you should also have a good understanding of the following:

- Basic system and network administration for either the AIX or NT operating system
- Internet TCP/IP protocols, including HTTP and SSL
- Web browser operations
- Web server administration

To create and customize your site, you may also require an understanding of the following, depending on the type of customization you intend to perform:

- Hypertext Markup Language (HTML), for creating and changing the appearance of the pages that are seen by shoppers
- A graphical software package, to create your site's multimedia content
- Structured Query Language (SQL), for writing database queries and updates
- DB2 Universal Database, for adding new tables to the Net.Commerce database and to perform database tuning
- The C++ programming language, for creating commands and overridable functions

# How This Book Is Organized

This book is organized into five major sections, as follows:

Part 1, *Getting Started*, introduces the underlying concepts of e-business, explains why Net.Commerce is an effective e-business solution, and suggests how to choose a starting point to create your e-commerce Web site.

Part 2, *Populating the Database*, covers the basics of how to set up your site and designate controlled access to the database. It also describes how to enter information about your store and its product catalog in the Net.Commerce database, using several different tools.

Part 3, *Creating Web Pages*, teaches you how to create dynamic Web pages that display the latest store pricing and product information to shoppers. It shows how to create these pages either from scratch or by modifying the pages supplied by the system.

Part 4, *Customizing the Site*, focuses on how to customize your site to meet your business and customer requirements. It covers the core Net.Commerce customization components: commands, tasks, and overridable functions, and describes how to program new commands and overridable functions so that you can change the way your site operates.

Part 5, *Appendixes*, contains detailed descriptions of the Product Advisor tool; the requirements to extend the Store Creator tool; the database schema; the supplied commands, tasks, and overridable functions; and the object model for creating new commands and overridable functions.

# Using the CD

The CD that accompanies this book contains a 60-day evaluation copy of Net.Commerce PRO version 3.1.1 for Windows NT. It also contains all the sample code presented in the chapters, stored in the \samples directory under the root, and the templates and graphics needed for the workshops, stored in the \workshops directory under the root.

To do the workshops, which guide you through the creation of a sample store, you first need to install Net.Commerce from the CD by following the instructions in the *Installing and Getting Started* guide, which is located in the \Docs directory under the root, and can be either printed or viewed online. It is available in both a Postscript file, ncinst.ps, and a PDF file, ncinst.pdf.

**Note:**
The workshops are not modular: that is, you must do them in the order in which they are presented. If you skip any, the store will not contain all of its intended features and functionality.

# Conventions Used in this Book

The following highlighting conventions are used in this book:

- File names, class names, function names, variable names, directories, and all the lines of sample code are shown in `monospace` font.

- Elements that you must select, such as buttons, hypertext links, drop-down list options, check boxes, and radio buttons are shown in **bold** type.

- Technical terms that are being introduced for the first time and important points that require emphasis are shown in *italics*.

- The images **WIN** and **AIX** are used to distinguish between the different commands and directories required by the Windows NT and AIX operating systems, respectively.

- Syntax diagrams, like the one shown in Figure P.1 below, are shown in a combination of *italics* and regular type. To read the diagrams, start in the upper left corner and follow the line from left to right, top to bottom. Data displayed on the line is mandatory, while data shown below the line is optional. Keywords and delimiters (shown in regular type) must be typed exactly as shown, while variables (shown in *italics*) must be replaced with the appropriate values. When a line contains more than one path, you may follow either one.

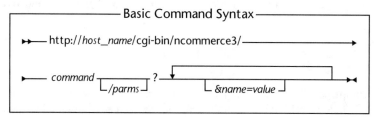

**Figure P.1** *An example of a syntax diagram.*

- Code that is being emphasized within a block of code or code that you type yourself is shown in **`bold monospace`** font. To help you identify where to insert or change code, comment blocks may be provided, between which you enter your code, as shown below:

```
<!------------------------------>
<!-     Your code begins here    ->
<!------------------------------>

Your code goes here.

<!------------------------------>
<!-     Your code ends here      ->
<!------------------------------>
```

- **bold monospace** font is also used to distinguish between code you must add and the code you have already added in a previous step, as in the following example:

```
<!----------------------------->
<!-    Your code begins here    ->
<!----------------------------->

<TR>
   <TD><A HREF="/cgi-bin/ncommerce3/ExecMacro/t_welcome.d2w/
    report" TARGET="main">
   <IMG SRC="/grocery/bb_log.gif" BORDER=0></A></TD>
   <TD><A HREF="/cgi-bin/ncommerce3/RegisterForm" NAME="register"
    TARGET="main"><IMG SRC="/grocery/bb_reg.gif" BORDER=0></A>
   </TD>
</TR>


<!----------------------------->
<!-    Your code ends here    ->
<!----------------------------->
```

# Acknowledgments

This book is the product of the combined efforts of many talented and dedicated individuals. First and foremost, I am indebted to Pawel Siarkiewicz, a hard-working co-op student who wrote and tested many of the code examples used in this book and produced the accompanying CD. It was a pleasure working with Pawel, and I wish him the best of luck in his future endeavors.

Special thanks too to Laurent Hasson, who wrote Chapter 10, provided significant content for Chapters 9, 11, 14, 17, and Appendix G, and spent considerable time and effort reviewing all the chapters that dealt with customization information. Those chapters would not exist if not for his technical expertise. Laurent also patiently provided answers to my endless questions and was able to simplify many complex concepts for me so that I could put them into meaningful words.

Thanks to Karl Salnoske for contributing the Executive Foreword, Peter Benton for writing Chapter 1, John Rofrano for writing Appendix A, and Leon Kuperman for both writing Appendix B and doing an invaluable overall technical review of the book. I am indebted as well to technical reviewers James Fong (Chapters 6, 7, and 8), Brenda Lam (Chapter 5), Hendra Suwanda (Chapters 2 and 4), Edward Salatovka (Chapter 3), and Don Bourne, who looked at last-minute additions.

A special acknowledgment goes out to Anne Stilman, my editor, whose title is an understatement of her enormous contributions to this book. Her expertise, attention to detail, and dedication were of great assistance while I was writing the chapters. I am also indebted to her for creating the index, for giving me advice on the layout, and for putting up with my panic attacks during those times when we encountered obstacles. Thanks Anne!

I would also like to extend my gratitude to Lynne Clancy, my manager, for giving me this incredible opportunity to write my first book; Sheila Richardson for coordinating with the folks at Prentice Hall; Terry McElroy for handling all the legal issues; Dr. Gabriel Silberman, Jim Caldwell, Melissa Fitzpatrick, Dave Liederbach, Roger Sage, Carol Zalger, and Mary McGarry for supporting me throughout the development of the book; Pamela Weedon, for doing the coordination work required for Chapter 1; Danielle Cumming, my media designer, for producing all the artwork in the book including the wonderful graphics for the workshops; Angelika Rother, for adding the final touches to the store graphics and for being there when I requested last-minute additions or changes; and Laurene Dong, for testing the workshops and formatting the draft manuscript. Finally, I thank Mike Meehan, Lisa Iarkowski, and Joan McNamara at Prentice Hall for their hard work in getting this book on the shelves.

And last but not least, thanks to Wellington, who kept me company on many a late night of writing.

# Part 1, Getting Started

More and more companies are using electronic business (e-business) to change the way they operate. With the help of networks, they are reaching out to new markets and new customers; making their operations more efficient; moving ideas and critical information across their enterprises faster; strengthening their relationships with customers, partners, suppliers, and distributors; and improving or completely transforming the ways in which they buy and sell products and serve customers.

For those who are not familiar with the phenomenon of "e-business", this part introduces the concept, describes the opportunities it presents to businesses of all sizes and purposes, and shows how to begin implementing an e-commerce site using the Net.Commerce product.

## Contents:

# Chapter 1, e-business and Net.Commerce

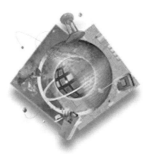

The pervasive connectivity of the Internet and the attractive graphical user interface of the World Wide Web present enormous opportunities for businesses of all kinds. Together, the Internet and the Web support growth opportunities in selling, customer relationships, product/service design, user support, geographic expansion, logistics, and supply chain integration. This chapter introduces you to electronic business (e-business) on the Internet and the benefits and opportunities that it presents, and describes the features and functionality of Net.Commerce that make it an effective e-business solution.

This chapter covers the following topics:

- What is e-business?
- Opportunities and Benefits of e-business
- Thinking About e-business Strategy
- Overview of IBM Net.Commerce
- Net.Commerce Features and Benefits
- How Net.Commerce Compares to Other Internet Commerce Solutions
- Customer Success Stories
- Components of Net.Commerce
- IBM Net.Commerce Enterprise Commerce Extension

# What is e-business?

e-business is about using Internet technologies to transform the way key business processes are performed. Its most visible form is online purchasing, both wholesale and retail. Every day, more companies and people gain access to the Web, and every day, more purchases are transacted electronically. Online purchasing became popular in 1996, when over 100,000 tickets for the Summer Olympics were ordered through the official Olympic Games Web site, which was created by IBM. By the end of 1996, business being conducted over the Web was running at the rate of US$60 billion annually. And the pace is quickening: it is estimated that the value of goods that will be ordered or purchased online by 2005 will be one trillion (1,000,000,000,000) US dollars.

# Opportunities and Benefits of e-business

e-business presents opportunities and benefits to companies of any size and purpose.

## Opportunities

There is a range of e-business opportunities that depend on the nature of the business and the customers it serves. Here are some opportunities of online business:

- Retail sellers on the Internet can sell high-quality, specialized products that appeal to an audience of affluent, well-educated, and well-informed people.

- Companies that sell their goods through catalogs and 1-800 numbers can expand their reach to additional global customers at a low marginal cost.

- Wholesalers, distributors, or service providers can sell to businesses that have embraced e-business and that demand the convenience and efficiencies of buying from a Web site.

- Companies holding comprehensive sets of digital assets (logos, image libraries, inventory information, and so forth) can sell and distribute their products electronically.

- Business-to-business sellers, the majority of whose customer base is already on the Internet, can build a closer relationship, electronically.

- Companies that already have a corporate Web site and an efficient network operation can establish subsidiary sites for related, ancillary, or consumable products.

- Businesses selling products that can readily be distributed over the Internet (for example, software, market research, industry and financial reports, news about local events, sports, travel and so on) can expand their customer bases.

- Businesses selling products that can be sampled on the Web (for example, books, magazines, and recorded music) can promote them economically.

- Businesses selling products that are subject to frequent changes (for example, airline tickets, financial instruments) can reduce production and obsolescence costs because they offer only current products on the site. They can also adjust pricing in real time in response to fluctuations in demand.

- Businesses that configure products to customer measurements or specifications (for example, custom-tailored garments, configured PCs, food shopping and delivery services or other just-in-time products) can expand made-to-order services to new markets.

# Benefits

The primary benefits of e-business are global accessiblity and sales reach, the prospect of increased profits from new markets and electronic channels, improved customer service and loyalty, shorter time-to-market, and supply chain integration.

## Global Accessibility and Sales Reach

An e-business can receive orders from just about any country in the world. The global reach of local companies that have become e-businesses may startle some firms that thought they were established in their markets.

For example, the Lehigh Valley Safety Supply Company in Pennsylvania distributes heavy-duty safety shoes to businesses. Direct sales to individual consumers are restricted to a specific geographic area under the terms of its agreement with the manufacturer. Mail order sales, however, are unrestricted, so using IBM Net.Commerce, Lehigh placed 50 items on the Web for sale. It began getting orders from all over the world and realized a 150 percent increase in revenue. Lehigh is now expanding its IBM Net.Commerce-based Web site to include safety shoes for a variety of other markets.

## Market Base Expansion

An e-business can open its critical information systems to entirely new groups of users, including employees, customers, suppliers, and business partners, who formerly did not have timely access to them. This ability enables companies to redesign and Web-enable their core business processes and extend them to anyone of their choosing, inside or outside a company, at any time of the day or night.

## Increased Profits

With e-business, companies reach more and different customers and gain exposure in new markets not covered by existing physical channels. Since the Internet is both a sales channel and a distribution channel (for example, for information, software, music, graphics, etc.), companies can sometimes leverage their existing customer relationships to offer new products and services.

By fully implementing e-business, a company can make every process that leads up to, surrounds, and follows an actual transaction more efficient and convenient. Companies are using the Internet to do the following:

- Advertise and create awareness for their products

- Promote and offer special deals that generate demand for their products

- Provide detailed information about their products

- Inform and influence the customer's choice
- Build brand loyalty by offering immediate and convenient service after the sale

What's more, businesses can cut selling costs by using the electronic channel and at the same time, free their sales personnel to focus on higher value activities, such as providing expert advice concerning a potential purchase or opening a new account.

## Improved Customer Service and Loyalty

e-business enables a company to be open for business whenever a customer needs it. This level of convenience is a differentiation today, but eventually it will be expected by customers. Up-to-date information about products can be offered on the Web, making it easier and more convenient for customers to serve themselves. In addition, combining the interactive nature of the Web with a proper understanding of a customer's needs helps a merchant to provide products and services built to order for each customer, and thus to build long-term relationships, increase loyalty, and sustain a competitive edge.

Futhermore, customers with questions about products can locate information themselves and solve their own problems, thereby reducing support headaches and costs. Better yet, they can select, configure, and order products themselves, from choosing safety shoes for hazardous work environments, to trading securities based on the underlying company's performance, to selecting electrical components to meet functional requirements, to configuring PCs for specific tasks.

## Shorter Time-to-Market

e-business makes for fast and flexible execution and response to market opportunities. The Web enables a company to introduce a new product into the market, get immediate customer reaction to it, and refine and perfect it, all without incurring huge investments in a physical distribution infrastructure or "buying" shelf space at a retailer or distributor. When the product is right, the company can launch it through traditional channels with much greater assurance of its success.

## Supply Chain Integration

e-business enables the full integration of a business, making the entire supply chain more efficient from the point of customer contact all the way back through physical distribution, warehousing, manufacturing, resource management, and purchasing. The resulting efficiencies reduce expenses, increase margins, facilitate flexible pricing strategies, and reduce costs by keeping inventories more in line with demand.

# Thinking About e-business Strategy

*The new mantra is growth, globalization, cycle times, speed and competitiveness ... e-business is not a technological change. It's a fundamental change in the way business will be done ... aided, abetted, supported and enabled by technology.*

–Lou Gerstner, Information Week 2/98

# The Impact of Extending the Enterprise

It is estimated that the number of worldwide business establishments with Web access will grow to 8 million by the year 2001. A substantial portion of these businesses will be interconnected over the Internet or private networks and will have two or more categories of electronic connections: selling to customers over the Internet (or to other businesses over a private network), and buying from suppliers over the Internet, private networks, or both. The typical business will extend out to encompass its supply chain, with goods and services moving towards end consumers and payments moving toward suppliers.

An e-business strategy should address both sides of the supply chain, because the company's total return can be more easily maximized when its linkages with business partners are efficient and swift. The combination of business process automation and Internet-enabled communications helps the business to compete on a higher level and gain share even in an established industry. For example, one start-up company with 35 employees made a very successful entrance into the European insurance industry by concentrating on its core competencies—product development and marketing—and obtaining policy administration, asset management, actuarial services, and other support from other world-class companies online. Linked online to independent brokers, it has gone from zero market share to 17 percent, with a cost structure that is 50 percent less than those of its competitors.

## Updating Operational Habits and Reducing Costs

The Internet is already profoundly influencing the structure of established companies through supply chain integration. By linking to suppliers through a Web-based network, major manufacturers can save the money spent on materials by shopping for better prices on standard components. They can also save on inventory and administrative costs for custom-designed components by integrating their purchasing systems with their suppliers' order processing systems. By integrating suppliers more closely for efficiency and cost savings, companies are giving rise to virtual enterprises in which it is difficult to tell where one organization ends and the next begins.

## Pressuring Resellers

The Internet's integration of the supply chain is pressuring resellers now that producers have a direct channel to the buyer. (And the Internet is a tempting channel indeed, when a bank, for example, can conduct an transaction online for five cents instead of conducting it through a teller for $1.50). Likewise, local distributors will feel more and more competitive pressure from online brokers who can operate independently of time and place. Resellers and distributors will have to find new ways of adding value to the supply chain if they are to survive—perhaps by delivering customization, configuration, and integration services.

## Transferring Power to Buyers

The Internet is transferring power to the buyer. Armed with information on price, quality, and availability, the customer now can easily compare items from a world of suppliers. With their competitors only a mouse click away, many businesses will have to rethink the value proposition they offer customers to ensure that it differentiates them from the rest of the field.

## Personalization

Among all the Internet-generated changes in commerce, the most exciting is the growing degree of personalization facilitated by this new medium. In the past, businesses focused on the product, designing it to appeal to a mass market. Now, using the information and processing power available to an e-business, they can gain a far more comprehensive knowledge of their clientele and use this knowledge to tailor their products and services specifically to the needs of the individual. Instead of the relationship with the customer ending after the transaction, it can span a lifetime because e-business technologies can help design goods and services that are uniquely relevant to that individual's needs and wants. With growing personalization, suppliers will begin to differentiate their brands as much on an understanding of the customer as on price and quality.

## Trust and Privacy

This new relationship with the customer and a thriving online commerce depend on the willingness of people to trust suppliers with large amounts of information about themselves, some of it very personal. People are enthralled by the prospect of buying and selling online, but at the same time, they are very conscious of the increased potential for their personal information being mishandled. Now that technology permits the gathering and analysis of so much information about so many millions of people, the creators of this new world of electronic commerce must act with a passionate respect for individual privacy. Anything less would open the way for consumer distrust and its consequent burdensome government regulation, undermining the most promising advance in global commerce since the Industrial Revolution.

## Requirements for e-business Platforms

Consider the trajectory of a successful Internet-based business. It may begin as a place for prospective customers to look up product information; progress to an online store; and from there evolve into a hub for business cycle automation, supporting Web-accessible transactions for a community of consumers or businesses. Because no one can reliably predict how quickly the site will grow or what future integration will be required to support it, technologies underlying e-business sites need to be extensible to encompass future requirements. They need flexibility to integrate with business-critical applications and suit a variety of operational configurations. They need the robustness to handle complex transactions reliably. They need scalability to grow with the business and transaction volume. Finally, they need the availability of technology in multiple national languages. The ideal e-business platform should also offer the following:

## Quick Startup

Merchants need to be able to get their sites up and running very quickly, either on their own systems or through a development and hosting service, without sacrificing long-term functionality or flexibility.

## Modularity

The key software components of an e-business Web site should be able to run on the same or different servers, which helps reduce expenses while matching capacity to the load. Specifically, merchants should have the flexibility to run the commerce server, the Web server, the payment server, the catalog server, the database, and a firewall on the same or different machines, depending on capacity required.

## Scalability and Variety of Upgrade Paths

Companies serving small markets or that are prototyping their sites should be able to set up a commerce system in a hosted environment (renting a storefront from an ISP) or on a small server (on Windows NT) for pilot purposes, and then, depending on performance requirements and availability of assets, migrate it to a variety of industrial-strength platforms such as UNIX servers (RS/6000 or Solaris), departmental or small business systems (AS/400), or mainframes (System 390). Net.Commerce is compatible with IBM load-balancing and system-clustering offerings, which provide both scalability and very high availability.

## Staff Familiarity

The underlying technologies should be already proven and well known, which allows the business to devote its existing staff (with their experience of the business) to developing the e-business site, while reducing the need to hire and train new staff for Internet-specialized technologies. Examples of operating system technologies familiar to many organizations include AIX (RS/6000), OS/400 (AS/400), and MVS (System 390). Familiar database technology includes relational DB2 with SQL access. Familiar integration technologies include Net.Data, MQSeries, and software development workbenches that generate executable code for dynamic link libraries (DLLs).

## Availability of End-to-End service

Timely business development sometimes requires supplemental skills (design, programming) or services (data preparation, conversion, hosting). It's important to know that skills and services surrounding the chosen e-business platform are available if needed to ensure swift achievement of objectives.

## Flexible Purchasing Processes

The purchasing process itself varies naturally from market to market, country to country, business-to-business, and merchant to merchant, as well as by type of product. The underlying purchasing process needs to be able to provide purchase orders, order lists, buyer groups, flexible pricing rules, variable discount rules, configurable shipping charges, and multiple tax rates—all at the same site or store.

## Strong Search and Product-Selection Capabilities

It's easier to sell when customers can find what they want quickly and easily. Customers who are unfamiliar with a product line need sales assistance; customers who know what they want need to be able to compare features of candidate products. These capabilities simplify a "buy" decision and foster repeat business.

## Open Architecture

In some scenarios, Internet commerce necessitates connectivity with the business's other applications as well as with trading partner systems. As a result, the e-business systems need to be readily integrated with other systems and architectures at the level of programming calls, operating system commands, transactions, database queries, and files.

# Overview of IBM Net.Commerce

Net.Commerce is a comprehensive package for creating not just attractive, high-performance Web sites, but *solutions* for e-business that are dynamic, scalable, and secure. Using Net.Commerce, merchants can design all features of the virtual storefront to create a unique product presentation that meets their business strategy. They can easily create Web pages that dynamically retrieve the most up-to-date product, pricing, and inventory availability information from the database. Net.Commerce provides a variety of tools for entering and managing the data related to the store, including products and prices, shipping information, taxes, and payment information. The predefined database schema can be extended to add new store functionality, such as special time-limited promotions. The purchasing process can be adapted to suit the business's patterns of interaction with shoppers and interface with their existing systems in the company and connect to trading partners.

Net.Commerce is available in two offerings: START and PRO. START is intended for customers who want to quickly set up an e-business site for a low entry price, while PRO is intended for more advanced customers who want to build a second-generation Web site with additional functionality.

# Successful e-business with IBM Net.Commerce

Successful e-businesses have many factors in common. Some of those key factors and how Net.Commerce supports them are described below.

### Get to know your customers—individually

Net.Commerce can expand your marketplace, and consequently your customer reach. By linking your Web site to your customer database, you can track visits, sales, buying trends and product preferences, all at the customer level. You can then present your customers with products they're most likely to buy, on an individual basis. It's a powerful direct marketing tool.

## Design an attractive environment that stimulates sales

Visualize a store or a whole mall on the Web. Now make it happen with IBM Net.Commerce. To set up a Web space, you start with a selection of flexible templates. You can create a site that complements your brand and provides a unique and powerful selling environment. With responsive tracking and powerful database capabilities, your store can be a dynamic environment tailored to the needs and established behavior of your customers.

## Generate pages dynamically

Net.Commerce makes it easy to keep sites "fresh." Dynamic page generation means you can keep current with any change in product, price, or service or deliver content that is based on customer behavior. The generated generated pages can be cached for fast retrieval. When data changes, the cached page is discarded so buyers see current data.

## Provide convenience to promote loyalty

Each customer can have access to a personal electronic address book of business associates, family, and friends anywhere in the world who can receive gifts. Once you know your customers' purchase patterns, you can target special promotions, savings, and incentives to them to increase your sales and their level of satisfaction. You earn their loyalty through exceeding their expectations.

## Deliver convenience 24 hours a day

To you, it may be the weekend, a holiday, or 3:00 in the morning—but somewhere in the world, it's the middle of a busy business day. With IBM Net.Commerce, your online store can be open to these customers 24 hours a day, seven days a week, 365 days a year.

## Manage selling from start to finish

IBM Net.Commerce delivers real-time data, so you have vital customer information available over every stage of the sales cycle. As prospects are converted into customers, as sales become repeat sales, and as orders become deliveries, you have a complete picture of what's happening with your customers.

## Track order routing intelligently

IBM Net.Commerce has tools to let you pinpoint location, availability, and timing of customer orders. When a customer orders an item, you know at each moment the status of that order, the cumulative actions of that customer's account, the payment and shipping information, and just about anything else of relevance. This allows you to provide the best possible information and to improve standards of customer service.

## Get meaningful feedback from customers

Selling effectively in today's market means acting fast on information. The built-in features of IBM Net.Commerce enhance your knowledge of your customer in ways that were never before possible. It's the equivalent of having an ongoing dialogue in which your customers participate directly in your market research.

## Adapt to changing transaction volumes

The price of success is the need to expand. Net.Commerce can grow from a single server on a departmental NT machine to a giant transaction engine, serving customers around the world. The load can be shared across multiple machines to provide reliability and scalability.

# Net.Commerce Features

The following are some of the key features of Net.Commerce:

- **Single or Multiple Storefront Support**. Net.Commerce supports a single site or multiple sites, such as a marketplace or mall. The seller can start with one virtual storefront and expand later on, serving different categories of buyers with dedicated storefronts. Alternatively, an Internet Services Provider or Internet entrepreneur can host storefronts for multiple clients on a stand-alone or marketplace basis.

- **Scalability**. Net.Commerce was designed to be scalable. The server and database components can be run on one or multiple machines, with Separate Internet addresses, in order to match the seller's particular operational loads and provide extremely high availability, if needed.

- **Multiple Platform Support.** Net.Commerce can run on anything from a laptop all the way up to clusters of IBM RS/6000 AIX machines containing many processors and disk drives, including Windows NT, UNIX Sun Solaris, and SP high availablity systems. It will also be available for IBM AS/400 mid-range and IBM System/390 mainframes, as well.

- **Database Extensibility.** The merchant can extend the DB2 database supplied by Net.Commerce to provide any transaction processing or information access needed to serve the customer base. Typical extensions include interfaces with inventory, shipping, and accounting systems, lists for buyers to plan future purchases and reminder calendars, and personal data (such as measurements) used to customize products.

- **System Integration Suppot**. Net.Commerce has multiple programming interface points to support integration with other business-critical systems, such as product inventory, pricing, shipping, tax calculations, and order-processing; supply-chain solutions such as EDI messaging and SAP; legacy environments such as IBM CICS and IMS; and transactional middleware such as IBM MQSeries.

- **IBM Catalog Architect Interfacing Capability.** Net.Commerce also accepts data from the separately available IBM Catalog Architect, a set of GUI tools running in Windows NT that is specifically designed for architecting, building, managing, and exporting rich electronic catalogs with a high degree of accuracy and productivity. IBM Catalog Architect is compatible with Net.Commerce's database schema, and can publish catalog data (or subsets) directly into Net.Commerce.

- **Dynamic Page Generation.** Net.Commerce provides the capabllity of generating Web pages that display up-to-the-minute pricing and inventory information from the database.

- **Data Import Capabilities.** A data import utility allows the seller to load catalogs and other data in bulk into the Net.Commerce database. Of course, sellers can use DB2 facilities to keep the data in Net.Commerce synchronized with a source product database, if needed.

- **Multiple Languages**. As an IBM global product, Net.Commerce is enabled for many national languages and can support Web sites in several of the world's major languages, including English, Spanish, French, German, Italian, Brazilian Portuguese, Japanese, Korean, Simplified Chinese, and Traditional Chinese.

- **Security**. Net.Commerce facilitates secure sessions and transactions over the Internet using the Secure Sockets Layer 3 (SSL3) protocol using the Domino Go Webserver or Netscape's Enterprise Server version 3 on AIX, NT or Solaris. IBM Net.Commerce also provides secure and confidential sessions between buyers and the supplier if the buyer uses a Secure Sockets Layer–equipped Web browser. Net.Commerce supports the SET Secure Electronic Transaction protocol for secure encrypted credit card payment over the Internet. VISA, MasterCard, IBM, and others developed the SET standard, and IBM has incorporated SET payment technology into its e-business products.

- **Product Advisor.** The Product Advisor, a component of Net.Commerce, allows merchants to build a knowledge base of sales questions and answers to help buyers who are unfamiliar with a product to select the product that is right for them; provide feature-based parametric search for product-knowledgeable buyers and help them find products that meet their criteria; and allow online buyers to make side-by-side product comparisons that highlight the similarities and differences between products.

# Net.Commerce Merchandising Capabilities

An e-commerce site is a lot more than simply a collection of Web pages; all the issues that are involved in setting up a physical store or catalog business need to be addressed in the design of an electronic commerce site as well. How will the buyer find the site? How will the site be laid out? What will the site look like? Can customers browse the site without identifying themselves? Must customers identify themselves in order to buy things? Will there be a customer service desk at the site? Will the site tell specific buying groups that a sale is coming up? What kind of after-purchase support will be provided? Will the site offer special services, such as buyer groups or a bridal registry? Can buyers try out the products before they buy them? What is the site's return policy?

Net.Commerce includes a range of capabilities and interfaces with other applications to provide merchandising features to address business-to-business and business-to-consumer opportunities:

- **Customer buying groups**. Net.Commerce provides functions to limit buyer access to catalogs, product information, and prices by buyer group. This can be controlled through a user ID and password, per account. Buyer groups enable the seller to customize what different buyers see, to conduct special promotions, and to sell using customer-specific contract prices.

- **Reorders**. Buyers can select a previous purchase event and reorder the items with a few mouse clicks. This dramatically improves ease of use, especially for repeat purchases for business.

- **Enrollment**. When a buyer is granted access to the store and signs on for the first time, he or she can self-enroll in a buying group. This simplifies the setup of business-to-business sites.

- **Buyer Account Administration**. Buyer account administration makes it possible for large businesses to monitor and control the purchasing contracts that they establish with the manufacturers, suppliers, and sellers who use Net.Commerce to sell their products over the Internet or a private or corporate intranet. The buyer's company can elect to administer the purchasing of the seller's goods and services by the buyer's employees. The chief buyer can control who gets enrolled in the buying group, can approve each purchase request, and can designate the ship-to and bill-to addresses used in all company purchases.

- **Volume-based pricing**. Net.Commerce supports volume-based pricing. Discounts can depend either on the quantity of a product purchased or on the total dollar volume of the order.

- **Flexible searching**. DB2 Text Extender adds word-search and string-search capabilities to queries run in the Net.Commerce Web environment by users who may want to track down products based on words or phrases, such as "tweed fabric."

- **Product Organization.** Net.Commerce allows merchants to organize product information in many different ways. Product categories, such as "Sensors" for the components manufacturer or "Women's Ski Jackets" for the catalog retailer, enable buyers to navigate to the subcategory where the products they want are located. Built into Net.Commerce is the distinction between a *product*, such as a woman's ski jacket of a certain style, and an *item,* such as a jacket in a particular size and color, which can be ordered as a SKU (stock-keeping unit). This distinction is made in the database design to ensure data consistency and facilitate administration.

- **Category Management.** Net.Commerce provides graphical drag-and-drop tools for the seller to change the location of a category within the category tree or to add new categories. For example, category management would enable the components manufacturer to create a new product category, "Connectors," and move all the connector products under it from their previous location under Wiring products.

- **Multiple Navigation Paths.** A product can appear under more than one category, so customers can follow more than one path and end up at the same "place." For example, a ski jacket product can appear under "Women's Coats" and "Winter Action Wear," as well as in the "Recommended Gear" section of an electronic brochure for a ski tour. Similarly, the components manufacturer could copy the connector product templates over to the new connector category so that customers could find connector products in either location.

- **Product data entry**. There are several ways to put product information into the Net.Commerce database. Small catalogs (dozens to hundreds of items) can be loaded by keying in the product data and storing graphics files in directories. This approach is effective for businesses whose products change infrequently. Large catalogs can be loaded by importing a file from another computer system. If product changes are infrequent, they can be made by keying in new items and changes using the

Net.Commerce product maintenance forms. If product changes are frequent, then the seller can set up a batch or continuous feed from the principal product database to maintain the company product catalog. Some sellers may find that the Net.Commerce product database has enough capability to become the principal product database, and may feed their other product systems (such as paper catalog preparation) from Net.Commerce.

- **Tax Calculation function.** Tax calculations are performed during the buying process. Sellers can develop their own tax calculations, interface to an existing online tax calculation system, or use the Sales Tax/Use System program which is available from Taxware International.

- **Shipping Selection and Charges function.** Net.Commerce provides great flexibility in selecting shipping services and calculating shipping costs. When setting up the site, the seller enters shipping codes for all shipping carriers and associated modes of shipment that can be used by the store. When a product is set up, the available shipping codes for the product are entered as well. When the customer orders a product, he or she selects from the available shipping codes. Additional fields are set aside for merchant customization.

# Net.Commerce START

The IBM Net.Commerce START offering includes all the capabilities required to create and operate a first generation e-business Web site.

Figure 1.1 shows the various components of the Net.Commerce START offering.

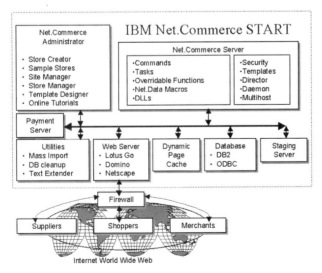

***Figure 1.1*** *The components of Net.Commerce START.*

## Net.Commerce Administrator

Net.Commerce Administrator contains the tools that you need to start creating virtual stores or malls for selling products and services over the World Wide Web. It consists of the following components:

- Store Creator, a wizard that is used to quickly create a framework on which to build a store.

- Sample stores that can be used as models for building a store or mall.

- Site Manager, which provides forms for setting up and managing the site for a store or mall.

- Store Manager, which provides forms for creating an interactive catalog for a store. The latest prices, product descriptions, and other key information are stored in the built-in relational database management system, DB2 from IBM. Using the Store Manager, you can also compile marketing statistics and track each individual customer's purchase patterns.

- Template Designer, a Java-based Web page design tool that offers a variety of fully customizable templates. The online help system for IBM Net.Commerce provides more information on this component.

## Net.Commerce Server

The Net.Commerce server is the heart of the Net.Commerce system. It controls the flow of information that is displayed to and provided by shoppers, as well as the flow of information that is accessed by merchant employees when they use the Administrator.

The architecture of the server is being integrated with IBM's Network Computing Framework. Over time, a set of common Commerce Objects will be used across all e-business products, including Net.Commerce and Domino Merchant. As object-oriented programming matures to support widely distributed networked applications, Net.Commerce will be ready. Components of the server include:

### Net.Commerce Security

The Net.Commerce base code has intrinsic security features built into its design. Access control has been extended to the level of individual commands, resources, and users. Commands and overridable functions that are added to Net.Commerce must be registered with the system to prevent unauthorized use.

### Net.Commerce Server Director and Server Daemon

The Server director and Server daemon work together to generate Web pages "on the fly" during a purchasing session by pulling product information and prices from the database, automatically filling in the fields on the template, and converting the result into Web pages that buyers see on their browsers.

## Multihost

Internet entrepreneurs and service providers can use the "Multihost" (Multiple Merchant Servers) feature to develop, operate, and host independent virtual storefronts within the same machine. Each storefront can have a unique Internet address (URL). The Multiple Merchant Servers feature provides an effective way to operate multilingual sites, because Web page templates can be prepared for each language while the product relationships can generate equivalent navigation paths for each language.

## Net.Commerce Commands

When a buyer who is browsing a virtual storefront or product page clicks on a button or hyperlink, this invokes a Uniform Resource Locator (URL) string containing a reference to a static HTML page or a Net.Commerce command. The command generally includes parameters that are used by other parts of Net.Commerce to complete the task. For example, if a buyer enters "sensor" in a product query field and then clicks the Search button, the term "sensor" is passed along to the search macro.

## Net.Commerce Tasks

A Net.Commerce task coordinates and sets up work that different parts of the system perform on behalf of the user.

## Net.Commerce Overridable Functions

Net.Commerce has an extensive set of overridable functions (also called Application Programming Interfaces or APIs), which are called at various times in during the buying cycle. While macros are optimized for accessing the database and generating report tables on Web pages, overridable functions are optimized for accessing remote systems and performing computations. To handle special requirements, the seller can prepare new overridable functions.

The overridable functions that are shipped with Net.Commerce perform specific functions, such as determining if a requested item is in stock, confirming a price, or performing a tax calculation and returning the result. The seller's programmer can access different resources in the buying cycle (such as a remote system) by replacing an overridable function with a custom-designed one.

## Net.Data Macros

Net.Data is a tool for making relational data accessible from a Web server, and is used to create Web pages dynamically using data from the Net.Commerce database. A Net.Data macro is a file that retrieves data from the Net.Commerce database and displays it as a formatted Web page. All mall and store functions interact with the shopper using Web pages created by Net.Data macros.

Net.Data macros play a critical role in reducing the maintenance of a site, because each can be used for hundreds or even thousands of Web pages. They are filled in automatically with data from the database by the Server director and Server daemon, resulting in a Web page. The system supplies many Net.Data macros to support mall and store design.

### Dynamic Link Libraries

Net.Commerce can be extended with executable programs (DLLs) that are stored in dynamic link libraries on the server. The programs need to be registered to prevent "Trojan Horse" attacks. Any software development tools that create DLLs that run in the physical server's operating environment can be used to create executable programs for Net.Commerce.

## IBM Payment Server

For credit card purchases, the Secure Sockets Layer (SSL) protocol in the Lotus Go Webserver and the end user's browser is used to scramble the credit card number when it is transmitted from the buyer's browser to the Web server. Secure Electronic Transaction (SET) was developed by VISA and MasterCard along with several technology partners, including IBM, to facilitate more secure credit card payment over the Internet. SET provides an end-to-end solution from consumer to merchant to credit card processor. IBM Payment Server, which is bundled with IBM Net.Commerce, enables the site to process SET-enabled credit card transactions for end users who pay with the SET wallet. (The Payment Server will eventually support other electronic payment vehicles as well, such as eCheck and eCash, as they become available.) One of the principal advantages of Payment Server is that the credit card information is encrypted, so that only the credit card issuer or bank (not the supplier or merchant) sees the payment card number: there is no credit card information stored at the merchant site. The existing authorization and payment processes mirror the credit card model used today. The online help system for IBM Net.Commerce provides more information on this component.

## Net.Commerce Utilities

Net.Commerce utilities make it easier to load an operating Net.Commerce-based site, and facilitate searching of the database by end users.

### Mass Import Utility

The Net.Commerce Mass Import utility can be used to load Net.Commerce product and category tables directly from files generated by the merchant's systems. This load may be one-time if Net.Commerce becomes the merchant's new repository for product information, or ongoing if the existing repository is maintained.

### Database Cleanup Utility

The Net.Commerce Database Cleanup utility is used for periodic removal of files in the cache and for removal of outdated product, category, price, and other records that have been superseded by normal maintenance or mass import processes. The online help system for IBM Net.Commerce provides more information on this component.

### DB2 Text Extender Utility

The DB2 Universal Database Text Extender utility enables the merchant to include synonyms, inexact matches, and proximity searches in the pages used by customers to find products or other information. Boolean and wild card searches can be used as well. The online help system for IBM Net.Commerce provides more information on this component.

## Web Server Options

Merchants have a choice of Web servers to use with Net.Commerce: Lotus Domino Go Webserver, Domino Web Server, or the open Netscape Enterprise Server for customers who prefer to use the Netscape product. The online help system for IBM Net.Commerce provides more information on these components.

### *Lotus Domino Go Webserver*

The Lotus Domino Go Webserver, a proven performer on the Web, establishes secure sessions across the Internet between the end user's browser and the Net.Commerce applications using the Secure Sockets Layer 3 protocol.

### *Domino Web Server*

Customers who use Lotus Domino 4.6 or above can use the Domino Web Server included in that package rather than installing the Lotus Go Webserver. Lotus Domino can be used when messaging between buyers and suppliers is to be built into the e-business site. Messaging is enabled when e-business participants are included in the Notes "Name and Address" book that underlies the Domino Server as well as in the Net.Commerce database.

### *Netscape Enterprise Web server*

The Netscape Enterprise Web server can be used instead of the Domino Go Webserver to control the flow of secure transactions to and from Net.Commerce. It implements the Secure Sockets Layer (SSL) protocol to protect the confidentiality of shopper transactions and ensure that only authorized users can perform Net.Commerce Administrator transactions.

## Dynamic Page Cache

Net.Commerce stores the dynamic Web pages in a cache after they have been created. When the data that is reflected in a page changes, the dynamic Web pages are automatically regenerated, so customers always see the correct information. Cached pages deliver much better performance than uncached ones. The online help system for IBM Net.Commerce provides more information on this component.

## DB2 Universal Database Platform

IBM Net.Commerce comes with the DB2 Universal Database, a robust, scalable relational database.

### *Open Database Connectivity*

Net.Commerce follows Microsoft's Open Database Connectivity standard, which gives access to ODBC-enabled databases, such as Oracle, in addition to DB2.

### *Net.Commerce Database Design*

The IBM Net.Commerce database design provides access to all product- and buyer-related data that is requested by Net.Commerce commands, macros, and overridable functions, as well as triggers in the database environment. For example, if a price update transaction reaches the database, and the new price is effective immediately, the database can update the active price.

Further, if the price has been cached in a product or item page, then that superseded page is discarded. The next time that Web page is requested, a new page will be generated with the new price and will be cached. The Net.Commerce database has been designed to support a range of products and merchandising techniques. Referential integrity is built-in with documented maintenance cascades. Merchants can extend functionality by adding tables and keying them to the Net.Commerce category, product, item and buyer tables.

The database design gives the merchant the flexibility to operate the site in many ways. The design provides the robustness and scalability expected of a relational database, while providing object-oriented characteristics for data updating and querying.

## Staging Server

Staging support enables you to test updates before going "live," so that errors or problems can be pinpointed before customers see them. The changes in the tested database are then promoted to go live. The online help system for IBM Net.Commerce provides more information on this component.

## Configuration Manager

The Configuration Manager tool has a graphical interface that lets you modify the way Net.Commerce is configured without dealing with the intricacies of syntax-sensitive configuration files. Configuration Manager also makes it easy to control many of the administration tasks associated with Net.Commerce.

# Net.Commerce PRO

The IBM Net.Commerce PRO offering includes all the capabilities of Net.Commerce START, plus the following:

- IBM Product Advisor, which offers advanced tools for catalog building and search (such as parametric search, a "virtual" sales person on the Web site, and comparison shopping thereby enabling different search strategies depending on the buyer's knowledge of a product)

- Tools for back-end integration to EDI messaging and SAP R/3 supply chain solutions

- Tools for integration with IBM application environments (CICS, IMS) transactional middleware to interface with other platforms (MQSeries)

Figure 1.2 shows the various components of the Net.Commerce PRO offering.

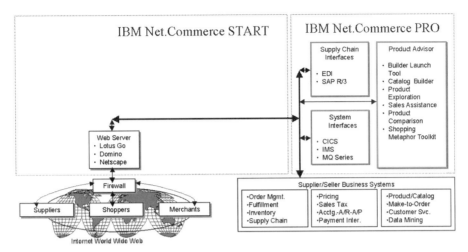

*Figure 1.2* *The components of Net.Commerce PRO.*

## Product Advisor

Merchants face special problems on the Web. Customers shop according to their needs and their product knowledge. Expecting them to find what they need by browsing by category assumes that they are familiar with the categorization system used, and expecting them to search by keywords assumes that they know the right words: if they don't, searches result in zero hits or irrelevant suggestions.

The Product Advisor (available only in Net.Commerce PRO) combines the marketing knowledge of a salesperson, the technical knowledge of a product specialist, and rich specifications into an easy-to-use format that contains product knowledge in addition to product data.

Product Advisor provides an interactive catalog environment that combines marketing and technical knowledge with different ways of finding the products, called "shopping metaphors." Buyers with little knowledge of a product category can use the Sales Assistance metaphor, which uses AI technology to leverage the knowledge of salespeople to guide buyers toward appropriate products through a series of questions and answers. In effect, you're a store's best salesperson is available to help customers, 24 hours a day, seven days a week. Buyers don't have to be familiar with the product they are looking for: they simply answer questions about how they plan to use it, and then are guided to appropriate products.

Those buyers with more knowledge can use the Product Exploration metaphor, which lets them select desired product attributes or features and then select the values that they want the product to have. Each time they select a value, all other values are adjusted so that only valid values are displayed. This ensures that products that meet the criteria are always selected and a buyer *never* comes up with an empty product list. The major frustration that shoppers have expressed with other search mechanisms (zero hits) is eliminated. Once the selection has been narrowed down through either method, shoppers can use the Product Comparison metaphor to compare similar products side by side in a variety of ways that show the differences and similarities between them.

Merchants can use the administrative tools provided to customize the shopping metaphors, including determining the features that will be displayed to buyers, the order in which the features will appear, the Graphical User Interface (GUI) controls that are used to display feature values, the templates that are used, and more. Metaphors can be further customized by Java programmers using the Product Advisor Metaphor Toolkit, which enables the creation of new GUI controls, new rendering tags, or whole new shopping metaphors.

## Supply Chain Interfaces

Net.Commerce PRO supports integration of Internet commerce with supply chain solutions. For example, the Internet can be used to deliver merchant orders or customer special orders to a supplier, and for suppliers to report order status. Net.Commerce's open architecture permits the supplier side of the connection to be Web-based (the supplier checks for new orders on private Web pages) or transaction-based (Net.Commerce transmits orders or an order file to the supplier's system). Net.Commerce can provide the Web order entry and payment interface for supply chain applications using Electronic Data Interchange (EDI) messaging, SAP R/3, and other supply chain solutions.

### Electronic Data Interchange

Net.Commerce PRO includes database tables and functions for Electronic Data Interchange (EDI) messaging integration. Net.Commerce can be configured to generate order data in a format that can be translated into a purchase order (EDI 850 message) by IBM's Global Services (IGS) EDI network. When a buyer places an order, the formatted order information is written to the EDI integration database table. Periodically, new orders are batched, encrypted and sent to IGS using a security-rich communications package. IGS translates the data into an EDI 850 message and forwards it to the next step in the supply chain. In return, Net.Commerce can accept a Functional Acknowledgment (EDI 997 message) from IGN.

### SAP R/3

Businesses using Systems, Applications and Products in Data Processing (SAP) R/3 version 3.1.G to run the back office can integrate it with Net.Commerce on Windows NT to create a World Wide Web front end for online global transactions. Net.Commerce automates and streamlines the Internet commerce process and provides additional advantages. By placing a copy of the SAP catalog on Net.Commerce, inquiry to SAP can be reduced as Net.Commerce passes only fully formatted orders to SAP. Net.Commerce can protect the SAP system from direct access by Internet users, acting as a firewall. Net.Commerce can present a substantially more attractive and interactive electronic catalog to Internet users than SAP. For example, graphics, animations or shopping metaphors can be used to improve and add value to shopping for items sold from the SAP system.

## System Interfaces

Net.Commerce PRO includes a variety of system integration tools that support interfaces to legacy platforms (CICS and IMS) and transactional middleware (MQSeries). Integration tools include database tables, sample code, and documentation to support transactions and message queues with other environments. The transactions and control methods can be extended by the merchants to incorporate whatever business data needs to be exchanged between Net.Commerce and the external application.

### CICS

Net.Commerce PRO provides sample code, database tables, and scripts that may be used to exchange transactions with a Customer Information Control System (CICS) transaction server running on a legacy system.

### IMS

Net.Commerce PRO provides sample code, database tables and scripts that may be used to exchange transactions with an Information Management System (IMS) application.

### MQSeries

Net.Commerce PRO provides sample code and database tables that may be used to integrate Net.Commerce as a front end to legacy systems using MQSeries. Outbound messages from Net.Commerce to the legacy system are enabled by overriding default Net.Commerce functions and routing them to the MQSeries message queue. Inbound messages from the legacy system are retrieved periodically from the message queue.

## Supplier/Seller Business Systems

It is easy to create an informational and promotional Web site from scratch, but efficient e-business, including transaction processing, typically requires integration with pre-existing systems. Net.Commerce's open architecture makes it the ideal Web commerce server for manufacturing, wholesaling, or merchandising businesses.

Often, the merchant can decide how the interface should operate based on the frequency of change in the data. For example, if prices change throughout the day, it may be appropriate for the pricing system to feed update transactions to Net.Commerce as they occur. In many situations, prices on the e-business site will mirror prices in the seasonal catalogs, so batch updates from the mainstream business system to Net.Commerce database may be used. Net.Commerce uses price effectivity dates so the new or replacement prices can be loaded in advance. Net.Commerce can associate prices with buyer groups, which gives merchants the flexibility to put negotiated prices into the database.

# How Net.Commerce Compares to Other Internet Commerce Solutions

Internet sellers are discovering that to succeed in e-commerce, they need tools and technologies with the flexibility to evolve with the business and the scalability to handle unprecedented growth. The problem that new Internet sellers face is that many Web commerce server solutions available today are acceptable only for "getting the feet wet," and lack the flexibility, scalability, robustness, extensibility, and global readiness to support the long-term growth of a flourishing Internet business. As the business ramps up, the seller discovers that it is necessary to start over with a new, more robust platform. This consequence of starting with a limited solution causes extra expense of reworking the site, wastes precious time-to-market and, if customers were poorly served by the site, generates a bad reputation.

e-business platforms are evolving rapidly, with new versions from one vendor or another being announced every quarter. However, the combination of skills, applications expertise, and systems integration knowledge required to produce a world-class e-business solution is beyond the reach of leading vendors, with the exception of IBM. Net.Commerce compares favorably with other Internet commerce solutions in the following areas:

- Application functionality. The Net.Commerce feature set is among the widest. It accommodates many different selling processes, including business-to-business and business-to-consumer applications; it supports single or multiple stores; it handles buyer groups; it provides variable pricing and discounting; and it has configurable calculations for shipping and taxes.

- Attractiveness. Net.Commerce supports a broad range of eye-catching features, from graphics and multimedia data to Java and extensible markup language applets. Virtual reality, audio, and video are easy to deliver with Net.Commerce.

- Quick site setup. Net.Commerce comes with Starter Store templates that can be readily adapted to quickly set up a new site incorporating illustrations and descriptions of the seller's products. From there, the Net.Commerce development tools (such as Template Designer) and the staging server feature enable the site administrator to add new features incrementally.

- Cross-platform support and scalability. Net.Commerce runs on departmental NT systems up through UNIX, AS/400, and System 390 mainframe systems. You can be sure that the small site you prototype internally will scale easily to handle the largest loads you may encounter.

- Global readiness. Net.Commerce has versions in several of the leading national languages, including English, Spanish, French, German, Italian, Brazilian Portuguese, Japanese, Korean, Simplified Chinese, and Traditional Chinese.

- Performance. Web pages are generated "on the fly" and then cached for faster presentation. Pages are updated automatically when the underlying data changes, which permits the merchant to update product information and prices through the day. The Net.Commerce database, running on DB2, has been optimized for performance, security, management, and scalability.

- Advanced catalog-production capabilities. Net.Commerce PRO includes catalog development tools that make short work of converting existing product legacy databases and files into searchable online catalogs.

- Merchandising and sales assistance. Net.Commerce PRO provides a unique range of catalog development, search, and shopping metaphors, including product navigation, parametric search and selection, and artificial intelligence–based sales assistance. Developers can extend the metaphors with the development tools in Net.Commerce.

- System integration/ legacy linkage. Net.Commerce PRO includes application programming interface (API) and connectivity tools enabling integration with a very wide range of operating environments, middleware, and enterprise resource planning applications. For those businesses that want to tailor every aspect of the online experience, Net.Commerce's open architecture provides the developer with all the access needed.

- End-to-end support. IBM and its business partners can sell Net.Commerce software as well as the services and hosting facilities to develop and deploy world-class Web sites.

- Strategic value. IBM developed the routing technology that enabled the Internet's dramatic expansion in the early '90s. IBM is the leading developer of standards-based technologies and products for e-business. Net.Commerce will continue to benefit from IBM's leadership in network computing in the years ahead.

# Net.Commerce Customer Success Stories

Net.Commerce is being used by some of the most innovative e-business–oriented companies around. In the success stories that follow, Net.Commerce has played a critical role in business-to-business and business-to-consumer Web sites and is tightly integrated into the existing transaction systems at these companies. This section describes how customers use IBM products. Note that many factors contribute to the results and benefits achieved, and IBM does not guarantee comparable results.

## Electronic Connectors Manufacturer

AMP, a leading manufacturer of electrical and electronic connectors and interconnection systems, uses Net.Commerce so that its customers and product distributors can place an immediate order for one or more parts through online shopping.

The company had been spending about US$8 million annually to publish and distribute its 400 product catalogs. Using the Web has not only saved a portion of this cost but has also provided AMP's customers with more timely product information. AMP adds or changes products at an astonishing rate of 200 product changes a day. In addition to the savings resulting from decreasing the print-runs of hardcopy catalogs, their Web service delivers other benefits: improved productivity, increased customer satisfaction, speedy order turnaround, and decrease in customer support personnel.

The solution enables the company's customers to do extensive parametric searches through the company's complicated technical products catalogs, thereby significantly reducing the time it takes to locate and order the desired product. The Internet is a new channel to AMP's market, and Net.Commerce enables users to access information and buy AMP products over the Internet. The company maintains an inventory of over 92,000 parts available on the Internet, with very specific identification numbers, product and usage characteristics, and packaging requirements that can now be quickly and efficiently found by their worldwide, multilingual customers.

## Accessories for Mobile Professionals

1-800-Batteries is a company that serves the needs of today's mobile professionals with rechargeable batteries and gear for laptop computers, cellular phones, and more. Its success is due in large part to an extensive inventory of products, a detailed cross-reference database, and excellent customer service. It carries almost 20,000 items, and ships products to the growing number of "road warriors" around the globe.

After a difficult experience with another e-business package, 1-800-Batteries worked with an IBM business partner to develop an advanced e-business Web site using Net.Commerce. This site is a perfect match between a robust, scalable e-commerce solution and a product line tailor-made for the Internet commerce market. The results have been phenomenal. Online sales from the 1-800-Batteries Internet site have jumped over 59% since the launch of the new solution based on IBM's Net.Commerce, and traffic to the site has increased more than 111%. Customer response has changed from dissatisfaction with the new system to enthusiasm for it. There has also been significant growth in cross-selling opportunities due to an additional function built by the integrator: when a customer searches for an accessory of a particular product, the database dynamically responds to the query and returns the whole range of accessories offered for that item.

1-800-Batteries is also exploring data-mining possibilities and identifying buyer trends with a commerce-specific metrics-reporting system built by the integrator. The Net.Commerce registration process gathers valuable demographic data, which is then pulled into a customized reporting program. Because Net.Commerce rides on IBM's DB2 relational database, the integrator was able to efficiently pull almost 20,000 items from legacy data as well as utilize the security of a DB2 system. Net.Commerce was also easily integrated with 1-800-Batteries' existing fulfillment system.

## Apparel Catalog Retailer

Recently, legendary catalog retailer L.L. Bean launched a completely functional Web shopping environment. Based on the IBM Net.Commerce software, this ambitious project was designed to fully integrate into L.L. Bean's existing business processes and inventory systems.

This site is an example of secure, reliable electronic commerce. It does not just duplicate the content of the catalog: it provides in-depth information for customers on outdoor-related topics as well as information on over 1,500 national parks.

As was anticipated for this project, the Web site "llbean.com" is cost-effectively attracting and retaining new customers that the company might not have reached through its traditional printed catalogs. The site has also expanded the company's reach into a younger audience, enabling the company to grow and to serve a whole new set of customers.

## Canadian Internet Service and Cable Service Provider

Videotron Ltd. of Montreal, Canada, is an Internet service and cable service provider that has extended its business to include operating online stores. It sells videos direct to consumers and hosts multiple online malls and stores, including Librarie Garneau, the largest French bookstore in the Americas with an inventory of over 250,000 titles. Videotron had already created a first-generation commerce Web site. For its second-generation commerce site, it needed flexible payment options with real-time credit card validation, and wanted a solution that would enable it to connect to any of several payment gateways. It is currently using National Bank of Canada's payment system (Securnat/Cybercash).

# European Wholesaler

Supervox, a wholesaler of electrical, sanitary, gardening, and automobile accessories with US$100 million in sales has numerous manufacturing, assembly, and distribution sites in France and Spain. Using the IBM Payment Suite family of Internet products and services, the company is making its catalog of 8,000 items available directly to customers. It is one of the first European commercial organizations to use electronic commerce to serve customers, and its interactive electronic warehouse on the Internet has caused a dramatic and extremely productive change in distribution methods for small retailers in France, Spain, Belgium, and Italy.

Working with IBM France, the company used IBM Net.Commerce to create an automated replenishment program, and created an Internet-based ordering, automatic restocking and distribution system. It uses the IBM Global Network to access the servers in Paris that check for authorized access and store the orders. The IBM Global Services Internet hosting service allows retailers to find products by name or category, displays them as on a shop shelf, and permits purchase at the click of a mouse.

The interactive electronic warehouse and IBM Net.Commerce save customers many hours of valuable time spent filling out order forms or scrolling through lists of 80,000 products. Customers save over 30 percent on the cost of ordering through traditional wholesale channels. Supervox provides an automated reordering process, accessible through the Internet, along with product sales statistics, manufacturer promotions, discounts, and coupons.

# IBM Catalog Architect and Net.Commerce

With the IBM Catalog Architect (CA), sellers can design, build, manage, and export rich electronic catalogs with a high degree of accuracy and productivity. IBM CA is available separately. It is a set of GUI tools running in Windows NT that is compatible with Net.Commerce's database schema, and can publish catalog data (or subsets) directly into Net.Commerce. CA works with both Net.Commerce START and PRO offerings.

CA was designed to do one thing: manage product data within a catalog. It is the perfect complement to the Net.Commerce PRO Product Advisor. While Product Advisor offers end users various ways to shop, search, or get sales assistance in selecting a product in a Net.Commerce Web site, CA makes it easier to ensure that the data describing the products is correct.

The CA incorporates a knowledge base that understands the relationships between catalog elements, including categories, products, stock-keeping units (SKUs), sets or kits of products, cross-sale items, and so on. Other tools for managing product data, such as spreadsheets and relational databases, cannot handle these relationships, and as a result the people who manage complex catalogs have to use manual clerical procedures to keep the details straight. The CA uses a variety of techniques to ensure that catalog data is complete, correct, and consistent. *Completeness* ensures that products belong to a category; that categories contain products; and that all required data entry fields are filled in. *Correctness* comes from spelling and grammar checking, validation of numeric fields and cross-checking of related data. *Consistency* comes from standardized word usage and spelling (for example, red vs. Red vs. scarlet; Pentium vs. 586, etc.).

CA increases the value of catalog data by making it easier for the seller to manage prices, sell kits, and up-sell or cross-sell, and for the buyers to find what they want. At the same time, it improves the efficiency of the catalog management effort, and enables staff to focus more on merchandising and less on clerical cross-checking.

# IBM Net.Commerce Enterprise Commerce Extension

With the IBM Net.Commerce Enterprise Commerce Extension (ECE), businesses can integrate their e-business Web sites based on Net.Commerce with their legacy business, transaction and Enterprise Resource Planning (ERP) systems far more swiftly and with better operational performance and maintainability than is otherwise possible today. IBM ECE is available separately.

The ECE enables exchange of information and transactions with existing systems using the most up-to-date interconnection technologies. This means that you can create whole new feature sets and introduce new functions more swiftly and easily. ECE is an open solution for simplifying and accelerating the implementation of applications that share information.

## Developer Advantages

The ECE architecture provides a simpler way to achieve tight integration between applications. It acts as an information switchboard, analyzing the data formats and transaction semantics of linked systems and properly transfering information between them. The ECE Formatter is a GUI tool that enables the developer to specify the precise characteristics of each side of a messaging connection. The ECE Rules tool enables the developer to define business logic, if needed, as part of the messaging connection. (An example might be to convert a zip code into a city-state combination.) ECE provides data synchronization, persistent guaranteed delivery, reformatting, and context-based routing to multiple destinations even when a process has temporarily failed. The advantages that it provides to developers include:

- Use of a standard method for transmitting order-related data between back-end systems.

- Modular, reusable components that work with many applications.

- A standard process by which business partners, ISV and integrators can access and update data elements in Net.Commerce.

- Incorporation of best-of-breed middleware technologies in a single package.

## ERP integration

The ECE will enable new orders to be passed from the e-business site to the supplier or manufacturer directly through your ERP package, shortening cycle time and processing expense. Likewise, information can be passed from your ERP systems back into the Net.Commerce system. Here are some benefits of ECE for ERP users:

- Save programming time by using prebuilt adapters to link Net.Commerce to ERP systems from a variety of vendors.

- Develop new adapters in Java to link to ERP systems developed in-house or by other vendors.

- Reduce system conversion effort when switching from one ERP system to another bysimply changing settings in the ECE Adapter Manager without having to reprogram in the new system's API.

## Legacy integration

The ECE can help you provide a richer e-business service by enabling Web users of Net.Commerce to query and transact with your transaction engines or databases. Here are some benefits of ECE for legacy system managers:

- Use ECE to connect Net.Commerce to CICS, IN4S, databases, or other transaction engines.

- Use Data Mapping Technology to customize the interfaces to traditional data stores associated with legacy or ERP systems without having to program in integration languages such as C, C++, or Java.

# The Network Computing Framework and IBM Net.Commerce

Users of computer technology welcome the advances of each new wave of technology, but bemoan the complexity of integrating it with their multi-generational applications and systems. The Web, with its standards-based network, browsers, servers, and presentation languages, points the way to a technology future that is more powerful than today's but is easier to maintain.

IBM and other leading technology vendors understand that customers want a simpler technology infrastructure, and are reaching agreement on what it should look like. IBM's name for this rationalized infrastructure is the Network Computing Framework, or NCF.

The elements of NCF include:

- A unifying programming model, based on Java, with cross-platform standards for enterprise Java Beans so that Web-based applications can employ the same degree of transactional functionality and security as "glass house" applications, and a much more efficient development environment

- Adoption of object and software component technologies compatible with future networks

- Criteria for selecting components and technologies to build the e-business

- Architectural guidelines and simpler approaches to developing and extending Web solutions

- Built-in support for standards-based communication, transaction and procedure call protocols, and integration points to facilitate maintenance and development

NCF is IBM's technology vision and strategy behind e-business. It provides a technology architecture and steps to take for designing and building e-businesses. Based on IBM's experience with thousands of customers, NCF incorporates the best practices that align existing IT systems with e-business goals:

- It helps IT managers move to e-business infrastructures that incorporate Web technologies and tight integration while leveraging their proven existing systems

- It helps developers quickly and cost-effectively Web-enable existing applications and build new ones, in heterogeneous, multi-vendor environments.

The design principles underlying Net.Commerce are based on NCF. As the enabling technologies are released on IBM and other vendors' transaction-processing platforms, Net.Commerce will be readily integrated with them. NCF will help to you tie together your e-business systems with those of your employees, partners, and customers to construct one tightly integrated e-business.

# Chapter 2, Getting Started with Net.Commerce

This chapter describes how to prepare for and start building an e-commerce site using the various site creation methods offered by Net.Commerce. It also contains the first of a set of workshops that are included in the book. In this workshop, you will create a pizza store using the Store Creator wizard as the starting point.

This chapter covers the following topics:

- Determining the Site to be Created
- Determining Site and Store Administrators
- Accessing Net.Commerce Administrator
- Creating or Connecting to a Database
- Choosing a Site Creation Method
- Workshop: Creating a Store Starting from the Store Creator

# Determining the Site to Be Created

Before you begin to use Net.Commerce, you must determine which type of site you will create: a single store or a mall. A single store exists independently of any other online store or mall, and shoppers access it by typing the URL of its home page. A mall contains a number of stores; shoppers access the mall by typing the URL of its home page, and from there, they click a link to enter a store. Stores within a mall can either share pages that represent common functions, such as registering or ordering, or each have pages with a unique look and feel. There are two levels of Web site management in a mall: *mall* and *store*. These levels will be discussed throughout this chapter.

> **Note:**
> Because of the two-tiered structure of a mall, some features in Net.Commerce apply only to stores that are part of a mall. For example, within a mall, stores may either be required to use the mall implementation of certain shopping functions or be allowed to implement their own, whereas for a single store this distinction does not exist.

# Determining Site and Store Administrators

Before you begin to create a store or mall, you need to determine who will act as site administrator and who will act as store administrator.

*Site administrators* are typically responsible for setting up and managing the high-level functions associated with the site, including the following:

- Creating a store using the Store Creator (after the store is created, the site administrator can then designate one or more store administrators to manage it)

- Designating store administrators and giving them access to specific data

- For a mall, adding and deleting stores

- Maintaining a list of available shipping carriers

- For a mall, defining whether some aspects of the shopping process, such as ordering, can be customized by the individual stores

- Activating customized store pages, overridable functions, and commands in the system

*Store administrators* are typically responsible for managing the day-to-day activities associated with running a store, including the following:

- Entering, updating, and deleting data about the store and its products or services

- Creating and updating the store pages, by writing or modifying Net.Data macros (which the site administrator must then activate)

- Changing the way that the system processes information, by creating new commands or replacing overridable functions (which the site administrator must then activate)

In a single-store site, the site administrator and the store administrator will likely be the same person. In a mall, there is typically one site administrator for managing the site and at least one store administrator for managing each store in the mall.

For the remainder of this chapter, you will take the role of the site administrator in order to start creating your store or mall.

# Accessing Net.Commerce Administrator

The first step in creating a store or mall is to open the Administrator, which contains all the tools you need.

## Specifying Computer and Browser Settings

It is advisable to make the following changes to your computer and Netscape Navigator to achieve optimal results while working with the Administrator.

### Computer Settings:

Ensure that you have set the following:

- Screen resolution: 1024 x 768 pixels or higher
- Number of colors: 256
- Fonts: small

### Netscape Settings:

Follow these steps to change your browser settings:

1. Start Netscape Communicator 4.04 and maximize the browser window.
2. From the **Edit** menu, select **Preferences...** to display the **Preferences** dialog box.
3. In the **Category** list, expand **Appearance**.
4. Click **Fonts**.
5. For **Variable Width Font**, select **Times New Roman 12** point.
6. For **Fixed Width Font**, select **Courier 10** point. If you want to use other fonts or font sizes, you should experiment to see which combination gives the best results. Be aware that other selections may affect the layout of the Administrator forms on your screen.
7. In the **Category** list, click **Advanced**.
8. Enable the **Java** and **JavaScript** languages.
9. Expand **Advanced,** and then under it click **Cache**.
10. Ensure that the **Memory Cache** and **Disk Cache** fields are greater than zero.
11. Under **Document in cache is compared to document on network**, enable **Once per session**.
12. Click **OK** to save these settings.

# Opening the Administrator

Follow these steps to open the Administrator.

1.  Type the following URL on your browser's command line:

    `http://<host_name>/ncadmin`

    where `<host_name>` is the fully qualified TCP/IP name of your Net.Commerce system.

2.  If you see messages concerning your site's certificate, respond affirmatively.

3.  If a pop-up window appears, accept the session cookie by clicking **OK**. The Net.Commerce server has assigned a temporary session ID, which is now being sent as part of a digitally signed Netscape cookie back to your browser to identify your user session. Your browser will send this cookie back to the server whenever that server is requested.

4.  When the Net.Commerce Administrator Logon page appears, enter the user name and password that were created during installation (they are both set to ncadmin) or, if they have been changed since then, enter the new ones.

5.  Click **Logon**. The Net.Commerce Administrator home page appears.

6.  If a window appears indicating that your session cookie has been updated with your shopper reference number, accept the new cookie by clicking **OK**. The Net.Commerce Administrator home page appears.

7.  Maximize your browser window.

8.  Add this page to your bookmark list, as you will be returning to it frequently throughout the store or mall creation process.

> **Note:**
> While using the Administrator, if you have loaded but not yet saved data, do not reload the browser window. If you do, your data will be lost.

# Changing the Site Administrator's Password

After you open Net.Commerce Administrator with the system-assigned password (ncadmin), you should change the password immediately to ensure that unauthorized individuals cannot access the program or the Net.Commerce database. (The steps below also apply when you want to change the password again later, or to change the password of a store administrator. Store administrators who want to change their own passwords can do so by using the registration form for their store.)

1.  From the task bar in the Administrator, click **Site Manager** and then **Access Control**. The Access Control form appears.

2.  Click **Clear** to clear all the fields in the form.

3.  Click **Search**. A list of all administrators for the site appears in the display area at the bottom of the form.

4.  Click the name of the administrator whose password you want to change.

5.  Scroll to see the current administrator logon IDs. (If you have not previously defined any other administrators or changed the site administrator's password, you will see only **ncadmin**.)

6.  Select the logon ID under the **Administrator Login ID** column that corresponds to the administrator whose password you want to change. If you are changing the default site password, select **ncadmin**. The fields fill with information about that administrator.

7.  In the **Password** and **Password Confirmation** fields, enter a new password. Only letters and numbers are allowed; you cannot use any special characters, such as an ampersand (&).

8.  In the appropriate fields, enter the administrator's last name and first name. You can also fill in other fields.

9.  Click **Save**.

10. Click **OK** in the confirmation window. The information is saved in the SHOPPER (Shopper Profile) and ACCTRL (Access Control) database tables.

# Creating or Connecting to a Database

Before you can begin to create any store or mall, you need to determine the database that you will use to store all the data related to it. You have the option of using the default database, which was automatically created during the installation of Net.Commerce; using the databases for the sample stores; or creating a new database. At any time, you can switch between the databases that you install.

## Using the Default Database

When Net.Commerce was installed, a database containing the default database tables was automatically created for your use. It contains the default data necessary for any store or mall to run, including the supplied Net.Data macros, commands, tasks, and overridable functions. You can replace any of this data with your own, and add your store data and product catalog data.

## Using the Sample Databases

If you decide to create your site based on one of the samples provided by Net.Commerce, a new database is automatically created when you install the sample. (For information about creating a store or mall based on a sample, see "Starting from a Sample" on page 44.) This database contains the sample data that is displayed in the sample store or mall. To use it for your production store, you will need to replace this data with your own. However, it is recommended that these databases be used only for viewing and testing the sample, not for a production store.

# Creating a New Database

You can manually create a new database containing either custom data or the same data that is contained in the default database.

## Creating a Custom Database

To create a database containing custom data or tables, do the following:

1.  Review the scripts that are provided with Net.Commerce in the following directory:

    **WIN**  \Ibm\NetCommerce3\nc_schema\db2
    **AIX**  /usr/lpp/NetCommerce3/nc_schema/db2

    The main script, schema.cmd or schema.sh, contains information about the other scripts.

2.  To change a script, create a new copy and edit the new copy.

    > **Note:**
    > Because the files in this directory are used by Net.Commerce, you must not edit them directly.

3.  Run the new script by following the instructions in the next section, "Creating a Default Database", but in Step 2 substituting the name of the default script, schema, with the name of your new script.

## Creating Another Default Database

To create another database that contains the default Net.Commerce data, including the supplied Net.Data macros, commands, tasks, and overridable functions, do the following:

1.  In a DB2 command window switch to the following drive:

    **WIN**  \Ibm\NetCommerce3\nc_schema\db2
    **AIX**  /usr/lpp/NetCommerce3/nc_schema/db2

2.  Type the following:

    Schema db_name S|N NCAdmin_password [log_file]

    where the values for each variable are as follows:

    db_name
    The name of your new database.

    S|N
    Type either S to create the database for a staging server, or N to create it for a production server.

`NCAdmin_password`

The encrypted default password of the Net.Commerce Administrator, enclosed in double quotation marks ( " " ). To determine the encrypted password, do the following:

a)  In a command prompt window on the machine on which you installed Net.Commerce, switch to the drive on which you installed Net.Commerce.

b)  Switch to the following directory:

**WIN** `\Ibm\NetCommerce3\bin`
**AIX** `/usr/lpp/NetCommerce3/bin`

c)  Type the following:

`nc3_crypt -e ncadmin <merchant_key>`

where `<merchant_key>` is the merchant key you used when you configured Net.Commerce. If you used the default merchant key, omit this parameter. The system responds with two character strings, one in ASCII and one in hexadecimal.

d)  Copy the ASCII character string to the clipboard, and paste it into the proper position in the Schema command.

`log_file`

The file into which you want the command to write log records as it populates the database.

After your new database is created, you need to connect to it by following the instructions in the next section, *"Connecting to a Database"*.

# Connecting to a Database

If you have installed more than one database (for example, you used more than one sample or you created a new database), you can switch between the databases using the Samples and Tutorials form in the Administrator.

1.  Open Net.Commerce Administrator, as described in "Opening the Administrator" on page 34.

2.  On the task bar, click **Site Manager** and then click **Samples and Tutorials**. The Samples and Tutorials form appears.

3.  Under **Switch to an Existing Sample/Tutorial Database**, in the **Database Name** drop-down list, select the name of the database to which you want to connect.

4.  Click **Switch**.

5.  After you have successfully connected to the database, follow the instructions on the screen to restart the Net.Commerce server.

6.  Restart the browser.

You are now connected to the selected database.

# Choosing a Site Creation Method

There are three ways to start creating your Net.Commerce site:

- Starting from the Store Creator (for stores only)

- Starting from the Site Manager and Store Manager

- Starting from a Sample

Which method you choose will depend largely on the size and nature of your business and on whether you are creating a store or a mall. Each of these methods is described below.

## Starting from the Store Creator

This method is the simplest and easiest, allowing you to create a completely functional store with basic features in as little as twenty minutes. (You cannot use it to create a mall.) It is ideal for the administrator who wants to get up and running quickly, or who does not have the programming experience necessary for creating a highly customized store. Absolutely no programming experience is required in order for you to use the Store Creator: the store's infrastructure, including the database, Net.Data macros, HTML files, commands, and overridable functions, is automatically generated.

The Store Creator consists of easy-to-use panels that present options and fields for entering specific information. To begin, it provides a choice of three pre-designed store models. After selecting the model that is most appropriate, you choose settings to define your store's appearance, and enter basic information including tax rates, payment methods, and shipping providers. You can also select sample product data so that you can view the store as it will appear to shoppers.

When you have completed the panels, the Store Creator builds a store based on your specifications. You can view this store, change any settings, and replace the sample data with your own. You can then further customize the store and add additional features, or use it as is.

The following browsers have been tested and successfully used to access stores created with the Store Creator: Internet Explorer versions 3 and 4, Netscape Navigator version 3, and Netscape Communicator version 4.

**Notes:**

- In order to use the Store Creator, you must be either a site administrator, or a store administrator who has been given access by a site administrator. For information on how to assign access to the Store Creator, see "Defining Access Control" on page 66.

- Do not create a store using the Store Creator when you are connected to the database for the East West Food Mart or the Office Window sample stores. These databases are reserved for those two samples only and do not support multiple stores. You must either create a new database or use the default that was created during the installation of Net.Commerce. For details, see "Creating or Connecting to a Database" on page 35.

- Stores created with the Store Creator will not work correctly if the Net.Commerce Server cache is on. By default it is off, and should remain off if you are using stores created by Store Creator. To ensure that it is off, open the file httpd.cnf in a text editor and check that the value of the CACHE parameter is set to "OFF".

- When the store is created by the Store Creator, an ISO 4217 currency code based upon your locale will automatically be created in the database. The locale is defined by the language version of Net.Commerce. For example, if you have installed the English version, the default ISO 4217 code would be USD. You can later change the currency using the Store Manager. (See "Specifying Store Contact, Currency, and Tax Rate Information" on page 83 for details.)

## Store Creator Models

The Store Creator provides a choice of three models upon which you can base your store. These models differ in terms of the types of pages that make up the store, its features, and how shoppers will interact with it. You also have the option of creating your own store models that will be used by the Store Creator. For more information, see "Appendix B, Creating Store Models" on page 497.

### The One-Stop Shop Store Model

The One-Stop Shop store model is very simple in structure and navigation, allowing shoppers to quickly find and order the products they want. It does not have a registration process or offer the option of an address book, so the only information that shoppers have to provide is a shipping address. This store does not keep a list of items in the shopping cart for future visits, so when the shopper leaves the store, any items still in the cart are removed.

This model is appropriate for stores that meet the following criteria:

- The merchant is targeting consumers

- The shoppers are usually one-time or occasional buyers

- The shoppers usually know what items they want to purchase and want to find them quickly

- All items that a shopper orders will be delivered to the same address

- The merchant does not want registration as part of the purchasing process

### The Personal Delivery Store Model

The Personal Delivery store model also has a simple navigation structure, but adds some features to help personalize the shopping experience. It requires shoppers to register before they can place an order, and to log on at return visits. This allows the merchant to track their buying habits and better serve them. Any items a shopper has placed in the shopping cart are kept there for future visits, until the shopper removes them. An address book is available so that shoppers can maintain a personal log of people to whom they frequently want to send goods.

This model is appropriate for stores that meet the following criteria:

- The merchant is targeting consumers

- The shoppers tend to repeat their purchases

- The shoppers usually know what items they want to purchase and want to find them quickly

- The shoppers may want items in an order to be shipped to different addresses

### The Business-to-Business Store Model

The structure of the Business-to-Business store model is geared for corporate purchasing, allowing merchants to group their business clients into different shopper groups, called *offices*, and target these groups with different product offerings and prices. The store manager is responsible for approving offices and for defining the product prices and product pages that will be available to each group. Before making a purchase, each shopper must register with an office and receive approval from the office manager.

This model is appropriate for stores that meet the following criteria:

- The merchant is targeting other businesses or groups of shoppers

- The merchant wants to be able to offer unique products or other incentives, such as discounts, to each business or group of shoppers

- The businesses or groups of shoppers tend to repeat their purchases

## Creating New Store Models

If the supplied store models do not meet your business needs, you can create your own upon which to base your store. For information on how to create a store model and integrate it into the Store Creator for use, see "Appendix B, Creating Store Models" on page 497.

## Assembling Your Information

Before you use the Store Creator, you should have ready the following information:

- Contact information: store name, address, e-mail address, and phone and fax numbers

- Store description

- Tax rates

- Credit cards accepted by the store

- A toll-free number that shoppers can call to place orders

- The names of supported shipping carriers, and their charges

## Creating the Store

To create a store base using the Store Creator, complete the following steps:

1. Open the Administrator. For information on how to do this, see "Opening the Administrator" on page 34.

2. On the task bar, click **Store Creator**.

3. Click **Load** at the bottom of the page that appears. After a few minutes the Store Creator appears, displaying its welcome panel.

4. Follow the instructions on each panel to build the store. To move to the next panel, click **Next**. To return to a panel in order to make changes, click **Back**.

5.  When you have entered or selected all the required information, click **Create Store** on the last panel.

6.  To view your new store, go to the URL indicated on the last panel.

## Changing Store Settings

After you have created and viewed your new store, you may want to make changes to its content or appearance. You can return to the Store Creator and change any settings, either while the Store Creator is still open or later.

**Notes:**

*   You can do this only with a store you created with the Store Creator; not with one you created with the Site Manager and Store Manager or with a sample store.

*   If you make any changes to the store using other tools in Net.Commerce, you cannot further change it in the Store Creator.

*   If you select a new sample product with which to view your store, you must restart your browser to see the change.

### Modifying the Store in the Current Session

To modify the store in the current session (that is, while the Store Creator is still open), do the following:

1.  On the last panel of the Store Creator, click **Back**.

2.  Go to the appropriate panels and make the changes.

3.  Return to the last panel and review your selections.

4.  When you are satisfied with the changes, click **Update Store** on the last panel.

5.  View the updated store at the URL provided.

6.  Repeat steps 1 to 5, as necessary.

### Modifying the Store in a Later Session

You can return to the Store Creator and change store options at any time, provided you have neither replaced the sample data with your own data nor customized your store using tools outside of the Store Creator. Do the following:

1.  Open the Store Creator.

2.  On the first panel, select the **Modify a previously created store** radio button.

3.  From the corresponding drop-down list, select the store that you want to modify.

4.  Go to the appropriate panels and make the changes.

5.  When you are finished, click **Update Store** on the last panel.

    The store is updated to reflect your changes.

## Deleting the Sample Products

Before you can enter your own products and categories in the database, you need to delete the sample products that are currently being displayed.

1.   In the Store Creator, go to the Add Sample Products and a Store Description panel.

2.   From the **Sample Products** drop-down list, select **No Sample Products**.

3.   Go to the last panel and click **Update Store**.

The sample products are deleted from the database and will not appear in your store.

> **Note:**
> Once you delete the sample products and replace them with your own, you cannot return to the Store Creator to make other changes. If you do, your products will be overwritten with the type of sample products selected in the Store Creator.

## Further Customizing the Store

The store you have built with the Store Creator may now meet all your needs, or you may want to further customize it. If you wish, you can now use the Store Manager to enter additional contact or merchant information, create complex shipping providers (such as ones that apply different charges to different products or use different calculation methods), create shopper groups, and implement discounts. For more information, see "Part 2, "Populating the Database" on page 61.

You can also customize the store pages or create additional ones to meet your business requirements. See "Part 3, Creating Web Pages" on page 147 for details.

Stores created from the Store Creator implement the supplied overridable function DoPayment_1.0 (IBM,NC), which during the placement of an order checks that the credit card type, number and expiry date are both provided and valid and then creates a record in the ORDPAYMTHD database table. You can replace this overridable function with one that passes the credit card information to a business critical system for authorization, using the SET protocol, Cybercash, or Verifone. For information on how to write overridable functions, see "Part 4, Customizing the Site" on page 255.

# Starting from the Site Manager and the Store Manager

If you prefer to create your store or mall from scratch, then instead of using the Store Creator, begin the creation process with the Site Manager and Store Manager. These tools provide you with forms for setting up a site and for entering the store and product catalog data in the database. Once the database information is entered, you create the store pages and customize them to meet your business needs.

The site administrator first uses the Site Manager to create the site for the store or mall. The tasks are outlined below; for detailed information, see "Chapter 3, Setting Up the Site" on page 63.

1. Define the store (for a single store) or define all the stores that will reside in the mall (for a mall), using the Store Records form.

2. Restrict access to the store's database (for a single store) or to the mall's database and the database of each store in the mall (for a mall) by assigning individuals to specific user groups, using the Access Groups forms.

3. Define the tax rates (for either the store or mall), using the Mall Information form.

4. Create a master list of the shipping providers that the store or stores can use.

5. If you are creating a mall, use the Task Management function to specify whether each Net.Commerce task can be managed and modified by individual stores in the mall or only by the site administrator using the Task Management form. (If you are creating a single store, you do not need to specify task scope; the default levels are sufficient.)

After the site has been created, the site administrator (or one or more designated store administrators) uses the Store Manager to add information about the products and other store data, for the store or for each of the stores within the mall. The tasks are outlined below; for detailed information, see "Chapter 4, Entering the Store Catalog" on page 79.

1. Define the currency to be used by the store, and the contact information (for example, the store's address and a contact person for customer service), using the Store Information form.

2. If a store in the mall wants to override the tax rates previously set by the site administrator, set new ones for the store using the Store and Merchant Information form.

3. Create categories for the store's products, either one at a time using the category forms in the Store Manager, or all at once using the Mass Import utility. The merchant uses categories to organize products into logical groups, and shoppers will use them as navigation routes to browse the store.

4. From the master list previously defined by the site administrator, select the shipping services to be used for the store, using the Shipping Service forms. You select the carriers you want to use, and create codes that specify carriers, charges, and calculation methods to be later assigned to products.

5. Enter information about your products into the database, including detailed descriptions, SKU numbers, prices, and the shipping codes that define how each product will be shipped. You can use either the product forms in the Store Manager to enter the products one at a time, or the Mass Import utility to enter them all at once.

6. Create and implement discounts for your products, using the Discounts forms. This involves creating discount codes based on your desired discount periods and calculation methods, and then assigning a discount code to individual products.

7. Create shopper groups for customizing the way product and category information will be displayed to different shoppers, or for offering special prices to different shoppers.

After you have set up your site and entered all the information related to the store, you will create the pages that display the store and catalog data. Typically, these include product and category pages, a shopping cart page, a registration page, and an order page. To create these pages, you can either customize the sample pages provided by Net.Commerce or write your own Net.Data macros. See "Part 3, Creating Web Pages" on page 147 for details.

# Starting from a Sample

Net.Commerce supplies several sample stores and a sample mall that you can use as starting points for creating your own store or mall. Each sample demonstrates different features or customization techniques and is intended to help you generate ideas for your business. Each sample uses a separate database and comes with its own unique sample products.

There are two ways to use a sample:

- You can start from the sample and customize it to suit your needs. The sample's database will be automatically generated when you install it, and you must delete the sample data from it before you add your own. This includes the products, categories, shipping providers, and other required store information. You can then modify the store pages to accommodate your own store data, and add additional ones if necessary.

- A quicker method is to first build your own database, and then pick and choose from one or more samples the pages and shopping flows that are appropriate for your business, and then customizing them to meet your needs. This way, you do not need to remove the sample data before adding your own, and you can build the store according to your specifications from the start. Once you have added your data, it will automatically be displayed on the store pages, and you can make the necessary changes for accommodating additional or modified data.

For information on how to create a database, see "Creating or Connecting to a Database" on page 35. For information on how to populate the database with your store data, see "Part 2, Populating the Database" on page 61. For information on how to create or customize the pages, see "Part 3, Creating Web Pages" on page 147.

The Net.Commerce sample stores are as follows. Detailed descriptions follow.

- **Metropolitan Mall**: demonstrates a mall scenario that implements the basic features of Net.Commerce with minimal customization.

- **East West Food Mart**: demonstrates a business-to-consumer scenario that has been customized to create a simple and expedient shopping flow.

- **Office Window**: demonstrates a business-to-business scenario that has been customized to allow a merchant to tailor the store catalog to specific groups of shoppers.

To view the samples, you install them and then browse them at their corresponding URLs.

**Note:**
The samples are for demonstration purposes only. Modifications are required if you want to use them for production. For example, some of the HTML and macro files require that you change the GET method in the HTML FORM statements to the POST method. For assistance, contact the IBM Net.Commerce Services and Support Team through the Net.Commerce Web site at: http://www.ibm.com/net.commerce.

## Metropolitan Mall Sample

The Metropolitan Mall is intended to demonstrate some of the features and functions that you can include in a mall without doing much customization, and to help you generate ideas for your own mall. You can use it as a starting point for creating your own mall, and you can also use any of the stores within it as a starting point for creating your own store.

The sample implements a wide variety of Net.Commerce features, including SET as a payment option and Lotus Domino for linking to a discussion database and for sending e-mail to confirm orders placed by shoppers. It uses almost all of the supplied commands and overridable functions provided by the Net.Commerce system to display store pages and perform specific business processes, such as adding items to the shopping cart and processing an order. It also includes some JavaScript. The mall comes complete with sample data, and when you install it, the current database is automatically populated with this data.

You can use any of the mall or store pages as they have been implemented, or modify them to meet your needs.

The Metropolitan Mall contains the following stores, which you can either modify or replace with your own:

- **6th Avenue**: A department store that sells hardware, computers, and clothing.

- **Basics**: A clothing store for men that features pants and tops.

- **Netaway**: A travel agency that offers travel packages.

- **Next Generation** (included only in the Net.Commerce PRO package): A store that sells computers. This store offers shoppers assistance in selecting products through its intelligent catalog, which was created with Product Advisor.

It also includes three stores that do not contain data and are provided only as placeholders: Nick's Nacks, Jim's Homeware, and Lorne's Lawncare.

The browsers that have been tested and successfully used to access the Metropolitan Mall and its stores are Internet Explorer versions 3 and 4, Netscape Navigator version 3, and Netscape Communicator version 4.

To explore this sample, you install it and go to its URL. To get started, see "Installing the Databases for the Samples" on page 47.

## East West Food Mart Sample

The East West Food Mart is an example of a retail store. It sells a variety of groceries, such as produce, beverages, frozen foods, and baked goods. This store features the simplest shopping process of all the samples. It bypasses certain Net.Commerce commands to achieve a navigational structure that is simple and expedient, allowing shoppers to get in and out with only a few clicks of the mouse. Many of its macros make use of JavaScript to enhance the dynamics of the store pages and to allow multiple functions to run simultaneously. You can use the store pages as they have been implemented, or modify them to meet your needs.

To access this store, shoppers must use a browser that supports the level of JavaScript used. Currently, Netscape Communicator Version 4.0 or later satisfies this requirement. Keep this in mind if you decide to use the East West Food Mart as a basis for your own store.

This sample store is ideal for merchants who meet the following criteria:

- They are targeting consumers

- Their products are familiar to shoppers

- Their shoppers usually know what items they want to purchase and want to find them quickly

- The shoppers often buy many items of the same product at one time

- Their shoppers tend to repeat their purchases

- All items in an order will be delivered to the same address

To explore this sample, install it and go to its URL. To get started, see "Installing the Databases for the Samples" on page 47.

## The Office Window Sample

The Office Window is an example of a wholesale store that targets specific business markets. It sells a variety of office supplies and computer equipment, and makes use of shopper groups to create customized catalogs for specific groups, called offices. An additional administrator group has been created for this purpose, whose members are called office administrators. An office administrator is typically a manager of a company who wants certain supplies to be ordered from this store. A shopper is typically an employee of that company who places orders on its behalf. The shopper must first enroll in an office, and the office administrator must approve the enrollment before the shopper can browse the store and make a purchase. Only the products and categories available for that office are displayed to the shopper. The office administrator must then approve the purchase before it is processed.

The roles of the various users are as follows:

### Merchant

- Creates the store pages

- Adds information about products and categories into the database

- Determines which categories and products will be accessible from each office

- Approves office administrators and their requested new offices

### Office Administrator

- Requests new offices

- Approves shopper enrollments in the office

- Approves orders placed by shoppers

- Browses the catalog available for the office

- Places orders for products

### Shopper

- Enrolls in an office

- Browses the catalog available for the office

- Places orders for products

Five users have already been created for this store for demonstration purposes: *merchant, admin1, admin2, shopper1*, and *shopper2*. Their passwords are the same as their user IDs.

Like the East West Food Mart, the Office Window makes use of JavaScript. Shoppers must therefore use a browser that supports JavaScript to access the store. Currently, Netscape Communicator Version 4.0 or later meets this requirement. Keep this in mind if you decide to use the Office Window as a basis for your own store.

To explore this sample, you install it and go to its URL. To get started, see "Installing the Databases for the Samples" on page 47.

# Installing the Databases for the Samples

Before you can view a sample, you must install its database.

> **Note:**
> You cannot use the sample databases of the East West Food Mart or the Office Window for storing more than one store's data. They can only be used for a single-store scenario.

1. For Net.Commerce PRO, if you use the Domino Web Server, you must copy the following files as described below before installing the Metropolitan Mall. When you copy these files, some files in the destination directory will be overwritten. You should therefore make a backup copy of the corresponding files in the destination directory beforehand.

   a) **WIN** Copy: `<drive>:\Ibm\NetCommerce3\domino\nc_schema\db2\`
   `demomall.cmd`
   to: `\Ibm\NetCommerce3\nc_schema\db2\`

   **AIX** Copy: `<drive>:/usr/lpp/NetCommerce3/domino/nc_schema/db2/`
   `demomall.cmd`
   to:`/usr/lpp/NetCommerce3/nc_schema/db2/`

   b) **WIN** Copy: `<drive>:\Ibm\NetCommerce3\domino\macro\en_US\`
   `demomall\mall_dir.d2w`
   to: `\Ibm\NetCommerce3\macro\en_US\demomall\`

   **AIX** Copy: `<drive>:/usr/lpp/NetCommerce3/domino/macro/en_US/`
   `demomall/mall_dir.d2w`
   to: `/usr/lpp/NetCommerce3/macro/en_US\demomall/`

   When asked to confirm that you wish to overwrite the existing file, click **Yes**.

2. Open Net.Commerce Administrator, as described in "Opening the Administrator" on page 34.

3. On the task bar, click **Samples and Tutorials**. The Samples and Tutorials form appears.

4. From the **Select Sample/Tutorial** drop-down list, select the sample that you want to install.

5. If desired, in the **Database Name** field, change the name of the database that will be created for the store. By default, the following database names will be created:

   - Metropolitan Mall: `demomall`

   - East West Food Mart: `grocery`

   - Office Window: `bus2bus`

6. Click **Install**. A progress window appears, indicating the progress of the installation.

7. After the database has successfully been installed, follow the instructions on the screen to restart the Net.Commerce server.

8. Restart the browser.

## Viewing the Samples

After you have installed a sample store, you can go to its URL to view it as it will appear to shoppers:

- **Metropolitan Mall**: `http://host_name/demomall/index.html`

- **East West Food Mart**: `http://<host_name>/grocery/index.html`

- **Office Window**: `http://host_name/bus2bus2/index.html`

  where `<host_name>` is the fully qualified name of your server.

Click the **Tell Me About This Page** button on each store page for a description of the page and the location of its source file. (Remember to remove these buttons if you intend to use the pages for your store.)

## Switching Between Samples

If you installed more than one sample store and you want to view one of them, you must be connected to its database beforehand. See "Connecting to a Database" on page 37 for the steps required to connect to the database of any of the samples.

# Workshop: Creating a Store Starting from the Store Creator

In this workshop you will use the Store Creator to create a store base, which in the workshops that follow, you will transform into a pizza delivery store. As the site administrator, you will be responsible for building and customizing the store to meet your business requirements. This store, called "OneStopPizza Shop", will sell a variety of homemade pizzas over the Internet.

The OneStopPizza Shop will have the following main features:

- **Pre-made or Custom Pizza:** Shoppers can select from a variety of the store's pre-made pizzas, or create their own pizza from a selection of toppings.

- **Free Delivery:** The store provides delivery at no extra charge to those customers living in the store's delivery radius.

- **Optional Registration:** Shoppers can choose to browse the store anonymously or, if they have previously registered, they can log on as a registered shopper. Either way, they can place an order. Registered shoppers are provided with the following conveniences:

  - They do not need to fill out their delivery address every time they place an order; it is automatically retrieved from the database and displayed at order time.

  - They can make "quick picks" from pizzas they have previously ordered, instead of having to search through the catalog each time. Once an order is placed, all items are recorded and are accessible when the shopper logs on during the next store visit.

- **Flexible Registration Process:** Shoppers do not need to go to a separate page to enter registration information: they can choose to register at the same time that they place an order.

- **One Delivery Address:** Shoppers are allowed to specify only one delivery address. Because of the nature of the products being sold (pizzas), people are not likely to ask for them to be sent to more than one address at one time, so there is no need for multiple addresses. This eliminates the need for the shopper too maintain a personal address book, and simplifies the ordering process. If a shopper has registered, the address will be the one that was specified during the placement of the last order; otherwise, the shopper provides it before submitting the order.

**Note:**
The workshops in this book run only on the Windows NT operating system and using a DB2 database. You cannot do the workshops using the AIX operating system and an Oracle database.

# Connecting to the Default Database

If you are not already connected to the default database that was created during the installation of Net.Commerce, do so now, following the instructions given in "Connecting to a Database" on page 37. Unless a new name was specified during installation, this database will have the default name **mser.** At the end of the workshops, you can delete the store data from the database.

# Opening the Store Creator

First, you will open the Store Creator.

1. Set up your computer and browser, as described in "Specifying Computer and Browser Settings" on page 33.

2. Open the Administrator, as described in "Opening the Administrator" on page 34.

3. On the task bar of the Administrator, click **Store Creator**.

4. At the bottom of the Store Creator page, click **Load**. The Store Creator begins to load, as indicated by its status window.

5. When the Welcome panel appears, ensure that the **Create a new store** radio button is selected and then click **Next**, as shown in Figure 2.1 below:

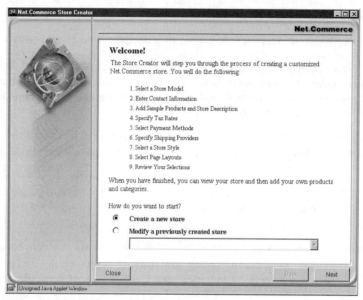

*Figure 2.1  The Store Creator Welcome panel.*

The Select a Store Model panel appears, as shown in Figure 2.2 below. From this panel, you will select the store model on which you will base your pizza delivery store.

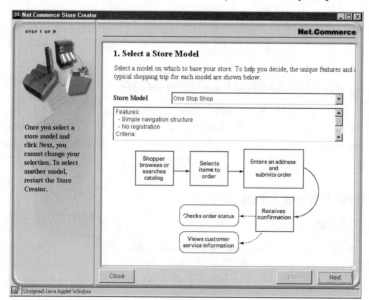

*Figure 2.2  The Select a Store Model panel.*

# Selecting a Store Model

The first and most important step in using the Store Creator is selecting the model on which to base your store. The store model will define the features for your store and the types of pages that will make it up, as well as how shoppers will interact with it to browse and place orders. You have a choice of three store models, and must carefully examine each to decide which one will be most suitable. Selecting the right model now will make it easier when you customize the store later.

1.  From the **Store Model** drop-down list, select **Business-to-Business**. A brief description of the store model's features and criteria is displayed, as well as a flow chart that shows a typical shopping trip in this store setup. As the description and diagram show, the Business-to-Business store model features a corporate purchasing structure, and is appropriate if your store meets the following criteria:

    - It is targeting other businesses or groups of shoppers

    - It will offer unique incentives, such as product discounts, to your customers.

    - Its shoppers tend to repeat their purchases

    It should be clear that this store model is not appropriate for your store, for the following reasons: First, you are targeting consumers, not other businesses. Second, using shopper groups is more appropriate for stores that offer a wide variety of products, not for ones like yours that specialize in a single product line. Third, the approval process is not required, since your customers are not ordering on behalf of a company; they are independent purchasers who require a simple purchasing structure.

2.  From the **Store Model** drop-down list, select **Personal Delivery**. This model features a simpler navigation structure and is appropriate if your store meets the following criteria:

    - It is targeting consumers

    - Its shoppers tend to repeat their purchases

    - Its shoppers usually know what items they want to purchase and want to find them quickly

    - Each item in an order can be shipped to a different address

    - Its shoppers must register before they can place an order, and must log on to the store at return visits

    - Any items the shopper has placed in the shopping cart are kept there for future visits, until the shopper removes them

    - An address book is available, for shoppers to maintain a personal log of the people to whom they frequently want to send goods

    Although this model is better suited to your pizza store than was the previous model, it still contains features that are not appropriate. First, it requires shoppers to be registered before they can place an order, whereas your store allows anonymous shopping. Second, it allows items in an order to be shipped to different addresses, which you do not permit in your store and most customers would not require. Third, the address book is not needed since you permit only one shipping address.

3.  From the **Store Model** drop-down list, select **One Stop Shop**. This model is very simple in structure and navigation, and is appropriate if your store meets the following criteria:

    -   It is targeting consumers

    -   Its shoppers are usually one-time or occasional buyers

    -   Its shoppers usually know what items they want to purchase and want to find them quickly

    -   Any items that the shopper selects but does not order will be removed from the order list when the shopper closes the browser

    -   All items that a shopper orders will be delivered to the same address

    -   It does not feature registration as part of the purchasing process

    -   It does not offer the option of using an address book. Shoppers can make their purchases without having to provide any information other than a shipping address at order time.

    This store model best fits your store design. Features that are lacking, such as the option to register and log on, will be added in later workshops; for now, the base is there, which is the most important requirement at this step of the store creation process.

4.  Click **Next**. It will take a few seconds for the Store Creator to set up the remaining panels for your selected store model. The Enter Contact Information panel then appears.

# Entering Store Information

You are now ready to go through the remaining panels of the Store Creator and enter the basic information that is required for your store to function, including contact information, taxes, shipping providers, and page layouts; and defining the appearance of the store.

1.  Ensure that the Enter Contact Information panel is still displayed.

2.  In the **Store Name (Mandatory)** field, enter `OneStopPizza Shop`. This name will appear on your store banner, and will also be used for the URL that shoppers will type to access the store.

3.  Fill in the other fields with a full store address, e-mail address, phone number, and fax number, and then click **Next**. The Add Sample Products and Store Description panel appears. Here, you will select sample products for testing your store later. They will appear as text and graphics on the store pages. You have a choice between clothing, tools and hardware, and grocery products. You can also select **No Sample Products**, which will not display text or images in the store. However, you would not be able to view the store end-to-end. This option is typically used to remove the sample products once you are ready to add your own.

4. From the **Sample Products** drop-down list, select **Grocery Products**. This is the most representative product type for your pizzas.

5. You will now add the text that will appear on your store's home page. In the **Store Description** field, change the text to the following:

```
<P>Welcome to the <B>OneStopPizza Shop</B>.
We specialize in the finest homemade pizzas, always delivered
fresh.</P>
```

6. Click **Next**. The Specify Tax Rates panel appears. On this panel, you will enter the tax rates that apply to orders.

7. In the first **Tax Name** field, enter `Sales Tax`.

8. In the corresponding **Tax Rate (%)** field, enter `6`.

9. In this example, a federal tax also applies. In the second **Tax Name** field, enter `Federal Tax`.

10. In the corresponding **Tax Rate (%)** field, enter 5.

11. Click **Next**. The Select Payment Methods panel appears. On this panel, you will select the credit cards that your store supports and the toll-free phone number that shoppers can call to place orders.

12. Select the checkboxes beside the **VISA** and **MasterCard** images.

13. In the **Toll-Free Phone Number** field, enter a number.

14. Click **Next**. The **Specify Shipping Providers** panel appears. From this panel, you will specify a shipping carrier that will be used to deliver pizzas to customers, and the fixed delivery charge that will be applied to their orders. To be competitive, you will provide service within thirty minutes of the customer placing an order or it is free of charge. In this example, only one shipping carrier entry is required, which is fulfilled by your store's delivery employees. (In other store scenarios you might require a delivery charge and provide the customer with more than one carrier option, such as delivery on the same day or overnight.)

15. In the first **Shipping Service Name** field, enter `Same Day`.

16. In the corresponding **Shipping Charge** field, enter `0`.

17. Click **Next**. The Select a Store Style panel appears. This panel presents a variety of store styles that you can use for your store's appearance. Each style consists of a color scheme, frame layout, and a style of navigation buttons. For the One Stop Store model, these buttons are displayed down the left side of the store, as indicated by (Side) beside each style name. Other store models display the navigation buttons at different locations (for example, along the top or bottom).

18. From the **Store Style** drop-down list, select each style name to see the styles that are available.

19. For your pizza store, you will choose a style that is colorful and bright. Select **Contemporary (Side)** from the list, as shown in Figure 2.3 below.

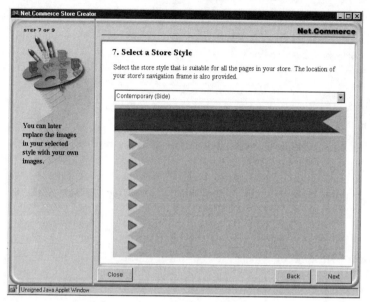

*Figure 2.3* *The Select a Store Style panel.*

20. Click **Next**. The Select Page Layouts panel appears. From this panel, you will select a page layout for your store's categories. You can choose to display the categories as text only or as a combination of images and text.

21. Select the **Image Layout** radio button, and then click **Next**. The Review Your Selections panel appears.

22. Examine the options you have selected for your store. This summary provides you with the opportunity to go back to a panel and change any store setting (except the store model). At this time, you will not change anything.

23. Click **Create Store** to build your store. A progress indicator displays while your store is created. When the store has been created, the Where To Go From Here panel appears, as shown in Figure 2.4. This panel provides suggestions on how to complete the store creation process. In the workshops that follow, you will transform the current store into your final pizza store.

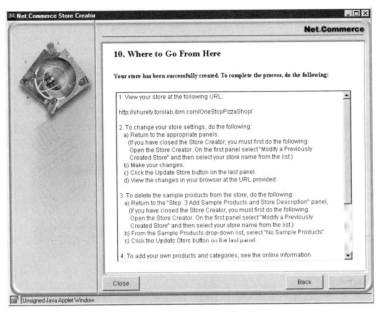

*Figure 2.4  The Where to Go From Here panel.*

# Viewing Your New Store

Now let's explore the store that has been produced by the Store Creator. You will browse each page to familiarize yourself with the content and to understand how your customers would currently interact with the store.

1.  Highlight and copy the URL that is provided on the Where to Go From Here panel. The URL is the following:

    ```
    http://<host_name>/OneStopPizzaShop/
    ```

    where <host_name> is the fully qualified name of your server. Shoppers will use this URL to access the store.

2.  Close the Store Creator and all browser windows. You are currently logged on as the site administrator, so you need to close the browsers and then enter the store in a new shopper session.

3.  Open a new browser window.

4.  Paste the URL on the browser's command line, and press Enter. The store appears, as shown in Figure 2.5 below. It is displayed in the style that you specified, including a banner with the store name across the top, a navigation bar down the left side, and the home page and the order list in the two main frames. The content of these two frames will change as the shopper moves through the store. Also note that the home page displays the store description that you entered.

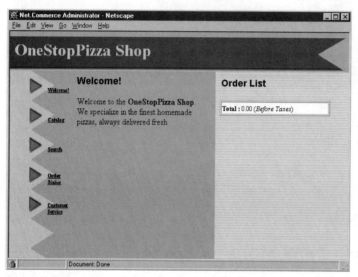

***Figure 2.5*** *How the home page of the OneStopPizza Shop initally looks after being generated by the Store Creator.*

5.  First, you will browse the store's catalog and find some products to purchase. On the navigation bar, click **Catalog**. A category page appears in the main left frame, displaying the store's top-level categories.

6.  Click **Beverages**. Remember that you will be viewing sample grocery store data, which was selected because it was the most appropriate for the pizza store. A page appears displaying the subcategories that belong to the *Beverages* category, as shown in Figure 2.6 on the next page:

*Figure 2.6  The subcategory page for the Beverages category.*

7.  Click **Water**.  A list of the different types of water products available is displayed.

8.  Scroll down the list and click **Mineral Water**.  The product page for mineral water appears, presenting different sizes to choose from.

9.  From the **Size** drop-down list, select **1.5 L** and then click **Add to Order List**.  The item is added to your Order List on the right, and its price is displayed, as shown in Figure 2.7 below:

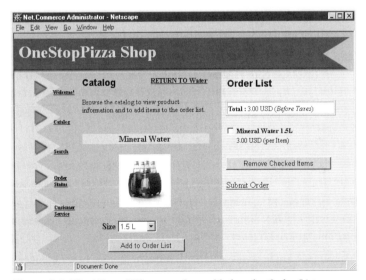

*Figure 2.7  The Mineral Water product added to the Order List.*

10. You will now add another product to your Order List. On the navigation bar, click **Catalog** to return to the top-level categories.

11. Click **Produce**.

12. On the resulting subcategory page, click **Squash**.

13. From the list of squash types, click **Butternut**.

14. On the resulting product page, click the button with the arrow to add this product to your Order List. Note that this product does not come in different sizes.

15. Let's add one more squash to your order. Click the arrow button on the product page again. Another squash is added to the Order List. The total price of all three items is displayed (before taxes), along with the individual prices.

16. Add a few more products of your choice to your Order List.

17. Now, you decide that you don't want to buy two squashes after all. In the Order List, select the check box beside one of the butternut squashes, and then click **Remove Checked Items**. The squash is removed from the list.

18. Now you are ready to place an order for the items in your Order List. At the bottom of the list, click **Submit Order**.

19. A new browser window appears, displaying your order. The page displays the subtotal cost of the order, the state and federal taxes, no charge for shipping, and the total cost of the order.

20. In the **Shipping Address** section of the form, enter a first and last name and a full address.

21. In the **Payment Information** section, select the type of credit card by which you want to pay for the order.

22. Enter a valid credit card number and expiry month and year.

23. Click **Purchase**. The order is sent to an order processing system, and a confirmation page appears. It displays your customer number, your order number, your shipping address, a summary of the items in the order, and contact information for inquiries.

24. Make a note of the customer number and the order number:

    Customer Number _____
    Order Number      _____

25. Close the browser window to reveal the original browser window.

26. Now let's view the status of your order. Shoppers may do this after an order has been placed or before they have submitted an order to view the contents of their order list. On the navigation bar, click **Order Status**.

27. In the fields provided, enter your customer number and your order number, and then click **Retrieve Order Status**. The Order Status page appears, showing your order in the completed state. The date and time at which it was completed and the items in the

order are also displayed. (If a shopper had not yet submitted an order, the order would be shown in the pending state.)

28. The last page that you will explore is the Customer Service page. On the navigation bar, click **Customer Service**. The Customer Service page appears, displaying the contact information that you previously entered in the Store Creator.

You have now completed your tour of the store you created based on the One Stop Shop store model.

# Deleting the Sample Products

You selected sample grocery text and graphics so that you could view your new store. You will now remove these products from the store, in preparation for adding your own products and categories in the workshop in Chapter 4.

1. Close the browser window.

2. Open the Administrator and then load the Store Creator.

3. On the first panel displayed, select the **Modify a previously created store** radio button.

4. From the drop-down list, select **OneStopPizza Shop**.

5. Click **Next** until you get to the Add Sample Products and Store Description panel.

6. From the **Sample Product** drop-down list, select **No Sample Products,** as shown in Figure 2.8 below:

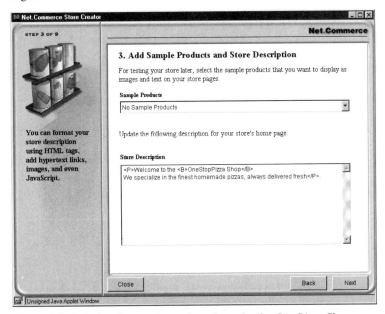

***Figure 2.8*** *Deleting the sample products from the OneStopPizza Shop.*

7.  Click next until you get to the Specify Shipping Providers panel.

8.  In the **Shipping Charge** field, reenter 0.

9.  Go to the last panel in the Store Creator (Review Your Selections) and click **Update Store**. When the Where to Go From Here panels appears, the sample grocery products have been successfully removed from the database, and will no longer appear in your store.

10. Close the Store Creator and all browser windows.

You have now completed this workshop. In the next workshop in Chapter 3, you will learn how to assign access to specific data in the store's database.

# Part 2, Populating the Database

One of the most time-consuming tasks involved in developing an e-commerce site is entering all the information into the database. This can amount to hundreds of thousands of entries, ranging from details about which administrators have access to the data, to the price of every item in the store.

To make this task easier, Net.Commerce provides an extensive suite of tools for setting up the site, for giving database access to authorized individuals, and for populating the database with information about the store or mall and its product catalog. This part shows you how to use these tools.

## Contents:

# Chapter 3, Setting Up the Site

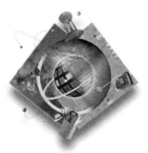

This chapter describes the main tasks involved in setting up a site for a store or mall. It shows you how to use the Site Manager to designate store administrators and give them access to data in the database, and how to set up the system with the basic data needed for the store or mall to run. In the workshop, you will designate database access to the pizza store that you built in the workshop in Chapter 2.

This chapter covers the following topics:

- The Site Manager
- Opening the Site Manager
- Creating a Store Record
- Setting Tax Rates for the Site
- Defining Access Control
- Setting Task Scope
- Assigning Tasks to Macros and Overridable Functions
- Specifying Shipping Providers
- Cookies and Session Management
- Specifying Command Security
- Workshop: Designating Access to the OneStopPizza Shop's Database

# The Site Manager

The Site Manager consists of a collection of online forms for managing the creation and maintenance of a store or mall site. A site administrator uses these forms to perform the following tasks:

- Create a store record for the store (or for each store within the mall)

- Define tax rates for the store or stores

- Maintain a list of shipping providers that will be available to the store or stores

- Designate store administrators and give them access to their respective store's database

- Maintain user IDs and passwords for the store administrators

- For a mall, assign scope to shopping tasks (such as shipping or ordering) to specify whether each task will function similarly for all the stores in the mall or vary from one store to the next

- Assign Net.Data macros or overridable functions to tasks, to customize certain shopping processes

- Assign security levels (SSL or authentication) to commands

For any store that was created using the Store Creator, the following site information has already been automatically created in the database, but can be modified using the Site Manager:

- A store record

- At least one tax rate

- At least one shipping provider

- The assignment of Net.Data macros to their corresponding tasks

For the remainder of this chapter, you will take the role of the site administrator in order to set up the site for your store or mall.

# Opening the Site Manager

To open the Site Manager, do the following:

1. Open the Administrator, as described in "Opening the Administrator" on page 34.

2. When prompted, enter your site administrator logon ID and password, and then click **Logon**.

3. On the task bar, click **Site Manager**.

    The Site Manager opens.

# Creating a Store Record

If you are creating a single store, you require one store record; if you are creating a mall, you require one store record for each store that will reside in the mall. A store record creates an entity in the MERCHANT (Merchant Profile) table in the database and "opens" the store. The record contains general information about the store, including its name, the company name, and contact information. A unique merchant reference number is also automatically generated for the store and stored in the MERCHANT table.

To create a store record, you use the Store Records form. (You will also use this form to add new stores to a mall and to remove any stores that are no longer in operation.)

To create a store record, do the following:

1.  On the task bar of the Site Manager, click **Store Records**. The Store Records form appears.

2.  Enter the appropriate information in the fields, and then click **Save**. Bold fields are mandatory.

3.  Click **OK** in the confirmation window. The information is saved as a new store record in the MERCHANT table in the database. Make sure that a confirmation message appears in the display area.

4.  If you are creating a mall, create a store record for each store in the mall by repeating steps 1 to 4 above.

From now on, if any changes to this form are necessary, they will be made using the Store and Merchant Information form in the Store Manager, and will typically be done by the store administrator. For more information, see "Specifying Store Contact, Currency, and Tax Rate Information" on page 83.

# Setting Tax Rates for the Site

To define a taxation rate that will be applied to the products in a single store or to the stores within a mall, do the following:

1.  On the task bar of the Site Manager, click **Mall Information**. The Mall Information form appears.

2.  In the **Tax Rate 1** field, enter the sales tax that will be applied to product prices. The rate is expressed as a percentage: for example, 8 means eight percent. The default is 0.

3.  If more than one tax applies (for example, state or provincial tax plus federal tax), enter their rates in the other tax fields.

4.  Click **Save**. The information is saved as a record in the MALL database table. Ensure that a confirmation message appears in the display area.

**Note:**
Any tax rates that have been defined by specific stores will take precedence over mall tax rates. For more information, see "Specifying Store Contact, Currency, and Tax Rate Information" on page 83.

# Defining Access Control

To facilitate database management and to ensure security, access to the Net.Commerce database must be restricted to specific individuals. As site administrator, you can designate store administrators and specify the data to which they will have access. (They should not have access to the data of stores that they do not manage.) You can also designate other site administrators, if you wish. You can assign a password to each administrator, to ensure that only authorized parties can access confidential information. This provides a way to control essential responsibilities, such as updating product information.

In the case of a mall, usually the site administrator manages the mall and performs site operations, and store administrators manage each store (although the site administrator also has automatic access to the database of every store in the site). In the case of a single-store site, the site administrator can either personally be responsible for both the site and the store data, or designate a store administrator to take care of the store data.

The way to designate which administrators have access to which data is to assign them to *access control groups*. Access control groups give users the authority to issue specific commands with respect to specific stores. Each command gives access to certain tables in the database; for example, the system admin commands provide access to the forms of the Administrator. The site administrator is authorized to use all commands with all stores, while each store administrator can be authorized to use only some commands with one specific store. (You can assign an administrator to more than one access group.) If a user attempts to issue a command for which an access group containing that combination of user, command, and store does not exist, the command cannot be executed. To assign site and store access, you first create an access control group and assign it to the store; then designate a store administrator; and then assign the store administrator to the access control group. These steps are detailed below.

You can also create access control groups that give certain shoppers access to only specific commands used in the store. For example, in a business-to-business scenario you would issue commands to shoppers that allow them to browse and order from the store and commands to administrators that allow them to approve the purchases made by the shoppers

## Creating Access Control Groups

You can create an original access control group, create one from an existing group that you have created, or base one on a predefined role. Any access group can be assigned to either a store or a mall, and can later be modified.

### Creating an Original Access Group

To create an access group that contains your choice of commands, do the following:

1.  On the task bar of the Site Manager, click **Access Groups**. The Access Group Assignment form appears.

2.  From the list of access group names, click **Add New Access Group**.

3. In the **Access Group Name** field, enter a name for the new access group.

4. In the **Store** drop-down list, either select the store you want to associate the group with, or select **Mall** to have the group apply to all stores in the mall.

5. In the **Description** field, enter a description of the new group.

6. From the **Commands** list, select the commands you want to include in this group. You can use the Shift and Control keys to select multiple commands. (For information about the commands, see "Appendix D, Net.Commerce Commands" on page 569.)

> **Note:**
> Although you are able to assign all commands in the list to either the store or the mall level, some commands are valid only at the mall level. If you assign a store administrator to a command that applies only at the mall level, the administrator will not be able to execute that command.

7. Click the **Add Commands** button. The commands you selected appear in the **Commands Assigned to Group** list.

8. Click **Update**. Ensure that **a** confirmation message appears in the display area.

## Creating a New Access Group from an Existing Group

You can create a new access group from an existing group that you have created, if the existing group contains the commands you want.

1. On the task bar of the **Site Manager**, click **Access Groups**. The Access Group Assignment form appears.

2. From the list of access group names, select the one you want. The fields fill with information about that group. (Store managers can only view access groups that are assigned to their own stores or to the mall. They cannot view access groups that are assigned to other stores.)

3. From the list of access group names, click **Add New Access Group**.

4. In the **Access Group Name** field, delete the name of the existing group and enter a name for the new one.

5. From the **Store** drop-down list, select the store you want to associate the group with, or select **Mall** to have the group apply to all stores in the mall.

6. In the **Description** field, enter a description of the new group.

7. Click **Update**. Ensure that a confirmation message appears. The new group has the same commands as the original.

## Creating an Access Control Group Based on a Predefined Role

The Net.Commerce system provides four predefined access groups, each of which contains commands that give the authority associated with a particular role. You can reuse a predefined role multiple times to create new access groups for different stores.

- **Site Administrator Role.** This role gives access to all the commands in the Net.Commerce system (both the default commands and any new ones that are created), so that the user has authority over the entire site.

- **Store Creator Role.** This role gives access to all the commands required for accessing the Store Creator, so that the user can create a store using the Store Creator.

- **Store Administrator Role.** This role gives access to the commands required for using the forms in the Store Manager, so that the user can manage the store's data.

- **Payment Administrator Role.** This role authorizes a user to perform commands dealing with payment activities for a specific store or for the entire mall.

> **Note:**
> Do not assign the predefined Store Admin (MALL) role to an administrator. This role should only be used as a template to create a store administrator role for a particular store.

To create an access control group based on one of the predefined roles, do the following:

1. On the task bar of the Site Manager, click **Access Groups**. The Access Group Assignment form appears.

2. From the list of access group names, select the predefined role you want. The fields fill with information about that group.

3. If you want to give the new access group a different name, click **Add New Access Group**.

4. In the **Access Group Name** field, delete the name of the predefined role and enter a new name.

5. From the **Store** drop-down list, select the store to which you want the role to apply, or select **Mall** to have the role apply to all stores in the mall.

6. In the **Description** field, enter a description of the new access group.

7. Click **Update**. Ensure that a confirmation message appears in the display area. The new group has the same commands as the predefined role, but you can modify it by adding or deleting commands.

> **Note:**
> Be careful not to delete the predefined roles that are installed by Net.Commerce. If you need to reload them, run the following SQL script in the database:
>
>    `\IBM\NetCommerce3\nc_schma\common\nc_access.sql`
> **AIX**   `/usr/lpp/NetCommerce3/nc_schma/common/nc_access.sql`

# Designating a Store Administrator

After you have created an access control group and assigned it to the store or mall, you need to designate one or more store administrators who will be assigned to that group. Do the following:

1. On the task bar of the Site Manager, click **Access Control**. The Access Control form appears.

2. In the **Administrator's ID** field, enter a logon ID for the store administrator. This ID will be used by the store administrator to log onto the Administrator.

3. In the appropriate fields, enter a password and password confirmation.

4. In the appropriate fields, enter the administrator's last name and first name. You can also fill in other fields.

5. Click **Save**.

6. Click **OK** in the confirmation window. The information is saved as a new record in the SHOPPER and ACCTRL database tables.

# Assigning Administrators to Access Control Groups

After you have created your access control groups and designated your administrators, you are ready to assign the administrators to these groups, thereby giving them authority to manage the data associated with particular commands. Do the following:

1. Ensure that you have already created the access control groups and designated the administrators.

2. On the task bar of the Site Manager, click **Access Control**. The Access Control form appears.

3. If the administrator you want to assign to a group is already registered in the database, display the information for that person; otherwise, enter the necessary information in the appropriate fields, and click **Save**.

4. Click **Access Assignment**. The Administrator - Access Group Assignment form appears.

5. In the **All Groups** list, select the group(s) to which you want the administrator to be assigned, and then click **Add Groups**.

6. Click **Save**. Ensure that a confirmation message appears in the display area.

## Changing an Administrator's Password

To change the password of an administrator, you can either use the Access Control form in the Site Manager or have the administrator change it himself or herself. For instructions on how to change the password using the Access Control form, see "Changing the Site Administrator's Password" on page 34.

Store administrators can also change their own passwords, by logging on to their store and changing the password on the registration form. If the store does not have registration, the site administrator must assign the password for the store administrator from the Site Manager.

# Setting Task Scope

In Net.Commerce, a *task* represents any process in the Net.Commerce system that you can customize; for example, checking inventory, calculating the price of an item, displaying a specific page, or handling an exception condition. A task is abstract in nature in that it defines the rules for a particular process, but the actual work is performed by an overridable function or Net.Data macro, which must be assigned to the task.

Net.Commerce defines the following types of tasks:

- **View tasks**, for calling overridable functions that execute Net.Data macros to display the pages that shoppers  normally see during the shopping process

- **Process tasks**, for calling overridable functions that process information

- **Exception tasks**, for calling overridable functions that handle exception conditions

For more information, see "Tasks" on page 266.

If you are creating a mall, you must determine which tasks in the system can be customized by the stores, by setting a *scope* for each task except the following tasks:

- Tasks that display product and category pages.  These are customized for each store, but you can perform additional customization by changing their macros.

- Tasks that display system error messages.  These are customizable only at the mall level.

- If you are creating a single store, you do not need to set task scope, since any scope level will apply to the store.

The scope of a task is set to either *store or mall.*  If a task has mall scope, only the site administrator can customize it, and the customization will affect every store in the mall.  You should set the scope to mall when you want certain shopping tasks, such as registration, to be the same for all stores within the mall.

If a task has store scope, each store in the mall can customize it, resulting in more variety in the shopping experience between stores.  For example, if the SHOPCART_DSP view task is set to store scope, each store in the mall will be able to implement its own shopping cart page.  If a store administrator decides not to customize a task that has store scope, the task assignment for the mall will apply to that store.

Each task also has a default implementation that applies if it is not customized.  For a detailed description of each task, see "Appendix E, Net.Commerce Tasks" on page 613.

Any task that can be customized at the store level can also be customized at the mall level.  If a task is customized at both levels and a merchant reference number is passed into the task, the store level customization takes precedence.  The following summarizes how precedence is determined:

1. If the scope of the task is store, and if the task has been customized for the store, the store's version of the task will be performed.

2. Otherwise, if the task is customized for the mall, the mall's version of the task will be performed.

3. Otherwise, the default version will be performed.

By default, all tasks (view, exception, and process) are set to store scope, meaning that stores can provide their own implementations of the task.

## Changing Task Scope

To change the scope of a task (for example, to change it to mall scope in order to provide the same implementation across a mall), do the following:

1. On the task bar of the Site Manager, click **Task Management**. The Task Management form appears.

2. From the **Select Task Type** drop-down list, select the task that you want to modify.

3. From the **Scope** drop-down list, select **Mall** if you want the task to be controlled at the site level and be the same for all stores in the mall. Select **Store** if you want the task to be controlled at the store level and be customized differently for each store.

4. In the **Comment** field, enter a description of the task, if desired.

5. Click **Save**. Make sure that a confirmation message appears in the display area.

# Assigning Tasks to Macros and Overridable Functions

The Task Management form in the Site Manager lets you assign new or customized macros and overridable functions to the tasks that they were designed to implement. Any time you replace a macro or overridable function that implements a task, you need to assign the name of the new file to its corresponding task in order to activate it in the system.

It is not necessary to do this when you are initially setting up the site; only after you or a store administrator has begun to customize the store. For example, if a store administrator creates a new shopping cart page, you (as the site administrator) will be asked to assign the name of the macro file to the task that it implements (the SHOPCART_DSP view task). If the store administrator creates a new overridable function to change the way that the system determines the price of each item before the shopping cart is displayed, you will be asked to replace the supplied overridable function (GetBaseUnitPrc_1.0 (IBM,NC) with the name of the new function and assign it to the task that it implements (the GET_BASE_UNIT_PRC process task). If the store administrator does not customize the store (modify or create new macros, or create new overridable functions), you do not need to use the Task Management form.

For information about the tasks or overridable functions that are supplied by Net.Commerce, see "Chapter 9, Commands, Tasks, and Overridable Functions" on page 257. For information about modifying Net.Data macros, see "Chapter 8, Modifying the Supplied Store Pages" on page 213. For information about creating new macros, see "Chapter 7, A Net.Data Tutorial" on page 169. For information about assigning a macro to the task that it implements, see "Step 9. Activating the Macro" on page 228. For information about assigning an overridable function to the task that it implements, see "Assigning an Overridable Functions to its Task" on page 400.

# Specifying Shipping Providers

The site administrator is responsible for creating and maintaining a master list of all the shipping companies and types of shipping services that will be available to shoppers. The store administrators then select from this list the companies and services they want to offer in their stores.

To create this list, do the following:

1. On the task bar of the Site Manager, click **Shipping Providers**. The Shipping Service Providers form appears.

2. From the **Select** list, select **Add New Carrier/Shipping Mode**. If the fields contain information about another carrier, you can clear the fields by clicking **Clear**.

3. In the **Carrier** field, enter the name of the shipping company that offers the shipping service.

4. In the **Shipping Mode** field, enter the type of shipping service (for example, "overnight delivery" or "priority").

5. In the **Description** field, enter a brief description of the shipping company, if desired.

6. In **Custom Field 1** and **Custom Field 2**, enter additional information, if desired.

7. Click **Save**. The information is saved as a new record in the SHIPMODE (Merchant Shipping Mode) database table. Make sure that a confirmation message appears in the display area. The new carrier should now appear in the **Select** drop-down list.

# Cookies and Session Management

Net.Commerce uses session cookies to identify shoppers and track their activities. The first time that a shopper invokes a Net.Commerce command on your site after starting the browser, or when a registered shopper logs on to the site, the Net.Commerce server generates a session cookie for that shopper and sends it to the browser. The cookie is stored in the browser's memory until the shopper closes the browser. The browser will send the cookie back to the server each time a shopper requests an activity from the server (that is, invokes a command).

A session cookie contains the following information:

- A name and value. Each cookie is identified with a name of "SESSION_ID" and a value of the shopper's reference number (if the shopper is registered), or an internally generated reference number (if the shopper is not registered), which is followed by an encrypted string.

- The path and domain to which the cookie will be returned. The cookie will be returned by the browser only to sites that are in the domain that originally issued the cookie.

- The life-cycle of the cookie. The cookie is called a "session cookie" because its existence is temporary: the browser stores the cookie in memory and discards it when the shopper shuts down the browser. Net.Commerce does not currently use cookies that are set to specific expiry dates.

- SSL enablement. You can specify whether or not the cookie should be transmitted back over a non-SSL connection.

Session cookies enable you to tailor the shopping trip according to who is shopping. When a registered shopper logs on, and at the start of each command that the shopper invokes thereafter, the system retrieves from the database the shopper record that corresponds to the shopper reference number stored in the cookie, and stores the record in the server environment. The shopper record, which is now accessible to the system for the duration of the currently invoked command, enables you to build custom sites for each registered shopper. For example, if you have assigned different shoppers to different shopper groups, which are linked to differently tailored product pages, the system uses the shopper reference number to determine which shopping group a given shopper belongs to, in order to generate the appropriate tailored product pages "on the fly". The system will also retrieve the appropriate pricing information based on the shopper reference number; for example, any discounts that you have granted to the shopper group.

For more information about session cookies, see "The Cookie Class" on page 303. To learn how to create shopper groups, see "Creating Shopper Groups" on page 105. For information about assigning the shopper groups to specific templates, see "Chapter 4, Entering the Store Catalog" on page 79.

> **Tip:**
> It is advisable to enable all commands for SSL that are invoked after a cookie is set. SSL encrypts the data contained in the cookie, so that if the cookie is intercepted during transmission by an unauthorized third party, the data in it cannot be extracted. For more information, see "Specifying Command Security" below.

# Specifying Command Security

As site administrator, you can secure the supplied commands or any new commands that you create (see "Part 4, Customizing the Site" on page 255 for information about creating new commands) in two ways: by enabling them for SSL (Secure Sockets Layer) or by enabling them for authentication.

## SSL

Commands that pass personal information about a shopper (such as address information or a password) between the browser and the server should be executed in conjunction with SSL, which encrypts the information, to prevent its exposure to unauthorized individuals.

> **Note:**
> SSL may decrease performance. However, if you choose not to enable it, you take the risk that unauthorized individuals will be able to access sensitive data during its transmission between the browser and the server.

If you do not specify whether or not SSL is to be enabled for a command either at the store level, mall level, or default level, the system will automatically enable the following commands for SSL:

| | |
|---|---|
| AddressAdd | OrderDisplay |
| AddressForm | OrderList |
| AddressUpdate | RegisterForm |
| InterestItemDisplay | RegisterNew |
| Logon | RegisterUpdate |
| LogonForm | OrderItemList |
| OrdertItemDisplay | OrderProcess |

# Authentication

You can enable any command for authentication, which requires that the shopper be registered or logged on before the command can be invoked. For example, you can ensure that shoppers are registered or logged on before they can add an item to their shopping carts. To do this, you enable the command that performs the store operation (in this case, adding the item to the shopping cart) for authentication. When the command is enabled, if the shopper is registered or logged on, the command is invoked as usual; otherwise, the shopper is prompted for a user ID and password before being allowed to proceed.

> **Note:**
> For security measures, once shoppers have logged on, they should also be in SSL mode, in order to protect their personal information and the cookie. Therefore, for security reasons, if the command is enabled for authentication, it should also be enabled for SSL.

# Specifying SSL or Authentication

To enable or disable a command for SSL or authentication or both, do the following:

1.  On the task bar of the Site Manager, click **Command Security**. The Command Security Assignment form appears.

2.  From the **Store** drop-down list, select either of the following:

    *   The name of the store for which you want to assign the command.

    *   **Default Assignment,** to specify a security level for commands that have not been assigned to a store.

    A list of all commands that have not been previously assigned to the store appears in the **Commands** list.

3.  From the **Commands** list, select the command to which you want to assign a level of security. To select multiple commands, hold down the Shift key while you select each one.

4. Click the **Add To List** button to add the commands to the **Assigned Commands (SSL)(Authentication)** list. The commands are removed from the **Commands** list.

5. To assign SSL, authentication, or both to the command, select the **Enable SSL** checkbox, the **Enable Authentication** checkbox, or both. To assign neither, leave both boxes unchecked.

6. Click **Update**. A confirmation message appears, indicating that the commands have been successfully updated.

**Notes:**

- By default, the OrderProcess command is the only command that requires a shopper to be registered or logged on before an order can be submitted.

- All commands that were added to the **Assigned Commands (SSL)(Authentication)** list are affected. To change the assignment of any command, simply select it and enable or disable the appropriate check box.

- To enable a command for SSL, you should also begin the URL containing the command with the https secure protocol.

# Workshop: Designating Access to the OneStopPizza Shop's Database

In this workshop, you will do the following:

- Create an access control group and assign it to the store

- Designate a store administrator

- Assign the store administrator to the access control group

## Creating an Access Control Group

In this step, you will create an access control group based on the Store Administrator role, which lets a user access the forms in the Store Manager and manage the store's data.

1. Open the Administrator, as described in "Opening the Administrator" on page 34.

2. On the task bar, click **Site Manager** and then click **Access Groups** to display the Access Group Assignment form.

3. From the **Access Group Name (Store)** drop-down list, select **Store Administrators (OneStopPizza Shop)**.

4. In the **Access Group Name** field, change the name to OneStopPizza Shop admin.

5. From the **Store** drop-down list, select **OneStopPizza Shop**.

6. In the **Description** field, enter Store Administrator for OneStopPizza Shop.

7.   Click **Update**.  Ensure that a confirmation message appears, as shown in Figure 3.1 below:

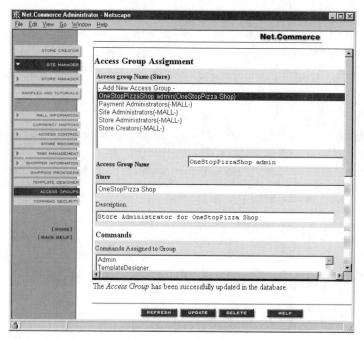

**Figure 3.1**  *The Access Group Assignment form.*

You have now successfully created an access group and assigned it to the store.

# Designating a Store Administrator

Now that you have created an access control group and assigned it to the store, you will designate a store administrator named John Smith.

1.   On the task bar, click **Access Control** to display the Access Control form.

2.   In the **Administrator's ID** field, type jsmith.

3.   In the corresponding fields, enter both the password and the password confirmation as smith.

4.   From the **Title** drop-down list, select **Mr**.

5.   In the **Last Name** field, enter Smith.

6.   In the **First Name** field, enter John.

7.   Click **Save**.

8. Click **OK** in the confirmation window. The information is saved as a new record in the SHOPPER and ACCTRL database tables. The form should look like Figure 3.2 below:

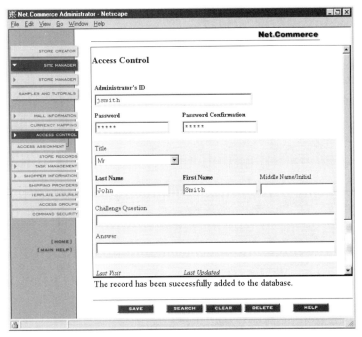

***Figure 3.2*** *The Access Control form.*

# Assigning the Store Administrator to Your Access Control Group

Now you will assign your new store administrator, John Smith, to the access control group that you created, to give him authority to manage the store's data.

1. On the task bar, click **Access Assignment** to display the Administrator - Access Group Assignment form.

2. From the **All Groups** drop-down list at the bottom of the form, select **OneStopPizza Shop admin (OneStopPizza Shop)**.

3. Click **Add Groups**. The store name now appears in the **Groups Assigned to Administrator** drop-down list.

4.  Click **Save** to update the database.  Ensure that a confirmation message appears.  The form should look like Figure 3.3 below:

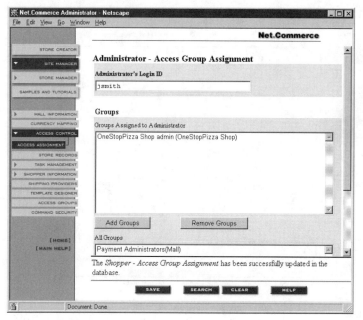

**Figure 3.3**  *Administrator - Access Group Assignment form.*

John Smith now has authority to manage the store's data using the Store Manager.

5.  Close the browser window.

You have now completed this workshop.  In the next workshop in Chapter 4, you will start to enter the store's products and categories in the database.

# Chapter 4, Entering the Store Catalog

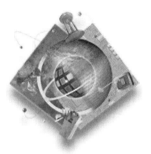

A store administrator who has been given write-access to the store's database by the site administrator can begin to populate the database with information about the store's catalog. This chapter describes how to use the Store Manager to enter all information about the store, including contact information; information about the store's categories, products, and items; pricing and applicable discount information; shipping and tax information; and any other data relevant to your business. In the workshop, you will enter product and category data for the pizza store.

This chapter covers the following topics:

- The Store Manager
- Opening the Store Manager
- Storing Images, HTML Files, and Templates
- Specifying Store Contact, Currency, and Tax Rate Information
- Creating Product Categories
- Defining Shipping Services
- Entering Product Information
- Implementing Discounts
- Creating Shopper Groups
- Creating an Interactive Catalog
- Workshop: Adding a New Catalog to the OneStopPizza Shop

# The Store Manager

The Store Manager consists of a collection of online forms that enables a store administrator to create and manage an interactive catalog without having to be familiar with the database schema. It provides a user interface to the database for quickly and easily entering the following information:

- **Currency and Contact Information.** Information about the currency in which prices are displayed, and the store's address and a contact person for customer inquiries.

- **Store Tax Rates.** A store administrator who is creating a store within a mall framework can override the tax rates previously defined by the site administrator with new tax rates that will apply only to the store.

- **Category Information.** The store's merchandise is organized into categories and subcategories that will serve as navigation routes for shoppers. Each category is entered into the database, along with a description, thumbnail and/or full-sized image, templates for displaying the images, and any other descriptive information that is required.

- **Shipping Services.** The shipping services and options that will be available to shoppers are defined, and the way that shipping charges will be calculated for the products (for example, by weight or by size) is determined.

- **Product Information.** Information about the store's products is entered into the database, including detailed descriptions, SKU numbers, prices, thumbnail and full-sized images, shipping codes for calculating the shipping charges, templates for displaying the products in the store, and any other descriptive information that is required.

- **Discount Information.** Discounts are defined and applied to selected products.

- **Shopper Groups.** Shoppers are assigned to shopper groups, and different prices are assigned to products based on the groups, in order to entitle certain shoppers to discounts or other incentives for purchasing from the store. The administrator can also arrange to display the store pages differently to certain shoppers, by assigning different templates to different groups.

For the remainder of this chapter, you will take the role of the store administrator, and it will be assumed that the site administrator has granted you access to the functions that enable you to populate the database with information related to the store's catalog.

**Notes:**
If your store was created using the Store Creator, note the following:

- At least one store tax rate and one shipping service have been automatically created in the database, and can be modified using the Store Manager. (For details on modifying store tax rates, see "Specifying Store Contact, Currency, and Tax Rate Information" on page 83. For details on shipping services, see "Defining Shipping Services" on page 88.)

- Once you start to add your own product catalog using the Store Manager, you cannot return to the Store Creator to change store settings. If you do, the modifications made in the Store Manager will be overwritten by the sample products selected in the Store Creator.

# Opening the Store Manager

To open the Store Manager, do the following:

1. Open the Administrator, as described in "Opening the Administrator" on page 34.

2. When prompted, enter the logon ID and password that were assigned to you by the site administrator, and then click **Logon**.

3. On the task bar, click **Store Manager**.

   The Store Manager opens.

# Storing Images, HTML Files, and Templates

When you enter product and category information in the database, you need to also specify the location of any images that the shopper will see, and the templates (Net.Data macros) that will be used to create the product and category pages. It is important that you properly define the directory now, in order to avoid having to change the location for hundreds of products and categories after they have been entered in the database. Normally, the directory that you define will also be used to store all other graphics required by your store, such as the store logo, background images, and navigation buttons, and any HTML files.

## Storing Images and HTML Files

When deciding on a storage place for your images and HTML files, you have two options: you can store them in the default location, which is under the Web server document root; or you can store them in a different directory and configure the Web server to look for them there.

### Using the Web Server Document Root

The Web server document root is the root directory that the store's URL (for example, `www.OneStopPizzaShop.com`) resolves to on the Web server. The Web server will automatically search in this directory for HTML files and images. For the Domino Go Webserver, the default Web server document root directory is:

> **WIN** `\ibm\www\html\`
> **AIX** `/usr/lpp/internet/server_root/pub/`

On the other hand, if you created your store using the Store Creator, the following directory was automatically created to store your images and HTML files:

> **WIN** `\ibm\www\html\<store_name>`
> **AIX** `/usr/lpp/internet/server_root/pub/<store_name>`

where `<store_name>` is the name of your store. To enter the name of the HTML files or images in the database or in macros or HTML files, you must prefix them with the `/<store_name>/` directory.

If you are using the Netscape Enterprise Web server, consult its documentation for its document root.

## Defining a New Directory

If you do not want to store your images and HTML files under the Web server's root directory, you can create a new directory and then add a `Pass` statement in the Web server configuration file. The `Pass` statement maps logical directory names to physical directory names. The configuration file is in the following directory:

> **WIN** `<drive>:WINNT/httpd.cnf`
> **AIX** `/etc/httpd.conf`

For example, say you want to store all your images in the following directory:

> **WIN** `\ibm\netcommerce3\html\en_US\store_name\images\`
> **AIX** `/usr/lpp/NetCommerce3/html/en_US/store_name/images/`

You must add the following `Pass` statement to the Web server configuration file so that the `/images/` directory will map to the directory above:

```
Pass /images/*
<drive>:\IBM\NetCommerce3\html\en_US\store_name\images\*
```

where `<drive>` is the machine on which Net.Commerce is installed.

Now when you enter in the database, or in Net.Data macros and HTML files, the names of images prefixed by `/images/`, the Web server will be able to find them.

# Storing Templates

You can store the templates (Net.Data macro files) for your product and category pages in any directory. Each directory that you create must be added to the `MACRO_PATH` statement in the `db2www.ini` configuration file, so that Net.Data can execute the macro. For more information, see "Storing Net.Data Macros and Include Files" on page 195.

If you created your store using the Store Creator, the following directories were automatically created to store the templates:

The category template `cat1.d2w` is stored in the following directory:

> **WIN** `\IBM\NetCommerce3\macro\en_US\category\<store_name>\`
> **AIX** `/usr/lpp/NetCommerce3/macro/en_US/category/<store_name>/`

The product template `prod1.d2w` is stored in the following directory:

> **WIN** `\IBM\NetCommerce3\macro\en_US\product\<store_name>\`
> **AIX** `/usr/lpp/NetCommerce3/macro/en_US/product/<store_name>/`

All other templates are stored in the following directory:

> **WIN** `\IBM\NetCommerce3\macro\en_US\<store_name>\`
> **AIX** `/usr/lpp/NetCommerce3/macro/en_US/<store_name>/`

where `<store_name>` is the name of your store.

To enter the names of these templates into the database, you must prefix them with the `/<store_name>/` directory.

# Specifying Store Contact, Currency, and Tax Rate Information

On the Store and Merchant Information form, you can enter a store address, and a contact person for customer inquiries. You can also specify the ISO 4217 currency code that will be used to indicate the currency used in your store. (If your store was created by the Store Creator, this code will have been automatically created in the database, based on your language version of Net.Commerce, but can be changed here. For the English version, the default code is USD.) If you are creating a store within a mall, you can also define store-level tax rates that will override the rates that were set at the mall level using the Site Manager. (If you are creating a single store, it does not make any difference whether the tax rates are set at the mall level or the store level.)

1. On the task bar of the Store Manager, click **Store Information**. The Store and Merchant Information form appears.

2. From the **Select Store** drop-down list, select the store you want to work with. The fields fill with any store information that is in the database.

3. To change the store name and store description, change the information in the corresponding fields.

4. In the **Currency** field, enter the appropriate ISO 4217 code to specify the currency that will be used for the product prices.

5. In the appropriate fields in the **Merchant Company Information** section, enter the company's street address, city, state or province, and country.

6. If you want to define store-level tax rates, do the following:

   a) Deselect the **Use Mall Tax Rates** check box (it is selected by default).

   b) In the **Tax Rate 1** field, enter the sales tax (expressed as a percentage) that will be applied to product prices. In the corresponding **Tax Name** field, enter the tax name.

   c) If more than one tax applies, enter the rates and names of the remaining taxes in the other fields.

   > **Note:**
   > If later you decide to use the tax rates that are defined at the mall level, you can select the **Use Mall Tax Rates** check box; however, you will lose the store-level rates you have defined.

7. Fill in any other fields, if desired. If you make an error, simply type over the incorrect information, or click **Clear** to clear the fields and start over.

8. Click **Save** to add the information to the database. Make sure that a confirmation message appears in the display area. If you have missed a mandatory field, a message will appear. If you receive a message, click **OK**; the cursor will reposition on the field that requires information. Enter the appropriate information, and click **Save** again.

9. To correct any mistakes made after saving the information, repeat the above steps.

# Creating Product Categories

To allow shoppers to easily browse your store and find what they are looking for with just a few clicks of the mouse, you need to organize your products into categories. Properly structured product categories lay out pathways for shoppers to surf through, starting at the home page and ending at a product page.

To create product categories, it is recommended that you first arrange your products in a hierarchy, or inverted *tree,* so that you can clearly see and control the navigation routes that shoppers may take to find products. The tree begins at a root category (which by default is the name of the store), and branches out into increasingly specific subcategories until it cannot be further divided into categories. Each lowest level category, which contains only products, is a *leaf.* A category is the *parent* to the categories immediately below it and a *child* of the one above it.

With certain product lines, you can place both products and categories in the same level of the tree. For example, within the category of *Woodworking Tools*, a hardware store may offer a brand of hand-powered drill that does not fall into any of the existing leaf categories (*Chisels*, *Planes*, and *Saws*). To accommodate this product, we could create another leaf category, *Drills*, under *Woodworking Tools*. But if this is the only hand-powered drill available, then the new leaf category would contain only one product. If you would rather avoid this, you can insert the name of the drill into the tree directly below *Woodworking Tools*, alongside the leaf categories. The parent category *Woodworking Tools* would then lead directly to three leaf categories and one product. The resulting Web page you create would contain information about the drill and descriptions of the three leaf categories (categories *Chisels*, *Planes*, and *Saws*) with links to their products.

It is also possible for a product to fall into more than one category. For example, some shoppers might look for a power drill under "power tools", while others would look for it under "machinery". To ensure that shoppers see this tool when they click either category, you can place it beneath both categories in the tree.

To help you organize your categories and to make entering them in the database easier, it is advisable to sketch a diagram of the tree on a sheet of paper beforehand. Figure 4.1 shows an example of a tree diagram for the hardware store.

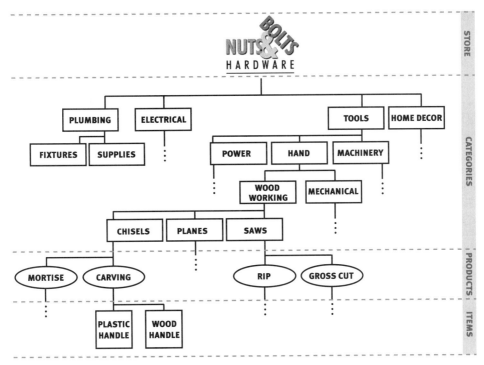

**Figure 4.1** *A tree diagram of the categories in a hardware store.*

**Note:**
At this step, you do not add the products that fall under the leaf categories. They have been included in the hand-drawn category tree as a reminder to add them later.

# Category Information Req uirements

Before you begin to create your categories, you should have ready all the information that you plan to enter for each one. It is recommended that you include all descriptive information when you create the categories, even if you have not yet created the images and templates that will display them (you need only enter the names of the image and macro files). This will prevent you from later having to update each category record, which could add up to thousands.

For each category you define, ensure that you have the following information:

- Its name (this is mandatory)
- Its sequence number (position relative to the other categories at the same level)
- One or more descriptions
- The name of the image file (thumbnail, full-sized, or both) that will visually describe it
- The name of its parent category

- The name of the template (Net.Data macro file) that will display it on a store page
- The name of shopper groups to which it will be shown (if you intend to show different categories to different groups of shoppers). If no shopper group is specified, the category can be viewed by all shoppers.

# Choosing a Category Creation Method

There are two ways to enter product categories in the database: with either the Store Manager or the Mass Import utility. The Store Manager provides forms for entering categories one at a time, and is ideal for entering small amounts of category data, updating individual categories once they have been added to the database, deleting individual categories, and adding a few categories at a time as the store's catalog grows. The Mass Import utility is faster for entering large amounts of category data or for importing data from another database, because it uses one text file to enter all the data.

## Using the Store Manager Forms

Creating each category for your store using the Store Manager is a two-step process. First you enter the category in the database, and then you assign the template that will display it in the store.

### Entering a Category

To enter a category in the database, do the following:

1.  Enable the caching feature on your browser. If you encounter an error when you create product categories, clear your browser's cache.

2.  On the task bar of the Store Manager, click **Product Categories**. The Product Categories form appears.

3.  From the **Select Store** drop-down list, select the store for which you want to add a category. Any existing categories will appear below the store name. Each time you create a new category, a category reference number appears, in brackets, beside the category name on the tree. You will later use this number to assign products to the category. You do not need to write it down, since you can display it again when you enter product information.

    > **Note:**
    > You cannot add items or products to the category tree. Products are linked to categories and items are linked to products using the Product/Item Information form. For information on how to add products and items, see "Entering Product Information" on page 92.

4.  Choose one of the following options:

    - To add your first categories beneath the root, click the store's name.
    - To add a child category, click the parent category under which it should appear.

    Your selection appears in italics.

5. From the action bar on the bottom, click **Add**. The Add New Category form appears.

6. In the **Name** field, enter the name of the category you want to add.

7. From the **Publish** drop-down list, select either **Yes** to display the category when your online store opens or **No** to delay its inclusion.

8. In the **Sequence Number** field, enter a number to indicate this category's position on the page in relation to the other categories of the same level in the tree. For example, enter 1 to position this category first on the page, 2 to position it second, and so forth.

9. If desired, enter descriptions in the fields provided.

10. To include thumbnail (miniature) and full-sized images for the category, enter the file names in the **Thumbnail Image** and **Full-sized Image** fields. If the image is stored on your Web server, enter its path and file name. (Make sure your image files are stored in a directory that your Web server has been configured to access. For more information, see "Storing Images and HTML Files" on page 81.) Otherwise, enter its URL.

11. If you make an error, you can type directly over the field, or click **Clear** to clear the fields and start over.

12. When you are done, click **Save**. A new record is inserted into the CATEGORY and CGRYREL tables in the database, and you are returned to the category tree. The category appears in the tree in the specified location.

13. Repeat these steps to create other categories in the store.

### *Assigning a Template to a Category*

Once you have created a category, you need to assign to it the template (Net.Data macro) that will display it in the store. If you have created shopper groups, you can assign different templates to different groups, allowing you to customize the way your categories will look to members of different groups. (For information on how to create shopper groups, see "Creating Shopper Groups" on page 105.)

1. On the category tree, select the category to which you want to assign the template. The selected category appears in red italics.

2. On the action bar below, click **Template.**

3. The Category Template Assignment form appears. Ensure that the category information is displayed.

4. To assign the same category template to all shoppers, select **None** from the **Shopper Group** drop-down list. To assign a template to a specific shopper group, select the group you want.

    a) In the **Template** field, enter the path and file name of the category template you want to use.

    b) Ensure that you have specified the macro path in the db2www.ini file. For more information, see "Specifying a Macro Directory" on page 195.

c) In the **Description** field, enter a brief description of the template, if desired.

d) If the template has already been created, you can click **View Template** to see it.

e) Click **Save**. A new record is inserted into the CATESGP (Shopper Group Category Template) table in the database. Make sure that a confirmation message appears in the display area.

5. Click **Return** to return to the Product Categories form.

6. Repeat these steps to assign templates to any other categories that you have created.

## Using the Mass Import Utility

The Mass Import utility offers you a fast way to import large amounts of product data into the database. For information on how to use it, see "Chapter 5, Mass-Importing Product and Category Data" on page 123.

# Defining Shipping Services

At some point in the catalog creation process, you must choose the shipping providers that will be used by your store and define how each product in the store will be shipped. Shoppers can then choose from the shipping services that you have made available. Defining shipping services is a three-step process. First, you select from the master list (which will have previously been created by the site administrator) all the shipping carriers and modes (for example, FastDelivery, Overnight) that you want to offer in your store. Next, you create shipping codes for each carrier and mode, with specific calculation methods and charges. Finally, you assign a shipping code to each product in the database, to define how it will be shipped and how its shipping charges will be calculated.

It is advisable to define the shipping services before you start entering products in the database; however, if you enter the products first, all you need is the name of the shipping code for each product, and you can define the details of the code later. Depending on how you have defined the codes, you can later change the way many products are shipped without having to enter new information for each product in the database.

If your store was created using the Store Creator, the site administrator has already defined up to three shipping services for it. Each service has a fixed shipping charge that is applied to each order. If required, you can change its details; for example, its calculation method. Or, you can select additional shipping services (if the site administrator has defined them using the Site Manager), assign to them new calculation methods to calculate the shipping charge, and assign them to different products.

The shipping functions provided in the Net.Commerce system are designed to suit many online purchasing applications and to maximize flexibility for merchants and options for shoppers. They can, however, be customized. You can also integrate an existing automated shipping application instead of using the one that is supplied, by creating an overridable function to modify the shipping process. For more information, see "Overridable Functions" on page 272.

# Selecting Shipping Carriers and Modes

The first step in defining shipping services for your store is to choose the carriers and modes that will be available in your store. Ensure that they have been previously defined by the site administrator.

1. On the task bar of the **Store Manager**, click **Shipping Services**. The Shipping Services form appears.

2. From the **Select Store** drop-down list, select the store for which you want to select shipping carriers and modes.

3. From the **Supported Shipping Mode** drop-down list, select **Add New Supported Shipping Mode**.

4. From the **Shipping Carrier and Mode** drop-down list, select the shipping carrier and mode you want.

5. In the **Start Date** and **End Date** fields, enter the start and end dates that you want this carrier to be available for your store. The date must be in the format year-month-day, but variations are acceptable: for example, 98-01-4, 98-01-04, 1998-01-4, or 1998-01-04. To modify the format, refer to the Net.Commerce online help.

6. Click **Save**. The information is saved as a new record in the MSHIPMODE (Merchant Shipping Mode) table. The new carrier now appears in the **Supported Shipping Mode** drop-down list, and will be available when you define shipping details. Make sure that a confirmation message appears in the display area.

# Creating Product Shipping Codes

After you have selected the shipping carriers and modes for your stores, you need to create the shipping codes that will later be assigned to each product. A shipping code is a name or number that identifies a particular set of shipping details, such as a shipping carrier, the effective dates that the carrier's services are offered, and how shipping costs are calculated (such as by weight or by unit). For each code, you can select the desired combination of the above details. By associating products with a shipping code, you can change the way those products are shipped by just redefining the code.

To offer your shoppers more options, you can define each code with more than one carrier, mode of service, and method for calculating the shipping cost. Shoppers can then choose the shipping option they want from the list you have created.

> **Note:**
> If a shopper does not select a shipping method, no shipping charge can be calculated. Therefore, if you create your own order forms, it is essential that you make this step compulsory. (The default order forms supplied with Net.Commerce system include this compulsory step.)

Using shipping codes also enables you to ship similar products in the same manner by linking them all to the same code. Any changes to the code will automatically be applied to all the products linked to it. Each shipping code defined is typically assigned to groups of products that share common shipping requirements. For example, all books could be assigned a shipping code called "printed matter," all compact discs could be assigned the code "small package," and so forth.

Products are linked to shipping codes on the Product/Item Information form. If a product is not given a shipping code on that form, then no shipping charge will be calculated. It is not necessary to define all the properties of shipping codes before you assign them to products: all you will require is a name for the shipping code you assign. However, you may prefer to define the shipping code before assigning it to products.

If your store was created using the Store Creator, a shipping code called SCSHP has already been created for each shipping service that was defined for the store. This shipping code can be modified; for example, you can change the calculation method (which is currently Quantity/ Range/Total).

To create a product shipping code, do the following:

1. On the task bar of the **Store Manager**, click **Shipping Services** and then **Product Codes**. The Product Shipping Codes form appears.

2. From the **Supported Product Shipping Code** drop-down list, select **Add New Code**.

3. In the **Product Shipping Code** field, enter a name for the code you are creating. It can be any name or number of your choice.

4. Select a calculation method from the drop-down list provided. You have the choices shown in Table 4.1 below:

*Table 4.1  The supplied shipping calculation methods.*

| Calculation Method | Description |
| --- | --- |
| Quantity/Cumulative/Total | The cost calculated for the total quantity of items within each specified range. For example, $2.00 for 1 to 5 books, and $1.00 for the next 5 (i.e., 6 to 10) books. A shipment of 7 books will cost $3.00 ($2.00 + $1.00). |
| Quantity/Cumulative/Unit | The cost for each item, calculated for each specified range. For example, $2.00 per book for 1 to 5 books, and $1.00 per book for the next 5 (i.e., 6 to 10) books. A shipment of 7 books will cost $12.00 ($2.00 x 5 + $1.00 x 2). |
| Quantity/Range/Total | The cost for the total order, falling within a specified range. For example, $1.00 per order for 1 to 5 books, and $2.00 per order for 6 to 10 books. A shipment of 7 books will cost $2.00. This calculation method is used by the Store Creator for all shipping services that are defined for the store. |
| Quantity/Range/Unit | The cost for each item, based on total quantity falling within a specified range. For example, $1.00 per book for 1 to 5 books, and $2.00 per book for 6 to 10 books. A shipment of 7 books will cost $14.00 (7 x $2.00). |

*Continued on next page*

*Table 4.1* *Continued*

| Calculation Method | Description |
|---|---|
| Weight/Cumulative/Total | The cost for total weight of shipment, calculated for each specified range. For example, $2.00 for 1 to 5 kg, $1.00 for the next 5 (i.e., 6 to 10) kg. A shipment weighing 7 kg will cost $3.00 ($2.00 + $1.00). |
| Weight/Cumulative/Unit | The cost for each unit of weight, calculated for each specified range. For example, $2.00 per kg for 1 to 5 kg, and $1.00 per kg for the next 5 (i.e., 6 to 10) kg. A shipment weighing 7 kg will cost $12.00 ($2.00 x 5 + $1.00 x 2). |
| Weight/Range/Total | The cost for total weight of shipment, falling within a specified range. For example, $1.00 for 1 to 5 kg, and $2.00 for 6 to 10 kg. A shipment weighing 7 kg will cost $2.00. |
| Weight/Range/Unit | The cost for each unit of weight, based on total weight within a specified range. For example, $1.00 per kilogram for 1 to 5 kg, and $1.00 per kilogram for 6 to 10 kg. A shipment weighing 7 kg will cost $14.00 (7 x $2.00). |

**Note:**
If you select calculation by weight, ensure that a weight is specified for the product on the Product/Item Information form; otherwise, no shipping cost will be charged to the customer. Also, in order for shipping charges to be calculated correctly, weight must be expressed in the same units for all products that use the same shipping codes.

5.   In the **Shipping Code Description** field, enter a brief description, if desired.

6.   Click **Save.** A new record is inserted into the PRSPCODE (Product Shipping Code) table in the database. Make sure that a confirmation message appears in the display area. The code also appears in the **Supported Product Shipping Code** drop-down list.

# Defining Shipping Code Details

After you have assigned a name and a calculation method to a shipping code, you need to specify which shipping mode (or modes—you can enter more than one) will be used to ship all products linked to that code, and the ranges for the calculation method.

1.   On the task bar of the **Store Manager**, click **Shipping Services** and then **Shipping Details**. The Shipping Details form appears.

2.   From the **Product Shipping Code** drop-down list, select the shipping code.

3.   From the **Shipping Mode** drop-down list, select the carrier and mode.

4. In the **Range: minimum** and **Range: maximum** fields, enter minimum and maximum ranges (of units or weight) for the shipping calculation. For example, if you want the cost to be applied for shipments of 0 to 5 items, enter 0 and 6 in these fields. The higher number is not included in the range; only the lower number. Thus, a range of "1 to 6 items" includes 1, 2, 3, 4, and 5; and a range of "6 to 10 items" includes 6, 7, 8, and 9. This is particularly useful when specifying weight ranges. For example, weight ranges of "0 to 5 kg" and "5 to 10 kg" would place a shipment weighing 4.999 kg in the first range, and one weighing 5.0 kg in the second.

5. In the **Charge (Total Cost)** field, enter the shipping charge for either the total cost or the unit cost, whichever applies.

> **Note:**
> Ensure that you enter information in the field for the same shipping calculation method, either total cost or unit cost, that you selected for this code on the Product Shipping Code form. The calculation method appears beside the code name.

6. In the **Start Date** and **End Date** fields, enter start and end dates for the specified link to be valid, if desired. The date must be in the format year-month-day, but variations are acceptable; for example, 98-01-4, 98-01-04, 1998-01-4, or 1998-01-04. To modify the format, refer to the product's online help.

7. In the **Country** field, enter the country that the carrier services.

8. In the **Jurisdiction** field, specify the jurisdiction (if applicable) for the shipping service.

9. Click **Create**. The information is saved as a new record in the SHIPPING table in the database. Make sure that a confirmation message appears in the display area. The shipping details record is now added to the database.

# Entering Product Information

Once you have created your product categories, you can begin populating the database with product information. You can also search for and modify information about products, and delete products that are no longer available. For information on how to do this, see the online information.

## Understanding Products Versus Items

Before you begin to enter your product information into the database, it is important that you understand the distinction between products and items, so that you can properly classify and store your products.

In the Net.Commerce system, a *product* is a tangible unit of merchandise or a service that has a specific name and manufacturer. An example would be a style and make of hammer, denim jeans, or automobile, or a service such as a particular wilderness tour or type of engine tune-up. Products are identified by product numbers. If a product is available in only one form (no variation in size, color, and so forth), such as a magazine, then it is identified by a SKU number.

Products have a parent category, but cannot be further divided into child categories. If, however, they are available in more than one format (different color, material, and so forth), then they are divided into these formats, called items.

An *item* is a product with specific set of attributes. For example, if a framer's hammer is available with either a wood or a plastic handle, then both these forms are items of the framer's hammer. Similarly, a particular size and color of a label of denim jeans is an item of that label; and a particular model of automobile in red, with an automatic transmission and air conditioning, is an item of that model. Each item has a unique SKU for stockkeeping purposes.

## Product Information Req uirements

Before you begin to enter information about the store's products, you should know exactly how you want to display and describe each one. It is recommended that you add all descriptive information at the same time, even if the images and templates that will display the products have not yet been created (you need only enter the names of the image and macro files). This will prevent you from later having to update each product record, which could add up to thousands.

For each product you define, ensure that you have the following required information:

- The name of the product
- Its unique product number and the SKU numbers for each of its items, to identify them (this is mandatory)
- Its price
- The parent reference number, to link it to its parent category
- One or more descriptions
- The name of the image files (thumbnail, full-sized, or both) that will visually describe the product
- The name of the template (Net.Data macro file) that will display the product on a store page
- Its shipping code, to define how it will be shipped. If the shipping code calculates shipping prices based on weight, you need to supply the weight, using the same unit (kilograms, pounds, and so forth) that is used in the shipping code. If you do not supply the weight, and the shipping code assigned to the product uses a weight calculation, then no shipping cost will be charged to the customer. The same will occur if you do not specify a shipping code.
- Its items and their attributes, including prices (if the product has variations)
- The names of shopper groups, if you intend to show different products or offer different product prices to different groups. (If you do not specify any shopper groups, the product will be displayed to all shoppers and always feature the same price.)

# Choosing a Product Creation Method

There are two ways to enter products in the database: with either the Store Manager or the Mass Import utility. The Store Manager provides forms for entering products one at a time, and is ideal for entering small amounts of product data, updating or deleting individual products, and adding a few products at a time as the store's catalog grows. The Mass Import utility is faster for entering large amounts of product data or for importing data from another database, because it uses one text file to enter all the data.

## Using the Store Manager Forms

Entering product information using the forms provided by the Store Manager is a three-step process. First, you define the product by providing high-level information about it, including a name and SKU number, parent category, and shipping code. Then, if the product does not have any variations, you enter its price; otherwise, you define the product items and their individual attributes and prices. The last step is to assign the template that will display the product and any items in the store. You also have the option of assigning a product to multiple parents, if it falls under more than one category or if you wish to expose it from more than one location in your store.

### Defining the Product

For each product, you must enter a unique SKU. You can also enter a name, parent category, one or more descriptions, a thumbnail and full-sized image, a shipping code, a tax code (if you are using Taxware International to calculate taxes), the inventory at hand, shipping dimensions, and any custom information required by your store. If the shipping code calculates shipping prices based upon weight, you must also specify a weight.

1.  On the task bar of the **Store Manager**, click **Product Information**. The Product/Item Information form appears.

2.  From the **Select Store** drop-down list, select the store for which you want to add products.

3.  From the **Input For** drop-down list, select **Product**.

4.  In the **Product Number or Item SKU** field, enter the product number. It can be any combination of numeric and alphanumeric characters.

    > **Note:**
    > Product numbers and item SKUs are case-sensitive in Net.Commerce. For example, product number BR-77-T is not the same as product number BR-77-t.

5.  Leave the **Product/Item Reference Number** field blank. Once you create and save the product in the database, the system will assign a number to it and fill this field.

6.  Click **Select Parent...** The Product Categories window appears. Note the number that is assigned to the parent category for this product from the category tree. Close the window.

7.  In the **Parent Reference Number** field, enter the reference number of the parent category.

8.  From the **Publish** drop-down list, select either **Yes** to display this product in your store as soon as the information is entered, or **No** to wait until later.

9.  In the **Thumbnail Image** and **Full-sized Image** fields, enter the path and file name of your thumbnail and full-sized image files (if available). If the image is stored on your Web server, enter its path and file name. (Make sure you have stored your image files in a directory that your Web server has been configured to access.) Otherwise, enter its URL.

10. From the **Product Shipping Code** drop-down list, select the shipping code.

11. If you are using Taxware International to calculate taxes, enter the number of the tax code that calculates the tax for this product in the **Tax Code** field. To see a list of available tax codes, click the **Tax Code List** button. Click a code in this list to place the code number in the **Tax Code** field.

12. Enter information in the other fields, if appropriate.

> **Note:**
> If you want to express inches in the **Unit of Measure** field, type  in. Do not use double quotes (").

13. If you make a mistake, type directly over the incorrect information, or click **Clear** to clear the fields and start over.

14. When you are satisfied that the product information is accurate and complete, click **Save**. The information is saved as a new record in the PRODUCT table in the database. Make sure that a confirmation message appears.

### *Entering a Price*

Once you have defined a product, you can enter its price. If the product does not have items, you specify its price at the product level; if it does, you typically define its items and then assign each item a price. For example, if you define a book in the database and it does not have variations, you would assign it a price. If however it comes in hardback and paperback versions that are priced differently, you must define these items and then assign a different price to each item. For information on defining items, see "Entering Items and their Attributes" on page 99.

You can enter and manage multiple prices for the same product or item; for example, a regular price, sale prices, and reduced prices for shopper groups. In such instances, the Net.Commerce server must have a way to determine which price to display when a shopper views the product or item. To determine the correct price of a product or item, the Net.Commerce server collects all the prices for that item that are valid for a shopper group (or for everybody, if no shopper group has been specified) at the current date and time. It then selects the one with the highest precedence value. Higher numbers represent higher precedence values. Suppose, for example, that on a particular day the valid prices are a regular price with precedence 0, a sale price with precedence 1, and a shopper group price with precedence 2. A member of the shopper group accessing the product page would see the shopper group price, while another shopper would see the sale price.

To enter a price, do the following:

1. On the task bar of the **Store Manager**, click **Product Information**. The Product/Item Information form appears.

2. If the product for which you want to define a price is not currently displayed, display it using one of the following methods:

3. If you know the product number or item SKU, enter it in **the Product Number or Item SKU** field, and click **Update Form**. The form fills with information about the product.

> **Note:**
> Some searchable fields in Net.Commerce are case-sensitive. To generate reliable search results, ensure that the product number or item SKU is accurate.

4. If you do not know the product number or item SKU, enter a piece of information that identifies it in one or more of the fields. From the **Input For** drop-down list, select **Product** to search for a product, or **Item** to search for an item, and then click **Search**. A list of all the products or items that satisfy your search criteria appears at the bottom of the screen. Click a product or item in this list to fill the fields of the form with information about it.

5. For example, if you select **Product** from the **Input For** drop-down list and enter a store name, a search will generate a list of all the products or items available for that store. If you select **Item** from the **Input For** drop-down list and enter a product reference number in the **Parent Reference Number** field, a search will display all the items that fall under that product.

6. On the task bar, click **Prices.** The Price Information form appears.

7. Choose from the following options:

   - To enter the regular price:

     a) Enter the regular price and currency of the product or item in the appropriate fields.

     b) In the **Precedence** field, enter a low number (for example, 1).

     c) To offer this price to all shoppers, select **None** from the **Shopper Group** drop-down list. You may leave the other fields blank.

     d) Click **Save**. A new record is inserted into the PRODPRCS (Product Price) table in the database. Ensure that a confirmation message appears in the display area.

   - To enter a sale price for all shoppers:

     a) Enter the price and currency in the appropriate fields.

     b) In the **Precedence** field, enter a number that is higher than the one you entered for the regular price (for example, 2). A higher number indicates that this price takes precedence over the regular price during the period that you will specify. Note that you can use floating decimal points, so that you can define the precedence of a new price in any position relative to existing prices. For example, you can enter 1.5 to give a price higher precedence than a price with a value of 1 and lower precedence than a price with a value of 2.

c) From the **Shopper Group** drop-down list, select **None**.

d) Enter the start and end dates that the sale price will be in effect.

e) Click **Save**. A new record is inserted into the PRODPRCS (Product Price) table in the database. Ensure that a confirmation message appears in the display area.

- To enter a reduced price for a shopper group, do the following. (Note that before you can assign shopper group prices, you must create shopper groups. For information on how to do this, see "Creating Shopper Groups" on page 105.)

a) Enter the price and currency in the appropriate fields.

b) To give this price precedence over both the regular price and the sale price, enter a number that is higher than the previous values (for example, 3) in the **Precedence** field. If you want the sale price to take precedence over the shopper group price, enter a number between the values for those two prices (for example, 1.5).

c) From the drop-down list, select the shopper group to which this price applies.

d) Enter the start and end dates that the shopper group price will be in effect.

e) Click **Save**. A new record is inserted into the PRODPRCS (Product Price) table in the database. Ensure that a confirmation message appears in the display area.

8. Repeat the above steps for other products or items to which you want to assign prices.

### Defining Attributes

After you have defined a product, you can enter its attributes into the database. For example, a product such as a particular brand of pants can have attribute types of size, color, fabric, and so forth.

> **Note:**
> Do not confuse product attributes with item attributes. Product attributes are attribute types assigned at the product level; item attributes are the corresponding attribute values assigned to the product's items. The item attributes for the pants could be blue, waist 36, length 38, and so forth. Shoppers select specific item attributes when they make online purchases. You must therefore create item attributes to allow them to make these selections. To create item attributes, you first have to define the attribute type at the product level.

You can also use the product attributes to assign key descriptive terms that can be used in product searches and for other data management purposes. Key words can reflect inventory classifications or suppliers' requirements, and be used for data management purposes. For example, a clothing distributor may find it useful to create an attribute type of "fabric," and then assign values such as "denim," "wool," and so forth to the various products in inventory. The merchant can then search the database for all products made of denim (using the Product

Attributes form), to determine the inventory levels of this line of merchandise. This task involves assigning attribute values at the product level. For this application, product attributes can be considered an enhanced method of describing products that allow for more sophisticated data management.

To define an attribute, do the following:

1.  On the task bar of the Store Manager, click **Product Information**. The Product/Item Information form appears.

2.  If the product is not currently displayed, display it using one of the following methods:

    *   If you know the product number or item SKU, enter it in **the Product Number or Item SKU** field, and click **Update Form**. The form fills with information about the product.

    > **Note:**
    > Some searchable fields in Net.Commerce are case-sensitive. To generate reliable search results, ensure that the product number or item SKU is accurate.

    *   If you do not know the product number or item SKU, enter a piece of information that identifies it in one or more of the fields. From the **Input For** drop-down list, select **Product** to search for a product, or **Item** to search for an item, and then click **Search**. A list of all the products or items that satisfy your search criteria appears at the bottom of the screen. Click a product or item in this list to fill the fields of the form with information about it. For example, if you select **Product** from the **Input For** drop-down list and enter a store name, a search will generate a list of all the products or items available for that store. If you select **Item** from the **Input For** drop-down list and enter a product reference number in the **Parent Reference Number** field, a search will display all the items that fall under that product.

3.  Click **Attributes.** The Product Attributes form appears.

4.  Enter the name of the first attribute type in the field provided (such as size) under **Create/Remove Attribute**.

5.  Click **Create**.

6.  Repeat steps 4 and 5 for all the attribute types for this product.

7.  To assign an attribute value, under **Define Attribute** select the first attribute type from the drop-down list (such as material).

    > **Note:**
    > Be sure to select only the attribute for which you want to specify a value at the product level. Attribute values for items must be selected on the Item Attributes form.

8.  Enter the attribute value for the product (such as denim) in the **Attribute Value** field.

9.  Click **Update**. The information is saved as a new record in the PRODATR (Product Attribute) and PRODDSTATR (Product Distinct Attribute) tables in the database. Make sure that a confirmation message appears.

10. Repeat steps 7 to 9 for each attribute type of this product. To define the attributes of all the other products under the same parent product without exiting the form, enter the product number in the field provided, click **Update Form**, and repeat these steps. Attribute types are retained in the drop-down list until you exit this form and select a new parent product.

You have now created a product attribute. Next, you will enter items and item attributes.

### Entering Items and their Attributes

To define the items and their attributes for each product, do the following:

1. Ensure that you have previously entered product attributes.

2. On the task bar of the Store Manager, click **Product Information**. The Product/Item Information form appears.

3. Display the product for which you want to enter items and attributes.

4. Check the fields, and make any required changes for the item.

5. From the **Input For** drop-down list, select **Item**.

6. In the **Product Number or Item SKU** field, change the product number to the item SKU.

   > **Note:**
   > Item SKUs are case-sensitive in Net.Commerce. For example, product number BR-77-T-01 is not the same as product number BR-77-t-01.

7. Clear the **Product/Item Reference Number** field. A new number will automatically be generated for this field after you create the item.

8. Click **Select Parent...**. In the window that is displayed, note the number of the product that is the parent to the item. Close the window.

9. Enter the number in the **Parent Reference Number** field.

10. Click **Save**. The information is saved as a new record in the PRODUCT table in the database. Make sure that a confirmation message appears.

11. Click **Attributes.** The Item Attributes form appears.

12. Under **Define Attribute**, select the first attribute type from the drop-down list (such as size.) These are the attribute types you created on the Product Attributes form.

13. Enter the attribute value for the item (such as *blue*, for color, or *small*, for size) in the **Attribute Value** field.

14. Click **Update**. The information is saved as a new record in the PRODATR (Product Attribute) and PRODDSTATR (Product Distinct Attribute) tables in the database. Make sure that a confirmation message appears.

15. Repeat steps 11 to 14 for each attribute type for this item.

16. To define the attribute values of all the other items of this product without exiting the form, enter the SKU for each item in the field provided, click **Update Form**, and repeat steps 12 to15. Attribute types are retained in the drop-down list until you exit this form and select a new parent product.

### Assigning a Template to a Product or Item

Once you have created a product or item, you need to assign to it the template (Net.Data macro) that will display it in the store. If you have created shopper groups, you can assign different templates to different groups, allowing you to customize the way your categories will look to members of different groups. For information on how to create shopper groups, see "Creating Shopper Groups" on page 105.

1. On the task bar of the Store Manager, click **Product Information**. The Product/Item Information form appears.

2. Display the information for a product or item that you want to work with.

3. On the task bar, click **Templates** to display the Product Template Assignment form, and ensure that the product number or item SKU is displayed.

4. To assign the same product template to all shoppers, select **None** from the **Shopper Group** drop-down list. To assign a product template to a specific shopper group, select the group you want.

5. In the **Template** field, enter the path and file name of the Net.Data macro that will display the product or item. (Ensure that you have specified the macro path in the db2www.ini file. For more information, see "Specifying a Macro Directory" on page 195.)

6. In the **Description** field, enter a brief description of the template, if desired.

7. If the template has been created, you can click **View Template** to see it.

8. Click **Save**. The information is saved as a new record in the PRODSGP (Shopper Group Product Template) table in the database. Make sure that a confirmation message appears.

9. Repeat steps 2 to 8 to assign templates to other products or items.

### Assigning Products to Multiple Parents

You can assign a product to more than one parent category. There are several reasons why you may want to do this. First, this gives the product increased exposure to customers, as they will be able to see it in more than one location in the store. You can position your product strategically so that customers who traditionally view certain categories will see it. Finally, to reduce the need for shoppers to search the store, you can ensure that all the categories that shoppers might associate with that product actually contain that product.

1. In the Store Manager, click **Product Information**. The Product/Item Information form appears.

2. Display the information for a product that you want to work with.

3.  Choose one of the following methods:

    - If you know the product number or item SKU, enter it in the **Product Number or Item SKU** field, and click **Update Form**. The form fills with information about the product.

    > **Note:**
    > Some searchable fields in Net.Commerce are case-sensitive. To generate reliable search results, ensure that the product number or item SKU is accurate.

    - If you do not know the product number or item SKU, enter a piece of information that identifies the product or item, in one or more of the fields. From the **Input For** drop-down list, select **Product** to search for a product or **Item** to search for an item, and then click **Search**. A list of all the products or items that satisfy your search criteria appears at the bottom of the screen. Click a product or item in this list to fill the fields of the form with information about it.

4.  Click **Parent Categories. The** Manage Parent Categories form appears.

5.  Choose one of the following:

    - To add a parent, enter the parent reference number in the field in the Add/Remove section, and click **Add**. If you do not know the parent reference number, click **Select Parent** and the category tree will appear in a separate window. Note the number and close the window.

    - To remove a parent, click the parent in the drop-down list in the Add/Remove section, and click **Remove**.

6.  From the **Define Sequence** section, select the name of the category from the drop-down list.

7.  Enter a number that indicates the position this product will have on the category template in relation to other products in the category (1=first, 2=second, etc.). Decimal values are accepted, enabling you to position a product between any two other products at any time without reassigning sequence numbers.

8.  Click **Update**. The information is added to the PRODUCT table in the database. Ensure that a confirmation message appears.

## Using the Mass Import Utility

The Mass Import utility offers you a fast way to import large amounts of product data into the database. For information on how to use it, see "Chapter 5, Mass-Importing Product and Category Data" on page 123.

# Implementing Discounts

With the increasing popularity of electronic commerce and online shopping, businesses must compete for customers. The Discounts function in the Store Manager allows you to offer shoppers incentives to buy from your store.

You can offer either percentage discounts (such as 10% off) or fixed-amount discounts (such as $15 off). Discounts can apply to entire orders or to specific products. For example, you can offer a 20% reduction to your staff members; or, if you have many red baseball caps in stock, you can offer a 25% discount on the caps for a limited time, in order to quickly sell overstocked inventory.

Implementing discounts is a three-step process. First, you define a scale code, which contains the actual value of the discount, the calculation method, and its range. Next, you create a discount code, which contains information about the discount, including its name, scope, effective dates, and the units on which it is based. Finally, if the discount will be applied to specific products, you assign the discount codes to them.

## Defining Scale Codes

A scale code can contain the following information about a discount:

- The numerical value of the discount.

- Whether the discount is calculated as a percentage or as a fixed amount.

- The discount *ranges* (the quantity, weight, or dollar value that the shopper must purchase in order to be eligible for the discount, and whether different discounts will apply to different sizes of orders). Each range indicates a minimum and maximum size of an order. Offering greater discounts on larger orders encourages your customers to order in bulk.

When defining ranges, you should consider the following:

- For each scale code, specify at least one range (minimum and maximum values) within which the discount applies. The units of the range will depend on whether you have defined the discount to apply to quantity, weight, or dollar value. For example, the range "20 to 30" could mean that the discount applies to 20 to 30 individual items, 20 to 30 kilograms, or 20 to 30 dollars.

- If you want the same discount to apply in all cases, create one large range with a maximum value that is high enough to cover all possibilities. The default start range is a value of zero.

- For each range, indicate the desired computation method. Possible methods are a fixed-amount discount applied to the total price (such as $5 off the total) or to each product or item (such as $5 off each baseball cap), or a percentage discount applied to the total price (such as 15% off the total). You must also specify a value of the discount. The meaning of this value depends on what you specify as the computation method. For example, a value of "5" could mean $5 off the entire order, $5 off each item, or 5% off the total price.

- You can specify a *scale* (set of ranges), whereby different discounts apply to different ranges. For example, you can offer shoppers a 10% discount if they buy one to five items, a 15% discount if they buy six to ten items, and a 20% discount if they buy more than ten items.

To define a scale code, do the following:

1. On the task bar of the Store Manager, click **Discounts** and then **Scale/Ranges**. The Define Scale/Ranges form appears.

2. From the **Select** drop-down list, select **Add New Scale**.

3. In the **Scale Code Name** field, enter a name that uniquely defines the scale code.

4. In the **Scale Code Description** field, enter a brief description of the scale code.

5. Enter additional information in the **Custom Field 1** field, if applicable.

6. From the **Current Ranges** drop-down list, select **Add Range** to specify a new range for the scale code. Only the range end is required to define a range.

7. In the **Range End** field, enter a maximum value for the first range. The minimum is always set to 0. For example, if you enter 5, the first range will be 0 - 5. (The units of the range depend on what you specify in the **Discount by** field on the Define Discount Codes form. For instance, the range "0 - 5" could mean that the discount applies to up to 5 individual items, up to 5 kilograms, or up to 5 dollars.). If you want only one range (that is, you want the same discount to apply to all orders, regardless of size), enter a value in the **Range End** field that is high enough to cover all possibilities.

   **Note:**
   You must enter at least one range when you create a scale code.

8. Click **Save.** The range is added to the **Current Ranges** drop-down list. Ensure that a confirmation message appears in the display area.

9. Repeat steps 6 and 8 to create a list of ranges, if desired. For each additional range, the minimum must be one unit higher than the maximum of the previous range.

10. From the **Computation Method** drop-down list, specify how you want the discount to be calculated for each range. Select either **On Total** to have a fixed-amount discount applied to the total price, **Per Unit** to have a fixed-amount discount applied to the price of each item, or **Percentage** to have a percentage discount applied to the total price.

11. In the **Computation Value/Rate** field, for each range, enter the value of the discount. The meaning of this value depends on what you entered in the **Computation Method** field. For example, a value of 5 could mean $5 off the entire order, $5 off each item, or 5% off the total price. If you use a customized computation method, or any other computation method that requires more than one value or rate, enter any additional values in the **Custom Value/Rate 1**, **Custom Value/Rate 2**, and **Custom Field 3** fields.

12. Click **Save**. The information is saved as a new record in the SCALE (Price Modifier Rate Scale) table and the RATE (Price Modifier Range/Rate) table in the database. The scale code is also added to the **Scale Code** drop-down list on the Define Discount Codes form.

# Creating Discount Codes

A discount code specifies the following details of a discount:

- A name and a description for the code

- Whether the discount applies to all shoppers or just to particular shopper groups. For instance, you can offer 15% off all orders placed by senior citizens, or reward frequent shoppers with a $10 savings for every $100 order.

- The start and end dates that the discount is in effect (a "limited time offer"). Specifying distinct promotion dates is an efficient way to reduce inventory that you want to move quickly, such as seasonal products or overstocked items. For instance, you can offer 50% off all calendars between January 15th and February 15th.

- The units on which the discount is based: either quantity, weight, or dollar value. For example, to encourage the purchase of large quantities, you can offer a 15% discount to shoppers who place orders for ten items at one time rather than five items now and five later.

- The scale code that determines the level of savings for different quantities of purchases.

To create a discount code, do the following:

1. On the task bar of the Store Manager, click **Discounts** and then **Define Codes**. The Define Discount Codes form appears.

2. From the **Select** drop-down list, select **Add New Code**.

3. In the **Discount Code Name** field, enter a name that uniquely defines the discount code.

4. In the **Discount Code Description** field, enter a brief description of the discount code.

5. Enter additional information in **Custom Field 1**, if applicable.

6. If you want a specific shopper group to be eligible for the discount, select that group from the **Shopper Group** drop-down list. (To learn how to create shopper groups, see "Creating Shopper Groups" on page 105.) To offer the discount to all shoppers, select **None**.

7. In the **Start Date** and **End Date** fields, specify the first and last days of the discount. The date must be in the format year-month-day, but variations are acceptable; for example, 98-01-4, 98-01-04, 1998-01-4, or 1998-01-04. To change the format, refer to the Net.Commerce online help.

8. In the **Discount by** field, specify what unit will be used for defining its size. You can have different discounts apply to different sizes of orders; that is, the larger the order, the greater the discount. "Size," however, can be defined in several ways. Select **Quantity** if you want to the discount to be based on the number of items ordered; **Weight** if you want it to be based on the total weight of the order; and **Dollar Value** if you want it to be based on the total price of the order. Depending on what you select here, the values of the ranges specified on the Define Scale/Ranges form will refer to either numbers, weights, or prices.

9. From the **Scale Code** drop-down list, select the scale code that you want to apply to the discount. The scale code determines the numerical value of the discount; whether it is calculated as a percentage or as a fixed amount; and the size of the order to which it applies.

10. Click **Save**. The information is saved in the DISCCODE (Product Discount Code) and the DISCCALC (Discount Calculation) tables in the database and added to the **Discount Code** drop-down list. Ensure that a confirmation message appears.

## Assigning Discount Codes

After you have created a discount code and defined its scale code, you are ready to assign the discount code to the products and items to which it applies. If your discount code applies only to orders, skip this step.

1. On the task bar of the Store Manager, click **Discounts**. The Discount Code Assignment form appears.

2. Conduct a search for the products or items to which you want to assign codes.

3. Click the search results you want, to add them to the **Selected Products/Items** list.

4. From the **Discount Code** drop-down list, select a discount code. This code will be applied to all the products and items listed in the **Selected Products/Items** drop-down list.

5. If you make a mistake or change your mind, do one of the following:

6. To undo a previous discount code assignment but keep the product or item in the **Select Products/Items** list, select the product or item, and then select **None** from the **Discount Code** drop-down list.

7. To delete a product or item from the **Select Products/Items**, select it and click **Remove**. To delete all the products and items, click **Empty**. (Note that when you click one of these buttons, you are removing or emptying the products or items from the list, not from the database.)

8. Click **Save.** The information is saved as a new record in the PRODUCT table in the database. Make sure that a confirmation message appears in the display area.

# Creating Shopper Groups

A shopper group is a collection, as defined by the merchant, of shoppers who share some common interest. For example, if market research has shown that certain shoppers repeatedly purchase a product in your store, you could assign those shoppers to the same group; or, you can create a group to reward frequent shoppers. You could also create groups that are based on demographic characteristics, such as a shopper group for seniors. Shopper groups are similar to the club memberships offered by some large stores to frequent or preferred customers. Being part of a shopper group can entitle a shopper to discounts or other bonuses.

You can assign different prices to products for different groups of shoppers. You can also customize the way products and categories appear to different groups. To do this, you create a separate template and assign it to the applicable shopper groups, using the Product Template Assignment and Category Template Assignment forms, respectively.

Perform the following steps to create shopper groups for your store:

1. In the Store Manager, click **Shopper Groups.** The Shopper Groups form appears.

2. From the **Select Store** drop-down list, select the store for which you want to create a shopper group.

3. From the **Shopper Group** drop-down list, select **Add New Shopper Group**.

4. In the **Shopper Group Name** field, enter a name for the shopper group.

5. In the **Description** field, enter a few sentences that describe the shopper group (for example, targeted customers, eligibility, policies, incentives).

6. If you make a mistake, type over the incorrect information in the fields, or click **Clear** and start over.

7. Click **Save** to add the new shopper group to the database. If after saving the shopper group you realize that you have made an error, delete the group and start over.

**Notes:**
- A shopper can belong to only one group per store.

- To enroll a shopper in a shopper group after it has been created, you must select the group from the Customer Information form.

# Creating an Interactive Catalog

You can create an interactive catalog that assists your shoppers in selecting products by prompting them with questions or providing feature comparisons. The Product Advisor tool provided with Net.Commerce enables you to add the following elements to your existing electronic catalog:

- Marketing knowledge, such as that possessed by a sales professional.

- Technical knowledge, such as that possessed by a product specialist or subject matter expert.

- "Shopping metaphors," to provide shoppers with different ways of finding what they want. Shoppers with little knowledge of a product category can use the Sales Assistance metaphor, which guides them toward appropriate products through a series of multiple-choice questions. Those with more knowledge can use the Product Exploration metaphor, which lets them select desired product features from a list. Once the selection has been narrowed down through either of the above methods, shoppers can use the Product Comparison metaphor to compare similar products side by side.

The Product Advisor consists of the following components:

- The Catalog Builder, which prepares the product data for use in the electronic catalog.

- Three shopping metaphor builders, which let you set up different presentations of the catalog data.

To use the Product Advisor, you first prepare a catalog by selecting the features you want to be displayed, and then you create any or all of the three types of shopping metaphors. For more information, see "Appendix A, Net.Commerce Product Advisor" on page 491.

# Workshop: Adding a New Catalog to the OneStopPizza Shop

In the workshop in Chapter 2, you deleted from the database the sample categories and products that were being displayed in the OneStopPizza Shop. In this workshop, you will begin to enter new categories and products in the database, using the Store Manager. The resulting hierarchical structure is shown in Figure 4.2 below:

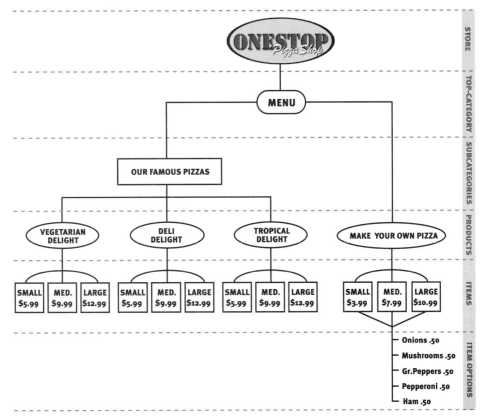

***Figure 4.2*** *The hierarchy of the categories and products in the OneStopPizza Shop.*

For simplicity, the menu for the OneStop Pizza Shop consists only of pizzas, so the categories span only two levels, *Menu* and *Our Famous Pizzas*. (In a production store that sells more than just pizzas, such as beverages and appetizers, you might add an additional layer under the top-level category *Menu* to include the *Pizzas, Beverages, and Appetizers* subcategories.)

It is important that you understand the navigation paths that the diagram will create for shoppers browsing your menu. When they first access the menu, they can do one of two things: view the store's ready-made pizzas or create their own. If they select *Our Famous Pizzas*, they will be presented with three product choices: *Vegetarian Delight*, *Deli Delight*, and *Tropical Delight*. After they make a selection, they will be connected to the product page for that type of pizza, from which they choose a size (small, medium, or large) and add the item to their Order List. If they take the other route and select *Make Your Own Pizza*, which is a product because it cannot be further divided into subcategories, they will be connected directly to its product page, from which they select a size, choose toppings, and add the item to their Order List.

For simplicity, the OneStop Pizza Shop does not use shopper groups or implement discounts. Since delivery is free in this store, you also do not need to modify or add additional shipping services; you will continue to use the default shipping service that was defined in the Store Creator.

# What You Will Do

In the following sections of this workshop, you will do the following:

- Store the images and templates that will display the categories and products in the store
- Create the top-level category *Menu*
- Add the subcategory *Our Famous Pizzas* under its parent *Menu*
- Add the product *Vegetarian Delight* under its parent *Our Famous Pizzas*
- Define the items and attributes for the *Vegetarian Delight* product

# Storing the Images and Templates

Before you begin to enter the new products and categories in the database, you need to specify where to store the product and category images and the templates that will display them in the store.

## Storing the Images

You will store all your custom images in the Web server document root, which eliminates the need to modify the configuration file.

Copy all the images in the `\workshops\images\` directory on the CD to the following directory:

**WIN** `\ibm\www\html\OneStopPizzaShop\`

(The `\OneStopPizzaShop\` directory was automatically created by the Store Creator when you created the store. It currently contains the `index.html`, to which the store URL resolves.)

When you enter the file names of the images in the database (and in later workshops, templates) you will also specify the /OneStopPizzaShop/ directory, so that the Web server will be able to map to the store's directory.

## Storing the Templates

You will continue to use the default directories that the Store Creator automatically created for storing the category and product templates, as follows:

**WIN** \IBM\NetCommerce3\macro\en_US\category\OneStopPizzaShop\

**WIN** \IBM\NetCommerce3\macro\en_US\product\OneStopPizzaShop\

When you enter the name of these templates in the database, you will also enter the /OneStopPizzaShop/ directory so that Net.Data can execute them at run-time. (The db2www.ini file has already been configured to point to this directory.)

# Opening the Store Manager

You will now use the Store Manager to enter the product and category data in the database. As mentioned in the previous workshop, "Designating Access to the OneStopPizza Shop's Database" on page 75, store data can be managed by either the site administrator or the store administrator. Here, you will enter the data as the store administrator John Smith. To access the Administrator as this person, follow these steps:

1. Ensure that all browser windows are closed, and then open the Administrator.

2. When prompted, enter the user name and password that you assigned to the store administrator, John Smith, in the workshop "Designating Access to the OneStopPizza Shop's Database" on page 75 (user name: jsmith and password: smith).

3. Click **Logon**. You now have access to the Store Manager component of the Administrator, but not to the Site Manager component. If you later need to update site data, you will have to close the browser and re-access Net.Commerce Administrator using your site administrator logon ID and password.

4. On the task bar, click **Store Manager**. You are now in the Store Manager and are ready to add the categories and products to the store.

# Creating the Top-Level Category

You will now create the top-level category *Menu,* which will be displayed when the shopper first starts browsing the catalog. This category, like all top-level categories, appears directly under the name of the store, as shown in Figure 4.3 below:

***Figure 4.3*** *The top-level category, Menu, in the OneStopPizza Shop.*

For this category, you will include the following descriptive information:

- Its name, for displaying as the title on its category page

- The template (the Net.Data macro file) that will display the category page.

Let's get started:

1. On the task bar of the Store Manager, click **Product Categories** to display the Product Categories form.

2. Make sure that **OneStop Pizza Shop** is selected in the **Select Store** drop-down list. Since you accessed the Store Manager as a store administrator, only this store should be available from the list (you granted John Smith access only to the East West Food Mart's data). The area underneath the selection list is where you will create a category tree depicting the navigational structure of your store's categories. At present, it is displaying the store name.

3. Click the triangle beside the store name to reveal its subcategories. Normally, when you create a store from scratch without using the Store Creator, the store name does not have any subcategories. When, however, you create it using the Store Creator and you delete the sample products, a category called *Top Category* is left in the database. This category represents the store's top-level category, which is mandatory and cannot be removed from the store because its reference number (displayed in parentheses) is being used to display the correct category page when the shopper first accesses the menu. The diamond symbol beside it indicates that it has no child categories.

4. You will now reuse this top-level category by changing its name to *Menu*. Click **Top Category,** and then on the action bar at the bottom of the form click **Edit**. The Edit Category form appears.

5. In the **Name** field, enter Menu.

6. On the action bar at the bottom, click **Save**. The information is saved in the CATEGORY and CGRYREL (Category Relationship) tables in the database. You return to the category tree, which now shows *Menu* as the top-level category for OneStopPizza Shop. Figure 4.4 shows the change:

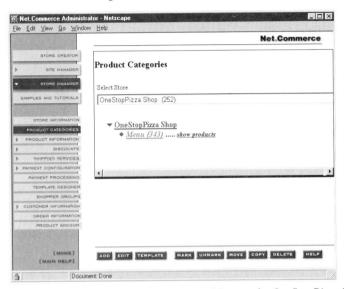

***Figure 4.4*** *Adding the top-level category Menu to the OneStopPizza Shop.*

The next step would normally be to specify the template (the Net.Data macro) that will display the category. However, since the category already exists, it also already has a template assigned to it, called `cat1.db2`. This macro will display the products and categories belonging to this category (*Our Famous Pizzas* and *Make Your Own Pizza*).

# Creating a Subcategory

Now you will create the subcategory *Our Famous Pizzas* under its parent *Menu*, as shown in Figure 4.5 below:

***Figure 4.5*** *The subcategory, Our Famous Pizzas, in the OneStopPizza Shop.*

For this subcategory, you will include the following descriptive information:

- The name of the subcategory, which will be displayed as the title on its page
- The sequence number, for specifying the position of this subcategory relative to the other categories at the same level
- The thumbnail image, to display on the category page
- The template (the Net.Data macro file) that will display the category page.

You will now add the subcategory:

1. In the category tree, click **Menu,** and then click **Add** on the action bar at the bottom. The Add New Category form appears.

2. In the **Name** field, enter Our Famous Pizzas.

3. Make sure that the **Publish** field displays **Yes**.

4. In the **Sequence Number** field, enter 1 to specify that the subcategory *Our Famous Pizzas* will appear first on its page.

5. In the **Thumbnail Image** field, enter /OneStopPizzaShop/ourfamous.gif, as shown in Figure 4.6 below:

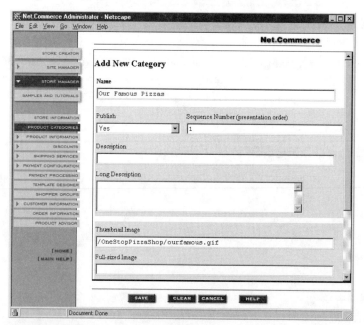

**Figure 4.6** *The Add New Category form.*

6. Click **Save**. The information is saved in the CATEGORY and CGRYREL tables in the database, and you are returned to the category tree. The category *Our Famous Pizzas* should appear under its parent *Menu*.

## Assigning a Template

Now you need to specify the template (the Net.Data macro) that will display the subcategory *Our Famous Pizzas*.

1.  In the category tree, click **Our Famous Pizzas**.

2.  On the action bar at the bottom, click **Template** to display the Category Template Assignment form.

3.  From the **Shopper Group** drop-down list, select **None (default template)**. (The OneStop Pizza Shop does not use shopper groups.)

4.  In the **Template** field, enter /OneStopPizzaShop/cat1.db2. This is the name of the default category macro that will display a listing of the products that belong to this category (*Vegetarian Delight*, *Deli Delight*, and *Tropical Delight*). Note that this is the same macro that is being used to display their parent category, *Menu*. In this store, all the code needed to display the different categories and product listings is included in this macro.

5.  Click **Save** to insert a new record in the CATESGP table in the database. Make sure that a confirmation message appears in the display area, as shown in Figure 4.7 below:

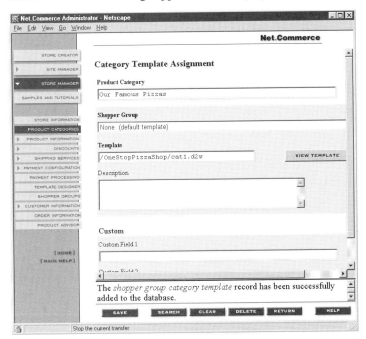

*Figure 4.7 The Category Template Assignment form.*

6.  At the bottom, click **Return** to return to the category tree. The category reference number for each category has been internally generated by the system and appears in parentheses beside each category name in the tree.

7. Make a note of the numbers for *Menus* and *Our Famous Pizzas*, as you will use them later to link the products to these parent categories.

Menu         _____

Our Famous Pizzas   _____

# Entering Product Information

In this step, you will add the *Vegetarian Delight* product under its parent category *Our Famous Pizza*s, as shown in Figure 4.8 below:

*Figure 4.8  The Vegetarian Delight product in the OneStopPizza Shop.*

For the product, you will enter the following descriptive information:

- The product number, to uniquely identify the product in the store

- The parent reference number, to link the product to its parent category

- The shipping code, to link it to a shipping calculation method

- The product name, for displaying on its product page

- The full-size image, for displaying on its product page

- The thumbnail image, for displaying on its preceding category page

- The template (Net.Data macro) to display the product

You are now ready to add the Vegetarian Delight product:

1. On the task bar, click **Product Information** to display the Product/Item Information form.

2. In the **Select Store** drop-down list, make sure that **OneStopPizza Shop** is selected.

3. From the **Input For** drop-down list, select **Product**.

4.  In the **Product Number or Item SKU** field, enter 10. Note that the **Product/Item Reference Number** field is blank. Once you create and save the product in the database, the system will assign a number to the product and fill this field.

5.  In the **Parent Reference Number** field, enter the number for the *Our Famous Pizzas* category. (If you did not make a note of this number, click **Select Parent** to get it. Then, close the window to return to the Product/Item Information form.)

6.  From the **Publish** drop-down list, select **Yes** to specify that this product is to be shown in the store.

7.  In the **Name/Short Description** field, enter: Vegetarian Delight.

8.  In the **Description Field 1**, enter the following:

    For you veggie lovers, mozzarella cheese and a fresh mix of mushrooms, onions, green peppers, tomatoes, and basil.

9.  In the **Thumbnail Image** field, enter: /OneStopPizzaShop/veg_pizza1.gif.

10. In the **Full-Sized Image** field, enter: /OneStopPizzaShop/veg_pizza2.gif.

11. From the **Product Shipping Code** drop-down list, select **SCSHP**. This shipping code was automatically generated by the Store Creator. It uses the value you entered for the shipping charge in the Store Creator as a fixed charge for each order placed. In our case, we entered 0 since delivery is free in the OneStopPizza Shop.

12. Click **Save**. The information is saved as a new record in the PRODUCT table in the database. Make sure that a confirmation message appears.

## Assigning a Template

You now need to assign the template (the Net.Data macro) that will display detailed information about the *Vegetarian Delight* product.

1.  On the task bar, click **Templates** to display the Product Template Assignment form. The SKU number for the product should be already filled in.

2.  From the **Shopper Group** drop-down list, select **None (default template)**.

3.  In the **Template** field, enter /OneStopPizzaShop/prod1.d2w. This is a default Store Creator macro, which will create the product pages.

4. Click **Save** to insert a new record into the PRODSGP (Shopper Group Product Template) table in the database. Make sure that a confirmation message appears, as shown in Figure 4.9 below:

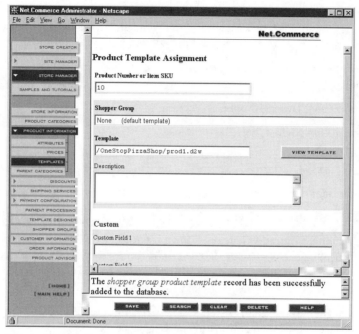

***Figure 4.9*** *The Product Template Assignment form.*

# Defining Items and Their Attributes

Now you are ready to define the items and their attributes for the *Vegetarian Delight* product. It is available in three sizes: *Small, Medium,* and *Large*, with each size sold at a different price, as shown in Figure 4.10 below:

***Figure 4.10*** *The items and attributes for the Vegetarian Delight product.*

For each item, you will include the following descriptive information:

- A SKU number, to uniquely identify the item in the store

- A parent reference number, to link the item to its parent product (*Vegetarian Delight*)

- The name of its attribute (size)

- The value of its attribute (small, medium, or large)

- A price

> **Note:**
> The items will be displayed using the **prod1.d2w** macro, which you previously assigned to their parent product *Vegetarian Delight*.

You are now ready to add the items and their attributes:

1. Click **Product Information** to return to the Product/Item Information form.

2. Click **Update Form** to make sure that all fields are filled in.

3. Make a note of the value in the **Product/Item Reference Number** field, as you will need this number to link the items to their parent product.

   Product Reference Number _____

4. From the **Input For** drop-down list, select **Item**.

5. In the **Product Number or Item SKU** field, enter 10-S.

6. Clear the **Product/Item Reference Number** field. A new number will automatically be generated for this field after you create the item.

7. In the **Parent Reference Number** field, enter the number that you noted in Step 3.

8. Click **Save** before continuing. The information is saved as a new record in the PRODUCT table. Make sure that a confirmation message appears, as shown in Figure 4.11 below:

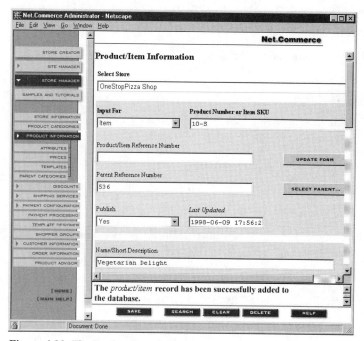

*Figure 4.11   The Product/Item Information form.*

9. On the task bar, click **Attributes** to display the Item Attributes form. The SKU number should be already filled in.

10. Under **Create/Remove Attribute**, enter `Size` in the **Attribute Name** field.

11. Beside the field, click **Create**.

12. Under **Define Attribute**, enter `Small` in the **Attribute Value** field.

13. Beside the field, click **Update**. The information is saved as a new record in the PRODATR (Product Attribute) and PRODDSTATR (Product Distinct Attribute) tables in the database. Make sure that a confirmation message appears, as shown in Figure 4.12 below:

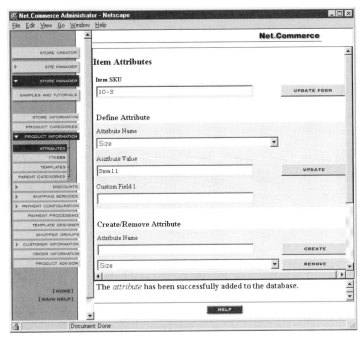

***Figure 4.12*** *The Item Attributes form.*

14. You now need to define a price for this particular item. On the task bar, click **Prices** to display the Price Information form.

15. In the **Price** field, enter 5.99, and verify that the **Currency** field is filled in. (The Store Creator automatically inserted the ISO currency code USD into the database when your store was created.)

16. To designate the price as the regular price, enter 0 in the **Precedence** field. (Additional prices with higher precedence values would indicate sale prices.)

17. To offer this price to all shoppers, select **None** from the **Shopper Group** list.

18. Enter 9999-01-12 as an expiry date for the price. Leave the effective date blank; the system will automatically insert the current date into the database.

19. Click **Save**. The information is saved as a new record in the PRODPRCS (Product Price) table. Make sure that a confirmation message appears in the display area, as shown in Figure 4.13 below:

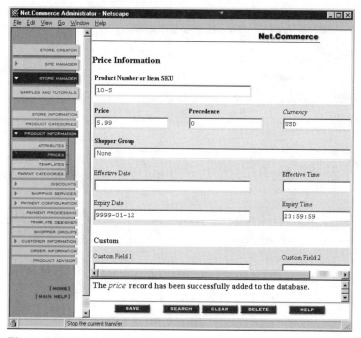

*Figure 4.13  The Price Information form.*

20. On the task bar, click **Product Information** to return to the Product/Item Information form.

21. Repeat steps 4 to 20 to create two more items for the *Vegetarian Delight* product using the following data. You do not need to redefine the attribute name *Size* (steps 10 and 11) each time. This name is retained in the database and will automatically appear each time that you assign a new attribute value.

- **SKU:** 10-M
- **size:** Medium
- **price:** 9.99

- **SKU:** 10-L
- **size:** Large
- **price:** 12.99

22. Close the Administrator.

# Testing the New Products and Categories

Before completing this workshop, let's see how the new categories, *Menu* and *Our Famous Pizzas*, and the new product, *Vegetarian Delight* and its items, appear in the store.

1.  Open a new browser window and type the following URL:

    `http://<host_name>/OneStopPizzaShop`

    where `<host_name>` is the fully qualified name of your server

2.  When the store appears, add it to your browser's bookmark list, for easy access later.

3.  On the store's navigation bar, click **Catalog** (which you will later rename **Menu**) to display its subcategory *Our Famous Pizzas*, as shown in Figure 4.14 below:

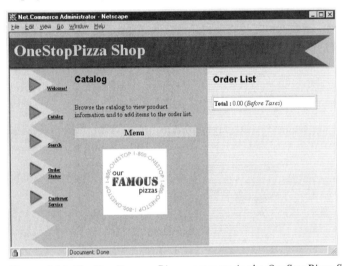

***Figure 4.14***  *The Our Famous Pizzas category in the OneStopPizza Shop.*

4.  Click **Our Famous Pizzas** to display its only child, *Vegetarian Delight*, as shown in Figure 4.15 below:

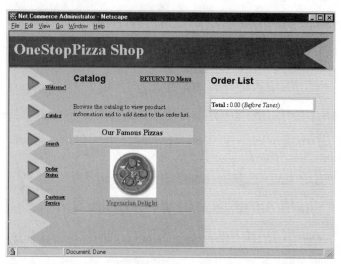

**Figure 4.15**  *The Vegetarian Delight pizza in the OneStopPizza Shop.*

5.  Click **Vegetarian Delight** to display its product page, along with its items (different sizes), as shown in Figure 4.16 below.  (You will later add the price for each size.)

**Figure 4.16**  *The Vegetarian Delight pizza in the OneStopPizza Shop.*

6.  Close the browser window.

This concludes this workshop.  In the next workshop in Chapter 5, you will learn how to use the Mass Import utility to add the remaining products and items to the store's database.

# Chapter 5, Mass-Importing Product and Category Data

If you are inserting or updating individual product and category records in the Net.Commerce database, it is best to use the forms provided by the Store Manager, as described in Chapter 4. However, if you have many products and categories to insert, using these forms to create a record for each one would be very time-consuming. The Mass Import utility provides an alternative method for populating the database tables, and is ideal for importing large quantities of data. This chapter explains how to use the Mass Import utility. In the workshop, you will use this utility to import data into the pizza store.

This chapter covers the following topics:

- The Mass Import Utility
- Creating an Import File
- Mass Import Utility Commands
- Invoking the Mass Import Utility
- Workshop: Adding the Remaining Products and Categories to the OneStopPizza Shop

# The Mass Import Utility

The Mass Import utility takes data from a delimited text file and imports it into the following product-related tables in the database:

- CATEGORY (Category)

- CATESGP (Shopper Group Category Template)

- CGRYREL (Category Relationship)

- PRODUCT (Product)

- PRODDSTATR (Product Distinct Attribute)

- PRODATR (Product Attribute)

- PRODPRCS (Product Price)

- PRODSGP (Shopper Group Product Template)

- CGPRREL (Category Product Relationship)

These tables contain information about categories, products, and items, and their relationships. For more information about them, see "Appendix C, Net.Commerce Database Tables" on page 511.

When the Mass Import utility inserts data into the tables, it automatically generates all reference numbers (for example, the product reference numbers) to prevent referential integrity errors. (The Store Manager also functions this way.) The utility also checks whether or not a record already exists in the database. If one exists, it updates the record; otherwise, it inserts a new record.

To process records more rapidly, the Mass Import utility stores certain common data, such as the reference number of the parent category, in a cache for re-use with subsequent related records. This reduces its need to query the database for each record. Table 5.1 shows the records that are cached by the utility:

*Table 5.1  Records cached by the Mass Import utility.*

| Records Cached | Group Cached | From Table |
| --- | --- | --- |
| prnbr, prrfnbr, and all ancestors | current set | PRODUCT |
| cgname, cgrfnbr and all ancestors | current set | CATEGORY |
| pscode, prpsnbr | all | PRODSGP |
| dcocode, prdcnbr | all | DISCODE |

**Note:**
Before you can use the Mass Import utility, you must have already created a store record. If your store was created using the Store Creator, a store record was automatically created for you. Otherwise, you must create the record manually using the Site Manager. To learn how, see "Creating a Store Record" on page 65.

# Creating an Import File

To use the Mass Import utility, you must first create an import file, which is an ASCII delimited file containing the commands and data with which to populate the product- and category-related tables. The file is treated as a continuous string of data, with the columns and rows of data separated by delimiters.

You can create an import file using any text editor, and can include any of the following commands in it. Each command will populate a different database table. For detailed descriptions of these commands, see "Mass Import Utility Commands" on page 130.

- #COLUMNDELIMITER - Defines the character that is used as a column delimiter
- #ROWDELIMITER - Defines the character that is used as a row delimiter
- #STORE - Specifies the name of the store for which the product and category records are being created
- #CATEGORY - Populates the Category table and the Category Relationship table
- #CATESGP - Populates the Shopper Group Category Template table
- #PRODUCT - Populates the Product table
- #PRODDSTATR - Populates the Product Distinct Attribute table
- #PRODATR - Populates the Product Attribute table
- #PRODPRCS - Populates the Product Price table
- #PRODSGP - Populates the Shopper Group Product Template table
- #CGPRREL - Populates the Category Product Relationship table

The following is an example of a portion of an import file for a single store (the East West Food Mart sample store). The commands in this file will add to the database the category *Softdrinks*, and its child products, *Cola* and *Lemon Lime*, along with their items.

```
#STORE;East West Food Mart
#CATEGORY;Softdrinks;;;;c1so_n.gif;;1;c1so_h.gif;;Beverages;2
#CATESGP;Softdrinks;;toc.d2w;;;;
#PRODUCT;110;;Cola;;;;soc1110a.gif;;1;;;;;;;;FD01;;;;
#PRODDSTATR;110;Size
#PRODPRCS;110;;1.00;USD
#PRODSGP;110;Frequent Shoppers;freqshp.d2w
#PRODSGP;110;Gold Club;goldclb.d2w;club for senior shoppers
#CGPRREL;Softdrinks;110;1
#PRODUCT;110-S;110;Cola;;;;soc1110a.gif;;1;;;;;;;;FD01;;;999;
#PRODATR;110-S;Size;500 mL
#PRODPRCS;110-S;;1;USD
#PRODSGP;110-S;Frequent Shoppers;freqshp.d2w
#PRODUCT;110-M;110;Cola;;;;soc1110a.gif;;1;;;;;;;;FD01;;;999;
#PRODATR;110-M;Size;1 L
#PRODPRCS;110-M;;2;USD
#PRODSGP;110-M;Frequent Shoppers;freqshp.d2w
```

```
#PRODSGP;100-M;Gold Club;goldclb.d2w;club for senior shoppers
#PRODUCT;110-L;110;Cola;;;;soc1110a.gif;;1;;;;;;;;FD01;;;999;
#PRODATR;110-L;Size;1.5 L
#PRODPRCS;110-L;;3;USD
#PRODSGP;110-L;Frequent Shoppers;freqshp.d2w
#PRODSGP;110-L;Gold Club;goldclb.d2w;club for senior shoppers
#PRODUCT;111;;Lemon Lime;;;;soc1111a.gif;;1;;;;;;;;FD01;;;;
#PRODDSTATR;111;Size
#PRODPRCS;111;;;USD
#PRODSGP;111;Frequent Shoppers;freqshp.d2w
#PRODSGP;111;Gold Club;goldclb.d2w;club for senior shoppers
#CGPRREL;Softdrinks;111;2
#PRODUCT;111-S;111;Lemon Lime;;;;soc1111a.gif;;1;;;;;;;;FD01;;;999;
#PRODATR;111-S;Size;500 mL
#PRODPRCS;111-S;;1;USD
#PRODSGP;111-S;Frequent Shoppers;freqshp.d2w
#PRODSGP;111-S;Gold Club;goldclb.d2w;club for senior shoppers
#PRODUCT;111-M;111;Lemon Lime;;;;soc1111a.gif;;1;;;;;;;;FD01;;;999;
#PRODATR;111-M;Size;1 L
#PRODPRCS;111-M;;2;USD
#PRODSGP;111-M;Frequent Shoppers;freqshp.d2w
#PRODSGP;111-M;Gold Club;goldclb.d2w;club for senior shoppers
#PRODUCT;111-L;111;Lemon Lime;;;;soc1111a.gif;;1;;;;;;;;FD01;;;999;
#PRODATR;111-L;Size;1.5 L
#PRODPRCS;111-L;;3;USD
#PRODSGP;111-L;Frequent Shoppers;freqshp.d2w
#PRODSGP;111-L;Gold Club;goldclb.d2w;club for senior shoppers
```

As shown in this example, each line in an import file begins with a Mass Import utility command (for example, #PRODATR), followed by a list of data representing a transaction that inserts a database record into a table. The transaction specifies the table that will be populated and the values for each column in the table. The column delimiter (the default is a semicolon) separates the columns. The row delimiter (the default is a new-line character) separates the rows (database records). Multiple transactions that begin with the same command name represent different records that will be inserted into the same table.

The following is an example of a transaction that populates the Product Attribute table (PRODATR) with information about a product's attributes. Each unit of data, separated by semicolons, corresponds to a value for a column in the PRODATR table.

```
#PRODATR;ACC12345-L;size;large
```

We will now examine the first nine transactions in the import file above, to identify the database columns and the values that will be populated when the Mass Import utility is invoked.

```
#STORE;East West Food Mart
```
> This transaction, located at the top of the file, specifies the name of the store for which the product and category data is being created. The store name must match the contents of the MESTNAME column in the MERCHANT table, which in this case is *East West Food Mart*. Note that the store name must be entered in the database prior to creating this file.

`#CATEGORY;Softdrinks;;;;clso_n.gif;;1;clso_h.gif;;Beverages;2`

This transaction populates both the CATEGORY table and the CGRYREL (Category Relationship) table with the following data:

- `Softdrinks`: Populates the CGNAME column (the name of the category).

- `clso_n.gif`: Populates the CGTHMB column (the thumbnail image file).

- `1`: Populates the CGPUB column (displays the category to the shopper).

- `clso_h.gif`: Populates the merchant-defined CGFIELD1 column (a merchant-defined field which, in this case, is used for the full-sized image file for the banner on the product page).

- `Beverages`: The name of the parent category.

- `2`: Populates the CRSEQNBR column (the category sequence number) in the CGRYREL table.

`#CATESGP;Softdrinks;;toc.d2w;;;;`

This transaction populates the CATESGP (Shopper Group Category Template) table with the following data:

- `Softdrinks`: The name of the category.

- `toc.d2w`: Populates the CSDISPLAY column (the macro that will display the category).

`#PRODUCT;110;;Cola;;;;soc1110a.gif;;1;;;;;;;;FD01;;;;`

This transaction populates the PRODUCT table with the following data:

- `110`: Populates the PRNBR column (the product number or item SKU).

- `Cola`: Populates the PRSDESC column (the name of the product).

- `soc1110a.gif`: Populates the PRTHMB column (the thumbnail image file).

- `1`: Populates the PRPUB column (displays the product to the public).

- `FD01`: The product shipping code, as defined in the PSCODE column in the PRSPCODE table.

`#PRODDSTATR;110;Size`

This transaction populates the PRODDSTATR (Product Distinct Attribute) table with the following data:

- `110`: The product number as defined in the PRODUCT table.

- `Size`: Populates the PDNAME column (the name of the attribute).

`#PRODPRCS;110;;1.00;USD`

This transaction populates the PRODPRCS (Product Price) table with the following data:

- `110`: The product number or item SKU as defined in the PRODUCT table.

- `1.00`: Populates the PPPRC column (the price of the item).

- `USD`: Populates the PPCUR column (the currency in which the item is expressed, as defined in the MERCHANT table).

```
#PRODSGP;110;Frequent Shoppers;freqshp.d2w
```
This transaction populates the PRODSGP (Shopper Group Product Template) table with the following data:

- `110`: The product number or item SKU as defined in the PRODUCT table.

- `Frequent Shoppers`: Populates the PSDESC column (the description of the shopper group).

- `Freqshp.d2w`: Populates the PSDISPLAY column (the macro that will display the product).

```
#CGPRREL;Softdrinks;110;1
```
This transaction populates the CGPRREL (Category Product Relationship) table with the following data:

- `Softdrinks`: The name of the category.

- `110`: The product number as defined in the PRODUCT table.

- `1`: Populates the CRSEQNBR column (the category sequence number).

# Conventions for Entering Commands

Follow these conventions when entering the Mass Import utility commands in your import file:

- Type each command name followed by the data that the command will be importing for a specific product or category all on one line.

- Separate each column value in the transaction with a column delimiter (the default is a semicolon).

- Separate each row (database record) with a row delimiter (the default is a new-line character).

- You can type the commands in uppercase, lowercase, or mixed case. For example, all the following formats are valid:

```
#PRODATR
#prodatr
#ProdAtr
```

- Specify each command as many times as required. For example, if you define the row delimiter as a comma (,) and then later in the file you need to add product data that contains this symbol, you can define a new row delimiter for the affected data.

- To leave a column in a row empty, ensure that you insert delimiters to create a placeholder for that column. If you insert a new record into the database and you leave a column empty, and a default value exists in the database schema, the Mass Import utility will automatically insert the default value into the column. If you update a record and you leave a column empty, the existing value for that column will remain. Columns are updated only when you specify new values.

- To prevent referential integrity problems, do not enter reference numbers (for example, the product and category reference numbers). They will be automatically generated by the utility.

- Do not use double quotes (") in the import file. If you need to specify inches as a unit of measurement, type in.

- The order of the records in the import file can have an impact on the speed with which the utility processes the records. To prevent referential integrity problems and to benefit from the performance advantages provided by the utility's automatic caching, after each #STORE command (there will be one for each store to be populated) add the commands in the following order:

```
#CATEGORY
#CATESGP
#PRODUCT
#PRODDSTATR
#PRODATR
#PRODPRCS
#PRODSGP
#CGPRREL
```

- Repeat for each product and category to be imported into the database.

- Enter the records pertaining to categories in the order presented above. The first record in the category group must be #CATEGORY. The category group consists of the CATEGORY and CATESGP tables.

- Enter the records pertaining to products as a group in the order presented above. The first record in the product group must be #PRODUCT. The product group consists of the PRODUCT, PRODDSTATR, PRODATR, PRODPRCS, and PRODSGP tables. Enter child products immediately after the parent product.

- Enter child categories immediately after the parent category.

- Enter category product relationship records (using the #CGPRREL command) after the corresponding product and category groups.

- To improve performance, adjust the commitcount parameter in the Mass Import utility run command. The higher the commitcount setting, the less frequently the database will be committed, which saves some time. The default commitcount is 1, which commits the database after each record is inserted. For more information, see "Invoking the Mass Import Utility" on page 139.

> **Note:**
> Ensure that the commitcount does not cause the transaction to exceed the database log size. If it does, a "database log full" error will occur.

# Mass Import Utility Commands

The following are detailed descriptions of the Mass Import utility commands, which each populate a specific table in the database.

## #COLUMNDELIMITER

The #COLUMNDELIMITER command, shown in Figure 5.1, defines the delimiter used to separate data that is to be imported into separate columns in the database. Each column corresponds to one unit of information, such as the name of a product, or the name of the GIF file you want to use to display it. You can specify any character except #, @, or a space or end-of-file character. The default is a semicolon (;). You can include any number of #COLUMNDELIMITER commands in an import file. Each column delimiter affects all records that follow it until another column delimiter is specified.

> **Note:**
> You can add any number of spaces after the column delimiter command.

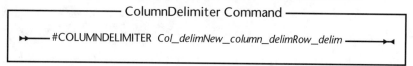

**Figure 5.1**  *The #COLUMNDELIMITER command.*

The values of each parameter are as follows:

`Col_delim`
    The column delimiter that is currently in effect.

`New_column_delim`
    The column delimiter that you want to take effect.

`Row_delim`
    The row delimiter.

## Example

To change the column delimiter from a semicolon to an ampersand (&), type:

```
#COLUMNDELIMITER;&
```

In this example, the row delimiter is a new-line character and cannot be seen. (Most text editors create a new-line character when you press Enter, and in most cases this character is not visible on the screen.)

## #ROWDELIMITER

The #ROWDELIMITER command, shown in Figure 5.2, defines the delimiter that is used to separate rows of data. Each row contains the data that you want to input into a specific database table, using one of the Mass Import commands. You can specify any character except #, @, or a space or end-of-file character. The default is a new-line character, which in most text editors is created by pressing Enter. You can include any number of #ROWDELIMITER commands in an import file. Each row delimiter affects all the records that follow it until another row delimiter is specified.

**Figure 5.2** *The #ROWDELIMITER command.*

The values of each parameter are as follows:

`Col_delim`
> The column delimiter.

`New_row_delim`
> The row delimiter that you want to take effect.

`Old_row_delim`
> The row delimiter that is currently in effect.

## Exam ples

The following are examples of how to change the row delimiter in the import file.

### Exam ple 1

To change the row delimiter from a new-line character to a dollar sign ($), type:

```
#ROWDELIMITER;$
```

In this example, the column delimiter is a semicolon. The original row character (a new-line character) is not visible.

### Exam ple 2

To change both the column and row delimiters from their default values to an ampersand (&) and a dollar sign ($), respectively, type:

```
#COLUMNDELIMITER;&
#ROWDELIMITER&$
```

**Note:**
In the second line, the column delimiter parameter takes the value that was specified in the first line. In both lines, the original row delimiter, a new-line character, is not visible.

## #STORE

The #STORE command, shown in Figure 5.3 on the next page, specifies the name of the store for which the product and category records are being created. All the transactions that follow are applied to that store, until another store is specified.

This command is mandatory. It must be inserted before the product and category records, and the import file must contain at least one #STORE command.

**Note:**
This transaction does not create a store record in the database. The store record must exist in the database before you can use this command. If you used the Store Creator to create your store, the store record will already exist. Otherwise, you must create the store record using the Store Records form in the Administrator. For details, see "Creating a Store Record" on page 65.

*Figure 5.3  The #STORE command.*

The values of each parameter are as follows:

`mestname`
> The name of the store, as defined in the MERCHANT table.

## Example

To specify that the records following the #STORE command will populate the database for the *Net.Commerce Retail Store,* type:

```
#STORE;Net.Commerce Retail Store
```

# #CATEGORY

The #CATEGORY command, shown in Figure 5.4, populates both the category table (CATEGORY) and the category relationship table (CGRYREL). You must type the entire record on one line. It is shown here on multiple lines for presentation purposes only.

**Notes:**
- If the CATEGORY table is empty before the Mass Import utility is run, all category-related records will be inserted into the database table without being checked. Therefore, you must ensure that there are no duplicate records in the import file. If there are, the subsequent inserts will fail.

- The CGDISPLAY column is reserved for merchant customization. Do not use it for the name of the macro file to display categories. The names of macro files must be stored in the CSDISPLAY column in the CATESGP table. For details, see the #CATESGP command on page 134.

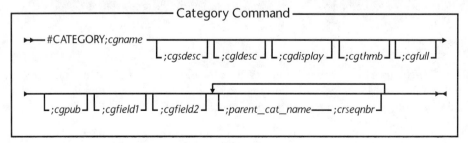

*Figure 5.4  The #CATEGORY command.*

The values of each parameter are as follows:

`parent_cat_name`
   The fully qualified name of a parent category. The format is as follows:

   ```
   top_level_category@2nd_level_category.........
   @parent_category_being_noted
   ```

   where @ is the separator. If the character @ is contained within a category name, type it as @@, to distinguish it from the @ separator.

   > **Note:**
   > If the category being specified has only one parent category, you can simply enter the name of the category without specifying its parent. For example, the unique parent category *Jeans*, which falls under the categories *Clothing@Pants@Jeans*, can be entered either as **Clothing@Pants@Jeans** or as **Jeans**. If the category has more than one parent category, you must enter the fully qualified name.

`crseqnbr`
   The category sequence number, as defined in the CGRYREL table.

`all other parameters`
   The value of the corresponding column in the CATEGORY or CGRYREL table.

## Exam ples

The following are examples of how to populate the CATEGORY and CGRYREL tables.

### Exam ple 1

To populate the CATEGORY and CGRYREL tables with the subcategory *Woodworking* under the parent categories *Power* and *Hand*, supplying all applicable parameters, type:

```
#CATEGORY;Woodworking;Woodworking for Professionals;A wide variety of
carefully handcrafted woodworking tools;;tool1.gif;tool2.gif;1;;;
Electrical@Power;469;Tools@Hand;765
```

In this example, the parent category *Power* has been previously defined under the category *Electrical*, and the parent category *Hand* has been previously defined under the category *Tools*. The utility looks for the subcategory *Woodworking* under *Electrical@Power*. If it finds it, it updates the record. If not, it creates a new record, even if the subcategory *Woodworking* is defined under *Tools@Hand*.

### Exam ple 2

To repeat the previous example, supplying only the required parameters and the parent category parameters, type:

```
#CATEGORY;Woodworking;;;;;;;;;Electrical@Power;;Tools@Hand;
```

In this example, the default values, as defined in the database schema, will be inserted into the empty columns. If however records already exist for the empty columns, the existing column values would not be changed.

# #CATESGP

The #CATESGP command, shown in Figure 5.5, populates the Shopper Group Category Template table, CATESGP.

**Note:**
This transaction does not create a shopper group in the database. To do this, use the Shopper Groups form in the Net.Commerce Administrator, as described in "Creating Shopper Groups" on page 105.

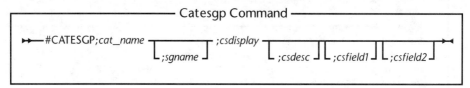

**Figure 5.5**  *The #CATESGP command.*

The values of each parameter are as follows:

cat_name
> The fully qualified name of the category.

sgname
> The name of the shopper group to which the category template applies.  This parameter corresponds to the SGNAME column n the SHOPGRP table.

all other parameters
> The value of the corresponding column in the CATESGP table.

## Example

To populate the CATESGP table with a record that displays the subcategory *Woodworking* to shoppers belonging to the shopper group *Seniors Shopper Club* using the cat3.d2w category template, type:

```
#CATESGP;Power Tools@Woodworking;Seniors Shopper Club;cat3.d2w;;;;
```

In this example, the subcategory *Woodworking* has been previously defined under its parent category, *Power Tools*.

# #PRODUCT

The #PRODUCT command, shown in Figure 5.6, populates the Product table, PRODUCT.  Type the entire command on one line.  It is shown on multiple lines here for presentation purposes only.

**Note:**
If the PRODUCT table is empty before the Mass Import utility is run, all product-related records will be inserted into the database table without being checked.  Ensure that there are no duplicate attributes in the input file.  If there are, the subsequent inserts will fail.

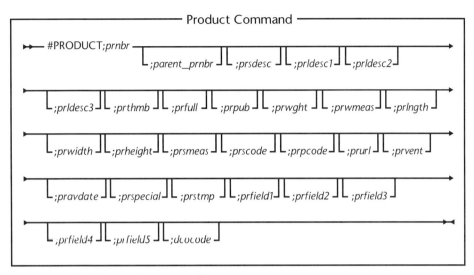

**Figure 5.6**  *The #PRODUCT command.*

**Note:**
The PRAVDATE column is defined as a date/time column type that accepts the following format: yyyy-mm-dd-hh.mm.ss.  For example: 1998-12-30-10.10.21

The values of each parameter are as follows:

`parent_prnbr`

> The product number of the parent product.  This parameter corresponds to the PRNBR column in the PRODUCT table.

`pscode`

> The product shipping code, as defined in the PRSPCODE table.  If a product or item SKU does not have a product shipping code, you can omit this parameter.

`dcocode`

> The product discount code, as defined in the DISCCODE table.  If a product or item SKU does not have a discount code, you can omit this parameter.

`all other parameters`

> The value of the corresponding column in the PRODUCT table.

# Example

To populate the PRODUCT table with a record that defines the product *V-Neck Sweater* with a product number of ACC1234, and supplying all applicable parameters, type:

```
#PRODUCT;ACC1234;;V-Neck Sweater;This comfortable all-natural
cotton lightweight sweater is perfect for the spring and fall
months.  It is available in navy blue, hunter green, ivory, cherry
red, and black, solid or striped.;;;sweater1.gif;sweater2.gif;1;
.4;Kg;;;;;PSE1;;;192;;S;;;;;;
```

# #PRODDSTATR

The #PRODDSTATR command, shown in Figure 5.7, populates the Product Distinct Attributes table, PRODDSTATR.

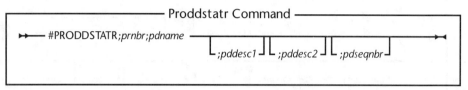

**Figure 5.7**  *The #PRODDSTATR command.*

The values of each parameter are as follows:

`prnbr`
> The product number, as defined in the PRODUCT table.

`all other parameters`
> The value of the corresponding column in the PRODDSTATR table.

## Example

To populate the PRODDSTATR table with a record that defines the distinct attribute "size" for the product *V-Neck Sweater* that has a product number of ACC1234, and supply all applicable parameters, type:

```
#PRODDSTATR;ACC1234;size;;;12
```

# #PRODATR

The #PRODATR command, shown in Figure 5.8, populates the Product Attributes table, PRODATR.

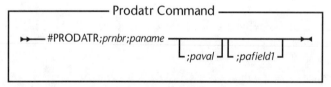

**Figure 5.8**  *The #PRODATR command.*

The values of each parameter are as follows:

`prnbr`
> The product number or item SKU, as defined in the PRODUCT table.

`all other parameters`
> The value of the corresponding column in the PRODATR table.

## Example

To populate the PRODATR table with a record that defines the attribute *size* with a value of *large* for the item with the SKU number ACC12345-L, type:

```
#PRODATR;ACC12345-L;size;large
```

# #PRODPRCS

The #PRODPRCS command, shown in Figure 5.9, populates the Product Price table, PRODPRCS. Type the entire transaction on one line. It is shown on two lines here for presentation purposes only.

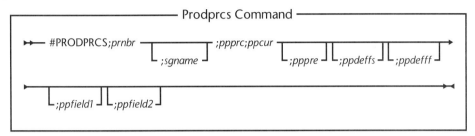

**Figure 5.9** *The #PRODPRCS command.*

**Notes:**

* Columns PPDEFFS and PPDEFFF are defined as date/time column types that accept the following format: yyyy-mm-dd-hh.mm.ss. For example, 1998-12-30-10.10.21

* You must enter the same currency that has already been defined in the MERCHANT table. (The currency is typically defined using the Store and Merchant Information form in Net.Commerce Administrator. For more information, see "Specifying Store Contact, Currency, and Tax Rate Information" on page 83.)

The values of each parameter are as follows:

`prnbr`
> The product number or item SKU, as defined in the PRODUCT table.

`sgname`
> The name of the shopper group to which this price information applies. This parameter corresponds to the SGNAME column in the SHOPGRP table. If the price applies to all shoppers, you can omit this parameter.

`all other parameters`
> The value of the corresponding column in the PRODPRCS table.

## Example

To populate the PRODPRCS table with a record that defines the price (with a precedence of 4) of the item with the SKU number ACC12345-L as 29.99 USD for shoppers belonging to the *Corporate Shopper Club 3*, supplying all applicable parameters, type:

```
#PRODPRCS;ACC12345-L;Corporate Shopper Club 3;29.99;USD;
4;1997-01-01-10.00.00;1999-12-30-12.00.00;;;
```

# #PRODSGP

The #PRODSGP command, shown in Figure 5.10, populates the Shopper Group Product Template table, PRODSGP.

**Note:**

This command does not create a shopper group in the database. To do this, use the Shopper Groups form in the Administrator, as described in "Creating Shopper Groups" on page 105.

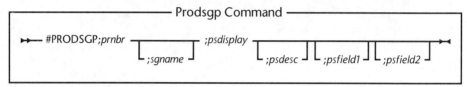

***Figure 5.10*** *The #PRODSGP command.*

The values of each parameter are as follows:

prnbr
> The product number or item SKU, as defined in the PRODUCT table.

sgname
> The name of the shopper group to which the product template applies. This parameter corresponds to the SGNAME column in the SHOPGRP table.

all other parameters
> The value of the corresponding column in the PRODSGP table.

## Example

To populate the PRODSGP table with a record that displays the item with the SKU number ACC12345-L to shoppers belonging to the *Seniors Shopper Club* using the sweater3.d2w product template, type:

```
#PRODSGP;ACC12345-L;Seniors Shopper Club;sweater3.d2w;
Discount Club for Seniors;;
```

# #CGPRREL

The #CGPRREL command, shown in Figure 5.11, populates the Category Product Relationship table, CGPRREL.

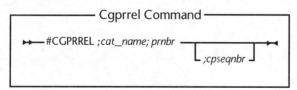

***Figure 5.11*** *The #CGPRREL command.*

The values of each parameter are as follows:

cat_name
> The fully qualified name of the category.

`prnbr`
> The product number, as defined in the PRODUCT table.

`cpseqnbr`
> The product sequence number, as defined in the CGPRREL table.

## Example

To populate the CGPRREL table with a record that places the product *V-Neck Sweater* with the product number ACC1234 and the sequence number 9 into the category:

*Clothing@Womens@Casual@Sweaters*, type:

```
#CGPRREL;Clothing@Womens@Casual@Sweaters;ACC1234;9
```

# Invoking the Mass Import Utility

After you have created an import file, you are ready to run the Mass Import utility to import the data contained in the file into the database.

1. Ensure that you are using the machine on which Net.Commerce is installed.

2. From any command window prompt, change to the following directory:

   **WIN** `\ibm\netcommerce3\bin\`
   **AIX** `/usr/lpp/NetCommerce3/bin/`

3. Type the command shown in Figure 5.12 all on one line (it is shown here on multiple lines for presentation purposes only).

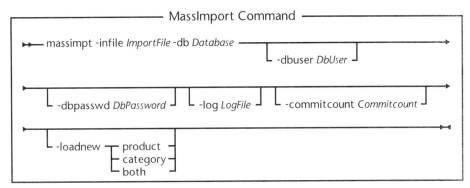

*Figure 5.12  The Mass Import utility command.*

The values of each parameter are as follows:

`ImportFile`
> The path and name of the text file that contains the product and category data to be imported.

`Database`
> The name of the database to which the data will be imported.  (The Mass Import utility uses ODBC to connect to the database.  This parameter actually refers to the ODBC data source name, which during the default installation of the Net.Commerce system is assigned the same name as the database.)

DbUser

The logon user ID of the administrator who has been assigned access to the database. If this parameter is not specified, the ID of the user currently running this utility will be used.

> **Note:**
> If your Net.Commerce database is Oracle, you must still include the logon user ID and password in the command, even if you are currently running this utility with the same user ID.

DbPassword

The password for the logon ID that is specified by the -DbUser parameter.

> **Note:**
> If your Net.Commerce database is Oracle, you must still include the logon user ID and password in the command, even if you are currently running this utility with the same user ID.

Logfile

The name of the file in which the Mass Import utility records its activities. If this parameter is not specified, the default log file, milog.txt, is created. Ensure that you specify a directory that can be written to. The current /bin directory is read-only.

Commitcount

The number of transactions within a commit scope. The default is 1. You can only enter integers for this parameter. If a value of 0 is specified, the data import will be committed after all the records are processed and the database connection is terminated.

loadnew

This parameter is used to load new products and/or categories into the database. Use it only if you are certain that your data has no duplicate records in the database. The Mass Import utility will not check the database tables for the existence of the records and will insert the records as new; this will create secondary table entries for any records that are duplicated. The -loadnew parameter has three levels:

product

Indicates that only the product records are new.

category

Indicates that only the category records are new.

both

Indicates that both the product and category records are new.

**Notes:**
- In previous versions of Net.Commerce, the Mass Import utility command contained an **-err** parameter for generating an error log file. If this parameter is specified in this version, it will be ignored.

- If you have installed the DB2 Text Extender for database searches, you will need to update the text indexes of the tables that have changed as a result of your using the Mass Import utility. For more information, refer to the Net.Commerce online help.

# Workshop: Adding the Remaining Products and Categories to the OneStopPizza Shop

In the previous workshop, "Adding a New Catalog to the OneStopPizza Shop" on page 107, you created the product *Vegetarian Delight* and its items (small, medium, and large sizes) under its parent *Our Famous Pizzas*. You will now create the products *Deli Delight* and *Tropical Delight*, also under the parent *Our Famous Pizzas*, and the *Make Your Own Pizza*, under the parent *Menus*, as shown in Figure 5.13 below:

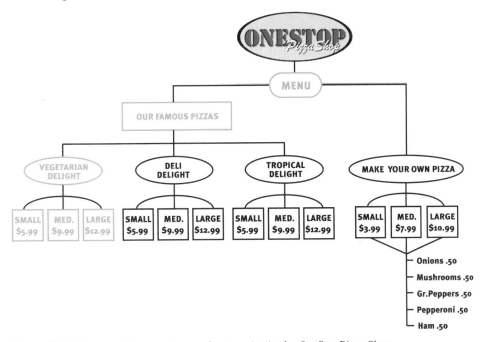

***Figure 5.13***  *The remaining products and categories in the OneStopPizza Shop.*

As you experienced in the previous workshop, creating the products and categories for a store one by one using the forms in the Store Manager is time-consuming. In this workshop, you will use the Mass Import utility to finish importing the remaining products and their items into the database for the OneStopPizza Shop.

To save you time, the import file that contains all the necessary commands for importing the remaining products has already been created for you. This file is called `pizza.in`.

1.  Copy the `pizza.in` import file from the `\workshops\massimpt\` directory on the CD to the following directory:

    **WIN**  `\ibm\netcommerce3\nc_schema\db2\`

2.  Open the file in a text editor.

Its content looks like this:

```
#STORE;OneStopPizza Shop
#PRODUCT;20;;Deli Delight;For you meat lovers, a generous helping
 of mozzarella cheese, pepperoni, sausage, and bacon.;;;/
 OneStopPizzaShop/deli_pizza1.gif;/OneStopPizzaShop/
 deli_pizza2.gif;1;;;;;;;SCSHP;;;;
#PRODDSTATR;20;Size
#PRODPRCS;20;;;USD
#PRODSGP;20;;/OneStopPizzaShop/prod1.d2w;
#PRODUCT;20-S;20;Deli Delight;For you meat lovers, a generous
 helping of mozzarella cheese, pepperoni, sausage, and bacon.;;;/
 OneStopPizzaShop/deli_pizza1.gif;/OneStopPizzaShop/
 deli_pizza2.gif;1;;;;;;;SCSHP;;;;
#PRODATR;20-S;Size;Small
#PRODPRCS;20-S;;5.99;USD
#PRODSGP;20-S;;/OneStopPizzaShop/prod1.d2w;
#PRODUCT;20-M;20;Deli Delight;For you meat lovers, a generous h
 helping of mozzarella cheese, pepperoni, sausage, and bacon.;;;/
 OneStopPizzaShop/deli_pizza1.gif;/OneStopPizzaShop/
 deli_pizza2.gif;1;;;;;;;SCSHP;;;;
#PRODATR;20-M;Size;Medium
#PRODPRCS;20-M;;9.99;USD
#PRODSGP;20-M;;/OneStopPizzaShop/prod1.d2w;
#PRODUCT;20-L;20;Deli Delight;For you meat lovers, a generous
 helping of mozzarella cheese, pepperoni, sausage, and bacon.;;;/
 OneStopPizzaShop/deli_pizza1.gif;/OneStopPizzaShop/
 deli_pizza2.gif;1;;;;;;;SCSHP;;;;
#PRODATR;20-L;Size;Large
#PRODPRCS;20-L;;12.99;USD
#PRODSGP;20-L;;/OneStopPizzaShop/prod1.d2w;
#CGPRREL;Our Famous Pizzas;20;2
#PRODUCT;30;;Tropical Delight;Hawaiian Heaven! Extra mozzarella
 cheese, pineapple, ham, and bacon.;;;/OneStopPizzaShop/
 trop_pizza1.gif;/OneStopPizzaShop/
 trop_pizza2.gif;1;;;;;;;SCSHP;;;;
#PRODDSTATR;30;Size
#PRODPRCS;30;;;USD
#PRODSGP;30;;/OneStopPizzaShop/prod1.d2w;
#PRODUCT;30-S;30;Tropical Delight;Hawaiian Heaven! Extra
 mozzarella cheese, pineapple, ham, and bacon.;;;/
 OneStopPizzaShop/trop_pizza1.gif;/OneStopPizzaShop/
 trop_pizza2.gif;1;;;;;;;SCSHP;;;;
#PRODATR;30-S;Size;Small
#PRODPRCS;30-S;;5.99;USD
#PRODSGP;30-S;;/OneStopPizzaShop/prod1.d2w;
#PRODUCT;30-M;30;Tropical Delight;Hawaiian Heaven! Extra
 mozzarella cheese, pineapple, ham, and bacon.;;;/
 OneStopPizzaShop/trop_pizza1.gif;/OneStopPizzaShop/
 trop_pizza2.gif;1;;;;;;;SCSHP;;;;
#PRODATR;30-M;Size;Medium
#PRODPRCS;30-M;;9.99;USD
```

```
#PRODSGP;30-M;;/OneStopPizzaShop/prod1.d2w;
#PRODUCT;30-L;30;Tropical Delight;Hawaiian Heaven! Extra
 mozzarella cheese, pineapple, ham, and bacon.;;;/
 OneStopPizzaShop/trop_pizza1.gif;/OneStopPizzaShop/
 trop_pizza2.gif;1;;;;;;;SCSHP;;;;
#PRODATR;30-L;Size;Large
#PRODPRCS;30-L;;12.99;USD
#PRODSGP;30-L;;/OneStopPizzaShop/prod1.d2w;
#CGPRREL;Our Famous Pizzas;30;3
#PRODUCT;40;;;Make Your Own Pizza;Create your own pizza from a
 selection of fresh and tasty toppings.;;/OneStopPizzaShop/
 make_pizza1.gif;/OneStopPizzaShop/
 make_pizza2.gif;1;;;;;;;SCSHP;;;;
#PRODDSTATR;40;Size
#PRODPRCS;40;;;USD
#PRODSGP;40;;/OneStopPizzaShop/prod2.d2w;
#PRODUCT;40-S;40;;Make Your Own Pizza;Create your own pizza from a
 selection of fresh and tasty toppings.;;/OneStopPizzaShop/
 make_pizza1.gif;/OneStopPizzaShop/
 make_pizza2.gif;1;;;;;;;SCSHP;;;;
#PRODATR;40-S;Size;Small
#PRODPRCS;40-S;;3.99;USD
#PRODSGP;40-S;;/OneStopPizzaShop/prod2.d2w;
#PRODUCT;40-M;40;;Make Your Own Pizza;Create your own pizza from a
 selection of fresh and tasty toppings.;;/OneStopPizzaShop/
 make_pizza1.gif;/OneStopPizzaShop/
 make_pizza2.gif;1;;;;;;;SCSHP;;;;
#PRODATR;40-M;Size;Medium
#PRODPRCS;40-M;;7.99;USD
#PRODSGP;40-M;;/OneStopPizzaShop/prod2.d2w;
#PRODUCT;40-L;40;;Make Your Own Pizza;Create your own pizza from a
 selection of fresh and tasty toppings.;;/OneStopPizzaShop/
 make_pizza1.gif;/OneStopPizzaShop/
 make_pizza1.gif;1;;;;;;;SCSHP;;;;
#PRODATR;40-L;Size;Large
#PRODPRCS;40-L;;10.99;USD
#PRODSGP;40-L;;/OneStopPizzaShop/prod2.d2w;
#CGPRREL;Menu;40;1
```

For an explanation of the commands used in this import file, see "Mass Import Utility Commands" on page 130.

3. Examine the commands used to import the *Make Your Own Pizza* product under its parent *Menu*, as follows:

```
#PRODUCT;40;;;Make Your Own Pizza;Create your own pizza from a
 selection of fresh and tasty toppings.;;/OneStopPizzaShop/
 make_pizza1.gif;/OneStopPizzaShop/
 make_pizza2.gif;1;;;;;;;SCSHP;;;;
#PRODDSTATR;40;Size
#PRODPRCS;40;;;USD
#PRODSGP;40;;/OneStopPizzaShop/prod2.d2w;
```

```
#PRODUCT;40-S;40;;Make Your Own Pizza;Create your own pizza from a
selection of fresh and tasty toppings.;;/OneStopPizzaShop/
make_pizza1.gif;/OneStopPizzaShop/
make_pizza2.gif;1;;;;;;;SCSHP;;;;
#PRODATR;40-S;Size;Small
#PRODPRCS;40-S;;3.99;USD
#PRODSGP;40-S;;/OneStopPizzaShop/prod2.d2w;
#PRODUCT;40-M;40;;Make Your Own Pizza;Create your own pizza from a
selection of fresh and tasty toppings.;;/OneStopPizzaShop/
make_pizza1.gif;/OneStopPizzaShop/
make_pizza2.gif;1;;;;;;;SCSHP;;;;
#PRODATR;40-M;Size;Medium
#PRODPRCS;40-M;;7.99;USD
#PRODSGP;40-M;;/OneStopPizzaShop/prod2.d2w;
#PRODUCT;40-L;40;;Make Your Own Pizza;Create your own pizza from a
selection of fresh and tasty toppings.;;/OneStopPizzaShop/
make_pizza1.gif;/OneStopPizzaShop/
make_pizza1.gif;1;;;;;;;SCSHP;;;;
#PRODATR;40-L;Size;Large
#PRODPRCS;40-L;;10.99;USD
#PRODSGP;40-L;;/OneStopPizzaShop/prod2.d2w;
#CGPRREL;Menu;40;1
```

These commands import the *Make Your Own Pizza* product and its sizes (small, medium, and large) into the database tables, just as the other products were imported. However, they do not import the pizza toppings (onions, mushrooms, green peppers, pepperoni, and ham) and their prices. This is because the default Net.Commerce database does not contain tables to store this type of information. In the workshop, "Planning New Overridable Functions for the OneStopPizza Shop" on page 362, you will learn how to add new tables to the database for storing this custom information and how to add the toppings and prices to those tables.

Another thing to note is that unlike the other products (*Vegetarian Delight, Deli Delight*, and *Tropical Delight*), which are displayed by the Store Creator's default prod1.d2w macro, the *Make Your Own Pizza* product is displayed by the prod2.d2w macro. The prod2.d2w macro is a custom macro that you will create in the workshop "Planning New Overridable Functions for the OneStopPizza Shop" on page 362. It will retrieve and display the toppings from the new tables you create, along with their prices.

4.  Now you will run the Mass Import utility to populate the database with the data contained in the pizza.in import file. Ensure that you are using the machine on which Net.Commerce is installed and then from any command prompt, change to the following directory:

    **WIN**    \ibm\netcommerce3\bin\

5. Type the following command all on one line (it is shown on more than one line for presentation purposes only):

```
massimpt -infile \ibm\netcommerce3\nc_schema\db2\pizza.in
-db <database>
-log \ibm\netcommerce3\macro\en_US\OneStopPizzaShop\pizza.log
-commitcount 0 -loadnew product
```

where `<database>` is the name of the database that you are using for the OneShopPizza Shop.

Note that you are using the `-commitcount` and the `-loadnew` parameters in order to enhance the performance of the Mass Import utility. The utility does not have to check the database tables for the existence of the product records, because you specified product for the `-loadnew` parameter, which indicates that the product records being imported are all new. Also, the data being imported will be committed only after all the records are processed and the database connection is terminated because you specified a value of 0 for the `-commitcount` parameter.

7. Before completing this workshop, examine the following import file (called `pizza2.in`). This file shows the commands needed to import all the product and category information into the database for the OneStopPizza Shop. You would create this file when you want to use only the Mass Import utility to import the data. The commands in bold font indicate the new commands that are needed to insert records for the top-level category *Top Category*, its subcategory *Our Famous Pizzas*, and its product *Vegetarian Delight*. (You have already entered these in the database using the Store Manager.)

```
#STORE;OneStopPizza Shop
#CATEGORY;Top Category;;;;;;1;;;
#CATESGP;Top Category;;/OneStopPizzaShop/cat1.d2w;;;;
#CATEGORY;Our Famous Pizzas;;;;/OneStopPizzaShop/
  pizza1.gif;;1;;;Top Category;1
#CATESGP;Our Famous Pizzas;;/OneStopPizzaShop/cat1.d2w;;;;
#PRODUCT;10;;Vegetarian Delight;For you veggie lovers, mozzarella
  cheese and a fresh mix of mushrooms, onions, green peppers,
  tomatoes, and basil.;;;/OneStopPizzaShop/veg_pizza1.gif;/
  OneStopPizzaShop/veg_pizza2.gif;1;;;;;;;SCSHP;;;;
#PRODDSTATR;10;Size
#PRODPRCS;10;;;USD
#PRODSGP;10;;/OneStopPizzaShop/prod1.d2w;
#PRODUCT;10-S;10;Vegetarian Delight;For you veggie lovers,
  mozzarella cheese and a fresh mix of mushrooms, onions, green
  peppers, tomatoes, and basil.;;;/OneStopPizzaShop/
  veg_pizza1.gif;/OneStopPizzaShop/
  veg_pizza2.gif;1;;;;;;;;SCSHP;;;;
#PRODATR;10-S;Size;Small
#PRODPRCS;10-S;;5.99;USD
#PRODSGP;10-S;;/OneStopPizzaShop/prod1.d2w;
```

```
#PRODUCT;10-M;10;Vegetarian Delight;For you veggie lovers,
mozzarella cheese and a fresh mix of mushrooms, onions, green
peppers, tomatoes, and  basil.;;;/OneStopPizzaShop/
veg_pizza1.gif;/OneStopPizzaShop/
veg_pizza2.gif;1;;;;;;;SCSHP;;;;
#PRODATR;10-M;Size;Medium
#PRODPRCS;10-M;;9.99;USD
#PRODSGP;10-M;;/OneStopPizzaShop/prod1.d2w;
#PRODUCT;10-L;10;Vegetarian Delight;For you veggie lovers,
mozzarella cheese and a fresh mix of mushrooms, onions, green
peppers, tomatoes, and basil.;;;/OneStopPizzaShop/
veg_pizza1.gif;/OneStopPizzaShop/
veg_pizza2.gif;1;;;;;;;SCSHP;;;;
#PRODATR;10-L;Size;Large
#PRODPRCS;10-L;;12.99;USD
#PRODSGP;10-L;;/OneStopPizzaShop/prod1.d2w;
#CGPRREL;Our Famous Pizzas;10;1
#PRODUCT;20;;Deli Delight;For you meat lovers, a generous helping
of mozzarella cheese, pepperoni, sausage, and bacon.;;;/
OneStopPizzaShop/deli_pizza1.gif;/OneStopPizzaShop/
deli_pizza2.gif;1;;;;;;;SCSHP;;;;
#PRODDSTATR;20;Size
#PRODPRCS;20;;;USD
#PRODSGP;20;;/OneStopPizzaShop/prod1.d2w;
```

.
.
.

This concludes this workshop.  In the next workshop, "Defining a Shopping Flow for the OneStopPizza Shop" on page 166, you will define the pages and the navigation paths in the store.

# Part 3, Creating Web Pages

Net.Commerce allows you to build Web pages that are capable of dynamically displaying up-to-the-minute information from the database, allowing a shopper to immediately know whether an item is in stock and the current price of that item. As well as displaying the data requested by the shopper, these pages serve to define the look and feel of your e-commerce site, thereby giving shoppers an impression of your overall business. Attractive, comprehensive, and intuitive pages enable shoppers to easily navigate to the products they are looking for, and ultimately encourage return visits.

This part provides the information you need to create all the Web pages for your store or mall. It introduces the concept of store and mall pages and describes the various methods that Net.Commerce provides for creating them.

## Contents:

- "Chapter 6, Store Pages" on page 149 introduces you to the most common types of store and mall pages and discusses different ways of defining the navigation paths that shoppers may take during their shopping trips.

- "Chapter 7, A Net.Data Tutorial" on page 169 shows you how to use the powerful Net.Data language to build Web pages that dynamically display the most recent information from the database.

- "Chapter 8, Modifying the Supplied Store Pages" on page 213 shows you how to modify the sample pages that are packaged with the Net.Commerce system and integrate them in your store or mall.

# Chapter 6, Store Pages

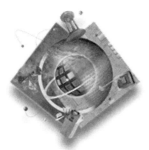

This chapter introduces the pages that most commonly appear in stores and malls, and shows how you can set them up to dynamically display information from the database. You will also learn how to combine these pages to define the navigation paths (the *shopping flow*) that shoppers may take as they browse your site. In the workshop, you will examine the store pages and the shopping flow that have been defined for the pizza store.

This chapter covers the following topics:

- Store and Mall Pages
- Common Store and Mall Pages
- Pages, Commands, and Tables: The Big Picture
- Creating the Shopping Flow
- Creating Store and Mall Pages
- Workshop: Defining the Shopping Flow for the OneStopPizza Shop

# Store and Mall Pages

*Store pages* are what shoppers see when they browse a store. They display information about the store and its products and services.

*Mall pages* display information about a mall. They typically include the mall home page; the mall directory, which lists all the stores within the mall; and any pages that are shared by all the stores, such as registration and order pages.

## Dynamic versus Static Pages

Before you begin to create pages, it is important that you understand the distinction between dynamic and static pages.

A *dynamic* page is created by a Net.Data macro. (Net.Data macros are discussed in detail in "Chapter 7, A Net.Data Tutorial" on page 169.) It contains information that is extracted from the database and displayed through a combination of SQL statements, Net.Data statements, and HTML. Typically, most of the pages in a store are dynamic, since most of the information—including the products, categories, prices, and shopper data—is subject to change. Dynamic store pages ensure that shoppers will always see the most up-to-date information.

A *static* page is created using only HTML. It is fixed in nature: that is, its content appears the same every time it is accessed. Typically, you use these pages for displaying information that is not likely to change or will change infrequently.

# Common Store and Mall Pages

Below are descriptions of the pages that are most commonly used in a store or mall. Their content and names are provided for illustrative purposes only and can be modified to meet your business requirements.

## Home Page

The home page acts as the virtual storefront (or mallfront), and is the first page that shoppers see when they access the site. It typically contains the name and logo of the store or mall, an introduction or welcome message, and links to the primary functions, such as the registration procedure, the mall directory (for a mall home page), the store catalog or departments (for a store home page), the administrative policies, copyright information, the terms and conditions for purchases and returns, customer service and other contact information, products or services that are currently being featured, the shopping cart (for repeat shoppers), the status of previously submitted orders, and the address book (if multiple shipping addresses are permitted).

Often a home page is divided into frames, consisting of at least a navigation frame and a main frame to display the page that is requested by the shopper.

## Creating Static versus Dynamic Home Pages

Home pages can be either dynamic or static, depending on how they are accessed. A home page that is displayed when the shopper types its URL on the command line must be static (HTML only), as it is displayed directly by the site's Web server. It can then be redirected to a dynamic page using a META tag or JavaScript. This typically applies to home pages for single stores and for malls. A home page can be dynamic if it will be accessed via a hypertext link: that is, it is preceded by another Web page. This typically applies to stores within a mall, which shoppers link to from a mall directory page. Creating a dynamic home page allows you to include up-to-date store information on the page.

# Mall Directory Page

A Mall Directory page lists the stores or main departments in a mall and provides links to their home pages, thereby allowing shoppers to easily locate the stores they want. It can be accessed via a hyperlink on the mall home page or from the mall's navigation frame, which makes it accessible from anywhere in the mall. You can choose to make it either static or dynamic.

# Registration Pages

There are typically two registration pages in a store: New Registration and Update Registration.

## New Registration Page

The New Registration page typically contains a blank form that a first-time shopper completes in order to register with the store. The form can contains fields for the following information:

- User logon ID
- Password
- Name
- Full address
- Title
- Employer
- Company name
- Telephone numbers (work and home) and type (listed or unlisted)
- Preferred method of communication and best time to call

- Fax Number
- e-mail address or URL
- Marital status
- Age
- Number of household members
- Annual household income
- Interests and hobbies
- Gender

The shopper's logon ID, password, last name, street address, city, state/province, zip/postal code, and country fields are mandatory.

## Update Registration Page

The Update Registration page typically contains a form that displays the registration information previously provided by the shopper, and allows the shopper to update it.

# Logon Page

The Logon page typically displays a form containing fields in which a registered shopper enters a user ID and password in order to log onto the store or mall.

# Address Pages

If your store supports multiple shipping addresses, the Address pages allow shoppers to maintain a personal log of the addresses of people (friends, family members, and so forth) to whom they frequently want to send goods. This log eliminates the need to retype addresses every time an order is placed: a shopper who wants to send an item to a third party merely has to enter the nickname (for example, "Mom") that he or she has chosen for that person.

There are typically three address pages in a store: the Main Address page, the Add Address page, and the Update Address page.

## Main Address Page

This page presents the options that are available for managing the address book. From here, the shopper can delete an address book entry, or connect to another page to add a new entry or update an existing one. To add an entry, the shopper usually has to first enter a nickname on this page. To update or delete an entry, the shopper usually has to first select the nickname of the entry to be updated or deleted on this page.

## Add Address Page

The Add Address page contains a blank form onto which the shopper can enter address information for a new person. This form contains fields for the following details:

- Person's title
- Full name (first, middle, and last)
- Daytime and evening telephone numbers
- Company name and fax number
- Full address
- E-mail address or URL

The last name, street address, city, state/province, country, and zip/postal code fields are mandatory.

The page typically contains a link to return the shopper to the Main Address page.

## Update Address Page

The Update Address page contains the address information of the person whose entry the shopper has selected to update. The shopper can update or add the following information:

- Person's title
- Full name (first, middle, and last)
- Daytime and evening telephone numbers
- Company name and fax number
- Full address
- E-mail address or URL

The last name, street address, city, state/province, country, and zip/postal code fields are mandatory.

The page typically contains a link to return the shopper to the Main Address page.

# Category Pages

Category pages help shoppers navigate through the various departments or groups of products or services available in a store. The first category pages lead to broad areas, and subsequent category pages narrow down the search. When a category cannot be further divided, its page contains links to product pages.

Category pages are typically dynamic in nature. They usually contain thumbnail images and brief descriptions to identify each category, and hypertext links to subcategories or products.

There are three types of category pages: those that list subcategories within a parent category, those that list products within a subcategory, and those that list both subcategories and products within a parent category.

You can create category pages to display to specific shopper groups, so that certain shoppers will see page styles or content that is likely to appeal to them. For example, pages with bold colors and designs may appeal more to a youth group than to a seniors' group.

# Product Pages

A Product page displays information about one particular product: typically, the product's name, a detailed description, a price, a full-sized image and, if the product has variations (for example, different sizes and colors), a form containing the choice of attributes. It also contains a form submit button so that the shopper can add the item with the chosen combination of attributes to the shopping cart.

Product pages are typically dynamic in nature. How many you create will depend on how much you want to vary the presentation of your products. For example, you may want to create a separate macro for each group of related products in your store (such as for brands of T-shirts), or just one macro for all your products. You may also want to display products differently to different shopper groups.

# Shopping Cart Page

The Shopping Cart page lists the products that the shopper has selected for possible purchase, including their names, prices, and other descriptive information. There are typically two types of shopping cart pages: the Interest List and the Order List. You can choose one or the other for your store or mall.

## Interest List

The Interest List displays all the products or items that the shopper has selected and is considering ordering. Items can be added to or removed from this list at any time. If the shopper is registered, the Interest List is permanent: that is, the items in it are retained until the shopper actively deletes them, and can be viewed on return visits. If the shopper is unregistered, any items in the list are not accessible once the shopper ends the browser session; the shopper is provided with a new empty Interest List on return visits.

This page typically contains a link to the Prepare Orders page, from which the shopper can select the items that he or she wishes to order.

## Order List

An Order List differs from an Interest List in that all the products and items contained in it are treated as one order and will be checked out together. Products and items can be added to or removed from this list at any time prior to checking them out. Before using the Order List, the shopper must register (on a first visit) or log on (on return visits). In addition to product descriptions, this list displays product quantities, and available shipping addresses and modes, all of which the shopper can update. The Order List is temporary: that is, once the items contained in it have been ordered, they are removed.

This page typically contains a link to the Checkout page, from which the shopper can place the order.

# Order Pages

The following are pages commonly associated with the order process. Which ones you choose to use will depend on whether you are creating a mall or store.

## Prepare Orders Page

This page is required if you use an Interest List. It is not necessary if you use an Order List, since it contains the same features. It lists all the items currently in the Interest List, along with descriptions, store names, product numbers, and prices. From it, the shopper can select the items to be ordered, and if multiple shipping addresses are supported, assign a shipping address to each item. Each address must be in the shopper's address book, and is specified using a nickname.

This page typically contains a link to the Shipping Details page, from which the shopper can change the quantity of items and any shipping information.

# Shipping Details Page

This page is required if you use an Interest List. If you use an Order List, you can include the following information either on the Order List page or on the Shipping Details page. It lists all items for which the shopper has specified shipping addresses. From this page, the shopper can update the quantity, the shipping address, and the shipping method, or remove an item from the order. The items are compiled according to the stores from which they were selected. A summary is also provided that includes the subtotal of the order, before taxes and shipping charges.

This page typically contains two links: one to display either the Checkout page (for a single store) or the Place Orders page (for a mall), from which the orders will be processed; and one to return the shopper to the Prepare Order page, from which additional items or shipping addresses can be selected.

# Place Orders Page

The Place Order page lists all pending orders (those that have been prepared but not placed) from one or more stores. It can also contain the nickname of the person to whom each order will be shipped; shipping carriers and modes; and the quantity of each item in each order. This page is only necessary for a mall, in which shoppers are able to prepare more than one order at a time. For a single store, in which shoppers can prepare only one order at a time, the Checkout page should be used instead.

From this page, the shopper can choose to process the orders one at a time by connecting to the Checkout page; remove an order (and all the items within it); or change shipping details.

# Checkout Page

The Checkout page is where the shopper confirms the details of an order and places the order. It contains detailed information about all the items in the order, including descriptions, shipping addresses, quantities, total prices, shipping charges, and taxes. The shopper can remove items from the order, view the details, and submit credit card information for payment.

# Order Confirmation Page

The Order Confirmation page informs the shopper that the order has been accepted by the system, and provides a reference number for it. In a mall, if the shopper has prepared other orders, he or she can either begin to process the next pending order or view a list of all pending orders.

# Order Status Page

The Order Status page lists all the orders that have been placed by the shopper. Each order description can consist of a reference number, store name, total price, date and time that the order was completed, and status (prepared, ordered, or canceled). The shopper can view the details of a completed order by connecting to the Completed Order Details page.

### Completed Order Details Page

The Completed Order Details page allows the shopper to confirm the details of an order that has been placed. It presents the shipping address(es), product descriptions, quantities, prices, shipping charges, sales taxes, and total charges for all items in the order, as well as the payment method (credit card type).

## Exception Pages

An exception page is displayed when a shopper does not interact correctly with the store or mall: for example, if the shopper types an incorrect password when logging on.

## System Error Pages

A system error message page is displayed when the system encounters a severe internal error that prevents it from performing the shopper's request. These pages are not usually seen by shoppers since they are caused by unforeseen system problems, not by user errors.

# Pages, Commands, and Tables: The Big Picture

Table 6.1 shows how commands and tables are typically used to invoke store pages and display their contents. Use this table as a guide to creating your store or mall pages.

For a description of the commands listed in the table, refer to "Appendix D, Net.Commerce Commands" on page 569. For a description of the database tables, see "Appendix C, Net.Commerce Database Tables" on page 511.

## Store/Mall Home Page

*Table 6.1* *The commands and database tables commonly used to create a mall or store home page.*

| Invoking Command | Features | Commands Used | Tables Used |
|---|---|---|---|
| N/A (If static, it is typically mapped to the index.html file. | Link to the Mall Directory page | ExecMacro | N/A |
| If dynamic, it is typically redirected to a macro from the index.html file using a META tag or JavaScript.) | Link to the category pages | CategoryDisplay | N/A |
| | Link to the Registration page | RegistrationForm | N/A |
| | Link to the Log On page | LogonForm | N/A |

*Continued on next page*

*Table 6.1* *Continued*

| Invoking Command | Features | Commands Used | Tables Used |
|---|---|---|---|
| | Link to the Interest List | InterestItemDisplay | N/A |
| | Link to the Order List | OrderItemDisplay | N/A |
| | Link to the Order Status page | OrderList?status=C | N/A |
| | Link to the address book pages | ExecMacro | N/A |

# Mall Directory Page

*Table 6.2* *The commands and database tables commonly used to create a Mall Directory page.*

| Invoking Command | Features | Commands Used | Tables Used |
|---|---|---|---|
| ExecMacro (only if dynamic; otherwise a hypertext link) | Links to the stores in the mall | CategoryDisplay | N/A |
| | Display information about each store | N/A | MERCHANT |

# New Registration Page

*Table 6.3* *The commands and database tables commonly used to create a New Registration page.*

| Invoking Command | Features | Commands Used | Tables Used |
|---|---|---|---|
| RegisterForm | Display a blank registration form for a new shopper to fill in | N/A | N/A |
| | Submit new registration information | RegisterNew | N/A |

# Update Registration Page

**Table 6.4** *The commands and database tables commonly used to create an Update Registration page.*

| Invoking Command | Features | Commands Used | Tables Used |
|---|---|---|---|
| RegisterForm | Display a shopper's registration information | N/A | SHOPPER SHADDR SHOPDEM |
| | Update registration information | RegisterUpdate | N/A |

# Logon Page

**Table 6.5** *The commands and database tables commonly used to create a Logon page.*

| Invoking Command | Features | Commands Used | Tables Used |
|---|---|---|---|
| LogonForm | Display fields for the user ID and password | N/A | N/A |
| | Log the shopper onto the store | Logon | N/A |

# Main Address Page

**Table 6.6** *The commands and database tables commonly used to create a Main Address page.*

| Invoking Command | Features | Commands Used | Tables Used |
|---|---|---|---|
| ExecMacro | Delete an entry from from the shopper's address book | AddressDelete | SHADDR |
| | Display the selected address entry for updating | AddressForm | SHADDR |
| | Display a blank form to add a new address entry | AddressForm | N/A |

# Add Address Page

*Table 6.7* *The commands and database tables commonly used to create an Add Address page.*

| Invoking Command | Features | Commands Used | Tables Used |
|---|---|---|---|
| AddressForm | Display a blank address form | N/A | N/A |
| | Add a new entry to the shopper's address book | AddressAdd | N/A |
| | Return to the Main Address page | ExecMacro | N/A |

# Update Address Page

*Table 6.8* *The commands and database tables commonly used to create an Update Address page.*

| Invoking Command | Features | Commands Used | Tables Used |
|---|---|---|---|
| AddressForm | Display the address information of a selected entry | N/A | SHADDR |
| | Update an entry in the shopper's address book | AddressUpdate | N/A |
| | Return to the Main Address page | ExecMacro | N/A |

# Category Page

*Table 6.9* *The commands and database tables commonly used to create a Category page.*

| Invoking Command | Features | Commands Used | Tables Used |
|---|---|---|---|
| CategoryDisplay | Display links to the subcategories | CategoryDisplay | CATEGORY CGRYREL |
| | Display category information | N/A | CATEGORY |
| | Display links to products or items | ProductDisplay | CATEGORY CGPRREL PRODUCT |
| | Display product or item information | N/A | PRODUCT PRODPRCS |

# Product Page

*Table 6.10* *The commands and database tables commonly used to create a Product page.*

| Invoking Command | Features | Commands Used | Tables Used |
|---|---|---|---|
| ProductDisplay | Display product or item information | N/A | PRODUCT PRODPRCS PRODDSTATR PRODATR |
| | Add a product or item to the Interest List | InterestItemAdd | N/A |
| | Add one or more products or items to the Order List | OrderItemProcess | N/A |

# Interest List

*Table 6.11* *The commands and database tables commonly used to create an Interest List.*

| Invoking Command | Features | Commands Used | Tables Used |
|---|---|---|---|
| InterestItemDisplay | Display the contents of Interest List, including descriptions and prices | N/A | SHOPPINGS PRODUCT PRODPRCS PRODATR |
| | Delete one or more products or items from the Interest List | InterestItemDelete | N/A |
| | Display the details of a product or item (link to its product page) | ProductDisplay | N/A |
| | Link to Prepare Orders page, to specify shipping addresses for each item to be ordered | OrderItemList | N/A |

# Order List/Shipping Details Page

*Table 6.12* *The commands and database tables commonly used to create an Order List or a Shipping Details page.*

| Invoking Command | Features | Commands Used | Tables Used |
|---|---|---|---|
| OrderItemDisplay | Display the products and items in an order, including quantities, shipping addresses, and shipping modes | N/A | SHIPTO<br>PRODUCT<br>PRODPRCS<br>PRODATR<br>SHADDR<br>SHIPMODE<br>MSHIPMODE<br>PRSPCODE |
| | Delete one or more products or items from the order | OrderItemDelete | N/A |
| | Change the quantity, shipping address, shipping mode, or all three for a single product or item | OrderItemUpdate | N/A |
| | For all items in the order, update the shipping address or shipping mode, or both | OrderShippingUpdate | N/A |
| | Link to the Checkout page | OrderDisplay?status=P | N/A |
| | Link to the Place Orders page (needed for a mall only) | OrderList?status=P | N/A |

# Prepare Orders Page

*Table 6.13* The commands and database tables commonly used to create a Prepare Orders page.

| Invoking Command | Features | Commands Used | Tables Used |
|---|---|---|---|
| OrderItemList | Display items selected for ordering, including available shipping addresses and shipping modes | N/A | SHOPPINGS PRODUCT PRODPRCS PRODATR SHADDR SHIPMODE MSHIPMODE PRSPCODE |
| | For each item to be ordered, specify a quantity, shipping address, or shipping mode | OrderItemProcess | N/A |
| | Link to the Shipping Details page | OrderItemDisplay | N/A |

# Place Orders Page

*Table 6.14* The commands and database tables commonly used to create a Place Orders page.

| Invoking Command | Features | Commands Used | Tables Used |
|---|---|---|---|
| OrderList | Display all pending orders for each store | N/A | ORDERS MERCHANT SHIPTO PRODUCT PRODPRCS PRODATR |
| | Remove an order | OrderCancel | N/A |
| | Place a selected order | OrderDisplay?status=P | N/A |

# Checkout Page

*Table 6.15* *The commands and database tables commonly used to create a Checkout page.*

| Invoking Command | Features | Commands Used | Tables Used |
|---|---|---|---|
| OrderDisplay?status=P | Display an order summary, including the items, the stores from which the items were ordered, shipping addresses, shipping modes, and the total cost with taxes | N/A | MERCHANT ORDERS SHIPMODE MSHIPMODE PRSPCODE SHADDR SHIPTO PRODUCT PRODΛTR |
| | Display payment options (credit card or C.O.D.) | N/A | N/A |
| | Submit the order | OrderProcess | N/A |
| | Cancel the order | OrderCancel | N/A |

# Order Confirmation Page

*Table 6.16* *The commands and database tables commonly used to create an Order Confirmation page.*

| Invoking Command | Features | Commands Used | Tables Used |
|---|---|---|---|
| OrderProcess | Display an order number, contact information, and the shipping details. | N/A | ORDERS MERCHANT |
| | Link to the Checkout page, to process the next pending order (for a mall only) | OrderDisplay?status=P | N/A |
| | Link to the Place Orders page, to view all pending orders (for a mall only) | OrderList?status=P | N/A |

## Order Status Page

*Table 6.17* *The commands and database tables commonly used to create an Order Status page.*

| Invoking Command | Features | Commands Used | Tables Used |
|---|---|---|---|
| OrderList?status=C | List all orders that have been placed, including a reference number, store name, total price, date and time that the order was completed, and status | N/A | ORDERS |
| | View details of an order (link to Completed Order Details page) | OrderDisplay?status=C | N/A |

## Completed Order Details Page

*Table 6.18* *The commands and database tables commonly used to create a Completed Order Details page.*

| Invoking Command | Features | Commands Used | Tables Used |
|---|---|---|---|
| OrderDisplay?status=C | Display the details of an order that has been placed, such as shipping aadress(es), product descriptions, shipping charges, and total charges | N/A | MERCHANT ORDERS SHIPMODE MSHIPMODE PRSPCODE SHADDR SHIPTO PRODUCT PRODATR |

# Creating the Shopping Flow

Once you are familiar with the types of pages that typically make up a store or mall, you are ready to define the shopping flow. The shopping flow indicates the pages that you will use and the paths by which shoppers can navigate to find products and make purchases.

Figures 6.1 and 6.2 show two shopping flows. Each uses different store pages and different commands to invoke each page. The dotted arrows indicate optional navigation paths, while the solid arrows indicate mandatory paths.

Note how much shorter and simpler Figure 6.2 is. Figure 6.1 shows how you can use most of the store pages and commands available, while Figure 6.2 shows how you can bypass certain pages and commands to create a simpler shopping flow. Use these examples as a guide to creating your own shopping flow.

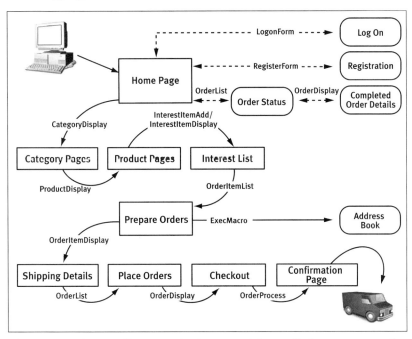

**Figure 6.1** *A shopping flow created using most of the supplied stores pages and commands.*

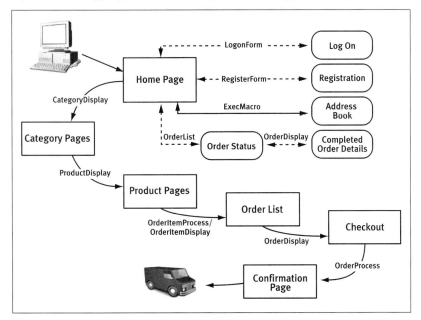

**Figure 6.2** *A shopping flow created using select store pages and commands.*

# Creating Store and Mall Pages

There are two ways to create store or mall pages: you can create them from scratch by writing your own Net.Data macros, or you can modify the pages that are supplied by Net.Commerce.

"Chapter 7, A Net.Data Tutorial" on page 169 provides a tutorial on how to write Net.Data macros for any store or mall page. "Chapter 8, Modifying the Supplied Store Pages" on page 213 describes how to modify any of the supplied store or mall pages and integrate them into your own site.

# Workshop: Defining a Shopping Flow for the OneStopPizza Shop

In this workshop, you will define the shopping flow for the OneStopPizza Shop. Although you will not be asked to perform any tasks, it is important that you read and understand the information presented, as it will be referred to in the workshops to follow.

Based on market research, you have determined that in order to be competitive in the pizza business you need to create a shopping flow that makes ordering over the Internet as fast and easy as ordering by phone. You want shoppers to be able to access the menu, select the pizzas they want, and place their orders with just a few clicks of the mouse. Figure 6.3 shows the shopping flow for the OneStopPizza Shop:

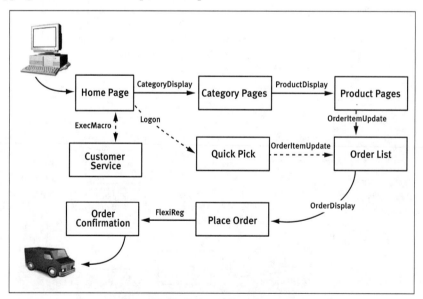

**Figure 6.3**  *The shopping flow for the OneStopPizza Shop.*

**Note:**
The store uses a new command, FlexiReg, which will either both register and process an order or just process an order, depending on the shopper's input. This eliminates the need to have a separate registration page, and simplifies the store's navigational structure. You will learn how to create this new command in the workshop "Writing the FlexiReg Command" on page 459.

# Store Pages

The following describes each page in the shopping flow:

## Home Page

The home page features the following:

- New customers can immediately start browsing the menu

- Return customers (those who have previously registered) can either log on or browse anonymously

## Navigation Bar

The shopper can do any of the following from the navigation bar:

- Return to the home page

- Browse the menu

- For registered shoppers who have logged on, view the types of pizzas that they have previously ordered and select any of them

- Access the Customer Services page for inquires or problems

## Quick Pick Page

The Quick Pick page, which is available only to registered shoppers, lists all types of pizzas that the shopper has ordered on previous occasions, and allows the shopper to add them directly to the Order List instead of having to browse the menu again. This makes the shopping trip more efficient, as shoppers can use it to quickly order pizzas that they purchase on a regular basis.

## Customer Service Page

The Customer Service page displays the store's address for customer inquiries or problems.

## Category Pages

From the menu, shoppers can either select a pre-made pizza or design one themselves.

## Product Pages

The store features the following product pages:

- One that displays the individual pre-made pizzas in the available sizes and toppings

- One that displays the options for making your own pizza

Both pages contain a description of the product, a full-sized image, sizes with prices, and a button to add the selection to the Order List.

## Order List

The Order List lists the pizzas that have been selected. If there is more than one, they are all part of the same order. From this page, shoppers can remove any items that they do not want, and connect to the Place Order page.

## Place Order Page

The Place Order page features the following:

- A summary of the shopper's order and the total charges, including taxes.

- A delivery address form, which is blank for new shoppers to fill out and pre-filled (but updateable) for registered shoppers.

- The option for new shoppers to register with the store by specifying a logon ID and password

- Payment options: either C.O.D. or credit card.

## Order Confirmation Page

The Order Confirmation page informs the shopper that the order was accepted, and provides a customer number and an order number for future inquiries.

You have now completed this workshop. In the next workshop in Chapter 7, you will learn how to create a new store page for the OneStopPizza Shop.

# Chapter 7, A Net.Data Tutorial

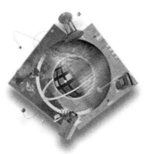

Net.Data is a powerful Web development tool for building dynamic store pages that extract up-to-date information from the database, such as catalog and pricing information, and display it to shoppers. This chapter introduces you to the Net.Data language and describes how to use it effectively. In the workshop, you will examine a Net.Data macro that was custom-built to meet a unique requirement of the pizza store.

This chapter covers the following topics:

- What is Net.Data?
- Invoking Net.Data Macros in Net.Commerce
- Writing Net.Data Macros
- Storing Net.Data Macros and Include Files
- Activating Net.Data Macros in the System
- Putting It All Together
- Workshop: Examining the Quick Pick Macro

# What is Net.Data?

Net.Data is a tool that allows you to quickly and easily create dynamic Web pages that interact with the Net.Commerce database. It uses language environments to access DB2 databases using ODBC. Net.Data has been integrated in Net.Commerce as an option for developing store pages. It is invoked as a Windows NT DLL or AIX shared library by the Net.Commerce daemon.

## Net.Data Macros

Net.Data macros are files that are parsed and executed by Net.Data. In Net.Commerce, they contain statements that retrieve information from the Net.Commerce database and display the results as a formatted Web page. They consist mostly of HTML with some Net.Data and SQL statements. The SQL statements search for and retrieve information from the database, the HTML defines the layout of the search results, and the Net.Data statements control the flow of the output.

In Net.Commerce, these macros perform three important store functions:

- They extract and display database information, such as products and categories for shoppers to select as they browse the store's catalog and make purchases

- They provide the interface for collecting information (such as a registration form for shoppers to fill out) that is required by commands to perform a specific store operation (such as registering)

- They display the result of the processing, whether it be a confirmation or an error message, back to the shopper as a store page.

# Invoking Net.Data Macros in Net.Commerce

You invoke a Net.Data macro either by calling a command that sets a view or exception task to display a store page as the final step of its execution (for example, the OrderDisplay or the CategoryDisplay command), or by calling the ExecMacro command.

## Calling a Command that Sets a View or Exception Task

All commands that set a view task as the final step of their execution invoke a Net.Data macro. By default all view tasks, except the CAT_DSP and PROD_DSP view tasks, call the TaskDisplay_1.0 (IBM,NC) overridable function, which determines from the database the file name of the macro to run. For example, the InterestItemDisplay command in its last step of execution sets the SHOPCART_DSP view task, which calls the TaskDisplay_1.0 (IBM,NC) overridable function. This function uses the reference number of the SHOPCART_DSP view task and the merchant reference number as the index to retrieve from the MACROS table the name of the Net.Data macro to execute, which by default is `shopcart.d2w`.

The CAT_DSP and PROD_DSP view tasks, which display category and product pages, respectively, call the MacroDisplay_1.0 (IBM,NC) overridable function. This function executes the %HTML_REPORT section of the macro that corresponds to the file name currently stored in the NC_Environment object. (The calling ProductDisplay or CategoryDisplay command retrieves the macro filename by querying the CSDISPLAY or PSDISPLAY column in the CATESGP or PRODSGP table for the merchant and category or product reference number that was passed to the command.) The category and product macros are stored in the CATESGP and PRODSGP tables, rather than the MACROS table, so that each product and category can be assigned to a different macro and to multiple shopper groups, for displaying a variety of category and product page layouts.

If a command calls an overridable function to do part of its processing, and the function encounters an exception condition, such as a shopper submitting incorrect information, the function sets an exception task to handle the error. By default, all exception tasks also call the TaskDisplay_1.0(IBM, NC) overridable function, which executes a Net.Data macro to display an error message. The function uses the reference number of the calling exception task and the merchant reference number as the index to retrieve from the MACROS table the name of the Net.Data macro to run.

All commands that set view or exception tasks invoke Net.Data macros starting from the %HTML_REPORT section, which is discussed in detail in "Creating a Web Page" on page 186.

# Calling the ExecMacro Command

The ExecMacro command is designed to call macros that are not assigned to a view or exception task and are therefore not stored in the database. It is also designed to call macros you create that are not designed for a specific command, such as search macros. It allows you to directly call a macro and specify whether it is to start executing from the %HTML_REPORT section or the %HTML_INPUT section. We will look at those sections in detail later; for now, you should just know that they are entry points into the macro.

The following is an example of using the ExecMacro command to invoke a macro starting from the %HTML_REPORT section:

```
To see the sample macro in action, <A HREF="/cgi-bin/ncommerce3/
ExecMacro/sample.d2w/input" TARGET="main"> click here</A>.
```

When executing a Net.Data macro, ensure that it is stored in one of the directories specified in the MACRO_PATH statement in the db2www.ini file. For more information, see "Specifying a Macro Directory" on page 195.

The following describes how a macro is invoked starting from a command in an online store:

1.  A shopper clicks a hypertext link or an HTML form button that calls a Net.Commerce command.

2.  The command is processed.

3.  The file name of the macro to execute is determined. If the command sets a view task to display a store page, or if an exception task is called to handle an error, the TaskDisplay_1.0 (IBM,NC) overridable function is called to retrieve from the database the file name of the Net.Data macro to execute. If the command is ExecMacro, the file name is determined from the command's URL.

4. The Net.Commerce daemon loads Net.Data as a DLL or shared library and passes the name of the macro to it. Net.Data expects two parameters: the name of the macro to process, and the HTML section to display. (All commands, except for the ExecMacro command, automatically specify the %HTML_REPORT section. For the ExecMacro command, you must explicitly specify the HTML section to be invoked; otherwise Net.Data will display an error in the browser.)

5. Net.Data searches for the macro name specified, using the MACRO_PATH statement in the db2www.ini file.

6. Input parameters are passed into the macro from HTML forms, command parameters, and other global variables, such as the SESSION_ID. These can be used in the macro to control processing.

7. Net.Data reads and parses through the macro and interprets the statements. Net.Data syntax controls the flow of the macro, and one or more SQL statements are executed to retrieve data from the database.

8. The results are formatted as an HTML page and returned to the browser.

# Writing Net.Data Macros

As mentioned earlier, Net.Data macros consist mostly of HTML, with some Net.Data statements to control the output and one or more SQL statements to retrieve information from the database. If you are familiar with HTML tagging, writing Net.Data macros simply involves adding the extra Net.Data and SQL statements that will be processed dynamically during run-time.

## Understanding the Macro Structure

To demonstrate how to create Net.Data macros for your store pages, we will first present an example. Once you understand the basic structure and functionality of a Net.Data macro, you will be able to write any macro required for your store.

The following code is a simple example of a Net.Data macro that illustrates most of the features you will want to include in your own macros. (Features that are not included here will be discussed later in the chapter.) When this macro is invoked by a command, it first displays an HTML form into which the shopper will enter his or her first name, last name, and phone number. Once the shopper submits this information, the macro displays a form that presents the shopper's challenge question, as well as fields in which to enter a new password and verification password.

Figures 7.1 and 7.2 illustrate the results of this macro:

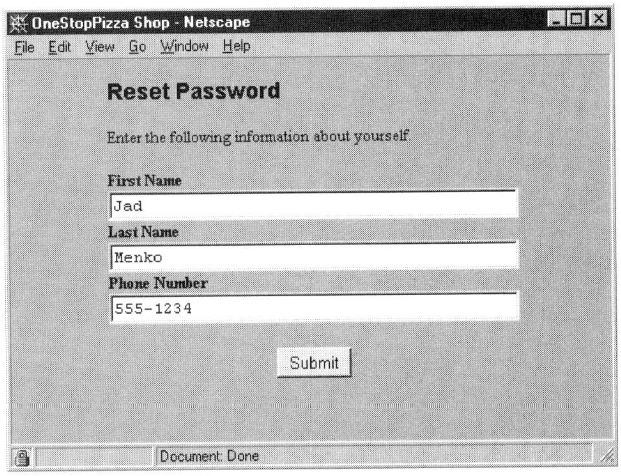

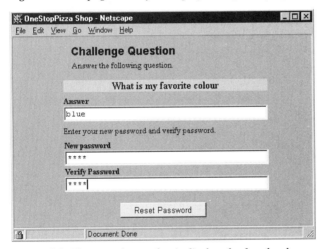

**Figure 7.1** *The page that is first displayed, requesting input from the shopper.*

**Figure 7.2** *The second page that is displayed, after the shopper submits the information.*

The source code for the macro is as follows:

```
%INCLUDE "OneStopPizzaShop\common.inc"

%{——————— Define Section ————————%}

%DEFINE {

  b_success = "true"
  s_loginid = ""

%}
```

```
%{————— Function Definition Section —————%}

%FUNCTION(DTW_ODBC) getQuestion() {

   select shchaque, shlogid
   from shopper, shaddr
   where salname='$(salname)'
   and shlogid = '$(SESSION_ID)'
   and safname='$(safname)'
   and saphone1='$(saphone1)'
   and sashnbr=shrfnbr
   and saadrflg='P'

   %REPORT {

      <TABLE WIDTH="300" CELLPADDING="0" CELLSPACING="0" BORDER="0">
        <TR>
           <TD ALIGN="left" VALIGN="center"><FONT FACE="helvetica"
           COLOR=$(TitleTxtCol)><H3>Challenge Question</H3></FONT></TD>
        </TR>
        <TR>
           <TD><FONT COLOR="black" SIZE="2">Answer the following
            question.</FONT></TD>
        </TR>
        <TR>
           <TD><BR></TD>
        </TR>

      %ROW {

         @DTW_ASSIGN(s_loginid, V_shlogid)
         <TR>
            <TD ALIGN="center" BGCOLOR=$(BodyColor2)>
            <FONT COLOR="$(TitleTxtCol)" SIZE="3">
            <B>$(V_shchaque)</B></FONT><BR></TD>
         </TR>
      %}
   %}

   %MESSAGE {

      100 : {
         <B>Your shopper record was not found in the database.  Please try
         again.</B>
         <BR><BR>
         @DTW_ASSIGN(b_success, "false")
      %}: CONTINUE

      DEFAULT : {
         <B>An unknown error occurred in the getQuestion() function.</B>
      %}
   %}
%}
```

```
%{——————— HTML Input Section ——————%}

%HTML_INPUT {

  <HTML>
  <HEAD><TITLE>Reset Password</TITLE></HEAD>
  <BODY BGCOLOR="$(BodyColor1)" TEXT="$(TextCol)" LINK="$(LinkCol)"
   VLINK="$(VLinkCol)" ALINK="$(ALinkCol)">

  <FORM METHOD="post" ACTION="/cgi-bin/ncommerce3/ExecMacro/
   $(STORENAME)/password.d2w/report">

  <TABLE WIDTH=250 CELLPADDING=0 CELLSPACING=0 BORDER=0>
    <TR>
      <TD ALIGN="left" VALIGN="center"><FONT FACE="helvetica"
      COLOR=$(TitleTxtCol)>
      <H3>Reset Password</H3></FONT></TD>
    </TR>
    <TR>
      <TD ALIGN="left"><FONT COLOR="black" SIZE="2">Enter the
      following information about yourself.</FONT></TD>
    </TR>
    <TR><TD><BR></TD></TR>
    <TR>
      <TD><B><FONT SIZE="-1">First Name</FONT></B></TD>
    </TR>
    <TR>
      <TD><INPUT TYPE="text" NAME="safname" SIZE="40"
       MAXLENGTH="30"></TD>
    </TR>
    <TR>
      <TD><B><FONT SIZE="-1">Last Name</FONT></B></TD>
    </TR>
    <TR>
      <TD><INPUT TYPE="text" NAME="salname" SIZE="40"
       MAXLENGTH="30"></TD>
    </TR>
    <TR>
      <TD><B><FONT SIZE="-1">Phone Number</B></FONT></TD>
    </TR>
    <TR>
      <TD><INPUT TYPE="text" NAME="saphone1" SIZE="40"
       MAXLENGTH="30"></TD>
    </TR>
    <TR>
      <TD><BR></TD>
    </TR>
    <TR>
      <TD ALIGN="center"><INPUT TYPE="submit" VALUE="Submit"></TD>
    </TR>

  </TABLE>
```

```
    </FORM>
    </BODY>
    </HTML>

%}


%{─────────── HTML Report Section ───────────%}


%HTML_REPORT{

  <HTML>
  <HEAD><TITLE>Reset Password</TITLE></HEAD>
  <BODY BGCOLOR="$(BodyColor1)" TEXT="$(TextCol)" LINK="$(LinkCol)"
   VLINK="$(VLinkCol)" ALINK="$(ALinkCol)">

  <FORM method=POST action="/cgi-bin/ncommerce3/PasswordReset">

@getQuestion()

  <INPUT TYPE = "hidden" NAME="merchant_rn" VALUE="$(MerchantRefNum)">
  <INPUT TYPE = "hidden" NAME="login_id" VALUE="$(s_loginid)">

%IF(b_success == "true")
  <TR>
    <TD><BR></TD>
  </TR>
  <TR>
    <TD><B><FONT SIZE="-1">Answer</FONT></B></TD>
  </TR>
  <TR>
    <TD><INPUT TYPE="text" NAME="chal_ans" SIZE="40"
    MAXLENGTH="254"></TD>
  </TR>
  <TR>
    <TD><BR></TD>
  </TR>
  <TR>
    <TD><FONT COLOR="black" SIZE="2">Enter your new password and
    verify password.</FONT></TD>
  </TR>
  <TR>
    <TD><BR></TD>
  </TR>
  <TR>
    <TD><B><FONT SIZE="-1">New password</FONT></B></TD>
  </TR>
  <TR>
    <TD><INPUT TYPE="password" NAME="new_pass" SIZE="40"
    MAXLENGTH="16"></TD>
  </TR>
  <TR>
    <TD><B><FONT SIZE=-1>Verify Password</FONT></B></TD>
```

```
    </TR>
    <TR>
      <TD><INPUT TYPE="password" NAME="newver_pass" SIZE="40"
      MAXLENGTH="16"></TD>
    </TR>
    <TR>
      <TD><BR></TD>
    </TR>
    <TR>
      <TD ALIGN="center"><INPUT TYPE="submit" VALUE="Reset Password">
      </TD>
    </TR>
    </TABLE>

  %ENDIF

    </FORM>
    </BODY>
    </HTML>

  %}
```

Note that this example consists of four main sections: the %DEFINE section, the %FUNCTION section, the %HTML_INPUT section, and the %HTML_REPORT section.

- The %DEFINE section contains the variables that you want to reference later in the macro.

- The %FUNCTION section contains SQL queries for retrieving information from the database, and HTML to display the results of the query.

- The %HTML_INPUT and %HTML_REPORT sections both contain HTML for displaying a complete HTML document, with the addition of Net.Data statements to call the SQL queries, control the flow of the macro's execution, and assign or reference variables.

You must have at least one HTML section defined in the macro. Net.Data executes the macro starting from either the %HTML_REPORT or %HTML_INPUT section, depending on which is specified. All the default commands that set view or exception tasks execute a macro from the %HTML_REPORT section, with the exception of the ExecMacro command, which allows you to specify the %HTML_INPUT or the %HTML_REPORT section.

 The %DEFINE section and the %FUNCTION section are optional, but to retrieve information from the database, you need to include at least one %FUNCTION section.  You can add multiple %DEFINE sections or %FUNCTION sections, if desired.

# Net.Data Variables

Using variables makes it easy to make global changes to your macros and is necessary for keeping your macros dynamic in nature.  Macros generally do not contain fixed values for data that exists in the database, because this information is constantly changing as different shoppers access the store and the business itself changes.  For example, as a store's product line expands and new products are introduced, updates to the database will be required to reflect this and to handle inventory changes.

You can explicitly define your own variables to reference the information in the database or to control the flow of the macro, or use the variables that have predefined values set by Net.Data. In addition, any input parameters that are passed into the macro from an HTML form or from data appended directly to a URL are implicitly defined as variables in the macro. For example, the OrderDisplay command, before invoking a macro to display a shopper's order, creates an order and passes the order reference number to the macro as an input parameter. This reference number can be used by the macro by referencing it as a variable.

**Note:**
Net.Data treats all variables as alphanumeric strings. You cannot define variables as integers.

## Defining Variables

In Net.Commerce, there are typically four ways to define variables in Net.Data macros: by using the %DEFINE section or the %DEFINE statement, by using Net.Data's built-in DTW_ASSIGN function, by using an HTML form, or by using a URL. We will examine each of these methods below.

### Using the %DEFINE Section or Statement

Using the %DEFINE section or the %DEFINE statement is the simplest way to define one or more variables that can be referenced from any part of the macro. In the example introduced at the beginning of the chapter, the %DEFINE section was used to define two variables, as follows:

```
%DEFINE {

    b_success = "true"
    s_loginid = ""


%}
```

The first variable that is defined, b_success, is assigned the string "true" and can be referenced anywhere in the macro using the syntax $(b_success). The second variable, s_loginid, is assigned an empty string for a value.

Another way to define a single variable is to use the %DEFINE statement alone, as follows:

```
%DEFINE b_success = "true"
%DEFINE s_loginid = ""
```

As you can see, the %DEFINE section is an easier to way to define multiple variables because you use only one %DEFINE statement.

Variable names must begin with a letter or underscore, and can contain any alphanumeric characters or an underscore. All variable names are case-sensitive, except N_columnName and V_columnName, which are table variables.

In addition to the simple string variables you have seen up to now, you can define within a %DEFINE section conditional variables, environment variables, list variables, table variables, and system variables. For information on how to define these variable types, consult the Net.Data documentation.

You can add multiple %DEFINE sections or %DEFINE statements to a macro as long as they are at the outermost macro level and they appear before any %FUNCTION or HTML sections that reference the macros. You can reference variables from any place in a Net.Data macro. If the variable has not yet been defined at the time it is referenced, Net.Data defines it and gives it an initial value of null. During parsing of the Net.Data macro, when a variable reference is found, it is evaluated and replaced inline with the current value of the variable.

### Using HTML Forms

You can use the INPUT and SELECT tags of an HTML form to define variables in a macro. The values of these variables are defined by the selection or input made by the shopper. You can then pass the variables as input parameters to another HTML section of the macro, to another macro, or to a command, depending on what you have defined as the URL for the form's ACTION tag.

Our example uses standard HTML form tags in the %HTML_INPUT section to define variables, as follows:

```
<FORM METHOD="post" ACTION="/cgi-bin/ncommerce3/ExecMacro/
$(STORENAME)/password.d2w/report">

<TABLE WIDTH=250 CELLPADDING=0 CELLSPACING=0 BORDER=0>
  <TR>
    <TD ALIGN="left" VALIGN="center"><FONT FACE="helvetica"
    COLOR=$(TitleTxtCol)>
    <H3>Reset Password</H3></FONT></TD>
  </TR>
  <TR>
    <TD ALIGN="left"><FONT COLOR="black" SIZE="2">Enter the
    following information about yourself.</FONT></TD>
  </TR>
  <TR><TD><BR></TD></TR>
  <TR>
    <TD><B><FONT SIZE="-1">First Name</FONT></B></TD>
  </TR>
  <TR>
    <TD><INPUT TYPE="text" NAME="safname" SIZE="40"
    MAXLENGTH="30"></TD>
  </TR>
  <TR>
    <TD><B><FONT SIZE="-1">Last Name</FONT></B></TD>
  </TR>
  <TR>
    <TD><INPUT TYPE="text" NAME="salname" SIZE="40"
    MAXLENGTH="30"></TD>
  </TR>
  <TR>
    <TD><B><FONT SIZE="-1">Phone Number</B></FONT></TD>
  </TR>
  <TR>
    <TD><INPUT TYPE="text" NAME="saphone1" SIZE="40"
    MAXLENGTH="30"></TD>
  </TR>
```

```
<TR>
   <TD><BR></TD>
</TR>
<TR>
   <TD ALIGN="center"><INPUT TYPE="submit" VALUE="Submit"></TD>
</TR>
</TABLE>

</FORM>
```

In this example, the values of the three variables `safname`, `salname`, and `saphone1` are defined when the shopper enters values into the corresponding form text input fields. When the shopper submits the information, the three variables, which now have values, are passed as name-value pairs to the `%HTML_REPORT` section of the macro, as defined in the URL for the form's ACTION tag.

You can use the INPUT and SELECT tags in the HTML sections and the `%FUNCTION` sections of macros. Note that the value of a variable that is received from an INPUT or SELECT tag overrides the value of a variable defined in the `%DEFINE` section or the `%DEFINE` statement in the macro.

### Using a URL

In the URL with which you call Net.Data, you can pass variables along with the command to send to Net.Data. All commands accept the parameters that were initially passed into them from a Net.Data macro, and pass them unchanged to any overridable functions and macros that are called downstream.

The following is an example of a URL for a hypertext link containing the CategoryDisplay command to execute a macro and pass to it variables for the selected category's reference number and the reference number of the merchant to which it belongs.

```
<A HREF="/cgi-bin/ncommerce3/CategoryDisplay?
cgrfnbr=$(V_cgrfnbr)&cgmenbr=$(V_cgmenbr)">Hardware</A>
```

The values for the two variables `cgrfnbr` and `cgmenbr` are referencing the rows in a query that was previously run in the macro. These variables are needed for the TaskDisplay_1.0 (IBM,NC) function, which is called by the CategoryDisplay command to determine in the database what Net.Data macro file to run. They are also passed unchanged to the macro that is executed. They can be referenced anywhere in the macro using the syntax `$(cgrfnbr)` and `$(cgmenbr)`.

### Using the DTW_ASSIGN Function

You can store the value of string variables in new string variable names using the built-in Net.Data function call `@DTW_ASSIGN`. It has the following syntax:

```
@DTW_ASSIGN(variable2,variable1)
```

In this example, the value of `variable1` is stored in `variable2`. You can assign a string variable using the `DTW_ASSIGN` function in the `%FUNCTION`, the `%HTML_INPUT`, or the `%HTML_REPORT` section of a macro. It is especially useful in the `%ROW` block of a `%FUNCTION` section in order to make a column value that is retrieved from an SQL query accessible from anywhere in the macro. (All database table value names defined as `V1` or `V_columnName` can be referenced only from within a `%ROW` block.)

In our example, the value of the shopper's login ID that is retrieved from the SQL query in the `%FUNCTION` section is assigned to a new variable, so that this variable can be referenced later in the macro from outside of the `%ROW` block.  The source code is as follows:

```
%FUNCTION(DTW_ODBC) getQuestion() {

    select shchaque, shlogid
    from shopper, shaddr
    where salname='$(salname)'
    and shlogid = '$(SESSION_ID)'
    and safname='$(safname)'
    and saphone1='$(saphone1)'
    and sashnbr=shrfnbr
    and saadrflg='P'

    %REPORT {

        <TABLE WIDTH="300" CELLPADDING="0" CELLSPACING="0" BORDER="0">
          <TR>
            <TD ALIGN="left" VALIGN="center"><FONT FACE="helvetica"
            COLOR=$(TitleTxtCol)><H3>Challenge Question</H3></FONT></TD>
          </TR>
          <TR>
            <TD><FONT COLOR="black" SIZE="2">Answer the following
             question.</FONT></TD>
          </TR>
          <TR>
            <TD><BR></TD>
          </TR>

        %ROW {

        @DTW_ASSIGN(s_loginid, V_shlogid)
        <TR>
          <TD ALIGN="center" BGCOLOR=$(BodyColor2)>
          <FONT COLOR="$(TitleTxtCol)" SIZE="3">
          <B>$(V_shchaque)</B></FONT><BR></TD>
        </TR>
      %}
    %}
```

The value of column shlogid retrieved from the query is referenced in the `%ROW` block using the syntax `V_shlogid`, and is then stored in the variable `s_loginid`.  The `%HTML_REPORT` section references the new variable `s_loginid` as a hidden input parameter for a form, as follows:

```
<INPUT TYPE="hidden" NAME="login_id" VALUE="$(s_loginid)">
```

## Referencing Variables

In Net.Data macros, variables are referenced by specifying the variable name inside `$(` and `)`; for example, `$(satitle)`.  When Net.Data finds a variable reference, it replaces the reference with the variable's value.  In this case, it would replace `$(satitle)` with the value stored in the database for the current shopper's title (Dr., Mr., Mrs., or Ms.).  You can reference variables from any part of the macro.  If the variable has not yet been defined at the time it is referenced, Net.Data defines it and gives it an initial value of null.  During parsing of the Net.Data macro, when a variable reference is found, it is evaluated and replaced inline with the current value of the variable.

Our examples use variable references extensively.  The following shows a few instances:

```
%HTML_REPORT{

  <HTML>
  <HEAD><TITLE>Reset Password</TITLE></HEAD>
  <BODY BGCOLOR="$(BodyColor1)" TEXT="$(TextCol)" LINK="$(LinkCol)"
   VLINK="$(VLinkCol)" ALINK="$(ALinkCol)">

  <FORM method=POST action="/cgi-bin/ncommerce3/PasswordReset">

@getQuestion()

  <INPUT TYPE = "hidden" NAME="merchant_rn" VALUE="$(MerchantRefNum)">
  <INPUT TYPE = "hidden" NAME="login_id" VALUE="$(s_loginid)">
```

The variable references $(BodyColor1), $(TextCol), $(LinkCol), $(VLinkCol), $(ALinkCol), and $(MerchantRefNum) will be replaced with the values of the corresponding variable names defined in the common.inc file that was imported into the macro.  The variable reference $(s_loginid) will get replaced with the value retrieved from the SQL query.

# Retrieving and Displaying Database Information

For almost every macro you create, you will need to retrieve information from the database to display to shoppers, to use for processing within the macro, or to pass as parameters to a command that will process the information.  For example, to enable catalog browsing, you will need one or more macros to retrieve and display information about the categories that shoppers select.  And when shoppers want to view a product of interest, the details of the product, including a price, description and maybe a picture or two, must be retrieved from the database and displayed.  When the shopper places an order, the total charges of the order and a summary of the items in it are commonly displayed.

To retrieve this information as well as other store information from the database for either displaying to the shopper as a Web page or passing as parameters to commands or other macros, you use the %FUNCTION section.  This section defines a function in the language environment you specify.  It has the following syntax:

```
%FUNCTION (DTW_ODBC) FunctionName(){

  ...SELECT statement to retrieve database information

  %REPORT {

    ...HTML to display header information
```

```
%ROW {

    ...HTML and database variable references to display each row

%}

%}

%MESSAGE {

  error_code : message_text : action

%}

%}
```

You can include as many functions in a macro as you like. You can even use the same name for different functions. When the macro calls the name, Net.Data will execute all the functions with the same name in the order in which they were defined in the macro. You must define all functions at the outermost macro level, and you must insert them before calling the function. To call a function, reference its name in an `%HTML_INPUT` section or `%HTML_REPORT` section and use the following syntax:

```
@FunctionName()
```

Because Net.Commerce uses ODBC to connect to the database, you must use the `DTW_ODBC` language environment statement to provide the interface between the database and Net.Data. The language environment statement must be configured in the db2www.ini file.

Let's look at the `%FUNCTION` statement defined in our macro example:

```
%FUNCTION(DTW_ODBC) getQuestion() {
```

This statement defines a function called `getQuestion` in the ODBC language environment.

After you have defined the function language environment and its name, you typically begin the function with an SQL SELECT statement to query the database and retrieve the information you need. The following is the SQL statement for the `getQuestion` function:

```
select shchaque, shlogid
from shopper, shaddr
where salname='$(salname)'
and shlogid = '$(SESSION_ID)'
and safname='$(safname)'
and saphone1='$(saphone1)'
and sashnbr=shrfnbr
and saadrflg='P'
```

This statement retrieves from the SHOPPER (Shopper Profile) table the challenge question and the logon ID for the shopper whose first name, last name, and phone number match the corresponding values that were passed into the macro as implicitly defined variables.

Since the `SESSION_ID` parameter is passed with all commands, you can use this parameter to select information from tables that are keyed off the session ID.

If the information is retrieved successfully, you use the `%REPORT` block to handle the results of the query. Typically, this block contains HTML to define how the data is displayed in the browser, but it can also contain variable references and function calls. It is processed and displayed once during the function call.

To specify how the function is to handle each matching row retrieved from the query, you use the `%ROW` block within the `%REPORT` block. The `%ROW` block is processed once for each row retrieved from the query. It can contain HTML, commands, and references to data in the current row being processed. To reference data from a row, you use the syntax `$(V2)` or `$(V_columnName)`. For example, `$(V2)` refers to the content of the second column in the row, and `$(V_PRRFNBR)` refers to the content of column PRRFNBR. Another useful implicitly defined variable is `ROW_NUM`, which stores the row number of the row currently being processed and, after the `%ROW` block has been processed, stores the total number of rows in the table. You can use `%IF`, `%ELSE`, and `%ENDIF` statements to handle each row differently. You can also use the built-in function call `%DTW_ASSIGN` to assign row values to variables that can be accessed from outside of the `%ROW` block.

If you do not want to display anything before or after the query results table (if the `%ROW` block is executed at least once, Net.Data treats everything it finds before the `%ROW` block as header information and everything it finds after as footer information), you can leave these "header" and "footer" sections empty.

The following is the `%REPORT` block for the `getQuestion` function:

```
%REPORT {

   <TABLE WIDTH="300" CELLPADDING="0" CELLSPACING="0" BORDER="0">
     <TR>
       <TD ALIGN="left" VALIGN="center"><FONT FACE="helvetica"
       COLOR=$(TitleTxtCol)><H3>Challenge Question</H3></FONT>
       </TD>
     </TR>
     <TR>
       <TD><FONT COLOR="black" SIZE="2">Answer the following
       question.</FONT></TD>
     </TR>
     <TR>
       <TD><BR></TD>
     </TR>

   %ROW {

   @DTW_ASSIGN(s_loginid, V_shlogid)
   <TR>
     <TD ALIGN="center" BGCOLOR=$(BodyColor2)>
     <FONT COLOR="$(TitleTxtCol)" SIZE="3">
     <B>$(V_shchaque)</B></FONT><BR></TD>
   </TR>
   %}
 %}
```

In this example, the %REPORT block displays the page title and introductory text as the header information. For each row retrieved, the %ROW first uses the @DTW_ASSIGN built-in function call to assign the value of the logon ID that was retrieved from the query (using the variable reference $(V_shlogid) to a variable called s_loginid. Now the logon ID can be referenced from outside of the %ROW block. The remaining HTML displays the retrieved challenge question using the variable reference $(V_shchaque).

When the function call completes, you use the %MESSAGE block to determine how to proceed, based on the function's return code. The %MESSAGE block is most useful for handling errors that are returned by the SQL statement. For example, if no matching rows are returned from the SQL query, an SQL error code of 100 is returned. You can add HTML in this block to provide a meaningful error message to the shopper for each type of error that could be encountered. You can also indicate the action that you want to take: either to exit the macro immediately by using the EXIT statement, or to continue processing the rest of the macro after displaying to the error message by using the CONTINUE statement. If no action is specified, the default is EXIT.

You can define a %MESSAGE block within each function defined, or define one at the outermost layer of the macro that will be used to handle the return codes of all functions in the macro.

The following is the %MESSAGE block for the getQuestion function:

```
%MESSAGE {

   100 : {
     <B>Your shopper record was not found in the database.  Please try
     again.</B>
     <BR><BR>
     @DTW_ASSIGN(b_success, "false")
   %}: CONTINUE

   DEFAULT : {
     <B>An unknown error occurred in the getQuestion() function.</B>
   %}
%}
```

This %MESSAGE block contains two message statements. If an SQL error code of 100 is returned by the function (no rows were found that matched the SELECT statement), the first statement is executed, which displays an error message in the shopper's browser and assigns the value "false" to the variable b_success. After the message is displayed, the CONTINUE statement is executed, which specifies to continue processing the remainder of the macro from where the function was called. For any other error codes returned from the SQL query that are not specified in the %MESSAGE block and if the return code is not 0, the second message statement will be executed, which displays a generic message in the shopper's browser. This statement does not specify an action to take once the message is displayed, so by default, Net.Data stops execution of the macro immediately. If you do not include the DEFAULT statement and an error code is returned that is not handled in the %MESSAGE block, Net.Data will display a default error message in the browser.

**Tip:**
When writing error messages, it is advisable to specify the name of the function that fails to facilitate debugging. (These error messages should never be seen by shoppers.)

# Creating a Web Page

You create a Web page by executing either the %HTML_INPUT or %HTML_REPORT section of a Net.Data macro. These sections are entry points into the macro, from which the flow and invocation of the other sections of the macro are controlled. HTML sections typically call functions in a specific order, which retrieve and display database information, along with any static graphics and text, as a Web page in the browser.

There is no difference between the %HTML_INPUT section and the %HTML_REPORT section of a Net.Data macro: they both are entry points into the macro, and they can both contain any valid HTML tags required for a displaying a Web page (<HTML><TITLE><HEAD><FORM>, <TABLE> tags, and so forth). In addition to containing HTML and function calls, both can contain %INCLUDE statements to import other files into the macro; %IF, %ELSE, and %ENDIF statements to control the flow of execution; variable references; and commands to process the input. When Net.Data processes the %HTML_INPUT or %HTML_REPORT section of a macro, anything not recognized as a Net.Data statement is assumed to be HTML and is sent to the browser to be displayed.

In most cases you will execute a macro starting from the %HTML_REPORT section, because by default all commands that set a view or exception task to display a Web page execute that section of the macro assigned to the task. You cannot use these commands to invoke the %HTML_INPUT section. A common use for the %HTML_REPORT section is to display a form in order to collect input from shoppers, such as registration information. Once the input is provided, the ACTION URL of the form can either call a command to process the input and call another macro to display the results, or it can execute the %HTML_INPUT section directly to process the input and display the results. Many macros contain only an %HTML_REPORT section (for example, product and category macros), in which case the %HTML_REPORT may simply run SQL queries to retrieve database information and display HTML based on the parameters passed in from the command that invoked the section, or display the results of a command's processing.

If, however, you create a macro for which there is no corresponding view or exception task, such as a search page or a page that features daily specials, you must execute it using the ExecMacro command. In this case, you can choose to execute the macro starting from either HTML section, by specifying the corresponding parameter in the command. For example, the following shows how a macro called specials.d2w can be invoked by the ExecMacro command, starting from either the %HTML_INPUT section or the %HTML_REPORT section:

```
ExecMacro/specials.d2w/input
ExecMacro/specials.d2w/report
```

The syntax of the %HTML_INPUT section is as follows:

```
%HTML_INPUT {

    ......
    @FunctionName()
    %INCLUDE "filename.inc"
    ......

%}
```

The syntax of the `%HTML_REPORT` section is as follows:

```
%HTML_REPORT {

   ......
   @FunctionName()
   %INCLUDE "filename.inc"
   ......

%}
```

In either HTML section, all HTML, commands, variable references, functions calls, `%INCLUDE` statements, and other valid data must be in between the `{` and `%}` tags, as shown in the above example.

Let's review the HTML sections of our example macro. The `%HTML_INPUT` section is as follows:

```
%HTML_INPUT {

   <HTML>
   <HEAD><TITLE>Reset Password</TITLE></HEAD>
   <BODY BGCOLOR="$(BodyColor1)" TEXT="$(TextCol)" LINK="$(LinkCol)"
    VLINK="$(VLinkCol)" ALINK="$(ALinkCol)">

   <FORM METHOD="post" ACTION="/cgi-bin/ncommerce3/ExecMacro/
    $(STORENAME)/password.d2w/report">

   <TABLE WIDTH=250 CELLPADDING=0 CELLSPACING=0 BORDER=0>
     <TR>
       <TD ALIGN="left" VALIGN="center"><FONT FACE="helvetica"
       COLOR=$(TitleTxtCol)>
       <H3>Reset Password</H3></FONT></TD>
     </TR>
     <TR>
       <TD ALIGN="left"><FONT COLOR="black" SIZE="2">Enter the
       following information about yourself.</FONT></TD>
     </TR>
     <TR><TD><BR></TD></TR>
     <TR>
       <TD><B><FONT SIZE="-1">First Name</FONT></B></TD>
     </TR>
     <TR>
       <TD><INPUT TYPE="text" NAME="safname" SIZE="40"
       MAXLENGTH="30"></TD>
     </TR>
     <TR>
       <TD><B><FONT SIZE="-1">Last Name</FONT></B></TD>
     </TR>
     <TR>
       <TD><INPUT TYPE="text" NAME="salname" SIZE="40"
       MAXLENGTH="30"></TD>
     </TR>
```

```
       <TR>
         <TD><B><FONT SIZE="-1">Phone Number</B></FONT></TD>
       </TR>
       <TR>
         <TD><INPUT TYPE="text" NAME="saphone1" SIZE="40"
         MAXLENGTH="30"></TD>
       </TR>
       <TR>
         <TD><BR></TD>
       </TR>
       <TR>
         <TD ALIGN="center"><INPUT TYPE="submit" VALUE="Submit"></TD>
       </TR>

    </TABLE>
    </FORM>
    </BODY>
    </HTML>

  %}
```

This %HTML_INPUT section displays a form to the shopper. After the shopper fills out the form and submits the information, the %HTML_REPORT section is executed to process the input.

Now, let's view the %HTML_REPORT section:

```
  %HTML_REPORT{

    <HTML>
    <HEAD><TITLE>Reset Password</TITLE></HEAD>
    <BODY BGCOLOR="$(BodyColor1)" TEXT="$(TextCol)" LINK="$(LinkCol)"
    VLINK="$(VLinkCol)" ALINK="$(ALinkCol)">

    <FORM method=POST action="/cgi-bin/ncommerce3/PasswordReset">

  @getQuestion()

    <INPUT TYPE = "hidden" NAME="merchant_rn" VALUE="$(MerchantRefNum)">
    <INPUT TYPE = "hidden" NAME="login_id" VALUE="$(s_loginid)">

  %IF(b_success == "true")
    <TR>
       <TD><BR></TD>
    </TR>
    <TR>
      <TD><B><FONT SIZE="-1">Answer</FONT></B></TD>
    </TR>
    <TR>
      <TD><INPUT TYPE="text" NAME="chal_ans" SIZE="40"
      MAXLENGTH="254"></TD>
    </TR>
    <TR>
       <TD><BR></TD>
```

```
    </TR>
    <TR>
       <TD><FONT COLOR="black" SIZE="2">Enter your new password and
       verify password.</FONT></TD>
    </TR>
    <TR>
       <TD><BR></TD>
    </TR>
    <TR>
       <TD><B><FONT SIZE="-1">New password</FONT></B></TD>
    </TR>
    <TR>
       <TD><INPUT TYPE="password" NAME="new_pass" SIZE="40"
       MAXLENGTH="16"></TD>
    </TR>
    <TR>
       <TD><B><FONT SIZE=-1>Verify Password</FONT></B></TD>
    </TR>
    <TR>
       <TD><INPUT TYPE="password" NAME="newver_pass" SIZE="40"
       MAXLENGTH="16"></TD>
    </TR>
    <TR>
       <TD><BR></TD>
    </TR>
    <TR>
       <TD ALIGN="center"><INPUT TYPE="submit" VALUE="Reset Password">
       </TD>
    </TR>
    </TABLE>

%ENDIF

    </FORM>
    </BODY>
    </HTML>

%}
```

This %HTML_REPORT section calls a function to perform a database query. Then, depending on the value of a variable that was previously defined, it displays a form into which the shopper may enter either additional information or nothing at all. If the form is submitted, a command is invoked to process the input.

# Using Conditional Statements

To do conditional processing in a macro, you must use the %IF, %ELIF, %ELSE, and %ENDIF statements. The %IF statement evaluates a condition based on the value of a variable and then processes the appropriate HTML or Net.Data statements. Note that %IF blocks cannot be nested.

Our example uses the %IF statement as follows:

```
%IF(b_success == "true")

   <TR>
     <TD><BR></TD>
   </TR>
   <TR>
    <TD><B><FONT SIZE="-1">Answer</FONT></B></TD>
   </TR>
   <TR>
     <TD><INPUT TYPE="text" NAME="chal_ans" SIZE="40"
     MAXLENGTH="254"></TD>
   </TR>
   <TR>
     <TD><BR></TD>
   </TR>
   <TR>
     <TD><FONT COLOR="black" SIZE="2">Enter your new password and
     verify password.</FONT></TD>
   </TR>
   <TR>
     <TD><BR></TD>
   </TR>
   <TR>
     <TD><B><FONT SIZE="-1">New password</FONT></B></TD>
   </TR>
   <TR>
     <TD><INPUT TYPE="password" NAME="new_pass" SIZE="40"
     MAXLENGTH="16"></TD>
   </TR>
   <TR>
     <TD><B><FONT SIZE=-1>Verify Password</FONT></B></TD>
   </TR>
   <TR>
     <TD><INPUT TYPE="password" NAME="newver_pass" SIZE="40"
     MAXLENGTH="16"></TD>
   </TR>
   <TR>
     <TD><BR></TD>
   </TR>
   <TR>
     <TD ALIGN="center"><INPUT TYPE="submit" VALUE="Reset Password">
     </TD>
   </TR>
   </TABLE>

%ENDIF
```

In this example, if the value of the variable b_success is equal to "true", an HTML form is displayed; otherwise, nothing is displayed.

> **Note:**
> The variable is not referenced using the syntax **$(b_success)** because this syntax is not needed inside the **%IF** statement.

# Importing Files

If some of the content of your macro will be used in other macros, you can store the information in a separate file and incorporate the file using the %INCLUDE statement into all the macros that will share the information. Using the %INCLUDE statement is an ideal way to share common global variables and common functions, the store's header or footer, background colors, and even your store's merchant reference number. Maintaining the shared information becomes easier when it is in include files: when the information must be updated, you simply update the one include file, rather than each macro.

In our example macro, an %INCLUDE statement was used to import a file containing a %DEFINE section for common background color variables and the merchant reference number. The statement looks like this:

```
%INCLUDE "OneStopPizzaShop\common.inc"
```

The %INCLUDE statement can be inserted at the beginning of the macro, in the HTML sections, and in the %REPORT and %ROW blocks in a %FUNCTION section. In this example, it was inserted at the beginning of the file, at the outermost macro level.

> **Note:**
> When you include a **%INCLUDE** statement in a macro, it will always be executed by Net.Data. Thus, you cannot insert the statement as part of a conditional statement (**%IF**, **%ELIF**, **%ELSE**, and **%ENDIF**) as it will be executed regardless of the condition that is true.

To include a file in a macro, you must ensure that the directory path that is specified for it in the %INCLUDE statement is relative to a path defined in the INCLUDE_PATH statement in the db2www.ini file. For more information, see "Specifying an Include File Directory" on page 197.

# Adding Comments

You can add comments to your macros by enclosing them in %{ and %}. You must insert the comments at the outermost level (not within a section or block) of the macro.

In our example, comments were inserted before each major section to indicate where they begin. The following is a comment inserted to identify the Define section of the example macro:

```
%{————————— Define Section ———————————%}

%DEFINE {

    b_success = "true"
    s_loginid = ""

%}
```

# Adding Commands

In Net.Commerce, a macro is not complete without the inclusion of a command. The command is needed to pass the information collected from the shopper via an HTML form, or the information retrieved from an SQL query to another macro or command to process. All commands are embedded in URLs associated with hypertext links or the ACTION tag of a form.

When you type a command in a macro, use the following conventions:

- Ensure that there are no spaces between keywords, delimiters, and variables.

- You may enter parameters in any order.

- Enter keywords exactly as they are shown: they are case-sensitive.

- Enter variables that represent column names and table names in lowercase.

- Replace spaces in values with plus signs (+).

- When entering a command in a hypertext link or as the value of a URL parameter (redirection URL), replace the symbols with the hex values shown in Table 7.1 below:

*Table 7.1  Command hex values.*

| Symbol | Hex Value |
| --- | --- |
| / | %2F |
| ? | %3F |
| & | %26 |
| = | %3D |

The above does not apply to commands contained in the URL of form submit buttons.

The following is an example of a command containing hex values in its URL parameter:

```
A HREF="/cgi-bin/ncommerce3/LogonForm?url=/cgi-bin/ncommerce3/
ProductDisplay%3Fprmenbr%3D123%26prrfnbr%3D234">Log On</A>
```

**Note:**
Do not duplicate name-value pairs in commands. This can result in an error if the name-value pair was used in an SQL query.

## Adding Commands to Hypertext Links

The simplest way to add a command to a macro is to embed it in the URL associated with a hypertext link. If you are not using a form in a macro, you would normally use this method to add commands. The following is an example of hypertext links in a macro used for a store's navigation bar. Each link calls a command to display a different store page.

```
<P><A HREF="/cgi-bin/ncommerce3/ExecMacro/home.d2w/report">Home</A>
<BR>
<P><A HREF="/cgi-bin/ncommerce3/
```

```
CategoryDisplay?cgmenbr=123&cgrfnbr=666">Catalog</A>
<BR>
<P><A HREF="/cgi-bin/ncommerce3/RegisterForm">Register</A>
<BR>
<P><A NAME="register" HREF="/cgi-bin/ncommerce3/
InterestItemDisplay?merchant_rn=123">Shopping Cart</A>
<BR>
<P><A HREF="/cgi-bin/ncommerce3/
OrderDisplay?merchant_rn=123&status=P">Place Order</A>
<BR>
<P><A HREF="/cgi-bin/ncommerce3/LogonForm?url=/cgi-bin/ncommerce3/
 ProductDisplay%3Fprmenbr%3D123%26prrfnbr%3D234">Log On</A>
```

## Adding Commands to Form Buttons

When the values for parameters required by a command can only be obtained by the shopper (for example, registration information to be processed by the RegisterNew command), you must use a form to collect the information and add the command to the URL associated with the form's ACTION tag. The options selected or the information entered into the form will be passed to the command as parameters when the shopper submits the form. The following is an example of how to use a form to collect address information from a shopper and pass this information to the AddressAdd command. All information entered in the form text input fields and the hidden input field will be passed as name-value pairs to the AddressAdd command to process. Use hidden input fields for passing information that cannot be entered by the shopper (in this case, the merchant reference number and the shopper's nickname) to the command.

```
<FORM ACTION="/cgi-bin/ncommerce3/
AddressAdd?merchant_rn=$(merchant_rn)" METHOD="post">

<INPUT TYPE="hidden" NAME="sanick" VALUE="$(nickname)">

<TABLE WIDTH="60" CELLPADDING="0" CELLSPACING="2" BORDER="0">
  <TR>
    <TD COLSPAN="3"><H2><CENTER>Address Form</CENTER></H2></TD>
  </TR>
  <TR>
    <TD COLSPAN="2" ALIGN="left"><FONT SIZE="2">Please fill in the
    following address information.</FONT></TD>
  </TR>
  <TR>
    <TD ALIGN="left"><B><FONT SIZE="-1">First Name</FONT></B></TD>
    <TD ALIGN="left"><B><FONT SIZE="-1">Last Name</FONT></B></TD>
  </TR>
  <TR>
    <TD COLSPAN="1"><INPUT TYPE="text" NAME="safname" SIZE="28"
    MAXLENGTH="30"></TD>
    <TD COLSPAN="1"><INPUT TYPE="text" NAME="salname" SIZE="28"
    MAXLENGTH="30"></TD>
  </TR>
  <TR>
    <TD ALIGN="left"><B><FONT SIZE="-1">Street Address</FONT></B>
      </TD>
```

```
    </TR>
    <TR>
      <TD COLSPAN="3"><INPUT TYPE="text" NAME="saaddr1" SIZE="58"
      MAXLENGTH="50"></TD>
    </TR>
    <TR>
       <TD ALIGN=left><FONT SIZE=2><b>City</FONT></b></TD>
       <TD ALIGN=left><FONT SIZE=2><b>State/Province</FONT></b></TD>
    </TR>
    <TR>
       <TD COLSPAN=1><INPUT TYPE="text" NAME="sacity" SIZE="28"
       MAXLENGTH="30"></TD>
       <TD COLSPAN=1><INPUT TYPE="text" NAME="sastate" SIZE="28"
       MAXLENGTH="20"></TD>
    </TR>
    <TR>
       <TD ALIGN=left><FONT SIZE=2><b>ZIP/Postal code</b></FONT></TD>
       <TD ALIGN=left><FONT SIZE=2><b>Country</b></FONT></TD>
    </TR>
    <TR>
       <TD COLSPAN=1><INPUT TYPE="text" NAME="sazipc" SIZE="28"
       MAXLENGTH="20"></TD>
       <TD COLSPAN=1><INPUT TYPE="text" NAME="sacntry" SIZE="28"
       MAXLENGTH="30"></TD>
    </TR>
   </TABLE>
```

> **Note:**
> Ensure that you enter the name portion of the name-value pairs exactly as it is defined for the command; otherwise, the command will fail.

## Adding Commands Using JavaScript

Using JavaScript in your macros allows you to further enhance the dynamics of your store pages. For example, you may want to add a command to a macro that will automatically be invoked when the macro is executed, rather than depending on the shopper to invoke it. In this case, you can use JavaScript to perform the dynamic invocation. Here is an example:

```
<script language="JavaScript">
   location.href = "/cgi-bin/ncommerce3/ExecMacro/OneStopPizzaShop/
   main.d2w/report";
</script>
```

When the macro containing this JavaScript function loads, it will automatically execute the `main.d2w` macro, without any interaction from the shopper.

You can also use JavaScript to customize the look of submit buttons for forms, which are rendered as gray buttons by default. The JavaScript `onClick` event handler lets you use an image for the button.

You can also use JavaScript to add multiple buttons to a form and specify that each one handle input differently. Each button builds a separate URL consisting of the data entered in the form and calls a specific command to process the input.

Here is an example:

```
<A HREF="#" onClick="update_shipto()">
<IMG SRC="/grocery/g_updt.gif" WIDTH=138 HEIGHT=24 BORDER=0></A>
```

When the shopper enters information into a preceding form and clicks this button, the update_shipto function is called, which builds and invokes a URL, as follows:

```
function update_shipto() {
   var pcounter = parseInt('$(productcounter)')
   var tempValue = ""
   var url1 = "/cgi-bin/ncommerce3/OrderItemUpdate?addr_rn="
   var url2 = "&url=/cgi-bin/ncommerce3/OrderItemDisplay
               &success3=true"
   var address_ref = document.forms[0].addr_rn.value;
   var shipto_ref = document.forms[0].shipto_rn.value;
   var quantity = document.forms[0].quantity.value;
   var shipmode_ref = document.forms[0].shipmode_rn.value;
       . . .

   var new_url = "https://" + window.location.host + url1 +
    address_ref + "&shipto_rn=" + shipto_ref + "&quantity=" +
    quantity + "&shipmode_rn=" + shipmode_ref + tempValue + url2

   window.location.href = new_url
```

# Storing Net.Data Macros and Include Files

In order for Net.Data to be able to execute the macros and import external files that you create for your store, you must indicate, in the db2www.ini file, the directory where they are stored. The db2www.ini configuration file contains directives that are used by Net.Data. You should not modify any of these directives, except the ones that are used for storing macros and include files, as discussed below.

You can edit the db2www.ini configuration file using any text editor. It is stored in the following directory:

**WIN** \<Domino_Go_Webserver_install_path>\html
**AIX** /usr/lpp/internet/server_root/pub

where <Domino_Go_Webserver_install_path> is the path in which you installed the Domino Go Webserver.

## Specifying a Macro Directory

To specify the directory in which your macro files are stored, you must add the directory to the MACRO_PATH statement in the db2www.ini configuration file. This statement lists one or more directories in which Net.Data will search for the macro file.

When you install Net.Commerce, the following paths are automatically appended to the `MACRO_PATH` statement:

```
MACRO_PATH
<drive>:\IBM\NetCommerce3\instance\<instance_name>\teditor;
<drive>:\IBM\NetCommerce3\macro\en_US;
<drive>:\IBM\NetCommerce3\macro\en_US\demomall;
<drive>:\IBM\NetCommerce3\macro\en_US\ncsample
```

where `<drive>` is the drive on which Net.Commerce was installed, and `<instance_name>` is the name you specified for your Net.Commerce instance during configuration of the Net.Commerce system.

> **Note:**
> In the configuration file, the paths above appear all on one line. They are shown here on multiple lines for presentation purposes only.

The first statement indicates the directory containing all the Template Designer macros. The second statement indicates the directory that contains the macros for the East West Food Mart sample store, the Office Window sample store, the Administrator forms, and the macros that are generated using the Store Creator. The macros for each store are stored in a separate subdirectory under this root directory. The third statement indicates the directory containing all the macros for the Metropolitan Mall sample. The last statement indicates the directory containing the default macros, which are automatically installed in the database during the installation of Net.Commerce.

You can use any of these directories to store your macros, in which case you do not need to edit the `MACRO_PATH` statement. For example, you could create a directory under the `/en_US` directory called `my_store` to store your macros. When you specify in the database where your macros are stored, you need only enter `/my_store/<macro_name>.d2w`, where `<macro_name>` is the name of each macro file.

Normally, however, you will want to create a new directory in which to store all your store macros. A suggested location is under the `/instance` directory, as follows:

**WIN**
```
<drive>:\IBM\NetCommerce3\instance\<instance_name>\<store_name>;
```
**AIX**
```
<drive>:/usr/lpp/NetCommerce3/instance/<instance_name>/<store_name>;
```

where `<drive>` is the drive on which Net.Commerce was installed, `<instance_name>` is the name you specified for your Net.Commerce instance during configuration of the Net.Commerce system, and `<store_name>` is the name of the store for which the macros were created. If you are creating only one store, you can omit this directory.

It is good practice to create different directories for each store that is being created for the same Net.Commerce instance. This facilitates file management and reduces the risk of files being accidentally deleted.

To specify this new directory path, add it to the `MACRO_PATH` statement separated by a semicolon, as follows:

```
MACRO_PATH
<drive>:\IBM\NetCommerce3\instance\<instance_name>\<store_name>;
<drive>:\IBM\NetCommerce3\instance\<instance_name>\teditor;
<drive>:\IBM\NetCommerce3\macro\en_US;
<drive>:\IBM\NetCommerce3\macro\en_US\demomall;
<drive>:\IBM\NetCommerce3\macro\en_US\ncsample
```

Note that the more directories you specify in the MACRO_PATH statement, the longer Net.Data will take to locate macros, and this impacts on performance. So, in a mall environment, you may want to specify only the path for the root directory, omitting the directories for each store. When you specify in the database the directory for each store's macros, you need to enter, for each macro file, /<store_name>/<macro_name>.d2w, where <store_name> is the directory containing the store's macros and <macro_name> is the name of the macro.

Net.Data will search through the paths in the MACRO_PATH statement in the order in which they are listed, so it is advisable to list your most important or most commonly used paths first, to enhance performance.

Also, if you do not require all the paths currently listed in the MACRO_PATH statement (for example, if you are not using the sample stores or the Template Designer), you can remove them from the statement. If you need them later you can always add them back.

Note also that a file created with Template Designer cannot be saved directly to your new directory. To store it there, you must first save it to the default directory and then move it to the new directory.

## Entering the Macro in the Database

When you specify in the database the file names of each macro in your store, you simply enter the name of the macro file; for example: catalog.d2w. Net.Data will automatically search the paths listed in the MACRO_PATH statement to find it. If the macro is stored in a subdirectory under a path listed in the MACRO_PATH statement, you must also enter the subdirectory: for example, /my_store/catalog.d2w.

# Specifying an Include File Directory

To specify the directory in which the files that are imported into a macro using the %INCLUDE statement will be stored, you must add the directory to the INCLUDE_PATH statement in the db2www.ini configuration file. This statement lists one or more directories in which Net.Data will search for the files referred to on Net.Data %INCLUDE statements. When you install Net.Commerce, the following paths are automatically appended to the INCLUDE_PATH statement:

```
INCLUDE_PATH
<drive>:\IBM\NetCommerce3\html\en_US;
<drive>:\IBM\NetCommerce3\instance\<instance_name>\teditor;
<drive>:\IBM\NetCommerce3\macro\en_US;
<drive>:\IBM\NetCommerce3\macro\en_US\ncsample
```

where <drive> is the drive on which Net.Commerce was installed, and <instance_name> is the name you specified for your Net.Commerce instance during configuration of the Net.Commerce system.

> **Note:**
> In the configuration file, the paths above appear all on one line.  They are shown here on multiple lines for presentation purposes only.

The first statement indicates the directory containing all the HTML files that are imported into the Metropolitan Mall sample macros, the East West Food Mart sample macros, the Office Window sample macros, the Administrator form macros, and the macros that are generated by the Store Creator.  The second statement indicates the directory containing the macro files that are imported into the Template Editor macros.  The third statement indicates the directory containing all the macro files that are imported into the Metropolitan Mall sample macros, the East West Food Mart sample macros, the Office Window sample macros, the Administrator form macros, and the macros that are generated by the Store Creator.  The last statement indicates the directory for the macros that are imported into the default macros, which are automatically installed in the database during the installation of Net.Commerce.

You can use any of these directories to store your include files, in which case you do not need to edit the INCLUDE_PATH statement.  For example, you could create a directory under the /en_US directory called my_store to store your include files.  When you specify in the database where your include files are stored, you need only enter  /my_store/<macro_name>.d2w, where <macro_name> is the name of each macro file.

Normally, however, you will want to create a new directory in which to store all your include files.  A suggested location is under the /instance directory, as follows:

**WIN**
```
<drive>:\IBM\NetCommerce3\instance\<instance_name>\<store_name>;
```
**AIX**
```
<drive>:/usr/lpp/NetCommerce3/instance/<instance_name>/<store_name>;
```

where <drive> is the drive on which Net.Commerce was installed, <instance_name> is the name you specified for your Net.Commerce instance during configuration of the Net.Commerce system, and <store_name> is the name of the store for which the include files will be imported.  If you are creating only one store, you can omit this directory.

It is good practice to create different directories for each store that is being created for the same Net.Commerce instance.  This facilitates file management and reduces the risk of files being accidentally deleted.

To specify this new directory path, add it to the INCLUDE_PATH statement separated by a semicolon, as follows:

```
INCLUDE_PATH
<drive>:\IBM\NetCommerce3\instance\<instance_name>\<store_name>;
<drive>:\IBM\NetCommerce3\html\en_US;
<drive>:\IBM\NetCommerce3\instance\<instance_name>\teditor;
<drive>:\IBM\NetCommerce3\macro\en_US;
<drive>:\IBM\NetCommerce3\macro\en_US\ncsample
```

Note that the more directories you specify in the INCLUDE_PATH statement, the longer Net.Data will take to locate the files, and this impacts on performance.  So, in a mall environment, you may want to specify only the path for the root directory, omitting the directories for each store.

Net.Data will search through the paths in the INCLUDE_PATH statement in the order in which they are listed, so it is advisable to list your most important or most commonly used paths first, to enhance performance.

Also, if you do not require all the paths currently listed in the INCLUDE_PATH statement (for example, if you are not using the sample stores or the Template Designer), you can remove them. If you need them later, you can always add them back.

### Importing the File in a Macro

When you specify in a macro the name of the file to be imported using the %INCLUDE statement, you simply enter the filename; for example:

```
%INCLUDE "common.inc"
```

Net.Data will automatically search the paths listed in the INCLUDE_PATH statement to find it. If the file is stored in a subdirectory under a path listed in the INCLUDE_PATH statement, you must also enter the subdirectory; for example:

```
%INCLUDE "MyStore\common.inc"
```

# Activating Net.Data Macros in the System

For each Net.Data macro that you create, you must activate it in the system so that shopper will be able to see the new page. See "Step 9. Activating the Macro" on page 228.

# Putting It All Together

Now that you are familiar with the structure of Net.Data macros and how to use them to create store pages, we will revisit the example that was introduced at the beginning of this chapter, to see how a macro is processed from beginning to end. This sample macro is called demo.d2w (located in the \samples directory on the CD) and it is invoked by a command in a hypertext link on a page, as follows:

```
If you have forgotten your password,
<A HREF="/cgi-bin/ncommerce3/ExecMacro/demo.d2w/input"
 TARGET="main">click here</A> to reset it.
```

The easiest way to understand a macro is to examine it from its point of execution. In this case, the macro begins in the %HTML_INPUT section, so we will look at that section first. Its source code is as follows:

```
%HTML_INPUT {

  <HTML>
  <HEAD><TITLE>Reset Password</TITLE></HEAD>
  <BODY BGCOLOR="$(BodyColor1)" TEXT="$(TextCol)" LINK="$(LinkCol)"
   VLINK="$(VLinkCol)" ALINK="$(ALinkCol)">

  <FORM METHOD="post" ACTION="/cgi-bin/ncommerce3/ExecMacro/
   $(STORENAME)/password.d2w/report">
```

```
<TABLE WIDTH=250 CELLPADDING=0 CELLSPACING=0 BORDER=0>
  <TR>
    <TD ALIGN="left" VALIGN="center"><FONT FACE="helvetica"
    COLOR=$(TitleTxtCol)>
    <H3>Reset Password</H3></FONT></TD>
  </TR>
  <TR>
    <TD ALIGN="left"><FONT COLOR="black" SIZE="2">Enter the
    following information about yourself.</FONT></TD>
  </TR>
  <TR><TD><BR></TD></TR>
  <TR>
    <TD><B><FONT SIZE="-1">First Name</FONT></B></TD>
  </TR>
  <TR>
    <TD><INPUT TYPE="text" NAME="safname" SIZE="40"
    MAXLENGTH="30"></TD>
  </TR>
  <TR>
    <TD><B><FONT SIZE="-1">Last Name</FONT></B></TD>
  </TR>
  <TR>
    <TD><INPUT TYPE="text" NAME="salname" SIZE="40"
    MAXLENGTH="30"></TD>
  </TR>
  <TR>
    <TD><B><FONT SIZE="-1">Phone Number</B></FONT></TD>
  </TR>
  <TR>
    <TD><INPUT TYPE="text" NAME="saphone1" SIZE="40"
    MAXLENGTH="30"></TD>
  </TR>
  <TR>
    <TD><BR></TD>
  </TR>
  <TR>
    <TD ALIGN="center"><INPUT TYPE="submit" VALUE="Submit"></TD>
  </TR>

</TABLE>
</FORM>
</BODY>
</HTML>

%}
```

This section contains HTML that will display a simple form with text input fields where the shopper will enter his or her first name, last name, and phone number. Note that variable references are used to display the page's background and text colors. The corresponding variables are defined in an include file that is inserted at the beginning of the file, using the following %INCLUDE statement:

```
%INCLUDE "OneStopPizzaShop\common.inc"
```

When the shopper clicks the form's submit button, the URL in the form's ACTION tag is invoked, as follows:

```
<FORM method=POST ACTION="/cgi-bin/ncommerce3/ExecMacro/
$(STORENAME)/password.d2w/report">
```

This URL contains the ExecMacro command, which executes the %HTML_REPORT section of this macro. The values entered into the form text input fields (first name, last name, and phone number) are passed as implicit input parameters to the %HTML_REPORT section.

Now let's look at the %HTML_REPORT section, which does the main work in the macro. Its source code is as follows:

```
%HTML_REPORT{

  <HTML>
  <HEAD><TITLE>Reset Password</TITLE></HEAD>
  <BODY BGCOLOR="$(BodyColor1)" TEXT="$(TextCol)" LINK="$(LinkCol)"
   VLINK="$(VLinkCol)" ALINK="$(ALinkCol)">

  <FORM method=POST action="/cgi-bin/ncommerce3/PasswordReset">

@getQuestion()

  <INPUT TYPE = "hidden" NAME="merchant_rn" VALUE="$(MerchantRefNum)">
  <INPUT TYPE = "hidden" NAME="login_id" VALUE="$(s_loginid)">

%IF(b_success == "true")
  <TR>
    <TD><BR></TD>
  </TR>
  <TR>
    <TD><B><FONT SIZE="-1">Answer</FONT></B></TD>
  </TR>
  <TR>
    <TD><INPUT TYPE="text" NAME="chal_ans" SIZE="40"
    MAXLENGTH="254"></TD>
  </TR>
  <TR>
    <TD><BR></TD>
  </TR>
  <TR>
    <TD><FONT COLOR="black" SIZE="2">Enter your new password and
    verify password.</FONT></TD>
  </TR>
  <TR>
    <TD><BR></TD>
  </TR>
  <TR>
    <TD><B><FONT SIZE="-1">New password</FONT></B></TD>
  </TR>
  <TR>
```

```
      <TD><INPUT TYPE="password" NAME="new_pass" SIZE="40"
       MAXLENGTH="16"></TD>
    </TR>
    <TR>
      <TD><B><FONT SIZE=-1>Verify Password</FONT></B></TD>
    </TR>
    <TR>
      <TD><INPUT TYPE="password" NAME="newver_pass" SIZE="40"
       MAXLENGTH="16"></TD>
    </TR>
    <TR>
      <TD><BR></TD>
    </TR>
    <TR>
      <TD ALIGN="center"><INPUT TYPE="submit" VALUE="Reset Password">
      </TD>
    </TR>
    </TABLE>

%ENDIF

    </FORM>
    </BODY>
    </HTML>


%}
```

After this section displays the page background and defines the beginning of a form and the URL for the form's ACTION tag, it calls the `getQuestion()` function using the following statement:

```
@getQuestion()
```

The function retrieves from the database the shopper's challenge question and logon ID, based on the information that the shopper provided (first name, last name, and telephone number). Its source code in the `%FUNCTION` section is as follows:

```
%FUNCTION(DTW_ODBC) getQuestion() {

   select shchaque, shlogid
   from shopper, shaddr
   where salname='$(salname)'
   and shlogid = '$(SESSION_ID)'
   and safname='$(safname)'
   and saphone1='$(saphone1)'
   and sashnbr=shrfnbr
   and saadrflg='P'

   %REPORT {

     <TABLE WIDTH="300" CELLPADDING="0" CELLSPACING="0" BORDER="0">
       <TR>
```

```
        <TD ALIGN="left" VALIGN="center"><FONT FACE="helvetica"
        COLOR=$(TitleTxtCol)><H3>Challenge Question</H3></FONT></TD>
      </TR>
      <TR>
        <TD><FONT COLOR="black" SIZE="2">Answer the following
        question.</FONT></TD>
      </TR>
      <TR>
        <TD><BR></TD>
      </TR>

  %ROW {

    @DTW_ASSIGN(s_loginid, V_shlogid)
    <TR>
      <TD ALIGN="center" BGCOLOR=$(BodyColor2)>
      <FONT COLOR="$(TitleTxtCol)" SIZE="3">
      <B>$(V_shchaque)</B></FONT><BR></TD>
    </TR>
  %}
%}

%MESSAGE {

  100 : {
    <B>Your shopper record was not found in the database.  Please try
    again.</B>
    <BR><BR>
    @DTW_ASSIGN(b_success, "false")
  %}: CONTINUE

  DEFAULT : {
    <B>An unknown error occurred in the getQuestion() function.</B>
  %}
 %}
%}
```

This function first runs an SQL query to retrieve the challenge question from the SHOPPER (Shopper Profile) table and the logon ID from the SHADDR (Shopper Address Book) table for the shopper whose first name, last name, and telephone number match the first name, last name, and phone number that were passed from the %HTML_INPUT section of the macro. If a record is found, the %REPORT section displays the page title and the introductory text. For each row retrieved, the %ROW block first uses the @DTW_ASSIGN built-in function call to assign the value of the logon ID that was retrieved from the query (using the variable reference $(V_shlogid) to a variable called s_loginid. Now the logon ID can be referenced outside of the %ROW block. The remaining HTML displays the retrieved challenge question using the variable reference $(V_shchaque). The source code is as follows:

```
%ROW {

  @DTW_ASSIGN(s_loginid, V_shlogid)
```

```
<TR>
  <TD ALIGN="center" BGCOLOR=$(BodyColor2)>
  <FONT COLOR="$(TitleTxtCol)" SIZE="3">
  <B>$(V_shchaque)</B></FONT><BR></TD>
  </TR>
%}
```

If a record is not found in the database, the %MESSAGE block displays an error message and assigns the value "false" to the variable b_success. This variable was initially assigned the value "true" in the %DEFINE section, as follows:

```
%DEFINE {

  b_success = "true"
  s_loginid = ""

%}
```

Now let's return to the remainder of the %HTML_INPUT section to see what occurs after the function completes. This section begins by defining two hidden input parameters containing name-value pairs for the shopper's logon ID and the merchant reference number, as follows:

```
<INPUT TYPE="hidden" NAME="merchant_rn" VALUE="$(MerchantRefNum)" >
<INPUT TYPE="hidden" NAME="login_id" VALUE="$(s_loginid)" >
```

The variable s_loginid, which was previously assigned by the getQuestion() function, is used for the value of the logon ID, and the variable MerchantRefNum is used for the value of the merchant reference number. The MerchantRefNum variable is defined in a file that is imported into the macro, and contains a fixed number. In this case, the value of the merchant reference number will always be the same, and is intended for the current store only. To dynamically retrieve the merchant reference number for a mall environment, you would need to add a function to the macro that retrieves the reference number for the current merchant and assigns it a variable that can be passed as a hidden input parameter to the FlexiReg command. The following is a function that you could use:

```
%FUNCTION(DTW_ODBC) getMerchantInfo()
  {
    select mestname, merfnbr
    from order_pend, merchant
    where orrfnbr=$(order_rn)
    and ormenbr=merfnbr

    %REPORT {
      %ROW {
        @DTW_ASSIGN(MerchantRefNum, V_merfnbr)
      %}
    %}
```

Next, if the value of b_success is equal to "true", which means that the query in the getQuestion() function successfully completed, the macro displays fields for entering the answer to the challenge question and a new password and verification password, as well as the form's submit button, as follows:

```
%IF(b_success == "true")

  <TR>
    <TD><BR></TD>
  </TR>
  <TR>
    <TD><B><FONT SIZE="-1">Answer</FONT></B></TD>
  </TR>
  <TR>
    <TD><INPUT TYPE="text" NAME="chal_ans" SIZE="40"
    MAXLENGTH="254"></TD>
  </TR>
  <TR>
    <TD><BR></TD>
  </TR>
  <TR>
    <TD><FONT COLOR="black" SIZE="2">Enter your new password and
    verify password.</FONT></TD>
  </TR>
  <TR>
    <TD><BR></TD>
  </TR>
  <TR>
    <TD><B><FONT SIZE="-1">New password</FONT></B></TD>
  </TR>
  <TR>
    <TD><INPUT TYPE="password" NAME="new_pass" SIZE="40"
    MAXLENGTH="16"></TD>
  </TR>
  <TR>
    <TD><B><FONT SIZE=-1>Verify Password</FONT></B></TD>
  </TR>
  <TR>
    <TD><INPUT TYPE="password" NAME="newver_pass" SIZE="40"
    MAXLENGTH="16"></TD>
  </TR>
  <TR>
    <TD><BR></TD>
  </TR>
  <TR>
    <TD ALIGN="center"><INPUT TYPE="submit" VALUE="Reset Password">
    </TD>
  </TR>
  </TABLE>

%ENDIF
```

When the shopper enters the information and clicks the button, the information, along with the merchant reference number and the logon ID, is sent in the URL defined in the form's ACTION tag, as follows:

```
<FORM method=POST action="/cgi-bin/ncommerce3/PasswordReset">
```

The PasswordReset command is not one of the commands supplied by Net.Commerce. In "Chapter 15, Planning Commands" on page 411, you learn how to create it and handle the information passed to it.

This concludes our Net.Data tutorial. To learn more about Net.Data, you can download the official Net.Data documentation at the following Net.Data Web site:

```
http://www.software.ibm.com/data/net.data/docs/v1.htm
```

> **Note:**
> Net.Commerce does not support the functionality in version 2.0 of Net.Data. Therefore, refer to the documentation for version 1.0 only, at the URL above.

# Workshop: Examining the Quick Pick Macro

In this workshop, you will examine the macro that will create the Quick Pick page in the OneStopPizza Shop. The Quick Pick page lets registered shoppers quickly select pizzas that they have ordered on previous occasions, instead of having to navigate each time through the category and product pages. It displays a maximum of four pre-made pizzas and four custom-made pizzas, for a total of eight choices. The custom-made pizzas are listed first, followed by the pre-made pizzas, with the groups ordered according to the date each pizza was last ordered, starting with the most recent date. Each listing consists of the pizza's name, its toppings (if it is custom-made), its price, and an **Add** button to add it to the shopper's Order List it.

The page will look something like the one shown in Figure 7.3 below:

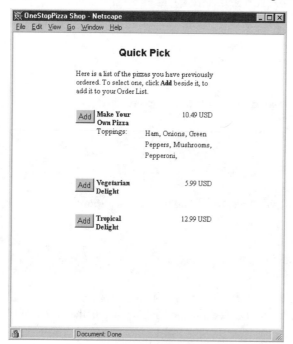

***Figure 7.3*** *An example of the Quick Pick page.*

In the example shown here, the shopper has previously placed an order for one custom-made pizza and two pre-made pizzas (*Vegetarian Delight* and *Deli Delight*).

1. Copy the macro that creates the page, `quickpick.d2w`, from the `\workshops\macros\` directory on the CD to the following directory:

   **WIN** `\ibm\netcommerce3\macro\en_US\OneStopPizzaShop\`

2. We will now briefly examine the content of the `quickpick.d2w` macro. Open the file in a text editor.

3. Go to the `%HTML_REPORT` section and look at its content, as follows:

```
%HTML_REPORT{

  <HTML>
  <HEAD><TITLE>The Quick Pick Page</TITLE></HEAD>
  <BODY BGCOLOR="$(BodyColor1)" TEXT="$(TextCol)"
  LINK="$(LinkCol)" VLINK="$(VLinkCol)" ALINK="$(ALinkCol)">

  <H3><CENTER><FONT FACE="helvetica">Quick Pick</FONT></CENTER>
  </H3>
  <P><FONT SIZE="-1">Here is a list of the pizzas you have
   previously ordered.  To select one, click <B>Add</B> beside it,
   to add it to your Order List.</FONT></P>

@findAddrRn()
@getShopperRefNum()

  <TABLE WIDTH="100%" CELLPADDING="0" CELLSPACING="0" BORDER="0">

@getPastOrders()
@getPastOrders2()

  </TABLE>
  </BODY>

  </HTML>
%}
```

The code to note here is the `@getPastOrders` and `@getPastOrders2` function calls, which display the custom-made and pre-made pizzas on the page.

4. Next, examine the `@getPastOrders` function, which displays the custom-made pizzas, as follows:

```
%FUNCTION(DTW_ODBC) getPastOrders(){

  select strfnbr, stsanbr, stshnbr, stmenbr, stprnbr,
  stprice, stquant, stcpcur, ststat, prrfnbr, prnbr,
  prldesc1, opdescr, oprefnum
  from shipto, product, options, optionrel
  where (stshnbr=$(SHOPPER_REF)
  and stmenbr=$(MerchantRefNum)
```

```
and stprnbr=prrfnbr
and ststat='C'
and oprlstrn=strfnbr
and oprloptrn=oprefnum)
order by stpstmp desc, oprloptrn desc

%REPORT{

  @DTW_ASSIGN (first_iteration, "true")
  @DTW_ASSIGN (counter, "0")

  %ROW{

    %IF (last_value != V_strfnbr)

      @DTW_ADD (counter, "1", "2", counter)

    %ENDIF

    %IF (last_value != V_strfnbr && first_iteration == "false" &&
     counter <= max_orders)

      </TD>
    </TR>
    </FORM>

    <FORM ACTION="/cgi-bin/ncommerce3/OrderItemUpdate"
     TARGET="list" METHOD="post">
    <INPUT TYPE="hidden" NAME="addr_rn" VALUE="$(addr_rn)">
    <INPUT TYPE="hidden" NAME="quantity" VALUE="1">
    <INPUT TYPE="hidden" NAME="url" VALUE="/cgi-bin/ncommerce3/
     OrderItemDisplay?merchant_rn=$(MerchantRefNum)">
    <TR>
      <TD>
    @DTW_ASSIGN (last_value, V_strfnbr)
      </TD>
    </TR>
      <TD HEIGHT="10"></TD>
    </TR>
    <TR>
      <TD ROWSPAN="2" VALIGN="top"><INPUT TYPE="submit"
       VALUE="Add"></TD>
      <TD> </TD>
      <TD ALIGN="left" VALIGN="top">
     <FONT SIZE="-1"><B>$(V_prldesc1)</B></FONT></TD>
      <TD ALIGN="right" VALIGN="top"><FONT SIZE="2">$(CURRENCY)
       $(V_stprice) $(V_stcpcur)</FONT></TD>
    </TR>
    <TR>
      <TD> </TD>
      <TD VALIGN="top"><FONT SIZE="-1">Toppings:</FONT></TD>
      <TD>
```

```
        <INPUT TYPE="hidden" NAME="product_rn"
         VALUE="$(V_prrfnbr)">
         <INPUT TYPE="hidden" NAME="option" VALUE="$(V_oprefnum)">

     %ELIF (last_value != V_strfnbr && first_iteration == "true"
      && counter <= max_orders)

     <FORM ACTION="/cgi-bin/ncommerce3/OrderItemUpdate"
      TARGET="list" METHOD="post">
     <INPUT TYPE="hidden" NAME="addr_rn" VALUE="$(addr_rn)">
     <INPUT TYPE="hidden" NAME="quantity" VALUE="1">
     <INPUT TYPE="hidden" NAME="url" VALUE="/cgi-bin/ncommerce3/
      OrderItemDisplay?merchant_rn=$(MerchantRefNum)">

     @DTW_ASSIGN (first_iteration, "false")
     @DTW_ASSIGN (last_value, V_strfnbr)

     <TR>
        <TD HEIGHT="10"></TD>
     </TR>
     <TR>
        <TD ROWSPAN="2" VALIGN="top"><INPUT TYPE="submit"
         VALUE="Add"></TD>
        <TD> </TD>
        <TD ALIGN="left" VALIGN="top">
        <FONT SIZE="-1"><B>$(V_prldesc1)</B></FONT></TD>
        <TD ALIGN="right" VALIGN="top"><FONT SIZE="2">$(CURRENCY)
         $(V_stprice) $(V_stcpcur)</FONT></TD>
     </TR>
     <TR>
        <TD> </TD>
        <TD VALIGN="top"><FONT SIZE="-1">Toppings:</FONT></TD>
        <TD>
        <INPUT TYPE="hidden" NAME="product_rn"
         VALUE="$(V_prrfnbr)">
         <INPUT TYPE="hidden" NAME="option" VALUE="$(V_oprefnum)">

  %ELIF (counter <= max_orders)

  <FONT SIZE="-1">$(V_opdescr)</FONT>,
  <INPUT TYPE="hidden" NAME="option" VALUE="$(V_oprefnum)">

  %ENDIF

  %}

     </TD>
  </TR>
  </FORM>

%}
```

This function displays the last four "Make Your Own" pizzas that were ordered by the current shopper. It does this as follows: First, for each pizza, it retrieves from the database all the information about its base and toppings. Next, for each topping that belongs to the current base (using the shipto reference number as the link between the topping and its parent base), it displays a form containing a description of the topping and its base, and the total price.

In other words, this function groups all toppings according to their base pizza and displays them in a form. The submit button for the form adds the product combination to the Order List, by invoking the OrderItemUpdate command. In the workshop "Planning New Overridable Functions for the OneStopPizza Shop" on page 362, you will learn how to replace the overridable functions that are called by this command, so that the command will add the pizza and toppings to the Order List. For now, you do not need to know the details. When the function encounters a topping from the database that does not belong to the current base (shipto reference number), a new form is displayed that contains every other option belonging to the new parent. This process is repeated until all four custom-made pizzas (the maximum) have been accounted for.

5. Now, examine the `getPastOrders2` function, which displays the pre-made pizzas, as follows:

```
%FUNCTION(DTW_ODBC) getPastOrders2(){

   select strfnbr, stsanbr, stshnbr, stmenbr, stprnbr, stprice,
   stquant, stcpcur, ststat, prrfnbr, prnbr, prsdesc
   from shipto, product
   where (stshnbr=$(SHOPPER_REF)
   and stmenbr=$(MerchantRefNum)
   and stprnbr=prrfnbr
   and ststat='C'
   and (select oprlstrn from optionrel where oprlstrn=strfnbr and
    oprloptrn=9999) is null)
   order by stpstmp desc

   %REPORT{

     @DTW_ASSIGN (first_iteration, "true")
     @DTW_ASSIGN (counter, "0")

    %ROW{

      @DTW_ADD (counter, "1", "2", counter)

     %IF (first_iteration == "false" && counter <= max_orders)

        </TD>
      </TR>
      </FORM>
```

```
<FORM ACTION="/cgi-bin/ncommerce3/OrderItemUpdate"
 TARGET="list" METHOD="post">
<INPUT TYPE="hidden" NAME="addr_rn" VALUE="$(addr_rn)">
<INPUT TYPE="hidden" NAME="quantity" VALUE="1">
<INPUT TYPE="hidden" NAME="url" VALUE="/cgi-bin/ncommerce3/
 OrderItemDisplay?merchant_rn=$(MerchantRefNum)">
<TR>
   <TD></TD>
</TR>
   <TD HEIGHT="10"></TD>
</TR>
<TR>
   <TD ROWSPAN="2" VALIGN="top"><INPUT TYPE="submit"
    VALUE="Add"></TD>
   <TD> </TD>
   <TD ALIGN="left" VALIGN="top">
   <FONT SIZE="-1"><B>$(V_prsdesc)</B></FONT></TD>

   <TD ALIGN="right" VALIGN="top"><FONT SIZE="2">$(CURRENCY)
   $(V_stprice) $(V_stcpcur)</FONT></TD>
</TR>
<TR>
   <TD> </TD>
   <INPUT TYPE="hidden" NAME="product_rn"
    VALUE="$(V_prrfnbr)">

%ELIF (first_iteration == "true" && counter <= max_orders)

<FORM ACTION="/cgi-bin/ncommerce3/OrderItemUpdate"
 TARGET="list" METHOD="post">
<INPUT TYPE="hidden" NAME="addr_rn" VALUE="$(addr_rn)">
<INPUT TYPE="hidden" NAME="quantity" VALUE="1">
<INPUT TYPE="hidden" NAME="url" VALUE="/cgi-bin/ncommerce3/
 OrderItemDisplay?merchant_rn=$(MerchantRefNum)">
@DTW_ASSIGN (first_iteration, "false")
<TR>
   <TD HEIGHT="10"></TD>
</TR>
<TR>
   <TD ROWSPAN="2" VALIGN="top"><INPUT TYPE="submit"
    VALUE="Add"></TD>
   <TD> </TD>
   <TD ALIGN="left" VALIGN="top">
   <FONT SIZE="-1"><B>$(V_prsdesc)</B></FONT></TD>
   <TD ALIGN="right" VALIGN="top"><FONT SIZE="2">$(CURRENCY)
    $(V_stprice) $(V_stcpcur)</FONT></TD>
</TR>
<TR>
   <TD> </TD>
   <TD><INPUT TYPE="hidden" NAME="product_rn"
    VALUE="$(V_prrfnbr)">
```

```
        %ENDIF
    %}

      </TD>
    </TR>
    </FORM>

%}
```

This function behaves similarly to the `getPastOrders` function, except that it does not display the pizzas according to each topping retrieved from the database (since the toppings cannot be individually selected) but rather according to each row retrieved from the database

6.  Close the file


You have now completed this workshop. In the next workshop, "Modifying the Store Pages in the OneStopPizza Shop" on page 236, you will modify the appearance of the existing pages in the OneStopPizza Shop.

# Chapter 8, Modifying the Supplied Store Pages

As an alternative to writing Net.Data macros from scratch, you can modify the macros that are supplied with the Net.Commerce system. These include macros for the sample stores; macros that are generated by the Store Creator; the default macros, which are automatically installed in the database when Net.Commerce is installed; and the system error pages, which are mostly HTML files. Each macro or HTML file is different and is intended to help you generate ideas for your store, as well as give you a headstart in creating your store pages.

> **Note:**
> With the exception of the system error pages, this chapter does not cover modifying the supplied HTML store pages, as that task involves straightforward HTML editing.

In the workshop, you will modify the store pages that were generated by the Store Creator, in order to create a unique look for the pizza store and to meet its business needs.

The chapter covers the following topics:

- Modifying the Default, Sample, and Store Creator–Generated Pages
- Modifying System Error Pages
- Workshop: Modifying the Store Pages in the OneStopPizza Shop

# Modifying the Default, Sample, and Store Creator-Generated Pages

You can modify any of the default and sample store pages that are provided by the Net.Commerce system, or the pages that are generated by the Store Creator. For example, you might find a page in the East West Food Mart sample that you want to use in your store, but it requires some modifications to meet your requirements.

You can perform any type of modification on the pages. You can change their look and feel, such as adding a store logo or rearranging the way information is displayed. You can also remove or add database information, as required by your business; for example, you may want to remove certain summary fields on an order page. You can remove any field from a page, as long as it is not required by either the Net.Commerce system or an overridable function.

The following are the general steps to follow when modifying any of the default, sample, or Store Creator-generated pages.

## Step 1. Storing Images

If you intend to add or change static images on the page, ensure that you first copy them to the directory in which you keep your store images and that you have configured the Web server to look for them in that directory. For information about storing and configuring a directory for your images, see "Storing Images and HTML Files" on page 81.

The following is a list of graphics that are typically used in online stores:

- General-purpose graphics (icons, image maps, backgrounds, etc.)
- Store logo (for store header and home page)
- Navigation icons (for store footer)
- Other multimedia files, such as sound, animation, plug-ins, and Java applets (optional)

**Note:**
The list above excludes the product and category full-sized and thumbnail images used for product and category pages. You normally enter these images into the database and then retrieve and display them on their corresponding pages using Net.Data database variable references.

## Step 2. Determining the Name of the Task that the Macro Implements

Before beginning to modify a macro, you must determine whether or not it implements a view or exception task. (Macros do not implement process tasks; those are implemented by overridable functions.) You need the name of the task to later activate the macro in the system.

If the macro is executed by the ExecMacro command, it does not implement a task. A product or category macro implements the CAT_DSP view task or the PROD_DSP view task, respectively.

All other macros are executed by the TaskDisplay_1.0 (IBM,NC) overridable function, which implements all of the other default view and exception tasks. To determine the name of the view or exception task, look up the description for the TaskDisplay_1.0 (IBM,NC) overridable function on page 671.

# Step 3. Determining the Name of the Macro that Creates the Page

To determine the name of the macro that you will be modifying, do one of the following:

- If your macro is executed by the ExecMacro command, look up the command on that page that invokes it. For example, let's say that you want to modify the search page created by the Store Creator. Upon looking at the store, you know that the navigation bar contains a link that, when clicked, displays the search page. You would then open the macro that creates the navigation bar and look for the link containing the ExecMacro command. The link will look like the following:

```
<TR>
<TD VALIGN="center" height=$(ButtonHeight) width=$(ButtonWidth)>
 <A HREF="/cgi-bin/ncommerce3/ExecMacro/$(STORENAME)/search.d2w/
  report" TARGET="main"><img src="$(Button3)" BORDER=0></A></TD>
<TD VALIGN="center">
 <A HREF="/cgi-bin/ncommerce3/ExecMacro/$(STORENAME)/search.d2w/
  report" TARGET="main"><FONT SIZE=1><B>Search</b></FONT></A></TD>
</TR>
```

This HTML shows that the ExecMacro command executes a macro called search.d2w, which is the name of the macro that you want to modify

- If your macro implements the CAT_DSP view task, do one of the following:

    - Use the Category Template Assignment form in the Store Manager to find the name of the macro that is associated with the categories that you want to display.

    - Use SQL to select column CSDISPLAY from table CATESGP. This column contains the path and name of the macro. You must qualify your selection by the category and merchant reference numbers (columns CSCGNBR and CSMENBR) and the shopper group reference number (column CSSGNBR). If there is no shopper group associated with the page, column CSSGNBR is null. The following is an example of an SQL statement that you can use:

    ```
    select cgrfnbr, cgname, csdisplay from category, catesgp
    where csmenbr = cgmenbr and cscgnbr = cgrfnbr
    ```

    For each category defined in the database, this statement displays its reference number, name, and the macro that displays it.

- If your macro implements the PROD_DSP view task, do one of the following:

    - Use the Product Template Assignment form in the Store Manager to find the name of the macro that is associated with the product that you want to display.

- Use SQL to select column PSDISPLAY from table PRODSGP. This column contains the path and name of the macro. You must qualify your selection by the product and merchant reference numbers (columns PSPRNBR and PSMENBR) and the shopper group reference number (column PSSGNBR). If there is no shopper group associated with the page, column PSSGNBR is null.

```
select prrfnbr, prsdesc, psdisplay from product, prodsgp
where psmenbr = prmenbr and psprnbr = prrfnbr
```

  For each product defined in the database, this statement displays its reference number, name, and the macro that displays it.

- If none of the above are true, refer to the TaskDisplay_1.0 (IBM,NC) overridable function description on page 671.

# Step 4. Determining the Macro's Input Parameters

All commands accept extra name-value pairs and pass them, along with the mandatory parameters, unchanged through the system to the macros that are called later. Ensure that your macro is not affected by unknown parameters, and that it forwards all such parameters unchanged to the appropriate commands. You can determine the calling command for your macro from the task that it implements. Refer to the calling command's description in "Appendix D, Net.Commerce Commands" on page 569 and the task description in "Appendix E, Net.Commerce Tasks" on page 613 for complete coverage of the input parameters that are passed to the macro.

# Step 5. Ensuring Authorization

If the macro implements a view or exception task, ensure that you are authorized to replace the macro. If you are the site administrator, you have the authority to replace all macros in the system and to set the scope of the tasks to which the macros are assigned to either *store* or *mall*.

- If a task is set to mall scope, the macro assigned to it is implemented for all the stores in the mall. Every macro that you replace affects every store in the mall.

- If a task is set to store scope, then store administrators can assign a different macro to the task, and have that macro applied to their store. If a store administrator chooses not to assign a different macro, then the macro assignment used for the mall will be applied to that store.

If you are a store administrator, you can only replace macros for which the site administrator has set the scope of the tasks to which they are assigned to *store*. To ensure that you are authorized to replace the macro, ask your site administrator whether or not the scope of the task is *store*. The site administrator can determine this as follows:

1. Open Net.Commerce Administrator as described in "Opening the Administrator" on page 34.

2. On the task bar, click **Site Manager** and then **Task Management**. The Task Management form appears.

3. From the **Select Task Type** drop-down list, select one of the following task types:

    - **ERROR**, for displaying error pages.

    - **VIEW**, for displaying the pages that shoppers normally see during the shopping process.

    A list of the tasks that are available for the selected task type appears in the bottom frame.

4. Select the desired task name from the list.

5. Look at the level that is displayed in the **Scope** drop-down list, to determine whether the task is set to *mall* or *store*.

# Step 6. Copying the Macro to Your Store's Macro Directory

If you have created a directory for your store's macros, you need to copy the macro to that directory. Ensure that you have configured Net.Data to look for the macro in this directory. For information on how to create and configure a new directory, see "Specifying a Macro Directory" on page 195.

## Default and Sample Macros

The following are the directories that contain the macros for each sample and default macro in the Net.Commerce system, as well as the directories that contain the sample images that display on the resulting store pages. Use this list to determine the directory in which your macro is stored.

### Default Macros (including the error macros for the Metropolitan Mall)

**WIN** \IBM\NetCommerce3\macro\en_US\ncsample\
**AIX** /usr/lpp/NetCommerce3/macro/en_US/ncsample/

### Metropolitan Mall

**WIN** \IBM\NetCommerce3\macro\en_US\demomall\
**AIX** /usr/lpp/NetCommerce3/macro/en_US/demomall/

### East West Food Mart

**WIN** \IBM\NetCommerce3\macro\en_US\grocery\
**AIX** /usr/lpp/NetCommerce3/macro/en_US/grocery/

### Office Window

**WIN** \IBM\NetCommerce3\macro\en_US\bus2bus\
**AIX** /usr/lpp/NetCommerce3/macro/en_US/bus2bus/

### Category Macros (for all samples)

**WIN** \IBM\NetCommerce3\macro\en_US\category\
**AIX** /usr/lpp/NetCommerce3/macro/en_US/category/

### Product Macros (for all samples)

**WIN**  \IBM\NetCommerce3\macro\en_US\product\
**AIX**  /usr/lpp/NetCommerce3/macro/en_US/product/

The location of the image files that are used in the default macros and the sample stores is as follows:

### Default Macros

**WIN**  \IBM\NetCommerce3\html\en_US\ncsample\
**AIX**  /usr/lpp/NetCommerce3/html/en_US/ncsample/

### Metropolitan Mall

**WIN**  \IBM\NetCommerce3\html\en_US\demomall\
**AIX**  /usr/lpp/NetCommerce3/html/en_US/demomall/

### East West Food Mart

**WIN**  \IBM\NetCommerce3\html\en_US\grocery\
**AIX**  /usr/lpp/NetCommerce3/html/en_US/grocery/

### Office Window

**WIN**  \IBM\NetCommerce3\html\en_US\bus2bus2\images\
**AIX**  /usr/lpp/NetCommerce3/html/en_US/bus2bus2/images/

## Store Creator Macros

If you created a store using the Store Creator, a unique set of macros was automatically generated for the model that you chose to use. The descriptions of each set are as follows:

### One Stop Shop Store Model Macros

Table 8.1 lists all of the macros that are generated for stores that are based on the One Stop Shop store model.

*Table 8.1* *The One Stop Shop store model macros.*

| Macro Name | Description |
| --- | --- |
| main.d2w | Creates a temporary address book entry for the shopper so that the shopper does not have to register in order to place an order. |
| frames.d2w | Builds the frameset for the store and loads the files (home.d2w, banner.d2w, nav_side.d2w, and shipto.d2w) into each frame. |
| home.d2w | Displays the home page, which welcomes the shopper to the store and displays the store description. |
| banner.d2w | Displays the store name on a banner background image (based on the store style that was selected in the Store Creator) across the top of the store. |
| nav_side.d2w | Displays the navigation bar down the left side of the store, which contains links to the primary store functions: Welcome, Catalog, Search, Submit Order, Order Status, and Customer Service. |

*Continued on next page*

*Table 8.1 Continued.*

| Macro Name | Description |
|---|---|
| cat1.d2w | Displays the category pages. |
| prod1.d2w | Displays the product pages. |
| contact.d2w | Displays the Customer Service page, which contains the store contact information. |
| search.d2w | Displays the Search page, which allows the shopper to search for a product in the store using keywords. |
| searchrslt.d2w | Displays the Search Results page, which displays all the products that match the shopper's search request. From this page, the shopper can view the product page of any product listed, add products to the Order List, or try another search. |
| shipto.d2w | Displays the Order List, from which the shopper can view the name and price of each item to be ordered and the total price (before taxes) of all items, or remove unwanted items from the list. |
| order.d2w | Displays the Place Order page, from which the shopper can view the details of the items in the order, including shipping charges and taxes; specify a shipping address; provide credit card information for payment; and submit the order. |
| orderlstc.d2w | Displays the Order Status page, which indicates the status of an order based on the order number and customer number specified by the shopper. |
| orderok.d2w | Displays an order confirmation page, which displays a summary of the order submitted, contact information, an order reference number, and a customer number for inquiries. |
| ordnone.d2w | Displays an error page, indicating that the shopper attempted to place an order without first adding an item to the Order List. |
| err_adrbk_up.d2w | Displays an error page, indicating that the system could not update the shopper's address record during the placement of an order. |
| err_shadd.d2w | Displays an error page, indicating that the shopper selected an incorrect combination of attributes on a product page. |

### *Personal Delivery Store Model Macros*

Table 8.2 lists all the macros that are generated for a store based on the Personal Delivery store model.

*Table 8.2 The Personal Delivery store model macros.*

| Macro Name | Description |
|---|---|
| main.d2w | Creates a temporary address book entry for the shopper so that the shopper can add items to the Order List without first having to register. |
| frames.d2w | Builds the frameset for the store and loads the files (home.d2w, banner.d2w, nav_top.d2w, and LeftSide.d2w) into each frame. |

*Continued on next page*

*Table 8.2 Continued.*

| Macro Name | Description |
|---|---|
| framescat.d2w | Builds the frameset for displaying the category pages and Order List in the main frame and loads the files (cat1.d2w and shiptolst.d2w) into each frame. |
| blank.d2w | Is used to properly display the Order List. |
| framesch.d2w | Builds the frameset for displaying the Search Results page and the Order List in the main frame, and loads the files (search.d2w and shiptolst.d2w) into each frame. |
| home.d2w | Displays the home page, which contains the store description and links for viewing the catalog, searching, and logging in or registering. |
| logon.d2w | Displays the Logon page, from which a registered shopper can log onto the store. If an error occurs at the time of logging on, an error message is displayed; otherwise, the top-level category page is displayed. |
| banner.d2w | Displays the store name on a banner background image (based on the store style that was selected in the Store Creator) across the top of the store. |
| nav_top.d2w | Displays the navigation bar under the store banner, which contains links to the primary store functions: Logon, Shopper Registration, Catalog, Search, Submit Order, Order Status, Customer Service, and Address Book. |
| LeftSide.d2w | Displays an image down the left side of the store. The image displayed depends on the store style that has been previously selected. |
| cat1.d2w | Displays the category pages. |
| prod1.d2w | Displays the product pages. |
| contact.d2w | Displays the Customer Service page, which contains the store contact information. |
| search.d2w | Displays the Search page, which allows the shopper to search for a product in the store using keywords. |
| searchrslt.d2w | Displays the Search Results page, which displays all the products that match the shopper's search request. From this page, the shopper can view the product page of any product listed, or add products to the Order List. |
| shiptolst.d2w | Displays the Order List, from which the shopper can view the name and price of each item to be ordered, the total price (before taxes) of all items, remove unwanted items from the list, or link to the product pages of the listed products. |
| shiptodsp.d2w | Displays the Order Details page, from which the shopper can specify shipping destinations and quantities for each item to be ordered, and specify a shipping service for each address. |
| order.d2w | Displays the Order Payment Information page, from which the shopper can view the details of the items in the order, including shipping charges and taxes; provide credit card information for payment; and submit the order. |
| orderlstc.d2w | Displays the Order Status page, which lists all orders that have been submitted. |

*Continued on next page*

***Table 8.2*** *Continued.*

| Macro Name | Description |
|---|---|
| orderok.d2w | Displays an order confirmation page, which displays a summary of the order submitted, and contact information for inquiries. |
| msregform.d2w | Displays the New Registration page, from which the shopper can register with the store. |
| msregupd.d2w | Displays the Update Registration page, from which a registered shopper can modify registration information. |
| adrbk.d2w | Displays the Address Book page, from which the shopper can add an entry to the address book, remove an existing entry, or update an entry. |
| adrbkad.d2w | Displays the New Address Book Entry page, from which the shopper can add an entry to the address book. |
| adrbkup.d2w | Displays the Update Address Book Entry page, from which the shopper can update an existing address book entry. |
| orderclup.d2w | After a guest shopper adds items to the Order List and then registers or logs on, transfers the selected items from the shopper's temporary ID to the new logon ID. |
| err_stdata.d2w | Displays an error page, indicating that the shopper entered an incorrect quantity for a product. |
| err_shadd.d2w | Displays an error page, indicating that the shopper selected an incorrect combination of attributes on a product page. |
| err_reg.d2w | Displays an error page, indicating that an error occurred when the shopper attempted to register or to update registration information. |
| err_do_payment.d2w | Displays an error page, indicating that the shopper entered incorrect payment information during the placement of an order. |
| err_adrbk.d2w | Displays an error page, indicating that an error occurred when the shopper attempted to add or update an address book entry. |

## Business-to-Business Store Model Macros

Table 8.3 lists all the macros that are generated for a store based on the Business-to-Business store model.

***Table 8.3*** *The Business-to-Business store model macros.*

| Macro Name | Description |
|---|---|
| main.d2w | Builds the frameset for the store and loads the files (home.d2w, nav_side.d2w, banner.d2w, and nav_bottom.d2w) into each frame. |
| home.d2w | Displays a page from which a user can register or log on; the store manager can approve any unapproved office groups; an office manager can approve shopper enrollments and orders placed or browse the catalog; and an approved shopper can browse the catalog. |

*Continued on next page*

**Table 8.3** *Continued.*

| Macro Name | Description |
| --- | --- |
| welcome.d2w | When the user first enters the store, displays the welcome page, which provides links to log on or to register. |
| banner.d2w | Displays the store name on a banner background image (based on the store style that was selected in the Store Creator) across the top of the store. |
| nav_bottom.d2w | Displays the navigation bar across the bottom of the store, which contains links to the primary store functions: Home, Register, Catalog, Search, Place Order, Order Status, and Customer Service. The Search, Place Order, and Order Status links are available only to office managers and approved shoppers. |
| nav_side.d2w | Displays an image down the left side of the store. The image displayed depends on the store style that was selected in the Store Creator. |
| cat1.d2w | Displays the category pages. |
| prod1.d2w | Displays the product pages. |
| contact.d2w | Displays the Customer Service page, which contains the store contact Information. |
| search.d2w | Displays the Search page to approved shoppers, which allows the shopper to search for a product in the store using keywords. |
| searchrslt.d2w | Displays the Search Results page, which displays all the products that match the shopper's search request. From this page, the shopper can view the product page of any product listed, add products to the Order List, or try another search. |
| shipto.d2w | Displays the Order List, from which the shopper can view the name and price of each item to be ordered, view the total price (before taxes) of all items, or remove unwanted items from the list. |
| order.d2w | Displays the Place Order page, from which an approved shopper can view the details of the items in the order, including shipping charges and taxes; provide credit card information for payment; and submit the order. |
| orderlstc.d2w | Displays the Order Status page, which lists all orders that have been placed and indicates whether or not each order has been approved by the office manager. |
| orderok.d2w | Displays an order confirmation page, which informs the shopper that the order has been submitted successfully and that the office administrator must now approve the order. It also displays the details of the order, store contact information, and the order reference number for inquiries. |
| grpaprv.d2w | Displays a page from which the store manager can approve office group enrollments that shoppers have requested. |
| orderaprv.d2w | Displays a page from which the office manager can approve orders that have been placed by shoppers. |
| regaccept.d2w | Displays a registration confirmation page, which informs the shopper that he or she has successfully enrolled in an existing or new office group and must now wait approval from the office manager. |
| regaprv.d2w | Displays a page that lists the shoppers who are waiting for office group enrollment approval, and from which the office manager can approve each shopper's enrollment. |

*Continued on next page*

*Table 8.3  Continued.*

| Macro Name | Description |
|---|---|
| regnew.d2w | Displays the New Registration page, from which the shopper can enroll in an existing office group or specify a new office group in which to enroll. |
| logon.d2w | Displays the Logon page, from which a registered user can log onto the store. If an error occurs at the time of logging on, this page is redisplayed with the appropriate message to indicate the type of error that occurred. |

The following are the directories that are created to store the macros generated by the Store Creator:

### Category macro cat1.d2w:

**WIN**  `\IBM\NetCommerce3\macro\cn_US\category\<store_name>\`

**AIX**  `/usr/lpp/NetCommerce3/macro/en_US/category/<store_name>/`

### Product macro prod1.d2w:

**WIN**  `\IBM\NetCommerce3\macro\en_US\product\<store_name>\`

**AIX**  `/usr/lpp/NetCommerce3/macro/en_US/producty/<store_name>/`

### All other macros:

**WIN**  `\IBM\NetCommerce3\macro\en_US\<store_name>\`

**AIX**  `/usr/lpp/NetCommerce3/macro/en_US/<store_name>/`

where `<store_name>` is the name that was assigned to your store using the Store Creator.

The sample images and HTML files for the store are in the following directory:

**WIN**  `\ibm\netcommerce3\html\en_US\ncadmin\StoreCreator\sggifs\`

**AIX**  `/usr/lpp/NetCommerce3/html/en_US/ncadmin/StoreCreator/sggifs/`

During installation of the Net.Commerce system, the following `Pass` statement was inserted into the Web server configuration file so that the `/sggifs/` directory will map to the directory above:

```
Pass /sggifs/*
<drive>:\IBM\NetCommerce3\html\en_US\ncadmin\StoreCreator\sggifs\*
```

You can either use this directory, use the Web server document root, or create a new directory to store your custom images and HTML files.  For more information, see "Storing Images and HTML Files" on page 81.

## Step 7. Renaming the Macro

Before you modify any macro, it is recommended that you first make a copy of it under a new name (if you have not copied it to another directory) or rename it (if you have copied it to another directory).  This way, you keep the original version for possible future reuse.

# Step 8. Editing the Macro

You are now ready to open the macro file in a text editor and perform the appropriate edits to it. If you intend to change the appearance or layout of the pages created by the macro (for example, add an image, hide an optional form field, or change static text), modify the HTML tags.

Remember that you can remove fields from any macro that are not required by the Net.Commerce system or by an overridable function. Fields that are required by the system correspond to table columns that are defined as NOT NULL. If the calling command sets a task that calls an overridable function to check or update specific fields in the database, you cannot remove these fields without replacing the overridable function that is assigned to the task. To determine whether or not the Net.Commerce system or an overridable function requires a field, do the following:

1.  Find the HTML tags that display the form field. If the field is to be pre-filled with database information, its value will be a Net.Data variable that references the contents of a column in the database. Note the column name. If the field is to display blank, note the type of information that the shopper is to enter in the field.

2.  Look up the column's corresponding table in "Appendix C, Net.Commerce Database Tables" on page 511, and then look up the column in the table. (A column name typically starts with the first two letters of the table to which it belongs.) If the column type is NOT NULL, the field is required by the system and cannot be removed.

3.  In "Appendix E, Net.Commerce Tasks" on page 613, check the descriptions of the tasks set by the macro's calling command, to determine which database fields are updated or checked. You cannot remove these fields without replacing the overridable function. (If you have replaced it, refer to your documentation or to the program itself, to determine whether or not it requires additional fields.)

To modify a command in the macro, edit the hypertext link or submit button that invokes the command. Refer to the command descriptions in "Appendix D, Net.Commerce Commands" on page 569 for information on what commands you can execute from the macro. For information on how to add commands to macros, see "Adding Commands" on page 192.

If you want to change the flow of how the macro is executed or to retrieve new information from the database, modify the Net.Data or SQL statements, respectively. See "Net.Data Variables" on page 177 for information on how to define and use variables. See "Retrieving and Displaying Database Information" on page 182 for information on retrieving and display database information in macros. Remember that all commands accept extra name-value pairs and pass them unchanged through the system to the overridable functions that are called later. Ensure that your macros are not affected by unknown parameters, and that they forward all such parameters unchanged. The SESSION_ID parameter is passed to all macros, so you can use this parameter to select information from tables that are keyed off the session ID.

When you finished editing the macro, save it under the new name that you have defined for it.

**Note:**
If you are running several Net.Commerce servers, copy the file to the other servers.

# Editing Macros Generated by the Store Creator

You can edit the macros that are generated by the Store Creator the same way that you edit the sample or the default macros provided by the Net.Commerce system. However, these macros differ from the sample or default macros in that they all reference common data, including background and text colors in an external file. You can modify this file, in order to change the appearance of the store pages. This file, which is imported into each macro, stores some of the information that was entered onto the panels of the Store Creator, including the following:

- Merchant reference number

- Payment methods used in the store (credit card types and a toll-free phone number)

- Category reference number of the top-level category in the store, to which the home page or the **Catalog** link on the navigation bar links

- Images and their dimensions used for the navigation buttons and the store banner

- Background colors and images for the different store frames

- Hypertext link colors

- Text colors

- The directory in which the macros are stored (based on the name of the store)

The file consists of a Net.Data `%DEFINE` section, which defines variable names and values extracted from the information specified on the panels of the Store Creator. These variables are individually referenced in the appropriate macros. Using this file is not mandatory, but it does provide an efficient way to display common information such as background and text colors on multiple store pages. Referencing this file for the merchant reference number is particularly useful because it eliminates the need to query the database for this number each time a macro needs to retrieve it. The merchant reference number is a common parameter for commands.

This file is called `<store_name>.inc`, and is in the following directory:

> **WIN** `\IBM\NetCommerce3\macro\en_US\<store_name>\<store_name>.inc/`
> **AIX** `/usr/lpp/NetCommerce3/macro/en_US/<store_name>/<store_name>.inc`

where `<store_name>` is the name that was entered in the **Store Name** field in the Store Creator.

The file is imported at the top of each macro using the following Net.Data statement:

```
%INCLUDE"<store_name_dir>\<store_name>.inc"
```

where `<store_name_dir>` is the directory that is automatically created to store your macros, based on the name of the store.

The following is an example of an "include" file that can be generated by the Store Creator:

```
%DEFINE {
EOF="EOF"
navigation="side"
CC_visa="NO"
```

```
HomeCategory="241"
ButtonHeight="31"
BannerLeftSpc="0"
title="Retro (Side)"
LinkCol="darkblue"
BckImageNavBar="/sggifs/f_leftbkg_s.gif"
Button1="/sggifs/f_butt1_s.gif"
TextCol="black"
Button2="/sggifs/f_butt2_s.gif"
Button3="/sggifs/f_butt3_s.gif"
VLinkCol="purple"
NavBarAlign="left"
CC_phone="YES"
Button4="/sggifs/f_butt4_s.gif"
NavLinkCol="darkblue"
STORENAME="newone"
Button5="/sggifs/f_butt5_s.gif"
TitleTxtCol="black"
BannerImage="/sggifs/f_banner.gif"
CC_master="NO"
Button6="/sggifs/f_butt6_s.gif"
MerchantRefNum="127"
Button7="/sggifs/f_butt7_s.gif"
BannerRightSpc="0"
CC_amex="YES"
Button8="/sggifs/f_butt8_s.gif"
BodyImage1="/sggifs/f_tablbkg.gif"
AddButton="/sggifs/f_add.gif"
CC_discover="NO"
LongStoreName="newone"
ButtonWidth="56"
BannerTxtCol="lightyellow"
ALinkCol="pink"
BodyColor1="#9CCECE"
BodyColor2="#6699CC"
BannerAlign="center"
gif="sggifs/retro_s.jpg"
BodyColor3="pink"
%}
```

To customize the appearance of some aspects of your store pages, you can edit this file to replace the variable values with custom store data. For example, you can change the background of all your store frames by simply changing the values of the corresponding variables defined in this file. If you change the directory in which you store your macros from the default, you can change the value of the STORENAME variable to the name of the new directory, and all references to this variable in the macros will automatically be updated. (Ensure that you also configure Net.Data to look for the macros in the new location. For details, see "Specifying a Macro Directory" on page 195.) You can add other credit cards that are not available in the file by editing the macro that will display the credit card image. You can edit the file using any text editor.

The following are the variables defined in the file that you can replace:

AddButton
> The path and file name of the image for the Add to Order List button on the product pages. Do not use this variable for form submit buttons; they are always rendered as gray buttons.

ALinkCol
> The color of all active links on the store pages (excluding the navigation bar).

BannerImage
> The path and file name of the image used as the store banner.

BannerLeftSpc
> Together with variable BannerRightSpc, controls the position of the store name on the banner image.

BannerRightSpc
> Together with variable BannerLeftSpc, controls the position of the store name on the banner image.

BannerTxtCol
> The text color of the store name on the banner.

BckImageNavBar
> The path and file name of the image used as the background for the navigation bar.

BodyColor1 to BodyColor3
> The color or path and file name of the image used as the background of the different frames in the store.

BodyImage1
> The path and file name of the image used as the background for a frame.

Button1 to Button8
> The path and file name of the images used as buttons on the navigation bar.

ButtonHeight
> The height, in pixels, of each button on the navigation bar. Each button must have the same height.

ButtonWidth
> The width, in pixels, of each button on the navigation bar. Each button must have the same width.

CC_amex
> An indicator as to whether or not the American Express credit card is to be displayed as a payment method in the store. Enter either Yes or No.

CC_discover
> An indicator as to whether or not the Discovery credit card is to be displayed as a payment method in the store. Enter either Yes or No.

CC_master
> An indicator as to whether or not the Master Card credit card is to be displayed as a payment method in the store. Enter either Yes or No.

CC_phone
> An indicator as to whether or not a toll-free phone number is to be displayed as a payment method in the store. Enter either Yes or No.

`CC_visa`
>An indicator as to whether or not the Visa credit card is to be displayed as a payment method in the store. Enter either `Yes` or `No`.

`HomeCategory`
>The category reference number of the top-level category in the store to which the home page or the **Catalog** link on the navigation bar links.

`LinkCol`
>The color of all hypertext links on the store pages (excluding the navigation bar).

`LongStoreName`
>The text for the store name that is displayed on the store banner.

`MerchantRefNum`
>The reference number of the merchant.

`NavLinkCol`
>The color of all the hypertext links on the navigation bar.

`TextCol`
>The color of all text that is not hyperlinked.

`TitleTxtCol`
>The color of all page titles.

`VLink`
>The color of all visited hypertext links on the store pages (excluding the navigation bar).

**Notes:**

- Do not reference the **StoreDescription** variable in any of your macros. It is not currently used in the store. The macros query the MESTDESC column in the MERCHANT database table instead.

- After editing the file, you cannot return to the Store Creator to make other changes; otherwise, the modifications you made here may be overwritten by the Store Creator's output.

When you have finished editing the file, save it under the same name. Now, the values that you replaced will dynamically appear on the store pages that reference the corresponding variable names.

# Step 9. Activating the Macro

If the macro implements a task, you need to ask your site administrator to activate it by assigning its name to the task. See the steps below for instructions.

If you are changing any of the macros that are executed by the ExecMacro command, you do not need to activate them. The change will take effect as soon as you change the macro name in the command's parameter. See page 579 for a description of the ExecMacro command's syntax.

If you have modified the macro for a category or product page, you need to assign the new macro to the categories or products in the database for which it is designed. To do this, you use the Category Template Assignment or Product Template Assignment form in the Administrator, respectively. See "Assigning a Template to a Category" on page 87 for information on how to assign the macro to categories, and "Assigning a Template to a Product or Item" on page 100 for information on how to assign it to products or items.

If you are the site administrator, do the following to assign a new macro to the task it implements:

1. Ensure that you know the name of the view or exception task that your new macro is designed to implement. If you do not know the name, refer back to "Step 2. Determining the Name of the Task that the Macro Implements" on page 214.

2. Open the Administrator as described in "Opening the Administrator" on page 34.

3. On the task bar, click **Site Manager** and then **Task Management**. The Task Management form appears.

4. From the **Select Task Type** drop-down list, select one of the following task types:

   - **ERROR**, for displaying error pages.

   - **VIEW**, for displaying the pages that shoppers normally see during the shopping process.

   **Note:**
   Do not select the **PROCESS** task type; this task is reserved for activating overridable functions that process information.

   A list of the tasks that are available for the selected task type appears in the bottom frame.

5. Select the desired task name from the list. The fields automatically fill with task information.

6. From the **Scope** drop-down list, change the task scope, if desired. If you are creating a single-store site, you do not have to change the scope. Both mall and store scope will function properly in this case.

7. If you changed the scope, click **Save** before proceeding.

8. On the task bar, click **Task Assignment**.

9. Click the **Macro** button at the bottom of the frame. The Macro Assignment form appears.

10. If the scope of the task has been assigned to *store*, select the store for which you want to assign the macro from the **Select Mall/Store** drop-down list.

11. In the **Macro Filename** field, change the name of the existing macro to the name of your new macro.

12. Click **Save**. A confirmation message appears, indicating that you have successfully assigned your new macro to the selected task.

# Step 10. Further Customizing the System

If your new macro contains additional parameters that are not directly handled by the Net.Commerce system, you may also need to do one of the following:

- Create one or more overridable functions to handle the new parameters. For details, see "Chapter 12, Planning Overridable Functions" on page 349.

- Extend the database to store any new parameters. For details, see "Step 4. Storing Custom Data in the Database" on page 353.

- Modify one or more additional macros by repeating the steps in this chapter. (Because macros are interconnected, your changes may affect other macros, such as error macros that are executed as a result of an exception condition.)

# Examples of Modifying the Default and Sample Pages

The following are examples of how to modify different macros in the Metropolitan Mall sample. All of these macros implement a view task. In each case, assume that your site administrator has set the scope of the tasks to *store,* thereby giving you authorization to customize the macro.

## Example 1: Replacing a Button on the Shopping Cart Page

In this example, you will replace the name of a button on the Metropolitan Mall's shopping cart page with your own text. (You can also use the steps that follow as a guide for changing graphics, text, and colors on any macro.)

1. Determine the name of the task that the macro implements, by referring to the description for the TaskDisplay_1.0 (IBM,NC) overridable function on page 671. The description indicates that the macro implements the SHOPCART_DSP view task.

2. Determine the name of the macro that creates the page, by referring to the TaskDisplay_1.0(IBM,NC) overridable function description. It indicates that the \macro\en_US\demomall\shopcart.d2w macro creates the page.

3. Copy the file to the directory in which you store your macro files.

4. Rename the macro to myshopcart.d2w.

5. Open the myshopcart.d2w macro in a text editor.

6. Look for the HTML tags that display the **Remove Item** button on the page. They are in the %REPORT block of the body function, as follows:

   ```
   <INPUT TYPE="submit" width=100 VALUE="Remove Items">
   ```

7. Change the text on the button to the following (bold type indicates the change):

   ```
   <INPUT TYPE="submit" width=100 VALUE="Remove Selected Products">
   ```

8. Save your work and close the file.

9. Ask your site administrator to activate your new macro (using the Task Management form) with the following information:

- **Task type:** VIEW

- **Task name:** SHOPCART_DSP

- **Macro name:** `myshopcart.d2w`

The next shopper who displays the shopping cart will see the page you updated.

## Example 2: Removing a Field from a Registration Page

In this example, you will remove from the Metropolitan Mall's Registration page the field that requests the shopper's middle name. You will not change the Update Registration page, so shoppers will still have the option of entering their middle names if they update their registration.

You can also use this example as a guide to removing fields from any macro.

1. Determine the name of the task that the macro implements, by referring to the description for the TaskDisplay_1.0 (IBM,NC) overridable function on page 671. It indicates that the macro implements the REG_NEW view task.

2. Determine the name of the macro that creates the page, by referring to the TaskDisplay_1.0(IBM,NC) overridable function description. It indicates that the `\macro\en_US\demomall\mallregform.d2w` macro creates the page.

3. Copy the file to the directory in which you store your macro files.

4. Rename the macro to `myregform.d2w`.

5. Open `myregform.d2w` in a text editor.

6. Perform the following steps to determine whether or not the field for the shopper's middle name is required by the Net.Commerce system or an overridable function:

   a) Find the HTML tags that display the field and its label. In this example, the HTML is in the `\ncsample\msregform.inc` file, which is imported into the macro, as follows:

   ```
   <TD><FONT SIZE=-1>$(1_samname)</FONT></TD><TD>
    <A NAME="samname">
   <INPUT TYPE="text" NAME="samname" VALUE="$(samname)" SIZE="20"
    MAXLENGTH="30">
   ```

   This HTML contains a database variable reference, `$(samname)`, which represents the value of the SAMNAME column in the database. (In this case, the column will be empty, since the shopper has not yet filled this field.) This column can be found in the SHADDR (Shopper Address Book) table.

   b) Look up the SHADDR table on page 515, and look up the column in the table. The column type is not defined as NOT NULL, which means that the system does not require the field. (The only columns that appear on the New Registration page that are defined as NOT NULL in table SHADDR are SHLOGID, the logon user ID of the shopper; SHLPSWD, the password; and SHLPSWDVER, the verification password.)

   c)  Read the descriptions of the tasks of the macro's calling command in "Appendix D, Net.Commerce Commands" on page 569 to determine which ones are called during the registration process. They indicate that the AUDIT_REG process task is called to check parameters that are passed from the new registration and update registration pages. Its default overridable function checks for the following fields:

- SALNAME: the shopper's last name

- SAADDR1: the first line of the address

- SACITY: the city

- SASTATE: the state or equivalent

- SACNTRY: the country

- SAZIPC: the zip code or equivalent

   You cannot remove the fields above without replacing the overridable function. Because the system and the function (the column is not listed above) do not require the SAFNAME column, you can remove it from the New Registration page.

7.   Hide or delete the HTML tags that display the shopper's first name. In this example, you will comment out the tags, as follows:

```
<!-
<TD><FONT SIZE=-1>$(l_samname)</FONT></TD>
<TD><A NAME="samname">
<INPUT TYPE="text" NAME="samname" VALUE="$(samname)" SIZE="20"
MAXLENGTH="30">
->
```

2.   Save and close the file.

3.   Ask your site administrator to activate your new macro (using the Task Management form) with the following information:

- **Task type:** VIEW

- **Task name:** REG_NEW

- **Macro name:** `myregform.d2w`

The next shopper who registers will see the page you updated. (Shoppers who update their registration information will still see the old page, because you did not change the task assignment for REG_UPDATE.)

## Example 3: Changing the Page that Follows Registration

In this example, you will change the page that is displayed after a shopper registers in the Metropolitan Mall. Currently, the shopping cart page is displayed. You will specify that the first category page in the first store in the mall is to be displayed instead.

(You will be able to use this example as a guide to changing which page is displayed after a shopper clicks a button or hyperlink on any store page.)

1. Determine the name of the task that the macro implements, by referring to the description for the TaskDisplay_1.0 (IBM,NC) overridable function on page 671. It indicates that the macro implements the REG_NEW view task.

2. Determine the name of the macro that creates the page, by referring to the TaskDisplay_1.0(IBM,NC) overridable function description. It indicates that the \macro\en_US\demomall\mallregform.d2w macro creates the page.

3. Copy the file to the directory in which you store your macros.

4. Rename the macro to myregform.d2w.

5. Open myregform.d2w in a text editor.

6. Examine the action that is associated with the **Submit Registration** button. Currently, when the shopper clicks this button, the ACTION URL of the form calls the RegisterNew command, as follows:

   ```
   <FORM METHOD=post ACTION="/cgi-bin/ncommerce3/RegisterNew">
   ```

   This command creates a new registration record for the shopper. After the command successfully completes, it calls a second URL. This URL is defined in a hidden input field called url, as follows:

   ```
   <INPUT TYPE = "hidden" NAME="url" VALUE="/cgi-bin/ncommerce3/
   ExecMacro/mallregform.d2w/input?mode=new&url=$(url_in)">
   ```

   This URL calls a second command, ExecMacro/mallregform.d2w/input?mode=new, which executes the HTML Input section of the current macro to retrieve the shopper's name from the SHADDR table and displays the name with a confirmation message.

7. Determine which command displays a category page, by referring to the command descriptions in "Appendix D, Net.Commerce Commands" on page 569. It indicates that the CategoryDisplay command displays a category page.

8. Determine the parameters for the CategoryDisplay command by reading its description. It requires two parameters: the merchant reference number and the category reference of the category page to display.

9. Change the value of the hidden input field, as follows:

   ```
   <INPUT TYPE = "hidden" NAME="url" Value="/cgi-bin/ncommerce3/
   ExecMacro/mallregform.d2w/input?mode=new
   &url=CategoryDisplay%3Fcgmenbr%3D1&cgrfnbr%3D0">
   ```

   > **Note:**
   > Type the value for the new URL all on one line. It is shown here on three lines for presentation purposes only.

10. Save your work and close the file.

11. Ask your site administrator to activate your new macro (using the Task Management form) with the following information:

- **Task type:** VIEW

- **Task name:** REG_NEW

- **Macro name:** myregform.d2w

The next shopper who registers will see the page you updated. (Shoppers who update their registration information will still see the old page, because you did not change the task assignment for REG_UPDATE.)

# Modifying System Error Pages

A system error page is displayed in the shopper's browser when a severe system error occurs and the system cannot perform the shopper's request. For most system error pages, a corresponding operator message also appears on the Net.Commerce operator console or in the log file.

Most system error pages are HTML files, making customization straightforward. You can change the graphics, text, and color of a system error message page by simply editing the HTML tags.

Each system error page is described below, along with the name of the HTML file or macro that displays it. The operator message number is provided as a cross-reference to the corresponding message that appears on the operator console.

The HTML files are stored in the following directory:

> **WIN**  \ibm\NetCommerce3\html\en_US\ncerror
> **AIX**  /usr/lpp/NetCommerce3/html/en_US/ncerror

The macro file (there is only one: tsslfail.d2w) is stored in the following directory:

> **WIN**  \ibm\NetCommerce3\macro\en_US\ncsample
> **AIX**  /usr/lpp/NetCommerce3/macro/en_US/ncsample

Table 8.4 lists the system error pages.

*Table 8.4*  *The system error pages.*

| File Name | Error Message | Operator Message No. |
| --- | --- | --- |
| cmdinc.html | COMMAND STRUCTURE FAILURE.<br><br>- Unable to complete command.<br>- The command syntax is not correct. | CMN0950E |
| datapop.html | DATA POPULATION FAILURE.<br><br>Data that is expected to be in the database, such as a macro or a task, is not found due to a system configuration problem. | CMN0953E |

*Continued on next page*

*Table 8.4* *Continued.*

| File Name | Error Message | Operator Message No. |
|---|---|---|
| default.html | An unknown error has occurred. Please try again later. | no operator message |
| config.html | CONFIGURATION/SETUP FAILURE.<br><br>- Unable to find or open a dynamic library specified by the merchant.<br>- Unable to find a function in a dynamic library specified by the merchant.<br>- The base page for the store is not valid or is unobtainable.<br>- The director is unable to communicate with the server. | CMN0958E |
| oom.html | MEMORY FAILURE.<br><br>Memory allocation failure. | CMN0959E |
| env.html | ENVIRONMENT FAILURE.<br><br>One or more values are missing in the file ncommerce.ini. | CMN0960E |
| cmdexe.html | COMMAND EXECUTION FAILURE.<br><br>Unable to complete command or a command could not execute. | CMN0961E |
| auth.html | AUTHORIZATION FAILURE.<br><br>A user has attempted to execute an administrative command without being logged on to an administrative user ID. | CMN0962E |
| noserver.html | SERVER NOT RESPONDING.<br><br>Server not responding.  A server could not be reached to service this request. | CMN0302E |
| passwd.html | PASSWORD INVALID.<br><br>Please check your password and try again. | no operator message |
| sql.html | SQL FAILURE.<br><br>An error occurred during the execution of an SQL statement.  DB2 may be down, or there may be a problem in the database. | CMN0957E |
| tsslfail.d2w | SECURITY VERIFICATION.<br><br>A shopper has accessed the site with a b browser that is not recognized by the system. (A page appears asking the shopper to indicate if the browser supports SSL.) | no operator message |

The following are the general steps to follow when modifying a system error page:

1.  Determine which file to change, by referring to the descriptions above.

2.  If appropriate, copy the file to the directory in which you store system error pages.

3.  Open the file in a text editor and save it immediately under a different name. This allows you to restore the original version if required.

4.  Make the appropriate changes. For example, type your text over the existing text and replace the generic error image and page background with your own.

5.  Save the file under its original name. (All system errors must be saved under their original names, because these names are hard-coded in the system.)

6.  If you copied the file to a new directory, add the following pass statement to the Web server configuration file so that the server can find the file:

    ```
    Pass /ncerror/* <drive>:\<directory>*
    ```

    where `<drive>` is the drive on which the directory is stored, and `<directory>` is the directory in which the error page is stored

    The next time the error occurs, your new text will be displayed on the system error message page.

# Workshop: Modifying the Store Pages in the OneStopPizza Shop

In this workshop, you will change the look of the OneStopPizza Shop by doing the following:

*   Replacing the navigation buttons

*   Changing the background color of each store frame

*   Changing the color of the hypertext links

*   Adding a new store banner

*   Removing unwanted links from the navigation bar

*   Adding the option for registered shopper to log on from the home page.

*   Creating an error page that will display when a shopper attempts to log on using an incorrect logon ID and password

All images required for this workshop are in the following directory. (You copied them to this directory in the workshop "Adding a New Catalog to the OneStopPizza Shop" on page 107.)

**WIN**   `\ibm\www\html\OneStopPizzaShop\`

# Viewing the Store

Before you begin to modify the macros in the store, let's review how the store currently looks.

1. Access the store at the following URL or by using your browser bookmark:

   `http://<host_name>/OneStopPizzaShop`

   where `<host_name>` is the fully qualified name of your server

2. Note the appearance of the store banner, the navigation bar, the background colors of each frame, and the color of the hypertext links, as shown in Figure 8.1 below:

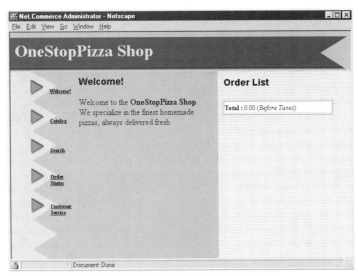

**Figure 8.1** *The home page of the OneStopPizza Shop, before the custom graphics are added.*

# Replacing the Navigation Buttons, Background Colors, Hypertext Colors, and Store Banner

You will now replace the navigation buttons, background colors, hypertext colors, and store banner by changing the values of the corresponding variables in the store's "include" file.

1. In a text editor, open the `OneStopPizzaShop.inc` file from the following directory:

   **WIN** `\IBM\NetCommerce3\macro\en_US\OneStopPizzaShop\`

   As you can see, the file consists of a list of variable names and their values, which are enclosed in a Net.Data `%DEFINE` section. It will look something like this:

   ```
   %DEFINE {
   EOF="EOF"
   navigation="side"
   CC_visa="YES"
   HomeCategory="343"
   ```

```
ButtonHeight="46"
BannerLeftSpc="0"
title="Contemporary (Side)"
LinkCol="black"
BckImageNavBar="/sggifs/c_leftbkg_s.gif"
Button1="/sggifs/c_butt1_s.gif"
TextCol="black"
Button2="/sggifs/c_butt2_s.gif"
Button3="/sggifs/c_butt3_s.gif"
VLinkCol="darkolivegreen"
NavBarAlign="left"
CC_phone="YES"
Button4="/sggifs/c_butt4_s.gif"
NavLinkCol="black"
STORENAME="OneStopPizzaShop"
Button5="/sggifs/c_butt5_s.gif"
TitleTxtCol="black"
BannerImage="/sggifs/c_banner.gif"
CC_master="YES"
Button6="/sggifs/c_butt6_s.gif"
MerchantRefNum="252"
Button7="/sggifs/c_butt7_s.gif"
BannerRightSpc="50"
CC_amex="NO"
Button8="/sggifs/c_butt8_s.gif"
BodyImage1="/sggifs/c_tablbkg.gif"
AddButton="/sggifs/c_add.gif"
CC_discover="NO"
LongStoreName="OneStopPizza Shop"
ButtonWidth="68"
BannerTxtCol="#FFCC00"
ALinkCol="yellow"
BodyColor1="#FF9933"
BodyColor2="#FFCC66"
gif="sggifs/cont_s.jpg"
BodyColor3="silver"
%}
```

2.  First, you will replace the navigation buttons, which currently appear as orange triangles, with black and white circles. The new images will be slightly larger, so you will also need to alter their width and height. Change the values of variables Button1, Button2, Button4, Button5, ButtonHeight, and ButtonWidth, as follows (bold type indicates the new values that you must enter):

    - ButtonHeight="**71**"

    - Button1="**/OneStopPizzaShop/home.gif**"

    - Button2="**/OneStopPizzaShop/menu.gif**"

    - Button4="**/OneStopPizzaShop/quickpick.gif**"

- `Button5="`**`/OneStopPizzaShop/custservice.gif`**`"`

- `ButtonWidth="`**`67`**`"`

`Button1` will link to your store's home page, `Button2` will link to your pizza menu, `Button4` will link to the Quick Pick page for registered shoppers, and `Button5` will link to your Customer Service page.

> **Note:**
> Variables **`ButtonHeight`** and **`ButtonWidth`** define the height and width of all the navigation buttons. Therefore, in order to use these variables, you need to keep the dimensions the same for each button.

Also note that you did not change the images for the variables `Button3`, `Button6`, `Button7`, and `Button8`. Although these variables are not required by your store, it is not necessary to remove them from this file. In a later step, you will remove all references to them.

3. Now you will replace the image used to display the background of the navigation frame. Change the value of variable `BckImageNavBar` to `/OneStopPizzaShop/ navbkgrnd.gif`, as follows:

   `BckImageNavBar="`**`/OneStopPizzaShop/navbkgrnd.gif`**`"`

4. Now, you will change the background color of the home page, category pages, product pages, and the order page from orange to white. Change the value of `BodyColor1` to `#FFFFFF`, as follows:

   `BodyColor1="`**`#FFFFFF`**`"`

5. Now you will change the background color of the Order List from a patterned yellow image to a solid pale yellow. Change the value of `BodyImage1` to `/OneStopPizzaShop/ yellow.gif`, as follows:

   `BodyImage1="`**`/OneStopPizzaShop/yellow.gif`**`"`

6. Next, you will change the color of the labels for the product and category pages to a brighter yellow. Change the value of `BodyColor2` to `#FFCC00`, as follows:

   `BodyColor2="`**`#FFCC00`**`"`

7. Next, you will change the color of all hypertext links on the store pages, except the links on the navigation bar, from black to deep red. Change the value of `LinkCol` to `#990000`, as follows:

   `LinkCol="`**`#990000`**`"`

8. Now you will change the color of all the active hypertext links on the store pages, except the links on the navigation bar, from yellow to bright red. Change the value of `ALinkCol` to `#FF0000`, as follows:

   `ALinkCol="`**`#FF0000`**`"`

9.  Now you will change the color of all visited hypertext links on the store pages, except the links on the navigation bar, from dark olive green to dark gray. Change the value of `VLinkCol` to `#666666`, as follows:

    `VLinkCol="`**`#666666`**`"`

10. Now you will change the color of the navigation hypertext links from black to white. Change the value of variable `NavLinkCol` to `#FFFFFF`, as follows:

    `NavLinkCol="`**`#FFFFFF`**`"`

11. Finally, you will change the image for the store banner to one that displays your store's logo. Change the value of `BannerImage` to `/OneStopPizzaShop/banner.gif`, as follows:

    `BannerImage="`**`/OneStopPizzaShop/banner.gif`**`"`

12. You are now finished editing the include file. Save your changes and close the file. Now, when shoppers view your store, the values that you replaced will dynamically appear on store pages that reference the corresponding variable names.

13. To see the results of your changes, reload the store in your browser. The home page should now resemble Figure 8.2 below:

**Figure 8.2** *Replacing the store's navigation buttons with custom buttons.*

New navigation buttons appear on the navigation bar. Note that one of the original buttons is still displaying. You will remove it and its corresponding text shortly. The background of the home page is now white, and the background of the Order List is a light yellow. Your store's logo appears as the store banner. Note that the store name still appears behind the logo. You will remove it in the next step.

# Editing the Store Banner

Editing the include file is ideal when you want to change the values of variables that are referenced in multiple macro files and you do not need to change the HTML formatting in the source files. However, there will be times when you need to do extensive editing of files that do not use the variables in the include file or in which you need to add or remove content. In these cases, you need to edit the corresponding macro directly. In this step, you will remove the store name that is currently displaying behind the store banner.

1. In a text editor, open the `banner.d2w` macro, which creates the store banner, from the following directory:

    **WIN** `\ibm\netcommerce3\macro\en_US\OneStopPizzaShop\`

2. Examine the contents. The code should look something like this:

```
%HTML_REPORT {

  <HTML>
  <HEAD><TITLE>$(LongStoreName)</TITLE></HEAD><META HTTP-
    EQUIV=Expires CONTENT="Mon, 01 Jan 1998 01:01:01 GMT">
  <BODY BACKGROUND="$(BannerImage)">

  <TABLE BORDER=0 WIDTH=650 HEIGHT=55 HSPACE=0 VSPACE=0
   ALIGN="left" VALIGN="top" CELLPADDING=0 CELLSPACING=0>
     <TR>
        <TD WIDTH=$(BannerLeftSpc)></TD>
        <TD ALIGN=$(BannerAlign) VALIGN="center" width=515>
         <B><FONT SIZE=6 COLOR=$(BannerTxtCol)>$(LongStoreName)
         </FONT></B></TD>
        <TD WIDTH=$(BannerRightSpc)></TD>
     </TR>
  </TABLE>
  </BODY>

  </HTML>
%}
```

    This file displays the background for the frame using the `$(BannerImage)` reference to the value of the `BannerImage` variable in the include file, and displays in a table the store name using other variables in the include file.

3. Remove the table from the file by removing the following HTML:

```
<TABLE BORDER=0 WIDTH=650 HEIGHT=55 HSPACE=0 VSPACE=0 ALIGN="left"
VALIGN="top" CELLPADDING=0 CELLSPACING=0>
  <TR>
    <TD WIDTH=$(BannerLeftSpc)></TD>
    <TD ALIGN=$(BannerAlign) VALIGN="center" width=515>
     <B><FONT SIZE=6 COLOR=$(BannerTxtCol)>$(LongStoreName)
     </FONT></B></TD>
    <TD WIDTH=$(BannerRightSpc)></TD>
  </TR>
</TABLE>
```

The file should now look like this:

```
%HTML_REPORT {

  <HTML>
  <HEAD><TITLE>$(LongStoreName)</TITLE></HEAD><META HTTP-
  EQUIV=Expires CONTENT="Mon, 01 Jan 1998 01:01:01 GMT">
  <BODY BACKGROUND="$(BannerImage)">
  </BODY>
  </HTML>
%}
```

4.  Save your changes and close the file.  Now the redundant store title is removed from the store banner, leaving only the logo image that you previously added.

5.  Reload the store in your browser to see the results, as shown in Figure 8.3:

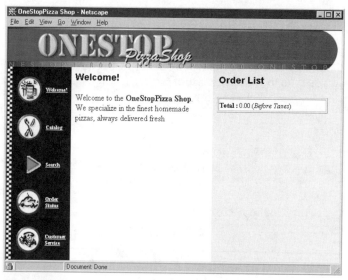

**Figure 8.3**  *The store with the modified store banner.*

# Modifying the Navigation Bar

You will now edit the macro that displays the navigation bar in the left frame.  You will change the text for the hypertext links and remove the links that are not required by your store.

1.  In a text editor, open the `nav_side.d2w` macro, which creates the navigation bar, from the following directory:

    **WIN**  `\ibm\netcommerce3\macro\en_US\OneStopPizzaShop\`

2.  Scan the file to examine its contents.  It consists of an HTML table that lists images and hypertext that link to the primary store functions: Home Page, Catalog, Search, Order Status, and Customer Service.  Each link contains a command that displays the appropriate store page.  The images, text colors, and background colors are defined by referencing variables in the `OneStopPizzaShop.inc` file.

3.  Now, you will remove the link to the Search page, which is not supported by your store. You do not require a Search page because your market research indicates that most of your shoppers prefer to browse the menu to find a pizza to order.

    Delete the following HTML, which displays links to the Search page:

```
<TR>
  <TD VALIGN="center" height=$(ButtonHeight)
  width=$(ButtonWidth)>
  <A HREF="/cgi-bin/ncommerce3/ExecMacro/$(STORENAME)/
    search.d2w/
    report" TARGET="main"><img src="$(Button3)" BORDER=0></A></TD>

  <TD VALIGN="center">
  <A HREF="/cgi-bin/ncommerce3/ExecMacro/$(STORENAME)/search.d2w/
   report" TARGET="main"><FONT SIZE=1><B>Search</b></FONT></A>
  </TD>
</TR>
```

4.  Now you will replace the link to the Order Status page with a link to the Quick Pick page. In review, this page is available to registered shoppers for quickly selecting pizzas that they have ordered on previous occasions, instead of searching each time through the category and product pages. You do not require an Order Status page because the Customer Service page that you already provide is sufficient.

    Find the following HTML:

```
<TR>
  <TD VALIGN="center" height=$(ButtonHeight)
  width=$(ButtonWidth)>
  <A HREF="/cgi-bin/ncommerce3/
   OrderList?merchant_rn=$(MerchantRefNum)&status=C"
   TARGET="main"><img src="$(Button4)" BORDER=0></A></TD>

  <TD VALIGN="center">
  <A HREF="/cgi-bin/ncommerce3/
   OrderList?merchant_rn=$(MerchantRefNum)&status=C"
   TARGET="main"><FONT SIZE=1><B>Order<BR>Status</b></FONT></A>
  </TD>
</TR>
```

    Make the following changes to it (indicated by bold type):

```
<TR>
  <TD VALIGN="center" height=$(ButtonHeight)
  width=$(ButtonWidth)>
  <A HREF="/cgi-bin/ncommerce3/ExecMacro/$(STORENAME)/
   quickpick.d2w/report" TARGET="main"><img src="$(Button4)"
   BORDER=0></A></TD>

  <TD VALIGN="center">
  <A HREF="/cgi-bin/ncommerce3/ExecMacro/$(STORENAME)/
   quickpick.d2w/report" TARGET="main"><FONT
   SIZE=1><B>Quick<BR>Pick</b></FONT></A></TD>
</TR>
```

You have just replaced the command for the links with the ExecMacro command, which will execute the `quickpick.d2w` macro. This macro will display a list of all of the shopper's previously ordered pizzas, from which the shopper can reselect for ordering. You also updated the text to reflect the new store function.

5. Now you need to change the text of the remaining links to text that is more suitable for your store. Change the label of the hypertext that links to your home page from "Welcome" to "Home", and the label of the hypertext that links to your pizza menu from "Catalog" to "Menu", as follows:

```
<TR>
  <TD VALIGN="center" height=$(ButtonHeight)
  width=$(ButtonWidth)>
  <A HREF="/cgi-bin/ncommerce3/ExecMacro/$(STORENAME)/home.d2w/
  report" TARGET="main"><img src="$(Button1)" BORDER=0></A></TD>
  <TD VALIGN="center" width=100>
  <A HREF="/cgi-bin/ncommerce3/ExecMacro/$(STORENAME)/home.d2w/
  report" TARGET="main"><FONT SIZE=1><B>Home</B></FONT></A></TD>
</TR>
<TR>
  <TD VALIGN="center" height=$(ButtonHeight)
  width=$(ButtonWidth)>
  <A HREF="/cgi-bin/ncommerce3/
  CategoryDisplay?cgmenbr=$(MerchantRefNum)&cgrfnbr=$(HomeCategory)"
  target="main"><img src="$(Button2)" BORDER=0></A></TD>
  <TD VALIGN="center" width=100>
  <A HREF="/cgi-bin/ncommerce3/
  CategoryDisplay?cgmenbr=$(MerchantRefNum)&cgrfnbr=$(HomeCategory)"
  target="main"><FONT SIZE=1><B>Menu</B></FONT></A></TD>
</TR>
```

Note that the ExecMacro command is used to execute the `home.d2w` macro, which displays the home page; and the CategoryDisplay command is used to display the store's top-level category, *Menu*. The merchant reference number and the reference number of the store's top-level category, which are both referenced from the values in the `OneStopPizzaShop.inc` file, are used as parameters so that the command can retrieve the correct macro from the database.

6. You have now finished editing the macro for the navigation bar. Save your work and close the file.

7. To view your changes, reload the store in your browser. The store should now resemble Figure 8.4.

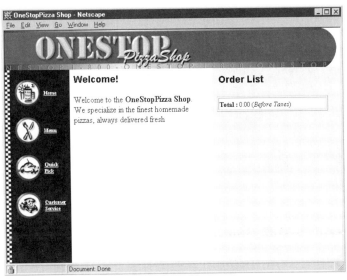

**Figure 8.4** *The store with the modified navigation bar.*

# Modifying the Category Pages

You will now remove the title "Catalog" and the introductory text from all of the category pages.

1. First, see how the category pages currently appear in the store by clicking **Menu** on the navigation bar. The top-level category page appears with the title and introduction. The title is redundant because you have a title below it called "Menu".

2. In a text editor, open the macro `cat1.d2w`, which creates the category pages, from the following directory:

   **WIN** `\ibm\netcommerce3\macro\en_US\category\OneStopPizzaShop\`

3. Find the beginning of the `%HTML_REPORT` section of the macro.

4. Remove the title by deleting the following HTML:

   ```
   <TD ALIGN="left"><FONT FACE="helvetica" COLOR="$(TitleTxtCol)">
   <H3>Catalog</H3></FONT></TD>
   ```

5. Remove the introduction by deleting the following HTML:

   ```
   <TR>
     <TD ALIGN="left" COLSPAN=2>
     <BR>
     <FONT COLOR="$(TitleTxtCol)" SIZE=2>Browse the catalog to view
      product information and to add items to the order list.</FONT>
     <BR><BR>
     </TD>
   </TR>
   ```

6. Save your work and close the file.

7. Test your changes by clicking **Menu** on the navigation bar of the store. The category page redisplays with only the title "Menu", as shown in Figure 8.5.

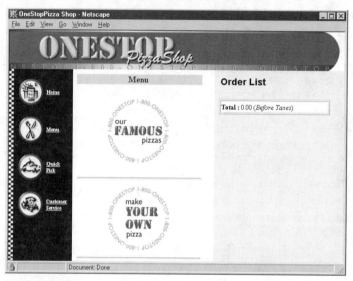

**Figure 8.5**  *The store with the modified category pages.*

# Modifying the Product Pages

For the product pages, you will remove the title "Catalog" and the introduction, add a price for each size of pizza, and move the product description to a new location on the page.

1. First, see how the product pages currently appear in the store by clicking **Our Famous Pizzas** on thecategory page, and then **Vegetarian Delight**. The product page for this pizza appears. It currently displays the title "Catalog" and an introduction. Note that the sizes listed in the drop-down list do not include a price, and that the description is at the bottom of the page.

2. In a text editor, open the macro `prod1.d2w`, which creates the product pages, from the following directory:

   **WIN** `\ibm\netcommerce3\macro\en_US\product\OneStopPizzaShop\`

3. Scroll down to find the beginning of the `%HTML_REPORT` section of the macro.

4. Repeat steps 4 and 5 in the previous section, "Modifying the Category Pages", to remove the title and introduction.

5. Now, you will move the description, which currently appears at the bottom of the product pages, to underneath the full-sized image of the product. In the `%HTML_REPORT` section of the macro, find the following three functions calls:

```
%IF (ATTRIBUTES == "TRUE")

    @DISPLAY_PRODUCT_IMAGE()
    @DISPLAY_PRODATTR_PRICE()
    @DISPLAY_PRODUCT_INFO()
```

This code does the following: if the value of variable ATTRIBUTES is equal to true, which is the case, the three functions are called to display the full-sized image, the drop-down list of available sizes, and the product's description, in that order.

6.  Move the function that displays the description, DISPLAY_PRODUCT_INFO(), so that it is called immediately after the image is displayed, as follows:

```
%IF (ATTRIBUTES == "TRUE")

  @DISPLAY_PRODUCT_IMAGE()
  @DISPLAY_PRODUCT_INFO()
  @DISPLAY_PRODATTR_PRICE()
```

7.  Next, you will add a price to the drop-down list, which currently contains only sizes (small, medium, and large).  Find the DISPLAY_PRODATTR_PRICE() function in the macro, as follows:

```
%function(dtw_odbc) DISPLAY_PRODATTR_PRICE(){

  SELECT distinct paname, paval
  FROM PRODUCT, PRODATR, PRODDSTATR
  WHERE pamenbr=$(MerchantRefNum)
  and prmenbr=$(MerchantRefNum)
  and paprnbr=prrfnbr
  and prprfnbr=$(prrfnbr)
  and paname=pdname

  %REPORT{

    <FORM ACTION="/cgi-bin/ncommerce3/OrderItemUpdate"
    TARGET="list" METHOD="post">

    <INPUT TYPE=hidden NAME=merchant_rn VALUE=$(MerchantRefNum)>
    <INPUT TYPE=hidden NAME=product_rn VALUE=$(prrfnbr)>
    <INPUT TYPE=hidden NAME=addr_rn VALUE=$(ADDRESS_REF)>
    <INPUT TYPE=hidden NAME=quantity VALUE=1>
    <INPUT TYPE=hidden NAME=shipmode_rn VALUE=$(SHIPPING_REF)>
    <INPUT TYPE=hidden NAME=url VALUE="/cgi-bin/ncommerce3/
    OrderItemDisplay?merchant_rn=$(MerchantRefNum)">

    <TR><TD><BR></TD></TR>

    %ROW{

      %IF (ITEM_ATTR_NAME != V_paname)

        </SELECT>
        </TD></TR>
        @DTW_assign(ITEM_ATTR_NAME, V_paname)
        <TR><TD ALIGN="right">
        <B>$(V_paname)</B>
        </TD>
```

```
        <TD>
        <SELECT NAME="$(V_paname)">
        <OPTION VALUE="$(V_paval)">$(V_paval)</OPTION>

    %ELSE

        <OPTION VALUE="$(V_paval)">$(V_paval)</OPTION>

    %ENDIF
  %}

</SELECT>
</TD></TR>
<TR><TD><BR></TD></TR>

<TR><TD ALIGN="center" COLSPAN=2><input type=submit value="Add
to Order List"></TD></TR>

</FORM>
<TR><TD><BR></TD></TR>
 %}


%MESSAGE{100:{ PROBLEM%} :continue %}

%}
```

This function first queries the database for all the names and values of each item belonging to the reference number of the parent product that was passed to the macro as an input parameter. It then displays all retrieved rows in one drop-down list with a label containing the name of the attribute (size). Following the drop-down list, it displays a form submit button, which calls the OrderItemUpdate command to add the size that is selected from the drop-down list to the Order List.

8.  Add the following statements to the function:

```
%function(dtw_odbc) DISPLAY_PRODATTR_PRICE(){

    SELECT distinct paname, paval, ppprc
    FROM PRODUCT, PRODATR, PRODDSTATR, PRODPRCS
    WHERE pamenbr=$(MerchantRefNum)
    and prmenbr=$(MerchantRefNum)
    and paprnbr=prrfnbr
    and prprfnbr=$(prrfnbr)
    and paname=pdname
    and ppprnbr=prrfnbr

    %REPORT{
      . . .

    %ROW{

      %IF (ITEM_ATTR_NAME != V_paname)
      </SELECT>
      </TD></TR>
```

```
@DTW_assign(ITEM_ATTR_NAME, V_paname)
<TR><TD ALIGN="right">
<B>$(V_paname)</B>
</TD>
<TD>
<SELECT NAME="$(V_paname)">
<OPTION VALUE="$(V_paval)">$(V_paval) @ $(V_ppprc)</OPTION>

%ELSE

   <OPTION VALUE="$(V_paval)">$(V_paval) @ $(V_ppprc)
   </OPTION>

%ENDIF
. . .
```

You have just added to the SQL statement the PPPRC (the product price) column and the PRODPRCS (Product Prices) table so that the query will also retrieve all prices whose product reference numbers in the PRODPRCS tables match the product reference numbers in the PRODUCT table. You also added a variable reference to the value of the drop-down list to display the price of each row retrieved from the query.

9.  Save your work and close the file.

10. To test your changes, reload the *Vegetarian Delight* product page in the store. The title and introduction to the page are now gone; the prices of each size now appears in the drop-down list; and the description now appears underneath the full-sized image, as shown in Figure 8.6 below:

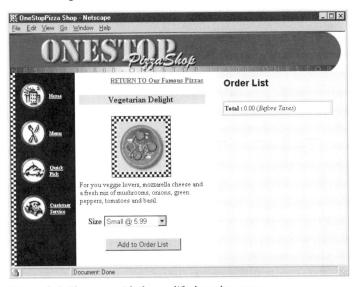

***Figure 8.6*** *The store with the modified product pages.*

# Modifying the Home Page

You will now add additional content to the home page. Currently, it displays only the store description that you entered using the Store Creator. You will now add the option for registered shoppers to log on, so that they can use your "Quick Pick" feature.

1. In a text editor, open the `home.d2w` macro, which creates the home page, from the following directory:

    **WIN** `\ibm\netcommerce3\macro\en_US\OneStopPizzaShop\`

2. Find the `%HTML_REPORT` section and examine its content. This macro currently calls the function `StoreDescription`, which displays the store description by querying the MERCHANT table in the database for the value of the MESTDESC column.

3. In a text editor, open the file `logon.txt` from the `\workshops\macros\` directory on the CD.

4. Copy all the code in the `logon.txt` file (except the legal disclaimer at the beginning) and paste it between the </TABLE> and </BODY> tags in the `%HTML_REPORT` section, as follows:

```
%HTML_REPORT {

  <HTML>
  <HEAD>
  <META HTTP-EQUIV=Expires CONTENT="Mon, 01 Jan 1996 01:01:01 GMT">
  </HEAD>
  <BODY BGCOLOR="$(BodyColor1)" TEXT="$(TextCol)"
   LINK="$(LinkCol)" VLINK="$(VLinkCol)" ALINK="$(ALinkCol)">

  @GETSHOPPER()

  <TABLE WIDTH=100% CELLPADDING=0 CELLSPACING=0 BORDER=0>

  <TR>
    <TD ALIGN="left" VALIGN="center">
    <FONT FACE="helvetica" COLOR=$(TitleTxtCol)><H3>Welcome!
    </H3></FONT></TD>
  </TR>
  <TR>
    <TD align="left" COLSPAN=3>
    <FONT SIZE=3>@StoreDescription()</FONT></TD>
    </TR>
  </TABLE>

  <FORM METHOD=get ACTION=/cgi-bin/ncommerce3/Logon>
  <INPUT TYPE=HIDDEN NAME="url" VALUE="/cgi-bin/ncommerce3/
   ExecMacro/$(STORENAME)/quickpick.d2w/report">
  <TABLE BORDER="0" WIDTH="100">
  <TR>
    <TD ALIGN="left" COLSPAN="2"><B><FONT SIZE="-1">Log on to
    <FONT COLOR="$(LinkCol)">QUICK PICK</FONT>!</FONT></B></TD>
  </TR>
```

```
 <TR>
    <TD ALIGN="left" COLSPAN="2"><FONT SIZE="-1"><P>If you are
    registered, log on to "quick pick" from any of your favorite
    pizzas that you have previously ordered.  <P>Just enter your
    logon ID and password below:</TD>
 </TR>
 <TR>
    <TD ALIGN="left"><B><FONT SIZE="-1">Logon ID</FONT></B></TD>
    <TD ALIGN="left"><INPUT TYPE="TEXT" NAME="name" SIZE="20">
    </TD>
 </TR>
 <TR>
    <TD ALIGN="left"><b><FONT SIZE="-1"> Password</FONT></b>:
    </TD>
    <TD ALIGN="left"><INPUT TYPE="PASSWORD" NAME="password"
    SIZE="20" MAXLENGTH="30"></TD>
 </TR>
 <TR>
    <TD ALIGN="center" COLSPAN="2"><BR><INPUT TYPE="SUBMIT"
    NAME="SUBMIT" VALUE="LOG ON"></TD>
 </TR>
 </TABLE>
 </FORM>

 </BODY>
 </HTML>
%}
```

You have just pasted code that displays a form for registered shoppers to log on. When they enter their logon ID and password and then click **LOG ON**, the URL in the ACTION tag of the form is invoked. This URL contains the Logon command, which logs the shopper on to the store by creating a digitally signed cookie, which is sent back to the browser to identify the user's session. The shopper is now in an authenticated session. When the command successfully completes, it redirects its flow of execution to the URL passed to the command, which in this case contains the ExecMacro command to execute the `quickpick.d2w`, which displays a list of pizzas previously ordered by the shopper.

5.   Save your work and close the file.

# Assigning the Logon_err.d2w macro to the LOGON_ERR Task

If a shopper enters an incorrect logon ID or password when attempting to log on, the Logon command will by default call the LOGON_ERR exception task to handle the error. This task will by default call the TaskDisplay_1.(IBM,NC) overridable function, which will execute the `mallogon.d2w` macro to display an error message to the shopper. The error code 300 is passed by the Logon command to this macro, to indicate the type of error that has occurred. In this step, you will replace the `mallogon.d2w` macro with a custom one made especially for the OneStopPizza Shop.

1.  Let's take a moment to examine this custom macro, which is called `logon_err.d2w`.
    Copy the `logon_err.d2w` macro from the `\workshops\macros\` directory on the CD
    to the following directory:

    **WIN** `ibm\netcommerce3\macro\en_US\OneStopPizzaShop\`

2.  In a text editor, open the file and examine its code.  It will look something like this:

```
%HTML_REPORT {

  <HTML>
  <HEAD><TITLE>Log On Failure</TITLE></HEAD>
  <BODY BGCOLOR="FFFFFF" TEXT="$(TextCol)" LINK="$(LinkCol)"
  VLINK="$(VLinkCol)" ALINK="$(ALinkCol)">
  <H3><FONT FACE="helvetica">Log On Failure</FONT></H3>

  %IF ( error_code == "300" )

    <P><FONT SIZE="-1">Your logon ID or password is incorrect.
     Please try again:</P>

  <FORM METHOD=get ACTION=/cgi-bin/ncommerce3/Logon>
  <INPUT TYPE=HIDDEN NAME="url" VALUE="/cgi-bin/ncommerce3/
  ExecMacro/$(STORENAME)/quickpick.d2w/report">

  <TABLE BORDER="0" WIDTH="100">
    <TR>
      <TD ALIGN="left"><B><FONT SIZE="-1">Logon ID</FONT></B>
      </TD>
      <TD ALIGN="left"><INPUT TYPE="TEXT" NAME="name"
       SIZE="20"></TD>
    </TR>
    <TR>
      <TD ALIGN="left"><b><FONT SIZE="-1"> Password</FONT></b>:
      </TD>
      <TD ALIGN="left"><INPUT TYPE="PASSWORD" NAME="password"
       SIZE="20" MAXLENGTH="30"></TD>
    </TR>
    <TR>
      <TD ALIGN="center" COLSPAN="2"><BR><INPUT TYPE="SUBMIT"
  NAME="SUBMIT" VALUE="LOG ON"></TD>
  </TR>
  </TABLE>
  </FORM>

  %ELSE

    <P>An unknown error occurred.  Please contact your Web server
      administrator.</P>
  %ENDIF
  </BODY>
  </HTML>
%}
```

This macro does the following: if the error code 300 is passed to it, it displays an error message indicating that the shopper entered an incorrect logon ID or password and provides fields for the shopper to retry; otherwise, it displays a generic error message.

3. To tell the system to start using the `logon_err.d2w` macro, you will now assign it to the LOGON_ERR task using the Task Management form in the Administrator. Open the Administrator.

4. Log on using your site administrator user ID and password. (Only site administrators can assign macros to tasks.)

5. On the task bar, click **Site Manager** and then **Task Management**. The Task Management form appears.

4. From the **Select Task Type** drop-down list, select **ERROR**.

5. In the bottom frame, scroll until you find **LOGON ERR,** and then select that task.

6. On the task bar, click **Task Assignment**.

7. Click the **Macro...** button at the bottom of the frame. The Macro Assignment form appears.

8. In the **Macro Filename** field, change `mallogon.d2w` to:

   `/OneStopPizzaShop/logon_err.d2w`

9. Click **Save**. A confirmation message appears, indicating that you have successfully assigned your new macro to the selected task, as shown in Figure 8.7 below:

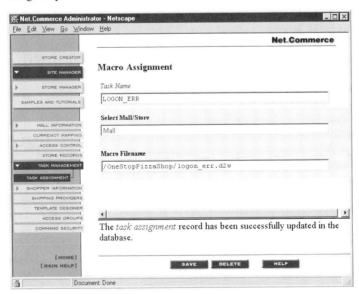

*Figure 8.7  The Macro Assignment form.*

**Note:**
The **Select Mall/Store** drop-down list shows **Mall** because your macro was assigned to the task as the default macro at the mall level. Your store is treated as a mall that contains only one store.

# Testing the Home Page

Let's see how your home page looks with all the additions you have made.

1.   Close the browser that is currently displaying the Adminstrator, and open the store in a new browser. Its home page now displays the fields for a registered shopper to log on, as shown in Figure 8.8 below:

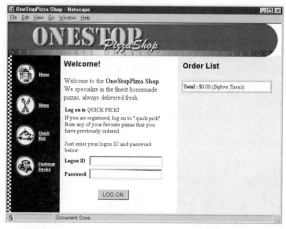

*Figure 8.8   The store home page with fields for the shopper to log on.*

At this point in the store creation process there is no way for the shopper to register, therefore any attempts to log on will fail. This is an ideal time to make sure that the `logon_err.d2w` macro is called by the LOGON_ERR exception task.

2.   To test the `logon_err.d2w` macro, enter test in both the **Logon ID** and **Password** field, and then click **LOG ON**. The `logon_err.d2w` macro displays the appropriate error message, as shown in Figure 8.9 below:

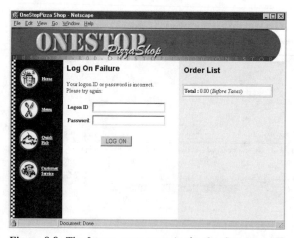

*Figure 8.9   The Logon error page in the OneStopPizza Shop.*

You have now completed this workshop. In the next workshop in Chapter 12, you will learn how to plan for creating the "Make Your Own Pizza" feature in the store.

# Part 4, Customizing the Site

What sets a truly successful e-business apart from its competitors is how closely its Web-based infrastructure matches the corporate strategy and how well it satisfies customer needs. A prominent feature of Net.Commerce is its flexibility, enabling merchants to implement unique product presentation strategies and create buying experiences that are consistent with their overall corporate strategies.

This part shows you how to customize a mall or store beyond the default Net.Commerce implementation. First, it shows you how to adapt the default purchasing process to suit business needs, such as interfacing with legacy systems. Next, it describes the extensive set of supplied commands, tasks, and overridable functions that perform store operations, such as adding an item to the shopping cart, and the corresponding business logic, such as determining if the requested item is in stock or confirming the price. Next, it teaches you how to program new commands to integrate new store operations, and how to replace overridable functions with ones that handle special business requirements such as accessing remote systems or performing custom computations. Finally, it describes how to extend the database schema, in order to store custom information and add new store functionality. Examples and sample code are provided.

## Contents:

- "Chapter 15, Planning Commands" on page 411 describes a suggested planning process for creating and implementing new commands.

- "Chapter 16, Writing Commands" on page 441 explains how to program commands.

- "Chapter 17, Activating and Testing Commands" on page 471 explains how to activate new commands in the system and test them.

# Chapter 9, Commands, Tasks, and Overridable Functions

This chapter introduces you to the core customization components of the Net.Commerce system: commands, tasks, and overridable functions, and describes the ones that are packaged with the Net.Commerce system. It also discusses ideas for creating new commands and overridable functions that will meet your needs and give you full control over how your site operates.

This chapter covers the following topics:

- Commands
- Tasks
- Overridable Functions
- Summary of Commands, Tasks, and Overridable Functions
- Putting It All Together: The Command/Task/Overridable Function Model
- Determining Whether to Create a Command or an Overridable Function

# Commands

A *command* performs a specific business operation, such as adding an item to the shopping cart, processing an order, or displaying a specific product page. All commands are executed as HTTP requests (or less frequently, they are executed internally by another command) which generate HTTP responses in the form of Web pages. Each command is imbedded in a URL associated with a button or hypertext link. When a shopper clicks the button or link, the URL containing the command and its parameters (as name-value pairs) is sent to the Net.Commerce system for processing.

## Supplied Commands

Table 9.1 summarizes the commands that are provided by the system. For a detailed description of each command, see "Appendix D, Net.Commerce Commands" on page 569.

*Table 9.1*  *The supplied commands.*

| Command Name | Description |
| --- | --- |
| Address Commands | Manipulate the shopper's address book. |
| CategoryDisplay Command | Displays a category page. |
| Exec Commands | Execute a specified Net.Data macro or task or redirects a URL. |
| InterestItem Commands | Manipulate the shopper's shopping cart. |
| Logon Commands | Allow the shopper to log on. |
| Order Commands | Manipulate the order process. |
| OrderItem Commands | Manipulate shipping information. |
| OrderShippingUpdate Command | Updates shipping information of order items records in an order. |
| ProductDisplay Command | Displays a product or item page. |
| Register Commands | Manipulate the registration process. |

## Command Types

Depending on the function that a command performs, it is classified as either a *display command* or a *process command*.

### Display Commands

Display commands retrieve information from the database and display it in the form of a store page. To achieve this, they set a view task, which calls an overridable function to display a specific store page. For example, the RegisterForm command displays a registration page. If the shopper is registered, the command sets the REG_UPDATE view task to display a registration page pre-filled with registration data; otherwise, it sets the REG_NEW view task to display a blank registration page.

Although not implemented for any of the supplied display commands, a display command can also directly invoke a store page, without setting a view task. This is done by hard-coding the HTTP response in the command's code (see "Hard-Coding an HTTP Response" on page 329 for details).

Display commands are repeatable: that is, they can be invoked consecutively. Each time that the command is executed, no changes are made to the database or the changes that are made are the same each time. For example, a shopper can execute the RegisterForm command as many times consecutively as desired. Each time it is executed, the page will display the same information.

## Process Commands

Process commands process and write information to the database. Most of them set one or more process tasks, which each call an overridable function to perform part of the processing. For example, the OrderProcess command processes an order that has been submitted by a shopper. The first process task that it sets is UPDATE_INV, which updates the inventory for each product and item being ordered. A process command can also directly update the database, without using an overridable function. For example, the OrderCancel command independently cancels the specified order by changing the status of its record in the database to X (for canceled).

Process commands are non-repeatable; that is, they cannot be invoked consecutively without updating the database each time the command is executed. Once a process command successfully completes, the updates to the database are committed. For example, once the shopper has placed an order, the database is updated and the shopper can no longer attempt to resubmit the order (it is no longer in the pending state). To indicate the change of state to the shopper (for example, a confirmation that the order has been successfully placed and is now in the completed state), a process command must eventually be chained to a display command through a redirection URL, which is used to display a store page. The command can be chained to other process command beforehand; for example, after the OrderProcess successfully completes, it could redirect to the AddressUpdate command to update the shoppers address and then finally redirect to a command to display the order confirmation page. The redirection URL is stored in a parameter called url, which is a required parameter for all process commands. (New commands do not have to follow this naming convention, but it is recommended for consistency.) This parameter consists of a display command or another process command and its parameters. After the process command successfully completes, the redirection URL is returned to the browser, which executes the display or process command. In the case of a display command, a store page is returned back to the browser, and in the case of a process command, the database is updated.

In summary, a chain of commands typically consists of one or more process commands followed by one display command. The ability to chain process and display commands together allows merchants to specify which page will eventually be displayed when one or more process commands successfully completes, and ultimately gives them complete control over the navigational flow and design of their stores.

If a process command encounters an exception condition (for example, a shopper entered an invalid credit card number), it typically sets an exception task, which calls an overridable function to display an error page to the shopper. All changes made to the database prior to the failure are also rolled back. The error page, depending on how it is customized, typically indicates the error that occurred and, when appropriate, provides fields for the shopper to correct the problem. For example, the error page that appears in response to an invalid credit card submission could display a field for allowing the shopper to enter another credit card number.

## The Command/Task Model

Figure 9.1 shows the two types of commands: display and process commands, and the tasks that they can call.

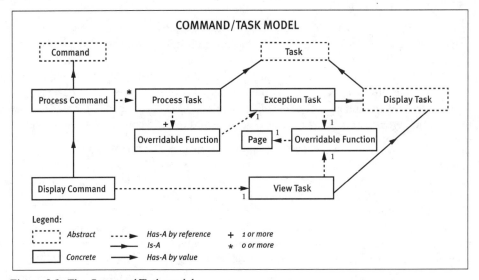

**Figure 9.1** *The Command/Task model.*

## Command Parameters

Some of the supplied commands have both mandatory and optional parameters. The parameters are used either by the command directly or by a command or overridable function that is later called. You can add or remove parameters as defined by the command syntax. You can also add extra custom parameters and modify the overridable functions assigned to its task to process this extra information. Net.Commerce will ignore these new parameters, as long as they do not conflict with the command's original parameters. You may also want to change the overridable functions assigned to the exception task, if one is defined for the command, to handle exception situations that can occur using your new parameters.

All commands accept extra name-value pairs and pass them unchanged through the system to any macros and overridable functions that are called downstream. Most parameter values are not passed to commands as static values, but rather as variable names that correspond to specific columns in the database.

If you are using Net.Data macros to create your store pages, you can find the correct variable name for a parameter as follows:

- The SQL statement within the macro that selects the corresponding column from the database
- The HTML tag within the macro that accepts the field as input on the page

## Parameter Types

Commands accept two types of required parameters and two types of optional parameters, as follows:

### Required Parameters:

- Parameters that are always required by the system. These parameters are shown in the command syntax diagrams and descriptions in "Appendix D, Net.Commerce Commands" on page 569.
- Parameters that are required by the default overridable functions. These parameters are covered in the command descriptions in "Appendix D, Net.Commerce Commands" on page 569. If you create your own functions, you determine what parameters are required.

### Optional Parameters:

- Parameters that are treated as optional by the system. These parameters are shown in the command syntax diagrams and descriptions in "Appendix D, Net.Commerce Commands" on page 569. If they are provided, the system processes them.
- Parameters that are treated as optional by macros. If you create your own macros, you determine what parameters are optional.

# The Command Manager

As its name indicates, the command manager manages commands. It is responsible for initializing, registering, and controlling a command's execution flow. It handles errors that are returned by the command, and calls the overridable functions assigned to the tasks that are used by the command.

## The Command Registration Model

Figure 9.2 illustrates how the command manager registers commands in the system when the server is initially started:

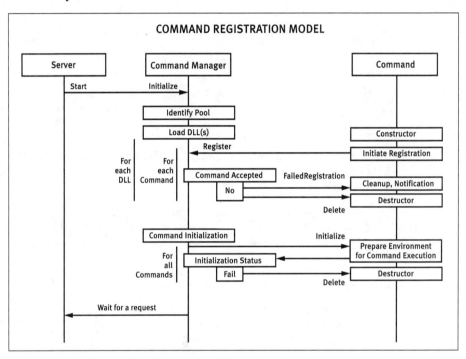

**Figure 9.2**  *The Command Registration model.*

The following are the steps involved in the command registration process:

1. The command manager retrieves the names of all the commands that are assigned to the server's pool, as defined in the database.

2. The command manager loads all of the DLLs or shared libraries in which the commands reside. In so doing, it activates each command.

3. Each command that is loaded calls the command manager in order to be dynamically registered in the system. If a command is not accepted by the command manager (for example, it is registered in the database under a different name), the command manager calls the `FailedRegistration` function in that command and then deletes the instance of the command.

4. For those commands that are successfully registered, the command manager calls the `Initialize` function in each command, to initialize it. If the `Initialize` function fails, the command manager deletes the instance of the command.

5. When the server has finished loading and initializing all commands, it waits to receive requests from the client (the browser).

# The Command Run-Time Model

Figure 9.3 shows how the command manager handles a shopper request and how it executes the command associated with the request:

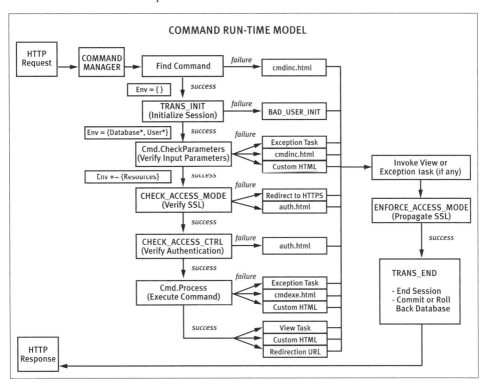

**Figure 9.3** *The Command Run-Time model.*

The following are the steps involved in the command run-time process:

1. A shopper clicks a button or hypertext link containing a command.

2. The command is passed as an HTTP request to the server director.

3. The director parses the command and creates an HttpRequest object containing the command, its parameters (as name-value pairs), cookies, and other information that is normally stored in an HTTP request.

4. The command manager retrieves the name of the command from the HttpRequest object, and begins initializing the command session by calling the TRANS_INIT system task. If the command name is not found, the command manager invokes the system error page, cmdinc.html, which indicates a command structure failure.

5. The TRANS_INIT system task obtains a database connection and identifies the shopper who is accessing the system. It returns a User object and a Database object to the NC_Environment object, making this information accessible to all commands and overridable functions that will be called during the request. (These objects should never be removed by a command or overridable function.) To return a User object,

the task calls its default overridable function. This function identifies the shopper based on whether or not a session cookie called SESSION_ID exists in the HttpRequest object, as follows:

- If a cookie exists (which means that the shopper has already accessed the system in the current browser session) and the value of the SESSION_ID matches the value of the shopper's logon ID in the database, the shopper's profile information is retrieved from the database and stored in the User object in the NC_Environment object. If the cookie is not recognized (which is typically a system problem), the function sets the BAD_USER_INIT exception task, which displays an error page indicating that the shopper was not accepted. The shopper should then close the browser and start a new session.

- If a cookie does not exist (which means that the shopper is accessing the system for the first time), the function creates a guest User object (containing a temporary ID) and adds it to the NC_Environment object. It also adds a new session cookie to the HttpResponse object, which will be sent back to the browser to start the user session. The cookie contains an internally generated reference number followed by a cipher (an encrypted piece of data). The cookie will be automatically discarded when the browser is closed.

6. If the TRANS_INIT system task returns successfully, the command manager calls the CheckParameters function in the command. This function checks that the command's required parameters exist in the HttpRequest object and that they contain correct values. It also creates a list of merchants for which the command can be accessed by the current shopper. If the CheckParameters function fails, it displays an error message in the browser by either:

- Returning false (in which case the command manager invokes the static system error page cmdinc.html, which indicates a command structure failure)

- Setting an exception task to display a custom error page

- Hard-coding the HTTP response

For more information about the CheckParameters function, see "The CheckParameters Function" on page 446.

7. If the CheckParameters function returns successfully, the command manager calls the CHECK_ACCESS_MODE system task. This task checks that if the SSL flag is enabled for the command and at least one of the merchants returned by the CheckParameters function requests SSL, the request is also in SSL mode; otherwise, it calls a function to set a redirection header in order to redirect the request as SSL (https). If the opposite occurs (the command is not enabled for SSL, but the request is) the function does not disable SSL for the command; it never removes SSL from an entity. The function also ensures that if a command is enabled for authentication, the shopper has registered or logged on prior to accessing the command; otherwise, it redirects to the system error page auth.html, which indicates that the user is not authorized to use the command.

For information about enabling or disabling commands for SSL or authentication, see "Specifying Command Security" on page 481.

8. If the CHECK_ACCESS_MODE system task returns successfully, the command manager calls the CHECK_ACCESS_CTRL system task to check whether the shopper is authorized to execute the command. The list of merchants generated by the CheckParameters function (in Step 6) defines the users who can access the command. Commands that are accessed by shoppers do not require access control. In this case, the CheckParameters function would return an empty merchant list, indicating that anyone can access the command. Only commands for internal use (for example, those used for the Administrator forms) require access control. If the CHECK_ACCESS_CTRL task fails, the command manager invokes the system error page auth.html, which indicates that the user is not authorized to use the command.

   For more information on access control, see "Defining Access Control" on page 66.

9. If the CHECK_ACCESS_CTRL system task returns successfully, the command manager calls the Process function in the command. This function performs the work for the command; for example, it calls one or more overridable functions to perform specific jobs. When the last function called returns successfully, the command displays a store page by either:

   - Setting a view task (if it is a display command)

   - Hard-coding the HTTP response (if it is a display command)

   - Redirecting to another command (if it is a process command)

   If the Process function fails, it displays an error page by either returning false (in which case the command manager invokes the system error page cmdexe.html indicating a command failure), setting an exception task to display a custom error page, or hard-coding an HTTP response.

   For more information about the Process function, see "The Process Function" on page 447.

10. If a view or exception task was set in any of the previous steps, the command manager invokes the task, to generate an HTTP document.

11. Before the command manager passes any of the HTTP responses generated in any of the above steps to the director to send back to the browser, it calls the following system tasks:

    a) ENFORCE_ACCESS_MODE system task, to reconstruct the URL in order to ensure that if the command is enabled for SSL, the return URL is also enabled for SSL (https). It also converts any relative URLs to absolute URLs.

    b) TRANS_END system task, to end the command session (if the command completed successfully) or to roll back the database (if the command failed).

# Tasks

A *task* is a "contract" between a command and an overridable function or between two overridable functions. It defines the rules that govern the relationship between the two. These rules dictate the following:

- The work that the caller (either a command or another overridable function) expects the overridable function to perform

- The parameters that the caller passes to the overridable function

- The parameters and other results that the caller expects the overridable function to return

The following is an example of defining a new process task, including the names and types of the input and output parameters to be exchanged between the implementing overridable function and the system:

**Task Name:** RESERVE_INV process task

**Expected Behavior:** Reserve a specified quantity of a specified product, for a given shopper. If unsuccessful, set the RESERVE_INV_ERR exception task.

**Explicit Input Parameters:**

| Variable Name | Variable Type | Description |
| --- | --- | --- |
| PRODUCT_REF_NUM | String* | The reference number of the product or item (integer). |
| QUANTITY | String* | The quantity requested (floating point number). |

**Explicit Output Parameters:** None

**Expected Return Codes:** For exceptions that are handled by setting the RESERVE_INV_ERR exception task, the expected return codes are the ones documented as input parameters for that exception task.

Tasks also provide a scope and security framework, which ensures that if a merchant customizes an overridable function for a task, the function is invoked for only that merchant. This enables merchants to provide their own implementations of the work to be done, by assigning their own versions of the overridable function to the task.

# Task Types

Net.Commerce defines two types of tasks: *display tasks* and *process tasks*. Display tasks can be further divided into view and exception tasks. These tasks are responsible for generating HTTP responses. A view task is invoked when a command or overridable function successfully completes, whereas an exception task is invoked when a command or overridable function fails. Process tasks define the rules for processing information or writing information to the database.

The following describe the supplied view, exception, and process tasks.

## View Tasks

View tasks define the rules for overridable functions that display the pages seen by shoppers, such as the product pages and registration pages. Table 9.2 lists the view tasks that Net.Commerce has defined for displaying each type of page. For a detailed description of each task, see "Appendix E, Net.Commerce Tasks" on page 613.

*Table 9.2* *The supplied view tasks.*

| Task Name | Description |
|-----------|-------------|
| ADDR_ADD | Defines the rules for displaying a blank address book page. |
| ADDR_UPDATE | Defines the rules for displaying an existing address book page for updating. |
| CAT_DSP | Defines the rules for displaying a category page. |
| LOGON_DSP | Defines the rules for displaying a page that allows registered shoppers to log on to the store or mall. |
| ORD_DSP_COM | Defines the rules for displaying a page showing the contents of the specified order, which has been already been placed. |
| ORD_DSP_PEN | Defines the rules for displaying a page showing the contents of the specified order, which has been prepared but not placed. |
| ORD_LST_COM | Defines the rules for displaying a list of orders that have already been placed. |
| ORD_LST_PEN | Defines the rules for displaying a list of orders that have been prepared but not placed. |
| ORD_OK | Defines the rules for displaying a page that indicates that an order has been accepted. |
| PROD_DSP | Defines the rules for displaying a product page. |
| REG_NEW | Defines the rules for displaying a blank registration page. |
| REG_UPDATE | Defines the rules for displaying an existing registration page for updating. |
| SHIPTO_ASSOC | Defines the rules for displaying a list of products and items in the Order List for which the shopper has specified any shipping address. |
| SHIPTO_DSP | Defines the rules for displaying a list of products and items in the Order List for which the shopper has specified a particular shipping address. |
| SHIPTO_LST | Defines the rules for displaying a list of products and items in the Order List, which shoppers can select for ordering. |
| SHOPCART_DSP | Defines the rules for displaying the shopper's Interest List. |

## Process Tasks

Process tasks are used for overridable functions that process information, such as calculating the total cost of an order. Table 9.3 lists the process tasks that Net.Commerce has defined, as well as suggestions for customizing each task. For a detailed description of each task, see "Appendix E, Net.Commerce Tasks" on page 613.

*Table 9.3  The supplied process tasks.*

| Task Name | Description and Customization Example(s) |
| --- | --- |
| AUDIT_ADDR_BOOK | Defines the rules for checking the parameters that are passed into the AddressAdd and AddressUpdate commands. This task can be modified to make the e-mail field a required field, check that a given postal code is valid, or confirm that a given address exists by looking it up in a postal address locator. |
| AUDIT_REG | Defines the rules for checking the parameters that are passed into the RegisterUpdate and RegisterNew commands. This task can be modified to make certain fields like the password and logon ID fields a different length, or to make a demographic field  mandatory. |
| CHECK_INV | Defines the rules for checking whether there is sufficient inventory in stock to process the OrderDisplay, OrderItemProcess, and OrderItemUpdate commands. This task can be modified so that it bypasses the inventory check or links to an external inventory checking system. |
| DO_PAYMENT | Defines the rules for processing the order specified by the OrderProcess command. This task can be modified so that if credit card data is received, it is passed to a business critical system for authorization. |
| EXT_ORD_PROC | Defines the rules for performing any additional processing required just prior to the completion of the OrderProcess command. This task can be modified to trigger external systems to process the order, or to transmit orders to a fulfillment system |
| EXT_SHIPTO_PROC | Defines the rules for performing any additional processing required just prior to the completion of the OrderItemProcess command. This task can be modified to trigger other systems to process the shipping instructions at the item level. |
| EXT_SHIPTO_UPD | Defines the rules for performing any additional processing required just prior to the completion of the OrderItemUpdate command. This task can be modified to trigger other systems to process the shipping instructions at the order level, to ask shoppers for additional information for overseas orders, or to generate log records. |
| GET_BASE_SPE_PRC | Defines the rules for calculating the price of an item (a product with a particular set of attributes), when requested by the OrderDisplay, OrderItemDisplay, OrderItemProcess, and OrderItemUpdate commands. This task can be modified to include charges for custom preparation or to retrieve prices from a business-critical system. |

*Continued on next page*

*Table 9.3* *Continued.*

| Task Name | Description and Customization Example(s) |
|---|---|
| GET_BASE_UNIT_PRC | Defines the rules for calculating the price of a product, when requested by the InterestItemAdd and InterestItemDisplay commands. This task can be modified to include applicable taxes in the displayed price or to retrieve prices from a business-critical system. |
| GET_ORD_PROD_TAX_TOT | Defines the rules for calculating the total cost of the products and items in an order, when requested by the OrderDisplay command. This task can be modified to use an external system to calculate taxes or to calculate them differently for certain shopper groups, such as tax-exempt groups. |
| GET_ORD_PROD_TOT | Defines the rules for calculating the total taxes payable on an order, when requested by the OrderDisplay command. This task can be modified to calculate discounts based on the total price or to obtain the total price from a remote system. |
| GET_ORD_SH_TOT | Defines the rules for calculating the total shipping charges for an order, when requested by the OrderDisplay command. This task can be modified to adjust shipping charges based on the total order volume or to retrieve the shipping charges from a business-critical system. |
| GET_SUB_ORD_PROD_TAX_TOT | Defines the rules for calculating the total tax payable on a part of an order that is to be shipped to a single address, when requested by the OrderDisplay command. This task can be modified to charge tax rates according to the shipping address or to retrieve taxes from a business-critical system. |
| GET_SUB_ORD_PROD_TOT | Defines the rules for calculating the total taxes payable on a part of an order that is to be shipped to a single address, when requested by the OrderDisplay command. This task can be modified to provide a discount on suborders whose total price exceeds a threshold, or to add surcharges associated with specific orders, such as foreign orders. |
| GET_SUB_ORD_SH_TOT | Defines the rules for calculating the total shipping charges for a part of an order that is to be shipped to a single address, when requested by the OrderDisplay command. This task can be modified to adjust shipping charges on suborders whose total price exceeds a threshold, to use alternative shipping rates for recipients who live in different shipping zones, or to retrieve the suborder shipping charges from a business-critical system. |
| RESOLVE_SKU | Defines the rules for resolving the item SKU for a parent product with a given set of attributes, when requested by the InterestItemAdd and OrderItemUpdate commands. For stores that do not use SKUs, this task can modified to bypass the SKU resolvement process. |
| UPDATE_INV | Defines the rules for reducing the amount of inventory in stock, when requested by the OrderProcess command. This task can be modified to bypass the inventory decrement, or to update the inventory quantity on a remote system. |

## Exception Tasks

Exception tasks define the rules for overridable functions that handle exception conditions, such as when a shopper tries to order an item that is not in stock. These exception conditions can be detected by commands or by overridable functions assigned to process tasks. Table 9.4 lists the tasks that handle exception conditions detected by commands. For a detailed description of each task, see "Appendix E, Net.Commerce Tasks" on page 613.

*Table 9.4 The supplied exception tasks.*

| Task Name | Description |
|---|---|
| BAD_ADDRESS_BOOK | Defines the rules for handling the condition where a parameter that was passed into the AddressAdd command contains an invalid character, or where a nickname has already been used. |
| BAD_ADRBK_MODIFY | Defines the rules for handling the condition where a parameter that was passed into the AddressUpdate command contains an invalid character, or where a nickname has already been used. |
| BAD_ORD_DATA | Defines the rules for handling the condition where a numeric parameter that was passed into the OrderProcess command contains non-numeric data or contains a number that is out of range. |
| BAD_REG | Defines the rules for handling the condition where an invalid parameter value was passed into the RegisterNew command. |
| BAD_REG_MODIFY | Defines the rules for handling the condition where an invalid parameter value was passed into the RegisterUpdate command. |
| BAD_ST_DATA | Defines the rules for handling the condition where a numeric parameter that was passed into the OrderItemUpdate or OrderItemProcess command contains non-numeric data or contains a number that is out of range. |
| LOGON_ERR | Defines the rules for handling the condition where a parameter required by the Logon command is missing or invalid. |
| ORD_NONE | Defines the rules for handling the condition where no orders were found that match the criteria specified on an OrderDisplay command. |
| ORD_UNLOCKED | Defines the rules for handling the condition where an order is unlocked and therefore cannot be processed by the OrderProcess command. |

*Continued on next page*

*Table 9.4 Continued.*

| Task Name | Description |
|---|---|
| The following exception tasks are designed to be set by overridable functions that are assigned to process tasks: | |
| AUDIT_ADDR_BOOK_ERR | Defines the rules for handling exception conditions encountered by the overridable function assigned to the AUDIT_ADDRESS_BOOK process task. |
| AUDIT_REG_ERR | Defines the rules for handling exception conditions encountered by the overridable function assigned to the AUDIT_REG process task. |
| BAD_PROD_ATTR | Defines the rules for handling the condition where the overridable function assigned to the RESOLVE_SKU process task detects an invalid product attribute-value combination. |
| CHECK_INV_ERR | Defines the rules for handling exception conditions encountered by the overridable function assigned to the CHECK_INV process task. |
| DO_PAYMENT_ERR | Defines the rules for r handling exception conditions encountered by the overridable function assigned to the DO_PAYMENT process task. |
| EXT_ORD_PROC_ERR | Defines the rules for handling exception conditions encountered by the overridable function assigned to the EXT_ORD_PROC process task. |
| EXT_SHIPTO_PROC_ERR | Defines the rules for handling exception conditions encountered by the overridable function assigned to the EXT_SHIPTO_PROC process task. |
| EXT_SHIPTO_UPD_ERR | Defines the rules for handling exception conditions encountered by the overridable function assigned to the EXT_SHIPTO_UPDATE process task. |
| GET_BASE_SPE_PRC_ERR | Defines the rules for handling exception conditions encountered by the overridable function assigned to the GET_BASE_SPE_PRC process task. |
| GET_BASE_UNIT_PRC_ERR | Defines the rules for handling exception conditions encountered by the overridable function assigned to the GET_BASE_UNIT_PRC process task. |
| GET_ORD_PROD_TAX_TOT_ERR | Defines the rules for handling exception conditions encountered by the overridable function assigned to the GET_ORD_PROD_TAX_TOT process task. |
| GET_ORD_PROD_TOT_ERR | Defines the rules for handling exception conditions encountered by the overridable function assigned to the GET_ORD_PROD_TOT process task. |

*Continued on next page*

**Table 9.4** *Continued.*

| Task Name | Description |
|---|---|
| GET_ORD_SH_TOT_ERR | Defines the rules for handling exception conditions encountered by the overridable function assigned to the GET_ORD_SH_TOT process task. |
| GET_SUB_ORD_PROD_TAX_TOT_ERR | Defines the rules for handling exception conditions encountered by the overridable function assigned to the GET_SUB_ORD_PROD_TAX_TOT process task. |
| GET_SUB_ORD_PROD_TOT_ERR | Defines the rules for handling exception conditions encountered by the overridable function assigned to the GET_SUB_ORD_PROD_TOT process task. |
| GET_SUB_ORD_SH_TOT_ERR | Defines the rules for handling exception conditions encountered by the overridable function assigned to the GET_SUB_ORD_SH_TOT process task. |
| MISSING_PROD_ATTR | Defines the rules for handling the condition where the overridable function assigned to the RESOLVE_SKU process task determines that a required product attribute was not provided. |
| UPDATE_INV_ERR | Defines the rules for handling exception conditions encountered by the overridable function assigned to the UPDATE_INV process task. |

# Overridable Functions

An *overridable function* is program code that implements a task. Specifically, it implements a behavior that is expected by the task, and handles input and output parameters as defined by the task. The input parameters that are passed by the calling command to an overridable function must be a subset of those defined by the task that the function implements. The output parameters (if any) returned by the overridable function must be a superset of those defined by the task and those expected by the command. This means that you can write an overridable function that does not use all of the input parameters sent by the caller (either a command or another overridable function), and that can return more parameters than expected back by the caller. This feature allows merchants to use one overridable function for multiple tasks. For example, Net.Commerce supplies the TaskDisplay_1.0 (IBM,NC) overridable function that is assigned, by default, to all the exception tasks and most of the view tasks.

When an overridable function is called, a task name and merchant reference number are provided to the overridable function manager. If the task is defined with a scope of 0, the merchant reference number is ignored, and the mall implementation (or default implementation) of the overridable function is invoked. If the scope is 1 and the merchant has provided an implementation, the merchant's implementation is invoked. If the merchant has not provided an implementation, the mall implementation is invoked. In a single-store scenario, either level of scope can be used.

Overridable functions that implement view or exception tasks must populate the HTTP response with a document that can be displayed in the browser. The system supplies two overridable functions, TaskDisplay_1.0 (IBM,NC) and MacroDisplay_1.0 (IBM,NC), which both use Net.Data to render the Web pages. TaskDisplay_1.0 (IBM,NC) is used by most view tasks and all exception tasks to invoke a Net.Data macro to display a store page or error message to the shopper. This function uses the reference number of the view or exception task and the merchant reference number as the index to retrieve from the MACROS table the file name of the Net.Data macro to execute. MacroDisplay_1.0 (IBM,NC) is used by the CAT_DSP or PROD_DSP view tasks to display a category or product page. It executes the %HTML_REPORT section of the macro that corresponds to the file name currently stored in the NC_Environment object. Because Net.Data is the default language for creating store pages, only the two overridable functions are needed for all view and exception tasks. If, however, you do not want to use Net.Data to create your store pages, you can code the HTTP response directly in the overridable function, or link to another language, such as Java, to create the pages.

Overridable functions that implement process tasks must process information, such as checking inventory, calculating a discount price, or invoking an external payment system. When the function successfully completes, it may return parameters to the calling command, such as the calculated discount price, and the calling command will continue to process the information. Alternatively, it may simply perform a direct database update and return no parameters to the calling command.

If the overridable function encounters an error, such as a product being out of stock, it typically sets an exception task in the same way that a command does to display an informative error page to the shopper. Moreover, like commands, all changes made to the database prior to the failure are rolled back.

When customizing your store or mall, you will typically replace the supplied overridable function that is assigned to a process task, to change the way that certain information is processed or to link to a legacy system. Net.Commerce also provides "extendable" process tasks, such as EXT_SHIPTO_PROC and EXT_SHIPTO_UPD, which are available to merchants for performing any additional processing required just prior to the completion of the OrderItemProcess or OrderItemUpdate commands. They both, by default, call the DoNothingNoArgs_1.0 (IBM,NC) overridable function, which returns without performing any work. You can replace this function for any requirements that are unique to your business. For example, you can create a function for the EXT_SHIPTO_PROC task that triggers an external system that requests special packing instructions on certain products.

**Note:**
When you create your own overridable function, you must follow the rules that are defined for the task that your function implements.

# Supplied Overridable Functions

Table 9.5 lists the overridable functions that are provided with Net.Commerce. For a detailed description of each function, see "Appendix F, Net.Commerce Overridable Functions" on page 665.

*Table 9.5* *The supplied overridable functions.*

| Overridable Function Name | Description |
|---|---|
| AuditAddrBook_1.0 (IBM,NC) | Verifies that the shopper provided the mandatory name and address fields when adding or updating an address book entry. |
| CheckInv_1.0 (IBM,NC) | Determines whether there is sufficient quantity in stock to order the item that corresponds to the specified order reference number. |
| DoNothingNoArgs_1.0 (IBM,NC) | Returns from any task that requires no explicit output parameters without performing any processing. |
| DoPayment_1.0 (IBM,NC) | Collects and validates the data needed to process a credit card payment, including ensuring that the credit card type, number and expiry date are provided and that they are valid. |
| GetBaseSpePrc_1.0 (IBM,NC) | Determines the price of the item that corresponds to the specified product reference number, based on extra features associated with the shipping address. |
| GetBaseUnitPrc_1.0 (IBM,NC) | Determines the price of an item that corresponds to the specified product reference number. |
| GetOrdProdTaxTot_1.0 (IBM,NC) | Calculates the total taxes payable on the order that corresponds to the specified order reference number. |
| GetOrdProdTot_1.0 (IBM,NC) | Calculates the total price of the order that corresponds to the specified order reference number. |
| GetOrdShTot_1.0 (IBM,NC) | Calculates the total shipping charges for the order that corresponds to the specified order reference number. |
| GetSubOrdProdTaxTot_1.0 (IBM,NC) | Calculates the total taxes payable on the suborder (multiple items that are sent to the same address) that corresponds to the specified order reference number and address reference number. |
| GetSubOrdProdTot_1.0 (IBM,NC) | Calculates the total price of the suborder (multiple items that are sent to the same address) that corresponds to the specified order reference number and address reference number. |
| GetSubOrdShTot_1.0 (IBM,NC) | Calculates the total shipping charges for the suborder (multiple items that are sent to the same address) that corresponds to the specified order reference number and address reference number. |

*Continued on next page*

*Table 9.5  Continued.*

| Overridable Function Name | Description |
| --- | --- |
| MacroDisplay_1.0 (IBM,NC) | Executes the HTML Report section of the Net.Data macro that corresponds to the filename specified. |
| ResolveSku_1.0 (IBM,NC) | Determines the SKU of the item that corresponds to the specified parent product reference number and item attributes. |
| TaskDisplay_1.0 (IBM,NC) | Executes the HTML Report section of the Net.Data macro in the MACROS table that corresponds to the calling task reference number and the merchant reference number. |
| UpdateInv_1.0 (IBM,NC) | Reduces the amount of inventory in stock for the product or item that corresponds to the specified product reference number. |

# The Overridable Function Manager

As its name indicates, the overridable function manager manages overridable functions. It is responsible for initializing, registering and controlling the flow of their execution. It also handles errors that are encountered by the overridable functions.

## The Overridable Function Registration Model

Figure 9.4 shows how the overridable function manager registers overridable functions in the system when the server is initially started:

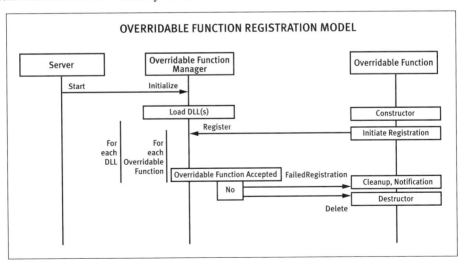

*Figure 9.4  The overridable function registration model.*

The following are the steps involved in the overridable function registration process:

1. The overridable function manager loads all of the DLLs or shared libraries in which the overrridable functions reside. In so doing, it activates each overridable function.

2. Each overridable function that is loaded calls the overridable function manager in order to be dynamically registered in the system. If a overridable function is not accepted by the overridable function manager (for example, it is registered in the database under a different name), the overridable function manager calls the `FailedRegistration` function in that overridable function and then deletes the instance of the overridable function.

3. For those overridable functions that are successfully registered, the overridable function manager calls the `Initialize` function in each overridable function, to initialize it. If the `Initialize` function fails, the overridable function manager deletes the instance of the overridable function.

4. When the server has finished loading and initializing all overridable function, it waits to receive calls from the command manager.

## The Overridable Function Run-Time Model

Figure 9.5 illustrates how the overridable function manager handles the execution of an overridable function that is called by a command:

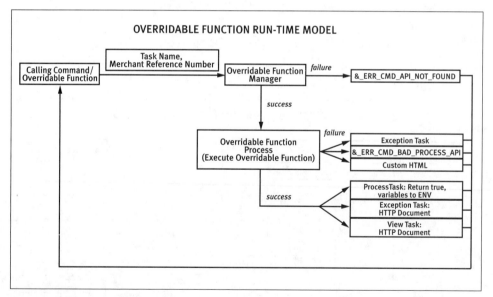

*Figure 9.5*  *The overridable function run-time model.*

The following are the steps involved in the overridable function run-time process:

1. The caller (either a command or overridable function) calls a task and passes to it the merchant reference number, to specify which implementation of the task is to be used.

2. The overridable function manager retrieves the name of the command from the `HttpRequest` object. If the command name is not found, the overridable function manager throws the `&_ERR_CMD_API_NOT_FOUND` exception.

3. The overridable function manager uses the merchant reference number to call the `Process` function of the corresponding overridable function. The `Process` function performs the work for the overridable function; for example, it updates the database. When the function successfully completes, it does one of the following:

- Returns a true value to the caller and, if applicable, returns variables to the `NC_Environment` object (if it is implementing an process task)

- Generates an HTTP document (if it is implementing a view or exception task). The supplied overridable functions execute Net.Data macros.

If the `Process` function fails, it displays an error page by either returning false and throwing the `&_ERR_CMD_BAD_PROCESS_API` exception (in which case the overridable function manager invokes the system error page `cmdexe.html` indicating a command failure), setting an exception task to display a custom error page, or hard-coding an HTTP response.

For more information about the `Process` function, see "The Process Function" on page 381.

# Summary of the Supplied Commands, Tasks, and Overridable Functions

Table 9.6 summarizes all of the default commands and their types, the tasks (if any) that each command calls (including those called when an exception condition is encountered), and the overridable functions that implement the tasks.

***Table 9.6*** *A summary of the commands, tasks, and overridable functions supplied by the system.*

| Command | Type | Task(s) | Overridable Function(s) |
|---|---|---|---|
| AddressAdd | Process | AUDIT_ADDR_BOOK | AuditAddrBook |
| | | **Exception Conditions:**<br>BAD_ADDRESS_BOOK<br>AUDIT_ADDR_BOOK_ERR | **Exception Conditions:**<br>TaskDisplay<br>TaskDisplay |
| AddressCheck | Process | N/A | N/A |
| AddressDelete | Process | N/A | N/A |
| AddressForm | Display | ADDR_UPDATE or ADDR_ADD | TaskDisplay |
| | | **Exception Conditions:**<br>None | **Exception Conditions:**<br>None |
| AddressUpdate | Process | AUDIT_ADDR_BOOK | AuditAddrBook |
| | | **Exception Conditions:**<br>BAD_ADRBK_MODIFY<br>AUDIT_ADDR_BOOK_ERR | **Exception Conditions:**<br>TaskDisplay<br>TaskDisplay |

*Continued on next page*

***Table 9.6*** *Continued.*

| Command | Type | Task(s) | Overridable Function(s) |
|---|---|---|---|
| CategoryDisplay | Display | CAT_DSP | MacroDisplay |
| | | **Exception Conditions:**<br>None | **Exception Conditions:**<br>None |
| ExecMacro | Display | N/A | N/A |
| ExecTask | Process | N/A | N/A |
| | | **Exception Conditions:**<br>BAD_EXEC_TASK | **Exception Conditions:**<br>TaskDisplay |
| ExecUrl | Process | N/A | N/A |
| InterestItemAdd | Process | RESOLVE_SKU<br>GET_BASE_UNIT_PRC | ResolveSku<br>GetBaseUnitPrc |
| | | **Exception Conditions:**<br>BAD_PROD_ATTR<br>MISSING_PROD_ATTR<br>GET_BASE_UNIT_PRC_ERR | **Exception Conditions:**<br>TaskDisplay<br>TaskDisplay<br>TaskDisplay |
| InterestItemDelete | Process | N/A | N/A |
| InterestItemDisplay | Display | GET_BASE_UNIT_PRC<br>SHOPCART_DSP | GetBaseUnitPrc<br>TaskDisplay |
| | | **Exception Conditions:**<br>GET_BASE_UNIT_PRC_ERR | **Exception Conditions:**<br>TaskDisplay |
| Logon | Process | N/A | N/A |
| | | **Exception Conditions:**<br>LOGON_ERR | **Exception Conditions:**<br>TaskDisplay |
| LogonForm | Display | LOGON_DSP | TaskDisplay |
| | | **ExceptionConditions:**<br>None | **Exception Conditions:**<br>None |
| OrderCancel | Process | N/A | N/A |
| OrderDisplay | Display | CHECK_INV<br>GET_BASE_SPE_PRC<br>GET_SUB_ORD_PROD_TOT<br>GET_SUB_ORD_PROD_TAX_TOT<br>GET_SUB_ORD_SH_TOT<br>GET_ORD_PROD_TOT<br>GET_ORD_PROD_TAX_TOT<br>GET_ORD_SH_TOT<br>ORD_DSP_PEN or ORD_DSP_COM | CheckInv<br>GetBaseSpePrc<br>GetSubOrdProdTot<br>GetSubOrdProdTaxTot<br>GetSubOrdShTot<br>GetOrdProdTot<br>GetOrdProdTaxTot<br>GetOrdShTot<br>TaskDisplay |
| | | **Exception Conditions:**<br>ORD_NONE | **Exception Conditions:**<br>TaskDisplay |

*Continued on next page*

**Table 9.6** *Continued.*

| Command | Type | Task(s) | Overridable Function(s) |
|---|---|---|---|
| OrderList | Display | ORD_LST_PEN or ORD_LST_COM | TaskDisplay |
| | | **Exception Conditions:**<br>None | **Exception Conditions:**<br>None |
| OrderProcess | Display | UPDATE_INV<br>DO_PAYMENT<br>EXT_ORD_PROC<br>ORD_OK<br>REVERSE_INV | UpdateInv<br>DoPayment<br>DoNothingNoArgs<br>TaskDisplay<br>ReverseInv |
| | | **Exception Conditions:**<br>None | **Exception Conditions:**<br>None |
| OrderUnlock | Process | N/A | N/A |
| OrderItemDelete | Process | N/A | N/A |
| OrderItemDisplay | Display | GET_BASE_SPE_PRC<br>SHIPTO_DSP or SHIPTO_ASSOC | GetBaseSpePrc<br>TaskDisplay |
| | | **Exception Conditions:**<br>None | **Exception Conditions:**<br>None |
| OrderItemList | Display | SHIPTO_LST | TaskDisplay |
| | | **Exception Conditions:**<br>None | **Exception Conditions:**<br>None |
| OrderItemProcess | Process | CHECK_INV<br>GET_BASE_SPE_PRC<br>EXT_SHIPTO_PROC | CheckInv<br>GetBaseSpePrc<br>DoNothingNoArgs |
| | | **Exception Conditions:**<br>BAD_ST_DATA<br>CHECK_INV_ERR<br>GET_BASE_SPE_PRC_ERR<br>EXT_SHIPTO_PROC_ERR | **Exception Conditions:**<br>TaskDisplay<br>TaskDisplay<br>TaskDisplay<br>TaskDisplay |
| OrderItemUpdate | Process | CHECK_INV<br>GET_BASE_SPE_PRC<br>RESOLVE_SKU<br>EXT_SHIPTO_UPD | CheckInv<br>GetBaseSpePrc<br>ResolveSku<br>DoNothingNoArgs |
| | | **Exception Conditions:**<br>BAD_PROD_ATTR<br>MISSING_PROD_ATTR<br>BAD_ST_DATA<br>CHECK_INV_ERR<br>GET_BASE_SPE_PRC_ERR<br>EXT_SHIPTO_PROC_ERR | **Exception Conditions:**<br>TaskDisplay<br>TaskDisplay<br>TaskDisplay<br>TaskDisplay<br>TaskDisplay<br>TaskDisplay |
| OrderShippingUpdate | Process | N/A | N/A |

*Continued on next page*

**Table 9.6** *Continued.*

| Command | Type | Task(s) | Overridable Function(s) |
|---|---|---|---|
| ProductDisplay | Display | PROD_DSP | MacroDisplay |
| | | **Exception Conditions:** None | **Exception Conditions:** None |
| RegisterForm | Display | REG_UPDATE or REG_NEW | TaskDisplay |
| | | **Exception Conditions:** None | **Exception Conditions:** None |
| RegisterNew | Process | AUDIT_REG | DoNothingNoArgs |
| | | **Exception Conditions:** BAD_REG AUDIT_REG_ERR | **Exception Conditions:** TaskDisplay TaskDisplay |
| RegisterUpdate | Process | AUDIT_REG | DoNothingNoArgs |
| | | **Exception Conditions:** BAD_REG_MODIFY AUDIT_REG_ERR | **Exception Conditions:** TaskDisplay TaskDisplay |

# Putting It All Together: The Command/Task/ Overridable Function Model

Figure 9.6 represents the basic model of how commands, tasks, and overridable functions work together in the Net.Commerce system:

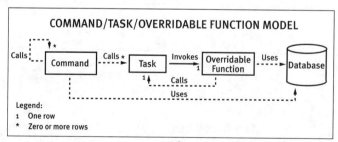

**Figure 9.6** *The Command/Task/Overridable Function model.*

When a shopper invokes a command from a store page requesting a specific operation to be performed, the command typically calls a task, which invokes an overridable function to do the work. The overridable function can also call a task; for example, an exception task to handle an error encountered by the function. If the overridable function returns successfully, the command can call another task to perform other work, and so on, until the command has successfully completed. Upon successful completion, the command will redirect its flow of execution to another command via a redirection URL (if it is a process command), or call a view task to display a store page (if it is a display command).

The main purpose of a command is to set up an environment in order to delegate work to tasks. The purpose of tasks is to enable different merchants to provide their own implementations of the work to be done, by assigning their own versions of the overridable function to the task. Thus, for each task that a command calls, there can be more than one implementation, depending on merchant requirements.

## Comparing Commands and Overridable Functions

Table 9.7 summarizes the main differences between a command and an overridable function:

*Table 9.7  Comparing commands and overridable functions.*

|  | Command | Overridable Function |
|---|---|---|
| **Purpose** | Performs a business operation; for example, adding an item to the shopping cart. | Performs a defined unit of work for the command; for example, ensuring sufficient inventory before the item can be added to the shopping cart. |
| **Invocation** | Invoked by the shopper via a button or hypertext link; for example, an **Add to Cart** button. | Invoked by a command or another overridable function via a task. |
| **Implementation** | Implemented at the system (mall) level. This does not mean that a store cannot implement a new command: it means that one URL cannot be mapped to multiple commands that are invoked based on the store. | Implemented at the store level. Each store can assign a custom overridable function to the tasks set by the command. |

# Determining Whether to Create a Command or an Overridable Function

Whether you create a command or an overridable function will depend on what you want to accomplish. The rule of thumb is to create a command if you want to implement a store operation or feature that the supplied commands do not support, and to create an overridable function if you want to change how a supplied command operates.

For example, Chapters 15 to 17 describe the planning, writing, and implementation process for creating a command that gives shoppers the ability to reset the logon password. The workshops in Chapters 15 to 17 describe how to plan and implement a command that implements a flexible registration process during the placement of an order, so that depending on the input from the shopper, the command will both register the shopper and process the order or just process the order.

You would create an overridable function if, for example, you wanted to change how the OrderProcess command updates inventory. Typically, you would replace the function that implements that operation (UpdateInv_1.0 (IBM,NC)) with a new one. This overridable function decrements the quantity of inventory in stock by the quantity ordered. This implementation is adequate for a stand-alone site in which all orders are placed from the Web. However, if the merchant sells through multiple channels, such as mail order and retail, it may be necessary to use a centralized inventory system. The merchant could replace the function with one that sends an item-hold transaction from the Web to the inventory system. If the transaction is accepted, the new function can indicate that the item is in stock; otherwise, it can indicate that the item is out of stock. When the shopper places the order, the function could send an item-commit transaction to the inventory system. If the shopper cancels the order, a customized function for the OrderCancel command could send an item-release transaction to the inventory system. As another example of creating an overridable function to incorporate legacy systems such as a payment system, you could replace the overridable function associated with payment processing (DoPayment_1.0 (IBM,NC) with one that links to your payment system.

The rule on when to create a command and when to create an overridable function is only a general guideline; depending on your business requirements, the reverse may be true. For example, merchants who sell items such as bicycles or computer hardware parts may specialize in "build your own" products, where shoppers choose different items, each with a different price, to form a product that can be ordered. These merchants can implement their products by replacing two overridable functions used by the OrderItemUpdate command. The workshops in Chapters 12 to 14 demonstrate how to replace these overridable functions in order to implement a "Make Your Own Pizza" product in the pizza store, allowing shoppers to create a pizza from a choice of different toppings.

For both new commands and overridable functions, you will typically have to also customize or create new error pages, so that they correctly use the new parameters.

The chapters that follow describe the planning, writing, activation, and testing process that is required to implement new commands and overridable functions in a store or mall.

# Chapter 10, The Net.Commerce Classes

Net.Commerce supplies a set of C++ classes for writing commands and overridable functions. This chapter describes the classes that you will use most often:

- The NC_Void Class
- The NC_Object Class
- The NC_Command Class
- The NC_OverridableFunction Class
- Stream Classes
- Container Classes
- Iterator Classes
- String-Related Classes
- The HttpDate Class
- The Cookie Class
- The HttpRequest Class
- The HttpResponse Class
- Name-Value Pair Related-Classes
- Configuration Related-Classes
- The NC_Environment Class
- The Misc Class
- The User Class
- Database Classes

283

> **Note:**
> At the time of this writing, IBM intends to maintain backward compatibility for only the following classes in Net.Commerce:
>
> - NC_Object
> - NC_Command
> - NC_OverridableFunction
> - Error, Status, and Debug (except for the nls member functions and nls messages)
> - List-related
> - Hash Table-related
> - String-related
> - HttpDate (as used in HttpResponse and HttpRequest only)
> - Cookie (as used in HttpResponse and HttpRequest only)
> - HttpRequest
> - HttpResponse
> - Name-Value Pair-related
> - NC_Environment
> - Misc
> - DataBase
> - SQL
> - Row
>
> All other classes documented in this chapter are subject to change in future versions of Net.Commerce. If you choose to use them, be aware that you may have to modify or recompile your commands or overridable functions if you migrate to future versions.

# The NC_Void Class

The NC_Void class is the base class from which all other classes in Net.Commerce derive. In order for a container to function, the class it contains must derive from this class. If you create a new class, make sure it derives, directly or indirectly, from the NC_Void class.

### Header File

 \IBM\NetCommerce3\adt\include\containers\ldh_misc.h
**AIX** /usr/lpp/NetCommerce3/adt/include/containers/ldh_misc.h

# The NC_Object Class

Every command and overridable function derives indirectly from the NC_Object class, which handles its registration. When a command or an overridable function is registered in the database, it may be rejected by the system when it is later executed. For example, an overridable function may not be stored in the correct DLL, or it may not be expected by the system. In such cases, the `FailedRegistration` function in the `NC_Object` class is called. In its default implementation, it returns without processing. After it is called, the overridable function manager (in the case of overridable functions) or the command manager (in the case of commands) will delete the instance of the command or function.

## Interface

```
class NC_Object : public NC_Void
{
   const NC_RegistrationID& getID(void) const;
   const String & getDllName(void) const;
   const String & getRefNum(void) const;
   const String & getGivenName(void) const;

   long getError(void ) const;
   bool setError(long E);

   public:
      virtual void FailedRegistration(NC_RegistrationID& RegID,
                                      const ErrorMsg_Reg* Err);
};
```

**Note:**
Use the member functions for retrieving information only; do not depend on the values returned to write your command or overridable function, as they could change depending on how Net.Commerce is set up.

### Header File

WIN `\IBM\NetCommerce3\adt\include\common\cmd_manager.h`
AIX `/usr/lpp/NetCommerce3/adt/include/common/cmd_manager.h`

# The NC_Command Class

All commands derive from the `NC_Command` class, which contains all the mandatory and optional functions for the command. This class derives from the `NC_Object` class.

## Interface

```
class NC_Command : public NC_Object
{
   virtual NC_Command* Clone(void) { return NULL; }
   virtual bool Initialize(void) { return true; }
   virtual bool CheckParameters(const HttpRequest& Req,
                     HttpResponse& Res,
                     NC_Environment& Env,
                     NC_Environment& Resources) = 0;
   virtual void FailedAccessControl(void) { };
```

```
    virtual bool Process(const HttpRequest& Req,
                         HttpResponse& Res,
                         NC_Environment& Env) = 0;
};
```

- The `Initialize` function is called when all commands in the system have been registered. It sets up the environment so that the command can begin receiving requests.

- The `CheckParameters` function is called when the command receives a request. It checks the validity of all the command's required parameters, and creates a list of merchant resources for controlling access to the command.

- The `FailedAccessControl` function is called when the user who is executing the command does not have access to the resources that the command will manipulate.

- The `Process` function performs the processing for the command.

For more information about any of the functions above, see "Understanding the Command Anatomy" on page 442.

### Header File

**WIN**  `\IBM\NetCommerce3\adt\include\common\cmd_manager.h`
**AIX**  `/usr/lpp/NetCommerce3/adt/include/common/cmd_manager.h`

# The NC_OverridableFunction Class

The `NC_OverridableFunction` class is the class from which all overridable functions derive. This class defines the `Process` function, which performs the function's logic. This class derives from the `NC_Object` class.

## Interface

```
class NC_OverridableFunction : public NC_Object
{
  public:
    NC_OverridableFunction() { }
    virtual ~NC_OverridableFunction(void);

  protected:
    String _TaskName; // The current task for which the overridable
                      // function is being implemented
    String _MerchantRefNum; // The current merchant for which the
                            // overridable is being used
    String _CallingCommand; // The current command for which the
                            // overridable function is being called
  public:
    // Execution function
    virtual bool Process(const HttpRequest& Req, HttpResponse& Res,
                         NC_Environment& Env)=0;
};
```

### Header File

**WIN** \IBM\NetCommerce3\adt\include\common\api_manager.h

**AIX** /usr/lpp/NetCommerce3/adt/include/common/api_manager.h

# Stream Classes

Net.Commerce provides logging facilities with three streams that behave in a similar fashion to standard C++ streams such as cout. These streams are debug, status, and error. They can be enabled or disabled at run-time. The system activates them according to the value of the INI file variable LOGLEVEL: a value of will activate all three streams, a value of 1 will activate the status and error streams, and a value of 0 will activate only the error stream. These streams are all directed to the same file in a directory specified by the INI variable LOGPATH. If the variable is not specified, the streams are directed to the cerr (aka stderr) stream.

All streams share the same interface and are typed to receive appropriately typed messages; for example, the error stream can retrieve only an error message. Text messages are compatible with all streams.

# Interface

```
class Error
{
  public:
    Error(void);

  public:
    bool Active(void);
    void Activate(void);
    void Deactivate(void);

  public:
    Error& operator <<(char v);
    Error& operator <<(int v);
    Error& operator <<(long v);
    Error& operator <<(float v);
    Error& operator <<(double v);
    Error& operator <<(const char* v);
    Error& nls(const ErrorMsg* v, ...);
    Error& nls(const TextMsg* v, ...);
};

inline Error& endl(Name& S);
inline Error& indent(Name& S);
inline Error& separator(Name& S);
```

- The indent function adds a specified number of spaces to the stream. The number is tracked by the Tracers when tracing is used and enabled. The function displays indentation and follows function calls in the log.

- The separator function inserts three blank lines in the log.

> **Note:**
> The **nls** member functions are subject to change in future versions of Net.Commerce. If you choose to use them, be aware that migrating to future versions of Net.Commerce may require modifying and recompiling your commands or overridable functions.

For information about tracing, see "Using the Tracing Facilities" on page 324.

### Header File

 \IBM\NetCommerce3\adt\include\containers\ldh_trace.h

**AIX** /usr/lpp/NetCommerce3/adt/include/containers/ldh_trace.h

# Container Classes

There are two types of containers in the Net.Commerce system: lists and hash tables. The hash table is the dominant data structure in Net.Commerce and many other classes use it, including the NameValuePairs, NC_Environment, and CookieMap classes. Containers contain pointers to objects, not objects themselves. It is important that you understand this distinction, since you are responsible for the ownership of these objects. When you create a container, you specify whether it will own its elements or not. If you want the container to own the objects you provide for it, it will take ownership of the pointers that you pass to the Add function, and it will delete the objects when it is itself destroyed. If an object is removed from the container, the container will lose ownership. By default, the ownership is false.

The following code example shows how to create a list of Strings. You have to instantiate a template of String* that can be accessed with a key of type String*. The second parameter in the template is the Key type that you want to use when you search the container.

```
typedef TemplateNC_PList<String, String> StringList;
```

The following shows how to instantiate two lists of strings. The SL list, by default, does not own any of the pointers supplied to it. The SL2 list does, and will delete all of its objects when it is destroyed.

```
StringList SL;
StringList SL2(true);
```

You now have two lists of String*, which you can search using String*. You can add strings to the newly created list of String pointers, as shown in the following example. When SL goes out of scope, it will discard only the pointer to LocalString that it was given. When SL2 goes out of scope, it will delete the "hello" string, and prevent a memory leak. If you reverse the two forms, you will have problems: SL will discard the pointer, and SL2 will try to delete a local object.

```
String LocalString("Local");
SL(&LocalString);
SL2.Append(new String("hello"));
```

For an object to be used by containers, it must publicly derive, directly or indirectly, from the NC_Void class, and implement the Compare function, which returns an int and takes a const Key* as its parameters, as follows:

```
int X::Compare(const Y* y) { /*...*/ }
```

The `int` returned is -1 if the key supplied is less than the key of the element being compared; 0 if it is equal; and +1 if it is larger. This behavior is similar to the standard C++ `strcmp` function. The code above illustrates such a function for a class X to be compatible with a container where the key type is Y.

# Interfaces

The following are the supported interfaces for the `TemplateNC_PList` and the `TemplateNC_PHash` classes. For simplicity, public functions of parent classes have been combined in this interface, which means that some functions listed below actually belong not to the class but to one of its ancestors.

> **Note:**
> Public functions that are listed in a header file but are not documented in this section are not supported.

## The List Class

The `List` class implements a doubly linked list, and does not perform any sorting on its elements.

```
template <class Element, class Key>
class TemplateNC_PList : public NC_PList
{
  public:
    typedef TemplateNC_PList_Iterator<E, K> Iterator;

  public:
    TemplateNC_PList(bool Own=false);

  public:
    Iterator getIterator(void) const;
    bool Prepend(E* ptr);
    bool Prepend(const Iterator& i, E* ptr);
    bool Append(E* ptr);
    bool Append(const Iterator& i, E* ptr);
    E* Remove(Iterator& i);
    E* getHead();
    bool Empty();
    void Clean(bool del);
    long Count();
};
```

- The `getIterator` function returns an iterator that points to the first element in the container (could be NULL if the container is empty).

- The `Prepend` function adds an element to the beginning of the list or before the supplied iterator.

- The `Append` function adds an element to the end of the list or after the supplied iterator.

- The `Remove` function removes the element that is pointed to by the iterator from the container, and returns that element. It is your responsibility to know whether this element should be deleted or discarded.

- The `getHead` function returns the first element in the list, or NULL if the list is empty.

- The `Empty` function returns a flag indicating whether or not the container is empty.

- The `Clean` function removes all the elements in the container. If `del` is true, it also deletes the elements. This behavior is independent of whether or not the container owns its objects.

- The `Count` function returns the number of elements in the container.

### Header File

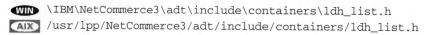
```
\IBM\NetCommerce3\adt\include\containers\ldh_list.h
/usr/lpp/NetCommerce3/adt/include/containers/ldh_list.h
```

## The HashTable Class

The `HashTable` class implements a hash table with a fixed number of buckets, where each bucket is a list. The element must provide a `Compare` function for the specified `Key` type, and the `Key` type provided must be able to return a `Hash` value with the following function:

```
UDWORD HashValue() const;
```

This function returns a `UDWORD` (defined as an unsigned long in the precompiled header file `containers.pch`).

Most of the hash tables in Net.Commerce use the `String` class as the key. The hashing function used by the `String` class is the ElfHash algorithm used in the UNIX elf utility. This algorithm expects a table with a primary number of buckets. If you use a table size that is not a primary number, the results of the `hash` function will deteriorate. The `String` class also caches the hash value; if you use the same String for many lookups, the hash value will be computed only once. For such Strings, using static constant `StringWithOwnership` instances is the best way to ensure that the hash value is reused as often as possible. See the description of the `StringWithOwnership` class on page 299 for details.

```
template <class Element, class Key>
class TemplateNC_PHash : public NC_PHash
{
  public:
    typedef TemplateNC_PHash_Iterator<E, K> Iterator;

  public:
    TemplateNC_PHash(UDWORD Size, bool Own=false, bool Unique=false);

  public:
    Iterator getIterator(void) const;
    bool Add(E* ptr, const K* Key);
    E* Get(const K* Key) const;
    E* Remove(Iterator& I);
```

```
      void Clean(bool del);
      long getCount(void) const;
};
```

- The `getIterator` function returns an iterator that points to the first element in the container (could be NULL if the container is empty).

- The `Add` function adds a new element with the key supplied.

- The `Get` function returns the first element that matches the key supplied, or NULL if no elements were found.

- The `Remove` function takes the element pointed to by the iterator out of the list, and returns that element. It is your responsibility to decide whether this element should be deleted or discarded.

- The `Clean` function removes all the elements from the container. If `del` is true, it also deletes the elements. This behavior is independent of whether or not the container owns its objects.

- The `getCount` function returns the number of elements in the container.

### Header File:

**WIN**  \IBM\NetCommerce3\adt\include\containers\ldh_hash.h

**AIX**  /usr/lpp/NetCommerce3/adt/include/containers/ldh_hash.h

# Iterators

Once you have populated your containers, or if you receive a container with elements, you can perform searches or iterate through the elements using iterators. Iterators are constructs borrowed from the standard C++ library. They operate like pointers, and provide the same type of logic across all containers.

The following example shows how to create an iterator in two different ways. `I1` is an iterator created separately and initialized with a container: the Iterator does not yet point to anything in the container. The `Begin` function sets the iterator to point to the first element. In the second case, `I2` is obtained directly from the container, and is already set to point to the first element.

```
StringList::Iterator I1(&SL);
I1.Begin();
StringList::Iterator I2 = SL.getIterator();
```

To search for an element, use the `Seek` function. It searches forward in the container starting from the place where the iterator points to. If an element is found, it will be returned; otherwise, NULL is returned, indicating the end of the container.

To retrieve the element to which an iterator points, you can either use the `getElement` function (Java style) or dereference the iterator (C++ style). To advance to the next element in the container, you can use either the `getNextElement` function (Java style) or the pre-increment operator (C++ style). For example, if you have an ordered list of Strings and you want to print all the ones that equal "hello", you would use the `Seek` function to locate the first element, and then use the pre-increment operator to get the next elements while they are equal to your key. The following code shows several ways to accomplish this:

### Advancing to the Next Element (Java Style):

```
StringList::Iterator I = SL.getIterator();
String Hello("Hello");
for (I.Seek(&Hello); I.getElement() != NULL; I.getNextElement())
{
   if (*I.getElement() != "hello")
   break;
   cout << *I.getElement() << endl;
}
```

### Advancing to the Next Element (C++ Style):

```
StringList::Iterator I(&SL);
I.Begin();
String Hello ("Hello");
for (I.Seek(&Hello); *I != NULL; ++I)
{
   if (**I != "hello")
   break;
   cout << (**I) << endl;
}
```

To make the code more generic, you may not want to assume that the list is ordered, and instead use the following type of code:

### Using an ordered list:

```
StringList::Iterator I = SL.getIterator();
String Hello("Hello");
for (I.Seek(&Hello); I.getElement() != NULL; I.Seek(&Hello))
{
   cout << *I.getElement() << endl;
}
```

### Iterating through each element in the list:

```
StringList::Iterator I = SL.getIterator();
I.Begin();
String Hello ("Hello");
while (I.getElement() != NULL)
{
   if (*I.getElement() == "hello")
   {
      cout << *I.getElement() << endl;
   }
I.getNextElement();
}
```

Lists benefit from bidirectional iterators, whereas hash tables' iterators can only move forward. Finally, iterating through a hash table is completely orderless: there is no relationship between the way elements are inserted and the way they are returned during an iteration.  By contrast, insertions in a list are positional: lists keep the elements in the order in which they were inserted.

# Iterator Interfaces

The following are the supported interfaces for the `TemplateNC_PListIterator` and the `TemplateNC_PHashIterator` classes.  For simplicity, public functions of parent classes have been combined in this interface, which means that some of the functions listed below actually belong not to the class but to one of its ancestors.

> **Note:**
> Public functions that are listed in a header file but not documented in this section are not supported.

## The List Iterator

```
template <class Element, class Key>
class TemplateNC_PList_Iterator : public NC_PList_Iterator
{
  public:
    TemplateNC_PList_Iterator(const TemplateNC_PList<E,K>*
                                                   List=NULL);
    void Init(const NC_PList* List=NULL);

  public:
    void Begin(void);
    void End(void);
    E* operator*(void);
    E* getElement(void);
    Self& operator++(void);
    E* getNextElement(void);
    Self& operator-(void);
    E* getPrevElement(void);
    void Seek(const K* Key);
};
```

### Header File:

**WIN** `\IBM\NetCommerce3\adt\include\containers\ldh_list.h`
**AIX** `/usr/lpp/NetCommerce3/adt/include/containers/ldh_list.h`

## The Hash Table Iterator

```
template <class Element, class Key>
class TemplateNC_PHash_Iterator : public NC_PHash_Iterator
{
  public:
    TemplateNC_PHash_Iterator(const TemplateNC_PHash<E,K>*
                                                   Hash=NULL);
    void Init(const NC_PHash* Hash=NULL);
```

```
    public:
      void Begin();
      E* operator*(void);
      E* getElement(void);
      Self& operator++(void);
      E* getNextElement(void);
      void Seek(const K* Key);
  };
```

### Header File:

**WIN** `\IBM\NetCommerce3\adt\include\containers\ldh_hash.h`

**AIX** `/usr/lpp/NetCommerce3/adt/include/containers/ldh_hash.h`

# String-Related Classes

The `string` class and its related classes are used consistently across the Net.Commerce programming environment. The `String` class implements a reference-counted `String` class with cached hashing. The `StringWithOwnership` class implements a constant String that is based on the `String` class. The `StringIterator` class implements an iterator for the `String` and `StringWithOwnership` classes.

> **Note:**
> Public functions that are listed in a header file but not documented in this section are not supported.

## The String Class

Most of Net.Commerce is based on or makes heavy use of the `string` class, which is derived from the `NC_Void` class. The class implements a rich interface and is reference-counted. Reference counting makes copying Strings very efficient. You can assign one String to another without actually performing a String copy; only if you modify one of the Strings will the copy be made. In many cases where Strings are passed between functions and not actually modified, a large amount of processing time is saved.

The following is an example of reference counting where one String makes a copy of another String only when the value of the second String changes:

```
    String S1("Hello");
    String S2;
    S2 = S1; // No copy is made.
    S1 << " and bye"; // Now a copy is made, before " and bye" is appended.
```

Strings also cache their own hash values, which makes both comparing Strings and using Strings in conjunction with hash tables very efficient. When you use a static String as a key to search an element in a hash table, the hash value does not have to be computed each time, which makes performing multiple lookups more efficient. The hash value is also used to short-circuit String comparisons (which are always case-sensitive). If two Strings each have a different cache value, then they must be different. In Net.Commerce, String mismatches occur more often than not, so caching the hash value in many cases can enable you to avoid performing a string comparison.

Each time you create a String that is based on a literal or a char*, a copy is made. In many cases, you might want to only declare constants without incurring the longer processing time associated with performing a copy. You can use the StringWithOwnership class to create a String by giving it a buffer. No copy will be made. This is the most efficient way to create a constant String based on a literal. The static constant value _STR_EMPTY_ is defined to be equal to StringWithOwnership(""").

The String class and its accompanying Iterator class provide a rich interface.

> **Note:**
> Do not bypass this interface to operate on the internal buffer through the **c_str()** function. If you cast away the const type of the pointer returned, you will bypass the reference-counting mechanism, the maintenance of the buffer, and the hash value.

The following is an example of how to search a hash table for a specific value.

```
bool CheckForHello(const NVPHash& NVP)
{
    static const StringWithOwnership S1("Hello");
    NVPHash::Iterator I = NVP.getIterator();
    I.Seek(&S1);
    return ((*I) == NULL) ? false : true;
}
```

## Constructors

```
// Constructs a new string based on the specified char*.  A copy of Str
// is made.
String(const char* Str = NULL);

// Copy constructor, which increments the reference count.
String(const String& rhs);

// Same as above but based on a String*.  The copy is reference counted.
String(const String* Str);

// Destructor, which decrements the reference count.
~String();
```

## String Iterators

```
typedef StringIterator Iterator;

// Get an iterator over this String.  The iterator is set to the
// beginning of the String.
Iterator getIterator(void) const;
```

## Assignment Operators

In the case of String*, reference counting takes effect; otherwise, a real copy is performed.

```
void operator = (const String& rhs);
void operator = (const char* rhs);
void operator = (long rhs);
void operator = (double rhs);
```

## Streaming Operators

The streaming operators append data at the end of the current string.

```
String& operator << (const char* rhs);
String& operator << (const String& rhs);
String& operator << (const String* rhs);
String& operator << (char rhs);
String& operator << (int rhs);
String& operator << (long rhs);
String& operator << (double rhs);

// Manipulator streamer.
void zero (void); // NULL terminator.
void endl (void); // end of line
```

## Comparison Operators

```
// Comparison operators on const char*.
bool operator == (const char* rhs) const;
bool operator != (const char* rhs) const;
bool operator <  (const char* rhs) const;
bool operator <= (const char* rhs) const;
bool operator >  (const char* rhs) const;
bool operator >= (const char* rhs) const;

// Comparaison operators on const String&.
bool operator == (const String& rhs) const;
bool operator != (const String& rhs) const;
bool operator <  (const String& rhs) const;
bool operator <= (const String& rhs) const;
bool operator >  (const String& rhs) const;
bool operator >= (const String& rhs) const;

// strcmp compatible comparisons.
int Compare(const String* rhs) const;
int Compare(const String& rhs) const;
int Compare(const char* rhs) const;
```

## Access Functions

The Access functions return a pointer to a char[] that contains the value of the String. In some cases, this is a copy of the value. In other cases, it is a pointer to the actual internal buffer.

```
const char* c_str() const;
```

**Note:**
Ensure that you never override the const type of objects and that you never attempt to modify this buffer in any way.

## Indexing Operators

The non-const version returns a `ProxyChar` to differentiate between reads (rhs) and writes (lhs) uses for `operator[]`. `ProxyChar` is just a detail of implementation, and should be used as a char. For a detailed discussion of this technique, refer to *More Effective C++* by Scott Meyers.

```
char operator[](long i) const;
ProxyChar operator[](long i);

// Length of the String (not counting NULL terminator).
long Len(void) const;

// Is any char* currently associated with the String?
bool IsNull(void) const;

// Is the String empty or does it consist of blank characters?
bool IsEmpty(void) const;

// Hashing.
UDWORD HashValue() const;
```

## Numeric Functions

```
bool IsLong() const // Is the string a representation of a long?
bool IsDouble() const // Is the string a representation of a double?
bool getVal(long& Val) const // Retrieve the string value as a long.
bool getVal(double& Val) const // Retrieve the string value as a
                              // double.

String& LocalizeCDouble(void);
String& UnlocalizeCDouble(void);
```

- The `Localize` function replaces the first occurrence of a period (.) with the locale decimal separator. Assume that the string contains an ASCII representation of a double and nothing else. This function does not check that the String is a representation of a double.

- The `Unlocalize` function replaces the first decimal separator for the current local with a period (.). This function does not check that the String is a representation of a double.

## Manipulation Functions

```
// Inserts a null terminator at the first char of the String.
String& Clean(void);
```

```
// Removes all trailing 'isspace' characters.
String& Trim(void);

// Converts all characters in the string to lower case.
String& ToLower(void);

// Converts all characters in the string to upper case.
String& ToUpper(void);

String& Resize(long Size, long CopySize=-1);
```

- The `Resize` function resizes the allocated buffer to handle `Size` characters and a null terminator. If the String's current size is greater than or equal to `Size`, no operation is performed. If `CopySize` is equal to -1 (the default value) or greater than or equal to the current size, the entire string is copied. Other values cause only the specified number of characters to be copied.

```
String& Delete (const StringIterator& i, long Len );
```

- The `Delete` function removes `Len` characters from the String, starting at the position indicated by `i`. If `i.Pos()+Len` is greater than the current size, null terminates the string at `Pos`; otherwise, the function moves all characters after `Pos+Len` into `Pos`.

```
// Inserts the given string into the current String, at the pos
// specified by the iterator.
String& Insert (const StringIterator& i, const char* Str );
String& Insert (const StringIterator& i, const String& Str);

// Starting at i.Pos(), replaces the next occurrence of Search by Rep.
// If All is true, replaces all occurrences.  There is also a version of
// that method optimized for a single char replacement.
String& Replace(const StringIterator& i, const char* Search,
                const char* Rep, bool All=false);
String& Replace(const StringIterator& i, char Search, char Rep,
                bool All=false);

// Copies the sub-string From to To into Dest.
String& Copy(const StringIterator& Dest, StringIterator From, const
             StringIterator& To);

// Copies Len characters from Src into the string.
String& Copy(const StringIterator& Dest, const char* Src, long Len);

// Copies Len characters from In into the string.
String& Copy(const StringIterator& Dest, istream& In, long Len);

// Copies a line or Len characters from In into the string.
String& GetLine(const StringIterator& Dest, istream& In, long Len);
```

### Header File:

**WIN**  \IBM\NetCommerce3\adt\include\containers\ldh_string.h

**AIX**  /usr/lpp/NetCommerce3/adt/include/containers/ldh_string.h

# The StringWithOwnership Class

The `StringWithOwnership` class allows you to efficiently manage buffers by passing a const char* to the `String` class. It will take the pointer without making a copy of the buffer. This is ideal for efficiently having the functionality of Strings from a const char*: you do not pay the price of allocating new space and making the copy. If the String gets modified in any way, then a copy will be made. Reference counting and hashing work the same way as for a real `String` object.

```
StringWithOwnership(const char* Str);
```

You will commonly use constant static instances of the `StringWithOwnership` class for constant Strings that are used as keys for hash tables. For example, in a command you will typically declare the names for the URL parameters (name-value pairs) as static instances of the `StringWithOwnership` class, as shown in the example below. Thus, the hash value for the string would be computed only once, and all subsequent lookups would be faster.

```
static const StringWithOwnership NVP_product_rn("product_rn");
String Value = Req.getNVPs().Get(&NVP_product_rn).getValue();
```

There are times when you need to allocate a buffer, perform processing on this buffer and then pass it to a `String` class to manage. The following constructor allows you to do that without having possibly two allocations and a buffer copy. First, obtain an allocated buffer using the `Allocate` function, perform processing on it for as long as you want, and then assign the buffer to a `StringWithOwnership` object using the constructor. After that, management of that buffer will be handled automatically. Do not use your char* afterwards; once you pass the buffer to the `String` class, you do not own it anymore. If you need a char*, use the `c_str()` functions, which returns only a const version of it. The size may be no larger than the size that is allocated.

```
StringWithOwnership(char* Str, long Size);
static char* Allocate(long Size);
static void DeAllocate(char* Buf);
```

The buffer returned by the `Allocate` function is destined to be given back to a `StringWithOwnership` object. Never delete that buffer directly; instead, ensure that you use the `DeAllocate` function.

## String Streamers

The Stream operators work with ostream and the standard Net.Commerce streams (`Trace`, `Debug`, `Status`, `Error`).

```
inline ostream& operator << (ostream& Out, const String& Str);
inline Trace& operator << (Trace& Out, const String& Str);
inline Debug& operator << (Debug& Out, const String& Str);
inline Status& operator << (Status& Out, const String& Str);
inline Error& operator << (Error& Out, const String& Str);
inline String& zero(String& S);
inline String& endl(String& S);
```

### Header File:

   **WIN** `\IBM\NetCommerce3\adt\include\containers\ldh_string.h`
   **AIX** `/usr/lpp/NetCommerce3/adt/include/containers/ldh_string.h`

# The StringIterator Class

The `StringIterator` class is an iterator for Strings. The iterators are index-based, meaning that they maintain their position as an index into the String, rather than a direct char*. A String can be modified (copied, resized, and so forth), and the iterator will maintain its position. There is, however, the possibility of an iterator being "pushed" out of bounds by a String that shrinks. Dereferencing the iterator is also not checked for bound validity. In such cases, "rewind" the iterator using the `Begin` function.

The following example shows how to interate through a String:

```
String X;

String::Iterator I = X.getIterator();
while (I.Pos() != I.Len())
{
  cout << *I;
  ++I;
}
```

The following shows how to search for a substring:

```
String X;

String::Iterator I = X.getIterator();
I.Seek('A');
if (I.Pos() != I.Len())
{
    // Found
}
```

The following shows how to delete a substring:

```
String X;

String::Iterator I = X.getIterator();
I.Seek("hello");
if (I.Pos() != I.Len())
X.Delete(I, 5); // Delete the "hello" found.
```

The following shows how to replace a substring:

```
String X;

String::Iterator I = X.getIterator();
X.Replace(I, "hello", "HELLO");
```

## Interface

```
StringIterator(const String* Str);

// Dereferences the iterator to return the current char.
char operator*() const;
```

```
// Returns that const char* from the pos.  As for the same method on the
// String class, NEVER cast away the const or try to modify the buffer.
// you get.
const char* c_str() const;

// Sets the iterator to the beginning of the string.
StringIterator& Begin();

// Sets the iterator to the end of the string.
StringIterator& End();

// Sets the iterator to position p.  If p is out of bound, the Iterator
// is set to the end of the string.
StringIterator& Set(long p);

// Returns the current position
long Pos() const;

// Returns the Len of the String.
long Len() const;

// Increments the position only if pos < Len.
StringIterator& operator ++ ();

// Decrements the position only if pos > 0.
StringIterator& operator — ();

// Increments Pos by i.  If that goes out of bound, sets iterator to the
// end of the string.
StringIterator& operator += (int i);

// Decrements Pos by i.  If that goes out of bound, sets iterator to the
// beginning of the string.
StringIterator& operator -= (int i);

// From the current position, advances the iterator to the next non
// 'space' character.
StringIterator& SkipBlanks(void);

// Advances the iterator to the first occurrence of Tok, or the end of
// the string is nothing is found.
StringIterator& Seek(const char* Tok);
StringIterator& Seek(const String& Tok);
StringIterator& Seek(char Tok);

// Two iterators are equal if their position are the same.  The
// iterators could actually be on two different strings.
bool operator == (const StringIterator& rhs) const;
bool operator != (const StringIterator& rhs) const;
)
```

```
// Provides a distance between 2 iterators.  Again the Iterators do not
// have to be on the same String.
long operator - (const StringIterator& rhs) const;
```

### Header File:

**WIN**  \IBM\NetCommerce3\adt\include\containers\ldh_string.h
**AIX**  /usr/lpp/NetCommerce3/adt/include/containers/ldh_string.h

## Utility Functions

When constructing an SQL statement, use the `sq` function to enclose all character literals in single quotes. This function operates with ostreams and the standard Net.Commerce streams, or in a standalone manner by returning a String. It accepts types such as long, char, String, char*, and double.

```
inline Stream& sq(Stream& s, const Type& t);
inline String sq(const Type& t);
```

When adding a floating point number to an SQL statement, use the `nl` function to ensure that the decimal separator is a period (.), regardless of the current locale. This function operates with ostreams and the standard Net.Commerce streams, or in a standalone manner by returning a String. In the case of Strings, it is assumed that they contain a text representation of a double (the function does not perform any checking for this). The function accepts the types double and String.

```
inline Stream& nl(Stream& s, double t);
inline Stream& nl(Stream& s, const String& t);
inline String nl(double t);
inline String nl(const String& t);
```

To insert a timestamp in the database using the INSERT statement, you need a special format, which is different from the format that you get from the database using a SELECT statement. The `ts` (time stamp) function converts from the SELECT format into the INSERT format. It expects a timestamp of the format 'YYYY-MM-DD HH:MM:SS.mmmmmm' and outputs the following format 'YYYY-MM-DD-HH.MM.SS.mmmmmm' to a stream. No check is performed.

```
inline Stream& ts(Stream& s, const String& t);
```

The system also provides a predefined empty string equivalent to "", as follows:

```
extern const StringWithOwnership _STR_EMPTY_;
```

## The HttpDate Class

The `HttpDate` class represents a date in the proper format for the HTTP protocol. It is linked to the time functions in C such as `gmtime`, and the time structure struct `tm`. This class is used mainly to set expiration dates for Web pages. See also the `Cookie` class on page 303, and the `HttpResponse` class on page 306.

# Interface

```
HttpDate();
HttpDate(int yyyy, int mm, int dd, int wday, int HH, int MM, int SS);
void setGMTime(int yyyy, int mm, int dd, int wday, int HH, int MM,
               int SS);
void getGMTime();
void Expire();
const struct tm& getTimeStruct() const;
bool IsEmpty() const;
```

- The default constructor invokes the `Expire` function and sets the `Empty` flag to false.

- The second constructor invokes the `setGMTime` function.

- The `getGMTime` function retrieves the date/time from the system and sets the date to that value.

- The `Expire` function sets the date as expired (January 1st 1970 at 00:00).

## Streamers

```
Stream& operator<<(Stream& S, const HttpDate& H);
SocketActiveStream& operator<<(SocketActiveStream& S,
                               const HttpDate& H);
SocketActiveStream& operator>>(SocketActiveStream& S, HttpDate& H);
```

# The Cookie Class

The `Cookie` class is an object that is often present in the HTTP protocol. It allows an application on a server to save certain data on the client (browser). When the client receives a cookie, it will send it back, when appropriate, to the server for each subsequent request. The total size of the cookie, including all its parameters, must be smaller than 4K. This class does not check the size.

A cookie can contain four pieces of data, as follows:

- A name and value (mandatory).

- The path and domain to which the cookie will be returned. You should leave the domain empty, so that the cookie will be sent back to only you. The path should be set for the entire site; however, you can also limit it to only the Net.Commerce URLs by setting it to "/cgi-bin/ncommerce3/". In this case, the cookies will be visible only to programs invoked through a URL that is prefixed with /cgi-bin/ncommerce3/.

- The life-cycle of the cookie. All cookies must be set to expire immediately. The browser will store the cookie in memory and discard it when the browser session ends. Net.Commerce does not use cookies that are set to specific expiry dates.

- SSL enablement. The HTTP protocol allows you to specify whether the cookie should be transmitted back over an SSL connection only.

> **Note:**
> If you enable a cookie for SSL, it will be sent back to the server only if the HTTP request is also enabled for SSL. For more information, refer to the HTTP standard.

## Interface

```
Cookie(const String& name, const String& value,
      const HttpDate& expires = HttpDate(),
      const String& path = StringWithOwnership("/"),
      const String& domain = StringWithOwnership(""),
      bool secure = false);

const String& getName(void) const;
const String& getValue(void) const;
const HttpDate& getExpires(void) const;
const String& getPath(void) const;
const String& getDomain(void) const;
bool isSecure(void) const;

void setName(const String& name);
void setValue(const String& value);
void setExpires(const HttpDate& expires);
void setPath(const String& path);
void setDomain(const String& domain);
void setSecure(bool secure);

// A cookie "equals" a string if the string equals the name of the
// cookie. The value is not taken into account.
int Compare(const String* rhs);
int Compare(const String& rhs);
int Compare(const char* rhs);
bool operator==(const String& S);
```

## Streamers

Streamers are provided for all standard Net.Commerce streams, as well as for the socket.

```
Stream& operator<<(Stream& S, const Cookie& C);
SocketActiveStream& operator<<(SocketActiveStream& S,
                               const Cookie& C);
SocketActiveStream& operator>>(SocketActiveStream& S, Cookie& C);
SocketActiveStream& operator>>(SocketActiveStream& s,
```

# The HttpRequest Class

The `HttpRequest` class is the input to a command. It contains all the information that is contained in an HTTP request, such as the cookies, the name-value pairs, and various CGI-type environment variables. For example, the `getAUTH_TYPE` function returns the value of the `AUTH_TYPE` variable that you would retrieve in the CGI type program. For more information, consult the HTTP and CGI standards.

# Interface

```
HttpRequest(void);
const String& getAUTH_TYPE(void) const;
const String& getCONTENT_LENGTH(void) const;
const String& getCONTENT_TYPE(void) const;
const String& getGATEWAY_INTERFACE(void) const;
const String& getHTTP_USER_AGENT(void) const;
const String& getHTTP_COOKIE(void) const;
const String& getHTTPS(void) const;
const String& getPATH_INFO(void) const;
const String& getPATH_TRANSLATED(void) const;
const String& getQUERY_STRING(void) const;
const String& getREMOTE_ADDR(void) const;
const String& getREMOTE_HOST(void) const;
const String& getREMOTE_IDENT(void) const;
const String& getREMOTE_USER(void) const;
const String& getREQUEST_METHOD(void) const;
const String& getSCRIPT_NAME(void) const;
const String& getSERVER_NAME(void) const;
const String& getSERVER_PORT(void) const;
const String& getSERVER_PROTOCOL(void) const;
const String& getSERVER_SOFTWARE(void) const;

void setAUTH_TYPE(const String& s);
void setCONTENT_LENGTH(const String& s);
void setCONTENT_TYPE(const String& s);
void setGATEWAY_INTERFACE(const String& s);
void setHTTP_USER_AGENT(const String& s);
void setHTTP_COOKIE(const String& s);
void setHTTPS(const String& s);
void setPATH_INFO(const String& s);
void setPATH_TRANSLATED(const String& s);
void setQUERY_STRING(const String& s);
void setREMOTE_ADDR(const String& s);
void setREMOTE_HOST(const String& s);
void setREMOTE_IDENT(const String& s);
void setREMOTE_USER(const String& s);
void setREQUEST_METHOD(const String& s);
void setSCRIPT_NAME(const String& s);
void setSERVER_NAME(const String& s);
void setSERVER_PORT(const String& s);
void setSERVER_PROTOCOL(const String& s);
void setSERVER_SOFTWARE(const String& s);

// Cookie functions.
CookieMap& getCookieNVPs();
const CookieMap& getCookieNVPs() const;

NameValuePairMap& getNVPs();
const NameValuePairMap& getNVPs() const;
```

```
HttpRequest& operator = (const HttpRequest& rhs);
void ReplacePathInfo(const String& NewPathInfo);
```

## Streamers

The Streamers allow you to stream the `req` to the standard Net.Commerce streams, such as, `ostream`, `Trace`, `Debug`, `Status` and `Error`. Streamers for sockets are also provided.

```
stream& operator << (stream& s, const HttpRequest& Req);
SocketActiveStream& operator << (SocketActiveStream& s,
                                const HttpRequest& Req);
SocketActiveStream& operator >> (SocketActiveStream& s,
                                HttpRequest& Req);
```

### Header File

**WIN**  \IBM\NetCommerce3\adt\include\common\cgi_envir.h

**AIX**  /usr/lpp/NetCommerce3/adt/include/common/cgi_envir.h

# The HttpResponse Class

The `HttpResponse` class is the output of a command. It contains all the information that is needed for returning a full HTTP document back to the browser, such as cookies, document type, expiration date, HTML, DHTML, VRML, JavaScript, and so on. Currently, only ASCII data can be sent back to the browser, and the document cannot be multi-part. For more information about the valid content for an HTTP response, consult the HTTP standard.

## Constructor and Assignment Operator

```
HttpResponse(void);
HttpResponse& operator = (const HttpResponse& rhs);
```

## Access Functions

```
void setHTTP_Version(const String& http_version);
void setStatus_Code(const String& status_code);
void setReason_Phrase(const String& reason_phrase);
void setContentEncoding(const String& content_encoding);
void setContentLength(const String& content_length);
void setContentLength(long content_length);
void setContentType(const String& content_type);
void setExpires(const HttpDate& http_date);
void setDate(const HttpDate& http_date);
void setExtraHeader(const String& extra_header);
void setDocument(const String& document);
const String& getHTTP_Version(void) const;
const String& getStatus_Code(void) const;
const String& getReason_Phrase(void) const;
const String& getContent_Encoding(void) const;
const String& getContent_Length(void) const;
```

```
const String& getContent_Type(void) const;
const HttpDate& getExpires(void) const;
const String& getLocation(void) const;
String& getLocation(void);
const HttpDate& getDate(void) const;
const String& getExtraHeader(void) const;
const String& getDocument(void) const;
String& getDocument(void);

// Use this function when you want to create an entire HTTP document,
// and not allow the system modify it in any way.  Instructs the system
// to send back the document as set by the setDocument function, back to
// the browser.
void setRawStatus(bool Status);
bool getRawStatus(void) const;

// Functions that manage the cookies in the document.
const TemplateNC_PHash<Cookie, String>& getCookies(void) const;
void AddCookie(const String& name, const String& value,
               const HttpDate& expires = HttpDate(),
               const String& path = StringWithOwnership("/"),
               const String& domain = StringWithOwnership(""),
               bool secure = false);
Cookie* getCookie(const String& name);
void RemoveCookie(const String& name);
void RemoveAllCookies(void);
```

The `HttpResponse` class provides several functions for setting a redirection header, which is a URL for the browser to call back automatically.

The following function sets the specified URL in a redirection header. If the URL is relative to the Web server document root, the function reconstructs a full URL based on the MS_HOST_NAME variable in the Web server configuration file. If `SslMode` is true, the function reconstructs the URL as https; otherwise, it uses the default http.

```
void setLocation(String Location, bool SslMode);
```

To set a redirection header based on parameters contained in an `HttpRequest` object, use the following function. It sets the hostname and the HTTP status from the request. If `useConfFile` is set to true (the default), it uses the configuration file like the previous function.

```
void setLocation(String Location, const HttpRequest& Req,
                 const bool& useConfFile=true);
```

To set a redirection to a specific host, either the current one or a new one, use the following function:

```
void setLocation(String Location, String& hostname, bool SslMode);
```

To construct a full URL that includes the name-value pairs and propagate the current name-value pairs, use the following function, which is most commonly used for commands:

```
void Redirect(const HttpRequest& Req, const String& UrlField,
              const NVPHash& NewNVPs);
```

This function constructs the return URL based on the data supplied. It first retrieves the original name-value pairs from the current `HttpRequest` object, then the name-value pairs stored in the variable `NewNVPs`, and finally the return URL. The return URL is retrieved from the current request using the `UrlField` parameter as the name-value pair name. When the name-value pairs are merged, the new values override the older values and multiple older values are replaced. Empty values override older values, allowing you to control which name-value pairs are propagated. The precedence level is as follows:

1. `Req`
2. `NewNVPs`
3. `UrlField`

> **Note:**
> The system automatically encrypts all name-value pairs in the redirection URL, to avoid a Netscape browser (version 4.0 and higher) problem that causes a redirection originating from a POST method to be erroneously redirected as a GET method. This problem would cause the redirected URL to appear in the Web server log and the Location window of the browser.

## Streamers

```
// Streams an HttpResponse to the standard Net.Commerce streams and
// sockets.
Stream& operator << (Stream& s, const HttpResponse& doc);
SocketActiveStream& operator << (SocketActiveStream& s,
                                 const HttpResponse& doc);
SocketActiveStream& operator >> (SocketActiveStream& s,
                                 HttpResponse& doc);
```

### Header File

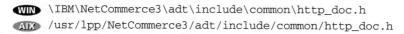

**WIN** `\IBM\NetCommerce3\adt\include\common\http_doc.h`
**AIX** `/usr/lpp/NetCommerce3/adt/include/common/http_doc.h`

# Name-Value Pair-Related Classes

The following are the supported interfaces for the name-value pair-related classes: `NameValuePair`, `NVPHash`, and `NVPHash::Iterator`, and `NameValuePairMap`. For simplicity, public functions of parent classes have been combined in this interface, which means that some of the functions listed below actually belong not to the class but to one of its ancestors.

> **Note:**
> Public methods in a header file that are not documented in this section are not supported.

## The NameValuePair Class

The `NameValuePair` class is a basic class that binds a name string and a value string together. Basic access and query functions are provided; for example, functions that query the type of the value string, whether it is a double or a long.

## Interface

```
// Constructor, that creates copies of the Strings passed to it.
NameValuePair(const String& Name, const String& Value);

// Copy constructor: that copies the rhs operand.
NameValuePair(const NameValuePair& rhs);

// Assignment Operator
void operator=(const NameValuePair& rhs);

// Access Functions
const String& getName() const;
const String& getValue() const;
bool getValueLong(long& Val) const;
bool getValueDouble(double& Val) const;
bool getRead() const;

void setName(const String& Name);
void setValue(const String& Value);
void setRead(bool Read);
```

The following are functions of the `NameValuePair` class that contain strings. The equality is done at the name value. The expression `NameValuePair("name", "value")=="name"` is true.

```
bool operator == (const String* rhs) const;
bool operator == (const String& rhs) const;
bool operator == (const char* rhs) const;

int Compare(const String* rhs) const;
int Compare(const String& rhs) const;
int Compare(const char*   rhs) const;
```

### Header File:

**WIN**  `\IBM\NetCommerce3\adt\include\containers\ldh_list.h`
**AIX**  `/usr/lpp/NetCommerce3/adt/include/containers/ldh_list.h`

# The NVPHash Class

The `NVPHash` class is a hash table of name-value pairs that takes in arguments by value rather than by pointers. Strings are cheap to copy (they are reference-counted), and are so pervasive in Net.Commerce that such a class makes manipulations easier. When you use the `NVPHash` class, you do not have to consider ownership, and the class will perform a copy of its own from the strings that you pass to it.

This class derives from `TemplateNC_PHash<NameValuePair, String>` and provides additional functions that are specialized for name-value pairs.

## Interface

```
class NVPHash : public TemplateNC_PHash<NameValuePair, String>
{
  public:
    typedef TemplateNC_PHash_Iterator<NameValuePair,
                                      String> Iterator;

  public:
    NVPHash(UDWORD Size=13, bool Unique=false);

  public:
    Iterator getIterator(void) const;
    bool Add(NameValuePair* ptr, const String* Key);
    NameValuePair* Get(const String* Key) const;
    NameValuePair* Remove(Iterator& I);
    void Clean(bool del);
    long getCount(void) const;

    bool setUnique(const String& Name, const String& Value);
    NVPHash& operator = (const NVPHash& rhs);
    bool Add(const String& Name, const String& Value);
    const String& Get(const String& Name,
                      const String& Default=_STR_EMPTY_) const;
    bool Remove(const String& Name, bool All=false);
};
```

- Functions in the first group are inherited from the parent classes. For details, see the interface definition for the `TemplateNC_PHash` class on page 308.

- The `setUnique` function operates like the `Add` function, except that it removes all name-value pairs with the same name already in the container first.

- The assignment operator allows you to copy all name-value pairs from one container to another.

- The `Add`, `Get`, and `Remove` functions are the same as the functions in the first group, except that they provide a simpler interface for name-value pairs.

- The `Get` function returns the value for a specified name. If the name is not found, the specified default value is returned.

### Header File:

(WIN)  `\IBM\NetCommerce3\adt\include\containers\ldh_hash.h`
(AIX)  `/usr/lpp/NetCommerce3/adt/include/containers/ldh_hash.h`

# The NVPHash::Iterator Class

The `NVPHash::Iterator` class does not exist per se: it is only a type defined as `NC_PHash_Iterator<NameValuePair, String>`. For details, refer to the interface of that class.

### Header File:

(WIN) \IBM\NetCommerce3\adt\include\containers\ldh_hash.h
(AIX) /usr/lpp/NetCommerce3/adt/include/containers/ldh_hash.h

## The NameValuePairMap Class

The `NameValuePairMap` class derives from the `NVPHash` class, and functions the same way as that class. It adds special functions for encoding and decoding HTTP name-value pairs.

### Interface

```
NameValuePairMap(const char* Str=NULL, bool Unique=false,
                 long PrimeNumber=23);
void AppendEncodedPairs(const char* Str);
void AppendEncodedPairs(const String& Str);
const String& getEncodedString(void) const;

void RenameAll(const String& Old, const String& New);
void Rename(NVPHash::Iterator& I , const String& New);
void setUnique(const String& name, const String& value);
void RemoveAll(const String& name);
void RemoveAll();
```

- The `AppendEncodedPairs` functions take a string of properly encoded name-value pairs and add them to the container.

- The `GetEncodedString` function encodes all the name-value pairs in the container, to make it suitable to add to a URL.

- The `RenameAll` function renames all name-value pairs from one specified name to another.

- The `Rename` function renames the name-value pair pointed to by the iterator to the new name.

- The `RemoveAll` functions remove all name-value pairs from the container or only those with the given name.

### Header File:

(WIN) IBM\NetCommerce3\adt\include\containers\nvp_util.h
(AIX) /usr/lpp/NetCommerce3/adt/include/containers/nvp_util.h

## Configuration-Related Classes

The classes that manipulate the `ncommerce.ini` file are `Confile` and `Confield`.

---

**Note:**
These classes are subject to change in future versions of Net.Commerce. If you choose to use them, be aware that migrating to future versions of Net.Commerce may require modifying and recompiling your commands or overridable functions.

# The ConFile Class

The `Confile` class contains all system variables that are either in an INI file, or in the registry (under Windows NT only), or from the command line. Therefore, anyone can add variables to the INI file, the command line, or the registry, and have access to it. There is only one instance of the `Confile` class in the entire system. It is implemented using a completely static interface. Therefore, every method is called as follows:

```
ConfFile::Method(.....);
```

## Interface

```
// Get an ini variable value based on the name of the variable.
static String GetConfValue(const ConfField& name,
                           bool UseNewEncryption=true);
static String GetNextValue(const ConfField& name);
```

### Header File:

**WIN**  \IBM\NetCommerce3\adt\include\containers\conf_file.h

**AIX**  /usr/lpp/NetCommerce3/adt/include/containers/conf_file.h

# The ConfField Class

To access name-value pairs, you must create a `Confield` object, which is a specification of a configuration variable: its name, whether it is an encrypted value, and, when it is a multi-value, the value separator.

```
ConfField(String Name, bool Encrypted = false, char sep=',');
String getName(void) const;
```

The following are predefined variables, which represent all the configuration values that are used in the Net.Commerce system.

```
static const ConfField _CONF_HOSTNAME;
static const ConfField _CONF_PORT;
static const ConfField _CONF_SERVICE;
static const ConfField _CONF_NUM_CHILD;
static const ConfField _CONF_TRANS_COUNT;
static const ConfField _CONF_HTML_MAX;
static const ConfField _CONF_CGI_LOG;
static const ConfField _CONF_DB_RETRY_LIMIT;
static const ConfField _CONF_DB_RETRY_INTERVAL;
static const ConfField _CONF_DBNAME;
static const ConfField _CONF_DBINST;
static const ConfField _CONF_DBPASS;
static const ConfField _CONF_MERCHANT_KEY;
static const ConfField _CONF_MACRO_PATH;
static const ConfField _CONF_HTML_PATH;
static const ConfField _CONF_SG_PATH;
static const ConfField _CONF_HTADMIN;
static const ConfField _CONF_HTPASS;
```

```
static const ConfField _CONF_MSLOGPATH;
static const ConfField _CONF_MSLOGNAME;
static const ConfField _CONF_MSLOGLEVEL;
static const ConfField _CONF_CONFIG_FILE;
static const ConfField _CONF_REGISTRY_KEY;
static const ConfField _CONF_DATABASE;
```

# The NC_Environment Class

Commands and overridable functions communicate with each other using the NC_Environment class. This class is based on the hash table and, like the NVPHash and String classes, is one of the classes that you will use most. The NC_Environment class is a hash table of pointers to generic objects derived from the NC_Void class.

This class has a dynamic untyped nature, and an Add function and a Seek function that allow you to add objects and search for objects of any type, based on a name. For example, when you write a command, you may have to call a task that takes a product reference number as a parameter. The following is the code for this scenario:

```
NC_Environment Env;
String ProducRefNum("123");
Env.AddRef("product_rn", ProductRefNum);
Env.Add ("product_rn", new String("124"));
```

The AddRef function adds a reference to the objects, which means that when the Env parameter goes out of scope, it will discard the pointer. With the Add function, however, we give a pointer to the Env parameter. When it goes out of scope, it will delete the String. As a rule, pointers to objects created with the new function should always be passed to the Add function. For pointers to local objects or objects that you do not own, use the AddRef function.

When you use the NC_Environment class, you have to manage ownership at the element level. (Other containers manage ownership at the container instance level.) The elements of the NC_Environment are typeless. In the example above, when the object named "product_rn" was added to the environment, a String was passed in. However, the receiving hand cannot rely on the compiler for the type: it has to know it is a string and cast.

```
String* Temp = (String*) Env.Seek("product_rn");
```

> **Note:**
> Do not delete a pointer that you retrieve from an **NC_Environment** object. If you need to delete an object, use the **Remove** function. This function checks whether it should delete the object or just discard the pointer.

You can also use iterators on the NC_Environment class, but remember that the class is a hash table of NameValuePair objects. Most often, you will insert Strings into the NC_Environment object. You can use the Add and Seek functions, which automatically handle the ownership by making a copy of the Strings and passing the copy to the NC_Environment object to own.

Since most of the time you will put Strings in this type of object, and since copying Strings is cheap, there are Add and Seek functions that automatically handle the ownership issue by making a copy of the string and giving that copy to the NC_Environment class to own.

The NC_Environment class is a generic container based on the hash table. As part of the class definition, we provide several predefined names used in a standard way throughout the system.

```
static const StringWithOwnership _VAR_Parameters;
static const StringWithOwnership _VAR_Shopper;
static const StringWithOwnership _VAR_Merchant;
static const StringWithOwnership _VAR_Macro_NVPHash;
static const StringWithOwnership _VAR_MainDatabase;
```

There are also traditional functions to manage the container, which are similar to those in the TemplateNC_PHash class, but with added functionality to manage ownership at the element level.

```
bool Add(const String& Name, NC_Void* Value);
bool AddRef(const String& Name, const NC_Void* Value);
bool AddIfUnique(const String& Name, NC_Void* Value);
bool AddRefIfUnique(const String& Name, const NC_Void* Value);

// Specialized methods for Strings, which are the dominant object
// stored in here.
bool Add(const String& Name, const String& Value);
bool AddIfUnique(const String& Name, const String& Value);

// Const and non const methods to get an element directly (if it exists)
const NC_Void* Seek(const String& Name) const;
NC_Void* Seek(const String& Name);

void Replace(const String& Name, NC_Void* Value);
void ReplaceRef(const String& Name, NC_Void* Value);
NameObjectPair* ReplacePair(const String& Name, NC_Void* Value);
NameObjectPair* ReplaceRefPair (const String& Name, NC_Void* Value);
bool Remove(const String& Name);
NameObjectPair* RemovePair(const String& Name);
```

# The NameObjectPair Class

This class behaves like the NameValuePair class, except that it manages pointers to all NC_Void derived objects, rather than just Strings. Additionally, the pair maintains data with respect to the ownership status of the object in the pair. If you delete a NameObjectPair instance, it will also delete the object it contains (if the ownership flag is true), or discard it (if the flag is false). Therefore, deleting a NameObjectPair is safe, whereas deleting the object directly is not.

## Interface

```
NameObjectPair(const String& Name, NC_Void* Value, bool Own);

bool getOwned(void) const;

const String& getName(void) const;
const NC_Void* getValue(void) const;
NC_Void* getValue(void);
void setValue(NC_Void* Value);
void setOwned(bool Own);
```

```
bool operator ==(const String& rhs) const;
int Compare(const String* rhs) const;
int Compare(const String& rhs) const;
```

**Header File:**

**WIN** \IBM\NetCommerce3\adt\include\common\environment.h

**AIX** /usr/lpp/NetCommerce3/adt/include/common/environment.h

# The Misc Class

The `Misc` class contains functions that you will most commonly call when creating commands and overridable functions. Using the functions in the class ensures that your commands and overridable functions operate like the default ones. All functions are static.

## Interface

```
class Misc : public NC_Void
{
  public:
    static bool CheckFieldExistence(const HttpRequest& Req,
                                    const String& Name, String& Value,
                                    bool CanBeEmpty);
    static bool CheckFieldExistenceLong(const HttpRequest& Req,
                                        const String& Name,
                                        String& Value,
                                        bool CanBeEmpty);
    static bool CheckFieldExistenceDouble(const HttpRequest& Req,
                                          const String& Name,
                                          String& Value,
                                          bool CanBeEmpty);
    static bool CheckFieldExistenceChar(const HttpRequest& Req,
                                        const String& Name,
                                        String& Value,
                                        bool CanBeEmpty);
    static bool CheckFieldExistence(const HttpRequest& Req,
                                    NC_Environment& Env,
                                    const String& TaskName,
                                    const String& MerchantRefNum,
                                    const String& ErrorCode,
                                    const String& Name, String& Value,
                                    bool CanBeEmpty);
    static bool CheckFieldExistenceLong(const HttpRequest& Req,
                                        NC_Environment& Env,
                                        const String& TaskName,
                                        const String& MerchantRefNum,
                                        const String& ErrorCode,
                                        const String& Name,
                                        String& Value,
                                        bool CanBeEmpty);
```

```
         static bool CheckFieldExistenceDouble(const HttpRequest& Req,
                                               NC_Environment& Env,
                                               const String& TaskName,
                                               const String&
                                               MerchantRefNum,
                                               const String& ErrorCode,
                                               const String& Name,
                                               String& Value,
                                               bool CanBeEmpty);
         static bool CheckFieldExistenceChar(const HttpRequest& Req,
                                             NC_Environment& Env,
                                             const String& TaskName,
                                             const String& MerchantRefNum,
                                             const String& ErrorCode,
                                             const String& Name,
                                             String& Value,
                                             bool CanBeEmpty);
         static bool CheckFieldForCommandLineInclusion (NC_Environment&
                                                          Env,
                                             const String& TaskName,
                                             const String& MerchantRefNum,
                                             const String& ErrorCode,
                                             const String& Name,
                                             const String& Value);
         static bool CheckFieldIsAlphaNum(NC_Environment& Env,
                                          const String& TaskName,
                                          const String& MerchantRefNum,
                                          const String& ErrorCode,
                                          const String& Name, String&
                                          Value);
         static bool SetErrorHandler(NC_Environment& Env,
                                     const String& TaskName,
                                     const String& MerchantRefNum,
                                     const String& ErrorCode,
                                     const String& ParamName=_STR_EMPTY_);
         static bool SetView (NC_Environment& Env,
                              const String& TaskName,
                              const String& MerchantRefNum,
                              const String& HandlerName=_STR_EMPTY_);
         static const NC_Void* CheckEnvironmentVariable(const
                                               NC_Environment& Env,
                                               const String& Name);
         static String CheckConfigurationVariable(const ConfField& Name,
                                               bool CanBeEmpty=false);
};
```

- The `CheckFieldExistence` functions allow you to check whether or not a name-value pair was passed in a URL to the command. If the specified field is found in the name-value pairs in the `Req` parameter, it sets `Value` to its value and returns true. An error occurs if the variable `CanBeEmpty` is false and the parameter is not present or its value is empty. In this case, false is returned. If the variable `CanBeEmpty` is true, a missing parameter or an empty value is permitted. Functions that do type checking are also provided. The second set of functions allows you to set up an error handler and related parameters in case you want an error handler to be invoked if a parameter is missing or not correct.

- The `CheckFieldForCommandLineInclusion` function checks that there are no double quotes in the value given. If any are found, it sets the error handler.

- The `CheckFieldIsAlphaNum` function checks whether the field is composed exclusively of alphanumeric characters, or whether it includes '@' or '.'.

- The `SetErrorHandler` function sets an exception task and returns false.

- The `SetView` function sets a view task and erroneously returns false, which will be corrected in future releases of Net.Commerce.

- The `CheckEnvironmentVariable` function checks for the specified variable in the `NC_Environment` object that is provided. If the variable is not found, the `&_ERR_CMD_ERR_BAD_SYSTEM` exception is thrown, which indicates a serious system error. If it is not caught, the system will terminate.

- The `CheckConfigurationVariable` function checks for the specified variable in the configuration file. If the variable is not found and the variable `CanBeEmpty` is false, the `&_ERR_CMD_ERR_BAD_SYSTEM` exception is thrown, which indicates a serious system error. If it is not caught, the system will terminate. If the variable `CanBeEmpty` is set to true, then not finding the variable will not result in an error.

# The User Class

The `User` class contains information needed to identify each shopper or user to the Net.Commerce system. Use this class to retrieve this profile information about the current shopper. For information on the interface for this class, see "The User Class" on page 683.

# Database Classes

Net.Commerce provides four classes for accessing and manipulating the database tables: `DataBase`, `NC_KeyManager`, `SQL`, and `Row`. These classes provide a wrapper around ODBC functionality so that you can issue queries to the database.

> **Tip:**
> As an alternative, consider using the Net.Commerce object model, which eliminates the need to use SQL statements in most cases. For details, see "Appendix G, Net.Commerce Object Model" on page 675.

# The DataBase Class

When you write a command or overridable function, the system will automatically create a DataBase object in the environment to which you can connect. This object derives from the DataBase class (note the uppercase 'B' in its name). The following are the functions that you can use:

```
const String& getName(void);
const String& getUser(void);
const String& getPasswd(void);
String getSQLState(void);
int ReportError(void);
SQLHENV Get_henv(void);
SQLHDBC Get_hdbc(void);

NC_KeyManager* getKeyManager(void);
```

- The getName function returns the name of the database.

- The getUser function returns the user under which the connection was made.

- The getPasswd function returns the database password.

- The getSQLState function returns the last SQL state that was generated.

- The ReportError function outputs an error message to the log.

- The Get_henv function returns the ODBC environment handle.

- The Get_hdbc function returns the ODBC database handle.

- The getKeyManager function returns the key manager for the database.

**Note:**
Although this class contains other functions, those that are not listed above are not supported. Most importantly, do not use the functions that create a new database connection or that commit or roll back the database. The Net.Commerce system is responsible for these actions.

*Header File:*

WIN  \IBM\NetCommerce3\adt\include\database\nc_dbc.h
AIX  /usr/lpp/NetCommerce3/adt/include/database/nc_dbc.h

# The NC_KeyManager Class

The key manager maintains primary keys for tables that have been registered in the KEYS table. You can obtain the values for primary keys by calling the GetNextKey function in the NC_KeyManager class. Do not use any other function to add primary keys to the system. If you code your SQL statements yourself, this is important to remember. If you use the object model discussed in "Appendix G, Net.Commerce Object Model" on page 675, this is done automatically for you.

```
long GetNextKey(const String& TableName);
```

# The SQL Class

After you have a `DataBase` object, you can issue SQL statements using the `SQL` class. You can use any of the following functions:

```
SQL(DataBase& db, const String& SQLStatement);
int getColCount(void);
int getNextRow(Row& row);
int getSQLrc(void);
String getSQLState(void);
int getError(String& x);
int ReportError(void);
```

- The constructor takes a database connection and a string that contains the SQL statement. Be aware that the maximum length of the SQL statement is 4K and that the constructor does not check this length.

- The `getColCount` function returns the number of columns in each row that result from the SQL statement.

- The `getNextRow` function retrieves the next row of data and returns an error code, as defined in the next section.

- The `getSQLrc` function returns the current error code.

- The `getSQLState` function returns the standard ODBC SQL state after an operation.

- The `getError` function returns the same value as the `getSQLrc` function and initializes the String with the ODBC error string.

- The `ReportError` function returns the same value as the `getSQLrc` function and prints to the 'error' stream the ODBC error string

**Note:**
Although this class contains other functions, only those that are listed above are supported.

### Header File:

**WIN**   `\IBM\NetCommerce3\adt\include\database\nc_sql.h`
**AIX**   `/usr/lpp/NetCommerce3/adt/include/database/nc_sql.h`

# The Row Class

After you issue an SQL statement, you can retrieve rows using the `Row` class. You can retrieve the type and value of a column through a 1-based index. This means that if you select two columns, the first column listed in the SQL statement corresponds to column 1 in the row returned, the second one corresponds to column 2, and so on.

```
Row();
void operator=(const Row& rhs);
String getColName(int ColNumber);
String getCol(int ColNumber);
String getCol(const String& ColName);
```

```
int getColType(int ColNumber);
int getColType(const String& ColName);
bool IsNull(int ColNumber);
bool IsNull(const String& ColName);
```

The types used are constants that are defined in the ODBC standard, as follows:

SQL_NO_TYPE, SQL_BIGINT, SQL_BINARY, SQL_BIT, SQL_CHAR, SQL_DATE, SQL_DECIMAL, SQL_DOUBLE, SQL_FLOAT, SQL_INTEGER, SQL_LONGVARBINARY, SQL_LONGVARCHAR, SQL_NUMERIC, SQL_REAL, SQL_SMALLINT, SQL_TIME, SQL_TIMESTAMP, SQL_TINYINT, SQL_VARBINARY, SQL_VARCHAR

### Header File:

**WIN** \IBM\NetCommerce3\adt\include\database\nc_row.h

**AIX** /usr/lpp/NetCommerce3/adt/include/database/nc_row.h

# Chapter 11, Net.Commerce Programming Conventions

This chapter describes the programming conventions you should follow when creating new commands and overridable functions. It is important that you understand these conventions before you begin to write, as a command or overridable function that is not coded properly can bring down the entire Net.Commerce system. Watch particularly for memory leaks, which accumulate each time your command or function is called and can eventually lead to a system problem that is difficult to diagnose.

This chapter covers the following programming conventions:

- General Conventions
- Using Booleans
- Using New and Delete Operators
- Using the Tracing Facilities
- Handling Exceptions
- Handling a Successful Return
- Handling Input and Output Parameters
- Checking a Command's Input Parameters
- Retrieving Objects from the Environment
- Calling an Overridable Function
- Invoking a Command
- Interacting with the Database
- Setting Up the Implementation File
- Compiling

# General Conventions

When writing a command or overridable function, ensure that you follow these general standards:

- Never commit or roll back the Net.Commerce database from within a command or overridable function. The Net.Commerce system is responsible for managing the commit scope of transactions.

- Do not use const objects for anything other than const access.

- Do not change the type of objects that are defined as const.

- If your overridable function uses the calling command ID, make sure that you do not use it for any processing. It should be used only during the test phase; for example, to print messages for debugging purposes.

- When you register your command or overridable function in the database, ensure that you specify the DLL or shared library either as a full path (under Windows NT) or as a path relative to the directory specified by your LIBPATH variable (under AIX).

- When accessing the database tables, use only the ODBC database classes or the new object model provided in Net.Commerce. *Do not* use embedded or static SQL, and do not use native database access or native ODBC. For more information, see "Interacting with the Database" on page 340.

- If you are creating an overridable function, respect the semantics of the task to which it is to be assigned. Do not insert, update, or delete records in the database that the task was not designed to handle.

- Ensure that you use a unique name for each new command or overridable function that you create. The tracing facilities provided by Net.Commerce can help you verify that a command or overridable function is called properly. For more information about the tracing facilities, see "Using the Tracing Facilities" on page 324.

- Ensure that all classes that you create are derived (directly or indirectly) from the NC_Void class, which is the base class from which all the default Net.Commerce classes derive. This class is empty and defines only a virtual destructor.

- Ensure that you derive classes for new commands or overridable functions from only the NC_Void (see the previous note), NC_Object, NC_Command, and NC_OverridableFunction classes.

- Do not create new classes for adding to the List- and Hash Table-related classes; these classes must be used as is.

# Using Booleans

The system makes heavy use of bool as a type. Since bool is not yet available on all the platforms, the system currently maps it to an int. Therefore, ensure that your boolean expressions are always complete.

Here is an example:

```
bool f(int i)
{
   return i > 0; // May cause problems with some compilers.
   return (i > 0) ? true : false; // Will work always.
}
void f(bool b)
{
   if (b) // May cause problems with some compilers.
{
   }
   if (b == true) // Will always work.
   {
}
```

# Using New and Delete Operators

Because the system is composed of DLLs or shared libraries, you must be careful when constructing an object in one DLL and destroying it in another. Many compilers provide different versions of their memory allocation subsystems for debug and non-debug builds. It is therefore possible for you to create an object in your DLL that is compiled in debug mode, and have the Net.Commerce system, which was compiled in release mode, destroy that object.

To avoid this problem, the classes that you define must override the new and delete operators using non-inlined functions, as follows:

*X.h*

```
class __DLL_XXX__ X : public NC_Void
{
   public:
      void* operator new (size_t tSize);
      void operator delete(void* p );

      // .... the remainder of the class

};
```

*X.cpp*

```
void* X::operator new (size_t tSize) { return ::operator new (tSize); }
void X::operator delete(void* p ) { ::operator delete(p ); }
```

Normally when you write commands or overridable functions, you will not need header files. However, you may need to create some supporting classes of your own that you will use in conjunction with the default Net.Commerce classes. In either case, ensure that you overload new and delete operators, and that if you use a header file, you do not include these functions inline.

# Using the Tracing Facilities

The Net.Commerce system provides compile-time tracers that allow you to debug your commands or overridable functions or to add run-time comments that will print to your log file or console. Tracers are a type of streamer, and are enabled or disabled at compile time. They provide a convenient way for you to add trace statements that can be removed automatically by the compiler, as opposed to your having to either delete the traditional `cout` lines or comment them out.

To define a tracer, add the following code to the appropriate CPP file:

```
#ifdef __MY_TRACE__
   typedef TraceYes Trace;
#else
   typedef TraceNo Trace;
#endif
static Trace trace("MY_TRACE ("__FILE__")");
```

> **Note:**
> Ensure that you define a tracer statically in the file and that you assign it a name. Streamer output is redirected to the same destination, so if you create several related classes, you can create several static tracers for each file, and have them share the same compiler flag (`__MY_TRACE__`) and the same name (`"MY_TRACE"`).

You can use the tracer anywhere in the file in which it has been defined. To enable tracing, add the flag _MY_TRACE_ to your make file. To disable it, remove this flag from the make file. The trace code will be compiled out. An object of type `TraceYes` will enable tracing, while an object of type `TraceNo` will disable tracing. For a quick check, you can also add the `#define__MY_TRACE__` statement just before the code above. Remember to remove it when you compile the command or overridable function for production.

Tracers also provide monitors to track the depth of function calls. If you want to trace a particular function call, you can use the following facilities:

```
void SomeClass::SomeMethod(void)
{
   Trace::Tracer T("SomeMethod", "SomeClass");
   trace  << indent << "This is a trace message."  << endl;
   debug  << indent << "This is a debug message."  << endl;
   status << indent << "This is a status message." << endl;
   error  << indent << "This is an error message." << endl;
}
```

When the `Tracer` function is called, it will print a banner in the log file and increment the indent count. When the function exits, the count is decremented. The `indent` function will always reflect the current value of the indent count.

# Handling Exceptions

For each command or overridable function that you create, you must determine how it will handle any exceptions that it encounters, in order to ensure that it returns the appropriate parameters to the system. (For example, a command may encounter a missing required input parameter, or a function may encounter a situation such as a product being out of stock.) There are three ways to handle an exception:

- Set an exception task to handle the error
- Let the system handle the error
- Let the command or overridable function handle the error

Each method is described below.

# Setting an Exception Task to Handle the Error

When an error occurs because a shopper fails to provide information that is a mandatory input parameter or enters an invalid value, you should set an exception task. Doing so allows you to provide a customized and meaningful error message. For example, if a shopper does not enter a logon ID when attempting to register (the logon ID is a mandatory input parameter for the RegisterNew command), you could set an exception task that displays an error page indicating the missing parameter, along with an input field where the shopper can resubmit the information. If you had returned false (let the system handle the error), the generic system error page that displays in the browser would not provide the shopper with a sufficient explanation of the problem.

In their default implementation, exception tasks call the TaskDisplay_1.0(IBM,NC) overridable function, which executes a Net.Data macro to display an error message to the shopper. The function uses the reference number of the calling task and the merchant reference number as the index to retrieve from the MACROS table the name of the Net.Data macro to execute. Unless you do not plan to call a Net.Data macro (for example, if you want to code the resulting Web page in another language, such as Java or C++), it is advisable to reuse the TaskDisplay_1.0(IBM,NC) overridable function to reduce redundant coding.

> **Note:**
> When an exception task is set, the database is also rolled back. For example, if a command calls three overridable functions and the third overridable function fails and returns false, the database changes made by the first two overridable functions will also be rolled back.

To set an exception task, you can use the built-in `SetErrorHandler` function. This function, which is from the `Misc` class, adds the parameters to the `NC_Environment` object that are required by the command manager to call the overridable function for the task and merchant reference number specified. You call the `SetErrorHandler` function as follows:

```
return Misc::SetErrorHandler(Env, "TaskName", MerchantRefNum,
                   "ErrorCode", "ParamName");
```

The values of the parameters are as follows:

`TaskName`
 A variable that stores the name of the exception task to be set.

`MerchantRefNum`
 A variable that stores the reference number of the merchant whose overridable function is to be called. To call the mall version of the overridable function, use the constant `_STR_EMPTY_` for the value of the merchant reference number.

`ErrorCode`
> The error code returned by the overridable function.

`ParamName`
> The name of the parameter to be used by the macro that will be called to display the error message.

Using the `SetErrorHandler` function is equivalent to the following:

```
Env.Add(NC_Environment::_VAR_HandlerTask, TaskName);
Env.Add(NC_Environment::_VAR_Merchant, MerchantRefNum);
Env.Add(NC_Environment::_VAR_ErrorCode, ErrorCode);
Env.Add(NC_Environment::_VAR_Field, ParamName);
return false;
```

> **Note:**
> The code above is shown for illustrative purposes only: it should not be used to set an exception task.

## Passing Extra Parameters

You can pass extra parameters to the macro that will display the error page (for example, an error code that will be used by the macro to display the appropriate error message) by passing to the `NC_Environment` object an `NVPHash` object that contains the parameters, as follows:

```
NVPHash* NVP = (NVPHash*)
Env.Seek(NC_Environment::_VAR_Macro_NVPHash);
if (NVP == NULL)
{
   NVP = new NVPHash;
   Env.Add(NC_Environment::_VAR_Macro_NVPHash, (NC_Void*) NVP);
}
NVP->Add("param1", "value1");
```

where `param1` is the name portion and `value1` is the value portion of a name-value pair to be received by the macro.

> **Notes:**
> - You must register the exception task in the database before you can test it. For information on registering tasks, see "Registering a Task" on page 474. You must also create the Net.Data macro that will display the Web page to the shopper and assign it to your exception task. For information on writing Net.Data macros, see "Chapter 7, A Net.Data Tutorial" on page 169. To assign the macro to its task, see "Registering and Assigning a Net.Data Macro to its Task" on page 478.
> - Ensure that you do not overwrite an **NVPHash** object that already exists in the environment.

## Letting the System Handle the Error

If a command or overridable function fails due to a system problem (for example, the name of a mandatory input parameter was typed incorrectly in the macro by the developer or the system was not set up properly), you should return a false value to the caller and output an error message to the log. This is the default error-handling implementation, which will display a generic static HTML page in the browser along with a message in the log. Because shoppers typically will not and should not see these pages (they are not a result of a shopper error), they can be used as a temporary way to handle the error, until it can be resolved.

If the false value is returned when a command is checking its input parameters (from its `CheckParameters` function), the command manager will invoke the default system error page `cmdinc.html`. This page indicates that the calling command syntax is not correct.

If the false value is returned during the processing of the command or overridable function (from its `Process` function), the command manager will invoke the system error page `cmdexe.html`, which indicates that the calling command could not execute or complete. The system will also roll back all database changes made by the command.

The system error pages can be customized for your store. For information on how to customize them, see "Modifying System Error Pages" on page 234.

## Letting the Command or Overridable Function Handle the Error

You can also handle an exception encountered by a command or overridable function by hard-coding the HTTP response directly in the command or function and then throwing the `&_ERR_CMD_ERR_HANDLED` exception. (Ensure that you throw the address of the object, not the object itself.) You would generally use this method as a temporary solution during the testing phase, or in cases when you want to ensure the error page is never overwritten by another merchant.

The HTTP response can contain any information that is valid within an ASCII HTTP document; for example, HTML, JavaScript, VRML, or a redirection header. You can overwrite the contents of the HTTP document, or append information to it as shown in the following example:

```
String& Doc = Req.getDocument();
Doc << "My error X occurred..." << endl;
throw &_ERR_CMD_ERR_HANDLED;
```

After the `&_ERR_CMD_ERR_HANDLED` exception is thrown, the calling command must then propagate the state to the command manager by re-throwing the exception. When the exception is caught, the command manager will send the contents of the HTTP response back to the browser.

This exception-handling method can also be used in cases where you want to bypass error-handling performed by the command manager.

## Handling a Successful Return

When your command or overridable function successfully completes, you need to determine how it will handle the successful return. The following describes how to handle a successful return in each case.

# For Commands

There are four ways that a command can handle a successful return, depending on its nature:

- Set a view task (for display commands)

- Hard-code an HTTP response (for display commands)

- Pass the flow of execution to another URL (for process commands)

- Redirect to another command and pass to it the current input parameters (for process commands)

These methods are described below.

## Setting a View Task

If you have created a display command (which will display a Web page to the shopper indicating that the command successfully completed), typically you set a view task. All the default display commands, which display a store page in their final step of execution, set view tasks. All the default view tasks, except the CAT_DSP and PROD_DSP view tasks, call the TaskDisplay_1.0 (IBM,NC) overridable function, which determines from the database the file name of the macro to run. For example, the InterestItemDisplay command in its last step of execution sets the SHOPCART_DSP view task, which calls the TaskDisplay_1.0 (IBM,NC) overridable function. This function uses the reference number of the SHOPCART_DSP view task and the merchant reference number as the index to retrieve from the MACROS table the name of the Net.Data macro to execute, which by default is `shopcart.d2w`.

The CAT_DSP and PROD_DSP view tasks, which display category and product pages, respectively, call the MacroDisplay_1.0 (IBM,NC) overridable function. This function executes the `%HTML_REPORT` section of the macro whose file name is currently stored in the `_VAR_HandlerName` parameter in the `NC_Environment` object.

Unless you do not plan to call a Net.Data macro (for example, if you want to code the resulting Web page in another language, such as Java or C++), it is advisable to also use the TaskDisplay_1.0(IBM,NC) or MacroDisplay_1.0(IBM,NC) overridable function to reduce redundant coding.

> **Note:**
> When a view task is set, the database is also committed.

Setting a view task is very similar to setting an exception task; the only difference being that you return a true value instead of a false value. You use the built-in `SetView` function. This function, which is from the `Misc` class, adds the parameters to the `NC_Environment` object that are required by the command manager to call the overridable function for the task and merchant reference number specified. You must call the `SetView` function as follows:

```
Misc::SetView(Env, TaskName, MerchantRefNum, HandlerName);
return true;
```

> **Note:**
> You must explicitly return a true value because in its default implementation, the `SetView` function returns false.

The values of each parameter are as follows:

TaskName

    A variable that stores the name of the exception task to be set.

MerchantRefNum

    A variable that stores the reference number of the merchant whose overridable function is to be called. To call the mall version of the overridable function, use the variable _STR_EMPTY_ for the value of the merchant reference number.

HandlerName

    The filename of the macro to be executed. This parameter is required only for the PROD_DSP or CAT_DSP view tasks.

Using the SetView function is equivalent to the following:

```
Env.Add(NC_Environment::_VAR_HandlerTask, TaskName );
Env.Add(NC_Environment::_VAR_Merchant, MerchantRefNum);
Env.Add(NC_Environment::_VAR_HandleName, HandlerName);
return true;
```

> **Note:**
> The code above is shown for illustrative purposes only: it should not be used to set a view task.

### Passing Extra Parameters

To pass extra parameters to the macro that will display the store page (for example, a database variable that will be used by a command in the macro), pass to the NC_Environment object an NVPHash object that contains the parameters, as follows:

```
NVPHash* NVP = (NVPHash*)
Env.Seek(NC_Environment::_VAR_Macro_NVPHash);
if (NVP == NULL)
{
  NVP = new NVPHash;
  Env.Add(NC_Environment::_VAR_Macro_NVPHash, (NC_Void*) NVP);
}
NVP->Add("param1", "value1");
```

where param1 is the name portion and value1 is the value portion of a name-value pair to be received by the macro.

> **Note:**
> After you set the view task, you must register it in the database before you can test it. For information on registering tasks, see "Registering a Task" on page 474 You must also create the Net.Data macro that will display the Web page to the shopper, and assign it to your new view task. For information on writing Net.Data macros, see "Chapter 7, A Net.Data Tutorial" on page 169. To assign the macro to its task, see "Registering and Assigning a Net.Data Macro to its Task" on page 478.

## Hard-Coding an HTTP Response

If you do not want to use Net.Data to display a Web page to the shopper when your display command successfully completes, you can hard-code the HTTP response directly in the command and return a true value to the system. The HTTP response can contain any information that is valid within an ASCII HTTP document; for example, HTML, JavaScript, or a redirection header. You can overwrite the contents of the HTTP document, or append information. The following is an example of overwriting the current HTTP document:

```
String& Doc = Req.getDocument();
Doc.Clean();
Doc << "<H1>HELLO WORLD</H1>" << endl;
return true;
```

## Setting a Redirection URL

If you have created a process command and a URL was passed to the command as a required parameter, you can pass the flow of execution to that URL. To do this, you need to obtain the following information:

- The original request that contains all the incoming name-value pairs.

- The name of the name-value pair in the `HttpRequest` object that contains the URL to which you want to redirect. By convention, the name `url` is used.

- The name-value pairs that you want to add to the redirection URL or override the existing name-value pairs.

The following are the steps required to set a redirection URL:

1. First, declare an `NVPHash` object for storing the name-value pairs that you want to pass with the redirection URL as part of the HTTP response, as follows:

   ```
   NVPHash NVP;
   ```

2. Do one or both of the following:

   - Add new name-value pairs to the `NVPHash` object. For example:
     ```
     static const StringWithOwnership MVP_param1 ("param1");
     NVP.Add(MVP_param1, "<val1>");
     ```
     where `<val1>` is the value of the parameter `MVP_param1`.

   - Override current (incoming) name-value pairs. For example, to hide a password that you do not want to redirect, store its value in the `NVPHash` object as an empty string, as follows:
     ```
     const StringWithOwnership MVP_password("password");
     NVP.Add(MVP_password, _STR_EMPTY_);
     ```

3. To set the redirection URL, use the `Redirect` function in the `Res` parameter, as follows:

   ```
   Res.Redirect(Req, "url", NVP);
   ```

   where `Req` contains the contents of the original HTTP Request, `url` is the name of the parameter that contains the return URL, and `NVP` contains the overriding name-value pairs.

   The `Redirect` function combines the name-value pairs from the three specified parameters (the original request, the overriding name-value pairs, and the return URL). The name-value pairs of each parameter override or eliminate previous name-value pairs. For example, consider the following: the current name-value pairs in the `Req` parameter are: `a=1, a=2, b=3, c=4, pwd=hello, url=/cgi-bin/ncommerce3/Xyz?e=7&a=&d=8`, the new name-value pairs stored in the `NVPHash` object `NewNVPs` are: `c=5, d=6, pwd=`, and the `url` parameter contains the return URL. When the `Redirect` function is called, it will do the following:

a) Retrieve the current name-value pairs from the `Req` parameter:: `a=1, a=2, b=3, c=4, pwd=hello, url=/cgi-bin/ncommerce3/Xyz?e=7&a=&d=8`

b) Remove the `url` parameter from the name-value pairs: `a=1, a=2, b=3, c=4, pwd=hello`

c) Merge the name-value pairs contained in `NewNVPs` with the current name-value pairs to yield the following results: `a=1, a=2, b=3, c=5, d=6`. (`d=6` was added, `c=4` was replaced with `c=5`, `pwd=hello` was removed.)

d) Merge the name-value pairs contained in `UrlFieldd` with the current name-value pairs to yield the following results: `b=3, c=5, d=8, e=7`. (all name-value pairs containing a name of "a" were removed, `e=7` was added, and `d=6` was replaced with `d=8`.

## Redirecting to Another Command

If you have created a process command and you want to redirect to another command, but the command to which you want to redirect is not contained in the `url` parameter that is associated with the process command, you can use the `SetLocation` function to call the command and pass to it the current input parameters. To use the `SetLocation` function, you must do the following in the `Process` function of your class:

1. Declare a String variable that stores all the parameters that are currently in the `Req` parameter (which was passed to the command), using the `getQUERY_STRING` function in the `Req` class, as follows:

   ```
   String string_name = Req.getQUERY_STRING();
   ```

   where `string_name` is the name of the string that contains the current input parameters.

2. Create a String variable that stores the fully qualified URL of the command to which you want to pass the current parameters, as follows:

   ```
   StringWithOwnership variable_name("command_URL");
   ```

   where `variable_name` is the name you assigned to the string that contains the command's URL, and `command_URL` is the fully qualified URL for the command.

3. Append the string that stores the current parameters to the string that stores the command URL, as follows:

   ```
   variable_name << string_name;
   ```

   where `variable_name` is the name you assigned to the string that contains the command's URL, and `string_name` is the name of the string containing the current input parameters.

4.  Call the `setLocation` function of the `Res` class to redirect to the command and enable it for SSL, as follows:

    ```
    Res.setLocation(variable_name, true);
    ```

    where `variable_name` is the name you assigned to the string that contains the command's URL.

For more information about the `setLocation` function and its variations, see "The HttpResponse Class" on page 306.

> **Note:**
> The command to which you redirect will always be called using the GET method, rather than the POST method. The system automatically encrypts all name-value pairs in the redirection URL, to avoid a Netscape browser (version 4.0 and higher) problem that causes a redirection originating from a POST method to be erroneously redirected as a GET method. This problem would cause the redirected URL to appear in the Web server log and the Location window of the browser.

The following is an example of a command that calls the RegisterNew command and passes to it the current input parameters:

```
String currentParams = Req.getQUERY_STRING();
StringWithOwnership commandURL("/cgi-bin/ncommerce3/RegisterNew");
commandURL << currentParams;
Res.setLocation(commandURL, true);
```

## For Overridable Functions

There are two ways that an overridable function can handle a successful return, depending on its nature:

*   Return a true value to the calling command and, if applicable, variables to the `NC_Environment` object (if it is implementing a process task)

*   Return an HTTP document to the system (if it is implementing a view or exception task). All of the supplied overridable functions execute Net.Data macros.

# Handling Input and Output Parameters

You handle input and output parameters for an overridable function and command using the `Process` function of the class and the `CheckParameters` function (for commands only). These functions contain the following objects, which are passed to them as parameters:

## HttpRequest

This object is a constant that contains the full information that was passed by the Web server to the Net.Commerce server. Use this object to check the cookies, the name value pairs, `PATH_INFO`, and so on. This parameter contains all the variables available through the CGI protocol. It is passed unchanged through all the commands and overridable functions that are called. For more information, see "The HttpRequest Class" on page 304.

# HttpResponse

This object is passed through all the commands and overridable functions that are called, but each command or overridable function can also modify the object. The object is returned to the Web browser when the calling command returns. Use this object to set cookies, redirection headers, or a full text HTTP document (HTML, VRML, Scripting, and so on). When you implement a process task, you normally do not set the HTTP document. For more information, see "The HttpResponse Class" on page 306.

# NC_Environment

This object is unique within a transaction and serves as a communication means between the various commands and overridable functions. For example, you can use it to communicate from a command to an overridable function and back. Input and output parameters defined by tasks are passed through this variable. The following example shows the Process function of an overridable function that is assigned to the GET_BASE_UNIT_PRC process task, for a store whose products each cost $1.00.

```
bool Process(const HttpRequest& Req, HttpResponse& Res,
NC_Environment& Env)
{
  // Retrieve input parameters and store them in constant local
  // variables
  const String& ProductRefNum = (const String&)
                               *Env.Seek("PRODUCT_REF_NUM");
  const String& Currency = (const String&)*Env.Seek("CURRENCY" );

  // Retrieve output parameters
  String& ProductPrice = (String&)*Env.Seek("PRODUCT_PRICE" );

  // Set the price equal to 1
  ProductPrice = 1;

  // If successful, return true
  return true;
}
```

The output parameters are passed to the command or overridable function by referencing the NC_Environment object. This concept is similar to the function having the following signature:

```
bool Process(const HttpRequest& Req, HttpResponse& Res,
          const String& ProductRefNum, const String& Currency,
          String& ProductPrice);
```

For more information about the NC_Environment object, see "The NC_Environment Class" on page 313.

> **Note:**
> Although all variables used are represented as Strings, they still have an underlying type. In this example, the type is a floating point number. If you set the price to "abc", an error will occur when the command or overridable function attempts to use the value.

# Checking a Command's Input Parameters

When checking the required input parameters for a command, you need only check that they exist and that they contain a value. The optional parameters may exist in the Req parameter but not contain a value, or they may simply not be present. You typically first specify the parameter to be looked up and specify whether it is optional or not, using the CheckFieldExistence function from the Misc class. If no parameter is found, or if a parameter is found that is mandatory but contains no value, you must handle the error in the usual ways: either by returning false (in which case a command structure failure message will be displayed in the browser), by hard-coding the HTTP response in the CheckParameters function, or by setting an exception task.

If the missing or empty parameter is a result of an incorrectly coded macro (for example, the name of the input parameter was typed incorrectly in the macro by the developer) or another type of system error occurred, you should return false to the system and output an error message to the log.

The following is an example of returning false and outputting an error message to the log, when the value of a required input parameter is missing or empty:

```
// The name of the name-value pair that you are searching for.
static const StringWithOwnership NVP_Name("xxx");

// A local variable to store the value of the retrieved name-value pair
// so that the Process function can later access the value.
String _LocalVar;

// If the value of the input parameter is missing or empty, return false
// and output an error message to the log.
if (Misc::CheckFieldExistence(Req, NVP_Name, _LocalVar, false) ==
    false)
  return false;
if (_LocalVar.IsLong() == false)
  {
  error << indent;
  error.nls(&_ERR_CMD_INVALID_PARAM, NVP_Name.c_str()) << endl;
  return false;
  }
```

The following parameters are passed to this function:

Req
> Contains the content of the HTTP request so that the name-value pair can be retrieved.

NVP_Name
> The name of the parameter to be checked.

LocalVar
> The local variable that stores the value of the parameter.

false
> A flag indicating whether or not the parameter is optional.

Setting exception tasks is more appropriate for errors that are caused by shoppers, because you can then provide the shoppers with meaningful explanations of their errors. If a shopper fails to provide information that is a mandatory input parameter for a command (for example, the shopper did not submit a logon ID on a registration form), you should set an exception task. If you return false, the generic system error page that appears will not give the shopper a sufficient explanation of the problem. When the command requires a merchant reference number to set an exception task but no value is available, you can use the variable _STR_EMPTY_.

The following is an example of setting an exception task if a parameter is not found or if a mandatory parameter does not contain a value. If any other error occurs, the CheckParameters function returns false, and the command manager returns the static HTML error page to the browser. This example only performs a syntax check; it does not interpret the value retrieved from each parameter.

```
// Local variable that stores the name of the exception task to be set.
static const StringWithOwnership ErrorTask("SAMPLE_XYZ_ERR");

// An error code that indicates that the parameter is missing.  The
// error code by default is "190".
static const StringWithOwnership _ERR_CODE_MISSING_PARAM("190");

// The name of the name-value pair that you are searching for.
static const StringWithOwnership NVP_Name("xxx");

// A local variable to store the value of the retrieved name-value pair
// so that the Process function can later access the value.
String _LocalVar;

// Use the CheckFieldExistence function from the Misc class to check
// each parameter in the HTTP request.
if (Misc::CheckFieldExistence(Req, Env, ErrorTask, _STR_EMPTY_,
                              _ERR_CODE_MISSING_PARAM, NVP_Name,
                              _LocalVar, false) == false)

   return false;

// If the value of the input parameter is empty or missing, set the
// exception task and output an error message to the log.
if (_LocalVar.IsLong() == false)
   {
   error << indent;
   error.nls(&_ERR_CMD_INVALID_PARAM,NVP_Name.c_str()) << endl;
   return Misc::SetErrorHandler(Env, ErrorTask, _STR_EMPTY_,
                                _ERR_CODE_MISSING_PARAM, NVP_Name);
```

The following parameters are passed to the CheckFieldExistence function:

Req
> Contains the content of the HTTP request so that the name-value pair can be retrieved.

Env
> For setting the exception task.

ErrorTask
> The variable containing the name of the exception task that will handle the error when no parameter is found or when a mandatory parameter contains no value.

_STR_EMPTY_
>    The merchant reference number required for invoking the exception task, which in
>    most cases for `CheckParameters` will not contain a value because the merchant
>    reference number will not have been retrieved yet. Here, the mall version of the task is
>    invoked.

_ERR_CODE_MISSING_PARAM
>    The variable containing the error code `190` to be used by the exception task.

NVP_Name
>    The name of the parameter to be checked.

LocalVar
>    The variable (previously declared) that will store the value of the parameter.

false
>    A flag indicating whether or not the parameter is optional.

To retrieve the value of a specific name-value pair in the `HttpRequest` object, use the following
example:

```
NameValuePair* NVP = Req.getNVPs().Get(&NVP_Name);

if (NVP == NULL || NVP->getValue().IsEmpty() == true)
  // Output an error message to the log.
  {
  error << indent; error.nls(&_ERR_CMD_MISSING_PARAM,
                             NVP_Name.c_str()) << endl;

  // Since no exception task was set, the commmand manager will invoke
  // the  default static HTML page to indicate a parameter failure.
  return false;

  }

_LocalVar = NVP->getValue();
```

If you need to iterate through all the name-value pairs, use the following logic (this function
applies to most containers in Net.Commerce):

```
NameValuePairMap::Iterator I = &Req.getNVPs().getIterator();
for (I.Begin(); I.getElement() != NULL; I.getNextElement())
  {
  // Dereferencing an iterator for NameValuePairMap.
  String NVP_Name = (*I)->getName();

  // Yields a NameValuePair*.
  String NVP_Value = (*I)->getValue();
  // Process the entry...
  }
```

In cases where you want to check multiple name-value pairs with the same name, use the
following logic. This code iterates through ten name-value pairs that have the same name, to
retrieve their values. The eleventh copy will result in an error.

```
NameValuePairMap::Iterator I2(&Req.getNVPs());
I.Begin();
```

```
I.Seek(&NVP_Name);

// If no parameter was found,
if (*I == NULL)
  // return false.
  return false;

int Counter=0;
while (*I != NULL && (*I)->getName() == NVP_Name)
  {
  if (++Counter > 10) // Retrieving the eleventh copy.
  return Misc::SetErrorHandler(Env, "MAX_ENTRIES", _STR_EMPTY_,
                              "1002", NVP_Name);
  String NVP_Value = (*I)->getValue(); //yields a NameValuePair*.
  // Process the entry...

  ++I;
  }
```

# Retrieving Objects from the Environment

The Env parameter (which is passed with the Process function in commands and overridable functions, and also with the CheckParameters function in commands) allows you to retrieve objects from the environment that are required for your command or overridable function.

You can retrieve from the environment the value of the Parameters variable, which is the part of the PATH_INFO variable that contains the parameters after the command name in a URL. For example, say the PATH_INFO variable contains the following command: /MyCommand/p1/ p2?a=1&b=2&c=3, the value of the Parameters variable is /p1/p2. To retrieve the value of the Parameters variable from the Env parameter, use the following code:

```
String& P = (const String&)*Misc::CheckEnvironmentVariable(Env,
                              C_Environment::_VAR_Parameters);
```

To retrieve environment variables and objects from the NC_Environment object, such as the current shopper or an overridable function, use the CheckEnvironmentVariable function. If the variable or object is not found, this function will send a message to the log and throw the _ERR_CMD_ERR_BAD_SYSTEM exception. This exception indicates a system failure, which should be thrown when mandatory objects, such as overridable functions, are not found in the environment. (Remember to always throw the address, not the object itself.) The following is an example of retrieving the current shopper from the environment:

```
User& U = (User&) *Misc::CheckEnvironmentVariable(Env,
                       NC_Environment::_VAR_Shopper);
```

You can also retrieve the current user of the current database connection, as follows:

```
DataBase& DB = (DataBase&)*Misc::CheckEnvironmentVariable(Env,
                          NC_Environment::_VAR_MainDatabase);
```

To retrieve an environment variable that may not exist (for example, it is optional) use the following construct:

```
SomeClass* X = (SomeClass*) Env.Seek("SOME_ENV_VARIABLE");
if (X != NULL)
{
    // Use X;
}
```

# Calling an Overridable Function

Many commands that you write will call one or more overridable functions to do some of its processing. Also, if your command performs a function that is common to multiple commands, you can write the function as a separate class and call it from all the commands, which reduces redundant coding.

You call an overridable function via a process task, which in turn calls the overridable function. The following example shows how to set the process task and also handle all possible error codes that can be returned by the overridable function when it encounters an exception condition:

```
const ErrorMsg_Cmd* Err;
Err = NC_OverridableFunctionManager::Call(Req, Res, Env, "<TaskName>",
                                          <MerchantRefNum>);

// If the error has already been handled by the overridable function,
if (Err == &_ERR_CMD_ERR_HANDLED)
{
    // Compose an error message,
    error << indent << "ERROR: <TaskName> called an overridable function
                        that generated its own error page." << endl;
    // and just propagate the error.
    throw Err;
}

// If the overridable function failed,
else if (Err == &_ERR_CMD_BAD_PROCESS_API)
{
    const String* ErrorHandler =
    Env.Seek(NC_Environment::_VAR_HandlerTask);
    if (ErrorHandler != NULL)
        error << indent << "ERROR: <TaskName> called an overridable
                            function that failed in its Process function."
                            << endl;
    else
        error << indent << "ERROR: <TaskName> called an overridable
                            function that set the exception task" << *X <<
                            endl;
    return false;
}

// If the system could not find an overridable function for the
// specified task,
else if (Err == &_ERR_CMD_API_NOT_FOUND)
```

```
{
    error << indent << "<TaskName> does not exist or does not map to any
                        overridable function" << endl;
    return false;
}

// Otherwise, return a false value to the calling command.
else if (Err != NULL)
{
    error << indent << "<TaskName> caused an error" << endl;
    return false;
}
return false;
```

where `<TaskName>` is a variable that stores the name of the process task to be set, and `<MerchantRefNum>` is the reference number of the merchant whose overridable function is to be called.

When you set a process task to call an overridable function, you must also handle the exception conditions that the overridable function may encounter. If the overridable function returns the `&_ERR_CMD_ERR_HANDLED` exception to the calling command, it indicates that the function handled the error by generating the appropriate HTTP response. In this case, your command only has to propagate the state to the command manager by re-throwing the exception. The command can output an error message to the log or perform some housekeeping, but the command must propagate the error state. When the error is caught, the command manager will send the contents of the HTTP response back to the browser.

If the overridable function returns either of the following errors, the command must handle the error in the usual ways that a command can handle an exception condition:

- `&_ERR_CMD_API_NOT_FOUND`, the system could not find an overridable function for the specified task.

- `&_ERR_CMD_BAD_PROCESS_API`, the `Process` function in the overridable function failed and either returned false or set an exception task. You can retrieve the exception task name from the `NC_Environment` object.

See "Handling Exceptions" on page 324 for information on how to handle exceptions encountered by a command.

# Invoking a Command

Although components, such as commands and overridable functions, cannot invoke each other directly by type, a command can call another command by name. For example, if you have created a new version of your command and you want to reuse your older version, you could do the following:

```
HttpRequest LocalReq = Req;
NC_RegistrationID ID("MyCompany", "MyProduct", "MyCmd", 1.0);
if (NC_CommandManager::Call(LocalReq, Res, Env, ID) != NULL)
                                            return false;
```

If the original command was to be replaced or modified (for example, to fix a defect), the new command would instantly benefit from these changes.

> **Note:**
> Ensure that you do not create cycles of commands: if command A invokes command B, which invokes command A again, you will have an infinite loop.

# Interacting with the Database

When your command or overridable function needs to interact with the database to perform a specific action, such as updating a shopper record or retrieving the price of a product, there are two ways to do this:

- Issue SQL statements
- Use the object model

## Issuing SQL Statements

If you want to use SQL statements when interacting with the database, you must use them in conjunction with the ODBC database classes (`DataBase`, `SQL`, and `Row`) supplied by the Net.Commerce system. For information about these classes and their public member functions, see "Database Classes" on page 317.

> **Note:**
> Do not use static or embedded SQL and do not use native database access or native ODBC.

The following are the steps required to issue an SQL statement using the ODBC classes:

### Step 1. Connect to the Database

Before you can issue an SQL statement, you need to connect to the current database. The Net.Commerce system will automatically set up a database object in the environment for you to use. This database connection is opened at server initialization and closes during the server shutdown. To access the database connection, use the following code:

```
DataBase* DB = (DataBase*) Env.Seek(NC_Environment::_VAR_Database);
```

### Step 2. Compose the Statement

Once you have a database connection, you are ready to issue your SQL statement. You create the statements using the `String` class. First, you declare a `String` variable and then allocate sufficient space to make your streaming efficient (that is, so you will not have to resize the string after each stream operation), as follows:

```
String Statement;
// Allocates a string large enough for a 1K SQL statement.
Statement.Resize(STRLEN_1K);
```

Use the standard streaming operators to compose your SQL statements.

Note that SQL requires that string data be enclosed in single quotes and that floating point values use a dot (.) as the decimal separator, regardless of the locale. Net.Commerce supplies two functions to accommodate these syntax requirements: sq, for SingleQuote, and nl, for NonLocale. The sq function ensures that a string is enclosed in the proper quotes, and the nl function ensures that the decimal separator in a floating point number appears as a dot, regardless of the locale. The following is an example of an SQL statement that uses the two functions:

```
String Data1("Paris's lights');
const char* Data2 = "The city's beautiful";
float Data3 = 5.6;
Statement << "INSERT INTO X VALUES (" << sq(Data1) << ", " << sq(Data2)
                                  << ", " << nl(Data3) << ")";
```

This SQL statement is syntactically correct, regardless of the locale, and is equivalent to the following:

```
INSERT INTO X VALUES ('Paris''s lights', 'The city''s beautiful', 5.6)
```

When generating SQL statements for the default tables, it is recommended that you minimize the use of native SQL statements by using the predefined variables in the classes of the object model, which map to the database tables and column names, and . Using native SQL statements binds you to the current database schema, which may change in future versions of Net.Commerce, and increases the risk of typing the table and column names incorrectly. Here is an example of using the predefined variables of the Merchant object:

```
Statement << "SELECT " << Merchant::_COL_CNTCT_LAST_NAME
          << ", " << Merchant::_COL_CNTCT_FIRST_NAME
          << ", " << Merchant::_COL_CNTCT_MAIL1
          << " FROM " << Merchant::_COL_TNAME;
          << " WHERE " << Merchant::_COL_REF_NUM << " = "
          << MerchantRefNum;
```

For information about the predefined variables in each object, refer to the corresponding header file in the following directory:

**WIN** \ibm\NetCommerce3\adt\include\objects\

**AIX** /usr/lpp/NetCommerce3/adt/include/objects/

For information about the interface of the object model, see "Appendix G, Net.Commerce Object Model" on page 675.

## Step 3. Execute the Statement

To execute the SQL statement, use the following code:

```
SQL Sql(*DB, Statement);
```

When this statement is executed, the results are stored in the Sql instance. Every time you want to run a new SQL query in the same Process function, a new SQL instance must be created to store the results.

Once the statement is executed, you can proceed to handle the data retrieved.  The following is an example of assigning the values of the columns retrieved in the previous SQL statement to Strings:

```
SQL Sql(*DB, Statement);
Row SqlRow;
int Count = 0;
for (_Error = Sql.getNextRow(SqlRow);
     _Error == ERR_DB_NO_ERROR;
     _Error = Sql.getNextRow(SqlRow)
   )
{
   ++Count;
   String LastName(SqlRow.getCol(1).Trim());
   String FirstName(SqlRow.getCol(2).Trim());
   String Mail(SqlRow.getCol(3).Trim());
}
```

## Step 4. Handle Database Errors

When you issue SQL statements, you also need to check the error codes.  The following is an example of using the two most common error codes:

```
// Basic error checking.
if (_Error != ERR_DB_NO_ERROR && _Error != ERR_DB_NO_DATA)
   {
      Sql.ReportError();
      return false;
   }
```

The error code ERR_DB_NO_DATA will be returned if an UPDATE or DELETE statement did not return successfully, and after the last row is retrieved.  If an UPDATE or DELETE statement did not return successfully, you must decide whether this represents an error for you.  If the error code was returned after the last row was retrieved, you cannot directly determine whether or not the statement returned a row; you must either count the rows yourself, as in the following example, or move the first retrieved row out of the loop and then test that row for an error.

To standardize error codes across different ODBC platforms, the Net.Commerce system maps SQL return codes and SQL states to the system's internal error codes.  The following are the internal error codes that are available for you to use:

```
const int ERR_DB_NO_ERROR = 0000;
const int ERR_DB_ROW_ALLOC =-1000;
const int ERR_DB_ROW_ALEADY_ALLOC =-1001;
const int ERR_DB_COL_RANGE =-1002;
const int ERR_DB_ALEADY_CONNECTED =-1003;
const int ERR_DB_ENV_ALLOC =-1004;
const int ERR_DB_CONNECT_ALLOC =-1005;
const int ERR_DB_CONNECT_FAIL =-1006;
const int ERR_DB_NOT_CONNECTED =-1007;
const int ERR_DB_COMMIT_FAIL =-1008;
```

```
const int ERR_DB_ROLLBACK_FAIL =-1009;
const int ERR_DB_SQL_ALLOC =-1010;
const int ERR_DB_FETCH_ON_UPDATE =-1011;
const int ERR_DB_NOT_PREPARED =-1012;
const int ERR_DB_NO_DATA =-1013;
const int ERR_DB_BAD_FETCH =-1014;
const int ERR_DB_PARMS =-1015;
const int ERR_DB_RECONNECT_FAILED =-1016;
const int ERR_DB_STR_TOO_LARGE =-1017;
const int ERR_DB_NOT_SET =-1018;
const int ERR_DB_PREPARE_FAILED =-1019;
const int ERR_DB_EXECUTE_FAILED =-1020;
const int ERR_DB_DESCRIBE_FAILED =-1021;
const int ERR_DB_COL_BIND_FAILED =-1022;
const int ERR_DB_NOT_AVAILABLE =-1023;

// The following error codes correspond to SQLSTATE:
const int ERR_DB_FEATURE =-1101;
const int ERR_DB_DATA_TRUNC =-1102;
const int ERR_DB_NULL_DATA =-1103;
const int ERR_DB_OUT_OF_RANGE =-1105;
const int ERR_DB_DATE_FORMAT =-1106;
const int ERR_DB_DIV_BY_ZERO =-1107;
const int ERR_DB_SYSTEM_FAIL =-1108;
const int ERR_DB_SQL_SYNTAX =-1109;
const int ERR_DB_UNDEF_COL =-1110;
const int ERR_DB_UNDEF_OBJ =-1111;
const int ERR_DB_DUPLICATE_ROW =-1112;
const int ERR_DB_NO_RC_FOUND =-7777;
```

If the values retrieved from the database were not as expected (for example, an integrity rule, such as the requirement that at least one merchant record exist in the database, is broken), you must throw a database exception, to indicate a database failure. The error message is displayed in the log. Here is an example:

```
if (Count == 0)
{
   error << indent << "ERROR : DB corruption: No merchant defined in the
                      database." << endl;
   throw &_ERR_CMD_ERR_BAD_DATABASE;
}
```

For more information about the error codes, refer to the following header file:

**WIN** \IBM\NetCommerce3\adt\include\database\database.pch

**AIX** /usr/lpp/NetCommerce3/adt/include/database/database.pch

# Using the Object Model

Net.Commerce provides an object model that you can use to manipulate the database as an alternative to using the ODBC classes and SQL statements. For information on how to use this object model, see "Appendix G, Net.Commerce Object Model" on page 675.

# Setting Up the Implementation File

You must write commands and overridable functions as inline C++ classes and include all the code in the CPP file. Commands and overridable functions are not referred to by type name directly. Every call is handled dynamically by the command or overridable function manager at run-time.

You do not need to create a header file for your commands or overridable functions in the CPP files. By not using header files, you ensure that you do not build dependencies between your components. A CPP file cannot contain a combination of commands and overridable functions classes in the same file; you must separate the two class types into at least two CPP files. You can, however, include multiple commands or overridable functions in the same file.

To access the standard Net.Commerce framework, ensure that you do the following:

- Include the following statement in the CPP file:

  ```
  #include "objects/objects.pch"
  ```

  The `objects.pch` precompiled header file contains all the Net.Commerce classes that you need in order to write commands and overridable functions.

- Include all the libraries that are stored in the `\bin` directory in your project.

- Define the project's include path as `\adt\include\`, which is the directory in which all the header files for the Net.Commerce classes are stored.

## Specifying a DLL or Shared Library

To specify whether your command or overridable function is stored in a DLL or shared library, it is recommended that you include the following constructs in your CPP file:

```
#if defined(WIN32)
   #define __EXPORT_MODE__ __declspec(dllexport) // this module must be
exported
#elif defined(AIX)
   #define __EXPORT_MODE__ // Under AIX, it does not matter
#endif
```

When the `__EXPORT_MODE__` flag is included in your class declaration line, the command or overridable function that is stored in a DLL will be exported properly.

The class declaration line for a command is as follows:

```
class __EXPORT_MODE__ ClassName : public NC_Command
```

The class declaration line for an overridable function is as follows:

```
class __EXPORT_MODE__ ClassName : public NC_OverridableFunction
```

In your makefile, you then need to define the flag (`-D__EXPORT_MODE__`).

# Compiling

You must compile your CPP file using the following compiler and release level:

- **WIN** Microsoft Visual C++ version 4.2

- **AIX** txlC++ version 4.1.x

When you compile your own DLL or shared library for your commands or overridable functions, ensure that you use make options that are compatible with the ones in the sample make file provided in the next section. Ensure that you are linking to the correct system DLLs or shared library. Most importantly, be careful with the threading flags. Net.Commerce is compiled in multithreaded mode and uses the multi-threaded version of the system libraries, so your DLLs or shared library should also be compiled in multi-threaded mode.

The compiler and linker flags are as follows:

## Windows NT

**Compiler:**
```
Debug: /Zi /Gm /Od /DEBUG
Release: /O2 /Og /Oi /Ot /Oy /Ob2 /Gs /Gf /Gy /G5
Common: cl /c /GX /MD /D_X86=1 /D_X86_ /D_CONSOLE /DWIN32
        /YX"objects/objects.pch" /Gi
```
**Linker:**
```
Debug : /DEBUG
Common: link /DLL /machine:IX86
```

## AIX

**Compiler:**
```
Debug: -g -w
Common: xlC_r -DAIX -qlistopt -qlist -qxref=full -c -D_BSD=43
```
**Linker:**
```
Common: /usr/lpp/xlC/bin/makeC++SharedLib_r -o -lld
```

**Note:**
Microsoft Visual C++ version 4.2 contains a bug that sometimes produces the following compiler error when you attempt to use templates with precompiled headers:

```
template_cmd.cpp(49) : fatal error C1001: INTERNAL COMPILER ERROR
(compiler file 'msc1.cpp', line 1089) Please choose the Technical
Support command on the Visual C++ Help menu, or open the Technical
Support help file for more information.
MAKE : fatal error U1077: 'cl' : return code '0x2' Stop.
NMAKE : fatal error U1077: 'c:\msdev\bin\NMAKE.EXE' : return code '0x2'
Stop.
```
To solve this problem, clean up your build and compile using the following command:

```
nmake -f makefile.nt cleanall
```

# Sample Makefiles (Windows NT Only)

Net.Commerce provides sample command and overridable function makefiles for the Microsoft Visual C++ version 4.2 compiler.  These files are located in the `\samples\cmds\` or `\samples\ofs\` directory on the CD, respectively.

To use either makefile, do the following:

- Change the `NC_ROOT` variable to the directory in which you installed Net.Commerce

- Change the name of `xxx_cmd.dll` (for commands) or `xxx_of.dll` (for overridable functions) to the name you have given to the DLL in which the command or overridable function resides.

- Use the skeleton CPP file for commands (described in "Understanding the Command Anatomy" on page 442), or the skeleton CPP file for overridable functions (described in "Understanding the Overridable Function Anatomy" on page 378), to create your commands or overridable functions.  Then, add each command or function to the makefile.

## Command Makefile

```
NC_ROOT             = c:\ibm\NetCommerce3

PCH                 = objects\objects.pch
INC                 = /I$(NC_ROOT)\adt\include
LIBS                = $(NC_ROOT)\bin\nc3_containers.lib \
                      $(NC_ROOT)\bin\nc3_messages.lib \
                      $(NC_ROOT)\bin\nc3_common.lib \
                      $(NC_ROOT)\bin\nc3_dbc.lib \
                      $(NC_ROOT)\bin\server_objs.lib

GCFLAGS             = /nologo /c /GX $(COMPILE_F) /MD /W1 /D_X86=1
                      / D_X86_ / /D_CONSOLE /DWIN32 $(INC) /YX"$(PCH)"
                      /Gi

GLFLAGS             = /nologo $(LINK_F) /DLL /machine:IX86

OBJS                = template_cmd.obj

debug:
  @nmake -f makefile.nt all "COMPILE_F=/Zi /Gm /Od /DEBUG" "LINK_F=/
  DEBUG" -NOLOGO

release:
  @nmake -f makefile.nt all "COMPILE_F =/O2 /Og /Oi /Ot /Oy /Ob2 /Gs /Gf
  /Gy /G5" -NOLOGO

all                 : xxx_cmd.dll

xxx_cmd.dll         : $(OBJS) link $(OBJS) $(GLFLAGS) $(LIBS)
```

```
                        /OUT:$(@R).dll /implib:$(@R).lib /PDB:$(@R).pdb

template_cmd.obj : $(@R).cpp $(GLBDEP)cl $(GCFLAGS) $(@R).cpp

cleanall          : del *.obj *.pdb *.idb *.ilk *.exp vc4?.*
```

## Overridable Function Makefile

```
NC_ROOT             = c:\ibm\NetCommerce3

PCH                 = objects\objects.pch
INC                 = /I$(NC_ROOT)\adt\include
LIBS                = $(NC_ROOT)\bin\nc3_containers.lib \
                       $(NC_ROOT)\bin\nc3_messages.lib \
                       $(NC_ROOT)\bin\nc3_common.lib \
                       $(NC_ROOT)\bin\nc3_dbc.lib \
                       $(NC_ROOT)\bin\server_objs.lib


GCFLAGS             = /nologo /c /GX $(COMPILE_F) /MD /W1 /D_X86=1
                      /D_X86_ /D_CONSOLE /DWIN32 $(INC) /YX"$(PCH)" /Gi

GLFLAGS             = /nologo $(LINK_F) /DLL /machine:IX86

OBJS                = template_of.obj

debug:
  @nmake -f makefile.nt all "COMPILE_F=/Zi /Gm /Od /DEBUG" "LINK_F=/
  DEBUG" -NOLOGO

release:
  @nmake -f makefile.nt all "COMPILE_F =/O2 /Og /Oi /Ot /Oy /Ob2 /Gs /Gf
  /Gy /G5" -NOLOGO

all            : xxx_of.dll

xxx_of.dll     : $(OBJS) link $(OBJS) $(GLFLAGS) $(LIBS)
                 /OUT:$(@R).dll /implib:$(@R).lib /PDB:$(@R).pdb

template_of.obj : $(@R).cpp $(GLBDEP) cl $(GCFLAGS) $(@R).cpp

cleanall          : del *.obj *.pdb *.idb *.ilk *.exp vc4?.*
```

# Chapter 12, Planning Overridable Functions

This chapter explains the planning that is typically required when you create overridable functions. To help you better understand the process, it presents a simple example, which will continue in the next two chapters. In the workshop, you will plan for two overridable functions for the pizza store.

This chapter covers the following topics:

- Sample Scenario
- Step 1. Determining the Business Logic
- Step 2. Determining the Task that Implements the Business Logic
- Step 3. Ensuring Authorization
- Step 4. Storing Custom Data in the Database
- Step 5. Determining the Function's Input and Output Parameters
- Step 6. Determining the Net.Commerce Classes You Will Use
- Step 7. Determining How to Handle Exceptions
- Step 8. Determining How to Handle a Successful Return
- Step 9. Creating the Interface to the Command
- Workshop: Planning New Overridable Functions for the OneStopPizza Shop

# Sample Scenario

As the store administrator of a hardware store, you want to create a shopping cart page that will provide the following features:

- List all the items that the shopper has selected

- Show the quantity selected for each item (carried over from the product pages)

- Contain an **Update Quantity** button for updating the quantity of multiple products in the cart

- Contain an **Empty Cart** button for removing all items from the cart

You will design the page to look like Figure 12.1 below:

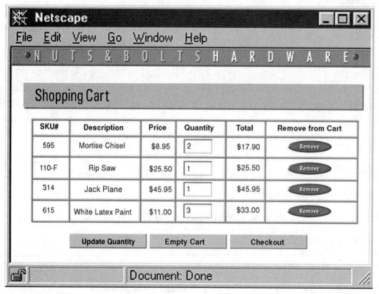

**Figure 12.1**  *A custom Shopping Cart page.*

Figure 12.1 shows the page with some products added to the cart by the shopper.

You have chosen to use the SHIPTO table for storing part of the contents of the shopping cart because it is the only table that stores product quantities and subsequently allows you to display them on the shopping cart page. As a prerequisite to using this table, you must generate an address reference number in order to fill the required STSANBR column. To satisfy this requirement, your store requires that shoppers log on or register before they can add products to the cart. The act of logging on or registering creates an address reference number that can be later inserted into the SHIPTO table.

Because you are using the SHIPTO table to store the contents of the shopping cart, you must use the OrderItemUpdate command for the **Update Quantity** and the **Empty Cart** buttons. However, in its default implementation, this command can update the quantity of only one product at a time—that is, it cannot update the quantities of multiple products; and it does not delete products from the SHIPTO table—that is, it cannot be used to empty the cart. You could use the OrderItemDelete command to empty the cart, but you want to be able to do both the update and the delete actions using the same command. Therefore, you must create a new overridable function that will extend the capabilities of the OrderItemUpdate command so that it will either update the quantities of multiple products in the shopping cart or remove all items from the cart, depending on the button clicked by the shopper.

# Step 1. Determining the Business Logic

The first step to planning how you will write an overridable function is to clearly define the business logic that you want to achieve.

## Sample Scenario:

In this case, you want to write an overridable function that will do the following on the shopping cart page:

- When the shopper changes a quantity for one or more products in the shopping cart and then clicks the **Update Quantity** button, the function will update the quantities of the products in the cart.

- When the shopper clicks the **Empty Cart** button, the function will remove all products from the cart.

# Step 2. Determining the Task that Implements the Business Logic

An overridable function serves one of two purposes: it replaces an existing overridable function that is called by a supplied command, or it performs some processing for a new command that has been created. Either way, you must follow the rules that are defined for the task that your overridable function will implement.

If you are intending to replace an overridable function for a command, supplied by the system, you need to determine the task (typically a process task) that it will implement. Do the following:

1. Review table Table 9.6 on page 277 to see a description of each command and the tasks that it sets, and determine which of these tasks is the one you want to implement.

2. Once you have determined which task you will be implementing, consult "Appendix E, Net.Commerce Tasks" on page 613 to understand the general behavior of this task and to see what overridable function implements it.

3. Once you have determined the task's implementing overridable function, go to "Appendix F, Net.Commerce Overridable Functions" on page 665 for a description of what this function does.

(If you are creating the function for a new command, consult the programmer who wrote the command in order to determine the task that it will implement. If you yourself are the programmer, ensure that you have defined a task that your function will implement. For information on defining tasks, see "Calling an Overridable Function" on page 338.)

## Sample Scenario:

In this example, you want to replace a function that is called by the OrderItemUpdate command. When you look this command up in Tabke 9.6 on page 277, you see that just before it completes, it calls the EXT_SHIPTO_UPD process task. This task is available for performing any additional processing that is required just prior to the completion of the OrderItemUpdate command. When you look at its description on page 644, you see that it is currently implemented by the DoNothingNoArgs_1.0(IBM,NC) overridable function, which returns without performing any processing. This is the function that you will be replacing.

# Step 3. Ensuring Authorization

Whenever you create an overridable function, you must ensure that you are authorized to replace the existing overridable function.

If you are the site administrator, you have the authority to replace all overridable functions and to set the scope of the task to which each function is assigned to either *mall* or *store*.

- If a task is set to mall scope, the overridable function assigned to it is implemented for all the stores in the mall, and will affect every store in the mall except stores that override the mall version of an overridable function with a store version.

- If a task is set to store scope, then each store administrator can assign a different overridable function or macro to the task and apply that for their store. If a store administrator chooses not to do this, then the overridable function assignment used for the mall will be applied to that store.

If you are a store administrator, you can only replace overridable functions and macros for which the site administrator has set the scope of the tasks to which they are assigned to *store*. To ensure that you are authorized to replace an overridable function or macro, ask your site administrator whether or not the scope of the task is *store*. The site administrator determines the task scope using the Task Management form, as follows:

1. Open the Administrator.

2. On the task bar, click **Site Manager** and then **Task Management**. The Task Management form appears.

3. From the **Select Task Type** drop-down list, select the appropriate task type.

   - **ERROR**, for overridable functions that handle exception conditions.

   - **PROCESS**, for overridable functions that process information.

   - **VIEW**, for overridable functions that display the pages that shoppers normally see during the shopping process.

   A list of all the tasks that are available for the selected task type appears in the bottom frame.

4.  Select the desired task name from the list. Typically, you will select **PROCESS**.The fields automatically fill with task information.

5.  Look at the level that is displayed in the **Scope** drop-down list, to determine whether the task is set to *mall* or *store*.

# Step 4. Storing Custom Data in the Database

If the current database schema does not provide a table in which you can store data required by your new overridable function, you will need to extend the database. There are two ways to do this:

*   Use a column that is reserved for merchant customization

*   Add a new table to the database, and link it to one or more existing tables through keys

These options also apply to new commands that are created that use custom data.

> **Note:**
> It is not advisable to add a new column to a table, because you may not be able to retrofit such changes into the database schema of future releases of Net.Commerce.

## Using the Merchant-Reserved Columns

You can use the columns that are designated as "Reserved for merchant customization" in the Net.Commerce database for your own data storage purposes. See "Appendix C, Net.Commerce Database Tables" on page 511 to determine which tables contain columns for merchant customization.

Before you enter your custom information in a merchant-reserved column, you must ensure the following:

*   Your information is of the same data type as the merchant-reserved column.

*   Your information can fit into the space that is allocated to the merchant-reserved column.

*   Your information corresponds to the kind of information for which the table was created.

See "Appendix C, Net.Commerce Database Tables" on page 511 for the information you need to make the above assessments.

If your data satisfies the above requirements, you can proceed to enter it into the column using the corresponding form in the Administrator or the appropriate SQL statements.

## Adding a New Table

If the columns reserved for merchant customization are not sufficient to store your custom data, you can add a new table to the database, using the appropriate SQL statements. To link this table into the existing database structure, you must define at least one column in it as a foreign key that is keyed off the primary key of an existing table. This ensures that you will be able to directly access the rows that are associated with a particular entity, such as a shopper, a merchant, or a product. (See "Appendix C, Net.Commerce Database Tables" on page 511 for an overview of the entities that are represented by the Net.Commerce database and the relationships between them.) For example, if you want to add a new table containing demographic information about shoppers that cannot be accommodated by table SHOPDEM, your new table must key off the shopper reference number in table SHOPPER, as does table SHOPDEM. Your macros and overridable functions can then select and update rows in the table that match the reference number of the shopper.

All primary keys are identified in the column descriptions in the database tables listed in Appendix C. You can use any of these keys for your new table. See also the descriptions below for the most common primary keys.

## Common Primary Keys

All primary keys are identified in the column descriptions in the database tables (see "Appendix C, Net.Commerce Database Tables on page 511). You can use any of these keys for new tables. Table 12.1 contains the keys that are most commonly used by the Net.Commerce system:

*Table 12.1  The most common primary keys in the Net.Commerce database.*

| Column Defined as Primary Key | Table Name | Description |
|---|---|---|
| SHRFNBR | SHOPPER | The shopper reference number. Use this key for tables whose rows correspond to individual shoppers. |
| MERFNBR | MERCHANT | The merchant reference number. Use this key for tables whose rows correspond to individual merchants. |
| CGRFNBR | CATEGORY | The category reference number. Use this key for tables whose rows correspond to individual categories in your store. |
| PRRFNBR | PRODUCT | The product reference number. Use this key for tables whose rows correspond to products and items in your store. |
| MMRFNBR | MSHIPMODE | The merchant shipping mode reference number. Use this key for tables whose rows correspond to individual shipping modes that are defined for your store. |
| SPRFNBR | SHIPPING | The shipping reference number. Use this key for tables whose rows correspond to rates for individual shipping modes. |
| STRFNBR | SHIPTO | The shipto reference number. Use this key for tables whose rows correspond to items in an order. |
| SBSHNBR SBPRNBR | SHOPPINGS | The shopper reference number and the product reference number, respectively. Use this key for tables whose rows correspond to items in the shopper's Interest List. |

*Continued on next page*

***Table 12.1*** *Continued.*

| Column Defined as Primary Key | Table Name | Description |
|---|---|---|
| ORRFNBR | ORDERS | The order reference number. Use this key for tables whose rows correspond to individual orders that are placed by shoppers. |

# Step 5. Determining the Function's Input and Output Parameters

You now need to determine 1) the input parameters that your overridable function will receive from the Net.Commerce system and 2) the output parameters that it will return to the system. Ensure that you do the following:

- Use any parameters that the system passes in if they are needed by your overridable function

- Pass the variables that the system expects to receive back to the system

- In case of an exception condition, return the parameters that are needed to handle the error

You send parameters to an overridable function by passing them into the command that invokes the task associated with the function. All commands forward parameters, unchanged, to the tasks that they set. For your new overridable functions, you will need to pass extra custom parameters. The system will not reject these new parameters, as long as they do not conflict with the command's original parameters.

The parameters can be treated as either mandatory or optional. Mandatory input parameters are always required by the overridable function, while optional input parameters are treated as optional by the function.

For overridable functions that implement process tasks, you may or may not return any parameters to the system, depending on the nature of the function. If the function performs a database update, it generally will not return any parameters. If it retrieves data or performs a database calculation, it generally returns this information to the system so that the calling command can handle this information; for example, to be used by another function that the command calls. For overridable functions that implement exception tasks, the output parameters include error codes that are used by a macro to display the appropriate error message to the shopper. For overridable functions that implement view tasks, the output parameters could be any parameter required by the macro that it calls to properly display a page.

In addition to the parameters that you pass to the overridable function through the invoking command, the task to which the function is assigned has defined the following:

- Explicit input parameters that the function expects to receive from the Net.Commerce system

- Explicit output parameters that the system expects to be returned.

To determine these input and output parameters, refer to the appropriate task description in "Appendix E, Net.Commerce Tasks" on page 613.

### Sample Scenario:

Let's look at the input and output parameters for our example overridable function. As defined by the EXT_SHIPTO_UPD process task on page 644, your overridable function will receive the reference number of the suborder as an explicit input parameter.

It also will receive the following optional input parameters from the system:

- The shipto reference number-quantity name-value pairs for each product in the shopping cart

- If the shopper clicks the **Empty Cart** button, the name-value pair `empty=1`

The function will not return any parameters to the system; it merely performs a database update.

# Step 6. Determining the Net.Commerce Classes You Will Use

Before you can write your overridable function, you need to understand the classes that are available for you to use. This section provides a review of some of the classes that you will most likely use when writing your overridable functions, based on the task that each class accomplishes. For more detailed information, review "Chapter 10, Net.Commerce Classes" on page 283.

## Checking or Retrieving Input Parameters

To check or retrieve the cookies, name-value pairs passed to the command or function as input parameters, `PATH_INFO`, and so forth, you use the `HttpRequest` object. This object is a constant that contains all the information that was passed to the Net.Commerce server by the Web server, including the variables available through the CGI protocol. It is passed unchanged through all the commands and overridable functions that are called.

For more information about the `HttpRequest` class, see "The HttpRequest Class" on page 304.

## Returning an HTTP Response

To set cookies, redirection headers, or a full-text HTTP document (HTML, VRML, Scripting, and so on) back to the browser, including the parameters returned by a command or overridable function, use the `HttpResponse` object. This object is passed through all the commands and overridable functions that are called, but each command or overridable function can also modify it. The object is returned to the Web browser when the calling command returns. Overridable functions that implement process tasks normally do not return HTTP documents.

For more information on the `HttpResponse` class, see "The HttpResponse Class" on page 306.

# Communicating With Other Commands or Overridable Functions

To communicate between the other commands and overridable functions in the system, and to retrieve environment variables and the explicit input and output parameters defined by tasks for overridable functions, you use the `NC_Environment` object. This object is unique per shopper transaction, and contains information about the Net.Commerce environment. It provides the communication means between the various commands and overridable functions. For example, you can use it to communicate from a command to an overridable function and back. Input and output parameters defined by tasks are passed through this class object.

For more information about the `NC_Environment` class, see "The NC_Environment Class" on page 313.

# Retrieving Information About the Current Shopper

To retrieve profile information about the current shopper, such as the logon ID, you use the `User` class. This class contains information needed to identify each shopper or user to the Net.Commerce system. It also contains some basic contact and classification information. It maps to the SHOPPER (shopper profile) table in the database.

For more information about the `User` class, see "The User Class" on page 683.

# Accessing the Database

To query, update, or delete information in the database, you can either issue SQL statements using the `DataBase`, `SQL`, and `Row` classes, or use the new object model (which does not require you to use SQL).

For more information about using the ODBC classes, see "Interacting with the Database" on page 340. For details about the object model, see "Appendix G, The Net.Commerce Object Model" on page 675.

# Step 7. Determining How to Handle Exceptions

You now need to plan how you will handle exception conditions that are encountered by your overridable function. You have the following options:

- Set an exception task to handle the error (either a new one or the supplied exception task that is currently set for the overridable function that you are replacing).

- Let the system handle the error, by returning a false value to the calling command.

- Let the overridable function handle the error, by hard-coding the HTTP response directly in the function and then throwing the `&_ERR_CMD_ERR_HANDLED` exception.

To review these methods, see "Handling Exceptions" on page 324.

## Sample Scenario:

The function must be able to handle the following two exception conditions:

- No record exists in the database for a shopper who is attempting to update the quantities of items in the shopping cart or to empty the cart.

- An error occurs when the overridable function attempts to interact with the database.

If any of the above errors occurs, you will let the system handle the error by returning a false value to the calling OrderItemUpdate command. Because the false value will be returned during the processing of the command (typically, command call overridable functions from their Process functions), the command manager will invoke the default system error page cmdexe.html, which indicates that the command could not execute, or in this case, complete. All updates made to the database by the OrderItemUpdate command, including those made by the process tasks that the command sets, will be rolled back.

# Step 8. Determining How to Handle a Successful Return

You need to plan what your overridable function will do when it successfully completes. Typically, you will be replacing an overridable function that implements a process task. In this case, you will return a true value to the calling command, and if applicable, variables to the NC_Environment object. If however, you are writing an overridable function that will implement a view or exception task, you will generate an HTTP document. The supplied overridable functions execute Net.Data macros.

## Sample Scenario:

When your overridable function successfully completes, you will return a true value to the OrderItemUpdate command.

# Step 9. Creating the Interface to the Command

Before you begin to write your overridable function, it is advisable to create the Net.Data macro that will invoke its calling command, to ensure that the command will receive all the parameters required for your function. For an overview of how to create Net.Data macros, see "Chapter 7, A Net.Data Tutorial" on page 169.

## Sample Scenario:

In review, the shopping cart page that invokes the OrderItemUpdate command, which in turn calls your custom function, looks like Figure 12.1 on page 350. The macro that creates this page has already been created. You will examine the code for only the **Update Quantity** and **Empty Cart** buttons at the bottom of the page. These buttons both contain the OrderItemUpdate command, which will invoke your function and pass to it its required parameters. The other elements on the page are created by standard Net.Data and HTML and do not require further explanation.

The following is the source code for the **Update Quantity** button. It is in the %HTML_REPORT section of the macro that creates the shopping cart.

```
<A HREF="#" onClick="update_shipto()">
<IMG SRC="/grocery/g_updt.gif" WIDTH=138 HEIGHT=24 BORDER=0></A>
```

When the shopper changes the quantity of one or more items in the cart and then clicks the **Update Quantity** button, the JavaScript function update_shipto in the %HTML_REPORT section is invoked. The source code for the this function is as follows:

```
function update_shipto() {
   var pcounter = parseInt('$(productcounter)')
   var tempValue = ""
   var url1 = "/cgi-bin/ncommerce3/OrderItemUpdate?addr_rn="
   var url2 = "&url=/cgi-bin/ncommerce3/OrderItemDisplay
              &success3=true"
   var address_ref = document.forms[0].addr_rn.value;
   var shipto_ref = document.forms[0].shipto_rn.value;
   var quantity = document.forms[0].quantity.value;
   var shipmode_ref = document.forms[0].shipmode_rn.value;

      for(i=0; i < pcounter; i++) {
      if(pcounter == 1) {

         if(document.forms[0].number.value <= 0) {
         alert("Please enter a valid quantity") return }
         tempValue +="&" + document.forms[0].refnum.value + "="
         + document.forms[0].number.value
      }

         else {
         if(document.forms[0].number[i].value <= 0) {
         alert(" Please enter a valid quantity") return }
         tempValue +="&" + document.forms[0].refnum[i].value + "="
         + document.forms[0].number[i].value
         }
      }
   var new_url = "https://" + window.location.host + url1 +
                 address_ref + "&shipto_rn=" + shipto_ref +
                 "&quantity=" + quantity + "&shipmode_rn=" +
                 shipmode_ref + tempValue + url2
   window.location.href = new_url
}
```

The update_shipto function does the following:

1.  If the shopper enters an invalid quantity (for example, a negative number), and then clicks the **Update Quantity** button, it displays a JavaScript alert box that informs the shopper of the error and prevents the update from occurring.

2.  Defines local variables that will be used by the function.

3.  Builds a URL that consists of the following parameters:

    a)  Variable `Url1`, which contains the OrderItemUpdate command and the command's required parameters: the address reference number, the shipto reference number, the quantity, and the shipping mode reference number. The values for these parameters are retrieved from the last product in the shopping cart table. (The OrderItemUpdate command by default can handle only one product at a time, so the last product is used.)

    b)  Variable `tempValue`, which stores a string of name-value pairs for the quantity and shipto reference number of each product in the shopping cart table. The function retrieves the values for these name-value pairs by referencing the value of the refnum and the number text input fields.

    c)  Variable `Ur2`, a redirection URL that contains the OrderItemDisplay command.

4.  Executes the URL, as follows:

    a)  The OrderItemUpdate command updates the SHIPTO table with the quantity of the last product in the table. At this point, the command is performing a "dummy" update, because the shopper may have changed the quantity not of the last product in the table, but of one or more of the other products. The "real" updating does not occur until the command calls the EXT_SHIPTO_UPD process task, as explained in the next step.

    b)  The OrderItemUpdate command calls the EXT_SHIPTO_UPD process task. By default this task does nothing, but its default overridable function, DoNothingNoArgs_1.0(IBM,NC), will be replaced with your custom function, which will update the SHIPTO table with the quantities of one or more products changed by the shopper. (Normally, the OrderItemUpdate command can update the quantity of only one product.)

    c)  When the update successfully completes, the redirection URL `Url2` is called, which executes the OrderItemDisplay command to redisplay the Shopping Cart page with the updated quantities.

    d)  Once the page is displayed, JavaScript displays a confirmation message in the status bar, indicating that the shopping cart has been successfully updated with the new quantities.

The following is the code for the **Empty Cart** button in the shopping cart macro:

```
<A HREF="#" onClick="empty_shipto()">
<IMG SRC="/grocery/g_empt.gif" WIDTH=138 HEIGHT=24 BORDER=0></A>
```

When the shopper clicks the **Empty Cart** button, the JavaScript function `empty_shipto` in the `%HTML_REPORT` section is invoked. Its source code is as follows:

```
function empty_shipto(form) {

  Ret = confirm("Are you sure you want to delete all items from the
               shopcart?")
```

```
if(!Ret)
return

var pcounter = parseInt('$(productcounter)')
var tempValue = ""
var url1 = "/cgi-bin/ncommerce3/OrderItemUpdate?addr_rn="
var url2 = "&empty=1&url=/cgi-bin/ncommerce3/OrderItemDisplay"
var address_ref = document.forms[0].addr_rn.value;
var shipto_ref = document.forms[0].shipto_rn.value;
var quantity = document.forms[0].quantity.value;
var shipmode_ref = document.forms[0].shipmode_rn.value;

  for(i=0; i < pcounter; i++) {

    if(pcounter == 1)
      tempValue += "&" + document.forms[0].refnum.value + "="
        + document.forms[0].number.value
    else
      tempValue += "&" + document.forms[0].refnum[i].value + "="
        + document.forms[0].number[i].value
  }

var new_url = "https://" + window.location.host + url1 + address_ref
+ "&shipto_rn=" + shipto_ref + "&quantity=" + quantity +
"&shipmode_rn=" + shipmode_ref + tempValue + url2

window.location.href = new_url
}
```

The `empty_shipto` function is similar to the function for the **Update Quantity** button. It does the following:

1.  Displays a JavaScript alert box, which asks the shopper to confirm that all items are to be deleted from the cart.

2.  After the shopper clicks **OK**, defines variables that will be used by the function.

3.  Builds a URL that consists of the same parameters that were contained in the URL for the `update_shipto` function, but with the addition of the name-value pair `empty=1`.

4.  Executes the URL, as follows:

    a)  The OrderItemUpdate command performs the usual "dummy" update on the SHIPTO table (using the input parameters for the last product in the cart).

    b)  The OrderItemUpdate command calls the EXT_SHIPTO_UPD process task. Again, this task's default overridable function, DoNothingNoArgs_1.0(IBM,NC), will be replaced with your custom one, which will remove all products from the shopping cart. The `empty=1` parameter is used to perform the delete.

    c)  When the products are successfully deleted, the Shopping Cart page is displayed with a message indicating that there are no items left in the cart.

In "Chapter 13, Writing Overridable Functions" on page 377 you will learn how to write the code for the function that will replace the DoNothingNoArgs_1.0(IBM,NC) overridable function.

# Workshop: Planning New Overridable Functions for the OneStopPizza Shop

In this workshop you will plan for implementing the feature that allows shoppers to build their own pizzas and add them to their Order List. Currently, the Net.Commerce system does not provide a way for shoppers to piece different attributes of a product together to form a single orderable product: instead, the merchant must group the attributes (in this case, pizza toppings) into predefined products. You have already done this for the store's ready-made pizzas: *Vegetarian Delight*, *Deli Delight*, and *Tropical Delight*. Each of these products has a set number of toppings and a set price for each available size. Shoppers cannot simply pick and choose different toppings for a pizza and get a total price based on the number of toppings selected, because if more than one topping is ordered, there is no mechanism in place for the system to determine which toppings belong to which pizza. There are three possible ways to implement the "Make Your Own Pizza" feature:

### Allow shoppers to order only one pizza at a time.

This is not an ideal solution, as shoppers should be able to order as many pizzas at one time as they want. It would also be difficult to implement a control mechanism that would ensure that shoppers do not attempt to order a second pizza before placing an order—not to mention that the restriction would likely deter them from returning to the store.

### Create a matrix of all the possible topping combinations and define each combination as a product.

This solution is also less than ideal. In this example alone, with each pizza having five toppings, the combinations would amount to 32 per size. It would be time-consuming to enter each combination in the database, and the process would be prone to error. And, if you decide to expand your toppings even by just one, it would be difficult to update the database records. Displaying all possible topping combinations would also be a challenge, since providing lengthy descriptions of the toppings for each pizza would be space-consuming, not to mention confusing for shoppers. Even saving space by using a table would make for a complex and perhaps unappealing product display.

### Define "Item Option" entity for each topping and link it to the product (pizza base).

This is the most realistic solution, and the one that you will implement in your store. Each pizza topping available will be defined in the database as a new entity called an "item option". Like products and items, each item option will have distinct properties, including a unique item option reference number, and will reside in the database independently of all other entities. Each item option will link to a unique shipto reference number, which is automatically created in the SHIPTO table when the shopper adds the chosen item options, along with the pizza base, to the Order List. The shipto reference number links to the PRODUCT table in the database, which contains information about the base product to which the item options belong.

Implementing this solution will involve replacing two default overridable functions associated with the command that adds the pizza and toppings to the shopper's Order List.

# Step 1. Determining the Business Logic

You want the system to do the following when the shopper selects one or more pizza toppings for a pizza base and adds the combination to the Order List:

- Calculate the total price of the selected pizza toppings and pizza base size

- Link the toppings to its pizza base, so that the pizza can be ordered as a single product

You will write two overridable functions to accomplish the above.

# Step 2. Determining the Tasks that Implement the Business Logic

Because the default Order List created by the Store Creator uses the SHIPTO table, which associates each product and item in a suborder with a shipping address, you must use one of the OrderItem commands to add a pizza with toppings to the list. You will use the OrderItemUpdate command, which will create a shipping record in the SHIPTO table, using the product reference number that you will pass to the command. In Table 9.6 on page 277, you see that this command sets the following tasks:

- CHECK_INV process task, to ensure there is enough inventory.

- GET_BASE_SPE_PRC process task, to get the special price associated with the product or item.

- RESOLVE_SKU process task, to determine the SKU for each product or item.

- EXT_SHIPTO_UPD process task, to perform additional processing to meet any unique requirements.

Of these four tasks, you will use the GET_BASE_SPE_PRC process task to implement the business logic for the function that calculates the total price of the selected toppings and pizza base size. The description on page 645 shows you that this task is currently implemented by the GetBaseSpePrc_1.0 (IBM,NC) overridable function, which retrieves a product or item price from the PRODPRCS table in the database, based on the shopper group and precedence, and returns the value to the calling command. You will replace this function with your own.

In addition, you will use the EXT_SHIPTO_UPD process task to implement the function that will link the toppings to a corresponding pizza base. The description on page 644 tells you that this task is currently implemented by the DoNothingNoArgs_1.0(IBM,NC) overridable function, which returns without performing any processing. Again, you will replace this function with your own.

For the remainder of this workshop, we will examine the planning required to implement the function for the EXT_SHIPTO_UPD task. The implementation of the function for the GET_BASE_SPE_PRC task will be examined in the next chapter.

# Step 3. Ensuring Authorization

Since the OneStopPizza Shop is an example of a single store scenario, the scope of the task is irrelevant. That is, the store administrator will be able to replace the overridable function whether the task is set to *mall* or to *store* scope.

# Step 4. Storing Custom Data in the Database

In the workshop, "Adding the Remaining Products and Categories to the OneStopPizza Shop" on page 141, you entered in the PRODUCT, PRODSGP, PRODATR, and PRODDSTATR tables the following information about the pizza base for the *Make Your Own Pizza* product:

- A name

- A description

- Its items and attributes (sizes at different prices)

- The name of the macro that will display the product page (`prod2.d2w`)

Now you need to enter information about the new item options that represent the toppings. Each item option will consist of the following information:

- A unique reference number.

- A price.

- A description (the name of the topping).

- One or more shipto reference numbers (internally assigned by the system). Each item option can be linked to multiple shipto reference numbers; for example, the shopper could order two pizzas with each containing the same mushroom topping.

The resulting hierarchy is shown in Figure 12.2.

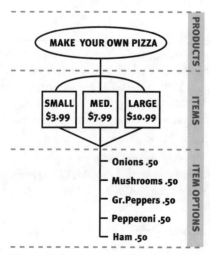

*Figure 12.2* The item options in the OneStopPizza Shop.

The tables in the database that store product item- and attribute-related information (PRODATR and PRODDSTATR) do not contain merchant-customizable fields for storing your item option information. Even it they did, it is advisable to create new tables to contain information about new entities, rather than combine the information into tables that are designed to store information for the existing entities. Therefore, you will create new tables to store the information required for the item options. You will create the following three tables:

## OPTIONS (Item Option) Table:

The OPTIONS table, shown in Table 12.2, describes all item options that are available in the store. Each row contains information about one item option.

*Table 12.2* *The OPTIONS table.*

| Column Name | Column Type | Column Description |
|---|---|---|
| OPREFNUM | INTEGER NOT NULL | Unique item option reference number. This is a primary key. |
| OPDESCR | CHAR (50) NOT NULL | Name of the item option. |

## OPTIONPRICE (Item option Price) Table:

The OPTIONPRICE table, shown in Table 12.3, stores the price of each item option that is available in the store. Each row contains the price of one item option.

*Table 12.3* *The OPTIONPRICE table.*

| Column Name | Column Type | Column Description |
|---|---|---|
| OPPRREFNUM | INTEGER NOT NULL | Price reference number. This is a foreign key that references the OPREFNUM column in the OPTIONS table. |
| OPPRPRICE | DECIMAL (10,2) NOT NULL | Price of the item option. |

## OPTIONREL (Item Option-Shipto Relationship) Table:

The OPTIONREL table, shown in Table 12.4, defines the relationships between the item options in the OPTIONS table and the shipto records in the SHIPTO table. Each row describes one relationship.

*Table 12.4* *The OPTIONREL table.*

| Column Name | Column Type | Column Description |
|---|---|---|
| OPRLSTRN | INTEGER NOT NULL | Shipto reference number, internally generated. This is a foreign key that references the STRFNBR column in the SHIPTO table. |

*Continued on next page*

**Table 12.4** *Continued.*

| Column Name | Column Type | Column Description |
|---|---|---|
| OPRLOPTRN | INTEGER NOT NULL | Item option reference number, internally generated. This is a foreign key that references the OPREFNUM column in the OPTIONS table. |

**Notes:**

- You can combine the contents of the OPTIONS and OPTIONPRICE tables into one table. In this example, we have chosen to create two separate tables, to follow the table structure that exists for products (PRODUCT and PRODPRCS tables).

- The merchant reference number is not defined as a column in any of the tables. Because the tables have been created for a single store, you do not require this column. However, if you were creating a mall, you would require the merchant reference number to identify which pizza toppings belong to which stores.

## Creating the Tables in the Database

You are now ready to create the three new tables in the OneStopPizza Shop's database.

1. Start a DB2 Command Line Processor window.

2. From the DB2 command prompt, connect to the database for the OneStopPizza Shop by typing the following:

   ```
   connect to <database_name>
   ```

   where <database_name> is the name of the database that you are using for the OneStopPizza Shop.

3. Create the OPTIONS table by typing the following DB2 command, all on one line (it is shown here on two lines for presentation purposes only):

   ```
   CREATE TABLE options (oprefnum INTEGER NOT NULL PRIMARY KEY,
   opdescr CHAR(50) NOT NULL)
   ```

4. Create the OPTIONPRICE table by typing the following command, all on one line:

   ```
   CREATE TABLE optionprice (opprrefnum INTEGER NOT NULL REFERENCES
   options(oprefnum), opprprice DECIMAL(10,2) NOT NULL)
   ```

5. Create the OPTIONREL table by typing the following command, all on one line:

   ```
   CREATE TABLE optionrel (oprlstrn INTEGER NOT NULL REFERENCES
   shipto(strfnbr), oprloptrn INTEGER NOT NULL REFERENCES
   options(oprefnum))
   ```

## Inserting Data into the Tables

You will now populate the OPTIONS and OPTIONPRICE table with information about the item options that will be available in your store. You will not insert data into the OPTIONREL table; the OrderItemUpdate command will automatically insert into this table a unique shipto reference number and item option reference number when the shopper adds a pizza with selected toppings to the Order List.

You will allow shoppers to build their own pizza with any of the following toppings:

- Pepperoni

- Mushrooms

- Green Peppers

- Onions

- Ham

For simplicity, each topping will cost 50 cents, but they can be priced differently if desired.

1. Ensure that you are still connected to the database for the OneStopPizza Shop.

2. From a DB2 command prompt, populate the OPTIONS table by typing the following five commands:

```
INSERT INTO options VALUES (1, 'Pepperoni')
INSERT INTO options VALUES (2, 'Mushrooms')
INSERT INTO options VALUES (3, 'Green Peppers')
INSERT INTO options VALUES (4, 'Onions')
INSERT INTO options VALUES (5, 'Ham')
INSERT INTO options VALUES (9999, 'Dummy')
```

3. Populate the OPTIONPRICE table by typing the following six commands:

```
INSERT INTO optionprice VALUES (1, .50)
INSERT INTO optionprice VALUES (2, .50)
INSERT INTO optionprice VALUES (3, .50)
INSERT INTO optionprice VALUES (4, .50)
INSERT INTO optionprice VALUES (5, .50)
INSERT INTO optionprice VALUES (9999, .0)
```

**Note:**
You added an additional record to the tables with a reference number of 9999. This is a "dummy" record, which will be used when a shopper selects a pizza base with no toppings. You can learn more about the use of this record in the workshop "Writing the Overridable Function for the EXT_SHIPTO_UPD Task" on page 391, when you examine how the selected pizza toppings are displayed in the Order List.

**Tip:**
During the test phase, it is a good idea to begin by only inserting a few records (two or three) into the OPTIONS and OPTIONPRICE tables, to ensure that all toppings are displayed correctly in your store and that the shopper is being charged for only those selected. Once this has been determined, you can add the remaining records.

4. Close the DB2 window.

# Step 5. Determining the Function's Input and Output Parameters

The overridable function that will implement the EXT_SHIPTO_UPD process task will receive the following required input parameter from the Net.Commerce system:

- Variable ORDERITEM_REF_NUM (shipto reference number), which is internally generated by the OrderItemUpdate command. This is an explicit input parameter defined by the EXT_SHIPTO_UPD task.

It may also receive from the system the following optional input parameter:

- Name-value pair option=<item_option_refnum>, which is the name and value of each item option (topping) selected by the shopper, where <item_option_refnum> is the reference number of the item option.

The function will not return any parameters to the system.

# Step 6. Determining How to Handle Exceptions

You now need to plan how you will handle exception conditions that are encountered by your overridable function. In this case, the function must be able to handle the following two exception conditions:

- The required input parameter, ORDERITEM_REF_NUM, has not been passed to the function by the calling OrderItemUpdate command, or it is syntactically incorrect.

- An error occurs when the overridable function attempts to interact with the database.

If either of the above errors occur, you will let the system handle the error by returning a false value to the calling the OrderItemUpdate command. Because the false value will be returned during the processing of the command (typically, commands call overridable functions from their Process functions), the command manager will invoke the default system error page cmdexe.html, which indicates that the command could not execute, or in this case, complete. All updates made to the database by the OrderItemUpdate command will be rolled back.

# Step 7. Determining How to Handle a Successful Return

When your overridable function successfully completes, you will return a true value to the OrderItemUpdate command.

# Step 8. Creating the Interface to the Command

You are now ready to create the *Make Your Own Pizza* product page, which will invoke the OrderItemUpdate command, which in turn will call your new overridable function. This page will contain the following information:

- The product's full-sized image of the pizza base

- The product's description

- A drop-down list of the three sizes to choose from (small, medium, and large), with each size priced differently

- A check box for each topping (pepperoni, ham, onions, green peppers, and mushrooms)

- A form submit button for the shopper to add the selected size and toppings to the Order List.

- A hypertext link for the shopper to return to the previous category page.

The resulting page will look similar to Figure 12.3 below:

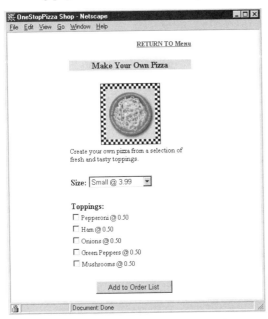

***Figure 12.3*** *The Make Your Own Pizza product page.*

To give you a head start, a skeleton of the macro that will create the page, `tmp_prod2.d2w`, has already been written for you.

1.  Copy the `tmp_prod2.d2w` macro from the `\workshops\macros\` directory on the CD to the following directory:

    **WIN**  `\ibm\netcommerce3\macro\en_US\product\OneStopPizzaShop\`

2.  Rename the file to `prod2.d2w`.

    This is the name of the macro that you entered in the database when you mass-imported the data for the *Make Your Own Pizza* product (in the workshop, "Adding the Remaining Products and Categories to the OneStopPizzaShop" on page 141).

3.  Open the macro in a text editor.

4.  You will first examine the existing code in the macro. Go to the beginning of the
    %HTML_REPORT section and look at its contents, as follows:

    %HTML_REPORT {

```
   <HTML>
   <HEAD><TITLE>Make Your Own Pizza</TITLE></HEAD>
   <BODY BGCOLOR="$(BodyColor1)" TEXT="$(TextCol)"
    LINK="$(LinkCol)" VLINK="$(VLinkCol)" ALINK="$(ALinkCol)">

   <TABLE WIDTH="100%" CELLPADDING="0" CELLSPACING="2" BORDER="0">
   <FORM ACTION="/cgi-bin/ncommerce3/OrderItemUpdate"
    TARGET="list" METHOD="post">

@findAddrRn()

      <INPUT TYPE="hidden" NAME="addr_rn" VALUE="$(addr_rn)">
      <INPUT TYPE="hidden" NAME="quantity" VALUE="1">
      <INPUT TYPE="hidden" NAME="url" VALUE="/cgi-bin/ncommerce3/
       OrderItemDisplay?merchant_rn=$(MerchantRefNum)">

@displayBackup()
@displayBanner()
@displayBase()
@displaySize()
@displayToppings()

      <TR><TD><BR></TD></TR>
      <TR>
        <TD ALIGN="center" COLSPAN="2"><INPUT TYPE="submit"
         VALUE="Add to Order List"></TD>
      </TR>
      </FORM>

   </TABLE>
   </BODY>
   </HTML>

%}
```

    This section begins by defining a table and form to display the product information on
    the page, and then calls six functions to display the different page elements and retrieve
    the parameters required by the OrderItemUpdate command. This command is defined
    as the ACTION for the form when the shopper clicks the **Add to Order List** button. All
    of the functions have already been written except the last, displayToppings, which
    has been left for you to write. This function will retrieve the information that you entered
    into the new item option-related tables, in order to display the pizza toppings.

5.  Examine the first function that is called, findAddrRn, as follows:

    %FUNCTION(DTW_ODBC) findAddrRn(){

```
select sarfnbr
from shaddr, shopper
where shlogid='$(SESSION_ID)'
and shrfnbr=sashnbr
and sanick=shlogid
and saadrflg='P'

%REPORT {

  %ROW{

    @DTW_ASSIGN(addr_rn, V_sarfnbr)
  %}
%}

%MESSAGE {
  100:{ %} :CONTINUE
%}
%}
```

This function retrieves from the SHADDR table the address reference number of the current shopper, and assigns its value to the global variable `addr_rn`. This variable is required by the OrderItemUpdate command, and is defined in the `%HTML_REPORT` section as a hidden input parameter that will be passed to the command when the shopper clicks the **Add to Order List** button.

6.   Next, examine the `displayBackup` function, as follows:

```
%FUNCTION(DTW_ODBC) displayBackup() {

  select distinct cgname
  from category
  where cgrfnbr=$(CGRY_NUM)
  and cgmenbr=$(MerchantRefNum)

  %REPORT{
    %ROW{

      <TR>
        <TD ALIGN="right"><FONT COLOR="$(TitleTxtCol)" SIZE="2">
        <B><A HREF="/cgi-bin/ncommerce3/
         CategoryDisplay?cgrfnbr=$(CGRY_NUM)&cgmenbr=$(MerchantRefNum)">RETURN
         TO $(V_cgname)</A></B></FONT></TD>
      </TR>
      <TR><TD><BR></TD></TR>
    %}
  %}

  %MESSAGE {
    100:{ %} :CONTINUE
  %}
%}
```

This function retrieves from the CATEGORY table the name of the category whose reference number is equivalent to the reference number of the product's parent category (stored in variable CGRY_NUM, which is passed to this macro by the ProductDisplay command when the page is first displayed). It then displays a hypertext link that contains the CategoryDisplay command to redisplay the category page. The CategoryDisplay command uses the CGRY_NUM variable to ensure that the correct category page is displayed.

7. Next, examine the displayBanner function, as follows:

```
%FUNCTION(DTW_ODBC) displayBanner() {

    select prrfnbr, prnbr, prldesc1
    from product
    where prrfnbr=$(prrfnbr)
    and prmenbr=$(prmenbr)

    %REPORT{

      %ROW{

        <TR>
              <TD ALIGN="center" VALIGN="top" BGCOLOR=$(BodyColor2)>
                  <FONT COLOR=$(TitleTxtCol)><B>$(V_PRLDESC1)</B>
                  </FONT></TD>
        </TR>
      %}
    %}

    %MESSAGE {
       100:{ %} :CONTINUE
    %}
%}
```

This function retrieves from the PRODUCT table the name of the product (stored in the merchant-customizable column PRLDESC1) and displays it at the top of the page as a banner.

8. Next, examine the displayBase function, as follows:

```
%FUNCTION(DTW_ODBC) displayBase() {

    select prrfnbr, prldesc2, prfull
    from product
    where prrfnbr=$(prrfnbr)
    and prmenbr=$(MerchantRefNum)

    %REPORT {

      %ROW {

        <TR>
```

```
         <TD ALIGN="center"><B><IMG SRC="$(V_prfull)"></TD>
       </TR>
       <TR>
         <TD ALIGN="left"><FONT SIZE="-1">$(V_prldesc2)</FONT>
         </TD>
       </TR>
   %}
   <TR><TD><BR></TD></TR>
 %}

 %MESSAGE {
   100:{ %} :CONTINUE
 %}
%}
```

This function retrieves from the PRODUCT table the product's long description and full-sized image and then displays the description underneath the image.

9. Now examine the `displaySize` function, as follows:

```
%FUNCTION(DTW_ODBC) displaySize() {

   select prrfnbr, paname, paval, ppprc
   from product, prodatr, prodprcs
   where ppprnbr=prrfnbr
   and paprnbr=prrfnbr
   and prprfnbr=$(prrfnbr)
   and prmenbr=$(MerchantRefNum)

   %REPORT {

     <TR>
       <TD ALIGN="left"><B>Size:</B>
       <SELECT NAME="product_rn">

       %ROW {

         <OPTION VALUE="$(V_prrfnbr)">$(V_paval) @ $(V_ppprc)
         </OPTION>
       %}

       </SELECT>
       </TD>
     </TR>
     <TR><TD><BR></TD></TR>
   %}

   %MESSAGE {
     100:{ %} :CONTINUE
   %}
%}
```

This function retrieves from the PRODUCT, PRODATR (Product Attributes), and PRODPRCS (Product Price) tables the product reference number, attribute name, attribute value, and unit price of each item belonging to the *Make Your Own Pizza* product.

For all rows retrieved from the query, the `%ROW` block displays the attribute value (small, medium, or large) and its corresponding price in a drop-down list. When the shopper clicks the **Add to Order List** button, the reference number of the item's parent product (pizza base) will be passed as an input parameter to the OrderItemUpdate command.

10. Now you will write the last function, `displayToppings`, which retrieves and displays the toppings available for the pizza. For each topping, you will display a checkbox and the topping name and its corresponding price. You will retrieve this information from the new OPTIONS and OPTIONPRICE tables.

   Add the following SQL statement after the function's declaration line, as follows:

```
%FUNCTION(DTW_ODBC) displayToppings() {

   <!--------------------------------->
   <!-       Your code begins here      ->
   <!--------------------------------->


      select oprefnum, opdescr, opprprice
      from options, optionprice
      where oprefnum=opprrefnum
      and oprefnum<$(dummyOption)
      order by opprprice


   <!--------------------------------->
   <!-       Your code ends here        ->
   <!--------------------------------->

%MESSAGE {
    100:{ %} :CONTINUE
  %}
%}
```

This SQL statement retrieves from the OPTIONS and OPTIONPRICE tables the item option reference number, item option description, and unit price for all options items whose reference number is less than the reference number stored in the variable dummyOption. The value of this variable is equivalent to the value of the "dummy" record (9999) that you entered in the OPTIONPRICE table earlier in this workshop.

11. You now need to define how each row that is retrieved from the OPTIONS and OPTIONPRICE tables will be displayed. To do this, you will create a `%REPORT` block that contains HTML and variables to reference the data retrieved from the query. Add the following:

```
%FUNCTION(DTW_ODBC) displayToppings() {
```

```
<!------------------------------->
<!-        Your code begins here      ->
<!------------------------------->

select oprefnum, opdescr, opprprice
from options, optionprice
where oprefnum=opprrefnum
and oprefnum<$(dummyOption)
order by opprprice
```

**%REPORT {**

```
  <TR>
    <TD ALIGN="left"><B>Toppings:</B></TD>
  </TR>

    %ROW {
      <TR>
        <TD><ALIGN="center"><FONT SIZE="-1">
        <INPUT TYPE="checkbox" NAME="option"
         VALUE="$(V_oprefnum)">$(V_opdescr) @ $(V_opprprice)
         </FONT></TD>
      </TR>
    %}
      <INPUT TYPE="hidden" NAME="option" VALUE="$(dummyOption)">
  %}

  <!------------------------------->
  <!-        Your code ends here       ->
  <!------------------------------->
```

```
%MESSAGE {
    100:{ %} :CONTINUE
  %}
%}
```

This HTML will first display the label "Toppings" for the check box group. Then, for each row retrieved from the query, it will display a checkbox with a label corresponding to its item option description (topping name) and price. When the shopper clicks the **Add to Order List** button, for each check box selected the name-value pair defined as "option" for the name and the item option reference number for the value will be passed as an input parameter to the OrderItemUpdate command.

Note that the value of variable dummyOption is defined as a hidden input parameter that will also be passed to the OrderItemUpdate command when the shopper clicks the **Add to Order List** button. You will learn more about this parameter when you examine the macro that creates the Order List, in the next workshop "Writing the Overridable Function for the EXT_SHIPTO_UPD Task" on page 391.

12. Remove the comment blocks from the file.

13. Save your work and close the file.

14. To test the macro in the store, do the following:

    a)   Open the OneStopPizza Shop in new browser window.

    b)   On the navigation bar, click **Menu**.

    c)   On the category page, click **Make Your Own Pizza**.

The Make Your Own Pizza product page appears, complete with the sizes and toppings to choose from, as shown in Figure 12.4 below.

***Figure 12.4***  *The Make Your Own Pizza product page in the OneStopPizza Shop.*

You have now completed this workshop. In the next workshop, "Writing the Overridable Function for the EXT_SHIPTO_UPD Task" on page 391, you will write the code for the overridable functions that will allow shoppers to add a "Make Your Own" pizza creation to the Order List.

# Chapter 13, Writing Overridable Functions

In the previous chapter, you learned how to plan for a new overridable function and create the Net.Data macro that will invoke its calling command and pass to it the required input parameters. This chapter describes how to write the code for an overridable function and how to activate it in the system. In the workshop, you will write the code for the overridable function that you planned in the workshop in Chapter 12.

Before proceeding, ensure that you have read "Chapter 11, Net.Commerce Programming Conventions" on page 321 so that you are familiar with the programming conventions you must follow.

This chapter covers the following topics:

- Understanding the Overridable Function Anatomy
- Adding Your Code
- Compiling the Overridable Function
- Displaying the Overridable Function Results
- Workshop: Writing the Overridable Function for the EXT_SHIPTO_UPD Task

# Understanding the Overridable Function Anatomy

Overridable functions are written as C++ classes, and all the code is included in the CPP file with no header file. Below is the class skeleton from which you should create any overridable function. It contains all the mandatory and optional functions for the overridable function.

> **Note:**
> All uses of the tracing facility are optional.

You can find this file on the CD in the following directory:

> **WIN**    \samples\ofs\skeleton.cpp

The code is as follows:

```
class __EXPORT_MODE__ MyOverridableFunction : public
                                        NC_OverridableFunction
{
   static const ClassName _STR_ThisClass;

   public:
     MyOverridableFunction()
     {
        Trace::Tracer T(_STR_CONSTRUCTOR, _STR_ThisClass);
     }

     virtual ~MyOverridableFunction()
     {
        Trace::Tracer T(_STR_DESTRUCTOR, _STR_ThisClass);
     }

     void operator delete(void* p) { ::delete p; }
     virtual NC_OverridableFunction* Clone(void)
     {
        return new MyOverridableFunction;
     }

   public:
     virtual void FailedRegistration(NC_RegistrationID& RegID,
                                  const ErrorMsg_Reg* Err)
     {
        Trace::Tracer T(_STR_FailedRegistration, _STR_ThisClass);
     }

     virtual bool Process (const HttpRequest& Req, HttpResponse& Res,
                        NC_Environment& Env)
     {
        Trace::Tracer T(_STR_Process, _STR_ThisClass);
     }
};
```

```
const ClassName MyOverridableFunction::_STR_ThisClass
                                   ("MyOverridableFunction");

static bool X = NC_OverridableFunctionManager::Register("Vendor",
                                      "Product",
                                  "MyOverridableFunction",
                                      Version,
                          new MyOverridableFunction);
```

We will now examine each section of the skeleton.

## The Class Declaration

The class declaration line is as follows:

```
class __EXPORT_MODE__ MyOverridableFunction : public
                              NC_OverridableFunction
```

## The Member Variables

The class begins by declaring an uninitialized static variable called _STR_ThisClass, which, if tracing is enabled, is used to trace your overridable function's execution path. It will later be initialized with the name of your class. Many compilers still cannot define a static member within the class declaration, so the initialization takes place outside of the class declaration.

The code is as follows:

```
static const ClassName _STR_ThisClass;
```

All other static variables that will be used by your function, such as those that will store the function's input parameter names, should be initialized here.

## The Constructor

A constructor is defined in which you can allocate storage, if required by your overridable function. The constructor also contains a tracer to trace the function call.

The code is as follows:

```
public:
   MyOverridableFunction()
   {
      Trace::Tracer T(_STR_CONSTRUCTOR, _STR_ThisClass);
   }
```

## The Destructor

The destructor will be called when the server is shut down or when your overrridable function fails to initialize. It also contains a tracer to trace the destructor call.

The code is as follows:

```
virtual ~MyOverridableFunction()
{
   Trace::Tracer T(_STR_DESTRUCTOR, _STR_ThisClass);
}
```

## The Delete Operator

When the server shuts down, the overridable function manager will call the delete operator, which in turn calls the function's destructor. Make sure that you have set your local delete operator so that the overridable function manager can delete this class. You also need to provide a clone function that the command manager can call to create new instances of your command if required; for example, in a multi-threaded environment. The command manager will automatically call the `Initialize` function after it calls the `Clone` function.

The code is as follows:

```
void operator delete( void* p ) { ::delete p; }
virtual NC_OverridableFunction* Clone(void)
{
   return new MyOverridableFunction;
}
```

## The FailedRegistration Function

During initialization of the server, if the overridable function manager cannot register your function, it calls the `FailedRegistration` function before it deletes the function instance. The `RegId` parameter passed to this function contains the Registration ID that was passed to the overridable function manager during the registration of your overridable function (for example, `DoPayment_1.0(IBM,NC)`.

The code is as follows:

```
public:
   virtual void FailedRegistration(NC_RegistrationID& RegID,
                                   const ErrorMsg_Reg* Err)
   {
      Trace::Tracer T(_STR_FailedRegistration, _STR_ThisClass);
   }
```

In this function, you normally output error messages to the log file to indicate the type of registration error that has occurred. The following example shows the exceptions that the overridable function manager may return when it fails to register the overridable function, and also shows how to output an error message to the log file.

```
if (Err == &_ERR_REG_UNEXPECTED_OBJ)
{
   error << indent << "ERROR: MyOverridableFunction not accepted by the
                        manager" << endl;
}

else if (Err == &_ERR_REG_DUPE_ID)
```

```
{
   error << indent << "ERROR: MyOverridableFunction: another
                      overridable function with the same name has
                      already been registered" << endl;
}

else if (Err == &_ERR_REG_OBJ_NOT_FROM_DLL)
{
   error << indent << "ERROR: MyOverridableFunction is packaged in a
                      different DLL than the one registered in the
                      database" << endl;
}

else
{
   error << indent << "ERROR: MyOverridableFunction unknown
                      registration error" << endl;
}

error << indent << "ERROR: MyOverridableFunction's registration
                   failed" << endl;
```

Implementing the `FailedRegistration` function is not mandatory. The default implementation returns true. It also contains a tracer to trace the function call.

## The Process Function

The `Process` function is where you do the processing for your overridable function, including accessing, retrieving information from, and updating the database; manipulating Net.Commerce objects; and so on. It also contains a tracer to trace the function call.

The code is as follows:

```
virtual bool Process (const HttpRequest& Req, HttpResponse& Res,
                      NC_Environment& Env)
{
   Trace::Tracer T(_STR_Process, _STR_ThisClass);
};
```

The `Process` function communicates with the Net.Commerce system through three classes that are passed to it as parameters:

- `HttpRequest Req` contains all the information that is contained in an HTTP request, including the input parameters that are passed to the calling command.

- `HttpResponse Res` contains all the information that is needed for returning a full HTTP document back to the browser. Overridable functions that implement process tasks normally do not return HTTP documents.

- `NC_Environment Env` contains information about the Net.Commerce environment, including the explicit input and output parameters for overridable functions (as defined by their tasks). It allows you to set exception tasks, and to pass the parameters that the overridable function returns to the environment.

One common operation that is performed in the `Process` function is retrieving information about the current shopper. To do this, use the `User` class, as follows:

```
User& U = (User&) *Misc::CheckEnvironmentVariable(Env,
                               NC_Environment::_VAR_Shopper);
```

When querying and updating the default database tables, you can either use SQL statements and the ODBC classes provided by Net.Commerce or, to eliminate the need to use SQL statements altogether, you can use the Net.Commerce object model. For information on both methods, see "Interacting with the Database" on page 340.

If the `Process` function encounters exception conditions, it must handle the error in the usual ways: either by setting an exception task; by returning false (in which case the command manager will invoke the `cmdexe.html` system error page, which indicates a command execution failure); or by hard-coding the HTTP response directly in the function. For a review of these methods, see "Handling Exceptions" on page 324.

> **Note:**
> If the **Process** function is successful, you must return a true value to the calling command; otherwise, the database will be rolled back and the command manager will invoke the static error page, **cmdexe.html**, indicating that the command could not complete.

## The Tracing Variable

The class contains a tracing variable, which allows you to identify calls to the function for your class, as follows:

```
const ClassName MyOverridableFunction::_STR_ThisClass
                               ("MyOverridableFunction");
```

## Instantiation and Registration

Each overridable function class must contain a unique static variable, which is used to instantiate the overridable function and dynamically register it in the system, as follows:

```
static bool X = NC_OverridableFunctionManager::Register("Vendor",
                               "Product",
                               "MyOverridableFunction",
                               Version,
                               new MyOverridableFunction);
```

The values for each parameter are as follows:

`Vendor`
> The name of the company for which the overridable function is being written. This may be a third-party vendor, a merchant or site administrator, or IBM itself.

`Product`
> The name of the product for which the overridable function is being implemented; for example, "NC" for Net.Commerce.

`MyOverridableFunction`
> The overridable function's "absolute" name, as it will be later registered in the database.

```
Version
```
    The version of the overridable function implementation.

```
new MyOverridableFunction
```
    Creates an instance of the overridable function.

This static variable is initialized when the server starts up and loads the DLL or shared library in which the overridable function resides. Prior to this, the overridable function manager has already queried the OFS (Overridable Function) table in the database for all the overridable functions that have been registered by merchants, and created an internal list of pointers to them. When this variable is initialized, it calls the `Register` function, which creates a unique instance of the overridable function as defined in the variable, and attempts to register the overridable function with the overridable function manager. The overridable function manager responds by comparing the overridable function definition with its internal list. If the definition matches a record in the database, the overridable function instance is registered in the system; otherwise, the overridable function manager cannot register the overridable function and calls the `FailedRegistration` function in this class before it deletes the overridable function instance.

> **Note:**
> If you implement multiple overridable functions in the same CPP file, you must assign a different name to the static boolean variable of each overridable function (for example, X1, X2, X3, and so forth).

# Adding Your Code

You are now ready to add your own skeleton code. You must first rename the skeleton CPP file, and replace every instance of `MyOverridableFunction` with the name of your own function. After that, you will be ready to add code to the `Process` function, and any other functions in the class that you want to customize.

> **Tip:**
> At this stage, it is advisable to compile the CPP file as it is, to ensure that it can be linked properly.

## Sample Scenario:

For our example overridable function, the skeleton CPP file has been renamed to `newof.cpp` and every instance of `MyOverridableFunction` has been replaced with the name `ExtendShiptoUpdate`.

You can find the file in the following directory on the CD:

    **WIN**    `\samples\ofs\newof.cpp`

The overridable function uses the default implementations for all functions in the class, except for the `Process` function, which does the following:

1.   Retrieves from the database the reference number of the current shopper.

2.   If the name-value pair `empty=1` exists in the `HttpRequest` object (when the shopper clicks the **Empty Cart** button), deletes all of the shipto reference numbers from the SHIPTO table that belong to the current shopper and that are in the pending state.

3.   Otherwise (when the shopper clicks the **Update** button) does the following:

a)   For every name-value pair in the `HttpRequest` object whose name is an integer, treats the name as a shipto reference number and the value as a quantity and retrieves them from the `HttpRequest` object.

b)   Updates the corresponding records in the SHIPTO table with the quantities stored in the retrieved name-value pairs.

c)   Upon successful completion, returns a true value to the OrderItemUpdate command.

The corresponding code is as follows (bold type indicates code that was added to or changed in the class skeleton):

```
class __EXPORT_MODE__ ExtendShiptoUpdate : public
                                          NC_OverridableFunction
{
   static const ClassName _STR_ThisClass;

public:
   ExtendShiptoUpdate()
   {
      Trace::Tracer T(_STR_CONSTRUCTOR, _STR_ThisClass);
   }

   virtual ~ExtendShiptoUpdate()
   {
      Trace::Tracer T(_STR_DESTRUCTOR, _STR_ThisClass);
   }

   void operator delete( void* p ) { ::delete p; }
   virtual NC_OverridableFunction* Clone(void)
   {
      return new ExtendShiptoUpdate;
   }

public:
   virtual void FailedRegistration (NC_RegistrationID& RegID,
                                    const ErrorMsg_Reg* Err)
   {
      Trace::Tracer T(_STR_FailedRegistration, _STR_ThisClass);
   }

   // The actual processing happens here.
   virtual bool Process (const HttpRequest& Req, HttpResponse& Res,
                         NC_Environment& Env)
   {
      // Retrieve the current shopper's reference number from
      // the environment by first getting the current user and
      // then that user's reference number.
      User* user = (User*) Misc::CheckEnvironmentVariable
                              (Env, NC_Environment::_VAR_Shopper);
```

```
DataBase* DB = (DataBase*) Misc::CheckEnvironmentVariable
                          (Env, NC_Environment::_VAR_MainDatabase);
String shopperRefNum = user->getValue(User::_COL_REF_NUM);
String where;
String emptyVal = Req.getNVPs().Get("empty");
OrderItemHome OIH(*DB);

if (emptyVal == "1")
{ // Delete all shipto reference numbers from the SHIPTO table
  where << OrderItem::_COL_SHOPPER_REF_NUM << "="
        << shopperRefNum << " AND " << OrderItem::_COL_STATUS
        << "= 'P'";
  OIH.Delete (where);

  if (OIH.getError() != ERR_DB_NO_ERROR && OIH.getError() !=
     ERR_DB_NO_DATA)
  {
    error << indent;
    error << "ERROR: Clearing the shopping cart";
    return false;
  }
}


else
{
  // Update the SHIPTO table with the product quantities.  Iterate
  // through all name-value pairs and for each one that contains an
  // integer for the name, treat it as a strfnbr-quantity pair.

  // Create an iterator and set it to the beginning.
  NVPHash::Iterator I = Req.getNVPs().getIterator();
  I.Begin();

   // Check every name-value pair.
  while (*I != NULL)
  {
    // Check if this pair's name is an integer.
    if ((*I)->getName().IsLong() == true)
      { // It's an integer, so update the table as needed.
      NVPHash changes;
      changes.Add(OrderItem::_COL_QUANTITY, (*I)->getValue());
      where.Clean();
      where << OrderItem::_COL_REF_NUM << "="
            << ((*I)-> getName())<< " AND "
            << OrderItem::_COL_SHOPPER_REF_NUM << "="
            << shopperRefNum << " AND " << OrderItem::_COL_STATUS
            << "= 'P'";
      OIH.Update(changes, where);

      if (OIH.getError() != ERR_DB_NO_ERROR)
```

```
            {
                error << indent;
                error << "ERROR: Updating quantities";
                return false;
            }
        }

        // Advance the iterator.
        ++I;

        }
    }

    return true;

    }
};

const ClassName ExtendShiptoUpdate::_STR_ThisClass
                                    ("ExtendShiptoUpdate");

static bool X2 = NC_OverridableFunctionManager::Register("IBM",
                                                "NC",
                                    "ExtendShiptoUpdate",
                                                1.0,
                                new ExtendShiptoUpdate);
```

We will now examine the new code. We will start at the Process function, since all of the other functions in the class use the default implementation.

The Process function begins by retrieving the shopper reference number of the current shopper. It does this by first calling the CheckEnvironmentVariable function in the Misc class, to retrieve a pointer to the current user and the current database. The Process function then calls the getValue(User::_COL_REF_NUM) function to retrieve from the User class the value of the SHRFNBR column in the SHOPPER table (by referencing the variable _COL_REF_NUM) and store it in the string shopperRefNum.

The code is as follows:

```
    virtual bool Process (const HttpRequest& Req, HttpResponse& Res,
                        NC_Environment& Env)
    {
        // Retrieve the current shopper's reference number from the
        // environment by first getting the current user and then that
        // user's reference number.
        User* user = (User*) Misc::CheckEnvironmentVariable(Env,
                                        NC_Environment::_VAR_Shopper);
        DataBase* DB = (DataBase*) Misc::CheckEnvironmentVariable(Env,
                                        NC_Environment::_VAR_MainDatabase);
        String shopperRefNum = user->getValue(User::_COL_REF_NUM);
```

The `Process` function then declares a String that will store the WHERE statement for the SQL statements that it will later execute. In this example, it declares a String called where, as follows:

```
String where;
```

To determine whether the `Process` function will empty the shopping cart or update the quantities of products entered by the shopper, it will use the value of the empty input parameter as the criterion. This parameter is stored in `HttpRequest Req`. If it is equal to "1", the shopping cart will be emptied; otherwise, the quantities of products will be updated. To retrieve the value of the empty parameter, the `Process` function calls the `getNVPs` function to retrieve the `NameValuePairMap` class stored in `HttpRequest Req`. It then calls the `Get("empty")` function to retrieve from the `NameValuePairMap` class instance the value of the name-value pair containing the name empty.

The source code is as follows:

```
String emptyVal = Req.getNVPs().Get("empty");
```

Then the `Process` function creates an instance of the `OrderItemHome` object called `OIH` that can access the SHIPTO table of the current database, as follows:

```
OrderItemHome OIH(*DB);
```

If the value of empty is equal to "1", the contents of the shopping cart will be emptied. To do this, the `Process` function first composes a WHERE statement that defines the criteria for deleting the records from the SHIPTO table: the records must belong to the current shopper and they must be in the pending state. It uses the predefined variables _COL_SHOPPER_REF_NUM and _COL_STATUS, which map to the STSHNBR (shopper reference number) and STSTAT (order status) columns in the SHIPTO table, respectively. Then, the `Process` function executes the WHERE statement to delete all records in the SHIPTO table that satisfy the criteria defined in the WHERE statement. If an error occurs, the function returns false and sends an error message to the log.

The source code is as follows:

```
if (emptyVal == "1")
{ // Delete all shipto reference numbers from the SHIPTO table.
  where << OrderItem::_COL_SHOPPER_REF_NUM << "=" << shopperRefNum
       << " AND " << OrderItem::_COL_STATUS << "= 'P'";
  OIH.Delete (where);

  if (OIH.getError() != ERR_DB_NO_ERROR && OIH.getError() !=
     ERR_DB_NO_DATA)
  {
    error << indent;
    error << "ERROR: Emptying the shopping cart";
    return false;
  }
}
```

The `Process` function must also be able to update the products in the shopping cart with new quantities when the shopper clicks the **Update** button. This will occur if the value of empty passed to the function is not equal to "1". The function will then update the SHIPTO table with the new quantities specified by the shopper, using the shipto reference number-quantity name-value pairs. These name-value pairs are stored in `HttpRequest Req`. To retrieve only them from `HttpRequest Req`, all name-value pairs whose names are integers will be treated as shipto reference numbers.

To perform the database update, the function does the following: first, it defines an `Iterator` `I` in order to retrieve the name-value pairs stored in `NameValuePairMap`, which is in `HttpRequest Req`. Then the Iterator is set to the beginning of the list. For every name-value pair stored in the `Iterator` `I`, if the name is an integer, the function does the following:

1.  Declares an `NVPHash` object called `changes` to store the changes that will be made to the database in the form of the name-value pair `<column>=<new value>`.

2.  Adds to the `NVPHash` object `changes` a name-value pair whose name is equal to the variable `_COL_QUANTITY` (which corresponds to the STQUANT column in the SHIPTO table) and whose value is equal to the value portion of the currently retrieved name-value pair (the quantity).

3.  Calls the `Clean` function to clear the WHERE statement. (This must be done for each iteration.)

4.  Composes a new WHERE statement in the where String that defines the following criteria for updating the quantities of records in the SHIPTO table: updates only those records which a) correspond to the currently retrieved shipto reference number, b) which belong to the current shopper, and c) whose state is pending.

5.  Inserts the retrieved quantity name-value pair stored in `changes` into the SHIPTO table by calling the `Update` function to execute the WHERE statement against the `OrderItemHome` instance `OIH`.

6.  If the SQL statement fails, returns false and outputs an error message to the log.

7.  Advances the iterator and processes the next name-value pair stored in the `Iterator` `I`, until all name-value pairs have been processed.

The source code is as follows:

```
else
{
    // Update the SHIPTO table with the product quantities by iterating
    // through all name-value pairs and for each one that contains an
    // integer for the name, treat it as a strfnbr-quantity pair.

    // Create an iterator and set it to the beginning.
    NVPHash::Iterator I = Req.getNVPs().getIterator();
    I.Begin();

    // Check each name-value pair.
    while (*I != NULL)
```

```
    {
      // Check if this pair's name is an integer.
      if ((*I)->getName().IsLong() == true)
      { // It's an integer, so update the table as needed.
        NVPHash changes;
        changes.Add(OrderItem::_COL_QUANTITY, (*I)->getValue());
        where.Clean();
        where << OrderItem::_COL_REF_NUM << "=" << ((*I)->getName())
              << " AND " << OrderItem::_COL_SHOPPER_REF_NUM << "="
              << shopperRefNum << " AND " << OrderItem::_COL_STATUS
              << "= 'P'";
        OIH.Update(changes, where);

        if (OIH.getError() != ERR_DB_NO_ERROR)
        {
          error << indent;
          error << "ERROR: Updating quantities";
          return false;
        }
      }

    // Advance the iterator.
    ++I;
    }
  }
```

If the `Process` function successfully completes, it returns a true value to the calling command (OrderItemUpdate), as follows:

```
    return true;

  }

};
```

The remaining code instantiates and registers the overridable function during the initialization of the server, as follows:

```
const ClassName ExtendShiptoUpdate::_STR_ThisClass
                                        ("ExtendShiptoUpdate");

static bool X2 = NC_OverridableFunctionManager::Register("IBM",
                                                         "NC",
                                          "ExtendShiptoUpdate",
                                                          1.0,
                                       new ExtendShiptoUpdate);
```

If the overridable function is successfully registered, a unique instance with the registration ID of `ExtendShiptoUpdate_1.0(IBM,NC)` will be created.

# Compiling the Overridable Function

Now you are ready to compile the CPP file and create the DLL or shared library for your overridable function. You must use the following compiler and release level:

**WIN** Microsoft Visual C++ version 4.2

**AIX** txlC++ version 4.1.x

## Sample Scenario:

For simplicity, a DLL has already been created for the ExtendShiptoUpdate_1.0(IBM,NC) function, which is called `newof.dll`. It is in the following directory on the CD:

**WIN** `\samples\ofs\`

# Storing the DLL or Shared Library

When you compiled the CPP file, you must copy the DLL or shared library to the following directory, so that the server can load it during initialization:

**WIN** `\ibm\netcommerce3\bin`

**AIX** `/usr/lpp/NetCommerce3/bin`

# Displaying the Overridable Function Results

For overridable functions that implement process tasks, their calling commands will handle a successful return and display the appropriate page to the shopper. If, however, your function sets exception tasks to handle errors, you need to modify the Net.Data macro that currently implements the task, in order to display an appropriate error page for your new function. You can also create a new macro.

For information on how to modify the default macros, see "Chapter 8, Modifying the Supplied Store Pages" on page 213. To create a new macro, see "Chapter 7, A Net.Data Tutorial" on page 169.

> **Note:**
> If you create a new macro or assign a new name to the default macro, you must also assign it to its corresponding task. See "Registering and Assigning a Net.Data Macro to its Task" on page 403 for details.

## Sample Scenario:

As shown in the code for the ExtendShiptoUpdate_1.0(IBM,NC) overridable function, when it successfully completes, it returns true to the OrderItemUpdate command. When an exception is encountered, the NCApiExtendShiptoUpdate_1.0(IBM,NC) overridable function returns false to the OrderItemUpdate command, which displays the default `cmdexe.html` error page in the browser. The macro that invokes the OrderItemUpdate command uses JavaScript to handle exception conditions, such as a shopper entering an invalid quantity. You can however, use an exception task to handle these type of errors. We have chosen not to in order to keep this example overridable function simple.

# Workshop: Writing the Overridable Function for the EXT_SHIPTO_UPD Task

In the last workshop, you planned how you were going to implement an overridable function that will be used by the EXT_SHIPTO_UPD process task, and you created the macro from which the shopper will invoke its calling command, OrderItemUpdate. Now you are ready to write the overridable function.

Your code will do the following:

1. Retrieve from the `NC_Environment` object the required variable `ORDERITEM_REF_NUM` and store its value in the string `shiptoRefNum`.

2. Retrieve all name-value pairs from the `HttpRequest` object.

3. For each name-value pair whose name is equal to "option", do the following:

    a) Retrieve its value (item option reference number) and store it in the string `value`.

    b) Insert into the OPTIONREL table the item option reference number (stored in the string `value`) and the shipto reference number (stored in the string `shiptoRefNum`).

    c) If an SQL error occurs, return a false value to the OrderItemUpdate command.

4. Upon successful completion, return a true value to the OrderItemUpdate command.

## Adding the Code

Now you are ready to write the code for the steps above. To save you some time, the skeleton code has already been written. All you have to do is add the remaining code to complete the class.

> **Note:**
> If you do not want to take the time to enter the code, you can just examine the code discussed here. A DLL has already been compiled using all the code, which you will use for your store.

1. Copy the template for the CPP file from the following directory to a temporary one:

    **WIN** `\workshops\ofs\oftemp.cpp`

2. Open the template in a text editor.

3. Change the name of the class to LinkItemOptions, by replacing every instance of `MyOverridableFunction` with `LinkItemOptions`.

4. Let's first examine the existing code in the `Process` function. It begins by retrieving the shipto reference number from the `NC_Environment` object. It does this by calling

the `CheckEnvironmentVariable` function in the `Misc` class to retrieve the value of the variable `ORDERITEM_REF_NUM`, and stores it in the string `shiptoRefNum`. It then declares a string called `optionName` to store the value "option", which will be referenced later in the `Process` function.

The code is as follows:

```
virtual bool Process (const HttpRequest& Req, HttpResponse& Res,
                      NC_Environment& Env)
{
  // Retrieve the shipto reference number from the environment.
  const String* shiptoRefNum = (const String*)
  Misc::CheckEnvironmentVariable (Env, "ORDERITEM_REF_NUM");

  static const StringWithOwnership optionName ("option");
```

5.  Now you will add the remaining code that will insert into the OPTIONREL table the item option reference number and shipto reference number for each name-value pair whose name is equal to "option". The `HttpRequest` object will a name-value pair for each topping that was selected by the shopper. Because the name-value pairs are not unique (they each have a name of "option" in the form of "option = <item_option_refnum>", you must iterate through each name-value pair to retrieve its value.

Add the following code to the `Process` function:

```
// For each item option in the request, insert a row in the
// OPTIONREL table. Because the parameter name 'option' is not
// unique, iterate through the name-value pairs.

//-------------------------------------------//
//-           Your Code Begins Here        -//
//-------------------------------------------//

NameValuePairMap::Iterator I = Req.getNVPs().getIterator();
String stmt;
I.Begin();

// Get the first option.
I.Seek(&optionName);

//-------------------------------------------//
//-           Your Code Ends Here          -//
//-------------------------------------------//
```

This code calls the `getNVPs` function to retrieve all the name-value pairs from the `HttpRequest` object instance `Req`. It then calls the `getIterator` function to retrieve the `Iterator` object from the `NameValuePairMap` object, and then creates an instance called `I`. Next, it declares the string `stmt` for storing the SQL statements that it will compose later. It then sets the iterator instance `I` to the first name-value-pair retrieved and advances to the first occurrence of the name-value pair with the name of "option".

6. Now you need to loop through all of the retrieved name-value pairs and retrieve the values only of those that are item options. Add the following code:

```
// For each item option in the request, insert a row in the
// OPTIONREL table. Because the parameter name 'option' is not
// unique, iterate through the name-value pairs.

//-----------------------------------------//
//-             Your Code Begins Here          -//
//-----------------------------------------//

NameValuePairMap::Iterator I = Req.getNVPs().getIterator();
String stmt;
I.Begin();

// Get the first option.
I.Seek(&optionName);

// Loop over every item in the request.
while ((*I) != NULL)
{
   if ((*I)->getName() == optionName)
   { // This is one of our parameters.
     String value = (*I)->getValue();

//-----------------------------------------//
//-             Your Code Ends Here            -//
//-----------------------------------------//
```

This code iterates through each name-value pair retrieved from the HttpRequest object. If the name of the current name-value pair is equal to "option", which indicates that it is an item option, retrieve its value using the getValue function in the NameValuePairMap object. The value (the item option reference number) is stored in the string value.

7. For each item option, you need to insert into the OPTIONREL table the item option reference number and the shipto reference number retrieved. This will link the item option to the shipto reference number, which in turn links it to its base pizza.

Add the following code:

```
// For each item option in the request, insert a row in the
// OPTIONREL table. Because the parameter name 'option' is not
// unique, iterate through the name-value pairs.

//-----------------------------------------//
//-             Your Code Begins Here          -//
//-----------------------------------------//

NameValuePairMap::Iterator I = Req.getNVPs().getIterator();
String stmt;
I.Begin();

// Get the first option.
I.Seek(&optionName);
```

```
// Loop over every item in the request.
while ((*I) != NULL)
{
  if ((*I)->getName() == optionName)
  { // This is one of our parameters.
    String value = (*I)->getValue ();
    stmt.Clean();
    stmt << "INSERT INTO optionrel (oprlstrn, oprloptrn) VALUES
       ("<< *shiptoRefNum << ", " << value << ")";
    SQL Sql((DataBase&)*Misc::CheckEnvironmentVariable (Env,
                 NC_Environment::_VAR_MainDatabase), stmt);
    if (Sql.getSQLrc() != ERR_DB_NO_ERROR)
    {
      Sql.ReportError();
      error << indent;
      error << "ERROR: Inserting NVP: " << *shiptoRefNum << ", " <<
               value << endl;
      return false;
    }
  }

//------------------------------------------//
//-            Your Code Ends Here        -//
//------------------------------------------//
```

For each item option contained in the array, this code first calls the `Clean` function in the String class instance `stmt` to clear the contents of the `stmt` variable. It then composes an SQL query in `stmt` to insert into the OPTIONREL table the value of string `shiptoRefNum` (the shipto reference number) and the value of string `value` (the item option reference number). It passes the statement to the constructor of the `SQL` class. The `SQL` class executes the query and stores the results in the `Sql` instance. Error checking is performed to ensure that the SQL statement executed properly. If an error occurs, the function sends to the log an error message containing the current shipto reference number that failed, and returns false to the OrderItemUpdate command.

8. Examine the remaining code in the class. It advances the iterator by one and repeats until all name-value pairs in the array have been looped through. If the function completes successfully, it returns true to the OrderItemUpdate command. The command will then redirect to the URL that was passed to it, which in this case contained the OrderItemDisplay command, to display the Order List with the selected pizza combination and total price.

The code is as follows:

```
    // Advance the iterator
    ++I;
  }
  return true;
  }
};
```

9. Now let's examine the code outside of the class, which is used to instantiate and register the overridable function during initialization of the server.

```
static bool X2 = NC_OverridableFunctionManager::Register("IBM",
                                                    "NC",
                                                "LinkItemOptions",
                                                          1.0,
                                            new LinkItemOptions);
```

This static variable X2 will be initialized when its DLL or shared library is loaded during the initialization of the server. An instance of the function will be created, and a call will be made to the overridable function manager in order to register the function as LinkItemOptions_1.0(IBM,NC).

10. Save your work and close the file.

You have now completed the LinkItemOptions overridable function. A final version of the code is stored in the of.cpp file on the CD, which you will use for the store.

# Examining the GetPizzaPrice Overridable Function

In the workshop "Planning New Overridable Functions for the OneStopPizza Shop" on page 362, you learned that in order to allow shoppers to make their own pizzas you had to replace the overridable function that is currently implementing the GET_BASE_SPE_PRC process task with a new one that will add the price of each topping selected by the shopper to the price of its corresponding pizza base. Without this function, the system would have no way of calculating the total price of these custom pizzas, since item option entities do not exist in the default Net.Commerce implementation. The OrderItemUpdate command calls this function before the LinkItemOptions function that you have just written is called.

The function is called GetPizzaPrice_1.0(IBM,NC) and is stored in the same CPP file as the LinkItemOptions function (of.cpp). It uses the default database objects to interact with the default database tables, and SQL statements to interact with the custom OPTIONREL and OPTIONPRICE tables. For any exceptions that it encounters (for example, an SQL failure), it returns a false value to the OrderItemUpdate command and outputs an error message to the log.

The following is the source code for the function's Process function:

```
virtual bool Process (const HttpRequest& Req, HttpResponse& Res,
                      NC_Environment& Env)
{
   // Retrieve the input parameters from the request.
   const String* merchantRefNum = (const String*)
         Misc::CheckEnvironmentVariable (Env, "MERCHANT_REF_NUM");
   const String* productRefNum = (const String*)
         Misc::CheckEnvironmentVariable (Env, "PRODUCT_REF_NUM");
   const String* shiptoRefNum = (const String*)
         Misc::CheckEnvironmentVariable (Env, "ORDERITEM_REF_NUM");
   String* price = (String*) Misc::CheckEnvironmentVariable (Env,
                                             "PRODUCT_PRICE");
   NVPHash NVP;
```

```
// Create the where string and make it large enough to avoid re-
// sizing.
String Where(STRLEN_1K);
Where << ProductPrice::_COL_MERCHANT_REF_NUM << " = "
      << *merchantRefNum << " AND "<< ProductPrice::_COL_PRICE
      << " IS NOT  NULL AND " << ProductPrice::_COL_PRODUCT_REF_NUM
      << " = " << *productRefNum;

// Retrieve the price of the base pizza.
ProductPriceHome ProdPrcHome((DataBase&)
                    *Misc::CheckEnvironmentVariable (Env,
                        NC_Environment::_VAR_MainDatabase));
ProductPriceHome::SchemaList* ProdPrcList =
 ProdPrcHome.Query(Where);

if (ProdPrcList == NULL)
{
   error << indent;
   error << "ERROR: Failed to get a list of potential product
           prices" << endl;
   return false;
}

ProductPriceHome::SchemaListIterator I(ProdPrcList);
I.Begin();
if (*I == NULL)
{
   error << indent;
   error << "ERROR: Failed to retrieve the price from the list of
           prices" << endl;
   return false;
}

double sumPrice = 0.0;
(*I)->getPrice().getVal(sumPrice);
ProdPrcHome.Destroy(ProdPrcList);

// Add the topping prices.
String stmt;

// First, get all toppings from the OPTIONREL table.
stmt << "SELECT oprloptrn FROM optionrel WHERE oprlstrn = "
      << *shiptoRefNum;

SQL Sql((DataBase&)*Misc::CheckEnvironmentVariable (Env,
                    NC_Environment::_VAR_MainDatabase), stmt);
Row SqlRow;
while (Sql.getNextRow(SqlRow) == ERR_DB_NO_ERROR)
{
   // For every topping, add its price to the base.
   stmt.Clean();
   stmt << "SELECT opprprice FROM optionprice WHERE opprrefnum = "
        << SqlRow.getCol (1);
```

```
      SQL Sql2 ((DataBase&)*Misc::CheckEnvironmentVariable (Env,
                        NC_Environment::_VAR_MainDatabase), stmt);
    Row SqlRow2;
    if (Sql2.getNextRow(SqlRow2) != ERR_DB_NO_ERROR)
    {
       error << indent;
       error << "ERROR: Can not retrieve price for option number "
              << SqlRow.getCol (1);
       return false;
    }

    double thisOption = 0.0;
    SqlRow2.getCol(1).getVal(thisOption);
    sumPrice += thisOption;
  }

  // Set the resulting price.
  price->Clean();
  *price << sumPrice;

  return true;
}
```

In summary, the above code for the GetPizzaPrice_1.0(IBM,NC) function does the following:

1.  Retrieves from the `NC_Environment` object the merchant reference number, the product reference number, the shipto reference number, and a pointer to the `price` variable, and stores their values in local variables.

2.  Retrieves from the PRODPRCS table the price that corresponds to the product reference number and merchant reference number previously retrieved from the environment.

3.  Declares the variable `sumPrice` for storing the total price of the item options and the product, and stores the retrieved price in this variable.

4.  Issues an SQL statement to retrieve from the OPTIONREL table all item option reference numbers that correspond to the shipto reference number previously retrieved from the environment.

5.  For each item option reference number that is retrieved, issues an SQL statement to retrieve its price from the OPTIONPRICE table and adds it to the variable `sumPrice`.

6.  Adds the value of `sumPrice` to the environment by inserting it into the `price` pointer.

## Compiling the Overridable Function

To save you some time, the CPP file for the LinkItemOptions and GetPizzaPrice overridable functions has already been compiled into the following DLL: `of.dll`.

## Storing the DLL

Copy of.dll from the \workshops\ofs following directory on the CD to the following directory:

> **WIN**    \ibm\netcommerce3\bin

## Displaying the Overridable Function Results

You do not need to create or modify macros to display the results of the GetPizzaPrice_1.0(IBM,NC) and LinkItemOptions_1.0(IBM,NC) overridable functions. Since they both implement process tasks, the calling OrderItemUpdate command will handle a successful return and display the appropriate page to the shopper. In this case, the command will redirect to the OrderItemDisplay command, which will refresh the Order List to display the pizza creation selected by the shopper. If either of the functions encounters an exception condition, they both return false to the command. The default system error page, cmdexe.html, is then displayed to the shopper, indicating that the command could not complete.

Currently, the Order List created by the Store Creator is not able to display the pizza and toppings selected by the shopper or its total price. Its macro needs to be modified so that it can retrieve from the custom OPTIONS, OPTIONPRICE, and OPTIONREL table the appropriate information for the shopper to view.

To save you some time, a replacement macro for the Order List has already been created, under the same name. All you have to do is copy it from the CD to the directory in which you store the macros for the OneStopPizza Shop.

Replace the shipto.d2w macro in the following directory with the shipto.d2w macro in the \workshops\macros\ directory on the CD:

> **WIN**    \ibm\netcommerce3\macro\en_US\OneStopPizzaShop\

If desired, you can open the macro in a text editor and examine what has been changed in it. The content is self-explanatory, so we will not stop to examine it in detail. The macro, does however, contain a new command, ItemOptionDelete, which replaces the original command, OrderItemDelete. When the shopper selects a pizza in the Order List and then clicks the **Remove Checked Items** button, this command first removes any toppings from the database and then calls the OrderItemDelete command to remove the pizza base from the database. The ItemOptionDelete command will be examined in greater detail in the workshop "Writing the FlexiReg Command" on page 459.

You have now completed this workshop. In the next workshop, "Activating and Testing the OneStopPizza Shop Overridable Functions" on page 407, you will learn how to activate the LinkItemOptions_1.0(IBM,NC) and the GetPizzaPrice_1.0(IBM,NC) overridable functions in the system and test them.

# Chapter 14, Activating and Testing Overridable Functions

After you have written your new overridable function, you must register it in the database and assign it to the task it implements, so that the system can execute it at run-time. If you have set a new exception task to handle errors encountered by the function, you will also need to register this task in the database and assign to it any macros that you have created or customized. You can then test the function. This chapter describes how to activate new overridable functions in the system and then test them to ensure that they function as intended. In the workshop, you will activate the overridable functions that you planned and wrote in the workshops in the previous two chapters.

> **Note:**
> Only site administrators have the authority to register new overridable functions. If you are a store administrator, you must ask your site administrator to perform the tasks described in this chapter.

This chapter covers the following topics:

- Registering an Overridable Function

- Assigning an Overridable Function to its Task

- Registering an Exception Task

- Registering and Assigning a Net.Data Macro to its Task

- Restarting the Net.Commerce Server

- Example of Activating the Sample Overridable Function

- Testing New Overridable Functions

- Disconnecting Default Overridable Functions

- Workshop: Testing and Activating the OneStopPizza Overridable Functions

# Registering an Overridable Function

To register an overridable function, you must insert a record into the OFS (Overridable Functions) table, as follows:

1.  From a DB2 command prompt, connect to the database in which you want to register the overridable function.

2.  Type the following command, all on one line:

    ```
    insert into ofs (refnum, dll_name, vendor, product, name,
    version, description) values ((select max(refnum)+1 from ofs),
    '<DLL/Shared_Library>', '<vendor>' , '<product>', '<name>',
    <version>, '<description>')
    ```

    The values for each field are as follows:

    `<DLL/Shared_Library>`
    > The name of the DLL or shared library in which the overridable function resides.

    > **Note:**
    > Ensure that you specify an extension for the DLL or shared library and that you specify the DLL or shared library either as a full path or as a path relative to the directory specified by your **LIBPATH** variable.

    `<vendor>`
    > The name of the company for which the overridable function is being written. This may be a third-party vendor, a merchant or site administrator, or IBM itself.

    `<product>`
    > The name of the product for which the overridable function is being implemented; for example, "NC" for Net.Commerce.

    `<name>`
    > The name of the overridable function.

    `<version>`
    > The version of the overridable function implementation.

    `<description>`
    > A brief description of the overridable function. If you do not want to insert a description, enter NULL.

# Assigning an Overridable Function to its Task

After you have registered your overridable function, you must assign it to the task that it implements. To do this, you must insert a record in the TASK_MER_OF table with your new overridable function. You can do this either manually or by using the Administrator forms. Both methods are described below.

## Manually

To manually insert a record into the TASK_MER_OF table, do the following for each task to be implemented:

1. From a DB2 command prompt, connect to the database in which you want to register the overridable function.

2. Type the following command, all on one line:

```
insert into task_mer_of (task_rn, merchant_rn, of_rn) values
((select tkrfnbr from tasks where tkname = '<task_name>'),
<merchant_rn>, (select refnum from ofs where name = '<name>'
and version = <version> and vendor = '<vendor>' and
product = '<product>'))
```

The values for each variable are as follows:

`<task_name>`
> The name of the task that the overridable function implements, as defined in the TASKS table.

`<merchant_rn>`
> The reference number of the merchant for which the function is being implemented. If the task is set to mall scope, (the overridable function will affect all stores in a mall), enter NULL.

`<name>`
> The name of the overridable function, as defined in the OFS table.

`<version>`
> The version of the overridable function implementation, as defined in the OFS table.

`<vendor>`
> The name of the company for which the overridable function is being written, as defined in the OFS table.

`<product>`
> The name of the product into which the overridable function is being implemented, as defined in the OFS table.

# Using the Administrator

To have the Administrator automatically insert a record in the TASK_MER_OF table, do the following for each task to be implemented:

1. Open the Administrator.

2. On the task bar, click **Site Manager** and then **Task Management**. The Task Management form appears.

3. From the **Select Task Type** drop-down list, select the appropriate task type.

   - **ERROR**, for overridable functions that handle exception conditions.

   - **PROCESS**, for overridable functions that process information.

   - **VIEW**, for overridable functions that display the pages that shoppers normally see during the shopping process.

   A list of all the tasks available for the selected task type appears in the bottom frame.

4. Select the desired task name from the list. Typically, you will select **PROCESS**. The fields automatically fill with task information.

5. From the **Scope** drop-down list, change the task scope, if desired. If you are creating a single-store site, you do not have to change the scope; both mall and store scope will function properly in this case.

6. If you changed the scope, click **Save** before proceeding.

7. On the task bar, click **Task Assignment**. If you selected a process task, the Overridable Function Assignment form appears. If you selected an exception or a view task, click the **Overridable Function** button at the bottom of the frame. The Overridable Function Assignment form appears.

8. From the **Store — Overridable Function(Product)(Vendor)(Version) Assignment** list, select the store or mall for which you want to assign your overridable function.

9. From the **Overridable Functions** list, select the overridable function that you want to assign to the selected task.

10. Click **Update**. A confirmation message appears, indicating that you have successfully assigned your new overridable function to the task for the selected store.

# Registering an Exception Task

If you created a new exception task to handle errors that are encountered by your overridable function, you must register the task in the database. For each exception task that your overridable function sets, insert a record in the TASKS table, as follows:

1. From a DB2 command prompt, connect to the database for your store.

2. Type the following command, all on one line:

```
insert into tasks (tkrfnbr, tkname , tkcomment , tkgroup , tkscope)
values ((select max(tkrfnbr)+1 from tasks), '<task_name>',
'<task_comment>', '<task_group>', <task_scope>)
```

The values for each field are as follows:

`<task_name>`
    The name of the task.

`<task_comment>`
    A brief description of the task.

`<task_group>`
    The task group to which the task belongs. Enter ERROR, which is the group for overridable functions that handle exception conditions.

`<task_scope>`
    The scope of the task. Enter 0 for mall scope or 1 for store scope. (The different stores residing in a mall can provide customized implementations by creating their own overridable functions.)

# Registering and Assigning a Net.Data Macro to its Task

If you have created a new macro or customized a supplied one for displaying an error page to shoppers, you must register the macro and assign it to the exception task that it implements. To do this, you must insert a record into the MACROS table. You can do this either manually or by using the Administrator forms provided.

## Manually

To manually insert a record into the MACROS table, do the following for each exception task to which the macro is to be assigned:

1. From a DB2 command prompt, connect to the database for your store.

2. Type the following command, all on one line:

   ```
   insert into macros (marfnbr, mamernbr, mafilename) values ((select
   tkrfnbr from tasks where tkname = '<task_name>'), <merchant_rn>,
   '<macro_name>')
   ```

   The values for each field are as follows:

   `<task_name>`
   > The name of the task for which the macro will be used, as defined in the TASKS table.

   `<merchant_rn>`
   > The reference number of the merchant for which the macro will be used. If the task is set to mall scope, (the macro will affect all stores in a mall), enter NULL.

   `<macro_name>`
   > The file name of the macro. Ensure that its path has been defined in the Net.Data `db2www.ini` configuration file. For more information, see "Specifying a Macro Directory" on page 195.

## Using the Administrator

To register the macro and assign it to its task using the Administrator, do the following:

1. Open the Administrator.

2. On the task bar, click **Site Manager** and then **Task Management**. The Task Management form appears.

3. From the **Select Task Type** drop-down list, select one of the following task types:

   - **ERROR**, for displaying error pages.

   - **VIEW**, for displaying the pages that shoppers normally see.

> **Note:**
> Do not select the **PROCESS** task type; this task is reserved for activating overridable functions that process information.

A list of the tasks that are available for the selected task type appears in the bottom frame.

4. Select the desired task name from the list. The fields automatically fill with task information.

5. From the **Scope** drop-down list, change the task scope, if desired. If you are creating a single-store site, you do not have to change the scope. Both mall and store scope will function properly in this case.

6. If you changed the scope, click **Save** before proceeding.

7. On the task bar, click **Task Assignment**.

8. Click the **Macro** button at the bottom of the frame. The Macro Assignment form appears.

9. If the scope of the task has been assigned to *store*, select the store for which you want to assign the macro from the **Select Mall/Store** drop-down list.

10. In the **Macro Filename** field, enter the file name of your new macro. Ensure that its path has been defined in the Net.Data db2www.ini configuration file. For more information, see "Specifying a Macro Directory" on page 195.

11. Click **Save**. A confirmation message appears, indicating that you have successfully assigned your new macro to the selected task.

# Restarting the Net.Commerce Server

After you register the infrastructure for your new overridable function, you must restart the Net.Commerce server in order for the database changes to take effect. Under Windows NT, you can easily stop and start the server from the Control Panel. Under AIX, you can do so from the Configuration Manager.

## Stopping and Starting the Server on Windows NT

To restart the Net.Commerce server from the Control Panel on Windows NT, do the following:

1. On a Windows NT user ID with Administrator authority, click **Start**, point to **Settings**, and then click **Control Panel**.

2. In the Control Panel window, double-click the **Services** icon.

3. For each Net.Commerce instance that you want to start, do the following:

   a) From the Service list, select **Net.Commerce – <instance_name>,** where **<instance_name>** is the name of the instance that you want to start. By default, the instance name is **mser** if you are running only one instance.

   b) Click **Stop** to stop the instance.

   c) When the instance has stopped successfully, click **Start** to start it again.

## Stopping and Starting the Server on AIX

To restart the Net.Commerce server from the Configuration Manager on AIX, do the following:

1.  If the Configuration Manager is not currently running, do the following to start it:

    a)  While logged on as user ID root, on an AIX command line, switch to the `/usr/lpp/NetCommerce3/server/bin` directory.

    b)  Type: `/start_admin_server`.

2.  Start your browser and go to `http://host_name:4444`.

3.  When prompted, enter your Configuration Manager user ID and password. If you have not yet changed them, your user ID is `webadmin`, and your password is `webibm`.

4.  From the list of instances, select the instance you want to restart and click **Stop**.

5.  When the instance has stopped successfully, click **OK** and then click **Start** to start it again.

# Example of Activating the Sample Overridable Function

The following describes the steps for activating the ExtendShiptoUpdate overridable function for the shopping cart page, which was initially introduced in "Chapter 12, Planning Overridable Functions" on page 349.

1.  Register the overridable function in the OFS table, as follows:

    ```
    insert into ofs (refnum, dll_name, vendor, product, name, version,
    description) values ((select max(refnum)+1 from ofs), 'newof.dll',
    'IBM', 'NC', 'ExtendShiptoUpdate', 1.0, 'Updates quantities or
    deletes products from the SHIPTO table')
    ```

2.  Assign the overridable function to the process task that it implements, EXT_SHIPTO_UPD, as follows:

    ```
    insert into task_mer_of (task_rn, merchant_rn, of_rn) values
    ((select tkrfnbr from tasks where tkname = 'EXT_SHIPTO_UPD'), NULL,
    (select refnum from ofs where name = 'ExtendShiptoUpdate' and
    version = 1.0 and vendor = 'IBM' and product = 'NC'))
    ```

3.  Since the overridable function does not set any exception tasks, there are no tasks that need to be registered or any macros to implement the task.

4.  Stop and start the Net.Commerce server, in order to activate the overridable function in the system.

# Testing New Overridable Functions

After you have registered your new overridable function in the database, along with the tasks and macros that it uses, you are ready to test it. You must first determine whether you will use a test environment within the Net.Commerce system, write your own, or use a combination of both.

The advantage to testing your implementation within the Net.Commerce system is that you can be sure it will run the same way in production. The disadvantage is that you must run the commands through a browser and determine whether they work as expected.

The advantage to writing your own test environment is that you have more control over your test cases and the ability to trace through your code. The disadvantage is that unless your test environment re-creates the Net.Commerce environment exactly, you cannot be sure that your changes will work the same way in production.

To gain the advantages of both environments while minimizing the disadvantages, you can start in your own test environment. When you believe that your changes are working properly, test them from within the Net.Commerce system.

Once you have created the scenario in which your overridable function will run, check for the following:

1. Ensure that the function responds as expected.

2. Ensure that the error pages are displayed when an exception condition is encountered by your function, and that the error parameters are passed as expected.

3. If it appears that your function is not being called, check the following:

   a) You have activated your function and macro (if applicable for displaying an error page), using the Administrator.

   b) If you are customizing a store, the task to which your overridable function is assigned is set to *store* scope.

   c) The Net.Commerce system does not display an error message in the log about your function or macro.

# Disconnecting Default Overridable Functions

You can disconnect any default overridable function that is not required by your business by replacing it with the DoNothingNoArgs_1.0 (IBM,NC) overridable function, as long as it is not assigned to any of the following tasks:

- An exception task or a view task; otherwise no page is displayed to the shopper.

- A process task that returns one or more values as output parameters; otherwise, all the output parameters will be empty strings.

When disconnecting an overridable function, you first need to determine the process task that is currently assigned to the overridable function. See "Appendix F, Net.Commerce Overridable

Functions" on page 665 for a description of the overridable function and the process task that it implements. Once you know the name of the task, ensure that you are authorized to disconnect the overridable function by examining the scope of the task to see whether it is set to *store* or *mall*. For details, see "Step 3. Ensuring Authorization" on page 352.

If you are authorized to disconnect the function, you can proceed to replace its task with the DoNothingNoArgs_1.0 (IBM,NC) overridable function using the Administrator, as follows:

1. Open the Administrator.

2. From the task bar, click Site Manager and then Task Management. The Task Management form appears.

3. From the **Select Task Type** drop-down list, select **PROCESS**.

   A list of all the tasks that belong to the PROCESS task group appears in the bottom frame.

4. Select the desired task name from the list. The fields automatically fill with task information.

5. On the task bar, click **Task Assignment.** The Overridable Function Assignment form appears.

6. From the **Store — Overridable Function(Product)(Vendor)(Version) Assignment** list, select the store or mall for which you want to assign your overridable function.

7. From the **Overridable Functions** list, select **DoNothingNoArgs(NC)(IBM)(1.0)**.

8. Click **Update**. A confirmation message appears, indicating that you have successfully assigned the DoNothingNoArgs_1.0 (IBM,NC) overridable function to the specified task for the selected store.

   The original function is now disconnected from the system.

# Workshop: Activating and Testing the OneStopPizza Shop Overridable Functions

In the previous workshop "Writing the Overridable Function for the EXT_SHIPTO_UPD Task" on page 391, you wrote the LinkItemOptions_1.0(IBM,NC) overridable function for the EXT_SHIPTO_UPD process task and examined the GetPizzaPrice_1.0(IBM,NC) overridable function for the GET_BASE_SPE_PRC process task. In this workshop, you will register both of these functions in the database and test them.

## Activating the Overridable Functions

To register and activate the LinkItemOptions_1.0(IBM,NC) and GetPizzaPrice_1.0(IBM,NC) overridable functions in the system, do the following:

1. Start a DB2 Command Line Processor window.

2.  From a DB2 command prompt, connect to the database for the OneStopPizza Shop by typing the following:

    ```
    connect to <database_name>
    ```

    where `<database_name>` is the name of the database that you are using for the OneStopPizza Shop.

3.  Register the LinkItemOptions_1.0(IBM,NC) overridable function in the OFS table by typing the following command all on one line:

    ```
    insert into ofs (refnum, dll_name, vendor, product, name, version,
    description) values ((select max(refnum)+1 from ofs), 'of.dll',
    'IBM', 'NC', 'LinkItemOptions', 1.0, 'Link item options to their
    base product')
    ```

4.  Register the GetPizzaPrice_1.0(IBM,NC) overridable function in the OFS table by typing the following command all on one line:

    ```
    insert into ofs (refnum, dll_name, vendor, product, name, version,
    description) values ((select max(refnum)+1 from ofs), 'of.dll',
    'IBM', 'NC', 'GetPizzaPrice', 1.0, 'Calculates total price of
    option items and base product')
    ```

5.  Assign the LinkItemOptions_1.0(IBM,NC) overridable function to the process task that it implements, EXT_SHIPTO_UPD, by typing the following command all on one line:

    ```
    insert into task_mer_of (task_rn, merchant_rn, of_rn) values
    ((select tkrfnbr from tasks where tkname = 'EXT_SHIPTO_UPD'),
    <merchant_rn>, (select refnum from ofs where name =
    'LinkItemOptions' and version = 1.0 and vendor = 'IBM' and product =
    'NC'))
    ```

    where `<merchant_rn>` is your merchant reference number. (If you do not know the number, type `select * from merchant` at the prompt. Then make a note of the merchant reference number that corresponds to the store name OneStopPizza Shop (column MESTNAME).)

6.  Assign the GetPizzaPrice_1.0(IBM,NC) overridable function to the process task that it implements, GET_BASE_SPE_PRC, by typing the following command all on one line:

    ```
    insert into task_mer_of (task_rn, merchant_rn, of_rn) values
    ((select tkrfnbr from tasks where tkname = 'GET_BASE_SPE_PRC'),
    <merchant_rn>, (select refnum from ofs where name = 'GetPizzaPrice'
    and version = 1.0 and vendor = 'IBM' and product = 'NC'))
    ```

    where `<merchant_rn>` is your merchant reference number.

7.  Since neither overridable function sets any exception tasks, there are no tasks that need to be registered or macros to implement the task.

8.  Close the DB2 window.

9.  To activate the overridable functions in the system, go to the Control Panel and stop and start the Net.Commerce server, as described in "Stopping and Starting the Server on Windows NT" on page 404.

## Testing the Overridable Functions

You are now ready to test the two overridable functions in the OneStopPizza Shop.

1.  Close any browser windows that are currently open.

2.  Open the OneStopPizza Shop in a new browser window.

3.  On the navigation bar, click **Menu**.

4.  On the category page, click **Make Your Own Pizza**. The Make Your Own Pizza page appears (created by the `prod.d2w` macro).

5.  From the **Size** drop-down list, select **Medium @ 7.99**.

6.  Select the checkboxes that correspond to **Ham @ 0.50**, **Green Peppers @ 0.50**, and **Mushrooms @ 0.50**.

7.  Click **Add to Order List**. Your pizza creation is added to the Order List, displaying the toppings and the total price of the pizza (before taxes), as shown in Figure 14.1.

***Figure 14.1*** *The Make Your Own Pizza page and the Order List.*

8.  Close the browser.

You have now completed this workshop. In the next workshop, "Planning a New Command for Flexible Registration" on page 424, you will learn how to plan for writing a new command that will provide flexible shopper registration in the store.

# Chapter 15, Planning Commands

Careful planning is required when creating new commands that will perform custom store operations. This chapter and the next present a simple example that will help you better understand the process of planning and creating commands. In the workshop, you will plan for a new command that implements a unique requirement in the pizza store.

This chapter covers the following topics:

- Sample Scenario
- Step 1. Determining the Store Operation
- Step 2. Determining the Command's Input and Output Parameters
- Step 3. Defining the Command Syntax
- Step 4. Determining the Scope of the Command
- Step 5. Determining How to Handle Exceptions
- Step 6. Determining How to Handle a Successful Return
- Step 7. Creating the Interface to the Command
- Workshop: Planning a New Command for Flexible Registration

# Sample Scenario

You are a store administrator who is responsible for managing and running a clothing store. Before a shopper can place an order, he or she must register (for the initial visit) or log on (for return visits). You have made registration mandatory in your store because you want to track the buying patterns of your shoppers and organize them into different shopper groups to which you can offer special discounts and other purchasing incentives. Lately, however, you have discovered that some shoppers are apparently forgetting the logon passwords that they specified when they first registered, meaning that on return visits they are re-registering each time instead of logging on. This response is causing you administrative problems, as such individuals are now registered as new shoppers and any previous activities are registered under their old shopper records, which are no longer active.

To solve this problem, you have decided to write a command that will allow a shopper who forgets the logon password to reset it. Before you begin, however, you need to do some planning.

**Note:**
The command described in this chapter is very simple in both nature and functionality, and is shown for illustrative purposes only. Issues such as security are not taken into consideration.

# Step 1. Determining the Store Operation

The first step in planning how you will write a command is to clearly define the store operation that you want to achieve.

## Sample Scenario:

In this case, you want to write a command that will let a shopper update his or her password in the database with a new one. To verify authenticity, the shopper must also provide the correct answer to the challenge question, which was defined during registration.

The command will have the execution flow shown in Figure 15.1 below:

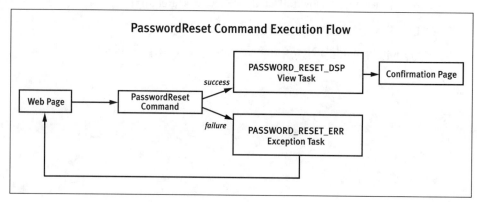

*Figure 15.1  The execution flow of the PasswordReset command.*

The parts of Figure 15.1 will be discussed throughout this chapter.

# Step 2. Determining the Command's Input and Output Parameters

You now need to determine: 1) the input parameters that your command will receive from the Net.Commerce system, and 2) the output parameters that it will return to the system. Ensure that you do the following:

- Use any parameters that the system passes in if they are needed by your command

- Pass the variables that the system expects to receive back to the system

- In case of an exception condition, return the parameters that are needed to handle the error

You can define as many input and output parameters as are required by your new command. The input parameters can be either used by the command directly or passed to any tasks that the command sets. All commands accept the parameters that were initially passed to them from a page or another command, and pass them unchanged to any overridable functions and macros that are called downstream.

Parameters can be treated as either mandatory or optional:

- Mandatory input parameters are always required by the command or by any overridable functions that the command calls downstream.

- Optional input parameters are treated as optional by the command or by any overridable functions that it calls.

- Mandatory output parameters are those that are required by the system and by the macros that display the resulting store page or error message.

- Optional output parameters are those treated as optional by the system and by any macros that are executed.

## Sample Scenario:

In our example, the command will receive the following mandatory input parameters from the system:

- The merchant reference number, for setting the correct view and exception task

- The shopper's logon ID, to retrieve the shopper's record from the database

- The shopper's answer to the challenge question, to verify his or her authenticity

- The new password and verification password submitted by the shopper

The command does not have any optional input parameters and it will not return any parameters to the system.

# Step 3. Defining the Command Syntax

Once you have determined the command's input parameters, you can define its syntax, which involves specifying its name and each of its mandatory and optional input parameters. This information will be coded in the page that invokes the command.

All Net.Commerce commands must have the basic syntax shown in Figure 15.2 below:

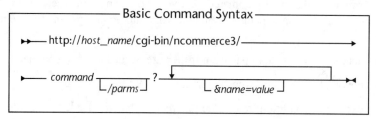

*Figure 15.2 The basic command syntax.*

The values of the parameters are as follows:

host_name
>    The fully qualified name of your Net.Commerce server.

cgi-bin
>    The directory in which Net.Commerce CGI executable files are stored.

command
>    The name of the command. It is case-sensitive, must be unique, and cannot contain forward slashes (/), spaces, or any character that is not valid within a URL.

parms
>    Additional parameters in the PATH_INFO portion of the URL that are required by the request.

name
>    The name portion of a name-value pair that is either a required or optional input parameter. It is part of the QUERY_STRING portion of the command URL.

value
>    The value portion of a name-value pair that is either a required or optional input parameter. It is part of the QUERY_STRING portion of the command URL.

You can pass custom name-value pairs that are required by one or more overridable functions, which are called by the command. The parameters can be passed in any order. All parameters must be defined in lowercase.

## Sample Scenario:

For our command example, we will call the command PasswordReset. It will have the syntax shown in Figure 15.3.

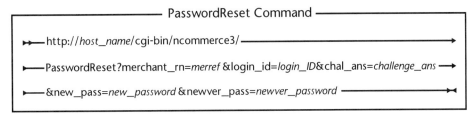

**Figure 15.3** *The PasswordReset command.*

You have defined all the parameters as mandatory. Their values are as follows:

`merref`
　　The merchant reference number

`login_ID`
　　The logon ID of the shopper

`challenge_ans`
　　The answer to the shopper's challenge question

`new_password`
　　The new password specified by the shopper

`newver_password`
　　The new verification password specified by the shopper

# Step 4. Determining the Scope of the Command

You now need to determine whether the command will call one or more overridable functions to do some of its processing. Commands that perform simple tasks, such as inserting or updating a record in the database, can generally do all the processing themselves. (An example would be the PasswordReset command.) Commands that are more complex could call one or more overridable functions to perform specific operations.

Also, if your command performs a function that is common to multiple commands, you can write the function as a separate class and call it from all the commands, which reduces redundant coding.

For a review of how to call an overridable function, see "Calling an Overridable Function" on page 338.

# Step 5. Determining How to Handle Exceptions

You now need to plan how you will handle exception conditions that are encountered by your command. You have the following options:

- Set an exception task to handle the error.
- Let the system handle the error, by returning a false value to the system.

- Let the command handle the error, by hard-coding the HTTP response directly in the function and then throwing the &_ERR_CMD_ERR_CMD_HANDLED exception.

To review these methods, see "Handling Exceptions" on page 324.

## Sample Scenario:

The PasswordReset command must be able to handle the following five exception conditions:

- One or more of the required input parameters are syntactically incorrect.

- An error occurs when the command attempts to interact with the database.

- The password and verification password submitted by the shopper do not match.

- The value of the logon ID is not valid.

- The challenge answer submitted by the shopper does not match the corresponding entry in the database.

If any of the required input parameters are syntactically incorrect, or if an error occurs when the command is interacting with the database, you will return a false value to the system, and in the case of the database error, you will output an error message to the log. The former error will be returned when the command is checking the input parameters, at which time the command manager will invoke the system error page cmdinc.html, indicating that the calling command syntax is not correct. The latter error will be returned from the command's Process function, at which time the command manager will invoke the system error page cmdexe.html, indicating that the command could not complete.

If the shopper's password does not match the verification password, the logon ID is not valid, or the shopper's challenge answer does not match the corresponding entry in the database, you will set an exception task called PASSWORD_RESET_ERR and pass to it a different error code for each exception condition (1000, 1001, and 1002, respectively). You will use the supplied overridable function, TaskDisplay_1.0(IBM,NC), to execute a Net.Data macro, which will display an error message that corresponds to the error code passed in, along with fields for the shopper to reenter the incorrect data.

# Step 6. Determining How to Handle a Successful Return

You need to plan what your command will do when it successfully completes. You have the following options:

- Set a view task to display a store page

- Pass the flow of execution to another URL

- Call another command and pass the current input parameters to it.

To review these methods, see "Handling a Successful Return" on page 327.

## Sample Scenario:

For the PasswordReset command, you will display a Web page by setting the view task PASSWORD_RESET_DSP. You will once again use the supplied TaskDisplay_1.0 (IBM,NC) overridable function, which will execute a custom macro called `pwdsuccess.d2w` to display a message indicating a successful password reset.

# Step 7. Creating the Interface to the Command

Before you begin to write your command, it is advisable to create the Net.Data macro that will invoke it, to ensure that it will receive all its required input parameters. For an overview of how to create Net.Data macros, see "Chapter 7, A Net.Data Tutorial" on page 169.

## Sample Scenario:

We will now look at the macro that has been created to invoke the PasswordReset command. This macro performs two important functions: it obtains from the shopper the information required for the command to perform the password reset, and it passes this information as parameters to the server in the form of an HTTP request, from which the command will retrieve them. In review, the command expects to receive the following as input parameters: the merchant reference number, the shopper's logon ID, the shopper's answer to the challenge question, and the new password and verification password.

Obtaining this information from the shopper can be done in many ways. In this example, you will do so in two stages. First, you will prompt the shopper for identifying information, and use that information to retrieve the challenge question from the corresponding shopper record in the database. You can ask for any information that the shopper specified during registration, but it should be something that can be easily recalled. In this example, we have decided to ask for the shopper's first name, last name, and telephone number. (Note that in a real store, you might ask for more challenging information to ensure authentication of the shopper.) Once the shopper has provided this information, the macro can retrieve the challenge question and the shopper's logon ID.

Second, you need to ask the shopper to answer the question and to provide a new password and verification password. When the shopper submits this information, you will pass it to the command, along with the logon ID that was retrieved from the database. The command will handle the rest of the processing.

The first page presented to the shopper will look something like Figure 15.4.

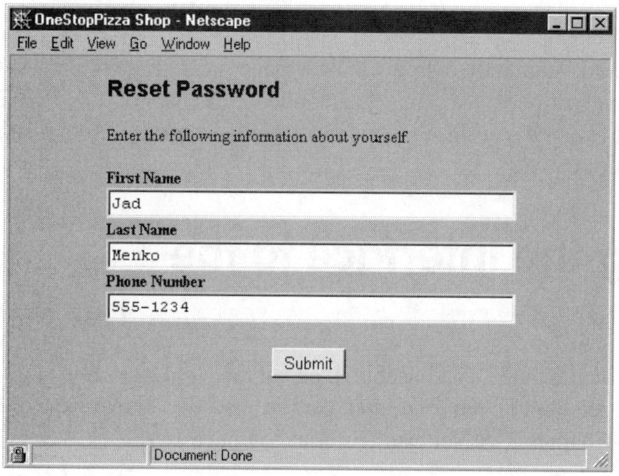

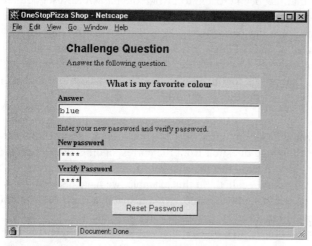

**Figure 15.4** *The first Reset Password page.*

After the shopper submits the information, the page shown in Figure 15.5, will appear:

**Figure 15.5** *The second Password Reset page.*

The source code of the macro is as follows:

```
%INCLUDE "OneStopPizzaShop\common.inc"

%DEFINE {

  b_success = "true"
  s_loginid = ""

%}

%FUNCTION(DTW_ODBC) getQuestion() {

  select shchaque, shlogid
  from shopper, shaddr
  where salname='$(salname)'
```

```
and shlogid = '$(SESSION_ID)'
and safname='$(safname)'
and saphone1='$(saphone1)'
and sashnbr=shrfnbr
and saadrflg='P'

%REPORT {

    <TABLE WIDTH="300" CELLPADDING="0" CELLSPACING="0" BORDER="0">
     <TR>
        <TD ALIGN="left" VALIGN="center"><FONT FACE="helvetica"
        COLOR=$(TitleTxtCol)><H3>Challenge Question</H3></FONT></TD>
     </TR>
     <TR>
        <TD><FONT COLOR="black" SIZE="2">Answer the following
         question.</FONT></TD>
     </TR>
     <TR>
        <TD><BR></TD>
     </TR>

    %ROW {

      @DTW_ASSIGN(s_loginid, V_shlogid)
      <TR>
        <TD ALIGN="center" BGCOLOR=$(BodyColor2)>
         <FONT COLOR="$(TitleTxtCol)" SIZE="3">
         <B>$(V_shchaque)</B></FONT><BR></TD>
      </TR>
    %}
  %}

  %MESSAGE {

    100 : {
       <B>Your shopper record was not found in the database.  Please try
        again.</B>
       <BR><BR>
       @DTW_ASSIGN(b_success, "false")
    %}: CONTINUE

    DEFAULT : {
       <B>An unknown error occurred in the getQuestion() function.</B>
    %}
  %}
%}

%HTML_INPUT{

  <HTML>
  <HEAD>
  <META HTTP-EQUIV=Expires CONTENT="Mon, 01 Jan 1996 01:01:01 GMT">
  </HEAD>
```

```
<BODY BGCOLOR="$(BodyColor1)" TEXT="$(TextCol)" LINK="$(LinkCol)"
VLINK="$(VLinkCol)" ALINK="$(ALinkCol)">

<FORM method=POST action="/cgi-bin/ncommerce3/PasswordReset">

@getQuestion()

<INPUT TYPE = "hidden" NAME="merchant_rn" VALUE="$(MerchantRefNum)">
<INPUT TYPE = "hidden" NAME="login_id" VALUE="$(s_loginid)" >

%IF(b_success == "true")

<TR>
  <TD><BR></TD>
</TR>
<TR>
  <TD><B><FONT SIZE="-1">Answer</FONT></B></TD>
</TR>
<TR>
  <TD><INPUT TYPE="text" NAME="chal_ans" SIZE="40"
  MAXLENGTH="254"></TD>
</TR>
<TR>
  <TD><BR></TD>
</TR>
<TR>
  <TD><FONT COLOR="black" SIZE="2">Enter your new password and
  verify password.</FONT></TD>
</TR>
<TR>
  <TD><BR></TD>
</TR>
<TR>
  <TD><B><FONT SIZE="-1">New password</FONT></B></TD>
</TR>
<TR>
  <TD><INPUT TYPE="password" NAME="new_pass" SIZE="40"
  MAXLENGTH="16"></TD>
</TR>
<TR>
  <TD><B><FONT SIZE=-1>Verify Password</FONT></B></TD>
</TR>
<TR>
  <TD><INPUT TYPE="password" NAME="newver_pass" SIZE="40"
  MAXLENGTH="16"></TD>
</TR>
<TR>
  <TD><BR></TD>
</TR>
<TR>
  <TD ALIGN="center"><INPUT TYPE="submit" VALUE="Reset Password">
  </TD>
```

```
    </TR>
  </TABLE>

%ENDIF

  </FORM>
  </BODY>
  </HTML>

%}

%HTML_REPORT {

  <HTML>
  <HEAD><TITLE>Reset Password</TITLE></HEAD>
  <BODY BGCOLOR="$(BodyColor1)" TEXT="$(TextCol)" LINK="$(LinkCol)"
   VLINK="$(VLinkCol)" ALINK="$(ALinkCol)">

  <FORM METHOD="post" ACTION="/cgi-bin/ncommerce3/ExecMacro/
   $(STORENAME)/password.d2w/input">

  <TABLE WIDTH=250 CELLPADDING=0 CELLSPACING=0 BORDER=0>
    <TR>
      <TD ALIGN="left" VALIGN="center"><FONT FACE="helvetica"
       COLOR=$(TitleTxtCol)>
      <H3>Reset Password</H3></FONT></TD>
    </TR>
    <TR>
      <TD ALIGN="left"><FONT COLOR="black" SIZE="2">Enter the
       following information about yourself.</FONT></TD>
    </TR>
    <TR><TD><BR></TD></TR>
    <TR>
      <TD><B><FONT SIZE="-1">First Name</FONT></B></TD>
    </TR>
    <TR>
      <TD><INPUT TYPE="text" NAME="safname" SIZE="40"
       MAXLENGTH="30"></TD>
    </TR>
    <TR>
      <TD><B><FONT SIZE="-1">Last Name</FONT></B></TD>
    </TR>
    <TR>
      <TD><INPUT TYPE="text" NAME="salname" SIZE="40"
       MAXLENGTH="30"></TD>
    </TR>
    <TR>
      <TD><B><FONT SIZE="-1">Phone Number</B></FONT></TD>
    </TR>
    <TR>
      <TD><INPUT TYPE="text" NAME="saphone1" SIZE="40"
       MAXLENGTH="30"></TD>
    </TR>
    <TR>
```

```
        <TD><BR></TD>
      </TR>
      <TR>
        <TD ALIGN="center"><INPUT TYPE="submit" VALUE="Submit"></TD>
      </TR>
    </TABLE>
    </FORM>
    </BODY>
    </HTML>
  %}
```

The macro contains an %HTML_INPUT section and an %HTML_REPORT section to create the two pages. The %HTML_REPORT section, which is invoked first, contains a simple HTML form with fields for the shopper to enter his or her first name, last name, and phone number. When the shopper clicks the submit button, the form's action URL is invoked, as follows:

```
<FORM METHOD="post" ACTION="/cgi-bin/ncommerce3/ExecMacro/
$(STORENAME)/password.d2w/input">
```

This URL contains the ExecMacro command, which executes the %HTML_INPUT section of this macro. The values entered into the form fields are passed as input parameters to this section. The %HTML_REPORT section does the main work in the macro. It calls the getQuestion function, which retrieves from the SHOPPER (Shopper Profile) table the challenge question and the logon ID for the shopper whose first name, last name, and phone number match the corresponding values that were passed from the %HTML_REPORT section of the macro. If an entry is not found in the database, an error message is displayed. If an entry is found, meaning that the shopper has registered with the store, the %REPORT block displays the page title and the introductory text. For each row retrieved (in this case there will be only one), the %ROW block first assigns the logon ID that was retrieved from the query to the variable s_loginid and then displays the challenge question.

The remainder of the %HTML_INPUT section defines two hidden input parameters containing name-value pairs for the shopper's logon ID and the merchant reference number. Note that these parameters must be named login_id and merchant_rn, as expected by the command; otherwise, the command will return an error when it checks for them. Next, fields for the answer to the challenge question and for a new password and verification password are displayed, as well as the submit button of the form. When the shopper enters the information and clicks the button, the password information, along with the merchant reference number and the logon ID, is sent in the URL that contains your command as an HTTP request to the server. The URL is defined in the form's action field as follows:

```
<FORM method=POST action="/cgi-bin/ncommerce3/PasswordReset">
```

Now the PasswordReset command will do the remaining processing to perform the password reset. You will learn how to write the actual command in the next chapter.

The password.d2w macro is stored in the following directory on the CD:

**WIN** \samples\macros\

**Tip:**
In this example, we use the ExecMacro command to call the **%HTML_REPORT** section of the
**password.d2w** macro, which then displays an HTML form to the shopper. As an alternative
to using this command, you could create a display command that sets a view task to call the macro.
The following is the source code for a display command called PasswordForm that sets the view
task PASSWORD_DSP, which in turn invokes the **password.d2w** macro:

```
class __DLL_EXPORT__ PasswordForm : public NC_Command
{
  static const PasswordForm _STR_ThisClass;

  public:
    PasswordForm() { }
    void operator delete( void* p ) { ::delete p; }
    virtual NC_Command* Clone(void) { return new PasswordForm; }

  protected:
    String _MerchantRefNum;

  public:
    virtual bool CheckParameters(const HttpRequest& Req,
                                 HttpResponse& Res,
                                 NC_Environment& Env,
                                 NC_Environment& Resources)
  {

    static const StringWithOwnership NVP_merchant_rn("merchant_rn");
    return Misc::CheckFieldExistence(Req, NVP_merchant_rn,
                                     _MerchantRefNum, true);

  }

  virtual bool Process(const HttpRequest& Req, HttpResponse& Res,
                       NC_Environment& Env)

  {

    static const StringWithOwnership TASK_PASSWORD_DSP
                                        ("PASSWORD_DSP");
    Misc::SetView(Env, TASK_PASSWORD_DSP, _MerchantRefNum);
    return true;
  }
};

static bool X2 = NC_CommandManager::Register("IBM", "NC",
                                              "PasswordForm", 1.0,
                                              new PasswordForm );
```

Another option is to use the ExecTask command, which behaves similarly to the above display
command: it calls a task based on the name of the task and the merchant reference number that
is passed to it. For more information about the ExecTask command, see page 580.

# Workshop: Planning a New Command for Flexible Registration

The OneStop Pizza shop lets shoppers get in and out of the store with only a few clicks of the mouse. To simplify the order process, shoppers can register at the same time that they place an order, rather than having to navigate to a separate registration page.

In this workshop, you will plan how to implement an order process that allows the shopper to do the following from one page:

- View a summary of the total charges of the order

- Enter a delivery address (for guest shoppers) or update the displayed address (for registered shoppers)

- Enter a logon ID and password (to register with the store) or update them (for registered shoppers)

- Select a payment method (C.O.D. or credit card)

- Submit the order

When the shopper submits the order, the following will happen:

- If the shopper entered only a delivery address and payment information, the address is updated in the database, the payment information is processed, and a confirmation page is displayed.

- If the shopper entered a delivery address, payment information, *and* a logon ID and password, the shopper is automatically registered in the database, the payment information is processed, and a confirmation page is displayed.

To implement this order process, you need to create a new command that will perform the appropriate operation based on the shopper's input. Let's begin the planning process for creating such a command.

## Step 1. Determining the Store Operation

You want to write a command that will do the following when a shopper places an order:

- If the shopper submits a logon ID and password in addition to the delivery address and payment method, the command will call either the RegisterUpdate command (if the shopper has previously registered) or the RegisterNew command (if the shopper has not registered).

- If the shopper submits only the delivery address and payment method, the command will call the AddressUpdate command to update the database with this delivery address.

In all cases, the OrderProcess command will be called when the RegisterUpdate, RegisterNew, or AddressUpdate command successfully completes, and will be passed to the command as a redirection URL.

The command will have the execution flow shown in Figure 15.6 below:

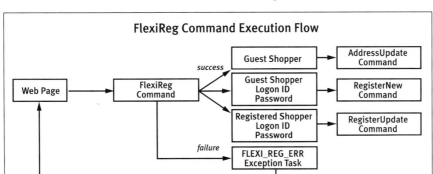

*Figure 15.6 The execution flow of the FlexiReg command.*

The parts of this flow diagram will be discussed throughout this workshop.

# Step 2. Determining the Command's Input and Output Parameters

Your command will receive the following required input parameter from the Net.Commerce system:

- The merchant reference number, for setting the correct exception task to handle errors that are encountered by the command.

It may also receive from the system the following optional input parameter:

- The shopper's logon ID and password, to call the RegisterNew or RegisterUpdate command.

The command will not return any parameters to the system: it will simply redirect the flow of execution to another command.

> **Note:**
> All parameters required by the RegisterNew, RegisterUpdate, or AddressUpdate command must also be passed as input parameters to the FlexiReg command; otherwise, these commands will fail and the order cannot be placed. These parameters are not required by the FlexiReg command, but will be forwarded to the command that it calls.

# Step 3. Defining the Command Syntax

You will call your command FlexiReg, and it will have the syntax shown in Figure 15.7 below:

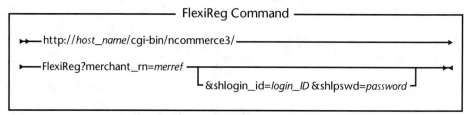

*Figure 15.7  The FlexiReg command.*

The values of the parameters are as follows:

merref
> The merchant reference number

login_ID
> The logon ID specified by the shopper

password
> The password specified by the shopper

newver_password
> The verification password specified by the shopper

> **Note:**
> Although not shown in the syntax diagram above, the parameters required by the RegisterNew, RegisterUpdate, or AddressUpdate command must also be included in the command. Again, these parameters are not required by the FlexiReg command, but will be forwarded to the command that it calls.

# Step 4. Determining the Scope of the Command

You now need to determine whether the command will call one or more overridable functions to perform some of its processing. Because your command simply passes the flow of control to another command, it does not need to call an overridable function to do any processing.

# Step 5. Determining How to Handle Exceptions

You now need to plan how you will handle exception conditions that are encountered by your command. In this case, three exception conditions need to be handled:

- One or more input parameters are syntactically incorrect.

- The shopper submits a logon ID but not a password.

- The shopper submits a password but not a logon ID.

If one or more input parameters are syntactically incorrect, you will return a false value to the system when the command is checking the input parameters.

If the shopper submits a logon ID but no password, or vice versa, you will set an exception task called FLEXI_REG_ERR, and pass an error code to it. You will use the default

TaskDisplay_1.0(IBM,NC) overridable function to execute a custom macro, which will display the error message and fields for the shopper to reenter the passwords (this will be the same page that originally requested the information).

# Step 6. Determining How to Handle a Successful Return

If your command completes successfully, it will redirect its flow of execution to another command and pass the current input parameters to it. To do this, you will use the `SetLocation` function, which is used when you want to redirect to a command that is not part of the URL of the current command. The implementation will be discussed in detail when you begin to write the command.

# Step 7. Creating the Interface to the Command

You will now customize the order page that was generated by the Store Creator so that it will invoke the FlexiReg command and pass to it its parameters, and the parameters that are required by the command to which it redirects (AddressUpdate, RegisterNew, or RegisterUpdate, and OrderProcess). Currently, the macro that creates the order page, `order.d2w`, simply calls the AddressUpdate and OrderProcess commands to process the shopper's address and order information.

To save you some time, a customized version of the `order.d2w` macro has already been created.

1. Replace the existing macro with this version by copying the order.d2w macro from the \workshops\macros\ directory on the CD to the following directory:

   **WIN** `\ibm\netcommerce3\macro\en_US\OneStopPizzaShop\`

2. Before you examine the new macro, you need to understand how shoppers are able to place an order without registering. Normally, the system requires that shoppers specify an address before they add items to their Order List. (The OrderItemUpdate command requires an address reference number in order to add the items to the SHIPTO table.) A simple way around this is to create and call a macro that generates a "dummy" address record, behind the scenes, when the shopper first enters the store. Now the shopper has the address record required to order from the store, without having to stop to register. The dummy address record gets updated at order time when the shopper provides a delivery address.

   The macro that creates the dummy address record can be executed any time before the shopper selects an item for purchasing. In your store, the dummy address record is already created by the `main.d2w` macro, which is called after the `index.html` file is accessed when the shopper first types the URL to your store. Let's examine this macro now.

3. In a text editor, open the `main.d2w` macro from the following directory:

   **WIN** `\ibm\netcommerce3\macro\en_US\OneStopPizzaShop\`

4. Examine the code. It first checks to see if an address record that matches the shopper's SESSION_ID exists in the database. A record will exist only if the shopper is currently logged on or registered. If an address book entry does not exist for the shopper, the macro inserts a "dummy" permanent record in the SHADDR table, using JavaScript and the AddressAdd command, as follows:

```
<SCRIPT LANGUAGE="javascript">
function AddShaddrEntry() {
location = "/cgi-bin/ncommerce3/AddressAdd?sanick=$(SESSION_ID)
&salname=empty&saaddr1=empty&sacity=empty&sastate=empty
&sacntry=empty&sazipc=empty&url=/cgi-bin/ncommerce3/ExecMacro/
$(STORENAME)/frames.d2w/report"
}
</SCRIPT>
```

This new address book entry consists only of the SESSION_ID as the nickname. Into all other required columns, the command inserts the text string "empty". (Those columns are mandatory, so they must contain a value.) Later, when the shopper orders and provides a "real" delivery address, a new record containing the specified address information will be inserted into the SHADDR table. The original record will be marked as temporary. When the AddressAdd command successfully completes, it executes the frames.d2w macro, which creates the storefront.

If an address book entry exists for the shopper (which means that the shopper is registered or logged on in the current browser session), the frames.d2w macro is executed to display the storefront (the AddressAdd command is not called).

5. Add the &safield2=T parameter to the AddressAdd command, as follows:

```
<SCRIPT LANGUAGE="javascript">
function AddShaddrEntry() {
location = "/cgi- bin/ncommerce3/
AddressAdd?sanick=$(SESSION_ID)&salname=empty&saaddr1=empty
&sacity=empty&sastate=empty&sacntry=empty&sazipc=empty&safield2=T&url=/
cgi-bin/ncommerce3/ExecMacro/$(STORENAME)/frames.d2w/report"
}
</SCRIPT>
```

Now when the AddressAdd command is executed, it will also insert the value T in the merchant-customizable column SAFIELD2. You will learn why this value is needed when you examine the macro that creates the Place Order page.

6. Save your changes and close the file.

7. Now that you know how the store has been customized to allow shoppers to place an order without having to first register, let's examine the new order macro that you replaced at the beginning of this section. This macro will create the page shown in Figure 15.8.

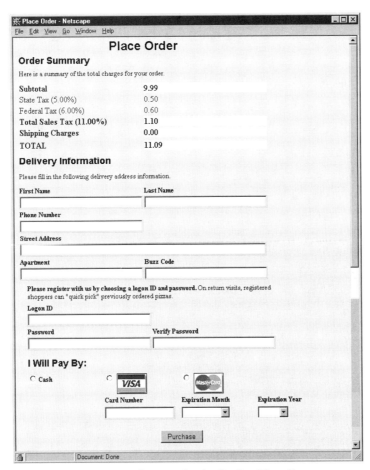

*Figure 15.8* *A custom order page for the OneStopPizza Shop.*

From this page, the shopper can do the following:

- View the total charges of the order

- Enter a delivery address (if a guest shopper) or update it if it differs from the one specified during registration (if a registered shopper)

- Select a payment method (either C.O.D. or credit card)

In Figure 15.8, the page has been accessed by a guest shopper, so the delivery address form is blank. If the shopper submits the order and then logs onto the store on a return visit, the form will display the delivery address information specified during the previous purchase. Pay particularly close attention to how the macro has been customized to display this dynamic address form.

8. In a text editor, open the `order.d2w` macro from the following directory:

    **WIN** `\ibm\netcommerce3\macro\en_US\OneStopPizzaShop\`

9. First, let's examine the variables that will be used by the macro. Like the other macros in the store, this macro imports the `OneStopPizzaShop.inc` file, which contains variables for common data including the page background colors, the text colors, the merchant reference number, and the store name. It uses the `%INCLUDE` statement to import the file, as follows:

```
%INCLUDE "OneStopPizzaShop\OneStopPizzaShop.inc"
```

The macro also defines a global variable in the `%DEFINE` section, as follows:

```
%DEFINE {

  guestShopper = ""

%}
```

This variable, `guestShopper`, is defined with no initial value. It will be used to control the information that is displayed in the delivery address form.

10. Now let's examine the `%HTML_REPORT` section and follow the macro's execution path. It first defines a form and table in which to display the shopper's order information, and then calls two functions, as follows:

```
%HTML_REPORT {

    <HTML>
    <HEAD><TITLE>Place Order</TITLE></HEAD>
    <BODY BACKGROUND="$(BodyImage1)" TEXT="$(TextCol)"
    LINK="$(LinkCol)" VLINK="$(VLinkCol)" ALINK="$(ALinkCol)">

    <FORM ACTION="/cgi-bin/ncommerce3/FlexiReg" METHOD="post">

    <TABLE WIDTH="60" CELLPADDING="0" CELLSPACING="2" BORDER="0">
      <TR>
        <TD COLSPAN="3"><H2><CENTER><FONT FACE="helvetica">Place
        Order</FONT></CENTER></H2></TD>
      </TR>

@getShopperInfo()
@displayOrderTotal()
```

11. Now let's examine the source code for the first function that is called, `getShopperInfo`:

```
%FUNCTION(DTW_ODBC) getShopperInfo()
{
    select sarfnbr, sanick, safield2
    from shaddr, shipto, shopper
    where sanick='$(SESSION_ID)'
    and saadrflg='P'
    and stsanbr=sarfnbr
    and sashnbr=shrfnbr
    and shlogid='$(SESSION_ID)'

    %REPORT {
```

```
%ROW {

   @DTW_ASSIGN(guestShopper, V_safield2)
   @DTW_ASSIGN(address_rn, V_sarfnbr)
   @DTW_ASSIGN(nickname, V_sanick)
%}
%}

%MESSAGE{

   100: { Could not retrieve your shopper information.<P>
   %}
   DEFAULT: {
      <FONT SIZE="+3"><B>Database Error 1:</B></FONT><BR>
      A database error occurred.  Please contact the merchant
      server administrator.<BR>
      SQL error code = $(SQL_CODE)
   %}
%}
%}
```

This function retrieves general information about the shopper who is placing the
order. It first runs an SQL query to retrieve from the SHADDR and SHIPTO tables the
shopper's address reference number and nickname, and the value for column
SAFIELD2.

Column SAFIELD2 is important, for its value will differ depending on whether or not
the shopper has registered.

- If the shopper has not registered, the value will be T. (In Step 3, you added the
  parameter safield2=T to the AddressAdd command, which creates a "dummy"
  address record when an unregistered shopper accesses the store.)

- If the shopper has registered, a new address book entry was created, consisting of
  the address information specified at order time. More importantly, no value is
  inserted into column SAFIELD2 (this column is reserved for merchant use, so it
  does not get updated automatically).

The %REPORT block of this function assigns a new variable name to each column value
that is retrieved from the query. The address reference number and the nickname are
mandatory parameters required by the command that is eventually called (AddressUpdate,
RegisterNew, or RegisterUpdate). The value of column SAFIELD2 is stored in the variable
isTempShopper, so that it can be used later in the macro.

12. Let's move to the next function, displayOrderTotal. The source code is as follows:

```
%FUNCTION(DTW_ODBC) displayOrderTotal()
{

   select sashnbr, sarfnbr, shrfnbr, oyprtot, oyshtot,
   oytax1, oytax2, oytxtot, oysanbr,
   (oyprtot+oyshtot+oytxtot) as total,
   mttaxrate1, mttaxname1, mttaxrate2, mttaxname2, mtmenbr,
```

```
(mttaxrate1+mttaxrate2) as mttax
from shaddr, shopper, orderpay, merchanttax
where shlogid='$(SESSION_ID)'
and oyornbr=$(order_rn)
and sashnbr=shrfnbr
and sarfnbr=oysanbr
and mtmenbr=$(MerchantRefNum)

%REPORT{

  <TR>
    <TD><H3><FONT FACE="helvetica">Order Summary</FONT></H3>
    </TD>
  </TR>
  <TR>
    <TD COLSPAN="2" ALIGN="left"><FONT SIZE="2">Here is a
    summary of the total charges for your order.</TD>
  </TR>
  <TR>
    <TD><BR></TD>
  </TR>

  %ROW {

    <TR>
      <TD ALIGN="left" VALIGN="top"><B>Subtotal</B></TD>
      <TD ALIGN="left" VALIGN="middle"
       BGCOLOR="white"><B>$(V_oyprtot)</B>
      </TD>
    </TR>
    <TR>
      <TD ALIGN="left" VALIGN="top">
       $(V_mttaxname1) ($(V_mttaxrate1)%)</TD>
      <TD ALIGN="left" VALIGN="middle">$(V_oytax1)</TD>
    </TR>
    <TR>
      <TD ALIGN="left" VALIGN="top">
       $(V_mttaxname2) ($(V_mttaxrate2)%)</TD>
      <TD ALIGN="left" VALIGN="middle">$(V_oytax2)</TD>
    </TR>
    <TR>
      <TD ALIGN="left" VALIGN="top">
      <B>Total Sales Tax ($(V_mttax)%)</B></TD>
      <TD ALIGN="left" VALIGN="middle"
       BGCOLOR="white"><B>$(V_oytxtot)</B></TD>
    </TR>
    <TR>
      <TD ALIGN="left" VALIGN="top"><B>Shipping Charges</B>
      </TD>
      <TD ALIGN="left" VALIGN="middle"
       BGCOLOR="white"><B>$(V_oyshtot)</B></TD>
    </TR>
```

```
    <TR>
      <TD></TD>
    </TR>
    <TR>
      <TD ALIGN="left" VALIGN="top"><B>TOTAL</B></TD>
      <TD ALIGN="left" VALIGN="middle"
       BGCOLOR="white"><B>$(V_total)</B></TD>
    </TR>
    <TR>
      <TD><BR></TD>
    </TR>
  %}
 %}

 %MESSAGE{

   100: { %}
   DEFAULT: {
     <FONT SIZE="+3">
     <B>Database Error 2:</B><P>A database error occurred when
      attempting to retrieve your order summary from the database.
      Please contact the merchant server administrator.</FONT>
      SQL error code = $(SQL_CODE)
   %}
 %}
%}
```

This function retrieves all the necessary data from the database for the subtotal price, shipping charge, sales tax, and total price of all items in the shopper's order. The %REPORT block displays the summary information in a table.

13. You will now see how the delivery address form is created. The form will be blank for guest shoppers to fill in, and will be filled in with address information for registered shoppers. The value of isTempShopper is used to display address information if the shopper has registered; empty fields otherwise. Examine the source code:

```
    <TR>
      <TD><H3><FONT FACE="helvetica">Delivery Information
       </FONT></H3></TD>
    </TR>
    <TR>
      <TD COLSPAN="2" ALIGN="left"><FONT SIZE="2">Please fill in
       the following delivery address information.</FONT></TD>
    </TR>
    <TR>
      <TD><BR></TD>
    </TR>

%IF (guestShopper == "T")

    <TR>
      <TD ALIGN="left"><B><FONT SIZE="-1">First Name</FONT></B>
```

```
        </TD>
        <TD ALIGN="left"><B><FONT SIZE="-1">Last Name</FONT></B>
        </TD>
      </TR>
      <TR>
        <TD COLSPAN="1"><INPUT TYPE="text" NAME="safname" SIZE="28"
        MAXLENGTH="30"></TD>
        <TD COLSPAN="1"><INPUT TYPE="text" NAME="salname" SIZE="28"
        MAXLENGTH="30"></TD>
      </TR>
      <TR>
        <TD ALIGN="left"><B><FONT SIZE="-1">Phone Number</FONT>
        </B></TD>
      </TR>
      <TR>
        <TD COLSPAN="1"><INPUT TYPE="text" NAME="saphone1"
        SIZE="28" MAXLENGTH="30"></TD>
      </TR>
      <TR>
        <TD ALIGN="left"><B><FONT SIZE="-1">Street Address</FONT>
        </B></TD>
      </TR>
      <TR>
        <TD COLSPAN="3"><INPUT TYPE="text" NAME="saaddr1" SIZE="58"
        MAXLENGTH="50"></TD>
      </TR>
      <TR>
        <TD ALIGN="left"><B><FONT SIZE="-1">Apartment</FONT></B>
        </TD>
        <TD ALIGN="left"><B><FONT SIZE="-1">Buzz Code</FONT></B>
        </TD>
      </TR>
      <TR>
        <TD COLSPAN="1"><INPUT TYPE="text" NAME="saaddr2" SIZE="28"
        MAXLENGTH="50"></TD>
        <TD COLSPAN="1"><INPUT TYPE="text" NAME="saaddr3" SIZE="28"
        MAXLENGTH="50"></TD>
      </TR>
      <TR>

        <TD><BR></TD>
      </TR>
      <TR>
        <TD COLSPAN="2" ALIGN="left"><FONT SIZE="-1"><B>Please
        register with us by choosing a logon ID and password.</B> On
        return visits, registered shoppers can "quick pick"
        previously ordered pizzas.</FONT></TD>
      </TR>
      <TR>
        <TD><BR></TD>
      </TR>
      <TR>
```

```
        <TD ALIGN="left"><B><FONT SIZE="-1">Logon ID</FONT></B>
        </TD>
      </TR>
      <TR>
        <TD COLSPAN="1"><INPUT TYPE="text" NAME="shlogid" SIZE="28"
        MAXLENGTH="30">
      </TR>
      <TR>
        <TD ALIGN="left"><B><FONT SIZE=-1>Password</FONT></B></TD>
        <TD ALIGN="left"><B><FONT SIZE=-1>Verify Password</FONT>
        </B></TD>
      </TR>
      <TR>
        <TD COLSPAN="1"><INPUT TYPE="password" NAME="shlpswd"
        SIZE="28" MAXLENGTH="16">
        <TD COLSPAN="1"><INPUT TYPE="password" NAME="shlpswdver"
        SIZE="28" MAXLENGTH="16">
      </TR>

%ELSE

@displayRegisteredShopper()

%ENDIF

<TR>
  <TD><BR></TD>
</TR>

</TABLE>
```

The %IF statement specifies that if the value of isTempShopper is T (which indicates that the shopper is a guest with a "dummy" address book entry), the macro is to display a blank delivery address information for the shopper to complete; otherwise, it is to run the displayRegisteredShopper function.

14. Now let's examine the displayRegisteredShopper function, which creates the delivery address form for registered shoppers. This function's source code is as follows:

```
%FUNCTION(DTW_ODBC) displayRegisteredShopper()
{
  select sarfnbr, shrfnbr, sanick, safname,
  salname, saphone1, saaddr1, saaddr2,
  saaddr3, shlogid, shlpswd
  from shaddr, shopper
  where sashnbr=shrfnbr
  and sanick='$(SESSION_ID)'
  and saadrflg='P'
  and shlogid='$(SESSION_ID)'

  %REPORT {

    %ROW {
```

```
<TR>
  <TD ALIGN="left"><B><FONT SIZE="-1">First Name</FONT>
  </B></TD>
  <TD ALIGN="left"><B><FONT SIZE="-1">Last Name</FONT>
  </B></TD>
</TR>
<TR>
  <TD COLSPAN="1"><INPUT TYPE="text" NAME="safname"
  VALUE="$(V_safname)" SIZE="28" MAXLENGTH="30"></TD>
  <TD COLSPAN="1"><INPUT TYPE="text" NAME="salname"
  VALUE="$(V_salname)" SIZE="28" MAXLENGTH="30"></TD>
</TR>
<TR>
  <TD ALIGN="left"><B><FONT SIZE="-1">Phone Number</FONT>
  </B></TD>
</TR>
<TR>
  <TD COLSPAN="1"><INPUT TYPE="text" NAME="saphone1"
  SIZE="28" VALUE="$(V_saphone1)" MAXLENGTH="30"></TD>
</TR>
<TR>
  <TD ALIGN="left"><B><FONT SIZE="-1">Street Address
  </FONT></B></TD>
</TR>
<TR>
  <TD COLSPAN="3"><INPUT TYPE="text" NAME="saaddr1"
  VALUE="$(V_saaddr1)" SIZE="58" MAXLENGTH="50"></TD>
</TR>
<TR>
  <TD ALIGN="left"><B><FONT SIZE=2>Apartment</FONT></B>
  </TD>
  <TD ALIGN="left"><B><FONT SIZE=2>Buzz Code</FONT></B>
  </TD>
</TR>
<TR>
  <TD COLSPAN="1"><INPUT TYPE="text" NAME="saaddr2"
  VALUE="$(V_saaddr2)" SIZE="28" MAXLENGTH="50"></TD>
  <TD COLSPAN="1"><INPUT TYPE="text" NAME="saaddr3"
  VALUE="$(V_saaddr3)" SIZE="28" MAXLENGTH="50"></TD>
</TR>
<TR>
  <TD><BR></TD>
</TR>
<TR>
  <TD COLSPAN="2" ALIGN="left"><FONT SIZE="-1"><B>B>If you
  haven't already done so, please register with us by
  choosing a logon ID and password.</B> On return visits,
  registered shoppers can "quick pick" previously ordered
  pizzas.</FONT></TD>
</TR>
<TR>
  <TD><BR></TD>
```

```
        </TR>
        <TR>
          <TD ALIGN="left"><B><FONT SIZE=-1>Logon ID</FONT></B>
          </TD>
        </TR>
        <TR>
          <TD COLSPAN="1"><INPUT TYPE="TEXT" NAME="shlogid"
          VALUE="$(V_shlogid)" SIZE="28" MAXLENGTH="30">
        </TR>
        <TR>
          <TD ALIGN="left"><B><FONT SIZE="-1">Password</FONT></B>
          </TD>
          <TD ALIGN="left"><B><FONT SIZE="-1">Verify Password
          </FONT></B></TD>
        </TR>
        <TR>
          <TD COLSPAN="1"><INPUT TYPE="password" NAME="shlpswd"
          VALUE="$(V_shlpswd)" SIZE="28" MAXLENGTH="16">
          <TD COLSPAN="1"><INPUT TYPE="password" NAME="shlpswdver"
          VALUE="$(V_shlpswd)" SIZE="28" MAXLENGTH="16">
        </TR>
    %}
  %}


  %MESSAGE{

    100: { No address was found.<p>
    %}

    DEFAULT: {
      <FONT SIZE="+3"><B>Database Error 3:</B></FONT><BR>
      A database error occurred.  Please contact the merchant
      server administrator.<BR>
      SQL error code = $(SQL_CODE)
    %}
  %}
%}
```

This function retrieves from the SHOPPER and SHADDR tables the registered shopper's information that must be displayed in the delivery address form (first name, last name, phone number, street address and, if previously provided, the logon ID and password). Because the database contains the shopper's address information (as opposed to a dummy entry for a guest shopper), the `%REPORT` block displays the information in the fields of the form, using variables that reference the corresponding database column values.

15. Let's return to the `%HTML_REPORT` section to examine its remaining code. After the appropriate address form has been successfully displayed, the macro displays the payment options, as follows.

```
<TABLE BORDER="0" CELLPADDING="0" WIDTH="600" COLS="4">
  <TR>
```

```
      <TD ALIGN="left" valign="top" COLSPAN="4"><h3>
       <FONT face="helvetica">I Will Pay By:</FONT></h3></TD>
    </TR>
    <TR>
      <TD valign="top" WIDTH="100"><INPUT TYPE="radio"
       NAME="Cash" VALUE="CASH"><FONT SIZE="2"><B>Cash</B></FONT>
       </TD>
      <TD WIDTH="250"><INPUT TYPE="radio" NAME="cctype"
       VALUE="VISA"> <img src="/sggifs/visa.gif" ALIGN="top"></TD>
      <TD COLSPAN="2" WIDTH="250"><INPUT TYPE="radio"
       NAME="cctype" VALUE="MAST"> <img src="/sggifs/mc.gif"
       ALIGN="top"></TD>
    </TR>
    <TR>
      <TD WIDTH="20"> </TD>
      <TD><FONT SIZE="2"><B>Card Number</B></FONT></TD>
      <TD><FONT SIZE="2"><B>Expiration Month</B></FONT></TD>
      <TD><FONT SIZE="2"><B>Expiration Year</B></FONT></TD>
    </TR>
    <TR>
      <TD WIDTH="20"> </TD>
      <TD WIDTH="20"><INPUT TYPE="text" SIZE="15"
      MAXLENGTH="20" NAME="ccnum" VALUE="$(ccnum)"></TD>
      <TD WIDTH="20"><SELECT NAME="ccxmonth" SIZE="1">
         <OPTION selected></OPTION>
         <OPTION VALUE="1">January</OPTION>
         <OPTION VALUE="2">February</OPTION>
         <OPTION VALUE="3">March</OPTION>
         <OPTION VALUE="4">April</OPTION>
         <OPTION VALUE="5">May</OPTION>
         <OPTION VALUE="6">June</OPTION>
         <OPTION VALUE="7">July</OPTION>
         <OPTION VALUE="8">August</OPTION>
         <OPTION VALUE="9">September</OPTION>
         <OPTION VALUE="10">October</OPTION>
         <OPTION VALUE="11">November</OPTION>
         <OPTION VALUE="12">December</OPTION>
      </SELECT></TD>
      <TD WIDTH="20"><SELECT NAME="ccxyear" SIZE="1">
         <OPTION selected></OPTION>
         <OPTION VALUE="1998">1998</OPTION>
         <OPTION VALUE="1999">1999</OPTION>
         <OPTION VALUE="2000">2000</OPTION>
         <OPTION VALUE="2001">2001</OPTION>
         <OPTION VALUE="2002">2002</OPTION>
         <OPTION VALUE="2003">2003</OPTION>
         <OPTION VALUE="2003">2004</OPTION>
      </SELECT></TD>
```

This is straightforward HTML for giving customers the option to either pay by C.O.D. or specify a credit card and provide the card details. The HTML simply constructs the table with fixed values for each form element within the table.

16. Now that you have seen how the macro creates the order page and displays the order summary information, a dynamic delivery address form, and payment options, let's examine how your new FlexiReg command has been incorporated into the macro. It is part of the URL contained in the form's ACTION tag, which is executed when the shopper clicks the **Purchase** button to place the order, as follows:

```
<FORM ACTION="/cgi-bin/ncommerce3/FlexiReg" METHOD="post">
```

When the shopper clicks **Purchase**, all the values entered into the delivery address form, a logon ID and password (if provided), the chosen payment method, and the following hidden input parameters are passed with the FlexiReg command as an HTTP request:

```
<INPUT TYPE="hidden" NAME="sanick" VALUE="$(nickname)">
<INPUT TYPE="hidden" NAME="sarfnbr" VALUE="$(address_rn)">
<INPUT TYPE="hidden" NAME="sacity" VALUE="This City">
<INPUT TYPE="hidden" NAME="sastate" VALUE="This State/Province">
<INPUT TYPE="hidden" NAME="sazipc" VALUE="A Zip/Postal Code">
<INPUT TYPE="hidden" NAME="sacntry" VALUE="This Country">
<INPUT TYPE="hidden" NAME="url" VALUE="/cgi-bin/ncommerce3/
 OrderProcess?merchant_rn=$(MerchantRefNum)">
<INPUT TYPE="hidden" NAME="order_rn" VALUE="$(order_rn)">
<INPUT TYPE="hidden" NAME="merchant_rn" VALUE="$(MerchantRefNum)">
```

There are a few things to note about these hidden input parameters. To start with, they are extra parameters that are required by the commands that later are called by your FlexiReg command.

- The values for the first two parameters, `sanick` and `sarfnbr`, were originally retrieved from the database by the `getShopperInfo` function, which we have already examined.

- The next four parameters, city, state/province, zip/postal code, and country, contain fixed "dummy" values. In this case, it is assumed that shoppers live in the store's neighborhood and that the pizzas will be hand-delivered to them, so we don't need to ask for this information. As an alternative, you could include the information on the form and create an overridable function for handling orders that are placed outside of the delivery region. Either way, you must pass these parameters, as they are required by the AddressUpdate, RegisterNew, or RegisterUpdate command.

- The next parameter, `url`, is a redirection URL containing the OrderProcess command. When the called command successfully completes, it will execute the OrderProcess command to process the order.

- The next parameter, `order_rn`, which is required by the OrderProcess command, was created and passed to this macro by the OrderDisplay command. (The OrderDisplay command invokes this macro.)

- The last parameter, `merchant_rn`, is required by the FlexiReg command, as you previously defined. It is also needed in a mall scenario when multiple stores use this macro. Here, the value is retrieved from the include file, which contains a fixed number. In this case, the value of the merchant reference number will always be the same, and is intended for the pizza store only. To dynamically retrieve the merchant reference number for a mall environment, you would need to add a function to the macro that retrieves the reference number for the current merchant and assigns it a variable that can be passed as a hidden input parameter to the FlexiReg command. The following is a function that you could use:

```
%FUNCTION(DTW_ODBC) getMerchantInfo()
{
    select mestname, merfnbr
    from order_pend, merchant
    where orrfnbr=$(order_rn)
    and ormenbr=merfnbr

    %REPORT {

      %ROW {

         @DTW_ASSIGN(MerchantRefNum, V_merfnbr)
      %}
    %}
%}
```

17.   Close the file.


You have now completed this workshop. In the next workshop, "Writing the FlexiReg Command" on page 459, you will write the code for the FlexiReg command.

# Chapter 16, Writing Commands

Now that you understand the planning required to write a new command and how to create the Net.Data macro that will invoke it and pass its mandatory and optional parameters to it, you are ready to write the code for the command. This chapter describes how to code a command according to how you planned for its implementation. In the workshop, you will code the command that you planned in the workshop in Chapter 15.

Before proceeding, ensure that you have read "Chapter 11, Net.Commerce Programming Conventions" on page 321 so that you are familiar with the programming conventions you must follow.

This chapter covers the following topics:

- Understanding the Command Anatomy

- Adding Your Code

- Compiling the Command

- Displaying the Command Results

- Workshop: Writing the FlexiReg Command

# Understanding the Command Anatomy

Commands, like overridable functions, are written as C++ classes, and all the code is included in the CPP file with no header file. Below is the class skeleton from which you should create any command. It contains all the mandatory and optional functions for the command. It is very similar to the skeleton for an overridable function class; the only difference is that it contains two extra functions, `Initialize` and `CheckParameters`.

> **Note:**
> All uses of the tracing facility are optional.

You can find this file on the CD in the following directory:

**WIN** \samples\cmds\skeleton.cpp

The code is as follows:

```cpp
class __EXPORT_MODE__ MyCommand : public NC_Command
{
    static const ClassName _STR_ThisClass;

public:
    MyCommand(void)
    {
        Trace::Tracer T(_STR_CONSTRUCTOR, _STR_ThisClass);
    }

    virtual bool Initialize(void)
    {
        Trace::Tracer T(_STR_Initialize, _STR_ThisClass);
    }

    virtual ~MyCommand(void)
    {
        Trace::Tracer T(_STR_DESTRUCTOR, _STR_ThisClass);
    }

    void operator delete( void* p ) { ::delete p; }
    virtual NC_Command* Clone(void)
    {
        return new MyCommand;
    }

public:
    virtual void FailedRegistration(NC_RegistrationID& RegID,
                                    const  ErrorMsg_Reg* Err)
    {
        Trace::Tracer T(_STR_FailedRegistration, _STR_ThisClass);
    }
```

```
   virtual bool CheckParameters(const HttpRequest& Req,
                                HttpResponse& Res,
                                NC_Environment& Env,
                                NC_Environment&  Resources)
   {
      Trace::Tracer T(_STR_CheckParameters, _STR_ThisClass);
   }

   virtual bool Process (const HttpRequest& Req, HttpResponse& Res,
                         NC_Environment& Env)
   {
      Trace::Tracer T(_STR_Process, _STR_ThisClass);
   }
};

const ClassName MyCommand::_STR_ThisClass("MyCommand");

static bool X = NC_CommandManager::Register("Vendor", "Product",
                                 "MyCommand", 1.0 ,
                                 new MyCommand);
```

We will now examine each section of the skeleton.

## The Class Declaration

The class declaration line is as follows:

```
class __EXPORT_MODE__ MyCommand : public NC_Command
```

## The Member Variables

The class begins by declaring an uninitialized static variable called `_STR_ThisClass`, which, if tracing is enabled, is used to trace your command's execution path. It will later be initialized with the name of your class. Many compilers still cannot define a static member within the class declaration, so the initialization takes place outside of the class declaration.

```
static const ClassName _STR_ThisClass;
```

All other static variables that will be used by your command, such as those that will store the command's input parameter names, should be initialized here.

## The Constructor

A constructor is defined in which you can allocate storage, if required by your command. The constructor also contains a tracer to trace the function call.

```
public:
   MyCommand(void)
   {
      Trace::Tracer T(_STR_CONSTRUCTOR, _STR_ThisClass);
   }
```

## The Initialize Function

The `Initialize` function is called during the initialization of the server and after all the DLLs or shared libraries for all the commands and overridable functions in the system have been registered and loaded. Use this function to initialize any resources and to set up the environment so that your command can start receiving requests. Assume that the Net.Commerce environment has been set up properly. For example, all commands and overridable functions in the system have been registered, a database connection exists, and you have access to the data in the configuration files. Do not, however, assume that any of the commands and overridable functions in the system have been initialized. The server initializes them in random order.

The `Initialize` function also contains a tracer to trace the function call.

The code is as follows:

```
virtual bool Initialize(void)
{
    Trace::Tracer T(_STR_Initialize, _STR_ThisClass);
}
```

To handle exception conditions that are encountered in the `Initialize` function, return false to the system and the command manager will automatically delete your command instance; otherwise, return true to indicate that the command is ready to be executed.

Implementing this method is not mandatory. The default implementation returns true.

## The Destructor

The destructor will be called when the server is shut down or when your command fails to initialize. It also contains a tracer to trace the destructor call.

The code is as follows:

```
virtual ~MyCommand(void)
{
    Trace::Tracer T(_STR_DESTRUCTOR, _STR_ThisClass);
}
```

## The Delete Operator

When the server shuts down, the command manager will call the delete operator, which in turn calls the command's destructor. Make sure that you have set your local delete operator so that the command manager can delete this class. You also need to provide a clone function that the command manager can call to create new instances of your command if required; for example, in a multi-threaded environment. The command manager will automatically call the Initialize function after it calls the Clone function.

The code is as follows:

```
void operator delete( void* p ) { ::delete p; }
virtual NC_Command* Clone(void)
{
    return new MyCommand;
}
```

## The FailedRegistration Function

During initialization of the server, if the command manager cannot register your command, it calls the `FailedRegistration` function before it deletes the command instance. The `RegId` parameter passed to this function contains the registration ID that was passed to the command manager during the registration of your command (for example, `PasswordReset_1.0(IBM,NC)`.

The code is as follows:

```
public:
  virtual void FailedRegistration(NC_RegistrationID& RegID, const
                                  ErrorMsg_Reg* Err)
  {
    Trace::Tracer T(_STR_FailedRegistration, _STR_ThisClass);
  }
```

In this function, you normally output error messages to the log file to indicate the type of registration error that has occurred. The following example shows the exceptions that the command manager may return when it fails to register the command, and also shows how to output an error message to the log file.

```
if (Err == &_ERR_REG_UNEXPECTED_OBJ)
{
  error << indent << "ERROR: MyCommand not accepted by the manager"
                  << endl;
}

else if (Err == &_ERR_REG_DUPE_ID)
{
  error << indent << "ERROR: MyCommand: another command with the same
                      name has already been registered" << endl;
}

else if (Err == &_ERR_REG_OBJ_NOT_FROM_DLL)
{
  error << indent << "ERROR: MyCommand is packaged in a different DLL
                      than   the one registered in the database, or is
                      listed as belonging to a different DLL" << endl;
}

else
{
  error << indent << "ERROR: MyCommand unknown registration error
                      occurred" << endl;
}

  error << indent << "ERROR: MyCommand's registration failed" << endl;
```

Implementing the `FailedRegistration` function is not mandatory. The default implementation returns without any processing. It also contains a tracer to trace the function call.

## The CheckParameters Function

The CheckParameters function, which is unique to commands, is used to check that the command's required input parameters exist and that they contain values. If only certain users can invoke the command (for example, for commands that are used for the Administrator forms) this function will also create a list of merchants that can access the command. The function also contains a tracer to trace the function call.

The code is as follows:

```
virtual bool CheckParameters(const HttpRequest& Req,
                             HttpResponse& Res,
                             NC_Environment& Env,
                             NC_Environment& Resources)
{
   Trace::Tracer T(_STR_CheckParameters, _STR_ThisClass);
}
```

The following three classes are passed as parameters to this function, which enable it to communicate with the Net.Commerce system:

- HttpRequest Req contains all the information that is contained in an HTTP request, including the input parameters that are passed to the command.

- HttpResponse Res contains all the information that is needed for returning a full HTTP document back to the browser, including the parameters that the command returns.

- NC_Environment Env contains information about the Net.Commerce environment.

- NC_Environment Resources returns the merchant reference numbers of those stores that can be accessed by the command for the current shopper, in order to be able to access the corresponding merchant resources (for example, product and order information).

Typically in this function, you will check the value of each required name-value pair in the Req parameter and save the value in a local variable so that it can be accessed later by the Process function. For more information on how to check the input parameters, see "Checking a Command's Input Parameters" on page 334.

If the CheckParameters function returns successfully and you want only certain individuals to be able to access the command, you must determine which merchant resouces the command can access for the current shopper, and populate the Resources object with the corresponding merchant reference numbers, as follows:

```
Resources.Add(NC_Environment::_VAR_Merchant, MerchantRefNum1);
Resources.Add(NC_Environment::_VAR_Merchant, MerchantRefNum2);
return true;
```

If you do not pass any parameters to the object (you do not want to enforce access control for the command), the system assumes that the command can be accessed by any shopper for any merchant. You typically do not pass any parameters when you are writing a command that will be invoked by shoppers when they are interacting with your store.

> **Note:**
> Do not use the **CheckParameters** function to manipulate the merchant resources (products, order information, payment information, and so forth); otherwise, any unauthorized users will have access to this information. At this stage, the command is responsible only for retrieving the merchant reference numbers and returning them to the system so that proper access control is enabled. If the shopper who is executing the command has not been granted access to the resource that is to be manipulated, the command manager will call the **FailedAccessControl** function; otherwise, the **Process** function is called, which performs the actual work for the command.

## The Process Function

The `Process` function is where you do the processing for your command, including accessing, retrieving information from, and updating the database; calling overridable functions; manipulating Net.Commerce objects; and so on. It also contains a tracer to trace the function call.

The code is as follows:

```
virtual bool Process(const HttpRequest& Req, HttpResponse& Res,
                     NC_Environment& Env)
{
   Trace::Tracer T(_STR_Process, _STR_ThisClass);
};
```

Like the `CheckParameters` function, the `Process` function also communicates with the Net.Commerce system through three classes that are passed to it as parameters:

- `HttpRequest Req` contains all the information that is contained in an HTTP request, including the input parameters that are passed to the command.

- `HttpResponse Res` contains all the information that is needed for returning a full HTTP document back to the browser.

- `NC_Environment Env` contains information about the Net.Commerce environment, including the explicit input and output parameters for the overridable functions that the command calls (as defined by their tasks). It allows you to set view, exception, and process tasks, and to pass the parameters that the command returns to the environment.

One common operation that is performed in the `Process` function is retrieving information about the current shopper. To do this, use the `User` class, as follows:

```
User& U = (User&) *Misc::CheckEnvironmentVariable(Env,
NC_Environment::_VAR_Shopper);
```

When querying and updating the default database tables, you can either use SQL statements and the ODBC classes provided by Net.Commerce or, to eliminate the need to use SQL statements altogether, you can use the object model. For information on how to use the ODBC classes or the object model to manipulate information in the database, see "Interacting with the Database" on page 340.

The `Process` function is also commonly used for calling one or more overridable functions via a process task. For information on how to call the overridable functions, see "Calling an Overridable Function" on page 338.

If the `Process` function encounters exception conditions, it must handle the error in the usual ways: by either setting an exception task; by returning false (in which case the command manager will invoke the `cmdexe.html` system error page, which indicates a command execution failure); or by hard-coding the HTTP response directly in the function. For a review of these methods, see "Handling Exceptions" on page 324.

If the `Process` function is successful, it can either set a view task to display a Web page to the shopper, redirect its flow of execution to another URL, or call another command. For more information, see "Handling a Successful Return" on page 327.

## The Tracing Variable

The class contains a tracing variable, which allows you to identify calls to the function for your class, as follows:

```
const ClassName MyCommand::_STR_ThisClass("MyCommand");
```

## Instantiation and Registration

Each command class must contain a unique static variable, which is used to both instantiate the command and dynamically register it in the system, as follows:

```
static bool X = NC_CommandManager::Register("Vendor", "Product",
                                            "MyCommand", Version,
                                            new MyCommand );
```

The values for each parameter are as follows:

`Vendor`
> The name of the company for which the command is being written. This may be a third-party vendor, a merchant or site administrator, or IBM itself.

`Product`
> The name of the product for which the command is being implemented; for example, "NC" for Net.Commerce.

`MyCommand`
> The command's name, as it will be later registered in the database.

`Version`
> The version of the command implementation.

`new MyCommand`
> Creates an instance of the command.

This static variable is initialized when the server starts up and loads the DLL or shared library in which the command resides. Prior to this, the command manager has already queried the CMD_POOL table in the database for all the commands that have been registered by merchants, and created an internal list of pointers to those commands. When this variable is initialized, it calls the `Register` function, which attempts to register the command with the command manager and create a unique instance of the command as defined in the variable. The command manager responds by comparing the command definition with its internal list. If the command definition matches a record in the database, the command instance is registered in the system; otherwise, the command manager cannot register the command and calls the `FailedRegistration` function in this class before it deletes the command instance.

> **Note:**
> If you implement multiple commands in the same CPP file, you must assign a different name to the static variable for each command (for example, X1, X2, X3, and so forth).

# Adding Your Code

You are now ready to add your own skeleton code. You must first rename the CPP file, and replace every instance of MyCommand with the name of your own command. At this stage, it is advisable to compile the CPP file as it is, to ensure that it can be linked properly. After that, you will be ready to add code to the CheckParameters and the Process functions in the class, as well as to any other function that you want to customize.

## Sample Scenario:

For our PasswordReset command, we will rename the CPP file passreset.cpp and then replace every instance of MyCommand with PasswordReset.

You can find the file in the following directory on the CD:

**WIN** \samples\cmds\newcmd.cpp

The command uses the default implementations for all functions in the class, except for the CheckParameters and the Process functions, which do the following:

1. Declare local variables to store the values of the input parameters.

2. Check that the HttpRequest object contains values for all the required input parameters (merchant reference number, logon ID, challenge answer, password, and verification password) and that their syntax is correct.

3. If the HttpRequest object does contain all the required values, retrieve the values and store them in local variables; otherwise, return a false value to the system.

4. Check that the new password and the verify password match. If they do not, set the PASSWORD_RESET_ERR exception task and return an error code of 1000.

5. Retrieve the shopper record from the database that corresponds to the logon ID. If the record cannot be retrieved due to an invalid logon ID, set the PASSWORD_RESET_ERR exception task and return an error code of 1001.

6. Retrieve the challenge answer for the shopper record from the database, and compare its value with the value of the challenge answer retrieved from the HttpRequest object.

   - If the values are the same, do the following:

     a) Update the shopper record with the password (the verification password is not stored in the database; it is used only to ensure that the shopper enters the desired password).

     b) Update the timestamp (the date and time that the record was last updated) for the shopper record.

     c) Set the PASSWORD_RESET_DSP to display a confirmation page.

- If the values are not the same, set the PASSWORD_RESET_ERR exception task and return an error code of `1002`.

The corresponding code is as follows. Bold type indicates code that was added to or changed in the class skeleton.

```
class __EXPORT_MODE__ PasswordReset : public NC_Command
{
    static const ClassName _STR_ThisClass;

    // Local variables used by the Process function
    String merchantRefNum;
    String loginId;
    String givenAnswer;
    String newPassword;
    String verifyPassword;

public:
    PasswordReset(void)
    {
        // Trace the function call.
        Trace::Tracer T(_STR_CONSTRUCTOR, _STR_ThisClass);
    }

    virtual bool Initialize(void)
    {
        // Trace the function call.
        Trace::Tracer T(_STR_Initialize, _STR_ThisClass);
        return true;
    }

    virtual ~PasswordReset(void)
    {

        // Trace the function call.
        Trace::Tracer T(_STR_DESTRUCTOR, _STR_ThisClass);
    }

    void  operator delete( void* p ) { ::delete p; }
    virtual NC_Command* Clone(void) { return new PasswordReset; }

public:
    virtual void FailedRegistration(NC_RegistrationID& RegID, const
                                    ErrorMsg_Reg* Err)
    {
        // Trace the function call.
        Trace::Tracer T(_STR_FailedRegistration, _STR_ThisClass);

        if (Err == &_ERR_REG_UNEXPECTED_OBJ)
        {
            error << indent << "ERROR: PasswordReset not accepted by the
                            manager" << endl;
        }
```

```
    else if (Err == &_ERR_REG_DUPE_ID)
    {
       error << indent << "ERROR: PasswordReset: another command with
                           the same name has already been registered" <<
                           endl;
    }
    else if (Err == &_ERR_REG_OBJ_NOT_FROM_DLL)
    {
       error << indent << "ERROR: PasswordReset is packaged in a
                           different DLL then the one registered in the
                           database" << endl;
    }
    else
    {
       error << indent << "ERROR: PasswordReset unknown registration
                           error" << endl;
    }
    error << indent << "ERROR: PasswordReset's registration failed" <<
                        endl;
}

virtual bool CheckParameters(const HttpRequest& Req,
                             HttpResponse& Res,
                             NC_Environment& Env,
                             NC_Environment& Resources)
{
   // Trace the function call.
   Trace::Tracer T(_STR_CheckParameters, _STR_ThisClass);

   static const StringWithOwnership NVP_Name1("merchant_rn");
   if (Misc::CheckFieldExistence(Req, NVP_Name1, merchantRefNum,
                                                 false) == false)
      return false;

   static const StringWithOwnership NVP_Name2("login_id");
   if (Misc::CheckFieldExistence(Req, NVP_Name2, loginId, false) ==
                                                             false)
      return false;

   static const StringWithOwnership NVP_Name3("chal_ans");
   if (Misc::CheckFieldExistence(Req, NVP_Name3, givenAnswer, false)
                                                           == false)
      return false;

   static const StringWithOwnership NVP_Name4("new_pass");
   if (Misc::CheckFieldExistence(Req, NVP_Name4, newPassword, false)
                                                           == false)
      return false;

   static const StringWithOwnership NVP_Name5("newver_pass");
   if (Misc::CheckFieldExistence(Req, NVP_Name5, verifyPassword,
                                                 false) == false)
```

```
      return false;

   // Return success if everything went OK.
   return true;
}

virtual bool Process (const HttpRequest& Req, HttpResponse& Res,
                      NC_Environment& Env)
{
   // Trace the function call.
   Trace::Tracer T(_STR_Process, _STR_ThisClass);


   // First, check if the new password matches the verify password.
   // If not, set an exception task.
   if (newPassword != verifyPassword)
   {
      error << indent << "ERROR:  Invalid verification password" <<
                         endl;
      return Misc::SetErrorHandler(Env, "PASSWORD_RESET_ERR",
                                   merchantRefNum, "1000",
                                   "newver_pass");
   }


   // Get the user from the database.
   NVPHash NVP;
   UserHome UH((DataBase&)*Misc::CheckEnvironmentVariable (Env,
                                NC_Environment::_VAR_MainDatabase));
   User* usr = UH.LookupByName(loginId, NVP);

   // Make sure that the user was retrieved.
   if (usr == NULL)
   {
      error << indent << "ERROR:  Invalid user login ID" << endl;
      return Misc::SetErrorHandler(Env, "PASSWORD_RESET_ERR",
                                   merchantRefNum, "1001",
                                   "login_id");
   }


   // Get the real challenge answer and the provided challenge answer
   // and compare them.
   String realAnswer = usr->getChallengeAnswer();

   if (realAnswer == givenAnswer)
   {
      // Overwrite the old password with the new one.
      usr->setPassword (newPassword,
                        Misc::CheckConfigurationVariable(
                        ConfField::_CONF_MERCHANT_KEY));
      usr->setLastVisit (SQL_Schema::_STR_CURRENT_TIMESTAMP_);

      // Write the update to the database
```

```
      if (usr->Write() != ERR_DB_NO_ERROR)
      {
        error << indent << "ERROR: Cannot update user record in the
                            database" << endl;
        return false;
      }
      static const StringWithOwnership
                          ViewTaskName("PASSWORD_RESET_DSP");
      Misc::SetView (Env, ViewTaskName, merchantRefNum);
      return true;
    }
    else
    {
      error << indent << "ERROR:  Invalid challenge answer" << endl;
      return Misc::SetErrorHandler(Env, "PASSWORD_RESET_ERR",
                                   merchantRefNum, "1002",
                                   "chal_ans");
    }
  }
};

// Tracing variable to identify calls to functions for your class.
const ClassName PasswordReset::_STR_ThisClass("PasswordReset");

ClassName PasswordReset::_STR_ThisClass("PasswordReset");

static bool X = NC_CommandManager::Register("IBM", "NC",
                                  "PasswordReset", 1.0,
                                  new PasswordReset);
```

We will now examine the new code.

The command class begins by declaring five uninitialized member variables, which will be used later to store the values of the mandatory input parameters. They are as follows:

```
// Local variables used by the Process function
String merchantRefNum;
String loginId;
String givenAnswer;
String newPassword;
String verifyPassword;
```

We will now skip to the CheckParameters function, which checks that each input parameter required by the command exists and that it contains a value. These input parameters were passed from the password.d2w macro and are accessible through the Req parameter. For each input parameter that is expected by the command, the CheckParameters function first assigns a string to store the parameter name. It then calls the CheckFieldExistence function in the Misc class to check that each parameter exists. If the parameter does exist, the function retrieves its value from the Req parameter; otherwise, it returns false and a command structure failure message is displayed in the browser. If all parameters are found and their values retrieved, the function returns true.

The code is as follows:

```
virtual bool CheckParameters(const HttpRequest& Req,
                             HttpResponse& Res,
                             NC_Environment& Env,
                             NC_Environment& Resources)
{
   // Trace the function call.
   Trace::Tracer T(_STR_CheckParameters, _STR_ThisClass);

   static const StringWithOwnership NVP_Name1("merchant_rn");
   if (Misc::CheckFieldExistence(Req, NVP_Name1, merchantRefNum,
                                                 false) == false)
      return false;

   static const StringWithOwnership NVP_Name2("login_id");
   if (Misc::CheckFieldExistence(Req, NVP_Name2, loginId, false) ==
                                                           false)
      return false;

   static const StringWithOwnership NVP_Name3("chal_ans");
   if (Misc::CheckFieldExistence(Req, NVP_Name3, givenAnswer, false)
                                                      == false)
      return false;

   static const StringWithOwnership NVP_Name4("new_pass");
   if (Misc::CheckFieldExistence(Req, NVP_Name4, newPassword, false)
                                                      == false)
      return false;

   static const StringWithOwnership NVP_Name5("newver_pass");
   if (Misc::CheckFieldExistence(Req, NVP_Name5, verifyPassword,
                                                 alse) == false)
      return false;

   // Return success if everything went OK.
   return true;
}
```

Now we will look at the `Process` function, in which the actual processing of the command occurs. This function begins by checking to see if the shopper's password and verification password, as stored in the local variables `newPassword` and `verifyPassword`, have the same value. If these values are not equal, the `Process` function sets the PASSWORD_RESET_ERR task to handle the error and outputs an error message to the log. The function stores the task in the `Env` parameter, along with the merchant reference number, the task reference number, and the error code that will be handled by the TaskDisplay_1.0(IBM,NC) function.

The code is as follows:

```
virtual bool Process (const HttpRequest& Req, HttpResponse& Res,
                      NC_Environment& Env)
{
```

```
// Trace the function call.
Trace::Tracer T(_STR_Process, _STR_ThisClass);

// First check if the new password matches the verify password
// If not, set an error task.
if (newPassword != verifyPassword)
{

   error << indent << "ERROR: Invalid verification password" << endl;
   return Misc::SetErrorHandler(Env, "PASSWORD_RESET_ERR",
                                    merchantRefNum, "1000",
                                    "newver_pass");

}
```

Next, the `Process` function retrieves from the database the shopper record that matches the value stored in the local variable `loginId` (which was initially retrieved from the `CheckParameters` function). It first creates a "dummy" `NVPHash` instance, which is needed by the `UserHome` class. It then connects to the current database and creates a `UserHome` instance to access the database. Then, it retrieves from the database the user record that corresponds to the logon ID, using the `LookupByName` function in the `UserHome` class. If the user record does not exist, which means that the logon ID retrieved is not valid, the function sets the PASSWORD_RESET_ERR exception task and outputs an error message to the log.

The code is as follows:

```
// Get the user from the database.
NVPHash NVP;
UserHome UH((DataBase&)*Misc::CheckEnvironmentVariable (Env,
                           NC_Environment::_VAR_MainDatabase));
User* usr = UH.LookupByName(loginId, NVP);

// Make sure that the user was retrieved.
if (usr == NULL)
   {
   error << indent << "ERROR:  Invalid user logon ID" << endl;
   return Misc::SetErrorHandler(Env, "PASSWORD_RESET_ERR",
                                 merchantRefNum, "1001", "login_id");
   }
```

The following code retrieves the challenge answer from the retrieved shopper record. The challenge answer is stored in the `usr` instance, and is retrieved using the `getChallengeAnswer` function. The results are stored in the String `realAnswer`.

```
// Get the real challenge answer and the provided challenge answer and
// compare them.
String realAnswer = usr->getChallengeAnswer();
```

If the value stored in `realAnswer` is equal to the value stored in `givenAnswer` (which was initially retrieved by the `CheckParameters` function), the `Process` function will update the password stored in the `usr` instance with the password retrieved by the `CheckParameters` function. To do this, it first sets the password in the `usr` instance to the value stored in `newPassword` and uses the merchant key to encrypt it. (The `setPassword` function needs the merchant key to encrypt the password. It is retrieved using the `CheckConfigurationVariable` function in the `Misc` class.) It then updates the current timestamp in the `usr` instance, using the `setLastChanged` function. (Note that the value of `_STR_CURRENT_TIMESTAMP_` stores a DB2 function call that will retrieve the current timestamp.) Then the `Process` function calls the `Write` function to insert the contents of `usr` into the database. If the return code is not equal to `ERR_DB_NO_ERROR` (which is a success code), the `Process` function composes an error string and returns false.

The code is as follows:

```
if (realAnswer == givenAnswer)
{
  // Overwrite the old password with the new one.
  usr->setPassword (newPassword,
  Misc::CheckConfigurationVariable(ConfField::_CONF_MERCHANT_KEY));
  usr->setLastChanged (SQL_Schema::_STR_CURRENT_TIMESTAMP_);

  // Write the update to the database
  if (usr->Write() != ERR_DB_NO_ERROR)
    {
    error << indent << "ERROR: Cannot update user record in the
                         database" << endl;
    return false;
    }
```

If the `Process` function returns successfully, it sets a view task to display a confirmation page to the shopper. To do this, it first stores the task name PASSWORD_RESET_DSP in the variable `ViewTaskName`, and then uses the `SetView` function to add it to the `Env` parameter, along with the variable storing the merchant reference number. The system will then look for the variable `ViewTaskName` and call the PASSWORD_RESET_DSP task to handle the success. If the value stored in `realAnswer` is *not* equal to the value stored in `givenAnswer` (meaning that the shopper's challenge answer does not match the one in the database), the `Process` function will set the PASSWORD_RESET_ERR task and output an error message to the log.

The code is as follows:

```
      static const StringWithOwnership ViewTaskName
        ("PASSWORD_RESET_DSP"); Misc::SetView (Env,
                                      ViewTaskName, merchantRefNum);
      return true;
  }
  else
  {
    error << indent << "ERROR:  Invalid challenge answer" << endl;
    return Misc::SetErrorHandler(Env, "PASSWORD_RESET_ERR",
                                 merchantRefNum, "1002", "chal_ans");
  }
```

The remaining class code registers the command during the initialization of the server, as follows:

```
// Tracing variable to identify calls to functions for your class.
const ClassName PasswordReset::_STR_ThisClass("PasswordReset");

ClassName PasswordReset::_STR_ThisClass("PasswordReset");
```

```
static bool X = NC_CommandManager::Register("IBM", "NC",
                                            "PasswordReset",
                                            1.0, new PasswordReset);
```

If the command is successfully registered, a unique command instance with the registration ID of `PasswordReset_1.0(IBM,NC)` will be created.

# Compiling the Command

Now you are ready to compile the CPP file and create the DLL or shared library for your command. You must use the following compiler and release level:

**WIN** Microsoft Visual C++ version 4.2
**AIX** txlC++ version 4.1.x

## Sample Scenario:

For simplicity, a DLL has already been created for the PasswordReset command, which is called `newcmd.dll`. It is in the following directory on the CD:

**WIN** `\samples\cmds\`

## Storing the DLL or Shared Library

When you compiled the CPP file, you must copy the DLL or shared library to the following directory, so that the server can load it during initialization:

**WIN** `\ibm\netcommerce3\bin`
**AIX** `/usr/lpp/NetCommerce3/bin`

# Displaying the Command Results

Once you have written your command and have defined the error codes and other parameters that will be used by the view and exception tasks to display the results of the command, you are ready to create the Net.Data macros that implement those tasks.

For a review on how to create Net.Data macros, see "Chapter 7, A Net.Data Tutorial" on page 169.

## Sample Scenario:

For the PasswordReset command, the `password.d2w` Net.Data macro (called by the PASSWORD_RESET_ERR exception task) is used to display an error message if any of the following occurs:

- The shopper submits a challenge question that does not match the one in the database
- The shopper submits a password and verification password that do not match
- An invalid logon ID is retrieved from the database.

If you recall, the `password.d2w` macro is the same macro that is used to initially get the above information from the shopper and pass it to the PasswordReset command. If any of the above exceptions occur, an error code is passed to the macro and it will display the appropriate error message, along with fields for the shopper to reenter the invalid data. The macro uses `%IF` statements in its `%HTML_REPORT` section to handle the different error codes that it may receive from the command, as follows:

```
%IF (error_code == "1000")

   <P><B>The new password does not match the verification password.<BR>
   Please try again.  </B></P>

%ELIF (error_code == "1001")
   <P><B>We were unable to find your user account in the database.
   Please try again.</B></P>

%ELIF (error_code == "1002")
   <P><B>We were unable to confirm your identity as the answer you have
   given does not match our records.<BR>Please try again.</B></P>


%ENDIF
```

As you can see, if the error code `1000` is passed to the macro, which means that the shopper did not enter the same value for both the new password and the verify password, the macro displays the appropriate error message. If the macro receives the error code `1001`, which means that the logon ID was not valid, it displays the appropriate error message. And, if the error code `1002` is passed to the macro, which means that the challenge answer provided by the shopper does not match the one in the database, it displays the appropriate error message.

The shopper was able to successfully reset his or her password, the `pwdsuccess.d2w` macro (called by the PASSWORD_RESET_DSP view task) is used to display a confirmation message, along with the shopper's logon ID for recording in a safe place.

It source code is as follows:

```
%HTML_REPORT{

<HTML>
<BODY BGCOLOR="$(BodyColor1)" TEXT="$(TextCol)"
LINK="$(LinkCol)" VLINK="$(VLinkCol)" ALINK="$(ALinkCol)">
<H3>PASSWORD RESET SUCCESS</H3>

<P>Your password has been successfully changed.  Your logon ID is:
<B>$(s_loginid)</B>.  Remember to record your logon ID and your new
password in a safe place.</P>

</BODY>
</HTML>
%}
```

In this example, a simple confirmation message is displayed to the shopper, but you can also display fields for the shopper to log on to the store using his or her logon ID and new password.

# Workshop: Writing the FlexiReg Command

In the previous workshop, "Planning a New Command for Flexible Registration" on page 424, you planned how you were going to implement the FlexiReg command, and you examined the `order.d2w` macro from which the shopper will invoke the command. Now you are ready to write the FlexiReg command.

Your code will do the following:

1. Declare local variables to store all possible input parameters.

2. Determine whether or not the `HttpRequest` object contains the required input parameter (the merchant reference number) and the optional parameters (the logon ID and password).

3. If the `HttpRequest` object contains the merchant reference number, store its value in a local variable; otherwise, return a false value to the system.

4. If the `HttpRequest` object does not contain both a logon ID and password, do the following:

   a) Assign the value "true" to the corresponding local boolean variables.

   b) Redirect to the AddressUpdate command, and pass to it all the parameters in the `HttpRequest` object.

5. If the `HttpRequest` object contains both a logon ID and password, do the following:

   a) Retrieve the values of the logon ID and password and store them in their local variables.

   b) Assign the value "false" to the corresponding local boolean variables.

   c) Determine whether a shopper record exists in the database that corresponds to the logon ID.

      • If a shopper record does not exist, redirect to the RegisterNew command and pass to it all the current input parameters.

      • If a shopper record does exist, determine whether the shopper is a guest or registered, based on the value of column SAFIELD2.

         1) If column SAFIELD2 contains the value "T" (the shopper is a guest), redirect to the RegisterNew command and pass to it all the current input parameters.

         2) If column SAFIELD2 does not contain the value "T" (the shopper is registered), redirect to the RegisterUpdate command and pass to it all the current input parameters.

6. If the `HttpRequest` contains a logon ID but no password, or vice versa, set the FLEXI_REG_ERR exception task to handle the error.

# Adding the Code

Now you are ready to write the code for the above steps. To save you some time, the skeleton code has already been written. All you have to do is add the remaining code to complete the class.

---

**Note:**
If you do not want to take the time to enter the code, you can just examine the code discussed here. A DLL has already been compiled using all the code, which you will use for your store.

---

1. Copy the template for the CPP file from the following directory to a temporary one:

   **WIN** `\workshops\cmds\cmdtemp.cpp`

2. Open the template in a text editor.

3. Change the name of the class to FlexiReg, by replacing every instance of `MyCommand` with `FlexiReg`.

4. We will now declare five uninitialized member variables that will later store the values of the input parameters retrieved by the command. After the class declaration line, add the following:

```
class __EXPORT_MODE__ FlexiReg : public NC_Command
{
    static ClassName _STR_ThisClass;

    //-----------------------------------------//
    //-           Your Code Begins Here       -//
    //-----------------------------------------//

    String merchantRefNum;
    String loginId;
    String password;
    bool noLogid;
    bool noPassword;

    //-----------------------------------------//
    //-           Your Code Ends Here         -//
    //-----------------------------------------//
```

   You have just declared three string variables to store the value of the merchant reference number, the shopper's logon ID, and the shopper's password, which are passed to the command as input parameters. You have also declared two boolean variables for indicating whether or not the shopper submitted a logon ID and password. All of these member variables will be used by the `Process` function.

5. We will now skip to the `FailedRegistration` function. (The command will use the default implementation for the constructor, the `Initialize` function, the destructor, and the delete operator.) The code for the `FailedRegistration` function has already been added. Let's examine it now:

```
public:
  virtual void FailedRegistration(NC_RegistrationID& RegID,
                                  const ErrorMsg_Reg* Err)
  {

    // Trace the function call.
    Trace::Tracer T(_STR_FailedRegistration, _STR_ThisClass);

    if (Err == &_ERR_REG_UNEXPECTED_OBJ)
    {
      error << indent << "ERROR: FlexiReg not accepted by the
                          manager" << endl;
    }
    else if (Err == &_ERR_REG_DUPE_ID)
    {
      error << indent << "ERROR: FlexiReg: another command with the
                          same name has already been registered" <<
                          endl;
    }
    else if (Err == &_ERR_REG_OBJ_NOT_FROM_DLL)
    {
      error << indent << "ERROR: FlexiReg is packaged in a
                          different DLL then the one registered in
                          the database" << endl;
    }
    else
    {
      error << indent << "ERROR: FlexiReg unknown registration
                          error"<< endl;
    }
    error << indent << "ERROR: FlexiReg's registration failed" <<
                        endl;

  }
```

This function uses the standard implementation for handling the errors when the command manager cannot register your command. The corresponding error message will be displayed in the log file.

6. Next, we will examine the CheckParameters function, which has also been written, as follows:

```
virtual bool CheckParameters(const HttpRequest& Req,
                             HttpResponse& Res,
                             NC_Environment& Env,
                             NC_Environment& Resources)
{
  // Trace the function call.
  Trace::Tracer T(_STR_CheckParameters, _STR_ThisClass);

  static const StringWithOwnership NVP_Name1("merchant_rn");
  if (Misc::CheckFieldExistence(Req, NVP_Name1, merchantRefNum,
                                false) == false)
```

```
        return false;

    static const StringWithOwnership NVP_Name2("shlogid");
    if (Misc::CheckFieldExistence(Req, NVP_Name2, loginId, false)
                                                    == false)
      noLogid = true;
    else
      noLogid = false;

    static const StringWithOwnership NVP_Name3("shlpswd");
    if (Misc::CheckFieldExistence(Req, NVP_Name3, password, false)
                                                    == false)
    {
      noPassword = true;
    }
    else
    {
      noPassword = false;
    }

  // If return successfully
  return true;
}
```

The `CheckParameters` function first calls the `CheckFieldExistence` function in the `Misc` class to check that the `HttpRequest` object contains a value for the merchant reference. If it does, it retrieves its value from the `Req` parameter and stores it in the local variable `merchandRefNum`; otherwise, it returns false and a command structure failure message is displayed in the shopper's browser. The function then checks for a logon ID. If one exists, it retrieves its value and stores it in the local variable `loginId`, and assigns to the local boolean variable `nologid` the value "false". Otherwise, it assigns to the local boolean variable `nologid` the value "true". The function performs the same logic when checking for the existence of a password in the `HttpRequest` object, using different variables to store the results of the parameter check. If the function completes successfully, it returns true and the `Process` function is called.

7.  In review, after the `CheckParameters` function completes successfully, there are three possible outcomes:

    •   The function did not retrieve a logon ID or password

    •   The function retrieved both a logon ID and password

    •   The function retrieved a logon ID but no password, or vice versa

Now you will write the code for each of these outcomes. Let's begin with the first outcome. If the `CheckParameters` function did not retrieve a logon ID or password, it means that the shopper did not want to register with the store and therefore did not submit a logon ID and password. In this case, you need to redirect to the AddressUpdate command and pass to it the current parameters in the `Req` parameter so that it can update the shopper's dummy address (which was created when the shopper initially entered the store) with the delivery address information submitted with the order.

Add the following code to the `Process` function:

```
virtual bool Process (const HttpRequest& Req, HttpResponse& Res,
                       NC_Environment& Env)
{
  // Trace the function call.
  Trace::Tracer T(_STR_Process, _STR_ThisClass);

  //-----------------------------------------//
  //-         Your Code Begins Here        -//
  //-----------------------------------------//

  String currentParams = Req.getQUERY_STRING();

  if ((noLogid == true) && (noPassword == true))
  {
    StringWithOwnership command("/cgi-bin/ncommerce3/
                                AddressUpdate?");
    command << currentParams;
    Res.setLocation(command, true);
  }

  //-----------------------------------------//
  //-          Your Code Ends Here         -//
  //-----------------------------------------//
```

This code first declares the `currentParams` String variable, which stores all the parameters that your command retrieved from the `Req` parameter, using the `getQUERY_STRING` function in the `Req` class. Then, if the value of the boolean variables `nologid` and `noPassword` are both equal to "true", it adds the current parameters to the AddressUpdate command by first creating a String variable that stores the fully qualified URL of the AddressUpdate command and then appending the `currentParams` variable to it. It then calls the `setLocation` function of the `Res` class to execute the AddressUpdate command and enable it for SSL.

8. Now, if the `CheckParameters` function retrieved both a logon ID and password, you need to determine whether a shopper record exists in the database that corresponds to the logon ID. Add the following code:

```
//-----------------------------------------//
//-         Your Code Begins Here        -//
//-----------------------------------------//

String currentParams = Req.getQUERY_STRING();

if ((noLogid == true) && (noPassword == true))
{
  StringWithOwnership command("/cgi-bin/ncommerce3/
                              AddressUpdate?");
  command << currentParams;
  Res.setLocation(command, true);
}
```

```
else if ((noLogid == false) && (noPassword == false))
{
   NVPHash NVP;
   UserHome UH((DataBase&)*Misc::CheckEnvironmentVariable (Env,
                              NC_Environment::_VAR_MainDatabase));
   User* usr = UH.LookupByName(loginId, NVP);

//-------------------------------------------//
//-             Your Code Ends Here         -//
//-------------------------------------------//
```

If the value of the boolean variables noLogid and noPassword are both equal to "false", your code first creates a "dummy" NVPHash instance, which is needed by the UserHome class. It then connects to the current database using the CheckEnvironmentVariable function and creates a UserHome instance to access the database. Then it retrieves from the database the shopper record that matches the value stored in the local variable loginId, using the LookupByName function in the UserHome class.

9.  Now, if a shopper record does not exist, which means that the shopper is a guest shopper, you need to redirect to the RegisterNew command and pass to it all the current input parameters so that it can register the shopper. Add the following code:

```
//-------------------------------------------//
//-             Your Code Begins Here       -//
//-------------------------------------------//

String currentParams = Req.getQUERY_STRING();

if ((noLogid == true) && (noPassword == true))
{
   StringWithOwnership command("/cgi-bin/ncommerce3/
                              AddressUpdate?");
   command << currentParams;
   Res.setLocation(command, true);
}

else if ((noLogid == false) && (noPassword == false))
{
   NVPHash NVP;
   UserHome UH((DataBase&)*Misc::CheckEnvironmentVariable (Env,
                              NC_Environment::_VAR_MainDatabase));
   User* usr = UH.LookupByName(loginId, NVP);

if (usr == NULL)
{
   String command;
   command.Resize(STRLEN_1K);
   command << "/cgi-bin/ncommerce3/RegisterNew?" << currentParams;
   Res.setLocation(command, true);
}

//-------------------------------------------//
//-             Your Code Ends Here         - //
//-------------------------------------------//
```

If the value in the `user` String is empty, your code redirects to the RegisterNew command in the same way that it called the AddressUpdate command. It first creates a String variable to store the fully qualified URL of the command, appends the string that was initially declared to store the current parameters to this string, and then calls the `setLocation` function to execute the command and enable it for SSL.

10. Now, if a shopper record that corresponds to the logon ID does exists in the database, you need to determine whether it is a guest shopper or a registered shopper. The simplest way to do this is to use the value of the SAFIELD2 column. If the SAFIELD2 column contains the value "T", which means that the shopper is a guest shopper, you must call the RegisterNew command and pass to it all the current input parameters so that it can register the shopper. Add the following code:

```
//-------------------------------------------//
//-           Your Code Begins Here        -//
//-------------------------------------------//

String currentParams = Req.getQUERY_STRING();

if ((noLogid == true) && (noPassword == true))
{
   StringWithOwnership command("/cgi-bin/ncommerce3/
                              AddressUpdate?");
   command << currentParams;
   Res.setLocation(command, true);
}

else if ((noLogid == false) && (noPassword == false))
{
   NVPHash NVP;
   UserHome UH((DataBase&)*Misc::CheckEnvironmentVariable (Env,
                              NC_Environment::_VAR_MainDatabase));
   User* usr = UH.LookupByName(loginId, NVP);

if (usr == NULL)
{
   String command;
   command.Resize(STRLEN_1K);
   command << "/cgi-bin/ncommerce3/RegisterNew?" << currentParams;
   Res.setLocation(command, true);
}

else
{
   String field = usr->getField2();
   if (field == "T")
   {
     String command;
     command.Resize(STRLEN_1K);
     command << "/cgi-bin/ncommerce3/RegisterNew?"
             << currentParams;
     Res.setLocation(command, true);
   }
```

```
//-------------------------------------------//
//-              Your Code Ends Here          -//
//------------------------------------------- //
```

This code first creates a String called `field`, which retrieves from the `user` instance the value of the SAFIELD2 column, using the `getField2` function from the `User` class. If the value is equal to "T", it redirects to the RegisterNew command and passes to it the current input parameters, using the `setLocation` function.

11. If column SAFIELD2 does not contain the value "T", which means that the shopper is already registered or logged on, you need to call the RegisterUpdate command and pass to it all the current input parameters so that it can update the shopper's registration record. Add the following code:

```
else
{
  String field = usr->getField2();
  if (field == "T")
  {
    String command;
    command.Resize(STRLEN_1K);
    command << "/cgi-bin/ncommerce3/RegisterNew?"
             << currentParams;
    Res.setLocation(command, true);
  }

    else
    {
      String command;
      command.Resize(STRLEN_1K);
      command << "/cgi-bin/ncommerce3/RegisterUpdate?" <<
       currentParams;
      Res.setLocation(command, true);
    }
  }
}


//-------------------------------------------//
//-              Your Code Ends Here          -//
//-------------------------------------------//
```

12. Now you need to handle the last outcome: the `CheckParameters` function retrieved a logon ID, but no password, or vice versa. In this case, you will set the FLEXI_REG_ERR exception task to handle the error. Add the following code to the `Process` function:

```
    else
    {
      String command;
      command.Resize(STRLEN_1K);
      command << "/cgi-bin/ncommerce3/RegisterUpdate?" <<
                                    currentParams;
      Res.setLocation(command, true);
    }
```

```
        }
    }

    else
    {
        return Misc::SetErrorHandler(Env, "FLEXI_REG_ERR",
                                    merchantRefNum, "10000");
    }

    return true;
    }
};

//-----------------------------------------//
//-          Your Code Ends Here        -//
//-----------------------------------------//
```

This code sets the FLEXI_REG_ERR exception task and passes to the `Env` parameter the merchant reference number and the error code `10000`.

The last statement indicates that the `Process` function will return true if it completes successfully.

13. Now let's examine the code outside of the command's class, which is used to instantiate and register the command during initialization of the server.

```
static bool X2 = NC_CommandManager::Register("IBM",
                                             "NC", "FlexiReg", 1.0,
                                             new FlexiReg);
```

This static variable will be initialized when the DLL is loaded during the initialization of the server. An instance of the FlexiReg command will be created and a call will be made to the command manager in order to register the command as `FlexiReg_1.0(IBM,NC)`.

You have now completed the FlexiReg command. A final version of the code is stored in the cmd.cpp file on the CD, which you will use for the store.

# Examining the ItemOptionDelete Command

In the workshops in Chapters 12 to 14 you implemented the "Make Your Own Pizza" feature in the OneStopPizza Shop. In summary, this feature required the following changes:

- Replacing two overridable functions that are called by the OrderItemUpdate command (GetBaseSpePrice and ExtShiptoUpdate) so that the command can add the pizza and its toppings selected on the product page to the Order List.

- Customizing the macro that creates the Order List by 1) modifying the SQL and Net.Data statements so that it displays the selected toppings and the pizza base along with the total price and 2) replacing the command used for the **Remove Checked Items** button with a new one called ItemOptionDelete so that when shoppers select one or more items to remove from the Order List and click this button, it removes both "Make Your Own" pizzas and the pre-made pizzas.

We will now examine the new ItemOptionDelete command further. To be able to remove both custom and pre-made pizzas, it does the following:

1. Checks that the `HttpRequest` object contains at least one value for the mandatory input parameter, shipto reference number.

2. If it does, for each shipto reference number in the `HttpRequest` object it removes the pizza toppings from the database by issuing an SQL statement to delete from the custom OPTIONREL table the shipto reference number that corresponds to the current shipto reference number.

3. Redirects to the `url1` parameter, which in this case, contains the OrderItemDelete command. This command deletes the base pizza (if it is a Make Your Own Pizza) or the pre-made pizza from the database by deleting the shipto reference number from the SHIPTO table that corresponds to the product reference number passed to the command.

The following is the source code for the steps above (which is in the same CPP file that contains the FlexiReg command (`cmd.cpp`)).

```
virtual bool Process (const HttpRequest& Req, HttpResponse& Res,
                      NC_Environment& Env)
{
   // Trace the function call.
   Trace::Tracer T(_STR_Process, _STR_ThisClass);

   // Get the current set of parameters passed.
   String currentParams = Req.getQUERY_STRING();
   static const StringWithOwnership shipto ("shipto_rn");

   // Do the database update.  One for every shipto reference number
   // passed in.
   NameValuePairMap::Iterator I = Req.getNVPs().getIterator();
   I.Begin();
   I.Seek(&shipto);
   String stmt;

   while ((*I) != NULL)
   {
      if ((*I)->getName() == shipto)
      { // This NVP is of shipto_rn=9999 format, so delete the given
         // shipto_rn.
         stmt.Clean();
         stmt << "DELETE from OPTIONREL WHERE oprlstrn="
              << (*I)->getValue ();
         SQL Sql((DataBase&)*Misc::CheckEnvironmentVariable (Env,
                          NC_Environment::_VAR_MainDatabase), stmt);
         if ((Sql.getSQLrc() != ERR_DB_NO_ERROR) && (Sql.getSQLrc() !=
                                            ERR_DB_NO_DATA))
         {
            Sql.ReportError();
            error << indent << "ERROR: Deleting shipto_rn: " <<
                          shiptoRefNum << " from optionrel table" <<
                          endl;
```

```
        return false;
      }
    }

    // Advance the iterator
    ++I;
  }
  // Execute OrderItemDelete.
  String command;
  command.Resize (STRLEN_1K);

  // Add the passed parameters.
  command << url << "?" << currentParams;
  // Set the redirection with SSL.
  Res.setLocation(command, true);
  return true;
}
```

## Compiling the Command

The CPP file for the FlexiReg and the ItemOptionDelete command has already been compiled into the following DLL: cmd.dll.

## Storing the DLL

Copy cmd.dll from the \workshops\cmds directory on the CD to the following directory:

     **WIN**   \ibm\netcommerce3\bin

## Displaying the Command Results

The FlexiReg command does not set a view task to display the results; it passes the flow of execution to another command. The command that it redirects to will display the results. It must however, display an error page when the shopper submits a logon ID but no password, or vice versa. To do this, the command sets the FLEXI_REG_ERR exception task, which executes the order.d2w macro and passes the error code 10000 to it. (This same macro initially invoked the command.) The order.d2w macro contains an %IF statement in its %HTML_REPORT section to handle the error code and display the appropriate error message, as follows:

```
%IF (error_code == "10000")

  <H3>ERROR: Missing the logon ID or password.</H3>

  <P>To register, you must provide both a logon ID and password.
  Please try again.</P>

%ENDIF
```

When the error code 10000 is passed to this macro, it simply displays an error message in the browser and requests that the shopper resubmit a logon ID and password using the fields provided on the order form.

You have now completed this workshop. In the next workshop, "Activating and Testing the OneStopPizza Shop Commands" on page 483, you will learn how to activate the FlexiReg and ItemOptionDelete commands in the system and test them in the store.

# Chapter 17, Activating and Testing Commands

After you have written your new command, you must register it in the database so that the system can execute it at run-time. You will also need to register any tasks that your command uses for handling exceptions and successful returns, as well as the macros and overridable functions that implement those tasks. In the workshop, you will activate the commands that you planned and wrote in the workshops in the previous two chapters.

> **Note:**
> Only site administrators have the authority to register new commands. If you are a store administrator, you must ask your site administrator to perform the tasks described in this chapter.

This chapter covers the following topics:

- Registering a Command
- Assigning a Command to a Server Pool
- Assigning a Command to an Access Control Group
- Registering a Task
- Registering an Overridable Function
- Assigning an Overridable Function to its Task
- Registering and Assigning a Net.Data Macro to its Task
- Restarting the Net.Commerce Server
- Example of Activating the Sample Command
- Specifying Command Security
- Testing the Command
- Workshop: Activating and Testing the OneStopPizza Shop Commands

# Registering a Command

To register the command, you must insert a record in the CMDS (Commands) table, as follows:

1. From a DB2 command prompt, connect to the database for your store.

2. Type the following command, all on one line:

```
insert into cmds (refnum, dll_name, vendor, product, name, version,
url, export, description) values ((select max(refnum)+1 from cmds),
'<DLL/Shared_Library>', '<vendor>', '<product>', '<name>',
<version>, '<URL>', <export>, '<description>')
```

The values for each field are as follows:

`<DLL/Shared_Library>`

> The name of the DLL or shared library in which the command resides.

> **Note:**
> Ensure that you specify an extension for the DLL or shared library and that you specify the DLL or shared library either as a full path or as a path relative to the directory specified by your **LIBPATH** variable.

`<vendor>`

> The name of the company for which the command is being written. This may be a third-party vendor, a merchant or site administrator, or IBM itself.

`<product>`

> The name of the product for which the command is being implemented; for example, "NC" for Net.Commerce.

`<name>`

> The command's "absolute" name. This name is defined in the command's static bool variable, which is used by the command manager to instantiate and register the command during server initialization.

`<version>`

> The version of the command implementation.

`<URL>`

> The name for the command that will be embedded in a URL, as defined by its syntax. This name can be the same as the command's absolute name. The name is case-sensitive, must be unique, and cannot contain forward slashes (/), spaces, or any character that is not valid within a URL.

`<export>`

> A flag indicating whether the command can be accessed from a URL. Enter 1 to make the command accessible from a URL, or 0 to make the command available internally only.

`<description>`

> A brief description of the command's functionality. If you do not want to insert a description, enter NULL.

# Assigning a Command to a Server Pool

Once you have registered your command, you must assign it to a server pool. A server pool is a collection of commands that is assigned to a specific server. It guarantees the command access to a server that has its own port on which it listens. Commands can be shared across pools. The sever pool that contains all of the default shopping commands is called **ncommerce**. Typically, this pool is used for new commands. To assign your command to a server pool, insert a record in the POOL_CMD (Pool-Command Association) table, as follows:

1.  From a DB2 command prompt, connect to the database for your store.

2.  Type the following command, all on one line:

    ```
    insert into pool_cmd (pool_rn, cmd_rn) values ((select refnum from
    pools where name = 'ncommerce'), ((select refnum from cmds where
    vendor = '<vendor>' and product = '<product>' and name = '<name>'
    and version = <version>)))
    ```

    The values for the fields are as follows:

    `<vendor>`
       The name of the company for which the command is being written, as defined in the CMDS table.

    `<product>`
       The name of the product into which the command is being implemented, as defined in the CMDS table.

    `<name>`
       The command's "absolute" name, as defined in the CMDS table

    `<version>`
       The version of the command implementation, as defined in the CMDS table.

# Assigning a Command to an Access Control Group

You must assign each command that you create to an access control group. An access control group consists of commands that allow shoppers to access a command for a specified merchant. You can create an original access control group for your command, or use one of the following predefined groups:

*   Site Administrators (super users)

*   Store Administrators

*   Store Creators

*   Dummy Group (no access control)

Normally, commands that you create to perform store operations do not need to be assigned to an access control group, as they will be used not by administrators to access the database but by shoppers who are interacting with your store. In this case, you should assign your command to the "Dummy Group" which makes it accessible to all users.

If the command is being created for administrators, you can use any of the predefined groups above or create new ones. For information on creating a new access control group and assigning commands and administrators to it, see "Defining Access Control" on page 66.

To assign your command to one of the predefined access control groups (most commonly the Dummy Group), insert a record into the ACC_CMDGRP (Access Command Group) table, as follows:

1. From a DB2 command prompt, connect to the database for your store.

2. Type the following command, all on one line:

```
insert into acc_cmdgrp (grpc_refnum, cmd_refnum) values ((select
refnum from acc_group where name='<access_grp_name>'), (select
refnum from cmds where name = '<name>' and version = <version> and
product = '<product>' and Vendor = '<vendor>'))
```

The values for each field are as follows:

`<access_grp_name>`
> The name of the access control group to which you want to assign the command, as defined in the ACC_GROUP table. The following are the predefined group names that you can choose from:
>
> - `Site Administrators`
> - `Store Administrators`
> - `Store Creators`
> - `Dummy Group`

`<name>`
> The command's "absolute" name, as defined in the CMDS table.

`<version>`
> The version of the command implementation, as defined in the CMDS table.

`<product>`
> The name of the product into which the command is being implemented, as defined in the CMDS table.

`<vendor>`
> The name of the company for which the command is being written, as defined in the CMDS table.

# Registering a Task

If your command sets one or more tasks to handle certain operations, such as exception conditions and successful returns, you need to register them in the database. For each task that your command sets, insert a record in the TASKS table, as follows:

1. From a DB2 command prompt, connect to the database for your store.

2. Type the following command, all on one line:

```
insert into tasks (tkrfnbr, tkname , tkcomment , tkgroup , tkscope)
values ((select max(tkrfnbr)+1 from tasks), '<task_name>',
'<task_comment>', '<task_group>', <task_scope>)
```

The values for each field are as follows:

`<task_name>`
> The name of the task.

`<task_comment>`
> A brief description of the task.

`<task_group>`
> The task group to which the task belongs. You must enter one of the following:
>
> - `ERROR`, for overridable functions that handle exception conditions.
>
> - `PROCESS`, for overridable functions that process information.
>
> - `VIEW`, for overridable functions that display the pages that shoppers normally see during the shopping process.

`<task_scope>`
> The scope of the task. Enter 0 for mall scope or 1 for store scope. (The different stores residing in a mall can provide customized implementations by creating their own overridable functions.)

# Registering an Overridable Function

If you have created a new overridable function to perform a specific piece of business logic for your command, you need to register it by inserting a record into the OFS (Overridable Functions) table, as follows:

1. From a DB2 command prompt, connect to the database in which you want to register the overridable function.

2. Type the following command, all on one line:

```
insert into ofs (refnum, dll_name, vendor, product, name, version,
description) values ((select max(refnum)+1 from ofs),
'<DLL/Shared_Library>', '<vendor>' , '<product>', '<name>',
<version>, '<description>')
```

The values for each field are as follows:

`<DLL/Shared_Library>`
> The name of the DLL or shared library in which the overridable function resides.

> **Note:**
> Ensure that you specify an extension for the DLL or shared library, and that you specify the DLL or shared library either as a full path or as a path relative to the directory specified by your **LIBPATH** variable.

`<vendor>`
> The name of the company for which the overridable function is being written. This may be a third-party vendor, a merchant or site administrator, or IBM itself.

`<product>`
>    The name of the product into which the overridable function is being implemented; for example, "NC" for Net.Commerce.

`<name>`
>    The name of the overridable function.

`<version>`
>    The version of the overridable function implementation.

`<description>`
>    A brief description of the overridable function. If you do not want to insert a description, enter NULL.

# Assigning an Overridable Function to its Task

You must assign each new overridable function that you register and each supplied overridable function that you use for your command (for example, TaskDisplay_1.0(IBM,NC)) to the task that it implements. (Ensure that you have already registered the task before doing this step.) To assign an overridable function to its task, you must insert a record in the TASK_MER_OF table, either manually or by using the Administrator forms provided. Both methods are described below.

## Manually

To manually insert a record into the TASK_MER_OF table, do the following for each task to be implemented:

1. From a DB2 command prompt, connect to the database in which you want to register the overridable function.

2. Type the following command, all on one line:

```
insert into task_mer_of (task_rn, merchant_rn, of_rn) values
((select tkrfnbr from tasks where tkname = '<task_name>'),
<merchant_rn>, (select refnum from ofs where name = '<name>'
and version = <version> and vendor = '<vendor>' and
product = '<product>'))
```

The values for each variable are as follows:

`<task_name>`
>    The name of the task that the overridable function implements, as defined in the TASKS table.

`<merchant_rn>`
>    The reference number of the merchant for which the function is being implemented. If the task is set to mall scope (that is, the overridable function will affect all stores in a mall), enter NULL.

`<name>`
>    The name of the overridable function, as defined in the OFS table.

```
<version>
```
The version of the overridable function implementation, as defined in the OFS table.

```
<vendor>
```
The name of the company for which the overridable function is being written, as defined in the OFS table.

```
<product>
```
The name of the product into which the overridable function is being implemented, as defined in the OFS table.

# Using the Administrator

To have the Administrator automatically insert a record into the TASK_MER_OF table, do the following for each task to be implemented:

1.  Open the Administrator.

2.  On the task bar, click **Site Manager** and then **Task Management**. The Task Management form appears.

3.  From the **Select Task Type** drop-down list, select the appropriate task type.

    *   **ERROR**, for overridable functions that handle exception conditions.

    *   **PROCESS**, for overridable functions that process information.

    *   **VIEW**, for overridable functions that display the pages that shoppers normally see during the shopping process.

    A list of all the tasks that are available for the selected task type appears in the bottom frame.

4.  Select the desired task name from the list. Typically, you will select **PROCESS**. The fields automatically fill with task information.

5.  From the **Scope** drop-down list, change the task scope, if desired. If you are creating a single-store site, you do not have to change the scope; both mall and store scope will function properly in this case.

6.  If you changed the scope, click **Save** before proceeding.

7.  On the task bar, click **Task Assignment**. If you selected a process task, the Overridable Function Assignment form appears. If you selected an exception or view task, click the **Overridable Function** button at the bottom of the frame. The Overridable Function Assignment form appears.

8.  From the **Store — Overridable Function(Product)(Vender)(Version) Assignment** list, select the store or mall for which you want to assign your overridable function.

9.  From the **Overridable Functions** list, select the overridable function that you want to assign to the selected task.

10. Click **Update**. A confirmation message appears, indicating that you have successfully assigned your new overridable function to the task for the selected store.

# Registering and Assigning a Net.Data Macro to its Task

If you have created a new macro or customized a supplied one to display to a Web page to the shopper, you must register the macro and assign it to the view or exception task that it implements. To do this, you must insert a record into the MACROS table. You can do this either manually or by using the Administrator forms provided. Ensure that you have already registered the view or exception task before doing this step.

## Manually

To manually insert a record into the MACROS table, do the following for each task to which the macro is to be assigned:

1. From a DB2 command prompt, connect to the database for your store.

2. Type the following command, all on one line:

   ```
   insert into macros (marfnbr, mamernbr, mafilename) values ((select
   tkrfnbr from tasks where tkname = '<task_name>'), <merchant_rn>,
   '<macro_name>')
   ```

   The values for each field are as follows:

   `<task_name>`
   > The name of the task for which the macro will be used, as defined in the TASKS table.

   `<merchant_rn>`
   > The reference number of the merchant for which the macro will be used. If the task is set to mall scope (that is, the macro will affect all stores in a mall), enter NULL.

   `<macro_name>`
   > The file name of the macro. Ensure that its path has been defined in the Net.Data db2www.ini configuration file. For more information, see "Specifying a Macro Directory" on page 195.

## Using the Administrator

To register the macro and assign it to its task using the Administrator, do the following:

1. Open the Administrator.

2. On the task bar, click **Site Manager** and then **Task Management**. The Task Management form appears.

3. From the Select Task Type drop-down list, select one of the following task types:

   - **ERROR**, for displaying error pages.

   - **VIEW**, for displaying the pages that shoppers normally see during the shopping process.

> **Note:**
> Do not select the **PROCESS** task type; this task is reserved for activating overridable functions that process information.

A list of the tasks that are available for the selected task type appears in the bottom frame.

4. Select the desired task name from the list. The fields automatically fill with task information.

5. From the **Scope** drop-down list, change the task scope, if desired. If you are creating a single-store site, you do not have to change the scope: both mall and store scope will function properly in this case.

6. If you changed the scope, click **Save** before proceeding.

7. On the task bar, click **Task Assignment**.

8. Click the **Macro** button at the bottom of the frame. The Macro Assignment form appears.

9. If the scope of the task has been assigned to *store*, select the store for which you want to assign the macro from the **Select Mall/Store** drop-down list.

10. In the **Macro Filename** field, enter the file name of your new macro. Ensure that its path has been defined in the Net.Data db2www.ini configuration file. For more information, see "Specifying a Macro Directory" on page 195.

11. Click **Save**. A confirmation message appears, indicating that you have successfully assigned your new macro to the selected task.

# Restarting the Net.Commerce Server

After you register the infrastructure for your new command, you must restart the Net.Commerce server in order for the database changes to take effect. Under Windows NT, you can easily stop and start the server from the Control Panel. Under AIX, you can do so from the Configuration Manager.

## Stopping and Starting the Server on Windows NT

To restart the Net.Commerce server from the Control Panel on Windows NT, do the following:

1. On a Windows NT user ID with Administrator authority, click **Start**, point to **Settings**, and then click **Control Panel**.

2. In the Control Panel window, double-click the **Services** icon.

3. For each Net.Commerce instance that you want to start, do the following:

   a) From the Service list, select **Net.Commerce – <instance_name>,** where **<instance_name>** is the name of the instance that you want to start. By default, the instance name is **mser** if you are running only one instance.

b)  Click **Stop** to stop the instance.

c)  When the instance has stopped successfully, click **Start** to start it again.

## Stopping and Starting the Server on AIX

To restart the Net.Commerce server from the Configuration Manager on AIX, do the following:

1.  If the Configuration Manager is not currently running, do the following to start it:

    a)  While logged on as user ID root, on an AIX command line, switch to the `/usr/lpp/NetCommerce3/server/bin` directory.

    b)  Type: `/start_admin_server`.

2.   Start your browser and go to `http://host_name:4444`.

3.  When prompted, enter your Configuration Manager user ID and password. If you have not yet changed them, your user ID is `webadmin`, and your password is `webibm`.

4.  From the list of instances, select the instance you want to restart and click **Stop**.

5.  When the instance has stopped successfully, click **OK** and then click **Start** to start it again.

# Example of Activating the Sample Command

The following describes the steps for registering the PasswordReset command and the tasks, overridable functions, and macros that it uses:

1.  Register the command in the CMDS table, as follows:

    ```
    insert into cmds (refnum, dll_name, vendor, product, name, version,
    url, export, description) values (select MAX(refnum)+1 from cmds,
    'newcmd.dll', 'IBM', 'NC', 'PasswordReset', 1.0, 'PasswordReset',
    1, 'Resets a logon password')
    ```

2.  Assign the command to the `ncommerce` server pool, as follows:

    ```
    insert into pool_cmd (pool_rn, cmd_rn) values ((select refnum from
    pools where name = 'ncommerce'), ((select refnum from cmds where
    vendor = 'IBM' and product = 'NC' and name = 'PasswordReset' and
    version = 1.0)))
    ```

3.  Assign the command to the `Dummy Group` access control group, as follows:

    ```
    insert into acc_cmdgrp (grpc_refnum, cmd_refnum) values ((select
    refnum from acc_group where name='Dummy Group'), (select refnum
    from cmds where name = 'PasswordReset' and version = 1.0 and product
    = 'NC' and Vendor = 'IBM')
    ```

4.  Since the macro sets two tasks, the PASSWORD_RESET_ERR exception task and the PASSWORD_RESET_DSP view task, the next step is to register them both by inserting two records into the TASKS table, as follows:

```
insert into tasks (tkrfnbr, tkname , tkcomment , tkgroup , tkscope)
values ((select max(tkrfnbr)+1 from tasks), 'PASSWORD_RESET_ERR',
'Display error page for mismatching new and verify password',
'ERROR', 1)

insert into tasks (tkrfnbr, tkname , tkcomment , tkgroup , tkscope)
values ((select max(tkrfnbr)+1 from tasks), 'PASSWORD_RESET_DSP',
'Display page to indicate a successful password reset', 'VIEW', 1)
```

5.  The supplied TaskDisplay_1.0(IBM,NC) overridable function implements both the PASSWORD_RESET_ERR and the PASSWORD_RESET_DSP tasks, so you must assign it to both those tasks. Here you will do this manually by inserting a record into the OFS_MER_TASK table for each task, but you can also assign it using the form provided in the Administrator. Assume a merchant reference number of 427.

```
insert into task_mer_of (task_rn, merchant_rn, of_rn) values
((select tkrfnbr from tasks where tkname = 'PASSWORD_RESET_ERR'),
427, (select refnum from ofs where name = 'TaskDisplay' and
version = 1.0 and vendor = 'IBM' and product = 'NC'))

insert into task_mer_of (task_rn, merchant_rn, of_rn) values
((select tkrfnbr from tasks where tkname = 'PASSWORD_RESET_DSP'),
427, (select refnum from ofs where name = 'TaskDisplay' and
version = 1.0 and vendor = 'IBM' and product = 'NC'))
```

6.  The `password.d2w` macro is used to display error pages and the `pwdsuccess.d2w` is used to display a success page, so you must now register these macros and assign them to their corresponding tasks (the PASSWORD_RESET_ERR exception task and the PASSWORD_RESET_DSP view task, respectively). Here you will do this by manually inserting a record in the MACROS table, but you can also do so using the form provided in the Administrator.

```
insert into macros (marfnbr, mamernbr, mafilename) values
((select tkrfnbr from tasks where tkname = 'PASSWORD_RESET_ERR'),
427, 'password.d2w')

insert into macros (marfnbr, mamernbr, mafilename) values
((select tkrfnbr from tasks where tkname = 'PASSWORD_RESET_DSP'),
427, 'pwdsuccess.d2w')
```

You are now finished registering the command infrastructure. Restart the Net.Commerce server to activate the command in the system.

# Specifying Command Security

For each new command that you create, you need to specify whether the command is to be enabled for SSL, for authentication, or for both. Enabling it for SSL encrypts the information that it passes between the browser and the server, to prevent its exposure to unauthorized individuals. Enabling it for authentication requires that shoppers log on before they can invoke the command.

> **Note:**
>
> For security measures, once shoppers have logged on, they should also be in SSL mode, in order to protect their personal information and the session cookie. Therefore, if you enable the command for authentication, you must also enable it for SSL.

For information on how to enable or disable your command for SSL, authentication, or both, see "Specifying SSL or Authentication" on page 74.

## Sample Scenario:

Because the PasswordReset command is dealing with the shopper's password, it should be enabled for SSL.

# Testing the Command

Once you have registered your command and its infrastructure in the database and created the necessary macros to display the results, you are ready to test your command. You must first determine whether you will use a test environment within the Net.Commerce system, write your own, or use a combination of both.

The advantage to testing your implementation within the Net.Commerce system is that you can be sure it will run the same way in production. The disadvantage is that you must run the commands through a browser and determine whether they work as expected.

The advantage to writing your own test environment is that you have more control over your test cases and the ability to trace through your code. The disadvantage is that unless your test environment re-creates the Net.Commerce environment exactly, you cannot be sure that your changes will work the same way in production.

To gain the advantages of both environments while minimizing the disadvantages, you can start in your own test environment. When you are confident that your changes are working properly, test them from within the Net.Commerce system.

Once you have created the scenario in which your command will run, check for the following:

- Ensure that the command responds as expected.

- Ensure that the error pages are displayed when an exception condition is encountered by your command, and that the error parameters are passed as expected.

- If it appears that your command is not being called, check the following:

  1.  You have registered the entire command infrastructure properly; for example, ensure that you have registered all tasks that your command uses, as well as the macros and overridable functions that implement them.

  2.  The Net.Commerce system does not display an error message in the log about the overridable function or macro that implements a task.

# Workshop: Activating and Testing the OneStopPizza Shop Commands

In the previous workshop "Writing the FlexiReg Command" on page 459, you wrote the FlexiReg command and examined the ItemOptionDelete command. In this workshop, you will register these commands in the database, including the FLEX_REG_ERR exception task that the FlexiReg command sets and the `order.d2w` macro that implements that task. Then, you will test both commands in the OneStopPizza Shop.

## Registering the Commands and their Infrastructure

Follow these steps to register the FlexiReg and ItemOptionDelete commands and the tasks, overridable functions, and macros that they use:

1. Open a DB2 Command Line Processor window.

2. From the DB2 command prompt, connect to the database for the OneStopPizza Shop.

3. Register the FlexiReg command and the ItemOptionDelete command in the CMDS table by typing the following two commands, each all on one line:

   ```
   insert into cmds (refnum, dll_name, vendor, product, name, version,
   url, export, description) values ((select max(refnum)+1 from cmds),
   'cmd.dll', 'IBM', 'NC', 'FlexiReg', 1.0, 'FlexiReg', 1, 'Processes
   an order and can register a shopper')
   ```

   ```
   insert into cmds (refnum, dll_name, vendor, product, name, version,
   url, export, description) values ((select max(refnum)+1 from cmds),
   'cmd.dll', 'IBM', 'NC', 'ItemOptionDelete', 1.0,
   'ItemOptionDelete', 1, 'Deletes custom and premade pizzas from the
   SHIPTO table')
   ```

4. Assign the commands to the `ncommerce` server pool by typing the following two commands:

   ```
   insert into pool_cmd (pool_rn, cmd_rn) values ((select refnum from
   pools where name = 'ncommerce'), ((select refnum from cmds where
   vendor = 'IBM' and product = 'NC' and name = 'FlexiReg' and version
   = 1.0)))
   ```

   ```
   insert into pool_cmd (pool_rn, cmd_rn) values ((select refnum from
   pools where name = 'ncommerce'), ((select refnum from cmds where
   vendor = 'IBM' and product = 'NC' and name = 'ItemOptionDelete'
   and version = 1.0)))
   ```

5. Assign the commands to the `Dummy Group` access control group, as follows:

   ```
   insert into acc_cmdgrp (grpc_refnum, cmd_refnum) values ((select
   refnum from acc_group where name='Dummy Group'), (select refnum
   from cmds where name = 'FlexiReg' and version = 1.0 and
   product = 'NC' and Vendor = 'IBM'))
   ```

```
insert into acc_cmdgrp (grpc_refnum, cmd_refnum) values ((select
refnum from acc_group where name='Dummy Group'), (select refnum
from cmds where name = 'ItemOptionDelete' and version = 1.0 and
product = 'NC' and Vendor = 'IBM'))
```

6.  For the FlexiReg command, register the FLEXI_REG_ERR exception task in the TASKS table, as follows:

```
insert into tasks (tkrfnbr, tkname , tkcomment , tkgroup , tkscope)
values ((select max(tkrfnbr)+1 from tasks), 'FLEXI_REG_ERR',
'Display error page for FlexiReg command', 'ERROR', 1)
```

7.  The default TaskDisplay_1.0(IBM,NC) overridable function implements the FLEXI_REG_ERR exception task, so you must assign it to the task. Here you will do it by manually inserting a record into OFS_MER_TASK table, but it can also be done using the form provided in the Administrator.

```
insert into task_mer_of (task_rn, merchant_rn, of_rn) values
((select tkrfnbr from tasks where tkname = 'FLEXI_REG_ERR'),
<merchant_rn>, (select refnum from ofs where name = 'TaskDisplay'
and version = 1.0 and vendor = 'IBM' and product = 'NC'))
```

    where <merchant_rn> is your merchant reference number.

8.  Register the order.d2w macro and assign it to the FLEXI_REG_ERR exception task by manually inserting a record in the MACROS table as follows (again, this can also be done using the form provided in the Administrator):

```
insert into macros (marfnbr, mamernbr, mafilename) values ((select
tkrfnbr from tasks where tkname = 'FLEXI_REG_ERR'), <merchant_rn>,
'order.d2w')
```

    where <merchant_rn> is your merchant reference number.

9.  To activate these database changes, restart the Net.Commerce server.

10. Close the DB2 Command window.

You have now completed the registration process for the FlexiReg command and the ItemOptionDelete command. Next, you will specify security for them.

## Specifying Command Security

You now need to specify whether you want to enable the FlexiReg command and the ItemOptionDelete command for SSL, for authentication, or for both. Since the FlexiReg command handles input parameters that contain personal information about the shopper (the logon ID, password, and address information), you will encrypt the information using SSL. You will not enable the ItemOptionDelete command for SSL, since it does not deal with sensitive data. Neither command will be enabled for authentication.

1.  Access Net.Commerce Administrator using your site administrator logon ID and password. (Only site administrators can enable or disable commands for SSL and authentication.)

2. On the task bar, click **Site Manager** and then **Command Security to display the** Command Security Assignment form.

3. From the **Store** drop-down list, select **Default Assignment**. All new commands need to have a default assignment for SSL and authentication. Then, if you are creating a mall, you can assign store versions by selecting the store from this list. For a single store like the one you are creating, you do not need to do the store assignment, as it is redundant once a default assignment is made.

4. From the **Commands** list at the bottom of the form, use the Shift key to select **FlexiReg** and **ItemOptionDelete**.

5. Click the **Add To List** button to add the commands to the **Assigned Commands (SSL)(Authentication)** list.

6. From the **Assigned Commands (SSL)(Authentication)** list, select **FlexiReg** (you will have to scroll to find it) and then select the **Enable SSL** check box.

7. On the action bar at the bottom of the form, click **Update**. The FlexiReg command is now enabled for SSL and disabled for authentication. It will appear in the format: **FlexiReg – (YES)(NO)**.

8. From the **Assigned Commands (SSL)(Authentication)** list, select **ItemOptionDelete – (YES)(NO)** and then disable the **Enable SSL** check box.

9. On the action bar at the bottom of the form, click **Update**. The ItemOptionDelete command is now disabled for both SSL and authentication. It appears in the format: **ItemOptionDelete – (NO,NO)**.

10. Close the browser window.

# Testing the ItemOptionDelete Command

You are now ready to test the ItemOptionDelete command in the OneStopPizza Shop. In review, this command removes both "Make Your Own" pizzas and the pre-made pizzas from the database, when requested from the Order List.

1. Ensure that you do not have any browser windows open.

2. Open the OneStopPizza Shop in a new browser window.

3. Navigate to the Deli Delight product page, and add one pizza to your Order List.

4. Navigate to the *Make Your Own Pizza* page, and add one pizza to your Order List.

5. On the Order List, select the check box beside *Make Your Own Pizza,* and then click **Remove Checked Items**. The product is removed from the list. The ItemOptionDelete command successfully removed the "Make Your Own" pizza and its toppings from the database.

6. On the Order List, select the check box beside **Deli Delight** and then click **Remove Checked Items**. The product is removed from the list. The ItemOptionDelete command successfully removed the pre-made pizza from the database.

# Testing the FlexiReg Command

Now let's test the FlexiReg command in the store. In review, this command will either register a shopper and process the order submitted or just process the order, depending on whether or not the shopper provides a logon ID and password when placing the order.

1.  Add another *Our Famous Pizza* to your Order List.

2.  On the Order List, click **Place Order**. The Place Order page appears in a new browser window. Note that the Delivery Address form is blank.

3.  Fill in the requested information, including a logon ID and password, to register.

4.  Select a credit card type and enter a valid number and expiry month and year, and then click **Submit Order**. The order confirmation page appears. You have now placed an order *and* registered with the store. Let's make sure that you have been registered.

5.  Close all browser windows and re-access the store.

6.  On the home page, enter your logon ID and password, and then click **LOG ON**. The Quick Pick page appears, displaying the pizza you just ordered. Seeing this page, which is only available to registered shoppers, proves that the FlexiReg command was successfully redirected to the RegisterNew command.

7.  Click **Add** beside the pizza to add it once again to your Order List.

8.  On the Order List, click **Place Order**. The order page appears again, but this time the Delivery Address form is filled the address you specified when you previously placed the order.

9.  Now let's test the FlexiReg command's redirection to the AddressUpdate command by *not* providing a logon ID and password during order time. Close the browser windows and open the store in a new one.

10. Add a pizza of your choice to your Order List.

11. On the Order List, click **Place Order**. The order page appears, displaying a Delivery Address form, which is once again blank because you have not logged on.

12. Fill in the information, but this time *without* providing a logon ID and password

13. Select a credit card and enter its details, and then click **Submit Order**. The order confirmation page appears. You have now placed an order, but you are not registered with the store.

You have now completed the workshops in this book.

# Cleaning Up

Now that you have completed the workshops in this book, you can remove the store and all of its data by first deleting the store record from the database and then deleting all the directories containing the store's macros, HTML files and images. This will allow others to do the workshops on the same Net.Commerce machine.

## Deleting the Store Record

To delete the store record for the OneStopPizza Shop, which will remove all the data associated with the store from the database, do the following:

1.  Open the Administrator, and log on using your site administrator logon ID and password. (The site administrator is the only person who can remove a store record from the database.)

2.  On the task bar, click **Site Manager** and then click **Store Records**. The Store Records form appears.

3.  Click **Search** to view a list of all store records that currently reside in the database.

4.  From the list at the bottom, select **OneStopPizza Shop**. The fields of the form fill with information about the selected store.

5.  Click **Delete**.

6.  Click **OK** in the confirmation window to complete the deletion. Ensure that a confirmation message appears in the display area.

    You have now successfully deleted the store record from the database.

## Removing the Store Macros, HTML Files, and Images

To remove all the files (macros, HTML files, and images) that were used to display the store pages, delete the following directories:

**WIN** `\ibm\netcommerce3\macro\en_US\OneStopPizzaShop`

**WIN** `\ibm\netcommerce3\macro\en_US\category\OneStopPizzaShop`

**WIN** `\ibm\netcommerce3\macro\en_US\product\OneStopPizzaShop`

**WIN** `\ibm\www\html\OneStopPizzaShop`

# Part 5, Appendixes

This part provides all the essential reference material required for building and customizing your e-commerce site.

## Contents:

# Appendix A, Net.Commerce Product Advisor

Companies face a unique problem when trying to sell products over the World Wide Web. First, it's not really possible to "sell" products in cyberspace. One can "present" products and product information, but there is no sales force to help out customers who are unsure of what they want. Second, customers shop differently based on their specific needs and their knowledge of the products they are looking to buy. In a physical storefront setting, a sales representative is available to help them find the answers they need and to make the proper product selections. In a storefront on the Web, however, customers have up until now been on their own.

## The "Intelligent" Way to Sell on the Web

Net.Commerce Product Advisor combines the marketing knowledge of a salesperson and the technical knowledge of a product specialist into an electronic catalog that contains not only product data but product "knowledge." It includes a set of easy-to-use tools that enable buyers to quickly find what they are looking for. Customers expect more from an electronic catalog than from a paper one: it must always contain the most recent information, and it must allow them to compare, search for, and retrieve items instantly. In order to enable users to do product comparisons, the data must be parameterized: that is, the specifications must be in separate fields, not run together in a paragraph. For users, the problem with such catalogs is that in order to perform a search, they must know something about the product area. If you're a camera expert, you may be able to perform a search on cameras; but if you're not and you are looking for a gift for a friend who likes photography, how do you search? If you don't know which key words to use, your options are to simply browse the electronic catalog or to navigate from an index through some categorization of products.

## How Do Customers Find Products on the Web?

There are several ways for customers to find products on the Web, each with its advantages and disadvantages. The goal is to get the customer to the right product and to do so quickly and easily. Making sure it's the "right" product is critical in reducing the number of returned items, which can be very costly. Making sure that the desired product can be found quickly increases the chance that the customer will return on future shopping trips.

## Category Navigation

The simplest way to find a product is through category navigation, where the buyer navigates through the seller's site, category by category. This works fine if both buyer and seller classify the product the same way, but not if the buyer can't figure out which category the seller has placed it under.

## Keyword Search

Another way of finding a product is by using a keyword search. However, this assumes that the buyer knows the appropriate keyword; also, it often yields either zero hits or a huge number of hits. In the former case, the buyer must think of another keyword that might be more relevant. In the latter case, the buyer is overwhelmed with the number of references that are returned and will often not bother to look at them at all, which may result in selecting the wrong product and later returning it.

# A More Efficient Approach

The Product Advisor function adds two ways of finding products: parametric search (also called feature-relevant shopping) and artificial intelligence assisted search (also called sales-assisted shopping).

## Parametric Search

A parametric search can quickly "weed out" products that are not of interest. This is good for buyers who know something about the products they are looking for. If a shopper is looking for a VCR that must be a stereo hi-fi system with four heads, there is no sense in him wasting his time paging through a selection of mono systems with two heads. By specifying the features they are interested in, buyers are guaranteed they will see only those products that meet their criteria. They will never get zero results, because Product Advisor will always keep a product in the search space.

## Artificial Intelligence (AI) Assisted Search

With AI assisted search, no assumptions are made about the customer's product knowledge. Many customers know the kind of product they want but are unfamiliar with a particular product line. Here, a "virtual salesperson" asks questions about how the product will be used, and then applies product knowledge to select the product that would be right for this buyer.

# Scenario

A company is selling cameras over the Web. For customers who are would-be or novice photographers, the company sets up a product-knowledgeable "sales assistant" that asks them about what type of photography they are interested in and how they plan to use the camera; relates their answers to the camera features they would most likely need; and then presents all the cameras that would be appropriate for the intended use.

For more experienced customers, the company sets up a list of features from which the buyers can select those that are important to them. For example, a customer could specify that she is looking for a waterproof Single Lens Reflex (SLR) camera with a built-in flash, and would be shown only those products that meet these criteria. She could then narrow down the selection even more by specifying additional relevant features, until the product selection is small enough to let her easily make a purchase decision.

# Product Advisor Components

Product Advisor includes tools that let product specialists enter data into the system from existing databases, and tools that let salespeople enter questions and answers based on their product knowledge and relate the answers back to product features. These tools all use a published application programming interface (API) which allows them to be interchangeable with customer-written and third-party tools. In this way, appropriate tools can be built for use by people with different levels of product knowledge or in different industries.

The administrative interface of Product Advisor is called from the Store Manager in the Administrator. There is also a rendering engine, which is used to present the different types of search strategies, called "shopping metaphors," to the customer. These interfaces are built on a catalog class library that abstracts the physical storage of objects into a model that is easy to manipulate and portable across releases and schema changes.

There are three types of shopping metaphors: Product Exploration, Sales Assistant, and Product Comparison. Each of these types is described below.

# Product Exploration Shopping Metaphor

With the Product Exploration shopping metaphor, customers select those features of a product that are important to them. It lists all the features of that product line and all the values that each feature may take. The customer selects the desired value for the first feature. Based on that selection, the system then constrains the product selection to only those products that have that feature and value, and displays all relevant features and their newly constrained values. The customer is then prompted to select another feature, and the system again constrains the product selection to only those products that satisfy both feature constraints. This process continues until either only one product is left or a small number of products is left, which the customer can now compare or browse.

## Product Exploration Tools Overview

The Product Exploration Builder tool allows merchants who have their product information in Net.Commerce format to quickly restructure it for use with the Product Exploration shopping metaphor.

- The first step is to identify the existing data that can be used in the electronic catalog. This data is then used by the collection tool to build the target exploration categories. Merchants can select features on which they would like their customer to explore by toggling the display flag. The tool gives some hints as to which features might be suitable for product exploration.  For example, a feature with hundreds of unique values is probably not a good candidate because customers will be overwhelmed by all the options.  Likewise, a feature that has a very long description (say, 200 characters) may not be a good one to show.

- The order in which features are displayed can be changed.  (It is probably best to keep the most popular features for a product near the top of the list.)

- The final step is to select a template from a list of predefined templates, in order to determine the overall look of the Web page.  Templates can be customized on a field-by-field basis, so you can use different graphical widgets to display the values of each feature.  With an HTML-driven template, you can select from edit fields, list boxes, and check boxes.  With a Java-driven template, you can select from more exotic dials and sliders that are not available with just HTML alone.  All this information is saved for use at run-time.

# Sales Assistant Shopping Metaphor

The Sales Assistant shopping metaphor presents customers who know relatively little about a product line with a set of multiple-choice questions that help determine which products might best meet their needs.  The questions are devised to reflect what a salesperson would be likely to ask in a real store.  The first question is the most general one.  The customer selects one of the answers provided and, based on this selection, the product count is reduced to the number of products that meet the criteria of this answer.  The customer is then asked another question, and the answer to that next question further subsets the product line.  The process continues until there are no more questions or until the customer requests to compare or view the remaining products.

The question-and-answer sequence is structured as a tree.  The first question, at the root of the tree, is seen by every customer.  The second and all subsequent questions may vary, depending on the answer given to the question before.  Thus, the customer sees only those questions that are relevant, based on previous answers and product availability.

## Sales Assistance Usage Scenario

The following is an example of how a shopper may use the Sales Assistant shopping metaphor from within a store.

1. The shopper requests sales assistance for a particular line (category) of products.

2. The Sales Assistant shopping metaphor presents the customer with a question and the possible answers to the question.

3. The shopper selects an appropriate answer to the question.

4. The Sales Assistant shopping metaphor applies any feature constraints that are associated with the answer to the product selection, reducing the product selection to only those products that satisfy these constraints.  It then determines if the answer has a follow-up question.  If there is one, it displays this next question and its possible

answers to the customer. If there is no further question, it displays a list of products that match the criteria specified by the answer.

5. The shopper either selects an appropriate answer to the next question or asks to see the list of remaining products.

6. The Sales Assistant shopping metaphor applies any feature constraints that are associated with this second answer, and the product selection is again reduced to only those products that satisfy all constraints.

7. The process is repeated until there are no more questions, at which point the shopper can view the remaining products and make a choice.

# Product Comparison Shopping Metaphor

The Product Comparison shopping metaphor allows customers to compare products in the same category side by side, to determine their similarities and differences. Products are shown in tabular format, with one feature per line. Common values are displayed in one color and unique values in a different color. At any time, the customer can click on a product part number to bring up a page with more information.

## Product Comparison Usage Scenario

The following is an example of how a shopper may use Product Comparisonfrom within a store:

1. The shopper requests to compare the current product selection.

2. The Product Comparison shopping metaphor creates a table that shows product features side by side, highlighting those that have different values.

3. The shopper selects a product to get further details on it.

4. The Product Comparison shopping metaphor passes the customer's selection to the merchant server's product details page.

## Product Comparison Tools Overview

Merchants can select the features they would like a customer to be able to compare. A good rule of thumb is that the same features that were used for the Product Exploration shopping metaphor will be included, but this is not compulsory. Once the features have been selected, the merchant can preview the results to get an idea of what the comparison will look like to the customer.

# Shopping Metaphor Framework

The functionality of the shopping metaphor framework is built on a Java framework that enables both IBM and third parties to plug in and build new shopping metaphors that include all the benefits of the first three, and add more functionality. There are several possible types of customization:

## Create New GUI Controls

Your Web site should look unique, not the same as everyone else's. Product Advisor provides you with the standard GUI controls plus a Java slider and dial, but you can also create and register new GUI controls. For example, if you are selling medical supplies, you might choose to use a thermometer as a slider control.

## Create New Metaphor Tags

Product Advisor uses its own rendering engine to map HTML tags to Java classes, so that users can place executable elements on HTML pages. New tags can be created and registered with Product Advisor to add new functionality that can be used in rendering Web pages.

## Create New Shopping Metaphors

Finally, merchants can create new shopping metaphors, along with corresponding administrative tools, and can collect information about a new metaphor they have created. This new information is available at run-time for your new tags to use in making discussions about rendering.

# Appendix B, Creating Store Models

The first and most important step in using the Store Creator is selecting a model on which to base your store. The store model defines the following:

- The features of the store (for example, registration and an address book)
- The types of pages that make up the store (for example, a registration page, product pages, category pages, a shopping cart page, order pages, and address pages)
- How shoppers interact with the store to browse and place orders (for example, all shoppers must register before placing an order)

The Store Creator provides three default store models: *One Stop Shop*, *Personal Delivery*, and *Business-to-Business*. For a detailed description of each, see "Store Creator Models" on page 39. If none of the supplied models is suitable, you can create a new one and configure the Store Creator to generate stores based upon it.

This appendix presents the steps that a site administrator must follow in order to create a new store model.

## Step 1. Creating a Store Model Directory

The first step in creating a store model is to create a directory for storing the Net.Data macros and the resource file (which will be discussed in a later step) that the Store Creator will use to generate a store.

The three default store models are stored in directories under the following directory:

> **WIN** `\ibm\netcommerce3\SmartGuide\`
> **AIX** `/usr/lpp/NetCommerce3/SmartGuide/`

For simplicity, it is recommended that you place your own store model directory under this directory as well. For example, the files associated with a *Gift Registry* store model could be stored in the following directory:

> **WIN** `\ibm\netcommerce3\SmartGuide\GiftReg`
> **AIX** `/usr/lpp/NetCommerce3/SmartGuide/GiftReg`

All the examples in this appendix will use the default directory. If you do not want to use this directory, you can create a new one and change the directory that is currently defined for the `SG_PATH` variable in the `ncommerce.ini` file.

During the store creation process, the Store Creator will copy all of the files stored in your store model directory to new directories for the store, one of which is named after the store being created. (For information on the location of the new directories, see "Store Creator Macros" on page 218.)

497

In addition, each Net.Data macro in the new store directories will import the `<store_name>.inc` file at the beginning of the macro, using the following Net.Data statement:

```
%include "<store_name_dir>\<store_name>.inc"
```

where `<store_name>` is the name that was entered in the **Store Name** field in the Store Creator, and `<store_name_dir>` is the directory that is automatically created to store your macros, based on the name of the store. The `<store_name>.inc` file stores some of the information that was entered onto the panels of the Store Creator. For more information about this file, see "Editing Macros Generated by the Store Creator" on page 225.

# Step 2. Adding the Store Model to the "Select a Store Model Panel"

The next step is to add the new store model to the list of models that appears on the Select a Store Model panel of the Store Creator, shown in Figure B.1 below:

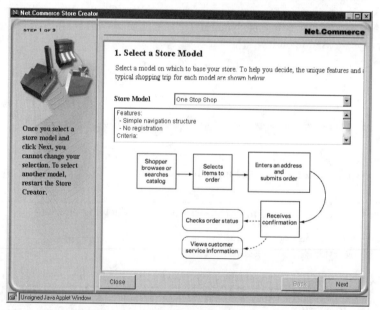

**Figure B.1** *The Select a Store Model panel.*

This panel contains a drop-down list from which to select a store model, a brief description of the model, and an image that shows a typical shopping trip for a store based on that model.

To add your store model to the Select a Store Model panel, do the following:

1.  Open the `template.list` file from the following directory:

    **WIN**  `\ibm\netcommerce3\SmartGuide\`
    **AIX**  `/ibm/NetCommerce3/SmartGuide/`

2.  Add the following to the end of the file:

```
#template
#path <GiftReg>
#title <Gift Registry>
#gif <sggifs/shopflow.gif>
#description <Features:
 - Not Available
Criteria:
 - Not Available>
#navigation <top>
```

In the above code, the variables are shown in angle brackets (<>). The values for each variable are based on our Gift Registry store model example, where each variable is defined as follows:

`#template`

> Defines the beginning of the store model. This variable does not require a value. Each variable after this one is mandatory and must contain a value.

`#path`

> The path in which the Store Creator will search to find the store model resource file (`<store_name>.rc`), relative to the store model directory defined for the `SG_PATH` variable in the `ncommerce.ini` file. (The resource file will be discussed in a later step.)

`#title`

> The name of the store model, which will appear in the **Store Model** drop-down list.

`#gif`

> The path and file name of a GIF image that represents a typical shopping trip for a store based on the model, which will display on the Select a Store Model panel. All images used by the Store Creator are stored in the following directory:

> **WIN** `\ibm\netcommerce3\html\en_US\ncadmin\StoreCreator` `\sggifs\`
> **AIX** `/usr/lpp/NetCommerce3/html/en_US/ncadmin/StoreCreator/` `sggifs/`

> You can either use this directory by prepending the image file name with the `\sggifs` directory as shown in the example above, use the Web server document root, or update the Web server configuration file to point to a custom directory. For more information, see "Storing Images and HTML Files" on page 81.

`#description`

> A brief description of the store model, which will display on the Select a Store Model panel. To remain consistent with the default store model descriptions, it is recommended that you list both the main features of your store model and the criteria required for merchants to choose the model. As an example to follow, here is a description for the *One Stop Shop* store model:

```
#description Features:
   - Simple navigation structure
   - No registration
Criteria:
```

```
- You are targeting consumers
- Shoppers are one-time or occasional buyers
- Each item in an order is delivered to the same address
```

`#navigation`

The location of the navigation frame in the store that is created. You have the following options:

`top`

Across the top of the store.

`bottom`

Along the bottom of the store.

`side`

Down the left side of the store.

3.   Save and close the file.

Your new store model will now appear on the Select A Store Model panel the next time the Store Creator is started.

# Step 3.  Adding Store Model Files to the Store Model Directory

Now you are ready to create all the files that will make up your store model (Net.Data macros and the resource file) and add them to the store model directory that you defined in step 1.  The simplest way to begin is to copy the files of the existing store model that most closely fits the look and feel of your desired store model.

Depending on which store model is the best starting point for you, you would copy all the files from one of the following directories to your store model directory:

### *One Stop Shop Store Model:*

WIN    `\ibm\netcommerce3\SmartGuide\OneStop`
AIX    `/ibm/NetCommerce3/SmartGuide/OneStop`

### *Personal Delivery Store Model:*

WIN    `\ibm\netcommerce3\SmartGuide\PDelivery`
AIX    `/ibm/NetCommerce3/SmartGuide/PDelivery`

### *Business-to-Business Store Model:*

WIN    `\ibm\netcommerce3\SmartGuide\BtoB`
AIX    `/ibm/NetCommerce3/SmartGuide/BtoB`

For information on the macros for the default store models, see "Store Creator Macros" on page 218.

# Editing the Store Model Macros

Once you have copied the macros of an existing store model to your store model directory, you are ready to edit them to meet your business requirements and, if applicable, to create new ones in order to extend the model.  For information on how to edit the macros, see "Chapter 8, Modifying the Supplied Store Pages" on page 213.  For information on how to create new macros, see "Chapter 7, A Net.Data Tutorial" on page 169.

## Store Model Macro Coding Conventions

The following are the coding conventions for Net.Data macros that all store models must adhere to in order to be compatible with the Store Creator's macro generation process.

- Each store model must assume one of three navigation frame styles: top, bottom, or side. The `frames.d2w` macro (called `main.d2w` in the Business-to-Business store model) is responsible for setting up the frames for the selected navigation style.  The following is the part of the `frames.d2w` macro for the side navigation frame style, which is used for the One Stop Shop store model:

```
<FRAMESET ROWS="80,*" BORDER="0" FRAMEBORDER="no">
  <FRAMESET COLS="100%"><FRAME NAME="banner" SRC="/cgi-bin/
  ncommerce3/ExecMacro/$(STORENAME)/banner.d2w/report"
  FRAMEBORDER="no" BORDERCOLOR="white" SCROLLING="no"
  RESIZE="no">
  <FRAMESET COLS="130,285,*"><FRAME NAME="navbar" SRC="/cgi-bin/
  ncommerce3/ExecMacro/$(STORENAME)/nav_side.d2w/report"
  FRAMEBORDER="no" SCROLLING="no"> <FRAME NAME="main" SRC="/cgi-
  bin/ncommerce3/ExecMacro/$(STORENAME)/home.d2w/report"
  FRAMEBORDER="no">  <FRAME NAME="list" SRC="/cgi-bin/
  ncommerce3/OrderItemDisplay?merchant_rn=$(MerchantRefNum)"
  FRAMEBORDER="no" BORDEr=2 RESIZE=YES>
  </FRAMESET>
</FRAMESET>
```

- When including the current store directory in a macro, use the $(STORENAME) Net.Data variable reference, as shown in the example above.  This value of this variable is defined in the <store_name>.inc file when the Store Creator generates the store.

- When including the merchant reference number in a macro, use the $(MerchantRefNum) Net.Data variable reference.  The value of this variable is  defined in the <store_name>.inc file when the Store Creator generates the store.

- When linking to the top-level category in the store (for example, from the navigation frame), use the $(HomeCategory) Net.Data variable reference; do not hard-code the number in the macro.  The category reference number of the top-level category is determined when the store is generated, and is stored in the $(HomeCategory) variable in the <store_name>.inc file.

- When adding the visual components of the page, such as backgrounds, navigation buttons, and hypertext link colors, reference the values of the corresponding variables that are defined in the `<store_name>.inc` file. For a list of all style variables available, see "Editing Macros Generated by the Store Creator" on page 225.

# Editing the Store Model Resource File

Included with the macros that you copied to your store model directory is the store model resource file. (If you did not copy the files from an existing store model, copy any resource file (`<store_name>.inc` ) to your store model directory now.) This file defines the Net.Data macros that make up the model. It describes each store page that is created and its purpose. You must now modify the file to reflect your store model, as follows:

1.  Rename the resource file to the name of your store model directory. For example, if the Gift Registry store model is using the One Stop Shop store model as a starting point, you would rename the file by issuing the following command:

    **WIN** Rename ibm/NetCommerce3/SmartGuide/GiftReg/OneStop.rc ibm/
    NetCommerce3/SmartGuide/GiftReg/GiftReg.rc

2.  Open your new resource file in a text editor.

3.  For each macro in the store model, include the following section:

    ```
    #resource
    #name <shipto>
    #description <image layout>
    #type <MACRO>
    #srcfile <shipto_image.d2w>
    #destfile <shipto.d2w>
    #task <SHIPTO_ASSOC>
    #selectable <YES>
    #gif <sggifs/spl_image.gif>
    #unique <YES>
    ```

    The values for each variable above (shown in angle brackets) are based on our Gift Registry store model example, where each variable is defined as follows:

    `#resource`
    > Defines the beginning of the section. This variable does not require a value.

    `#name`
    > A descriptive name for the macro. It must be unique for all macros that are not available in different page layouts (those that do not contain a value of YES for the `#selectable` variable).

    `#type`
    > The resource type, which identifies the type of macro and the directory in which it will be published at the time of store generation. The following resource types are available:

    HOME
    >> The first macro to be invoked when the shopper accesses the store. This macro is often responsible for setting up the store's frames. This resource type must have the file name `main.d2w` defined for the `#destfile` variable. There

can be only one HOME resource type for a given store model, and it will be published in the store macro directory (named after the store being created).

CATEGORY

Represents a category macro that will be published in the `\macro\en_US\category` directory.

PRODUCT

Represents a product macro that will be published in the `\macro\en_US\product` directory.

MACRO

Represents any macro that is not of the HOME, CATEGORY, or PRODUCT resource type. It will be published in the store macro directory.

#srcfile

The source macro, which represents the resource (stored in the store model directory). This file may or may not be the same as the destination file. In a given store model, there may be only one destination file, with potentially many source files pointing to it. This relationship between source files and destination files allows for selectable "plug-in" store pages layouts within a model. See "Adding Page Layouts" on page 504 for information on creating different page layouts.

#destfile

The published name of the macro, which the merchant has access to. The other macros in the store model depend upon this name.

#selectable

Indicates whether or not the macro is available in more than one page layout. Enter YES if you want to include this macro in the Select Page Layouts panel of the Store Creator; otherwise, enter NO.

#unique

Not currently used.

#gif

A GIF image representing a page layout. Use this variable only when the #selectable variable is set to YES.

#description

A description of the store page that is created by the macro, which will appear as a layout option on the Select Page Layouts panel of the Store Creator. Use this variable only when the #selectable variable is set to YES.

#task

The name of the view or exception task that the macro is implementing. To determine whether or not the macro implements a view or exception task, look up its invoking command in Table 9.6 on page 277, and see what tasks, if any, are used by the command.

4. Save and close the file.

# Step 5. Adding Page Layouts

The Store Creator allows you to make specific store pages in a store model available in more than one page layout. For example, you could provide three layout options for a shopping cart page: one that lists the images and prices of each item in the cart, one that displays them in a table format, and one that displays only text in a list format. Or, for a registration page, you could provide the option of either showing or hiding demographic information on the form. Providing different page layouts for a given store page gives you the opportunity to provide customization options to the merchant. The default store models provide two layout options for the category pages in the stores: one that shows images and one that shows only text, as illustrated in Figure B.2 below:

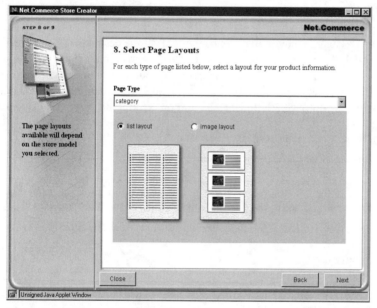

***Figure B.2***   *The Select Page Layouts panel.*

The following are the steps required to create different page layouts for a store page in your store model:

1. Create a macro for each page layout that will be available for the store page.

2. Enter each macro in the store model resource file, as described in the previous section, "Editing the Store Model Resource File." The following is an example for a category page that is available in two different page layouts:

```
#resource
#name category
#description list layout
#type CATEGORY
#srcfile cat_list.d2w
#destfile cat1.d2w
#selectable YES
```

```
#gif sggifs/spl_list.gif
#unique NO

#resource
#name category
#description image layout
#type CATEGORY
#srcfile cat_image.d2w
#destfile cat1.d2w
#selectable YES
#gif sggifs/spl_image.gif
#unique NO
```

In this example, there are two page layouts available for the category pages of a store model: "List Layout" and "Image Layout". As described in the previous section, in order to make a store page available in more than one page layout, you must set the #selectable variable to YES, which will display the page in the drop-down list on the Select Page Layouts panel of the Store Creator. Note also that the value for the #destfile variable in both sections points to the same file: cat1.d2w. This is the name of the destination file, which the other macros in the store model depend upon. The source files cat_list.d2w and cat_image.d2w are intermediate files that will assume the name cat1.d2w if selected by the user. Only one of the two source files will be published when the store is created.

# Step 6. Adding a New Product Bundle

For each new store model you create, you can create a product bundle (also known as a mass import file), which contains sample products and categories for displaying in the store that is based on your store model. This step is optional; if the existing sample products (*Clothing*, *Tools and Hardware*, and *Groceries*) are sufficient for your store model, you do not need to create another product bundle. New product bundles will be displayed as an option on the Add Sample Products and Store Description panel shown in Figure B.3.

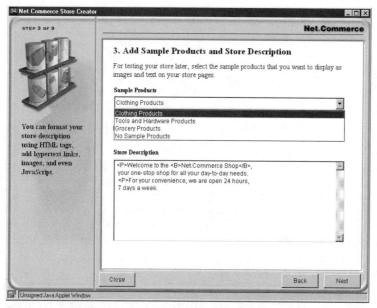

**Figure B.3**  *The Add Sample Products and Store Description panel.*

To add a new product bundle to the Store Creator, do the following:

1. Create an import file.  (Do not include the #STORE command in the import file, since the store name is not known until the merchant specifies it.  The Store Creator will insert this command at store generation time.)  For information on how to create an import file, see "Chapter 5, Mass-Importing Product and Category Data" on page 123.

2. Copy the import file to the following directory:

   **WIN**  `\ibm\netcommerce3\SmartGuide\bundles`
   **AIX**  `/ibm/NetCommerce3/SmartGuide/bundles`

3. Open the `bundles.list` file (stored in the above directory) in a text editor.  This file is used by the Store Creator to both display your sample products as an option in the Store Creator and to associate the sample products with an import file.

4. At the end of the file, add the following section:

   ```
   #bundle
   #path <stat.in>
   #title <Stationery Products>
   ```

   The values for each variable above, shown in angle brackets, are based on our Gift Registry store model example, where each variable is defined as follows:

   `#bundle`
   > Defines the beginning of the product bundle.  This variable does not require a value.

   `#path`
   > The file name of the mass import file containing your sample data, relative to the `\SmartGuide\bundles` directory.

```
#title
```
The name of the sample products, which will appear in the **Sample Products** drop-down list on the Add Sample Products and Store Description panel of the Store Creator.

5.  Save and close the file.

Your new product bundle will now appear as an option in the Store Creator and, when selected by the user, will be imported into the database using the corresponding import file.

# Step 7. Adding a New Store Style

If you want to extend the list of store styles that are available on the Select a Store Style panel of the Store Creator (shown in Figure B.4 below), you can create your own and add it to the Store Creator.

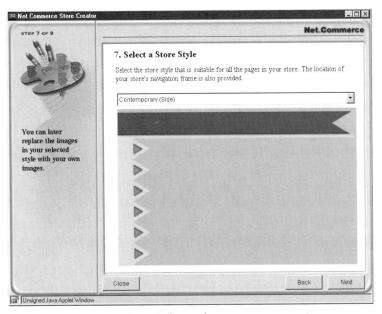

***Figure B.4*** *The Select a Store Style panel.*

The following are the steps required to create and integrate a new store style for the Store Creator:

1.  Open the `styles.list` file from the following directory:

    **WIN** `\ibm\netcommerce3\SmartGuide\styles`
    **AIX** `/ibm/NetCommerce3/SmartGuide/styles`

2.  At the end of the file, add a new style section, using the following example as a guide:

    ```
    #style
    #gif <sggifs/retro_s.jpg>
    #title <Retro (Side)>
    #navigation <side>
    ```

```
#BannerTxtCol <lightyellow>
#BannerImage </sggifs/f_banner.gif>
#BannerRightSpc <0>
#BannerLeftSpc <0>
#BannerAlign <center>
#NavLinkCol <darkblue>
#NavBarAlign <left>
#BckImageNavBar </sggifs/f_leftbkg_s.gif>
#BodyColor1 <##9CCECE>
#BodyColor2 <##6699CC>
#BodyColor3 <pink>
#BodyImage1 </sggifs/f_tablbkg.gif>
#TitleTxtCol <black>
#TextCol <black>
#LinkCol <darkblue>
#VLinkCol <purple>
#ALinkCol <pink>
#Button1 </sggifs/f_butt1_s.gif>
#Button2 </sggifs/f_butt2_s.gif>
#Button3 </sggifs/f_butt3_s.gif>
#Button4 </sggifs/f_butt4_s.gif>
#Button5 </sggifs/f_butt5_s.gif>
#Button6 </sggifs/f_butt6_s.gif>
#Button7 </sggifs/f_butt7_s.gif>
#Button8 </sggifs/f_butt8_s.gif>
#AddButton </sggifs/f_add.gif>
#ButtonWidth <56>
#ButtonHeight <31>
```

The values for each variable above, shown in angle brackets, are based on our Gift Registry store model example, where each variable is defined as follows:

`#style`

Defines the beginning of the store style. This variable does not require a value.

`#gif`

An image representing the store style, which will appear on the Select a Store Style panel of the Store Creator.

`#title`

The name of the store style, which will appear in the drop-down list on the Select a Store Style panel of the Store Creator.

`#navigation`

The location of the navigation frame in the store. You have the following options:

`top`

Across the top of the store.

`bottom`

Along the bottom of the store.

`side`

Down the left side of the store.

The remaining variables, which define the visual elements of the pages (such as background colors and hypertext link colors), are described in detail in "Editing the Macros Generated by the Store Creator" on page 225. These Net.Data variables will be replaced with your specified values during the store generation process. In the example above, the Net.Data variable `$(Button6)` will be replaced by `/sggifs/f_butt6_s.gif`. In this way, it is possible to design a store model without having information about color, buttons, and so forth.

3. Save and close the file.

   You have now finished defining a new store style. The next time the Select a Store Style panel is accessed, your style will appear as an option.

# Appendix C, Net.Commerce Database Tables

This appendix provides an overview of the database tables that are part of the default schema and the relationships between them.

## Overview

The Net.Commerce database contains all the information that is used by the Net.Commerce system, from basic information needed to run the server to data that pertains to individual shoppers, items, and prices. It also includes pointers to images, macros, overridable functions, and HTML files.

The database is a relational database that consists of a collection of tables. Some of the tables contain customizable columns that are reserved for merchants, and merchants can further customize the database by adding new tables.

## Functional Groups

The tables are organized into the following functional groups:

- Tables about shoppers and users
- Tables about merchants, stores, shopper groups, and customers
- Tables about categories, products and items
- Tables about price discounting
- Tables about shipping
- Tables about tax calculations
- Tables about orders
- Tables about system functions
- Tables about Net.Commerce commands
- Tables about access control

# Tables About Shoppers and Users

This group of tables contains information about shoppers and users. (A user is a merchant employee who is authorized to use the Net.Commerce Administrator.) It includes basic and demographic information, information about address books, and (for users) the level of access granted to Net.Commerce resources.

- SHOPPER: Shopper Profile

- SHOPDEM: Shopper Demographics

- SHADDR: Shopper Address Book

- ACCTRL: Access Control

The relationships between the tables in this group are shown in Figure C.1 below:

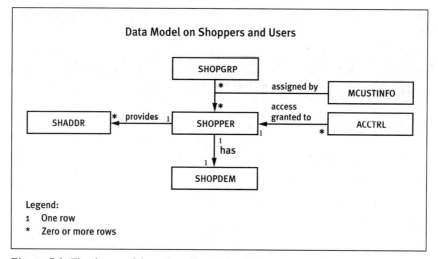

***Figure C.1*** *The data model on shoppers and users.*

# SHOPPER: Shopper Profile Table

The table SHOPPER contains information needed to identify each shopper and user to the Net.Commerce system. It also contains some basic contact and classification information. (More contact and classification information is in tables SHOPDEM and SHADDR.)

When the database is initially installed, a row is inserted into the table SHOPPER (and tables ACCTRL, SHOPDEM, and SHADDR) defining the site administrator. In the table, SHLOGID is set to ncadmin, and SHLPSWD is set to the encrypted form of ncadmin. The administrator should change this password immediately after installing the system.

One row is defined for each shopper (whether or not the shopper is registered), and for each user.

*Table C.1* *The SHOPPER table.*

| Column Name | Column Type | Column Description |
|---|---|---|
| SHRFNBR | INTEGER NOT NULL | Shopper's or user's reference number. This is a primary key. |
| SHLOGID | CHAR (31) NOT NULL (for DB2) RAN (32) (for Oracle) | The registered shopper's or user's logon ID (unique). You can limit the input length by using the HTML tags in the store page macro. |
| SHLPSWD | CHAR (32) FOR BIT DATA | The registered shopper's or user's logon password (encrypted). By default, the input length is restricted to 16 bytes. You can change the input length by using the HTML tags in the store page macro. |
| SHSHTYP | CHAR (4) NOT NULL | Shopper or user type: **R** - Registered shopper **G** - Guest shopper (not registered, default) **A** - Administrator |
| SHCOMM | CHAR (2) | Shopper's preferred method of communication: **E1** - Email or URL address 1 **E2** - Email or URL address 2 **P1** - Phone number 1 **P2** - Phone number 2 The actual e-mail addresses and phone numbers are defined in table SHADDR. |
| SHPHLST | SMALLINT | Reserved for IBM use. |
| SHLVSTMP | TIMESTAMP (for DB2) DATE (for Oracle) | The date and time that the shopper last visited the store. |
| SHLOSTMP | TIMESTAMP (for DB2) DATE (for Oracle) | The date and time that the shopper last placed an order. |
| SHRSTMP | TIMESTAMP (for DB2) DATE (for Oracle) | The date and time that the shopper registered or was assigned a session ID. |
| SHCSTMP | TIMESTAMP(for DB2) DATE (for Oracle) | The date and time that the shopper cancelled the registration. |
| SHLUSTMP | TIMESTAMP (for DB2) DATE (for Oracle) | The date and time the shopper last changed any registration information. |
| SHCNTCT | INTEGER | Reserved for IBM use. This is not a foreign key. Note that no foreign key is enforced on column SHCNTCT because this table cannot be defined as a dependent of table SHADDR. |
| SHCHAQUE | VARCHAR (254) | Challenge question for verbal confirmation of the shopper's or user's identity. |
| SHCHAANS | VARCHAR (254) | Answer to the challenge question. |
| SHFIELD1 | VARCHAR (254) | Reserved for merchant customization. |
| SHFIELD2 | VARCHAR (254) | Reserved for merchant customization. |

# SHOPDEM: Shopper Demographics Table

The table SHOPDEM contains demographic information about each registered shopper. The information is provided by the shopper during registration. Each row contains information about one shopper.

*Table C.2* *The SHOPDEM table.*

| Column Name | Column Type | Column Description |
| --- | --- | --- |
| SDSHNBR | INTEGER NOT NULL | Shopper reference number. This is a primary key, and a foreign key that references column SHRFNBR in table SHOPPER. |
| SDGENDR | CHAR (1) | Shopper'sgender:<br>**F** - Female<br>**B** - Male<br>**N** - Not provided (default) |
| SDAGE | INTEGER | Shopper's age:<br>**0** - Not provided (default)<br>**1** - 0-9 years<br>**2** - 10-19 years<br>**3** - 20-29 years<br>**4** - 30-39 years<br>**5** - 40-49 years<br>**6** - 50-59 years<br>**7** - 60 years or older |
| SDINCOM | INTEGER | Shopper's annual income:<br>**0** - Not provided (default)<br>**1** - $0 - $19,999<br>**2** - $20,000 - $39,999<br>**3** - $40,000 - $59,999<br>**4** - $60,000 or more |
| SDMSTAT | CHAR (1) | Shopper's marital status:<br>**S** - Single<br>**M** - Married<br>**C** - Common Law<br>**P** - Separated<br>**D** - Divorced<br>**W** - Widowed<br>**0** - Other<br>**N** - Not Provided |
| SDCHNBR | INTEGER | Number of children. If not provided, the default is 0. |
| SDHHNBR | INTEGER | Number of people in the shopper's household. If not provided, the default is 1. |
| SDCOMP | CHAR (30) | The company for which the shopper works. |
| SDINTRS | VARCHAR (254) | The shopper's main interests and hobbies. |

*Continued on next page*

*Table C.2* *Continued.*

| Column Name | Column Type | Column Description |
|---|---|---|
| SDPREORD | CHAR (1) | Indicator of whether or not the shopper has previously placed an order. Supplied by the shopper. |
| SDBRWER | CHAR (64) | Reserved for IBM use. |
| SDFIELD1 | CHAR (1) | Reserved for merchant customization. |
| SDFIELD2 | CHAR (1) | Reserved for merchant customization. |
| SDFIELD3 | CHAR (1) | Reserved for merchant customization. |
| SDFIELD4 | CHAR (1) | Reserved for merchant customization. |
| SDFIELD5 | VARCHAR (254) | Reserved for merchant customization. |
| SDFIELD6 | INTEGER | Reserved for merchant customization. |

# SHADDR: Shopper Address Book Table

The table SHADDR serves as an address book for each registered shopper. At the time of registration, the shopper provides the contact address information for the shopper, and this entry is flagged as permanent.

When a shopper moves, the shopper can provide new contact address information, and a new entry is added to the table. The old address information is not discarded, but it is flagged as a temporary address. Temporary rows are also created if a shopper provides new address information for a specific order without updating the address book.

Shoppers can also add address information for other individuals, such as relatives, or places to this table. All such entries are flagged as permanent addresses.

*Table C.3* *The SHADDR table.*

| Column Name | Column Type | Column Description |
|---|---|---|
| SARFNBR | INTEGER NOT NULL | Unique address reference number, internally generated. This is a primary key. |
| SASHNBR | INTEGER NOT NULL | Shopper reference number. This is a foreign key that references column SHRFNBR in table SHOPPER. |
| SANICK | CHAR (31) NOT NULL | The nickname of another individual, such as a relative, to whom the address information applies. |
| SATITLE | CHAR (5) | Individual's title:<br>**Dr**<br>**Mr**<br>**Mrs**<br>**Ms**<br>**N** - Not provided (default) |

*Continued on next page*

*Table C.3* *Continued.*

| Column Name | Column Type | Column Description |
|---|---|---|
| SAADRFLG | CHAR (1) | Flag to indicate whether or not this is a temporary or permanent address.<br>**T** - Temporary address information for a specific order, or old address information for the shopper.<br>**P** - Permanent address information. |
| SALNAME | CHAR (30) | Individual's last name. |
| SAFNAME | CHAR (30) | Individual's first name. |
| SAMNAME | CHAR (30) | Individual's middle name or initial. |
| SAREPCOM | CHAR (80) | Company that the individual represents. |
| SAPHONE1 | CHAR (30) | Individual's phone number 1 (For example, Daytime Phone). |
| SAPHONE2 | CHAR (30) | Individual's phone number 2 (For example, Evening Phone). |
| SAFAX | CHAR (30) | Individual's facsimile number. |
| SAADDR1 | CHAR (50) NOT NULL | Individual's address line 1. |
| SAADDR2 | CHAR (50) | Individual's address line 2. |
| SAADDR3 | CHAR (50) | Individual's address line 3. |
| SACITY | CHAR (30) NOT NULL | Individual's city name. |
| SASTATE | CHAR (20) NOT NULL | Individual's state, province, or equivalent, abbreviated. |
| SACNTRY | CHAR (30) NOT NULL | Individual's country. |
| SAZIPC | CHAR (20) | Individual's zip code or equivalent. |
| SAEMAIL1 | CHAR (254) | Individual's email or URL address 1. |
| SAEMAIL2 | CHAR (254) | Individual's email or URL address 2. |
| SASTMP | TIMESTAMP (for DB2) | The date and time the row was created. |
| SADPHTYP | CHAR (3) | The type of daytime phone, such as TTY for a teletypewriter for people who have a hearing impairment, or PHN for a standard telephone. |
| SADPHLST | SMALLINT | **1** - Daytime phone number is listed.<br>**0** - Daytime phone number is unlisted. |
| SAEPHTYP | CHAR (3) | The type of evening phone, such as TTY for a teletypewriter for people who have a hearing impairment, or PHN for a standard telephone. |
| SAEPHLST | SMALLINT | **1** - Evening phone number is listed.<br>**0** - Evening phone number is unlisted. |

*Continued on next page*

*Table C.3* *Continued.*

| Column Name | Column Type | Column Description |
| --- | --- | --- |
| SABTCALL | CHAR (1) | Best time to call indicator:<br>**D** - Daytime<br>**E** - Evening |
| SAPKGSUP | SMALLINT | Package inserts suppression flag: indicates the shopper's preference for including package inserts in orders shipped.<br>**1** - Include<br>**0** - Do not include |
| SAFIELD1 | CHAR (3) | Reserved for merchant customization. |
| SAFIELD2 | CHAR (1) | Reserved for merchant customization. |

## ACCTRL: Access Control Table

The table ACCTRL contains information about the resources and access authority that have been granted to users. More than one row can be defined for each user. This table is kept for backward compatibility with previous versions of Net.Commerce.

*Table C.4* *The ACCTRL table.*

| Column Name | Column Type | Column Description |
| --- | --- | --- |
| ACSHNBR | INTEGER NOT NULL | User's reference number. Together with ACRES and ACRESID, this is a primary key. This is a foreign key that references column SHRFNBR in table SHOPPER. |
| ACRES | CHAR (4) NOT NULL | Resource type granted to the user. Together with ACSHNBR and ACRESID, this is a primary key.<br>**M** - Mall Level<br>**S** - Store Level |
| ACRESID | INTEGER NOT NULL | Merchant reference number. Together with ACRES and ACSHNBR, this is a primary key. |
| ACPERM | INTEGER | Level of access granted to the user. |

# Tables About Access Control

This group of tables contains information that control access within the Net.Commerce system: which users are in which groups and which commands can be used by which groups.

- ACC_GROUP: Access Group
- ACC_CMDGRP: Access Command Group
- ACC_USRGRP: Access User Group
- ACC_MODE: Access Mode

The relationships between the tables in this group are shown in Figure C.2 below:

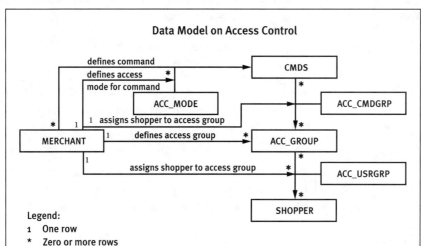

**Figure C.2**  *The data model on access control.*

# ACC_GROUP: Access Group Table

The table ACC_GROUP describes the access groups created for a merchant.  This table can be used to restrict or allow access to resources, such as commands, at the mall or store level.  A merchant can have more than one group, and a group can be created at the mall level by simply leaving the merchant reference number field null.  While it is possible to use the Access Group table to restrict category or product information to certain shoppers, this table is more commonly used to restrict access to administrative functions such as pricing, payment and inventory.  Each row in this table defines an access group and assigns a merchant to that group or, by not assigning a merchant, defines the group as being mall-wide.

**Table C.5**  *The ACC_GROUP table.*

| Column Name | Column Type | Column Description |
| --- | --- | --- |
| REFNUM | INTEGER NOT NULL | Unique access group reference number.  This is the primary key. |
| MER_REFNUM | INTEGER | Reference number of the merchant for whom the access group is defined.  This is a foreign key that references column MERFNBR in table MERCHANT.  A NULL value indicates that the group is mall-wide and not owned by a specific merchant. |
| NAME | CHAR (32) NOT NULL | Name of the access group.  This is a unique index. |
| DESCRIPTION | CHAR (128) | Detailed description of the access group. |

# ACC_CMDGRP: Access Command Group Table

The table ACC_CMDGRP assigns a command to an access group. Each group may be able to access multiple commands, and each command may be used by multiple groups. For each row in the table, a command is designated as being accessible to the users in a particular group.

**Table C.6** *The ACC_CMDGRP table.*

| Column Name | Column Type | Column Description |
|---|---|---|
| GRPC_REFNUM | INTEGER NOT NULL | Reference number of the access group for which the group/command relationship is defined. This is a foreign key that references column REFNUM in table ACC_GROUP. Together with column CMD_REFNUM, this is a unique index. |
| CMD_REFNUM | INTEGER NOT NULL | Reference number of the command for which the group/command relationship is defined. This is a foreign key that references column REFNUM in table CMDS. Together with column GRPC_REFNUM, this is a unique index. |

# ACC_USRGRP: Access User Group Table

The table ACC_USRGRP assigns a user to an access group. Each user may belong to more than one group, and each group may contain more than one user. Users reference the table SHOPPER, but the access groups are normally used to restrict access for administrative functions, not for product or category pages. (As registered users themselves, site and store administrators have entries in the SHOPPER table.) For instance, an access user group would be created and assigned to an administrator to ensure that administrator has access only to a particular store's administrative functions. Each row in this table defines a relationship between a user and an access group.

**Table C.7** *The ACC_USRGRP table.*

| Column Name | Column Type | Column Description |
|---|---|---|
| USR_REFNUM | INTEGER NOT NULL | Reference number for the user for which this relationship is defined. This is a foreign key that references column SHRFNBR in table SHOPPER. Together with column GRPU_REFNUM, this is a unique index. |
| GRPU_REFNUM | INTEGER NOT NULL | Reference number for the access group for which this relationship is defined. This is a foreign key that references column REFNUM in table ACC_GROUP. Together with column USR_REFNUM, this is a unique index. |

# ACC_MODE: Access Mode Table

The table ACC_MODE defines the relationship between a merchant and a command. Access groups are used to designate which users are to be allowed access to which sets of commands. The Access Mode table determines how and whether access control is to be enabled for a particular command. Each row in this table contains either information about the relationship between a single command and a single merchant or, if the merchant field is null, indicates that the command can access all resources.

*Table C.8*  *The ACC_MODE table.*

| Column Name | Column Type | Column Description |
| --- | --- | --- |
| REFNUM | INTEGER NOT NULL | Unique access mode reference number. This is the primary key. |
| MER_REFNUM | INTEGER | Reference number of the merchant for which the relationship is defined. This is a foreign key that references column MERFNBR in table MERCHANT. Together with column CMD_REFNUM, this is a unique index. |
| CMD_REFNUM | INTEGER NOT NULL | Reference number of the command for which this relationship is defined. This is a foreign key that references column REFNUM in table CMDS. Together with column MER_REFNUM, this is a unique index. |
| SSL | SMALLINT NOT NULL | SSL flag. If this field is not zero, SSL is enabled for commands using this merchant's resources. |
| PROTECT | SMALLINT NOT NULL | Web server security flag. If this field is not zero, basic web server security (msprotect) is enabled for commands using this merchant's resources. |
| ACCESS | SMALLINT NOT NULL | Access control flag. If this field is not zero, access control is enabled for this command using this merchant's resources. |

# Tables About Merchants, Stores, Shopper Groups, and Customers

This group of tables contains information about merchants, their stores, the shopper groups that the merchants define, the unique product templates that are presented to shopper groups, and the merchants' shoppers.

- MERCHANT: Merchant Profile
- STRCGRY: Store Category
- SHOPGRP: Shopper Group
- MCUSTINFO: Merchant Customer Info
- SG_STORES: Merchant-User

The relationships between the tables in this group are shown in Figure C.3 below:

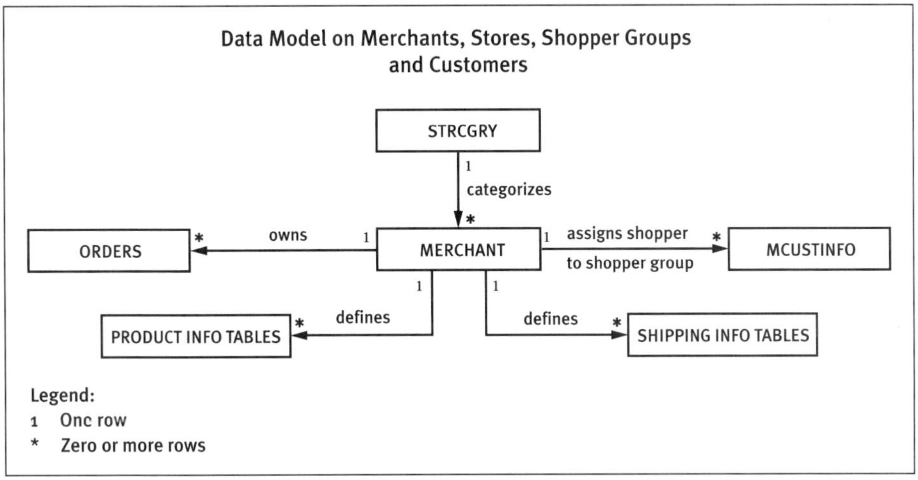

**Figure C.3**  *The data model on merchants, stores, shopper groups, and customers.*

# MERCHANT: Merchant Profile Table

The table MERCHANT describes each merchant, including information on the primary contact for the merchant. Each row corresponds to one merchant. For a one-merchant mall, this table contains only one row.

**Note:**
No foreign key is enforced for this table.

*Table C.9*  *The MERCHANT table.*

| Column Name | Column Type | Column Description |
| --- | --- | --- |
| MERFNBR | INTEGER NOT NULL | Unique merchant reference number, internally assigned. This is a primary key. |
| MENAME | CHAR (80) | Merchant's company name. If no name is provided when the store is created, this column contains the store name of the merchant as defined in column MESTNAME in this table. |
| MECLNAM | CHAR (30) NOT NULL | Merchant contact's last name. |
| MECFNAM | CHAR (30) NOT NULL | Merchant contact's first name. |
| MECMNAM | CHAR (30) | Merchant contact's middle name or initial. |
| MECTITLE | CHAR (30) | Merchant contact's title. |
| MECPH1 | CHAR (30) NOT NULL | Merchant contact's primary phone number. |
| MECPH2 | CHAR (30) | Merchant contact's secondary phone number. |

*Continued on next page*

**Table C.9** *Continued.*

| Column Name | Column Type | Column Description |
|---|---|---|
| MECFAX | CHAR (30) | Merchant contact's facsimile number. |
| MECMAIL1 | CHAR (254) | Merchant contact's primary email or URL address. |
| MECMAIL2 | CHAR (254) | Merchant contact's secondary email or URL address. |
| MEPHONE | CHAR (30) NOT NULL | Merchant's company phone number. |
| MEADDR1 | CHAR (50) | Merchant's company street address line 1. |
| MEADDR2 | CHAR (50) | Merchant's company street address line 2. |
| MEADDR3 | CHAR (50) | Merchant's company street address line 3. |
| MECITY | CHAR (30) NOT NULL | Merchant's company city name. |
| MESTATE | CHAR (20) NOT NULL | Merchant's company state, province, or equivalent, abbreviated. |
| MECNTRY | CHAR (30) NOT NULL | Merchant's company country. |
| MEZIPC | CHAR (20) | Merchant's company zip code or equivalent. |
| MESTNAME | CHAR (80) NOT NULL | Name of the store. Unique across the mall. |
| MESTDESC | VARCHAR (1000) | Brief description of the store. |
| MESCNBR | INTEGER | Store category reference number. A list of category choices is provided from which the merchant can choose, or the merchant can create a new one. This column is not used for malls that contain only one store. This is a foreign key that references column SCRFNBR in table STRCGRY. |
| METHMB | CHAR (254) | Thumbnail image file path and name for merchant's store logo. |
| METHEAD | CHAR (254) | Relative path off the HTML root for the file name of the HTML text used as the default header on store pages. |
| METFOOT | CHAR (254) | Relative path off the HTML root for the file name of the HTML text used as the default footer on store pages. |
| METBASE | CHAR (254) | Relative path off the HTML root for the file name of the HTML text that is displayed when no parameters are provided to the Web interface program. |
| MECUR | CHAR (10) NOT NULL | Currency in which prices for this store are expressed. The format of the currency must adhere to ISO 4217 standards. |
| MEFIELD1 | VARCHAR (254) | Reserved for merchant customization. |
| MEFIELD2 | VARCHAR (254) | Reserved for merchant customization. |

# STRCGRY: Store Category Table

The table STRCGRY defines categories into which stores within a mall are classified. It contains one row per category.

**Table C.10** *The STRCGRY table.*

| Column Name | Column Type | Column Description |
|---|---|---|
| SCRFNBR | INTEGER NOT NULL | Store category reference number. This is a primary key. |
| SCGRY | CHAR (50) | Name of the store category. Unique across the mall. |
| SCREMARK | VARCHAR (254) | Remarks. |

# SHOPGRP: Shopper Group Table

The table SHOPGRP describes the shopper groups that are defined for each store. Each row contains information on one shopper group.

**Table C.11** *The SHOPGRP table.*

| Column Name | Column Type | Column Description |
|---|---|---|
| SGRFNBR | INTEGER NOT NULL | Unique shopper group reference number. This is a primary key. |
| SGMENBR | INTEGER NOT NULL | Reference number of the merchant for whom the group is defined. This is a foreign key that references column MERFNBR in table MERCHANT. Together with column SGNAME, this is a unique index. |
| SGNAME | CHAR (50) NOT NULL | Name of the shopper group. Together with column SGMENBR, this is a unique index. |
| SGTEXT | VARCHAR (1000) | Text that describes the shopper group. |
| SGFIELD1 | VARCHAR (254) | Reserved for merchant customization. |
| SGFIELD2 | VARCHAR (254) | Reserved for merchant customization. |

# MCUSTINFO: Merchant Customer Information Table

The table MCUSTINFO has two purposes:

- It associates shoppers with shopper groups.
- It holds additional information about shoppers who have special relationships with the merchant. For example, if a particular shopper has a customer number with the merchant, the number can be identified in this table.

**Note:**

Each shopper and customer can belong to a maximum of one shopper group.

*Table C.12* *The MCUSTINFO table.*

| Column Name | Column Type | Column Description |
| --- | --- | --- |
| MCSHNBR | INTEGER NOT NULL | Shopper reference number. Together with column MCMENBR, this is a primary key. This is a foreign key that references column SHRFNBR in table SHOPPER. |
| MCMENBR | INTEGER NOT NULL | Reference number of the merchant for which the group is defined. Together with column MCSHNBR, this is a primary key. This is a foreign key that references column MERFNBR in table MERCHANT. |
| MCSGNBR | INTEGER | Shopper group reference number. This is not a foreign key. No foreign key is enforced on column MCSGNBR so that no customer information is lost when the corresponding shopper group in table SHOPGRP is deleted. |
| MCUSTID | VARCHAR (30) | Customer identifier (assigned by the merchant). |
| MCFIELD1 | VARCHAR (254) | Reserved for merchant customization. |

# SG_STORES: Merchant-User Table

The table SG_STORES defines the relationship between a user and a store. Each row in the table describes a relationship between a single merchant and a single user. A user can be registered with more than one merchant in the same mall.

*Table C.13* *The SG_STORES table.*

| Column Name | Column Type | Column Description |
| --- | --- | --- |
| SG_SHLOGID | CHAR (31) NOT NULL | The login ID of the user. This is the same value as in column SHLOGID in table SHOPPER. |
| SG_MERFNBR | INTEGER NOT NULL | Merchant reference number. This is a foreign key that references column MERFNBR in table MERCHANT. This is a unique index. |

# Tables About Categories, Products, and Items

These tables contain information that describes the categories and products and their relationships with one another.

- CATEGORY: Category

- CGRYREL: Category Relationship

- PRODUCT: Product

- CGPRREL: Category Product Relationship

- PRODPRCS: Product Price

- PRODATR: Product Attribute

- PRODDSTATR: Product Distinct Attribute

- PRODSGP: Shopper Group Product Template

- CATESGP: Shopper Group Category Template

The relationships between the tables in this group are shown in Figure C.4 below:

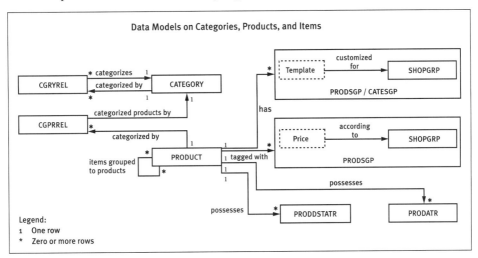

***Figure C.4*** *The data model on categories, products, and items.*

# CATEGORY: Category Table

The table CATEGORY contains information that describes the product categories and subcategories for each store. Each row describes one category.

The column CGLDESC and CGDISPLAY are available for merchant customization. The content, path and name of the template that displays the category information, subcategory information, and images that were originally stored in these fields, are now stored in the table CATESGP.

*Table C.14  The CATEGORY table.*

| Column Name | Column Type | Column Description |
|---|---|---|
| CGRFNBR | INTEGER NOT NULL | Category reference number, internally generated. This is a primary key. |
| CGMENBR | INTEGER NOT NULL | Merchant reference number. This is a foreign key that references column MERFNBR in table MERCHANT. |
| CGNAME | CHAR (200) NOT NULL | Name of the category. |
| CGSDESC | CHAR (254) | Brief description of category. |
| CGLDESC | LONG VARCHAR (for DB2) VARCHAR (2000) (for Oracle) | Reserved for merchant customization. |
| CGDISPLAY | CHAR (254) | Reserved for merchant customization. |
| CGTHMB | CHAR (254) | Category or subcategory thumbnail image file path and name. |
| CGFULL | CHAR (254) | Category or subcategory full-sized image file path and name. |
| CGPUB | SMALLINT | Should this category be displayed to the public? **1** - Yes **0** - No |
| CGFIELD1 | VARCHAR (254) | Reserved for merchant customization. |
| CGFIELD2 | VARCHAR (254) | Reserved for merchant customization. |
| CGSTMP | TIMESTAMP (for DB2) DATE (for Oracle) | The time and date the category entry was last updated. |

# CGRYREL: Category Relationship Table

The table CGRYREL defines the relationships between the categories and subcategories for each store. This information is used to structure the product categories that are presented to shoppers. Each row describes one relationship.

**Table C.15** *The CGRYREL table.*

| Column Name | Column Type | Column Description |
|---|---|---|
| CRMENBR | INTEGER NOT NULL | Merchant reference number. This is a foreign key that references column MERFNBR in table MERCHANT. Together with columns CRPCGNBR and CRCCGNBR, this is a unique index. |
| CRPCGNBR | INTEGER | Category reference number of the parent. This is a foreign key that references column CGRFNBR in table CATEGORY. Together with columns CRMENBR and CRCCGNBR, this is a unique index. If null, this category has no parents. |
| CRCCGNBR | INTEGER | Category reference number of the child, or subcategory. This is a foreign key that references column CGRFNBR in table CATEGORY. Together with columns CRMENBR and CRPCGNBR, this is a unique index. |
| CRSEQNBR | FLOAT | Category sequence number. This governs the order of presentation. |

# PRODUCT: Product Table

The table PRODUCT describes all the products and items available at all stores. An item is a product that must be qualified by one or more attributes to be resolved into a SKU. A SKU (Stock Keeping Unit) is an orderable item. In this table, items are distinguished by having a non-null PRPRFNBR. Each row contains information on one product or item.

**Note:**
No foreign key is enforced so that no product information is lost when the product shipping code in table PRSPCODE is deleted.

**Table C.16** *The PRODUCT table.*

| Column Name | Column Type | Column Description |
|---|---|---|
| PRRFNBR | INTEGER NOT NULL | Product reference number. This is a primary key. |
| PRMENBR | INTEGER NOT NULL | Merchant reference number. This is a foreign key that references column MERFNBR in table MERCHANT. Together with column PRNBR, this is a unique index. |
| PRPRFNBR | INTEGER | Product number of the parent. This is a foreign key that references column PRRFNBR in table PRODUCT. If null, this is the topmost product. |
| PRNBR | CHAR (64) NOT NULL | Product number or item SKU. Together with column PRMENBR, this is a unique index. |
| PRSDESC | VARCHAR (254) | Short description of the product, including its name. |

*Continued on next page*

***Table C.16*** *Continued.*

| Column Name | Column Type | Column Description |
|---|---|---|
| PRLDESC1 | LONG VARCHAR (for DB2) VARCHAR (2000) (for Oracle) | Detailed description 1 of the product. |
| PRLDESC2 | LONG VARCHAR (for DB2) VARCHAR (2000) (for Oracle) | Detailed description 2 of the product. |
| PRLDESC3 | LONG VARCHAR (for DB2) VARCHAR (2000) (for Oracle) | Detailed description 3 of the product. |
| PRTHMB | CHAR (254) | Product thumbnail image file path and name. |
| PRFULL | CHAR (254) | Product full-sized image file path and name. |
| PRPUB | SMALLINT | Should this product be displayed to the public? **0** - No **1** - Yes **2** - Marked for deletion |
| PRKNUTAG | CHAR (64) | Reserved for IBM use. |
| PRWGHT | NUM (15,4) | Weight of the item for determining the shipping charges. The default is 0. |
| PRWMEAS | CHAR (20) | Unit of measurement for the weight (for example, kilograms or ounces). |
| PRLNGTH | NUM (15,4) | Length of the item, can be used for shipping. The default is 0. |
| PRWIDTH | NUM (15,4) | Width of the item, can be used for shipping. The default is 0. |
| PRHEIGHT | NUM (15,4) | Height of the item, can be used for shipping. The default is 0. |
| PRSMEAS | CHAR (20) | Unit of measurement for the dimensions (for example, meters or inches). |
| PRPSNBR | INTEGER | Product shipping code for shipping charges. The default is null. This is not a foreign key. |
| PRPCODE | CHAR (25) | Product code for taxation purposes as defined by the Taxware Sales/Use Tax System. The default is null. This is a foreign key (delete rule = set null) that references column TPCODE in table TAXPRCODE. |
| PRURL | VARCHAR (254) | URL for soft goods or links. |
| PRVENT | INTEGER | Number of items in stock. The default is null, meaning the merchant has not yet stocked the product. This field is not used for a product that has items associated with it. |

**Table C.16** *Continued.*

| Column Name | Column Type | Column Description |
|---|---|---|
| PRAVDATE | TIMESTAMP (for DB2) DATE (for Oracle) | Availability date of the product. If the item is out of stock or is not yet stocked, the merchant can specify the availability date. |
| PRSPECIAL | CHAR (4) | Special information about the product:<br>**S** - on sale |
| PRSTMP | TIMESTAMP (for DB2) DATE (for Oracle) | The date and time the product information was last updated. |
| PRFIELD1 | INTEGER | Reserved for merchant customization. |
| PRFIELD2 | INTEGER | Reserved for merchant customization. |
| PRFIELD3 | NUM (15,2) | Reserved for merchant customization. |
| PRFIELD4 | VARCHAR (254) | Reserved for merchant customization. |
| PRFIELD5 | VARCHAR (254) | Reserved for merchant customization. |
| PRDCONBR | INTEGER | Product discount code. This is a foreign key that references column DCORFNBR in table DISCCODE. |

# CGPRREL: Category Product Relationship Table

The table CGPRREL defines the relationships between the categories and products. Each row describes one relationship.

**Table C.17** *The CGPRREL table.*

| Column Name | Column Type | Column Description |
|---|---|---|
| CPMENBR | INTEGER NOT NULL | Merchant reference number. This is a foreign key that references column MERFNBR in table MERCHANT. Together with columns CPCGNBR and CPPRNBR, this is a unique index. |
| CPCGNBR | INTEGER | Category reference number, or null if the product does not belong to a category. This is a foreign key that references column CGRFNBR in table CATEGORY. Together with columns CPMENBR and CPPRNBR, this is a unique index. |
| CPPRNBR | INTEGER NOT NULL | Product reference number of the topmost product. This is a foreign key that references column PRRFNBR in table PRODUCT. Together with columns CPMENBR and CPCGNBR, this is a unique index. |
| CPSEQNBR | FLOAT | Product sequence number. This governs the order of presentation. |

# PRODPRCS: Product Price Table

The table PRODPRCS contains the prices of all products and items in all stores. Each product (with a SKU) and item has at least one row in this table. Additional rows may be added if different prices are offered to shoppers in different groups, and if an item has a different price for a defined period of time. To determine the correct price of an item, the Net.Commerce system collects all the price entries for the item that are valid for the appropriate shopper group (or for all shoppers if no shopper group is applicable) at the current date and time. The correct price is the one with the highest precedence value from column PPPRE.

> **Note:**
> This table replaces the Version 1 table PRODPRC, and includes a view PRODPRC containing all the columns from the Version 1 table.

*Table C.18  The PRODPRCS table.*

| Column Name | Column Type | Column Description |
|---|---|---|
| PPRFNBR | INTEGER NOT NULL | Unique reference number for this price, internally generated. This is a primary key. |
| PPMENBR | INTEGER NOT NULL | Merchant reference number. This is a foreign key that references column MERFNBR in table MERCHANT. Together with PPPRNBR, PPSGNBR and PPPRE, this forms a unique index. |
| PPPRNBR | INTEGER NOT NULL | Product reference number. This is a foreign key that references column PRRFNBR in table PRODUCT. |
| PPSGNBR | INTEGER | Shopper group reference number to which the price applies. This is a foreign key that references column SGRFNBR in table SHOPGRP. The default is null, which means the price applies to all shoppers. |
| PPPRC | NUM (15,2) | Price of the item. |
| PPCUR | CHAR (10) NOT NULL | Currency in which the price is expressed. The format of the currency must adhere to ISO 4217 standards. |
| PPPRE | INTEGER | Precedence for this price. The default is 0. The precedence is unique within a shopper group for a product or item. If the shopper group is null, the precedence is unique within a product. |
| PPDEFFS | TIMESTAMP (for DB2) DATE (for Oracle) | Date that the item price becomes effective. The default is the current date and time. |
| PPDEFFF | TIMESTAMP (for DB2) DATE (for Oracle) | Date that the item price expires. The default is 9999-12-31 at 24:00:00. |
| PPFIELD1 | CHAR (30) | Reserved for merchant customization. |
| PPFIELD2 | CHAR (1) | Reserved for merchant customization. |

# PRODATR: Product Attribute Table

The table PRODATR associates attribute names with attribute values for products. Each product can have any number of associations defined in this table. Each row describes one attribute and one attribute value.

**Table C.19** *The PRODATR table.*

| Column Name | Column Type | Column Description |
| --- | --- | --- |
| PAMENBR | INTEGER NOT NULL | Merchant reference number. This is a foreign key that references column MERFNBR in table MERCHANT. |
| PAPRNBR | INTEGER NOT NULL | Product reference number. This is a foreign key that references column PRRFNBR in table PRODUCT. |
| PANAME | CHAR (200) NOT NULL | Name part of the name-value pair. |
| PAVAL | CHAR (254) | Value part of name-value pair. |
| PAFIELD1 | INTEGER | Reserved for merchant customization. |

# PRODDSTATR: Product Distinct Attribute Table

The table PRODDSTATR contains the names of all the attributes that qualify an item as a distinct SKU. The SKU (Stock Keeping Unit) is the specific, orderable item. Attributes contained in this table, such as size, color or style, are used to distinguish items from other similar items. Each product can have any number of distinct SKU-level attribute names. This table should contain only attributes for SKU-level items. Table PRODATR takes an attribute from this table, such as color, and matches it with a value for a specific item, such as red.

**Table C.20** *The PRODDSTATR table.*

| Column Name | Column Type | Column Description |
| --- | --- | --- |
| PDMENBR | INTEGER NOT NULL | Merchant reference number. This is a foreign key that references column MERFNBR in table MERCHANT. |
| PDPRNBR | INTEGER NOT NULL | Product reference number. This is a foreign key that references column PRRFNBR in table PRODUCT. It refers to the product reference number of the product which is the parent of a SKU. |
| PDNAME | CHAR (200) NOT NULL | Name of the attribute. |
| PDDESC1 | CHAR (254) | Miscellaneous. |
| PDDESC2 | CHAR (254) | Miscellaneous. |
| PDSEQNBR | FLOAT | Attribute sequence number. This governs the order of presentation. |

# PRODSGP: Shopper Group Product Template Table

The table PRODSGP contains information that the Net.Commerce system needs to display product and item information to shoppers in different shopper groups. Each row associates one shopper group with one template for one product. A product template defines the format in which products and items are displayed.

Net.Commerce now also allows custom templates for category pages using the table CATESGP.

*Table C.21  The PRODSGP table.*

| Column Name | Column Type | Column Description |
| --- | --- | --- |
| PSMENBR | INTEGER NOT NULL | Merchant reference number. This is a foreign key that references column MERFNBR in table MERCHANT. |
| PSPRNBR | INTEGER NOT NULL | Product reference number. This is a foreign key that references column PRRFNBR in table PRODUCT. |
| PSSGNBR | INTEGER | Shopper group reference number. This is a foreign key that references column SGRFNBR in table SHOPGRP. The default is null, which means the template applies to shoppers who are not members of a shopper group. |
| PSDISPLAY | CHAR (254) NOT NULL | Path and name of the custom template that displays product and item information for this group. |
| PSDESC | LONG VARCHAR (for DB2) VARCHAR (2000) (for Oracle) | Description of the shopper group that is to appear on the product/item page. |
| PSFIELD1 | VARCHAR (254) | Reserved for merchant customization. |
| PSFIELD2 | VARCHAR (254) | Reserved for merchant customization. |

# CATESGP: Shopper Group Category Template Table

The table CATESGP contains information that the Net.Commerce system needs to display category information to shoppers in different shopper groups. Each row associates one shopper group with one template for one category. A category template defines the format in which categories are displayed.

Template customization by category was introduced in Version 2 of Net.Commerce. It functions similarly to the existing shopper group product template customization, which uses the table PRODSGP.

*Table C.22*  *The CATESGP table.*

| Column Name | Column Type | Column Description |
|---|---|---|
| CSMENBR | INTEGER NOT NULL | Merchant reference number. This is a foreign key that references column MERFNBR in table MERCHANT. |
| CSCGNBR | INTEGER NOT NULL | Category reference number. This is a foreign key that references column CGRFNBR in table CATEGORY. |
| CSSGNBR | INTEGER | Shopper group reference number. This is a foreign key that references column SGRFNBR in table SHOPGRP. The default is null, which means the template applies to shoppers who are not members of a shopper group. |
| CSDISPLAY | CHAR (254) NOT NULL | Path and name of the custom template that displays category and subcategory information for this group, and images. Note that in Version 1, the information in this column was stored in table CATEGORY as column CGDISPLAY. |
| CSDESC | LONG VARCHAR (for DB2) VARCHAR (2000) (for Oracle) | Description of the shopper group that is to appear on the category page. Note that in Version 1, the information in this column was stored in table CATEGORY as column CGLDESC. |
| CSFIELD1 | VARCHAR (254) | Reserved for merchant customization. |
| CSFIELD2 | VARCHAR (254) | Reserved for merchant customization. |

# Tables About Pricing and Discounting

These tables contain information that is needed for discount pricing and for determining which products and items are to be discounted at what rates for which shopper groups.

- SCALE: Price Modifier Rate Scale
- RATE: Price Modifier Rate
- DISCCODE: Product Discount Code
- DISCCALC: Discount Calculation

The relationships between the tables in this group are shown in Figure C.5.

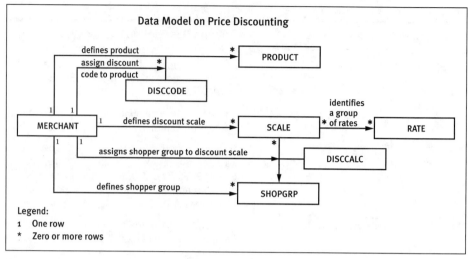

**Figure C.5**  *The data model on pricing and discounting.*

# SCALE: Price Modifier Rate Scale Table

The table SCALE is a container for the entities that comprise a rate scale for discount pricing. A scale is composed of one or more rates or ranges. Together, they set the various rates at which products will be discounted depending on quantity of purchase, shopper group, or both. Each row associates one scale code with one merchant or, if the merchant column is NULL, defines a scale code that can be used globally.

*Table C.23*  *The SCALE table.*

| Column Name | Column Type | Column Description |
|---|---|---|
| SCLRFNBR | INTEGER NOT NULL | Scale code reference number. This is a primary key. |
| SCLCODE | CHAR (15) NOT NULL | Unique identifier of a group of related rates or, in some cases, an individual rate. Unique within a merchant. |
| SCLMENBR | INTEGER | Merchant who defines the scale code. This is a foreign key that references column MERFNBR in table MERCHANT. The attribute is NULL when the scale code is defined for global use. |
| SCLDESC | VARCHAR (254) | Scale code description. |
| SCLFIELD1 | VARCHAR (254) | Reserved for merchant customization. |

# RATE: Price Modifier Range/Rate Table

The table RATE contains the information about a specific rate or range on which a product may be discounted. A range or rate includes the ending amount of the range on which the pricing will apply, plus the computation rate or value and the computation method. Each row contains a single rate associated with a scale from table SCALE. A scale comprises one or more rates.

*Table C.24* *The RATE table.*

| Column Name | Column Type | Column Description |
|---|---|---|
| RATSCLNBR | INTEGER NOT NULL | Scale code reference number. This is a foreign key that references column SCLRFNBR in table SCALE. |
| RATRANGEEND | NUM (15,4) NOT NULL | The ending amount of a range. The amount will be calculated in the same units as defined for the products or items being discounted. The range value will be interpreted as number of units, weight or monetary value depending on column DCCSCLTYPE in table DISCCALC. Only the ending amount is specified as a range. The system presumes the starting amount of the first range will be set to zero. For example, if there are 3 records for the same scale code in table RATE, with range ends of 10, 100, 1000000, then the 3 ranges are 0 to 10, 10.0001 to 100, and 100.0001 to 1000000. Since the column RATRANGEEND is a decimal number supporting 4 decimal places, the start of a range is the previous range end plus 0.0001. Therefore, the implicit range origin is 0. |
| RATVALUE | NUM (15,2) NOT NULL | Computational rate or computational value. The numerical value that will be applied to calculate the discount. |
| RATMTHD | CHAR (4) NOT NULL | Computation method to be applied on the computational rate or value to calculate the result. Can be one of:<br>**R1** - Range-based, used as Total Fixed Value<br>**R2** - Range-based, used as Unit Value<br>**R3** - Range-based, rate in Percentage<br>**C1** - Cumulative-based, used as Total Fixed Value<br>**C2** - Cumulative-based, used as Unit Value<br>**C3** - Cumulative-based, rate in Percentage |
| RATFIELD1 | NUM (15,2) | Reserved for merchant customization. |
| RATFIELD2 | NUM (15,2) | Reserved for merchant customization. |
| RATFIELD3 | VARCHAR (254) | Reserved for merchant customization. |

**Note:**
Only the ending amount is specified as a range. The system presumes the starting amount of the first range will be set to zero.

# DISCCODE: Product Discount Code Table

The table DISCCODE contains the discount codes used to group products and items that will be discounted on common rate scales. Each discount code is unique within a merchant, but multiple items can have the same discount code. Each row contains a single discount code.

***Table C.25***  *The DISCCODE table.*

| Column Name | Column Type | Column Description |
|---|---|---|
| DCORFNBR | INTEGER NOT NULL | Discount code reference number. This is a primary key. |
| DCCODE | CHAR (15) NOT NULL | A product discount code. The code is assigned to a product or a group of products to define them for discounting on a common rate scale. Each discount code is unique within a merchant. |
| DCOMENBR | INTEGER NOT NULL | The reference number of the merchant who defines the discount code. This is a foreign key that references column MERFNBR in table MERCHANT. |
| DCODESC | VARCHAR (254) | Product discount code description. |
| DCOFIELD1 | VARCHAR (254) | Reserved for merchant customization. |

# DISCCALC: Discount Calculation Table

The table DISCCALC contains the information used by Net.Commerce to enact discounted pricing based on a discount code, a shopper group, and a rate scale. The table also contains information about the quantitative type (weight, number of units or monetary value) for the discount, and the discount start and end dates.

***Table C.26***  *The DISCCALC table.*

| Column Name | Column Type | Column Description |
|---|---|---|
| DCCDCONBR | INTEGER | Product discount code reference number. This is a foreign key that references column DCORFNBR in table DISCCODE. If the attribute is NULL, the discount is not defined for a product but will be applied to the entire order. |
| DCCMENBR | INTEGER NOT NULL | Merchant reference number. This is a foreign key that references column MERFNBR in table MERCHANT. |
| DCCSGNBR | INTEGER | The shopper group that can receive the discount. This is a foreign key that references column SGRFNBR in table SHOPGRP. If this attribute is NULL, the discount can be offered to everybody. |
| DCCSCLNBR | INTEGER NOT NULL | Rate scale reference number. This is a foreign key that references column SCLRFNBR in table SCALE. |

*Continued on next page*

*Table C.26  Continued.*

| Column Name | Column Type | Column Description |
|---|---|---|
| DCCSCLTYPE | CHAR (5) | Rate scale quantitative type. This column determines that the discount will be applied based on one of the following types:<br>**Q** - Quantity (units)<br>**D** - Dollars (monetary)<br>**W** - Weight |
| DCCDEFFS | TIMESTAMP (for DB2)<br>DATE (for Oracle) | The date and time at which the discount becomes effective. |
| DCCDEFFF | TIMESTAMP (for DB2)<br>DATE (for Oracle) | The date and time at which the discount is no longer effective. |
| DCCFIELD1 | NUM (15,2) | Reserved for merchant customization. |
| DCCFIELD2 | VARCHAR (254) | Reserved for merchant customization. |

# Tables About Shipping

These tables contain information that is needed for shipping orders and for calculating the shipping charges, such as shipping modes, shipping codes, and calculation methods.

- SHIPMODE: Shipping Mode

- MSHIPMODE: Merchant Shipping Mode

- PRSPCODE: Product Shipping Code

- SHIPPING: Shipping

The relationships between the tables in this group are shown below.

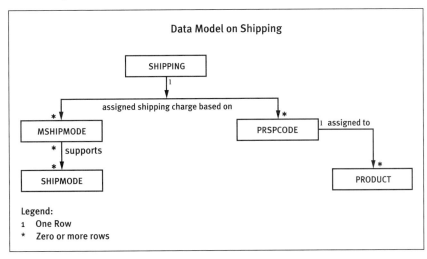

*Figure C.6  The data model on shipping.*

# SHIPMODE: Shipping Mode Table

The table SHIPMODE contains the names of the carriers, such as Federal Express, and the shipping service arrangements (shipping modes) that each carrier provides. Each row associates one shipping mode with one carrier.

*Table C.27  The SHIPMODE table.*

| Column Name | Column Type | Column Description |
| --- | --- | --- |
| SMRFNBR | INTEGER NOT NULL | Shipping mode reference number. This is a primary key. |
| SMCARRID | CHAR (30) | Carrier identifier, such as Federal Express. |
| SMSPMODE | CHAR (30) | Carrier service shipping mode, such as FedEx Express Overnight. |
| SMSPDESC | VARCHAR (254) | Shipping mode description. |
| SMFIELD1 | VARCHAR (254) | Reserved for merchant customization. |
| SMFIELD2 | INTEGER | Reserved for merchant customization. |

# MSHIPMODE: Merchant Shipping Mode Table

The table MSHIPMODE indicates the shipping modes that each merchant supports. Each row associates a shipping mode with a merchant.

*Table C.28  The MSHIPMODE table.*

| Column Name | Column Type | Column Description |
| --- | --- | --- |
| MMRFNBR | INTEGER NOT NULL | Merchant shipping mode reference number. This is a primary key. |
| MMSMNBR | INTEGER NOT NULL | Shipping mode reference number. This is a foreign key that references column SMRFNBR in table SHIPMODE. |
| MMMENBR | INTEGER NOT NULL | Merchant reference number. This is a foreign key that references column MERFNBR in table MERCHANT. |
| MMDEFFS | TIMESTAMP (for DB2) DATE (for Oracle) | The date that the shipping mode becomes available. |
| MMDEFFF | TIMESTAMP (for DB2) DATE (for Oracle) | The date that the shipping mode becomes unavailable. |
| MMFIELD1 | VARCHAR (254) | Reserved for merchant customization. |
| MMFIELD2 | INTEGER | Reserved for merchant customization. |

# PRSPCODE: Product Shipping Code Table

The table PRSPCODE contains the shipping codes that a merchant can assign to a product. The shipping code can be used to determine the method for calculating the shipping charges.

The Net.Commerce system provides an overridable function that supports eight shipping charge calculation options. These options are described in column PSSPMTHD. You can change them by coding an overridable function. Each row contains a shipping charge calculation method for each product shipping code.

***Table C.29*** *The PRSPCODE table.*

| Column Name | Column Type | Column Description |
| --- | --- | --- |
| PSRFNBR | INTEGER NOT NULL | Product shipping code reference number. This is a primary key. |
| PSCODE | CHAR (5) NOT NULL | Product shipping code. Together with PSMENBR and PSSPMTHD, this is a unique index. |
| PSMENBR | INTEGER NOT NULL | Merchant reference number. This is a foreign key that references column MERFNBR in table MERCHANT. Together with PSCODE and PSSPMTHD, this is a unique index. |
| PSSPMTHD | CHAR (2) | Shipping charge calculation method. Together with PSMENBR and PSSPMTHD, this is a unique index. The default overridable function recognizes the following methods: **Q1** - The shipping model is "RANGE." The charge in SHIPPING is used as a total fixed shipping cost and is based on the total quantity. **Q2** - The shipping model is "RANGE." The charge in SHIPPING is used as a unit shipping cost and is based on the total quantity. **Q3** - The shipping model is "CUMULATIVE." The charge in SHIPPING is used as a total fixed shipping cost and is based on the total quantity. **Q4** - The shipping model is "CUMULATIVE." The charge in SHIPPING is used as a unit shipping cost and is based on the total quantity. **W1** - The shipping model is "RANGE." The charge in SHIPPING is used as a total fixed shipping cost and is based on the total weight. **W2** - The shipping model is "RANGE." The charge in SHIPPING is used as a unit shipping cost and is based on the total weight. **W3** - The shipping model is "CUMULATIVE." The charge in SHIPPING is used as a total fixed shipping cost and is based on the total weight. |

*Continued on next page*

**Table C.29** *Continued.*

| Column Name | Column Type | Column Description |
|---|---|---|
| | | **W4** - The shipping model is "CUMULATIVE." The charge in SHIPPING is used as a unit shipping cost and is based on the total weight. |
| PSSPDESC | VARCHAR (254) | Shipping code description. |
| PSFIELD1 | VARCHAR (254) | Reserved for merchant customization. |

# SHIPPING: Shipping Table

The table SHIPPING assigns a shipping charge or rate to each shipping calculation method that a merchant uses based on any one or more of the following factors:

- Shipping mode, or freight arrangement.

- Shipping charge calculation method. The default overridable function recognizes the following methods:

  - **Q1**: Quantity-based, range, fixed charge

  - **Q2**: Quantity-based, range, unit cost

  - **Q3**: Quantity-based, cumulative, fixed charge

  - **Q4**: Quantity-based, cumulative, unit cost

  - **W1**: Weight-based, range, fixed charge

  - **W2**: Weight-based, range, unit cost

  - **W3**: Weight-based, cumulative, fixed charge

  - **W4**: Weight-based, cumulative, unit cost

- Address jurisdiction (region and country).

The default overridable function applies the first two factors.

If columns SPSTRAMT and SPENDAMT contain the weight amount, the unit of measurement is the same as the unit that is used in the table PRODUCT for the corresponding product. Each row in this table describes a shipping calculation method and its associated shipping charge or rate.

*Table C.30* *The SHIPPING table.*

| Column Name | Column Type | Column Description |
|---|---|---|
| SPRFNBR | INTEGER NOT NULL | Shipping reference number. This is a primary key. |
| SPMENBR | INTEGER NOT NULL | Merchant reference number. This is a foreign key that references column MERFNBR in table MERCHANT. |
| SPMMNBR | INTEGER | Merchant shipping mode reference number. This is a foreign key that references column MMRFNBR in table MSHIPMODE. |
| SPPSNBR | INTEGER | Product shipping code reference number. This is a foreign key that references column PSRFNBR in table PRSPCODE. |
| SPADDRJR | CHAR (20) | Address jurisdiction indicator. This is the jurisdiction on which the price is based. |
| SPCNTRY | CHAR (30) | Country identifier. This is the country on which the price is based. |
| SPSTRAMT | NUM (15,2) NOT NULL | Starting amount of a range. If used for a weight, the weight must be in the same units as defined for the product in table PRODUCT. |
| SPENDAMT | NUM (15,2) NOT NULL | Ending amount of a range. If used for a weight, the weight must be in the same units as defined for the product in table PRODUCT. |
| SPCHRGE | NUM (15,2) | Shipping charge. |
| SPRATE | NUM (8,2) | Shipping rate. |
| SPDEFFS | TIMESTAMP (for DB2) DATE (for Oracle) | The date that the shipping calculation method becomes effective. |
| SPDEFFF | TIMESTAMP (for DB2) | The date that the shipping calculation method is no longer valid. |
| SPFIELD1 | VARCHAR (254) | Reserved for merchant customization. |
| SPFIELD2 | NUM (15,2) | Reserved for merchant customization. |

# Tables About Orders

These tables contain information about the products and items in the shopping carts, the orders that are placed by shoppers, the suborders that are destined for different shipping addresses, the payment methods, and the links between suborders and entries in the shoppers' address books.

- SHOPPINGS: Shopping Cart
- ORDERS: Order
- ORDERPAY: Order Payment
- ORDPAYMTHD: Order Payment Method
- SHIPTO: Shipping Association

The relationships between the tables in this group are shown in Figure C.7 below:

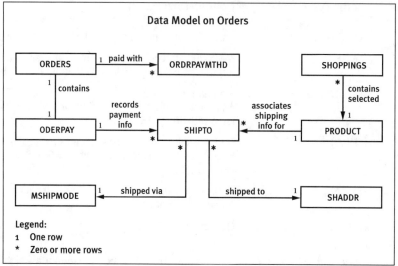

**Figure C.7** *The data model on orders.*

# SHOPPINGS: Shopping Cart Table

The table SHOPPINGS describes the contents of the shopping carts. Each row corresponds to one item in one shopping cart for one shopper.

**Table C.31** *The SHOPPINGS table.*

| Column Name | Column Type | Column Description |
| --- | --- | --- |
| SBSHNBR | INTEGER NOT NULL | Shopper reference number. Together with SBPRNBR, this is a primary key. This is a foreign key that references column SHRFNBR in table SHOPPER. |
| SBMENBR | INTEGER NOT NULL | Merchant reference number. This is a foreign key that references column MERFNBR in table MERCHANT. |
| SBPRNBR | INTEGER NOT NULL | Product reference number. Together with SBSHNBR, this is a primary key. This is a foreign key that references column PRRFNBR in table PRODUCT. |
| SBPRICE | NUM(15,2) | Unit price of the product or item. This column is updated when the shopper places the order (in case the price has changed). |
| SBCPCUR | CHAR (10) | Currency in which the price is expressed. The format of the currency must adhere to ISO 4217 standards. |
| SBDATE | TIMESTAMP (for DB2) DATE (for Oracle) | The date the row was created or last updated. |
| SBFIELD1 | INTEGER | Reserved for merchant customization. |

*Continued on next page*

*Table C.31 Continued.*

| Column Name | Column Type | Column Description |
|---|---|---|
| SBFIELD2 | NUM (15,2) | Reserved for merchant customization. |
| SBFIELD3 | VARCHAR (254) | Reserved for merchant customization. |

# ORDERPAY: Orderpay Table

The table ORDERPAY contains information about the order payment, the tax payable and shipping charges for each suborder. (A suborder is a part of an order to be shipped to a single address.) Each row contains the payment information for one suborder. For information about the tax categories used in this table, see the tax jurisdiction table.

*Table C.32 The ORDERPAY table.*

| Column Name | Column Type | Column Description |
|---|---|---|
| OYORNBR | INTEGER NOT NULL | Order reference number. Together with OYSANBR, this forms a primary key. This is a foreign key that references column ORRFNBR in table ORDERS. |
| OYSANBR | INTEGER NOT NULL | Address reference number. Together with OYORNBR, this forms a primary key. This is a foreign key (delete rule = no action) that references column SARFNBR in table SHADDR. |
| OYTAX1 | NUM (15,2) | Tax amount in category 1. Used for US Federal Tax. The default is 0. |
| OYTAX2 | NUM (15,2) | Tax amount in category 2. Used for US State Tax and Canadian GST. The default is 0. |
| OYTAX3 | NUM (15,2) | Tax amount in category 3. Used for US County tax and Canadian PST. The default is 0. |
| OYTAX4 | NUM (15,2) | Tax amount in category 4. The default is 0. |
| OYTAX5 | NUM (15,2) | Tax amount in category 5. The default is 0. |
| OYTAX6 | NUM (15,2) | Tax amount in category 6. The default is 0. |
| OYCNTAX | CHAR (30) | Country for which the tax calculation applies. It is used for determining the definitions of the preceding tax amount columns. |
| OYPRTOT | NUM(15,2) | Total product price for this shipment. |
| OYTXTOT | NUM(15,2) | Total sales tax for this shipment. |
| OYSHTOT | NUM(15,2) | Total shipping charges for this shipment. |
| OYSHTXTOT | NUM(15,2) | Total tax on shipping charges for this order. |
| OYCPCUR | CHAR (10) | Currency in which the price is expressed. The format of the currency must adhere to ISO 4217 standards. |

*Continued on next page*

**Table C.32** *Continued.*

| Column Name | Column Type | |
|---|---|---|
| OYFIELD1 | INTEGER | Reserved for merchant customization. |
| OYFIELD2 | NUM (15,2) | Reserved for merchant customization. |
| OYFIELD3 | VARCHAR (254) | Reserved for merchant customization. |

The tax amount columns in the preceding table correspond to the tax jurisdictions in the U.S. and Canada. To implement Net.Commerce in other countries, you must establish your own definitions based on the requirements of your jurisdiction and of the taxation package that you use to calculate the amounts.

# ORDERS: Orders Table

The table ORDERS contains information about orders that are placed by shoppers. Each row corresponds to a single order. The products and items in an order may have different shipping information, that is the products and items can be shipped to different locations.

**Table C.33** *The ORDERS table.*

| Column Name | Column Type | Column Description |
|---|---|---|
| ORRFNBR | INTEGER NOT NULL | Unique order reference number, internally generated. This is a primary key. |
| ORSHNBR | INTEGER NOT NULL | Shopper reference number. This is a foreign key (delete rule = no action) that references SHRFNBR in table SHOPPER. |
| ORMENBR | INTEGER NOT NULL | Merchant reference number. This is a foreign key that references column MERFNBR in table MERCHANT. |
| ORMORDER | CHAR (30) | Order reference number generated by the merchant. Unique within a merchant store. |
| ORBLLTO | INTEGER | Address reference number for the billing address. This is a foreign key (delete rule = no action) that references column SARFNBR in table SHADDR. |
| ORPRTOT | NUM(15,2) | Total product price for this order. |
| ORTXTOT | NUM(15,2) | Total sales tax for this order. |
| ORSHTOT | NUM(15,2) | Total shipping charges for this order. |
| ORSHTXTOT | NUM(15,2) | Total tax on shipping charges for this order. |
| ORCPCUR | CHAR (10) | Currency in which the price is expressed. The format of the currency must adhere to ISO 4217 standards. |
| ORSTAT | CHAR (1) | Order status:<br>**P** - Order in pending state<br>**C** - Order in completed state (order was placed)<br>**X** - Order was cancelled |

**Table C.33**   *Continued.*

| Column Name | Column Type | Column Description |
|---|---|---|
| | | **I** - Inventory updated pending (order no longer pending) <br> **M** - Ready for authorization (order passed inventory update) **Note:** All single upper case letters are reserved for Net.Commerce. |
| ORLOCK | CHAR(1) | Lock indicator for disallowing any updates to the order. |
| ORPSTMP | TIMESTAMP (DB2) <br> DATE (for Oracle) | The date and time the order was placed. |
| ORUSTMP | TIMESTAMP (DB2) <br> DATE (for Oracle) | The date and time the order entry was last updated. |
| ORFIELD1 | INTEGER | Reserved for merchant customization. |
| ORFIELD2 | NUM (15,2) | Reserved for merchant customization. |
| ORFIELD3 | VARCHAR (254) | Reserved for merchant customization. |

# ORDPAYMTHD: Order Payment Method Table

The table ORDPAYMTHD contains order payment methods selected for an order.

**Table C.34**   *The ORDPAYMTH table.*

| Column Name | Column Type | Column Description |
|---|---|---|
| OMORNBR | INTEGER NOT NULL | Order reference number. This is a foreign key that references column ORRFNBR in table ORDERS. Together with OMPAYMTHD and OMPAYDEVC, this is a primary key. |
| OMPAYMTHD | CHAR (5) NOT NULL | Payment method identifier for the payment method, such as a credit card, coupon, or gift certificate. Together with OMORNBR and OMPAYDEVC, this is a primary key. |
| OMPAYDEVC | CHAR (64) NOT NULL | Payment device identifier. Together with OMORNBR and OMPAYMTHD, this is a primary key. |
| OMDEFFS | TIMESTAMP (for DB2) <br> DATE (for Oracle) | Expiration date for the payment method. |
| OMDEFFF | TIMESTAMP (for DB2) <br> DATE (for Oracle) | Issue date for the payment method. |
| OMMAXAAMT | NUM (15,2) | Payment maximum authorization amount. |

# SHIPTO: Shipping Association Table

The table SHIPTO associates each product and item in a suborder with a shipping address. Each row corresponds to one product or item.

**Table C.35**  *The SHIPTO table.*

| Column Name | Column Type | Column Description |
|---|---|---|
| STRFNBR | INTEGER NOT NULL | Unique shipto reference number, internally generated. This is a primary key. |
| STORNBR | INTEGER | Order reference number. This is a foreign key that references column ORRFNBR in table ORDERS. |
| STSANBR | INTEGER NOT NULL | Address reference number for the shipping address. |
| STSHNBR | INTEGER NOT NULL | Shopper reference number. This is a foreign key that references column SHRFNBR in table SHOPPER. |
| STMENBR | INTEGER NOT NULL | Merchant reference number. This is a foreign key that references column MERFNBR in table MERCHANT. |
| STPRNBR | INTEGER NOT NULL | Product reference number. This is not a foreign key. Note that no foreign key is defined on column STPRNBR so that no information on any order is lost when the product in table PRODUCT is deleted. |
| STPRICE | NUM(15,2) | Unit price of the item. |
| STCPCUR | CHAR (10) | Currency in which the price is expressed. The format of the currency must adhere to ISO 4217 standards. |
| STPCODE | CHAR (5) | Product code for taxation purposes as defined by the Taxware Sales/Use Tax System. This is a foreign key (delete rule = set null) that references column TPCODE in table TAXPRCODE. |
| STCMT | VARCHAR (254) | Comments from shopper, such as a greeting for a gift. |
| STQUANT | INTEGER NOT NULL | Quantity ordered. |
| STSTAT | CHAR (1) NOT NULL | Order Status:<br>**P** - In pending state<br>**C** - In past state<br>**X** - Cancelled<br>**I** - Inventory update pending (shipto no longer pending)<br>**M** - Ready for authentication (shipto passed inventory update) |
| STPSTMP | TIMESTAMP (for DB2) DATE (for Oracle) | The date and time the shipto entry was made. |
| STUSTMP | TIMESTAMP (for DB2) DATE (for Oracle) | The date and time the shipto entry was last updated. |
| STSMNBR | INTEGER | Merchant shipping mode reference number (refer to table MSHIPMODE). |
| STFIELD1 | INTEGER | Reserved for merchant customization. |
| STFIELD2 | VARCHAR (254) | Reserved for merchant customization. |

# Tables About Tax Calculations

The following tables contain information about the tax categories and codes, and information about the codes that are used to represent different states or tax jurisdictions.

- TAXCGRY: Tax Category
- TAXPRCODE: Tax Product Code
- STATCODE: State Code
- MERCHANTTAX: Merchant Tax
- WTMERINFO: Merchant World Tax Information

The relationships between the tables in this group are shown in Figure C.8 below:

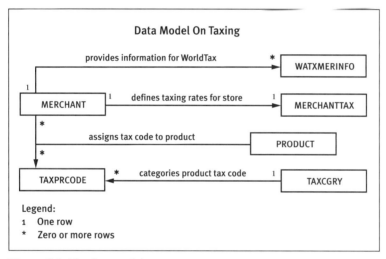

**Figure C.8** *The data model on taxing.*

## TAXCGRY: Tax Product Category Table

The table TAXCGRY associates tax categories with product codes. The information is compatible with the Sales/Use Tax System. Each row associates one tax category with one product code.

**Table C.36** *The TAXCGRY table.*

| Column Name | Column Type | Column Description |
|---|---|---|
| TCRFNBR | INTEGER NOT NULL | Tax category reference number. This is a primary key. |
| TCAT | CHAR (70) | Tax product code category. |

## TAXPRCODE: Tax Product Code Table

The table TAXPRCODE describes the types of products associated with each applicable Sales/ Use Tax System product code. The information is compatible with the Sales/Use Tax System. Each row defines one product code.

*Table C.37  The TAXPRCODE table.*

| Column Name | Column Type | Column Description |
| --- | --- | --- |
| TPCODE | CHAR (25) NOT NULL | Unique product code. This is a primary key. The product code must correspond to a Sales/Use Tax System product code. |
| TPTCNBR | INTEGER | Tax category reference number. This is a foreign key that references column TCRFNBR in table TAXCGRY. |
| TPCNAME | CHAR (30) | Name of the product code. |
| TPCDESC | LONG VARCHAR | Detailed description of the product code. |

## STATCODE: State Code Table

The table STATCODE associates states or other geographic regions with state codes. The information is used internally for calculating the tax payable on orders. Each row associates one code with one state or geographic region.

*Table C.38  The STATCODE table.*

| Column Name | Column Type | Column Description |
| --- | --- | --- |
| STACODE | CHAR (3) NOT NULL | Unique code assigned to a state or other geographic region, indexed. |
| STAABBR | CHAR (20) NOT NULL | Abbreviated name of state or region. |
| STANAME | CHAR (40) NOT NULL | Full name of state or region. |
| STACNTRY | CHAR (30) | Country in which state or region is located. |

## MERCHANTTAX: Merchant Tax Table

The table MERCHANTTAX contains information that can be used by a merchant to calculate tax on products. Each row in this table associates a piece of tax information with a single merchant. Each merchant can define only one entry.

*Table C.39* *The MERCHANTTAX table.*

| Column Name | Column Type | Column Description |
|---|---|---|
| MTMENBR | INTEGER NOT NULL | Merchant reference number. This is a foreign key that references column MERFNBR in table MERCHANT. |
| MTTAXRATE1 | NUMERIC (4,2) NOT NULL | A definable rate that can be applied on a level of taxation, such as local or value-added. |
| MTTAXNAME1 | VARCHAR (30) | The name of the tax rate defined in the associated column above. |
| MTTAXRATE2 | NUMERIC (4,2) NOT NULL | A definable rate that can be applied on a level of taxation, such as local or value-added. |
| MTTAXNAME2 | VARCHAR (30) | The name of the tax rate defined in the associated column above. |
| MTTAXRATE3 | NUMERIC (4,2) NOT NULL | A definable rate that can be applied on a level of taxation, such as local or value-added. |
| MTTAXNAME3 | VARCHAR (30) | The name of the tax rate defined in the associated column above. |
| MTTAXRATE4 | NUMERIC (4,2) NOT NULL | A definable rate that can be applied on a level of taxation, such as local or value-added. |
| MTTAXNAME4 | VARCHAR (30) | The name of the tax rate defined in the associated column above. |
| MTTAXRATE5 | NUMERIC (4,2) NOT NULL | A definable rate that can be applied on a level of taxation, such as local or value-added. |
| MTTAXNAME5 | VARCHAR (30) | The name of the tax rate defined in the associated column above. |
| MTTAXRATE6 | NUMERIC (4,2) NOT NULL | A definable rate that can be applied on a level of taxation, such as local or value-added. |
| MTTAXNAME6 | VARCHAR (30) | The name of the tax rate defined in the associated column above. |
| MTFIELD1 | NUMERIC (4,2) | Reserved for merchant customization. |
| MTFIELD2 | NUMERIC (4,2) | Reserved for merchant customization. |
| MTFIELD3 | VARCHAR (254) | Reserved for merchant customization |

# WTMERINFO: Merchant WorldTax Information Table

The table WTMERINFO is used to provide merchant-specific information required by WorldTax, a stand-alone application that can calculate and apply taxes in a number of countries, including those in the European Common Market. Each row in this table contains information about a single merchant. A merchant uses only one row in the table per location, and only if that merchant is using WorldTax for tax calculations. However, a merchant who does business from more than one country can use a row to provide tax information from each country from which it docs business.

> **Note:**
> Version 3 of Net.Commerce supports only a single location.

*Table C.40  The WTMERINFO table.*

| Column Name | Column Type | Column Description |
| --- | --- | --- |
| WTMENBR | INTEGER NOT NULL | Merchant reference number. This is a foreign key that references column MERFNBR in table MERCHANT. This column and column WTREGNBR together form a unique index. |
| WTREGNBR | CHAR (25) | Merchant registration number, as mapped from the WorldTax menu. This field determines the type of tax to be calculated and the location at which to calculate the tax. This column and column WTMENBR together form a unique index. |
| WTCOMPANYID | CHAR (20) | Merchant company identification |
| WTBUSLOC | CHAR (10) | Business location, as mapped from the WorldTax menu. |
| WTCNTRYCODE | CHAR (3) | Country code, as mapped from the WorldTax menu. |
| WTFIELD1 | INTEGER | Reserved for merchant customization. |
| WTFIELD2 | VARCHAR (50) | Reserved for merchant customization. |

# Tables About System Functions

This group of tables contains basic information that the Net.Commerce system needs to function.  It includes the tables listed below.

- MALL: Mall
- BROWSER: Browser
- KEYS: Keys
- CACHLOG: Caching log
- STAGLOG: Staging Server log
- DAEMON: Daemon Administration

## MALL: Mall Table

The table MALL contains the basic information needed to run the mall.  It also contains the mall-wide tax rates that are applied to any stores for which no customized tax rates are found. The table contains only one row.  See the tax jurisdiction table for details about the tax categories.

**Table C.41**  *The MALL table.*

| Column Name | Column Type | Column Description |
|---|---|---|
| MHTHEAD | CHAR (254) | Relative path off the HTML root for the file name of the HTML text used as the default header on the mall display page. |
| MHTFOOT | CHAR (254) | Relative path off the HTML root for the file name of the HTML text used as the default footer on the mall display page. |
| MHTBASE | CHAR (254) | Relative path off the HTML root for the file name of the HTML text displayed when no parameters are provided to the Web interface program. |
| MHMAXID | CHAR (31) | Reserved for IBM use. |
| MHDVERSION | CIIAR (30) | Heserved for IBM use.  Defines which version of Net.Commerce and of the database system is installed. |
| MHTAXRATE | NUM (4,2) NOT NULL | Default tax rate for category 1 for all the stores in the mall, multiplied by 100.  For example, 8 per cent is represented as 8.00, not 0.08.  The default is 0.  Use this field if you want to use a simple tax calculation method, such as charging 6% of the total price as tax |
| MHTAXRATE2 | NUM (4,2) NOT NULL | Default tax rate for category 2 for all the stores in the mall, multiplied by 100.  For example, 8 per cent is represented as 8.00, not 0.08.  The default is 0. |
| MHTAXRATE3 | NUM (4,2) NOT NULL | Default tax rate for category 3 for all the stores in the mall, multiplied by 100.  For example, 8 per cent is represented as 8.00, not 0.08.  The default is 0. |
| MHTAXRATE4 | NUM (4,2) NOT NULL | Default tax rate for category 4 for all the stores in the mall, multiplied by 100.  For example, 8 per cent is represented as 8.00, not 0.08.  The default is 0. |
| MHTAXRATE5 | NUM (4,2) NOT NULL | Default tax rate for category 5 for all the stores in the mall, multiplied by 100.  For example, 8 per cent is represented as 8.00, not 0.08.  The default is 0. |
| MHTAXRATE6 | NUM (4,2) NOT NULL | Default tax rate for category 6 for all the stores in the mall, multiplied by 100.  For example, 8 per cent is represented as 8.00, not 0.08.  The default is 0. |
| MHFIELD1 | VARCHAR (254) | Reserved for merchant customization. |

# BROWSER: Browser Table

The table BROWSER contains information about the Web browsers that can be used to access Net.Commerce stores and malls.  Each browser is described in a different row.

***Table C.42***  *The BROWSER table.*

| Column Name | Column Type | Column Description |
|---|---|---|
| BRAGENT | CHAR (254) NOT NULL | Agent for the browser.  This is a primary key. |
| BRHITS | INTEGER | The cumulative total number of hits on this browser. |
| BRSET | SMALLINT | **0** - SET is not supported.<br>**1** - SET is supported. |
| BRSSL | SMALLINT | **0** - SSL is not supported.<br>**1** - SSL is supported. |
| BRSHTTP | SMALLINT | **0** - SHTTP is not supported.<br>**1** - SHTTP is supported. |
| BRTABLE | SMALLINT | **0** - The table function is not supported.<br>**1** - The table function is supported. |
| BRGET | SMALLINT | **0** - The get function is not supported.<br>**1** - The get function is supported. |
| BRPOST | SMALLINT | **0** - The post function is not supported.<br>**1** - The post function is supported. |
| BRFRAME | SMALLINT | **0** - The frame function is not supported.<br>**1** - The frame function is supported. |
| BRFIELD1 | SMALLINT | Reserved for merchant customization. |
| BRFIELD2 | SMALLINT | Reserved for merchant customization. |

# KEYS: Keys Table

The table KEYS contains the current maximum values of the primary keys of the following tables.

- ORDERS
- SHIPTO
- SHOPPER
- SHADDR
- TASK
- STAXCGRY
- SHIPMODE
- STRCGRY

- MERCHANT

- MSHIPMODE

- ACC_GROUP

- PRSPCODE

- SHIPPING

- SHOPGRP

- PRODUCT

- PRODPRCS

- CATEGORY

- SCALE

- DISCCODE

- STAGLOG

- ACC_MODE

The Net.Commerce system uses this information to set primary keys for new rows. If you populate the database without using Net.Commerce Administrator, you must update this table manually to include the highest keys you use for each table.

*Table C.43* *The KEYS table.*

| Column Name | Column Type | Column Description |
|---|---|---|
| KEYRFNBR | INTEGER NOT NULL | Key reference number. This is a primary key. |
| KEYTABLE | CHAR (18) NOT NULL | The name of the table to which the key belongs. |
| KEYCOLUMN | CHAR (18) NOT NULL | The column on which the key is defined. |
| KEYMAXID | INTEGER NOT NULL | The current highest value of the key. |

# CACHLOG: Caching Log Table

The table CACHLOG is a system table with columns and rows. A row (record) is created every time a change is made in a PRRFNBR (product) or CGRFNBR (category) row, or in any other row specified by the mall or a merchant as "significant." The Net.Commerce daemon queries this table for new rows at specified intervals, and uses this information to purge files that may be obsolete from the cache.

*Table C.44*  *The CACHLOG table.*

| Column Name | Column Type | Column Description |
|---|---|---|
| CACNAME | VARCHAR (64) NOT NULL | The parameter name in a command URL used to generate a file in the cache. This is typically PRRFNBR or CGRFNBR, but can be any other column name specified in the system configuration file as "significant." |
| CACVALUE | INTEGER | The value of the parameter. The name and value are used together to create the file names in the cache. The daemon purges the cache based on file names. |
| CACMENBR | INTEGER NOT NULL | The merchant ID. This is a foreign key that references column MERFNBR in table MERCHANT. |
| CACSTMP | TIMESTAMP(for DB2) DATE (for Oracle) NOT NULL | The date and time at which the row was created. |

# STAGLOG: Staging Log Table

The table STAGLOG contains information about records that are changed in the staging database. For each table or record that is changed in the staging database, a trigger inserts a record into the STAGLOG table.

*Table C.45*  *The STAGLOG table.*

| Column Name | Column Type | Column Description |
|---|---|---|
| STGRFNBR | INTEGER NOT NULL | Unique reference number for a staging log entry, internally generated. This is a primary key. |
| STGSTMP | TIMESTAMP (for DB2) DATE (for Oracle) NOT NULL | Date and time the STAGLOG record is created. This is the same date and time the changed record was captured by the trigger. |
| STGTABLE | CHAR (18) NOT NULL | The name of the table in which the change occurs. |
| STGOP | CHAR (1) NOT NULL | The type of change: **I** - Insert **U** - Update **D** - Delete **T** - Create a table in the destination database and copy all data **V** - Create a view in the destination database **C** - Copy all data to the destination database. |
| STGMENBRNAME | CHAR (18) | Name of the column that stores the merchant reference number in the changed table, if the changed table stores merchant data. If the table is used mall-wide, this column is NULL. |

*Continued on next page*

*Table C.45* *Continued.*

| Column Name | Column Type | Column Description |
|---|---|---|
| STGMENBR | INTEGER | Merchant reference number of the changed record, if applicable. |
| STGPKEYNAME | CHAR (18) | Name of the primary key of the changed table, if applicable. |
| STGPKEY | INTEGER | Value of the primary key of the changed record, if applicable. |
| STGKEY1NAME | CHAR (18) | Name of the first column that forms a unique index in the changed table, if there is no primary key. |
| STGKEY2NAME | CHAR (18) | Name of the second column that forms a unique index in the changed table, if applicable. |
| STGKEY3NAME | CIIAR (18) | Name ot the third column that forms a unique index in the changed table, if applicable. |
| STGKEY4NAME | CHAR (18) | Name of the fourth column that forms a unique index in the changed table, if applicable. |
| STGOKEY1 | INTEGER | Old value of the first column of the unique index in the changed record. Applicable only if column STGOP contains U or D. |
| STGOKEY2 | INTEGER | Old value of the second column of the unique index in the changed record. Applicable only if column STGOP contains U or D. |
| STGOKEY3 | VARCHAR (200) | Old value of the third column of the unique index in the changed record. Applicable only if column STGOP contains U or D. |
| STGOKEY4 | INTEGER | Old value of the fourth column of the unique index in the changed record. Applicable only if column STGOP contains U or D. |
| STGNKEY1 | INTEGER | New value of the first column of the unique index in the changed record. Applicable only if column STGOP contains I or U. |
| STGNKEY2 | INTEGER | New value of the second column of the unique index in the changed record. Applicable only if column STGOP contains I or U. |
| STGNKEY3 | VARCHAR (200) | New value of the third column of the unique index in the changed record. Applicable only if column STGOP contains I or U. |
| STGNKEY4 | INTEGER | New value of the fourth column of the unique index in the changed record. Applicable only if column STGOP contains I or U. |
| STGPROCESSED | INTEGER, default 0 | Indicates whether or not the Propagate utility has processed the changed record.<br>**0** - Not processed<br>**1** - Processed |
| STGRESERVED1 | INTEGER, default 0 | Reserved field for internal use. |

## DAEMON: Daemon Administration Table

The table DAEMON contains information regarding cache purging and password synchronization for the multi-machine environment.

*Table C.46   The DAEMON table.*

| Column Name | Column Type | Column Description |
|---|---|---|
| HOSTNAME | CHAR (254) | The hostname of the machine. |
| SYNCUPDT | TIMESTAMP (for DB2) DATE (for Oracle) | The date and time that the password sync was updated. |
| CACHUPDT | TIMESTAMP (for DB2) DATE (for Oracle) | The date and time that the cache was updated. |

# Tables About the Command Infrastructure

This group of tables contains information that control the commands, server pools, functions, tasks and macros within Net.Commerce.

- POOLS: Pools

- CMDS: Commands

- POOL_CMD: Pool-Command Association

- OFS: Overridable Functions

- PARAMS: Parameters

- CMD_PARAM: Command-Parameter

- OF_PARAM: Overridable Functions/Parameters

- TASKS: Tasks

- APIS: APIs

- MACROS: Macros

- CMD_TASK: Commands-Tasks Association

- TASK_MER_OF: Task-Overridable Functions

- TASK_MER_MACRO: Tasks-Macro

- OF_TASK: Overridable Function-Tasks

The relationships between the tables in this group are shown in Figure C.9:

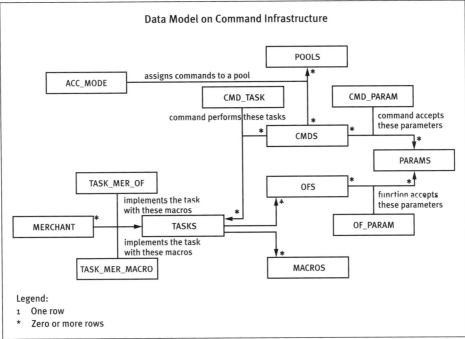

**Figure C.9** *The data model on the command infrastructure.*

# POOLS: Pools Table

The table POOLS contains information about all server pools that will be accessing this database for initialization. Each row in this table contains the ID number and the name of a server pool.

**Table C.47** *The POOLS table.*

| Column Name | Column Type | Column Description |
|---|---|---|
| REFNUM | INTEGER NOT NULL | The pool's ID number. This is the primary key. |
| NAME | CHAR (127) | The name of the server pool. This name is unique in the database. |

# CMDS: Commands Table

The table CMDS contains information about all the commands that are available within the system.

**Table C.48** *The CMDS table.*

| Column Name | Column Type | Column Description |
|---|---|---|
| REFNUM | INTEGER NOT NULL | The command's ID number. This is the primary key. |
| DLL_NAME | CHAR (32) | The name of the DLL that owns this command. |
| VENDOR | CHAR (32) NOT NULL | The name of the vendor of the command. |
| PRODUCT | CHAR (32) NOT NULL | The name of the product to which the command belongs. |
| NAME | CHAR (32) NOT NULL | The command's "absolute" name. |
| VERSION | NUM (15,2) NOT NULL | The version number of the command. The combination of VENDOR, PRODUCT, NAME and VERSION values must be unique. |
| URL | CHAR (32) NOT NULL | The name of the command's URL. This field is case-sensitive and must be unique. |
| EXPORT | INTEGER NOT NULL | A flag indicating whether the command can be accessed from a URL. |
| DESCRIPTION | CHAR (127) | A description of the command's basic functionality. |

**Note:**
Net.Commerce reserves the reference numbers 1 - 9999 in this table.

# POOL_CMD: Pool-Command Association Table

The table POOL_CMD matches the server pools to the various commands they can accept. Each row in this table identifies a single pool-command relationship. A server pool can accept multiple commands, and a command can be used by multiple server pools.

**Table C.49** *The POOL_CMD table.*

| Column Name | Column Type | Column Description |
|---|---|---|
| POOL_RN | INTEGER NOT NULL | Pool reference number. This is a foreign key that references column REFNUM in table POOLS. |
| CMD_RN | INTEGER NOT NULL | Command reference number. This is a foreign key that references column REFNUM in table CMDS. |

# OFS: Overridable Functions Table

The table OFS contains information about default overridable functions and about any functions that are provided by a merchant or the site administrator. Each row in this table contains information about a single function and the DLL that contains it. You can replace the default overridable functions in this table by either:

- Writing new functions

- Installing third-party software, such as Taxware's World Tax, and mapping its functions to the appropriate functions in Net.Commerce

*Table C.50  The OFS table.*

| Column Name | Column Type | Column Description |
| --- | --- | --- |
| REFNUM | INTEGER NOT NULL | The unique reference number of the function. This is the primary key. |
| DLL_NAME | CHAR (32) | The name of the DLL file that contains the function. |
| VENDOR | CHAR (32) NOT NULL | The name of the vendor of the overriding function. This may be a third-party vendor, a merchant or site administrator, or Net.Commerce itself. Together with the PRODUCT, NAME, and VERSION columns, this is a unique index. |
| PRODUCT | CHAR (32) NOT NULL | The name of the product that contains the function. This may be Net.Commerce. Together with the VENDOR, NAME, and VERSION columns, this is a unique index. |
| NAME | CHAR (32) NOT NULL | The name of the function. Together with the VENDOR, PRODUCT, and VERSION columns, this is a unique index. |
| VERSION | NUM (15,2) NOT NULL | The version number of the function. Together with the VENDOR, PRODUCT, and NAME columns, this is a unique index. |
| DESCRIPTION | CHAR (127) | A description of the function. |

**Note:**
Net.Commerce reserves the reference numbers 1 - 9999 in this table.

# PARAMS: Parameters Table

The table PARAMS contains information describing the parameters that will be assigned to a command. A parameter can be applied to more than one command, and a command have more than one parameter assigned to it.

*Table C.51  The PARAMS table.*

| Column Name | Column Type | Column Description |
| --- | --- | --- |
| REFNUM | INTEGER NOT NULL | The parameter's ID number.  This is the primary key. |
| NAME | CHAR (32) NOT NULL | The unique name of the parameter. |
| TYPE | CHAR (32) NOT NULL | The type of parameter. |
| MIN | NUM (15, 2) | The minimum value of the parameter. |
| MAX | NUM (15,2) | The maximum value of the parameter. |
| DESCRIPTION | CHAR (127) | A description of the parameter's basic purpose. |

# CMD_PARAM: Command-Parameter Table

The table CMD_PARAM describes a relationship between a command and a single parameter. Each command may accept more than one parameter, and each parameter may be assigned to more than one command.  Therefore, this table may contain multiple rows for each command and for each parameter.

*Table C.52  The CMD_PARAM table.*

| Column Name | Column Type | Column Description |
| --- | --- | --- |
| CMD_RN | INTEGER NOT NULL | Command reference number.  This is a foreign key that references column REFNUM in table CMDS.  This field and PARAM_RN together form a unique index. |
| PARAM_RN | INTEGER NOT NULL | Parameter reference number.  This is a foreign key that references column REFNUM in table PARAMS. This field and CMD_RN together form a unique index. |
| CARDINALITY | INTEGER NOT NULL | The number of times a command-parameter relationship may be used.  Must be one of the following:<br>**0** - 0 or 1 instances (the relationship is optional)<br>**1** - 1 instance (the relationship is mandatory)<br>**2** - 0 or more instances<br>**3** - 1 or more instances |

# OF_PARAM: Overridable Function Parameters Table

The table OF_PARAM defines the relationship between an overridable function and its parameters.  Each row in the table describes a single Overridable Function/parameter relationship.  A function can have more than one parameter, and a parameter can be assigned to more than one function.

*Table C.53* *The OF_PARAM table.*

| Column Name | Column Type | Column Description |
|---|---|---|
| OF_RN | INTEGER NOT NULL | Overridable Funtion reference number. This is a foreign key that references column REFNUM in table OFS. Together with column PARAM_RN, this is a unique index. |
| PARAM_RN | INTEGER NOT NULL | Parameter reference number. This is a foreign key that references column REFNUM in table PARAMS. Together with column OF_RN, this is a unique index. |
| CARDINALITY | INTEGER NOT NULL | The number of times an overridable function-parameter relationship may be used. Must be one of the following:<br>**0** - 0 or 1 instances (the relationship is optional)<br>**1** - 1 instance (the relationship is mandatory)<br>**2** - 0 or more instances<br>**3** - 1 or more instances |

# TASKS: Tasks Table

The table TASKS defines the name and scope of each task.

*Table C.54* *The TASKS table.*

| Column Name | Column Type | Column Description |
|---|---|---|
| TKRFNBR | INTEGER NOT NULL | Task reference number, internally assigned. This is a primary key. |
| TKNAME | CHAR (32) NOT NULL | Name of the task, unique. |
| TKCOMMENT | CHAR (254) | Comment for the task. |
| TKGROUP | CHAR (8) | The task group to which the task applies, such as PROCESS, VIEW, and ERROR. |
| TKSCOPE | INTEGER NOT NULL | Scope for the task:<br>**0** - Mall<br>**1** - Store |

**Note:**
Starting with Version 3, Net.Commerce reserves the following reference numbers in this table: 1-9999

# APIS: APIs Table

The table APIS contains information about the APIs (application programming interfaces) in Net.Commerce. It is primarily used to store APIs from Versions 1 and 2 of Net.Commerce. Version 3 functions are usually stored in the OFS (overridable functions) table.

*Table C.55  The APIS table.*

| Column Name | Column Type | Column Description |
|---|---|---|
| APIRFNBR | INTEGER NOT NULL | Task reference number. This is a foreign key that references column TKRFNBR in table TASKS. |
| APIMERNBR | INTEGER | Merchant reference number. This is a foreign key that references column MERFNBR in table MERCHANT. If NULL, it applies to all merchants. |
| APIDLLNAME | CHAR (254) | **WIN** DLL name for the API. Can be absolute or relative, i.e. \ibm\NetCommerce3\bin\myapi.dll or myapi.dll. In second case, be sure that LIBPATH is set.<br>**AIX** Shared library name for the API. Can be absolute or relative, i.e. /usr/lpp/NetCommerce3/bin/myapi.so or myapi.so. In second case, be sure that LIBPATH is set. |
| APIFUNCNAME | CHAR (254) | API function name. |

# MACROS: Macros Table

The table MACROS contains information about the macros that are defined in the Net.Commerce system. The macros are Net.Data files that provide a database-web interface by querying the database and creating the HTML page that the visitor sees.

*Table C.56  The MACROS table.*

| Column Name | Column Type | Column Description |
|---|---|---|
| MARFNBR | INTEGER NOT NULL | Macro reference number. This is a foreign key that references column TKRFNBR in table TASKS. Together with column MAMERNBR, this is a unique index. |
| MAMERNBR | INTEGER | Merchant reference number. This is a foreign key that references column MERFNBR in table MERCHANT. Together with column MARFNBR, this is a unique index. |
| MAFILENAME | CHAR (254) | File name of the macro. |

**Note:**
Starting with Version 3, Net.Commerce reserves the following reference numbers in this table: 1-9999

# CMD_TASK: Commands-Tasks Association Table

The table CMD_TASK matches the server commands to the various tasks they perform. Each row in this table identifies a single command-task relationship. A command can perform multiple tasks, and the same task can be assigned to more than one command.

*Table C.57 The CMD_TASK table.*

| Column Name | Column Type | Column Description |
|---|---|---|
| CMD_RN | INTEGER NOT NULL | Command reference number. This is a foreign key that references column REFNUM in table CMDS. This field and TASK_RN form a unique index. |
| TASK_RN | INTEGER NOT NULL | Task reference number. This is a foreign key that references column TKRFNBR in table TASKS. This field and CMD_RN form a unique index. |

# TASK_MER_OF: Task-Overridable Functions Table

The table TASK_MER_OF describes a relationship between a task, a merchant and an overridable function. Each row in this table defines a specific overridable function used by a particular merchant to perform a certain task. A merchant can have multiples entries in this table to describe how a task is implemented using a combination of override functions. Each function should only be specified to a task once.

*Table C.58 The TASK_MER_OF table.*

| Column Name | Column Type | Column Description |
|---|---|---|
| TASK_RN | INTEGER NOT NULL | Task reference number. This is a foreign key that references column TKRFNBR in table TASKS. Together with columns MERCHANT_RN and OF_RN, this is a unique index. |
| MERCHANT_RN | INTEGER | Merchant reference number. This is a foreign key that references column MERFNBR in table MERCHANT. Together with columns TASK_RN and OF_RN, this is a unique index. |
| OF_RN | INTEGER NOT NULL | Overridable function reference number. This is a foreign key that references column REFNUM in table OFS. Together with columns TASK_RN and MERCHANT_RN, this is a unique index. |

# TASK_MER_MACRO: Task-Macro Table

The table TASK_MER_MACRO identifies the relationship between a merchant, a task and the macro the merchant uses to perform the task. A merchant can have only one defined implementation for each task. Each row in this table contains information about a single merchant using a single macro to perform a single task.

*Table C.59* *The TASK_MER_MACRO table.*

| Column Name | Column Type | Column Description |
|---|---|---|
| TASK_RN | INTEGER NOT NULL | Task reference number. This is a foreign key that references column TKRFNBR in table TASKS. |
| MERCHANT_RN | INTEGER | Merchant reference number. This is a foreign key that references column MERFNBR in table MERCHANT. |
| MACRO_RN | INTEGER NOT NULL | Macro reference number. This is a foreign key that references column MARFNBR in table MACROS. |

# OF_TASK: Overridable Function-Tasks Table

The table OF_TASK defines the relationship between overridable functions and the tasks they perform. Each row in the table describes a single Overridable Function/task relationship.

*Table C.60* *The OF_TASK table.*

| Column Name | Column Type | Column Description |
|---|---|---|
| OF_RN | INTEGER NOT NULL | Overridable Function reference number. This is a foreign key that references column REFNUM in table OFS. Together with column TASK_RN, this is a unique index. |
| TASK_RN | INTEGER NOT NULL | Task reference number. This is a foreign key that references column TKRFNBR in table TASKS. Together with column OF_RN, this is a unique index. |

# Referential Integrity Relationships

The Net.Commerce system implements delete cascades to preserve the referential integrity of the database. If you add a new table to the database, you may want to establish a referential integrity mechanism for it to ensure that it remains synchronized with other tables.

Each table in the database is linked to at least one other, in order to connect information in different tables. For example, if a unique template exists for displaying a particular product to a particular shopper group, a record in the Shopper Group table, SHOPGRP, contains a link to a record in the Shopper Group Template table, PRODSGP. If a record in table SHOPGRP is deleted, its corresponding record in table PRODSGP will be automatically deleted as well.

The diagrams at the end of this chapter illustrate this system of referential integrity relationships.

The referential integrity relationships for the Oracle database are similar to those for the DB2 database, with a few exceptions. Refer to the Oracle database schema for details.

# Triggers for Database Tables

Triggers are used to enforce certain business rules and to ensure the integrity of the database. For example, if the status of an order changes from P to C in table ORDERS, the database automatically updates the corresponding column in table ORDERPAY.

You can establish new triggers, by using the appropriate SQL statements, to enforce your own business rules. . Do not remove any existing triggers, or you may compromise the integrity of the database.

The following table shows the triggers that are provided with the Net.Commerce system for the base database tables:

*Table C.61* *Database triggers.*

| Database Trigger | Trigger Action |
| --- | --- |
| Delete on SHOPGRP | SIGNAL SQLSTATE or Raise Application error when the shopper group is referenced in table MCUSTINFO. |
| Update on SHOPGRP (SGRFNBR) | SIGNAL SQLSTATE or Raise Application error when the shopper group is referenced in table MCUSTINFO. |
| Delete on MSHIPMODE | SIGNAL SQLSTATE or Raise Application error when the merchant shipping mode is referenced in table SHIPTO. |
| Update on MSHIPMODE (MMRFNBR) | SIGNAL SQLSTATE or Raise Application error when the merchant shipping mode is referenced in table SHIPTO. |
| Delete on PRSPCODE | SIGNAL SQLSTATE or Raise Application error when the product shipping code is referenced in table PRODUCT. |
| Update on PRSPCODE (PSRFNBR) | SIGNAL SQLSTATE or Raise Application error when the product shipping code is referenced in table PRODUCT. |
| Delete on PRODUCT | SIGNAL SQLSTATE or Raise Application error when the product is referenced in table SHIPTO. |
| Update on PRODUCT (PRRFNBR) | SIGNAL SQLSTATE or Raise Application error when the product is referenced in table SHIPTO. |
| Delete on PRODUCT | SIGNAL SQLSTATE or Raise Application error when the product is referenced in table SHOPPINGS. |
| Update on PRODUCT (PRRFNBR) | SIGNAL SQLSTATE or Raise Application error when the product is referenced in table SHOPPINGS |
| Delete on PRODDSTATR | Delete the corresponding entries in PRODATR. |
| Update on PRODDSTATR (PDNAME) | Update the corresponding entries in PRODATR. |

*Continued on next page*

*Table C.61  Continued.*

| Database Trigger | Trigger Action |
|---|---|
| Update on SHOPPER (SHSHTYP) | SIGNAL SQLSTATE 'N9010' if the shopper type is changed from registered to guest. |
| Update on ORDER (ORSTAT) | Update column STSTAT in table SHIPTO to the same state. |
| Update on ORDER (ORSTAT) | SIGNAL SQLSTATE or Raise Application error if the status X is changed back to C or P, and if the status C is changed back to P. |
| Update on SHIPTO (STSTAT) | SIGNAL SQLSTATE or Raise Application error if the status X is changed back to C or P, and if the status C is changed back to P. |
| Insert on DISCCALC | SIGNAL SQLSTATE or Raise Application error if the dates collide. |
| Update on DISCCALC | SIGNAL SQLSTATE or Raise Application error if the dates collide. |
| Delete on DISSCODE | Update the corresponding field (PRDCONBR) to NULL in PRODUCT. |

# Diagram of Referential Integrity Relationships (1) for DB2

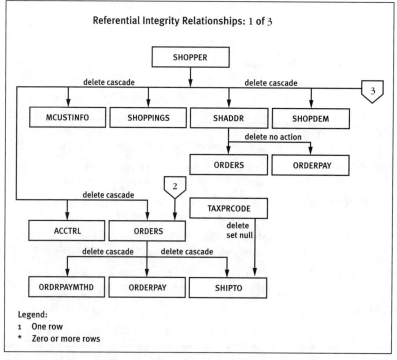

**Figure C.10**  *Referential integrity relationships (1 of 3).*

# Diagram of Referential Integrity Relationships (2) for DB2

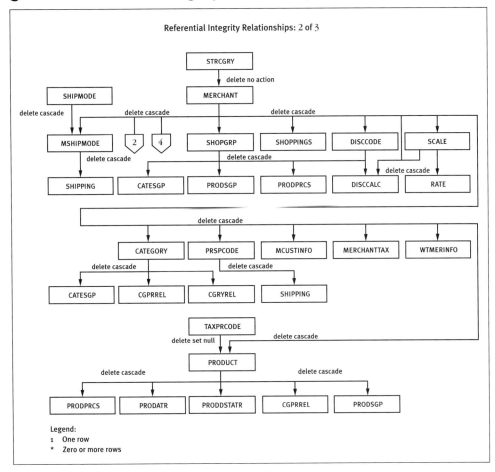

**Figure C.11** *Referential integrity relationships (2 of 3).*

# Diagram of Referential Integrity Relationships (3) for DB2

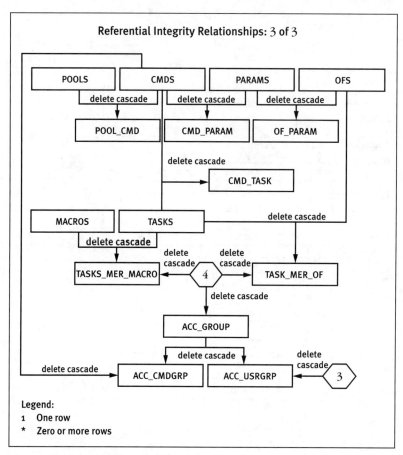

**Figure C.12** *Referential integrity relationships (3 of 3).*

# Appendix D, Net.Commerce Commands

This appendix describes all of the commands that are packaged with the Net.Commerce system.

## AddressAdd Command

The AddressAdd command, shown in Figure D.1, adds a new address entry to the shopper's address book.

> **Note:**
> It is recommended that this command be used in conjunction with SSL (Secure Sockets Layer), to ensure that the shopper's logon password and personal information are encrypted. To do this, both type the command with the HTTPS secure protocol and use Net.Commerce Administrator to assign the command as well as the AddressForm command, which initially displays the address page, to the SSL protocol. For more information, see "Specifying Command Security" on page 481.

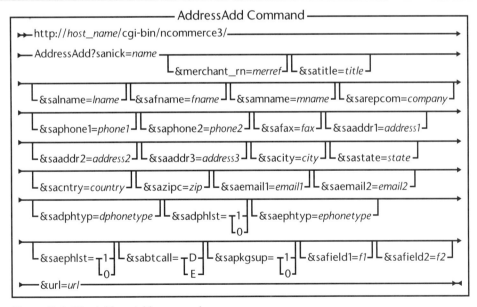

***Figure D.1*** *The AddressAdd command.*

### Parameter Values

host_name
> The fully-qualified name of your Net.Commerce server.

name
> The nickname that represents the new entry.

`merref`
>The reference number of the merchant for which the address entry is to be created.

`title`
>The title of the individual. For example, Mr. or Ms.

`lname`
>The last name of the individual.

`fname`
>The first name of the individual.

`mname`
>The middle name or initial of the individual.

`company`
>The company that the individual represents.

`phone1`
>The main phone number of the individual.

`phone2`
>The additional phone number of the individual.

`fax`
>The facsimile number of the individual.

`address1`
>The first address line of the individual's street address.

`address2`
>The second address line of the individual's street address.

`address3`
>The third address line of the individual's street address.

`city`
>The name of the city in which the individual resides.

`state`
>The name of the state, province, or equivalent in which the individual resides.

`country`
>The name of the country in which the individual resides.

`zip`
>The zip code or equivalent of the individual's address.

`email1`
>The e-mail or URL address 1 of the individual.

`email2`
>The e-mail or URL address 2 of the individual.

`dphonetype`
>The type of daytime phone of the individual.

`sadphlst`
>1
>>An indicator that the daytime phone number is listed.

>0
>>An indicator that the daytime phone number is unlisted.

`ephonetype`
> The type of evening phone of the individual.

`saephlst`
> `1`
>> An indicator that the evening phone is listed.
>
> `0`
>> An indicator that the evening phone is unlisted.

`sabtcall`
> `D`
>> An indicator that daytime is the best time to call.
>
> `E`
>> An indicator that evening is the best time to call.

`sapkgsup`
> `1`
>> An indicator to include package inserts in the order shipped.
>
> `0`
>> An indicator to not include package inserts in the order shipped.

`f1`
> Merchant-customizable field.

`f2`
> Merchant-customizable field.

`url`
> The URL to be called when the command successfully completes.

**Note:**

To determine the data type and maximum length of each parameter value, refer to the SHADDR (Shopper Address Book) table on page 515.

### Behavior

1. Checks the specified nickname.

2. Calls the AUDIT_ADDR_BOOK process task to perform additional parameter checking.

3. Creates an address book record in the SHADDR (Shopper Address Book) table.

4. Upon successful completion, calls the specified URL.

### Exception Conditions

- If the nickname specified already exists in the shopper's address book or a required parameter is invalid, sets the BAD_ADDRESS_BOOK exception task to handle the error.

- If the overridable function assigned to the AUDIT_ADDR_BOOK process task fails, the function sets the AUDIT_ADDR_BOOK_ERR exception task to handle the error.

## Example of the AddressAdd Command

```
AddressAdd?sanick=jeff&saaddr1=7+Elm+St.&sacity=Toronto
&sastate=Ontario&sacntry=Canada&sazipc=M4M+2T1&salname=Lee
&url=/cgi-bin/ExecMacro/success.d2w/report
```

This example adds an entry to the address book of the shopper with the nickname jeff, including all information that is required by the default overridable function, and then calls the ExecMacro command.

# AddressCheck Command

The AddressCheck command, shown in Figure D.2, determines whether or not a permanent address book entry exists for the shopper and displays a page that you specify.

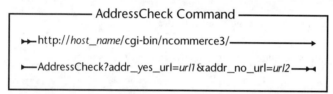

*Figure D.2  The AddressCheck command.*

### Parameter Values

host_name
>    The fully-qualified name of your Net.Commerce server.

url1
>    The URL that is called if a permanent address reference number exists.

url2
>    The URL that is called if a permanent address reference number does not exist.

### Behavior

If at least one permanent address reference number exists for the shopper, calls the URL specified for addr_yes_url. If none exists, calls the URL specified for addr_no_url.

### Exception Conditions

None

# AddressDelete Command

The AddressDelete command, shown in Figure D.3, deletes an entry from the shopper's address book.

*Figure D.3*  *The AddressDelete command.*

## Parameter Value

host_name
> The fully-qualified name of your Net.Commerce server.

adrbkref
> The reference number of the address book entry to be deleted.

url
> The URL to be called when the command successfully completes.

## Behavior

1. Marks the specified address record as temporary, using the T flag.

2. Upon successful completion, calls the specified URL.

**Note:**
If the address record is already marked as temporary, the address reference number specified does not belong to the shopper or the address reference number is invalid, the command still calls the URL specified.

## Exception Conditions

None

# Example of the AddressDelete Command

    AddressDelete?sarfnbr=128&url=/cgi-bin/ExecMacro/success.d2w/report

This example marks the address book entry with reference number 128 as temporary and then calls the ExecMacro command.

# AddressForm Command

The AddressForm command, shown in Figure D.4, displays an address page.

> **Note:**
> It is recommended that this command be used in conjunction with SSL (Secure Sockets Layer), to ensure that the shopper's logon password and personal information are encrypted. To do this, type the command with the HTTPS secure protocol and use Net.Commerce Administrator to assign the command to the SSL protocol.

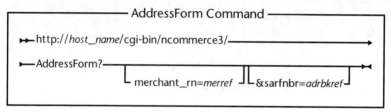

**Figure D.4** *The AddressForm command.*

## Parameter Values

`host_name`
> The fully-qualified name of your Net.Commerce server.

`merref`
> The reference number of the merchant whose address page is to be displayed.

`adrbkref`
> The reference number of the shopper's address book entry.

## Behavior

If the address reference number is specified, sets the ADDR_UPDATE view task to display the shopper's address information; otherwise, sets the ADDR_ADD view task to display a blank address page.

## Exception Conditions

None

# Example of the AddressForm Command

    AddressForm?merchant_rn=4

This example displays a blank address form for the merchant whose reference number is 4.

# AddressUpdate Command

The AddressUpdate command, shown in Figure D.5, updates an entry in the shopper's address book.

> **Note:**
> It is recommended that this command be used in conjunction with SSL (Secure Sockets Layer), to ensure that the shopper's logon password and personal information are encrypted. To do this, both type the command with the HTTPS secure protocol and use Net.Commerce Administrator to assign the command as well as the AddressForm command, which initially displays the address page, to the SSL protocol. For more information, see "Specifying Command Security" on page 481.

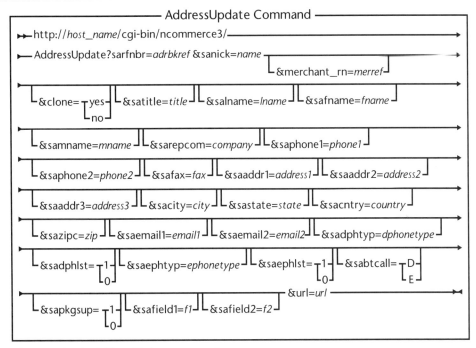

**Figure D.5** *The AddressUpdate command.*

## Parameter Values

host_name
> The fully-qualified name of your Net.Commerce server.

adrbkref
> The reference number of the address book entry to be updated.

name
> The nickname that represents the address book entry to be updated.

merref
> The reference number of the merchant for which the address entry is to be updated.

`clone`

   `yes`

      If a new nickname is specified, an indicator to not mark the old entry as temporary; otherwise, the old entry is marked as temporary.

   `no`

      An indicator to mark the old entry as temporary. This is the default behaviour.

`title`

   The title of the individual. For example, Ms. or Mr.

`lname`

   The last name of the individual.

`fname`

   The first name of the individual.

`mname`

   The middle name or initial of the individual.

`company`

   The company that the individual represents.

`phone1`

   The main phone number of the individual.

`phone2`

   The additional phone number of the individual.

`fax`

   The facsimile number of the individual.

`address1`

   The first address line of the individual's street address.

`address2`

   The second address line of the individual's street address.

`address3`

   The third address line of the individual's street address.

`city`

   The name of the city in which the individual resides

`state`

   The name of the state, province, or equivalent in which the individual resides.

`country`

   The name of the country in which the individual resides.

`zip`

   The zip code or equivalent of the individual's address.

`email1`

   The e-mail or URL address 1 of the individual.

`email2`

   The e-mail or URL address 2 of the individual.

`dphonetype`

   The type of daytime phone of the individual.

sadphlst

   1

      An indicator that the daytime phone number is listed.

   0

      An indicator that the daytime phone number is unlisted.

ephonetype

   The type of evening phone of the individual.

saephlst

   1

      An indicator that the evening phone is listed.

   0

      An indicator that the evening phone is unlisted.

sabtcall

   D

      An indicator that daytime is the best time to call.

   E

      An indicator that evening is the best time to call.

sapkgsup

   1

      An indicator to include package inserts in the order shipped.

   0

      An indicator to not include package inserts in the order shipped.

   f1

   Merchant-customizable field.

   f2

   Merchant-customizable field.

   url

   The URL to be called when the command successfully completes.

**Note:**

To determine the data type and maximum length of each parameter value, refer to the SHADDR (Shopper Address Book) table on page 515.

## *Behavior*

1. Calls the AUDIT_ADDR_BOOK process task to check the address book information parameters.

2. Inserts a new address book entry into the SHADDR table with the specified nickname. The old permanent address book entry for the nickname is marked as temporary, and the new address is marked as permanent. If clone is set to yes, and a new nickname is specified, the old entry remains unchanged, and a new entry with the new nickname is created. If a shopper attempts to update a temporary entry for which there is already a permanent entry, (for example, the shopper bookmarked an address page containing old address information and then tried to change that information again), the command automatically checks the database for the permanent address entry using the specified nickname, and marks that address entry as temporary.

3.    When the command successfully completes, calls the URL specified.

### Exception Conditions

- If a required parameter is an invalid character or the nickname is not unique, sets the BAD_ADRBK_MODIFY exception task.

- If the function assigned to the AUDIT_ADDR_BOOK process task fails, the function sets the AUDIT_ADDR_BOOK_ERR exception task to handle the error.

## Example of the AddressUpdate Command

```
AddressUpdate?sarfnbr=128&sanick=jeff&safname=Jeffery
&url=/cgi-bin/ExecMacro/success.dtw/report
```

This example creates a new permanent address book entry with reference number 128 and nickname jeff so that it includes the first name Jeffery, and then calls the ExecMacro command.

# CategoryDisplay Command

The CategoryDisplay command, shown in Figure D.6, displays a category page based on the shopper group—if any—of which the shopper is a member.  Merchants can assign category templates to specific shopper groups using Net.Commerce Administrator.

**Figure D.6**  *The CategoryDisplay command.*

### Parameter Values

`host_name`
> The fully-qualified name of your Net.Commerce server.

`merref`
> The merchant's reference number that defines the category.

`catref`
> The reference number of the category that you want to display.

### Behavior

Sets the CAT_DSP view task to display the category page that corresponds to the specified merchant reference number and category reference number.  If the shopper does not belong to a shopper group, the category page that is assigned to the shopper group with the "NULL" reference number is displayed.

### Exception Conditions

None

## Example of the CategoryDisplay Command

```
CategoryDisplay?cgmenbr=1&cgrfnbr=16
```

This example displays information about the category with reference number 16 which belongs to the merchant with reference number 1.

# ExecMacro Command

The ExecMacro command, shown in Figure D.7, executes the Net.Data macro that you specify. The macro can be one that is provided by the system or one that you create.

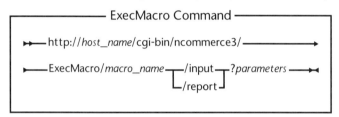

**Figure D.7**  *The ExecMacro command.*

### Parameter Values

host_name
    The fully-qualified name of your Net.Commerce server.

macro_name
    The name of the Net.Data macro.

input
    Starts executing the macro at the %HTML_INPUT section.

report
    Starts executing the macro at the %HTML_REPORT section.

parameters
    Name-value pairs that the macro uses.

### Behavior

Executes the specified Net.Data macro, starting at the specified HTML section.

### Exception Conditions

None.

## Example of the ExecMacro Command

```
ExecMacro/mall_dir.d2w/report
```

This example executes the mall_dir.d2w macro, starting execution at the %HTML_REPORT section.

# ExecTask Command

The ExecTask command, shown in Figure D.8, calls a view or exception task that you specify.

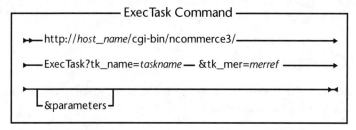

**Figure D.8**  *The ExecTask command.*

## Parameter Values

`host_name`
> The fully-qualified name of your Net.Commerce server.

`taskname`
> The name of the view or exception task that you want to call.

`merref`
> The reference number of the merchant whose macro is to be executed.

`parameters`
> Parameters that the macro uses.

## Behavior

Calls the specified task for the specified merchant.

## Exception Condition

If the task specified does not exist, sets the BAD_EXEC_TASK exception task to handle the error.

## Example of the ExecTask Command

```
ExecTask?tk_name=REG_NEW&tk_mer=112
```

This example calls the REG_NEW view task for the merchant whose reference number is 112.

# ExecUrl Command

The ExecUrl comman, shown in Figure D.9, redirects a URL that is specified as an HTML form input parameter to a URL that you specify, allowing you to pass the flow of control to your specified URL.

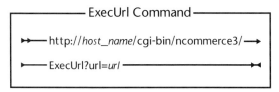

**Figure D.9**  *The ExecUrl command.*

### Parameter Values
host_name
>    The fully-qualified name of your Net.Commerce server.

url
>    The destination URL.

### Exception Condition

None

## Example of the ExecUrl Command

```
ExecUrl?url=ExecTask?tk_name=SHIPTO_LST&tk_mer=112
```

This example redirects to a URL that contains the ExecTask command.

# InterestItemAdd Command

The InterestItemAdd command, shown in Figure D.10, adds a product or item to the shopper's shopping cart.

> **Note:**
> It is recommended that this command be used in conjunction with SSL (Secure Sockets Layer), to ensure that the shopper's logon password and personal information are encrypted. To do this, type the command with the HTTPS secure protocol and use Net.Commerce Administrator to assign the command to the SSL protocol. For more information, see "Specifying Command Security" on page 481.

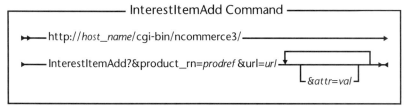

**Figure D.10**  *The InterestItemAdd command.*

## Parameter Values

`host_name`

> The fully-qualified name of your Net.Commerce server.

`prodref`

> The reference number of the product to be added.

`url`

> The URL that is called when the command successfully completes.

`attr`

> Any attribute name that is defined for the product in the PRODATR (Product Attribute) table.

`val`

> The attribute value that corresponds to the product in the PRODATR (Product Attribute) table.

> **Note:**
> To determine the data type and maximum length of each parameter value, refer to the PRODATR (Product Attribute) table on page 531.

## Behavior

1. Calls the RESOLVE_SKU process task to determine the SKU for the product or item.

2. Adds the product or item to the SHOPPINGS (Shopping Cart) table.

3. Calls the GET_BASE_UNIT_PRC process task to determine the price of the product or item.

4. On successful completion, calls the URL specified.

## Exception Conditions

- If the overridable function assigned to the RESOLVE_SKU process task determines that a required product attribute is missing, it sets the BAD_PROD_ATTR exception task to handle the error.

- If it determines that a product with the specified attributes does not exist in the database, it sets the MISSING_PROD_ATTR exception task to handle the error.

- If the overridable function assigned to the GET_BASE_UNIT_PRC process task fails, it sets the GET_BASE_UNIT_PRC_ERR exception task to handle the error.

# Example of the InterestItemAdd Command

```
InterestItemAdd?merchant_rn=1&product_rn=9
&url=/cgi-bin/ncommerce3/InterestItemDisplay&version=deluxe
```

This example adds the deluxe version of the product with reference number 9 sold by the merchant with reference number 1 to the shopper's shopping cart, and then calls the InterestItemDisplay command. The attribute *version* must be a valid attribute for the product as defined in the PRODATR table.

# InterestItemDelete Command

The InterestItemDelete command, shown in Figure D.11, deletes one or more products, items, or both from the shopping cart.

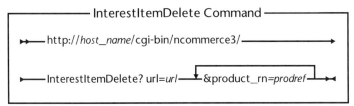

***Figure D.11*** *The InterestItemDelete command.*

## Parameter Values

```
host_name
```
The fully-qualified name of your Net.Commerce server.

```
url
```
The URL that is called when the command successfully completes.

```
prodref
```
The reference number of the product to be deleted.

## Behavior

1.  Deletes the product or item from the SHOPPINGS (Shopping Cart) table. The product is not deleted from any order. If a product or item is not in the shopping cart, or if no product reference number is specified, the command does nothing.

2.  When the command successfully completes, it calls the URL specified.

## Exception Conditions

None

# Example of the InterestItemDelete Command

```
InterestItemDelete?url=/cgi-bin/ncommerce3/
InterestItemDisplay&product_rn=3&product_rn=17
```

This example deletes the products with reference numbers 3 and 17 from the shopper's shopping cart, and then calls the InterestItemDisplay command.

# InterestItemDisplay Command

The InterestItemDisplay command, shown in Figure D.12, displays a list of all the products and items in the shopping cart.

**Note:**
It is recommended that this command be used in conjunction with SSL (Secure Sockets Layer), to ensure that the shopper's logon password and personal information are encrypted. To do this, type the command with the HTTPS secure protocol and use Net.Commerce Administrator to assign the command to the SSL protocol. For more information, see "Specifying Command Security" on page 481.

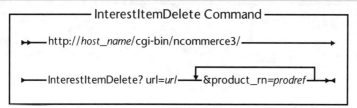

**Figure D.12**   *The InterestItemDisplay command.*

## Parameter Values

host_name
>    The fully-qualified name of your Net.Commerce server.

merref
>    The reference number of the merchant whose products and items are to be displayed.

## Behavior

1.   For each product and item in the shopping cart, sets the GET_BASE_UNIT_PRC process task to obtain the current price, and updates the record in the SHOPPINGS (Shopping Cart) table. Depending on the mall or store policies, if a merchant reference number is specified, this step may be performed only for the products and items being purchased from the specified merchant.

2.   Sets the SHOPCART_DSP view task to display a shopping cart page.

## Exception Condition

If the overridable function assigned to the GET_BASE_UNIT_PRC process task fails, the function sets the GET_BASE_UNIT_PRC_ERR exception task to handle the error.

## Example of the InterestItemDisplay Command

```
InterestItemDisplay
```

This example displays a list of all the products and items in the shopper's shopping cart for the entire mall.

# Logon Command

The Logon command, shown in Figure D.13, logs a registered shopper on to a store or mall.

> **Note:**
> It is recommended that this command be used in conjunction with SSL (Secure Sockets Layer), to ensure that the shopper's logon password is encrypted and that the cookie created cannot be captured by unauthorized individuals. To do this, begin the command with the HTTPs secure protocol and use Net.Commerce Administrator to assign the command to the SSL protocol. For more information, see "Specifying Command Security" on page 481.

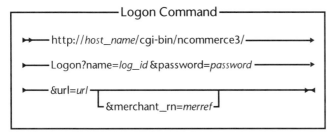

*Figure D.13   The Logon command.*

## Parameter Values

`host_name`
  The fully-qualified name of your Net.Commerce server.

`log_id`
  The registered shopper's logon ID.

`password`
  The registered shopper's password.

`merref`
  The reference number of the merchant whose store the shopper is logging on to.

`url`
  The URL that is called when the command successfully completes.

## Behavior

1.  Ensures that the shopper's logon ID and password are correct.

2.  Creates a digitally signed cookie which is sent back to the browser to identify the user's session. The shopper is now in an authenticated session. The cookie contains the following information:

    * The name. A flag that indicates whether or not the shopper is registered

    * The date and time (timestamp) that the shopper logged on

    * A digital signature

3.  If a URL is specified, the URL is called when the command successfully completes.

### Exception Condition

If the shopper entered an incorrect logon ID or password, or the URL is missing, sets the LOGON_ERR exception task to handle the error.

### Example of the Logon Command

```
Logon?SESSION_ID=henry&pwd=hsmith&url=http://grocery/
home.htm"&merchant_rn=4
```

This example logs the shopper with the logon ID henry the and password hsmith on to the store with reference number 4, and then displays the store home page.

# LogonForm Command

The LogonForm command, shown in Figure D.14, displays a page that allows a registered shopper to log on to the store or mall.

> **Note:**
> It is recommended that this command be used in conjunction with SSL (Secure Sockets Layer), to ensure that the shopper's logon password is encrypted and that the cookie created cannot be captured by unauthorized individuals. To do this, begin the command with the HTTPS secure protocol and use Net.Commerce Administrator to assign the command to the SSL protocol. For more information, see "Specifying Command Security" on page 481.

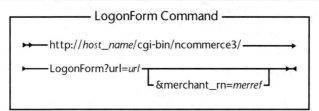

*Figure D.14  The LogonForm command.*

### Parameter Values

`host_name`
> The fully-qualified name of your Net.Commerce server.

`merref`
> The reference number of the merchant whose logon page is to be displayed.

`url`
> The URL that is called after the shopper has successfully logged on.  This is a hidden input parameter that must be included on the logon page so that it can be passed as a parameter to the Logon command when the shopper submits the information.

### Behavior

Sets the LOGON_DSP view task to display a logon page.  If a merchant reference number is specified, the logon page that is assigned to that merchant is displayed.

### Exception Conditions

None.

## Example of the LogonForm Command

```
LogonForm?merchant_rn=2
```

This example displays the logon page belonging to the merchant whose reference number is 2.

# OrderCancel Command

The OrderCancel command, shown in Figure D.15, cancels the specified order by changing its order status to X. This command does not remove the order from the database.

**Figure D.15**  *The OrderCancel command.*

### Parameter Values

```
host_name
```
    The fully-qualified name of your Net.Commerce server.
```
ordref
```
    The reference number of the order to be canceled.
```
url
```
    The URL that is called when the command successfully completes.

### Exception Conditions

If the order_rn specified is invalid or if the order status is not in the pending state, no processing occurs and the URL specified is called.

## Example of the OrderCancel Command

```
OrderCancel?order_rn=1&url=/cgi-bin/ncommerce3/InterestItemDisplay
```

This example cancels the order whose reference number is 1 and displays the shopping cart.

# OrderDisplay Command

The OrderDisplay command, shown in Figure D.16, displays the contents of the specified order. If no order reference number is specified, this command displays the first order that was created that matches the order status and merchant reference number (if any) that is specified.

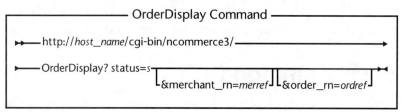

**Figure D.16**  *The OrderDisplay command.*

## Parameter Values

`host_name`
> The fully-qualified name of your Net.Commerce server.

`s`
> The status of the order to be displayed.  This can be any value other than `x`.

`merref`
> The reference number of the merchant for which the shopper's orders are to be listed.  If you omit the `merchant_rn` parameter and do not specify an order reference number, the first order created that matches the specified status for any merchant appears.

`ordref`
> The reference number of the order to be displayed.

## Behavior

If the order status is **P**, this command does the following:

1. Calls the CHECK_INV process task for each product and item to ensure that there is enough quantity in stock.

2. Calls the GET_BASE_SPE_PRC process task for each product and item to obtain its price, and stores the values returned in column STPRICE in table SHIPTO.

3. For each *suborder* (the items in an order that are associated with a single shipping address):

   a) Creates a new suborder entry in the ORDERPAY table.

   b) Calls the GET_SUB_ORD_PROD_TOT process task to find the total price of all the products and items in the suborder.

   c) Calls the GET_SUB_ORD_PROD_TAX_TOT process task to find the total tax payable on the suborder.

   d) Calls the GET_SUB_ORD_SH_TOT process task to find the total shipping charges for the suborder.

e) Updates the ORDERPAY table with the calculated amounts as follows:

- The GET_SUB_ORD_PROD_TOT result is inserted into column OYPRTOT.

- The GET_SUB_ORD_PROD_TAX_TOT results are inserted into the tax columns.

- The GET_SUB_ORD_SH_TOT result is inserted into column OYSHTOT.

4. Calls the GET_ORD_PROD_TOT process task to find the total price of all the products and items in the order.

5. Calls the GET_ORD_PROD_TAX_TOT process task to find the total tax payable on the order.

6. Calls the GET_ORD_SH_TOT process task to find the total shipping charges for the order.

7. Creates or updates the entry in the ORDERS table with the calculated amounts as follows:

- The GET_ORD_PROD_TOT result is inserted into column ORPRTOT

- The GET_ORD_PROD_TAX_TOT result is inserted into column ORTXTOT

- The GET_ORD_SH_TOT result is inserted into column ORSHTOT

8. Creates an order reference number and stores it in the global variable order_rn.

9. Locks the order.

10. Sets the ORD_DSP_PEN view task to display the pending order.

If the status is not **P** (and not **X**, which is considered a command error,) the order is a completed order. No preparation is required for completed orders. The command sets the ORD_DSP_COM view task to display the completed order.

**Note:**
If an order reference number is specified, the order status must match the status that is specified. A mismatch is an exception condition.

## Exception Conditions

- If no orders match the specified parameters, the command sets the ORD_NONE exception task to handle the error.

- If an overridable function assigned to any process task fails, the function sets the exception task of the same name.

# Example of the OrderDisplay Command

```
OrderDisplay?status=P&order_rn=1
```

This example displays the contents of the pending order whose reference number is 1.

# OrderList Command

The OrderList command, shown in Figure D.17, displays a list of the shopper's orders that have been prepared but not placed.

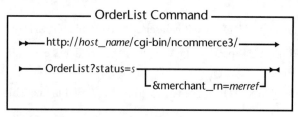

**Figure D.17**  *The OrderList command.*

### Parameter Values

host_name

> The fully-qualified name of your Net.Commerce server.

s

> The status of the orders to be listed.

merref

> The reference number of the merchant for the orders to be listed.  If you omit this parameter, the shopper's orders for all merchants are listed.

### Behavior

- If **status** is P, sets the ORD_LST_PEN view task to display the list of pending orders.  If a merchant reference number is also provided, the list contains only one entry, because a shopper can have only one pending order per merchant.

- If **status** is not P (and not X, which is considered a command error), sets the ORD_LST_COM view task to display the list of orders that match the specified status for a merchant (if specified).

### Exception Conditions

None

## Example of the OrderList Command

```
OrderList?status=P
```

This example lists all the shopper's orders that are in pending status for all merchants.

# OrderProcess Command

The OrderProcess command, shown in Figure D.18, processes an order that has been submitted.

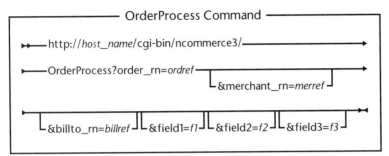

**Figure D.18** *The OrderProcess command.*

## Parameter Values

host_name
> The fully-qualified name of your Net.Commerce server.

ordref
> The reference number of the order to be placed.

merref
> The reference number of the merchant with which the order is to be placed. This value is ignored unless an error occurs before the order is resolved. It is used only then to call the correct merchant's exception handler.

billref
> The reference number of the address to be billed.

f1, f2, and f3
> Merchant-customizable fields.

> **Note:**
> To determine the data type and maximum length of each parameter value, refer to the ORDERS table on page 544.

## Behavior

1. Ensures that the shopper is logged on as a registered shopper.

2. Ensures that the order is pending and locked.

3. Updates the order to reflect the billing address and the merchant-customizable fields.

4. Calls the UPDATE_INV process task to update the inventory for each product and item.

5. Calls the DO_PAYMENT process task to perform additional error checking and process the payment.

6. Calls the EXT_ORD_PROC process task to perform additional processing that is needed for any unique requirements.

7. Sets the ORD_OK view task to indicate acceptance of the order.

### Exception Conditions

- If the order is not locked, sets the ORD_UNLOCKED exception task to handle the error.
- If the shopper typed incorrect data, sets the BAD_ORD_DATA exception task to notify the shopper.
- If the overridable function assigned to the UPDATE_INV process task fails, the function sets the UPDATE_INV_ERR exception task to handle the error.
- If the overridable function assigned to the DO_PAYMENT process task fails, the function sets the DO_PAYMENT_ERR exception task to handle the error.

## Example of the OrderProcess Command

```
OrderProcess?order_rn=3
```

This example processes the placing of order whose reference number is 3.

# OrderUnlock Command

The OrderUnlock command, shown in Figure D.19, both unlocks an order that was previously locked by the OrderDisplay command and calls the URL specified. If the order is not locked, or if the order reference number is not correct, the command only calls the URL.

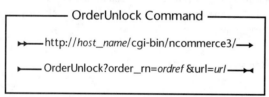

**Figure D.19** *The OrderUnlock command.*

### Parameter Values

host_name
> The fully-qualified name of your Net.Commerce server.

ordref
> The reference number of the order to be unlocked.

url
> The URL that is called when the command successfully completes.

### Exception Conditions

None

## Example of the OrderUnlock Command

```
OrderUnlock?order_rn=2&url=/cgi-bin/ncommerce3/
OrderDisplay?status=P&order_rn=2
```

This example unlocks the order whose reference number is 2 and displays the contents of the order.

# OrderItemDelete Command

The OrderItemDelete command, shown in Figure D.20, deletes the association between a shipping address and an item to be shipped to that address, and calls the URL specified. To delete multiple item/address associations, use multiple parameters.

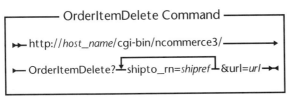

**Figure D.20**  *The OrderItemDelete command.*

### Parameter Values

host_name
> The fully-qualified name of your Net.Commerce server.

shipref
> The shipping reference number that corresponds to the association to be deleted.

url
> The URL that is called when the command successfully completes.

### Exception Conditions

None

## Example of the OrderItemDelete Command

```
OrderItemDelete?addr_rn=2&url=/cgi-bin/ncommerce3/OrderItemList
```

This example deletes the nickname that corresponds to address reference number 2 from the shopper's order, including the corresponding products and items, and then calls the OrderItemList command.

# OrderItemDisplay Command

The OrderItemDisplay command, shown in Figure D.21, lists all items for which the shopper has specified shipping addresses.

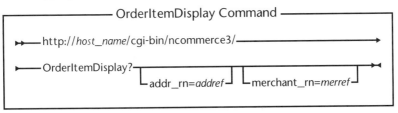

**Figure D.21**  *The OrderItemDisplay command.*

### Parameter Values

host_name
> The fully-qualified name of your Net.Commerce server.

addref
> The reference number of the address book entry for the items to be displayed.

merref
> The reference number of the merchant whose version of the page is to be displayed. If it is omitted (or if the merchant has no version of the page), the mall version is used.

### Behavior

1.  Calls the GET_BASE_SPE_PRC process task for each product and item to obtain their prices.

2.  If `addr_rn` is specified, the command sets the SHIPTO_DSP view task to display a specific shipping details page; otherwise, it sets the SHIPTO_ASSOC view task to display a general shipping details page.

### Exception Conditions

None

## Example of the OrderItemDisplay Command

```
OrderItemDisplay?addr_rn=2
```

This example displays all the products and items that correspond to address reference number 2.

# OrderItemList Command

The OrderItemList command, shown in Figure D.22, displays a list of products and items in the shopping cart, from which shoppers can select the ones they want to order.

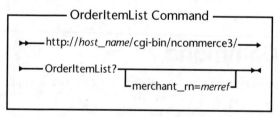

*Figure D.22  The OrderItemList command.*

### Parameter Values

host_name
> The fully-qualified name of your Net.Commerce server.

merref
> The reference number of the merchant whose Web page is to be used to display the products and items. If it is omitted, or if the merchant has no version of the page, the mall version is used.

### Behavior

Sets the SHIPTO_LST view task to list all the shipping addresses that correspond to the shopper's orders.

### Exception Conditions

None

## Example of the OrderItemList Command

```
OrderItemList
```

This example lists all the nicknames that correspond to the shopper's orders.

# OrderItemProcess Command

The OrderItemProcess command, shown in Figure D.23, adds a quantity of products and items to the list of products and items to be shipped to the address corresponding to the address reference number specified.

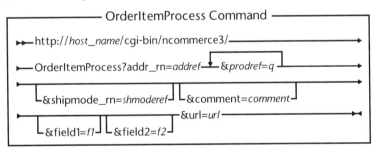

*Figure D.23*  *The OrderItemProcess command.*

### Parameter Values

host_name
: The fully-qualified name of your Net.Commerce server.

addref
: The reference number of the address to which the products and items are to be shipped.

prodref
: The reference number of the product or item to be shipped.

q
: The quantity of the product or item to be shipped.

shmoderef
: The reference number of the shipping mode to be used for the product or item.

comment
: A comment to be included with the order.

f1
: A merchant-reserved integer value.

```
f2
```
A merchant-reserved text value. Accepts up to 256 characters.
```
url
```
The URL that is called when the command successfully completes.

### Behavior

1.  Checks the validity of the address book reference number and updates it, if necessary. The number is incorrect if it refers to an address book entry that the shopper has changed after creating the shipping association.

2.  For each product or item and quantity that is provided, does the following:

    a)  If the quantity is 0, the product or item is ignored.

    b)  If the order is locked, unlocks it.

    c)  Calls the CHECK_INV process task to check the inventory for the product or item.

    d)  Calls the GET_BASE_SPE_PRC process task to get the special price of the product or item.

    e)  Creates the association between the product or item and the shipping address

    f)  Calls the EXT_SHIPTO_PROC process task to perform additional processing to meet any unique requirements.

    g)  Commits the database.

3.  After all products and items are processed, calls the URL that is specified.

### Exception Conditions

*   If the shopper has entered incorrect information, sets the BAD_ST_DATA exception task to handle the error.

*   If the shopper enters a negative value for the quantity of a product or item, sets the BAD_ST_DATA exception task to handle the error.

*   If the overridable function assigned to the CHECK_INV process task fails, the function sets the CHECK_INV_ERR exception task to handle the error.

*   If the overridable function assigned to the GET_BASE_SPE_PRC process task fails, the function sets the GET_BASE_SPE_PRC_ERR exception task to handle the error.

*   If the overridable function assigned to the EXT_SHIPTO_PROC process task fails, the function sets the EXT_SHIPTO_PROC_ERR exception task to handle the error.

## Example of the OrderItemProcess Command

```
OrderItemProcess?addr_rn=2&url=cgi-bin/ncommerce3/OrderItemList&24=3
```

This example adds three units of the product whose reference number is 24 to the shopper's order, indicating that they are to be shipped to the address that corresponds to address reference number 2, and then calls the OrderItemList command.

# OrderItemUpdate Command

The OrderItemUpdate command, shown in Figure D.24, updates or creates a shipping record, depending on whether the shipto_rn or product_rn is passed to it respectively.

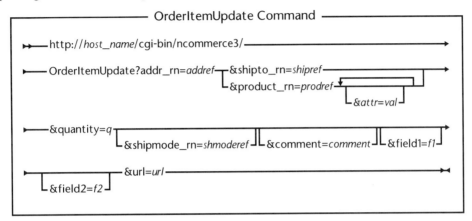

**Figure D.24**  *The OrderItemUpdate command.*

## *Parameter Values*

host_name
> The fully-qualified name of your Net.Commerce server.

addref
> The reference number of the address to which the products and items are to be shipped.

shipref
> The reference number of the shipping association.

prodref
> The reference number of the product whose attributes are to be updated.

attr
> Any distinct attribute that is defined for the product in the table PRODDSTATR.

value
> The value of the distinct attribute.

q
> The quantity of the product or item to be shipped.

shmoderef
> The reference number of the shipping mode to be used for the product or item.

comment
> A comment to be included with the order.

f1
> A merchant-reserved integer value.

f2
> A merchant-reserved text value.  Accepts up to 256 characters.

url
> The URL that is called when the command successfully completes.

### Behavior

- If `shipto_rn` is specified, updates the entry with the specified quantity.

- If `product_rn` is specified, determines the SKU number based on the specified attributes, and creates a shipto entry for the specified quantity of the item.

1. Checks the validity of the address book reference number and updates it if necessary. The number is incorrect if it refers to an address book entry that the shopper has changed after creating the shipping association. Then, for both shipto_rn and product_rn, this command performs the following steps:

2. If the order is locked, unlocks it.

3. Calls the CHECK_INV process task to ensure there is enough inventory.

4. Calls the GET_BASE_SPE_PRC process task to get the special price associated with the product or item.

5. Calls the RESOLVE_SKU process task to determine the SKU for each product or item.

6. Updates the comment, field1, and field2 fields.

7. Calls the EXT_SHIPTO_UPD process task to perform additional processing to meet any unique requirements.

8. On successful completion, calls the URL specified.

### Exception Conditions

- If the overridable function assigned to the RESOLVE_SKU process task determines that a required product attribute is missing, it sets the BAD_PROD_ATTR exception task to handle the error.

- If it determines that a product with the specified attributes does not exist in the database, it sets the MISSING_PROD_ATTR exception task to handle the error.

- If the quantity specified is not numeric or a positive value or errors are detected in the values `comment`, `f1`, or `f2`, sets the BAD_ST_DATA exception task to handle the error.

- If the overridable function assigned to the CHECK_INV process task fails, it sets the CHECK_INV_ERR exception task to handle the error.

- If the overridable function assigned to the GET_BASE_SPE_PRC process task fails, it sets the GET_BASE_SPE_PRC_ERR exception task to handle the error.

- If the overridable function assigned to the EXT_SHIPTO_UPD process task fails, it sets the EXT_SHIPTO_PROC_ERR exception task to handle the error.

## Example of the OrderItemUpdate Command

```
OrderItemUpdate?addr_rn=2&product_rn=18&monogram=CJK
&quantity=1&shipmode_rn=4&url=cgi-bin/ncommerce3/OrderItemList
```

This example updates the product whose reference number is 18 and which is destined for the address with reference number 2, so that the following is true:

- It includes the monogram "CJK";

- One unit of the item is shipped;

- The mode of shipping has reference number 4;

and when the command completes, calls the OrderItemList command.

# OrderShippingUpdate Command

The OrderShippingUpdate command, shown in Figure D.25, updates the shipping address or shipping mode information, or both, of all the order items records for a specified order.

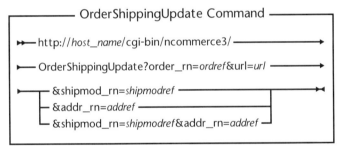

**Figure D.25** *The OrderShippingUpdate command.*

### Parameter Values

ordref

    The reference number of the order containing the order items whose shipping address and shipping mode information are to be updated.

addref

    The reference number of the address to which all the order items records are being shipped to.

shipmodref

    The reference number of the shipping mode to be used for all the order item records.

url

    The URL that is called when the command successfully completes.

### Behavior

1. Checks the validity of the address book reference number and updates it, if necessary. The number is incorrect if it refers to an address book entry that the shopper changes after creating the shipping association.

2. Checks the validity of the address book reference number and updates it for all pending order items in the order.

3.  For each order item record in the order, does one of the following:

    - If only `shipmod_rn` is specified, updates the shipping mode reference number with the specified value.

    - If only `addr_rn` is specified, updates the address reference number with the specified value.

    - If both are supplied, then updates the shipping mode reference number for all order items being shipped to the given address reference number.

4.  Unlocks the order.

5.  On successful completion, calls the URL specified.

### Exception Conditions

None

### Example of the OrderShippingUpdate Command

```
OrderShippingUpdate?order_rn=45&addr_rn=113
&url=cgi-bin/ncommerce3/OrderItemList
```

This example updates all the order item records for the order with the reference number of 45 with address information that corresponds to the address reference number 113. When the command successfully completes, it calls the OrderItemList command.

# ProductDisplay Command

The ProductDisplay command, shown in Figure D.26, displays a product or item page based on the shopper group—if any—of which the shopper is a member. Merchants can assign product templates to specific shopper groups using the Net.Commerce Administrator.

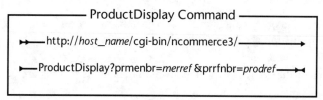

**Figure D.26**  *The ProductDisplay command.*

### Parameter Values

`host_name`
  The fully-qualified name of your Net.Commerce server.

`merref`
  The reference number of the merchant that sells the product or item.

`prodref`
  The reference number of the product or item that you want to display.

### Behavior

Sets the PROD_DSP view task to display the product or item page that corresponds to the merchant reference number and product reference number specified. If the shopper does not belong to a shopper group, the category page that is assigned to the shopper group with the "NULL" reference number is displayed.

### Exception Conditions

None

## Example of the ProductDisplay Command

```
ProductDisplay?prmenbr=1&prrfnbr=123
```

This example displays information about the product with reference number 123 that belongs to the merchant with reference number 1.

# RegisterForm Command

The RegisterForm command, shown in Figure D.27, displays a registration page.

> **Note:**
> It is recommended that this command be used in conjunction with SSL (Secure Sockets Layer), to ensure that the shopper's logon password and personal information are encrypted. To do this, type the command with the HTTPS secure protocol and use Net.Commerce Administrator to assign the command to the SSL protocol. For more information, see "Specifying Command Security" on page 481.

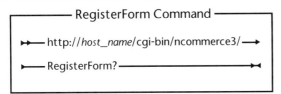

**Figure D.27** *The RegisterForm command.*

### Parameter Values

```
host_name
```
    The fully-qualified name of your Net.Commerce server.

### Behavior

If the shopper is registered, sets the REG_UPDATE view task to display their registration page. If the shopper is not registered, sets the REG_NEW view task to display a blank registration page.

### Exception Conditions

None

## Example of the RegisterForm Command

```
RegisterForm?
```

This example displays the mall version of the registration form.

# RegisterUpdate Command

The RegisterUpdate command, shown in Figure D.28, modifies the shopper's registration record.

> **Note:**
> It is recommended that this command be used in conjunction with SSL (Secure Sockets Layer), to ensure that the shopper's logon password and personal information are encrypted. To do this, type the command with the HTTPS secure protocol and use Net.Commerce Administrator to assign the command as well as the RegisterForm command, which initially displays the shopper's registration information, to the SSL protocol. For more information, see "Specifying Command Security" on page 481.

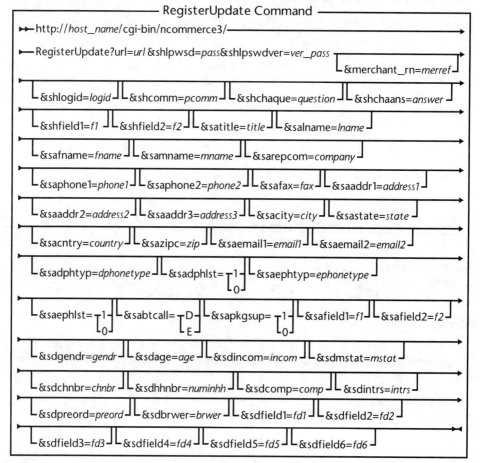

*Figure D.28* *The RegisterUpdate command.*

## Parameter Values

`host_name`
> The fully-qualified name of your Net.Commerce server.

`url`
> The URL that is called when the command successfully completes.

`pass`
> The shopper's password.

`ver_pass`
> The verification password.

`merref`
> The reference number of the merchant for which the registration record is to be updated.

`logid`
> The logon ID of the shopper.

`pcomm`
> The preferred method of communication for the shopper.

`question`
> The challenge question used by the administrator to verbally confirm the shopper's identity.

`answer`
> Answer to the challenge question which the shopper has to provide when confirming identity.

`f1`
> Merchant-customizable field.

`f2`
> Merchant-customizable field.

`title`
> The title of the shopper. For example, Mr. or Ms.

`lname`
> The last name of the shopper.

`fname`
> The first name of the shopper.

`mname`
> The middle name or initial of the shopper.

`company`
> The company that the shopper represents.

`phone1`
> The main phone number of the shopper.

`phone2`
> The additional phone number of the shopper.

`fax`
> The facsimile number of the shopper.

`address1`
> The first address line of the shopper's street address.

`address2`

The second address line of the shopper's street address.

`address3`

The third address line of the shopper's street address.

`city`

The name of the city in which the shopper resides.

`state`

The name of the state, province, or equivalent in which the shopper resides.

`country`

The name of the country in which the shopper resides.

`zip`

The zip code or equivalent of the shopper's address.

`email1`

The e-mail or URL address 1 of the shopper.

`email2`

The e-mail or URL address 2 of the shopper.

`dphonetype`

The type of daytime phone of the shopper.

`sadphlst`

  1

An indicator that the daytime phone number is listed.

  0

An indicator that the daytime phone number is unlisted.

`ephonetype`

The type of evening phone of the individual.

`saephlst`

  1

An indicator that the evening phone is listed.

  0

An indicator that the evening phone is unlisted.

`sabtcall`

  D

An indicator that daytime is the best time to call.

  E

An indicator that evening is the best time to call.

`sapkgsup`

  1

An indicator to include package inserts in the order shipped.

  0

An indicator to not include package inserts in the order shipped.

  `f1`

Merchant-customizable field.

  `f2`

Merchant-customizable field.

gendr
>   The gender of the shopper.

age
>   The age of the shopper.

incom
>   The income of the shopper.

mstat
>   The marital status of the shopper.

chnbr
>   The number of children the shopper has.

numinhh
>   Number of members in the shopper's household.

comp
>   The company for which the shopper works.

intrs
>   The shopper's main interests and hobbies.

preord
>   Indicator of whether or not the shopper has previously placed an order. Supplied by
>   the shopper.

brwer
>   Reserved for IBM use.

fd1
>   Merchant-customizable field.

fd2
>   Merchant-customizable field.

fd3
>   Merchant-customizable field.

fd4
>   Merchant-customizable field.

fd5
>   Merchant-customizable field.

fd6
>   Merchant-customizable field.

**Note:**

To determine the data type and maximum length of each parameter value, refer to the SHADDR table on page 515 (for parameters that begin with sa) and to the SHOPPER table on page 512 (for parameters that begin with sh).

## *Behavior*

1.  Checks the required parameters.

2.  Calls the AUDIT_REG process task to check the shopper parameters (the parameters that begin with sh).

3. Modifies the registration record. The shopper's old address is marked as temporary, and the new address is marked as permanent. If a shopper attempts to update a temporary entry for which there is already a permanent entry, (for example, the shopper bookmarked an registration page containing old address information and then tried to change that information again), the command automatically checks the database for the permanent address entry using the specified nickname, and marks that address entry as temporary.

4. When the command successfully completes, calls the URL specified.

5. Updates the cookie which is sent back to the browser for identifying the user's session. The cookie contains the following information:

   - The SESSION_ID

   - A flag that indicates whether or not the shopper is registered

   - The date and time (timestamp) that the shopper registered

   - A digital signature

6. On successful completion, calls the URL specified.

### Exception Conditions

- If a required parameter is missing or incorrect, sets the BAD_REG_MODIFY exception task to handle the error.

- If the overridable function assigned to the AUDIT_REG process task fails, the function sets the AUDIT_REG_ERR exception task to handle the error.

## Example of the RegisterUpdate Command

```
RegisterUpdate?&url=/cgi-bin/ncommerce/InterestItemDisplay
&shlpswd=butter&shlpswdver=butter&salname=Kohl
&saaddr1=255+Consumers+Road
&sacity=North+York&sastate+Ontario&sacntry=Canada&sdmstat=M
```

This example changes the marital status of the shopper, including all parameters required by the default

# RegisterNew Command

The RegisterNew command, shown in Figure D.29, creates a registration record for the shopper.

**Note:**
It is recommended that this command be used in conjunction with SSL (Secure Sockets Layer), to ensure that the shopper's logon password and personal information are encrypted. To do this, both type the command with the HTTPS secure protocol and use Net.Commerce Administrator to assign the command as well as the RegisterForm command, which initially displays the registration page, to the SSL protocol. For more information, see "Specifying Command Security" on page 481.

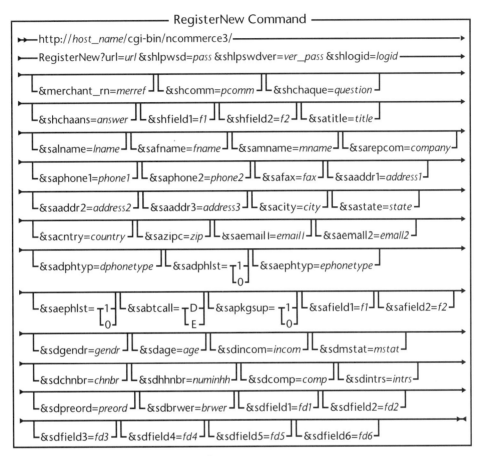

**Figure D.29** *The RegisterNew command.*

## Parameter Values

`host_name`

The fully-qualified name of your Net.Commerce server.

`url`

The URL that is called when the command successfully completes.

`pass`

The shopper's password.

`ver_pass`

The verification password.

`logid`

The logon ID of the shopper.

`merref`

The reference number of the merchant for which the registration record is to be created.

`pcomm`

The preferred method of communication for the shopper.

`question`
> Challenge question for verbal confirmation of the shopper's identity.

`answer`
> Answer to the challenge question.

`f1`
> Merchant-customizable field.

`f2`
> Merchant-customizable field.

`title`
> The title of the shopper.

`saadrflg`
> `T`
>> A flag to indicate that the new entry is temporary.
>
> `P`
>> A flag to indicate that the new entry is permanent.

`lname`
> The last name of the shopper.

`fname`
> The first name of the shopper.

`mname`
> The middle name or initial of the shopper.

`company`
> The company that the shopper represents.

`phone1`
> The main phone number of the shopper.

`phone2`
> The additional phone number of the shopper.

`fax`
> The facsimile number of the shopper.

`address1`
> The first address line of the shopper's street address.

`address2`
> The second address line of the shopper's street address.

`address3`
> The third address line of the shopper's street address.

`city`
> The name of the city in which the shopper resides.

`state`
> The name of the state, province, or equivalent in which the shopper resides.

`country`
> The name of the country in which the shopper resides.

`zip`
> The zip code or equivalent of the shopper's address.

email1
> The e-mail or URL address 1 of the shopper.

email2
> The e-mail or URL address 2 of the shopper.

dphonetype
> The type of daytime phone of the shopper.

sadphlst
> 1
>> An indicator that the daytime phone number is listed.
>
> 0
>> An indicator that the daytime phone number is unlisted.
>
> ephonetype
>> The type of evening phone of the individual.

saephlst
> 1
>> An indicator that the evening phone is listed.
>
> 0
>> An indicator that the evening phone is unlisted.

sabtcall
> D
>> An indicator that daytime is the best time to call.
>
> E
>> An indicator that evening is the best time to call.

sapkgsup
> 1
>> An indicator to include package inserts in the order shipped.
>
> 0
>> An indicator to not include package inserts in the order shipped.

f1
> Merchant-customizable field.

f2
> Merchant-customizable field.

gendr
> The gender of the shopper.

age
> The age of the shopper.

incom
> The income of the shopper.

mstat
> The marital status of the shopper.

chnbr
> The number of children the shopper has.

numinhh
> The number of members in the shopper's household.

`comp`
> The company for which the shopper works.

`intrs`
> The shopper's main interests and hobbies.

`preord`
> Indicator of whether or not the shopper has previously placed an order. Supplied by the shopper.

`brwer`
> Reserved for IBM use.

`fd1`
> Merchant-customizable field.

`fd2`
> Merchant-customizable field.

`fd3`
> Merchant-customizable field.

`fd4`
> Merchant-customizable field.

`fd5`
> Merchant-customizable field.

`fd6`
> Merchant-customizable field.

**Note:**

To determine the data type and maximum length of each parameter value, refer to the SHADDR table on page 515 (for parameters that begin with sa) and to the SHOPPER table on page 512 (for parameters that begin with sh).

### Behavior

1. Checks the required registration information parameters.

2. Calls the AUDIT_REG process task to check the shopper parameters (the parameters that begin with sh).

3. Updates the registration record.

4. Logs the shopper on by creating a digitally signed cookie which is sent back to the browser for identifying the user's session. The shopper is now in an authenticated session. The cookie contains the following information:

   - The SESSION_ID

   - A flag that indicates whether or not the shopper is registered

   - The date and time (timestamp) that the shopper registered

   - A digital signature

5. On successful completion, calls the URL specified.

### Exception Conditions

- If a required parameter is missing or incorrect, sets the BAD_REG exception task to handle the error.

- If the overridable function assigned to the AUDIT_REG process task fails, the function sets the AUDIT_REG_ERR exception task to handle the error.

## Example of the RegisterNew Command

```
RegisterNew?&url=/cgi-bin/ncommerce/
;InterestItemDisplay&shlogid=jennyk&shlpswd=butter
&shlpswdver=butter&salname=Kohl&saaddr1=255+Consumers+
Road&sacity=North+York&sastate=Ontario&sacntry=Canada
```

This example creates a registration record for the shopper, including all parameters required by the default overridable function, and then calls the InterestItemDisplay command.

# Appendix E, Net.Commerce Tasks

This appendix describes all of the tasks that are packaged with the Net.Commerce system.

## AUDIT_ADDR_BOOK_ERR Exception Task

### Designed to be called by:
The function assigned to the AUDIT_ADDR_BOOK process task.

### Explicit Input Parameters:

*Table E.1* *Explicit input parameters for the AUDIT_ADDR_BOOK_ERR exception task.*

| Variable Name | Variable Type | Description |
| --- | --- | --- |
| MACRO_NVP | NVPHash* | A collection of name-value pairs that supercede any equivalent name-value pairs found in the http request. For this task, the collection is empty. |
| ERROR_CODE | String* | A string identifying the reason for the exception condition. See below for descriptions of the exception conditions. |

### Exception Conditions:

*Table E.2* *Exception conditions for the AUDIT_ADDR_BOOK_ERR exception task.*

| Error Code | Description | Additional Input Parameters | | |
| --- | --- | --- | --- | --- |
| | | String | Value | Description |
| 190 | A required parameter was not provided. | FIELD | String* | Name of the invalid field. |

### Expected Behavior of Overridable Function:
Generate a page that informs the shopper of the error.

### Expected Return Values:
None

### Default Overridable Function:
TaskDisplay_1.0 (IBM,NC)

# AUDIT_REG_ERR Exception Task

### Designed to be called by:

The function assigned to the AUDIT_REG process task.

### Explicit Input Parameters:

*Table E.3  Explicit input parameters for the AUDIT_REG_ERR exception task.*

| Variable Name | Variable Type | Description |
|---|---|---|
| MACRO_NVP | NVPHash* | A collection of name-value pairs that supercede any equivalent name-value pairs found in the http request. For this task, the collection is empty. |
| ERROR_CODE | String* | A string identifying the reason for the exception condition. See below for descriptions of the exception conditions. |

### Exception Conditions:

*Table E.4  Exception conditions for the AUDIT_REG_ERR exception task.*

| Error Code | Description | Additional Input Parameters | | |
| | | String | Value | Description |
|---|---|---|---|---|
| 190 | A required parameter was not provided. | FIELD | String* | Name of the invalid field. |

### Expected Behavior of Overridable Function:

Generate a page that informs the shopper of the error.

### Expected Return Values:

None

### Default Overridable Function:

TaskDisplay_1.0 (IBM,NC)

# BAD_ADDRESS_BOOK Exception Task

### Calling Command:

AddressAdd

## Explicit Input Parameters:

**Table E.5** *Explicit input parameters for the BAD_ADDRESS_BOOK exception task.*

| Variable Name | Variable Type | Description |
|---|---|---|
| MACRO_NVP | NVPHash* | A collection of name-value pairs that supercede any equivalent name-value pairs found in the http request. For this task, the collection includes the parameters shown below. |
| ERROR_CODE | String* | A string identifying the reason for the exception condition. See below for descriptions of the exception conditions. |

## MACRO_NVP Parameters:

**Table E.6** *MACRO_NVP parameters for the BAD_ADDRESS_BOOK exception task.*

| Variable Name | Variable Type | Description |
|---|---|---|
| ADDRESS_REF_NUM | String | The updated address reference number. If the address reference number passed into the command refers to a temporary address book entry, and a permanent address book entry exists for the same nickname, this string is set to the reference number of the permanent address book entry. |

## Exception Conditions:

**Table E.7** *Exception conditions for the BAD_ADDRESS_BOOK exception task.*

| Error Code | Description | Additional Input Parameters | | |
| | | String | Value | Description |
|---|---|---|---|---|
| 160 | A value contains an invalid character. | FIELD | String* | Name of the invalid field. |
| 210 | The nickname has already been used. | FIELD | String* | Name of the invalid field. |

## Expected Behavior of Overridable Function:

Generate a page that informs the shopper of the error.

## Expected Return Values:

None

## Default Overridable Function:

TaskDisplay_1.0 (IBM,NC)

# BAD_ADRBK_MODIFY Exception Task

### Calling Command:

AddressUpdate

### Explicit Input Parameters:

*Table E.8*  *Explicit input parameters for the BAD_ADRBK_MODIFY exception task.*

| Variable Name | Variable Type | Description |
|---|---|---|
| MACRO_NVP | NVPHash* | A collection of name-value pairs that supercede any equivalent name-value pairs found in the http request. For this task, the collection includes the parameters shown below. |
| ERROR_CODE | String* | A string identifying the reason for the exception condition. See below for descriptions of the exception conditions. |

### MACRO_NVP Parameters:

*Table E.9*  *MACRO_NVP parameters for the BAD_ADRBK_MODIFY exception task.*

| Variable Name | Variable Type | Description |
|---|---|---|
| ADDRESS_REF_NUM | String | The updated address reference number. If the address reference number passed into the command refers to a temporary address book entry, and a permanent address book entry exists for the same nickname, this string is set to the reference number of the permanent address book entry. |

### Exception Conditions:

*Table E.10*  *Exception conditions for the BAD_ADRBK_MODIFY exception task.*

| Error Code | Description | Additional Input Parameters | | |
| | | String | Value | Description |
|---|---|---|---|---|
| 160 | A value contains an invalid character. | FIELD | String* | Name of the invalid field. |
| 210 | The nickname has already been used. | FIELD | String* | Name of the invalid field. |

### Expected Behavior of Overridable Function:

Generate a page that informs the shopper of the error.

**Expected Return Values:**

None

**Default Overridable Function:**

TaskDisplay_1.0 (IBM,NC)

# BAD_ORD_DATA Exception Task

**Calling Command:**

OrderProcess

**Explicit Input Parameters:**

*Table E.11  Explicit input parameters for the BAD_ORD_DATA exception task.*

| Variable Name | Variable Type | Description |
|---|---|---|
| MACRO_NVP | NVPHash* | A collection of name-value pairs that supercede any equivalent name-value pairs found in the http request. For this task, the collection is empty. |
| ERROR_CODE | String* | A string identifying the reason for the exception condition. See below for descriptions of the exception conditions. |

**Exception Conditions:**

*Table E.12  Exception conditions for the BAD_ORD_DATA exception task.*

| Error Code | Description | Additional Input Parameters | | |
| | | String | Value | Description |
|---|---|---|---|---|
| 220 | A numeric field contains a non-numeric character, or a number is out of range. | FIELD | String* | Name of the invalid field. |

**Expected Behavior of Overridable Function:**

Generate a page that informs the shopper of the error.

**Expected Return Values:**

None

**Default Overridable Function:**

TaskDisplay_1.0 (IBM,NC)

# BAD_PROD_ATTR Exception Task

### *Designed to be called by:*

The function assigned to the RESOLVE_SKU process task.

### *Explicit Input Parameters:*

**Table E.13** *Explicit input parameters for the BAD_PROD_ATTR exception task.*

| Variable Name | Variable Type | Description |
|---|---|---|
| MACRO_NVP | NVPHash* | A collection of name-value pairs that supercede any equivalent name-value pairs found in the http request. For this task, the collection is empty. |
| ERROR_CODE | String* | A string identifying the reason for the exception condition. See below for descriptions of the exception conditions. |

### *Exception Conditions:*

**Table E.14** *Exception conditions for the BAD_PROD_ATTR exception task.*

| Error Code | Description | Additional Input Parameters | | |
|---|---|---|---|---|
| | | String | Value | Description |
| 100 | A required product attribute is missing. | N/A | N/A | N/A |

### *Expected Behavior of Overridable Function:*

Generate a page that informs the shopper of the error.

### *Expected Return Values:*

None

### *Default Overridable Function:*

TaskDisplay_1.0 (IBM,NC)

# BAD_REG Exception Task

## Calling Command:

RegisterNew

## Explicit Input Parameters:

**Table E.15** *Explicit input parameters for the BAD_REG exception task.*

| Variable Name | Variable Type | Description |
|---|---|---|
| MACRO_NVP | NVPHash* | A collection of name-value pairs that supercede any equivalent name-value pairs found in the http request. For this task, the collection is empty. |
| ERROR_CODE | String* | A string identifying the reason for the exception condition. See below for descriptions of the exception conditions. |

## Exception Conditions:

**Table E.16** *Exception conditions for the BAD_REG exception task.*

| Error Code | Description | Additional Input Parameters | | |
|---|---|---|---|---|
| | | String | Value | Description |
| 4 | An error occurred while saving the password. | FIELD | String* | Name of the invalid field. |
| 160 | A parameter value contains an invalid character. | FIELD | String* | Name of the invalid field. |
| 170 | The verification password does not match the initial password. | FIELD | String* | Name of the invalid field. |
| 180 | The user ID already exists. | FIELD | String* | Name of the invalid field. |
| 190 | A parameter that is required by the system is missing. | FIELD | String* | Name of the invalid field. |
| 200 | The shopper is already registered. | FIELD | String* | Name of the invalid field. |
| 210 | The user ID has already been used as an address book nickname. | FIELD | String* | Name of the invalid field. |
| 270 | The password is not alphanumeric. | FIELD | String* | Name of the invalid field. |
| 280 | The user ID is not alphanumeric. | FIELD | String* | Name of the invalid field. |

**Expected Behavior of Overridable Function:**

Generate a page that informs the shopper of the error.

**Expected Return Values:**

None

**Default Overridable Function:**

TaskDisplay_1.0 (IBM,NC)

# BAD_REG_MODIFY Exception Task

**Calling Command:**

RegisterUpdate

**Explicit Input Parameters:**

*Table E.17  Explicit input parameters for the BAD_REG_MODIFY exception task.*

| Variable Name | Variable Type | Description |
|---|---|---|
| MACRO_NVP | NVPHash* | A collection of name-value pairs that supercede any equivalent name-value pairs found in the http request. For this task, the collection is empty. |
| ERROR_CODE | String* | A string identifying the reason for the exception condition. See below for descriptions of the exception conditions. |

**Exception Conditions:**

*Table E.18  Exception conditions for the BAD_REG_MODIFY exception task.*

| Error Code | Description | Additional Input Parameters | | |
|---|---|---|---|---|
| | | String | Value | Description |
| 4 | An error occurred while saving the password. | FIELD | String* | Name of the invalid field. |
| 160 | A parameter value contains an invalid character. | FIELD | String* | Name of the invalid field. |
| 170 | The verification password does not match the initial password. | FIELD | String* | Name of the invalid field. |
| 190 | A parameter that is required by the system is missing. | FIELD | String* | Name of the invalid field. |
| 210 | The user ID has already been used as an address book nickname. | FIELD | String* | Name of the invalid field. |

*Continued on next page*

*Table E.18 Continued.*

| Error Code | Description | Additional Input Parameters | | |
| | | String | Value | Description |
| --- | --- | --- | --- | --- |
| 270 | The password is not alphanumeric. | FIELD | String* | Name of the invalid field. |
| 280 | The user ID is not alphanumeric. | FIELD | String* | Name of the invalid field. |

### Expected Behavior of Overridable Function:

Generate a page that informs the shopper of the error.

### Expected Return Values:

None

### Default Overridable Function:

TaskDisplay_1.0 (IBM,NC)

# BAD_ST_DATA Exception Task

### Calling Commands:

OrderItemUpdate, OrderItemProcess

### Explicit Input Parameters:

*Table E.19  Explicit input parameters for the BAD_ST_DATA exception task.*

| Variable Name | Variable Type | Description |
| --- | --- | --- |
| MACRO_NVP | NVPHash* | A collection of name-value pairs that supercede any equivalent name-value pairs found in the http request. For this task, the collection includes the parameters shown below. |
| ERROR_CODE | String* | A string identifying the reason for the exception condition. See below for descriptions of the exception conditions. |

### MACRO_NVP Parameters:

**Table E.20** *MACRO_NVP parameters for the BAD_ST_DATA exception task.*

| Variable Name | Variable Type | Description |
|---|---|---|
| ADDRESS_REF_NUM | String* | The updated address reference number. If the address reference number passed into the command refers to a temporary address book entry, and a permanent address book entry exists for the same nickname, this string is set to the reference number of the permanent address book entry. |

### Exception Conditions:

**Table E.21** *Exception conditions for the BAD_ST_DATA exception task.*

| Error Code | Description | Additional Input Parameters | | |
|---|---|---|---|---|
| | | String | Value | Description |
| 220 | A numeric field contains a non-numeric character, or a number is out of range. | FIELD | String* | Name of the invalid field. |

### Expected Behavior of Overridable Function:
Generate a page that informs the shopper of the error.

### Expected Return Values:
None

### Default Overridable Function:
TaskDisplay_1.0 (IBM,NC)

# CHECK_INV_ERR Exception Task

### Designed to be called by:
The function assigned to the CHECK_INV process task.

### Explicit Input Parameters:

**Table E.22** *Explicit input parameters for the CHECK_INV_ERR exception task.*

| Variable Name | Variable Type | Description |
|---|---|---|
| MACRO_NVP | NVPHash* | A collection of name-value pairs that supercede any equivalent name-value pairs found in the http request. For this task, the collection is empty. |
| ERROR_CODE | String* | A string identifying the reason for the exception condition. See below for descriptions of the exception conditions. |

## Exception Conditions:

*Table E.23* *Exception conditions for the CHECK_INV_ERR exception task.*

| Error Code | Description | Additional Input Parameters | | |
| --- | --- | --- | --- | --- |
| | | String | Value | Description |
| 2 | An SQL statement returned more than one row. | FIELD | String* | Name of the invalid field. |
| 3 | A system error occurred. No additional parameters are passed in. | N/A | N/A | N/A |
| 1001 | Insufficient inventory. | PRODUCT _REF_NUM | String* | Product reference number. |
| | | QUANTITY | String* | Quantity requested. |

## Expected Behavior of Overridable Function:

Generate a page that informs the shopper of the error.

## Expected Return Values:

None

## Default Overridable Function:

TaskDisplay_1.0 (IBM,NC)

# DO_PAYMENT_ERR Exception Task

## Designed to be called by:

The function assigned to the DO_PAYMENT process task.

## Explicit Input Parameters:

*Table E.24* *Explicit input parameters for the DO_PAYMENT_ERR exception task.*

| Variable Name | Variable Type | Description |
| --- | --- | --- |
| MACRO_NVP | NVPHash* | A collection of name-value pairs that supercede any equivalent name-value pairs found in the http request. For this task, the collection is empty. |
| ERROR_CODE | String* | A string identifying the reason for the exception condition. See below for descriptions of the exception conditions. |

## Exception Conditions:

*Table E.25* *Exception conditions for the DO_PAYMENT_ERR exception task.*

| Error Code | Description | Additional Input Parameters | | |
| --- | --- | --- | --- | --- |
| | | String | Value | Description |
| 1 | An SQL statement did not complete successfully. | N/A | N/A | N/A |
| 2 | An SQL statement returned more than one row. | N/A | N/A | N/A |
| 190 | A parameter that is required by the system is missing. | FIELD | String* | Name of the missing parameter. |
| 1005 | The credit card number is not valid. | N/A | N/A | N/A |
| 1006 | The credit card expiration date has passed. | N/A | N/A | N/A |
| 1007 | An error occurred creating a row in table ORDPAYMTHD. | ORDER | String* | Order reference number. |

## Expected Behavior of Overridable Function:

Generate a page that informs the shopper of the error.

## Expected Return Values:

None

## Default Overridable Function:

TaskDisplay_1.0 (IBM,NC)

# EXT_ORD_PROC_ERR Exception Task

## Designed to be called by:

The function assigned to the EXT_ORD_PROC process task.

## Explicit Input Parameters:

*Table E.26* *Explicit input parameters for the EXT_ORD_PROC_ERR exception task.*

| Variable Name | Variable Type | Description |
| --- | --- | --- |
| MACRO_NVP | NVPHash* | A collection of name-value pairs that supercede any equivalent name-value pairs found in the http request. For this task, the collection is empty. |

### Expected Behavior of Overridable Function:

Generate a page that informs the shopper of the error.

### Expected Return Values:

None

### Default Overridable Function:

TaskDisplay_1.0 (IBM,NC)

# EXT_SHIPTO_PROC_ERR Exception Task

### Designed to be called by:

The function assigned to the EXT_SHIPTO_PROC process task.

### Explicit Input Parameters:

*Table E.27  Explicit input parameters for the EXT_SHIPTO_PROC_ERR exception task.*

| Variable Name | Variable Type | Description |
| --- | --- | --- |
| MACRO_NVP | NVPHash* | A collection of name-value pairs that supercede any equivalent name-value pairs found in the http request. For this task, the collection includes the parameters shown below. |

### MACRO_NVP Parameters:

*Table E.28  MACRO_NVP parameters for the EXT_SHIPTO_PROC_ERR exception task.*

| Variable Name | Variable Type | Description |
| --- | --- | --- |
| ADDRESS_REF_NUM | String* | The updated address reference number. If the address reference number passed into the command refers to a temporary address book entry, and a permanent address book entry exists for the same nickname, this string is set to the reference number of the permanent address book entry. |

### Expected Behavior of Overridable Function:

Generate a page that informs the shopper of the error.

### Expected Return Values:

None

### Default Overridable Function:

TaskDisplay_1.0 (IBM,NC)

# EXT_SHIPTO_UPD_ERR Exception Task

### Designed to be called by:

The function assigned to the EXT_SHIPTO_UPD process task.

### Explicit Input Parameters:

*Table E.29  Explicit input parameters for the EXT_SHIPTO_UPD_ERR exception task.*

| Variable Name | Variable Type | Description |
|---|---|---|
| MACRO_NVP | NVPHash* | A collection of name-value pairs that supercede any equivalent name-value pairs found in the http request. For this task, the collection includes the parameters shown below. |

### MACRO_NVP Parameters:

*Table E.30  MACRO_NVP parameters for the EXT_SHIPTO_UPD_ERR exception task.*

| Variable Name | Variable Type | Description |
|---|---|---|
| ADDRESS_REF_NUM | String* | The updated address reference number. If the address reference number passed into the command refers to a temporary address book entry, and a permanent address book entry exists for the same nickname, this string is set to the reference number of the permanent address book entry. |

### Expected Behavior of Overridable Function:

Generate a page that informs the shopper of the error.

### Expected Return Values:

None

### Default Overridable Function:

TaskDisplay_1.0 (IBM,NC)

# GET_BASE_SPE_PRC_ERR Exception Task

## Designed to be called by:

The function assigned to the GET_BASE_SPE_PRC process task.

## Explicit Input Parameters:

*Table E.31* *Explicit input parameters for the GET_BASE_SPE_PRC_ERR exception task.*

| Variable Name | Variable Type | Description |
|---|---|---|
| MACRO_NVP | NVPHash* | A collection of name-value pairs that supercede any equivalent name-value pairs found in the http request. For this task, the collection is empty. |
| ERROR_CODE | String* | A string identifying the reason for the exception condition. See below for descriptions of the exception conditions. |

## Exception Conditions:

*Table E.32* *Exception conditions for the GET_BASE_SPE_PRC_ERR exception task.*

| Error Code | Description | Additional Input Parameters | | |
| | | String | Value | Description |
|---|---|---|---|---|
| 1 | An SQL statement did not complete successfully. | N/A | N/A | N/A |
| 1002 | The price could not be found. | PRODUCT _REF_NUM | String* | Product reference number. |
| | | QUANTITY | String* | Quantity requested. |

## Expected Behavior of Overridable Function:

Generate a page that informs the shopper of the error.

## Expected Return Values:

None

## Default Overridable Function:

TaskDisplay_1.0 (IBM,NC)

# GET_BASE_UNIT_PRC_ERR Exception Task

### Designed to be called by:

The function assigned to the GET_BASE_UNIT_PRC process task.

### Explicit Input Parameters:

**Table E.33** *Explicit input parameters for the GET_BASE_UNIT_PRC_ERR exception task.*

| Variable Name | Variable Type | Description |
|---|---|---|
| MACRO_NVP | NVPHash* | A collection of name-value pairs that supercede any equivalent name-value pairs found in the http request. For this task, the collection is empty. |
| ERROR_CODE | String* | A string identifying the reason for the exception condition. See below for descriptions of the exception conditions. |

### Exception Conditions:

**Table E.34** *Exception conditions for the GET_BASE_UNIT_PRC_ERR exception task.*

| Error Code | Description | Additional Input Parameters | | |
| | | String | Value | Description |
|---|---|---|---|---|
| 1 | An SQL statement did not complete successfully. | N/A | N/A | N/A |
| 1002 | The price could not be found. | PRODUCT_REF_NUM | String* | Product reference number. |
| | | QUANTITY | String* | Quantity requested. |

### Expected Behavior of Overridable Function:

Generate a page that informs the shopper of the error.

### Expected Return Values:

None

### Default Overridable Function:

TaskDisplay_1.0 (IBM,NC)

# GET_ORD_PROD_TAX_TOT_ERR Exception Task

### Designed to be called by:

The function assigned to the GET_ORD_PROD_TAX_TOT process task.

### Explicit Input Parameters:

**Table E.35** *Explicit input parameters for the GET_ORD_PROD_TAX_TOT_ERR exception task.*

| Variable Name | Variable Type | Description |
|---|---|---|
| MACRO_NVP | NVPHash* | A collection of name-value pairs that supercede any equivalent name-value pairs found in the http request. For this task, the collection is empty. |
| ERROR_CODE | String* | A string identifying the reason for the exception condition. See below for descriptions of the exception conditions. |

### Exception Conditions:

**Table E.36** *Exception conditions for the GET_ORD_PROD_TAX_TOT_ERR exception task.*

| Error Code | Description | Additional Input Parameters | | |
|---|---|---|---|---|
| | | String | Value | Description |
| 1 | An SQL statement did not complete successfully. | N/A | N/A | N/A |
| 1004 | The order contains no suborders. | ORDER _REF_NUM | String* | Order reference number. |

### Expected Behavior of Overridable Function:

Generate a page that informs the shopper of the error.

### Expected Return Values:

None

### Default Overridable Function:

TaskDisplay_1.0 (IBM,NC)

# GET_ORD_PROD_TOT_ERR Exception Task

### Designed to be called by:

The function assigned to the GET_ORD_PROD_TOT process task.

### Explicit Input Parameters:

*Table E.37* *Explicit input parameters for the GET_ORD_PROD_TOT_ERR exception task.*

| Variable Name | Variable Type | Description |
|---|---|---|
| MACRO_NVP | NVPHash* | A collection of name-value pairs that supercede any equivalent name-value pairs found in the http request. For this task, the collection is empty. |
| ERROR_CODE | String* | A string identifying the reason for the exception condition. See below for descriptions of the exception conditions. |

### Exception Conditions:

*Table E.38* *Exception conditions for the GET_ORD_PROD_TOT_ERR exception task.*

| Error Code | Description | Additional Input Parameters | | |
|---|---|---|---|---|
| | | String | Value | Description |
| 1 | An SQL statement did not complete successfully. | N/A | N/A | N/A |
| 1004 | The order contains no suborders. | ORDER _REF_NUM | String* | Order reference number. |

### Expected Behavior of Overridable Function:

Generate a page that informs the shopper of the error.

### Expected Return Values:

None

### Default Overridable Function:

TaskDisplay_1.0 (IBM,NC)

# GET_ORD_SH_TOT_ERR Exception Task

### Designed to be called by:

The function assigned to the GET_ORD_SH_TOT process task.

### Explicit Input Parameters:

*Table E.39* *Explicit input parameters for the GET_ORD_SH_TOT_ERR exception task.*

| Variable Name | Variable Type | Description |
|---|---|---|
| MACRO_NVP | NVPHash* | A collection of name-value pairs that supercede any equivalent name-value pairs found in the http request. For this task, the collection is empty. |
| ERROR_CODE | String* | A string identifying the reason for the exception condition. See below for descriptions of the exception conditions. |

### Exception Conditions:

*Table E.40* *Exception conditions for the GET_ORD_SH_TOT_ERR exception task.*

| Error Code | Description | Additional Input Parameters | | |
| | | String | Value | Description |
|---|---|---|---|---|
| 1 | An SQL statement did not complete successfully. | N/A | N/A | N/A |
| 1004 | The order contains no suborders. | ORDER _REF_NUM | String* | Order reference number. |

### Expected Behavior of Overridable Function:

Generate a page that informs the shopper of the error.

### Expected Return Values:

None

### Default Overridable Function:

TaskDisplay_1.0 (IBM,NC)

# GET_SUB_ORD_PROD_TAX_TOT_ERR Exception Task

### Designed to be called by:

The function assigned to the GET_SUB_ORD_PROD_TAX_TOT process task.

### Explicit Input Parameters:

*Table E.41* *Explicit input parameters for the GET_SUB_ORD_PROD_TAX_TOT_ERR exception task.*

| Variable Name | Variable Type | Description |
|---|---|---|
| MACRO_NVP | NVPHash* | A collection of name-value pairs that supercede any equivalent name-value pairs found in the http request. For this task, the collection is empty. |
| ERROR_CODE | String* | A string identifying the reason for the exception condition. See below for descriptions of the exception conditions. |

### Exception Conditions:

*Table E.42* *Exception conditions for the GET_SUB_ORD_PROD_TAX_TOT_ERR exception task.*

| Error Code | Description | Additional Input Parameters | | |
| | | String | Value | Description |
|---|---|---|---|---|
| 1 | An SQL statement did not complete successfully. | N/A | N/A | N/A |
| 2 | Table MALL does not contain exactly one row. | N/A | N/A | N/A |

### Expected Behavior of Overridable Function:

Generate a page that informs the shopper of the error.

### Expected Return Values:

None

### Default Overridable Function:

TaskDisplay_1.0 (IBM,NC)

# GET_SUB_ORD_PROD_TOT_ERR Exception Task

### Designed to be called by:

The function assigned to the GET_SUB_ORD_PROD_TOT process task.

### Explicit Input Parameters:

*Table E.43* *Explicit input parameters for the GET_SUB_ORD_PROD_TOT_ERR exception task.*

| Variable Name | Variable Type | Description |
|---|---|---|
| MACRO_NVP | NVPHash* | A collection of name-value pairs that supercede any equivalent name-value pairs found in the http request. For this task, the collection is empty. |
| ERROR_CODE | String* | A string identifying the reason for the exception condition. See below for descriptions of the exception conditions. |

### Exception Conditions:

*Table E.44* *Exception conditions for the GET_SUB_ORD_PROD_TOT_ERR exception task.*

| Error Code | Description | Additional Input Parameters | | |
| | | String | Value | Description |
|---|---|---|---|---|
| 1 | An SQL statement did not complete successfully. | N/A | N/A | N/A |
| 1003 | The suborder contains no items. | PRODUCT _REF_NUM | String* | Product reference number. |
| | | QUANTITY | String* | Quantity requested. |

### Expected Behavior of Overridable Function:

Generate a page that informs the shopper of the error.

### Expected Return Values:

None

### Default Overridable Function:

TaskDisplay_1.0 (IBM,NC)

# GET_SUB_ORD_SH_TOT_ERR Exception Task

### Designed to be called by:

The function assigned to the GET_SUB_ORD_SH_TOT process task.

### Explicit Input Parameters:

**Table E.45**  *Explicit input parameters for the GET_SUB_ORD_SH_TOT_ERR exception task.*

| Variable Name | Variable Type | Description |
|---|---|---|
| MACRO_NVP | NVPHash* | A collection of name-value pairs that supercede any equivalent name-value pairs found in the http request. For this task, the collection is empty. |
| ERROR_CODE | String* | A string identifying the reason for the exception condition. See below for descriptions of the exception conditions. |

### Exception Conditions:

**Table E.46**  *Exception conditions for the GET_SUB_ORD_SH_TOT_ERR exception task.*

| Error Code | Description | Additional Input Parameters | | |
| | | String | Value | Description |
|---|---|---|---|---|
| 1 | An SQL statement did not complete successfully. | N/A | N/A | N/A |
| 1007 | Unrecognized shipping calculation method. | N/A | N/A | N/A |
| 1008 | No shipping calculation method is currently in effect, or more than one is currently in effect, for the range specified. | N/A | N/A | N/A |
| 1009 | For a cumulative shipping calculation methods, the ranges specified are not contiguous. | N/A | N/A | N/A |
| 1010 | No shipping calculation method is defined for the quantity or weight specified. | N/A | N/A | N/A |

### Expected Behavior of Overridable Function:

Generate a page that informs the shopper of the error.

**Expected Return Values:**

None

**Default Overridable Function:**

TaskDisplay_1.0 (IBM,NC)

# LOGON_ERR Exception Task

**Calling Command:**

Logon

**Explicit Input Parameters:**

*Table E.47  Explicit input parameters for the LOGON_ERR exception task.*

| Variable Name | Variable Type | Description |
|---|---|---|
| MACRO_NVP | NVPHash* | A collection of name-value pairs that supercede any equivalent name-value pairs found in the http request. For this task, the collection is empty. |
| ERROR_CODE | String* | A string identifying the reason for the exception condition. See below for descriptions of the exception conditions. |

**Exception Conditions:**

*Table E.48  Exception conditions for the LOGON_ERR exception task.*

| Error Code | Description | Additional Input Parameters | | |
| | | String | Value | Description |
|---|---|---|---|---|
| 300 | Login attempt was unsuccessful. | N/A | N/A | N/A |

**Expected Behavior of Overridable Function:**

Generate a page that informs the shopper of the error.

**Expected Return Values:**

None

**Default Overridable Function:**

TaskDisplay_1.0 (IBM,NC)

# MISSING_PROD_ATTR Exception Task

### Designed to be called by:

The function assigned to the RESOLVE_SKU process task.

### Explicit Input Parameters:

*Table E.49  Explicit input parameters for the MISSING_PROD_ATTR exception task.*

| Variable Name | Variable Type | Description |
| --- | --- | --- |
| MACRO_NVP | NVPHash* | A collection of name-value pairs that supercede any equivalent name-value pairs found in the http request. For this task, the collection is empty. |
| ERROR_CODE | String* | A string identifying the reason for the exception condition. See below for descriptions of the exception conditions. |

### Exception Conditions:

*Table E.50 Exception conditions for the MISSING_PROD_ATTR exception task.*

| Error Code | Description | Additional Input Parameters | | |
| --- | --- | --- | --- | --- |
| | | String | Value | Description |
| 260 | A product with the specified attributes cannot be found in the database. | N/A | N/A | N/A |

### Expected Behavior of Overridable Function:

Generate a page that informs the shopper of the error.

### Expected Return Values:

None

### Default Overridable Function:

TaskDisplay_1.0 (IBM,NC)

# ORD_NONE Exception Task

### Calling Command:

OrderDisplay

### Explicit Input Parameters:

*Table E.51* *Explicit input parameters for the ORD_NONE exception task.*

| Variable Name | Variable Type | Description |
|---|---|---|
| MACRO_NVP | NVPHash* | A collection of name-value pairs that supercede any equivalent name-value pairs found in the http request. For this task, the collection is empty. |
| ERROR_CODE | String* | A string identifying the reason for the exception condition. See below for descriptions of the exception conditions. |

### Exception Conditions:

*Table E.52* *Exception conditions for the ORD_NONE exception task.*

| Error Code | Description | Additional Input Parameters | | |
| | | String | Value | Description |
|---|---|---|---|---|
| 230 | No orders that match the display request were found. | FIELD | String* | Name of the invalid field. |

### Expected Behavior of Overridable Function:

Generate a page that informs the shopper of the error.

### Expected Return Values:

None

### Default Overridable Function:

TaskDisplay_1.0 (IBM,NC)

# ORD_UNLOCKED Exception Task

### Calling Command:

OrderProcess

### Explicit Input Parameters:

*Table E.53* *Explicit input parameters for the ORD_UNLOCKED exception task.*

| Variable Name | Variable Type | Description |
|---|---|---|
| MACRO_NVP | NVPHash* | A collection of name-value pairs that supercede any equivalent name-value pairs found in the http request. For this task, the collection is empty. |
| ERROR_CODE | String* | A string identifying the reason for the exception condition. See below for descriptions of the exception conditions. |

## Exception Conditions:

**Table E.54** *Exception conditions for the ORD_UNLOCKED exception task.*

| Error Code | Description | Additional Input Parameters | | |
| --- | --- | --- | --- | --- |
| | | **String** | **Value** | **Description** |
| 240 | The order is unlocked, and therefore cannot be processed. | FIELD | String* | Name of the invalid field. |

## Expected Behavior of Overridable Function:

Generate a page that informs the shopper of the error.

## Expected Return Values:

None

## Default Overridable Function:

TaskDisplay_1.0 (IBM,NC)

# REVERSE_INV_ERR Exception Task

## Designed to be called by:

The function assigned to the REVERSE_INV process task.

## Explicit Input Parameters:

**Table E.55** *Explicit input parameters for the REVERSE_INV_ERR exception task.*

| Variable Name | Variable Type | Description |
| --- | --- | --- |
| MACRO_NVP | NVPHash* | A collection of name-value pairs that supercede any equivalent name-value pairs found in the http request. For this task, the collection is empty. |
| ERROR_CODE | String* | A string identifying the reason for the exception condition. See below for descriptions of the exception conditions. |

## Exception Conditions:

**Table E.56** *Exception conditions for the REVERSE_INV_ERR exception task.*

| Error Code | Description | Additional Input Parameters | | |
| --- | --- | --- | --- | --- |
| | | **String** | **Value** | **Description** |
| 2 | An SQL statement returned more than one row. | PRODUCT _REF_NUM | String* | Product reference number. |

## Expected Behavior of Overridable Function:

Generate a page that informs the shopper of the error.

*Expected Return Values:*

None

*Default Overridable Function:*

TaskDisplay_1.0 (IBM,NC)

# UPDATE_INV_ERR Exception Task

*Designed to be called by:*

The function assigned to the UPDATE_INV process task.

*Explicit Input Parameters:*

**Table E.57** *Explicit input parameters for the UPDATE_INV_ERR exception task.*

| Variable Name | Variable Type | Description |
|---|---|---|
| MACRO_NVP | NVPHash* | A collection of name-value pairs that supercede any equivalent name-value pairs found in the http request. For this task, the collection is empty. |
| ERROR_CODE | String* | A string identifying the reason for the exception condition. See below for descriptions of the exception conditions. |

*Exception Conditions:*

**Table E.58** *Exception conditions for the UPDATE_INV_ERR exception task.*

| Error Code | Description | Additional Input Parameters | | |
|---|---|---|---|---|
| | | String | Value | Description |
| 2 | An SQL statement returned more than one row. | PRODUCT _REF_NUM | String* | Product reference number. |
| 2 | Insufficient inventory. | PRODUCT _REF_NUM | String* | Product reference number. |
| | | QUANTITY | String* | The quantity requested. |

*Expected Behavior of Overridable Function:*

Generate a page that informs the shopper of the error.

*Expected Return Values:*

None

*Default Overridable Function:*

TaskDisplay_1.0 (IBM,NC)

# AUDIT_ADDR_BOOK Process Task

### Calling Commands:

AddressAdd, AddressUpdate

### Expected Behavior:

Check the validity of the name-value pairs that are passed into the calling command. If any are invalid, either set an exception task, return a false value to the calling command, or handle the exception by writing an http response.

### Explicit Input Parameters:

None

### Explicit Output Parameters:

None

### Expected Return Codes:

For exceptions that are handled by setting the AUDIT_ADDR_BOOK_ERR exception task, the expected return codes are the ones documented as input parameters for that exception task.

### Default Overridable Function:

AuditAddrBook_1.0 (IBM,NC)

### Usage Examples:

- Turn an optional field, such as the email address, into a required field.

- Perform syntax checking on parameters, such as ensuring that the zip code field corresponds to the format that is used for postal codes in your country.

- Perform semantic checking on parameters, such as ensuring that the zip code or equivalent is valid for the city.

- Ensure that additional parameters you pass in when a shopper updates the address book are correct.

# AUDIT_REG Process Task

### Calling Commands:

RegisterUpdate, RegisterNew

### Expected Behavior:

Check the validity of the name-value pairs that are passed into the calling command. If any are invalid, either set an exception task, return a false value to the calling command, or handle the exception by writing an http response.

### Explicit Input Parameters:

None

### Explicit Output Parameters:

None

### Expected Return Codes:

For exceptions that are handled by setting the AUDIT_REG_ERR exception task, the expected return codes are the ones documented as input parameters for that exception task.

### Default Overridable Function:

DoNothingNoArgs 1.0 (IBM,NC)

### Usage Examples:

- Turn an optional field into a required field, such as the email address

- Perform syntax checking on parameters, such as ensuring that the zip code field corresponds to the format that is used for postal codes in your country

- Perform semantic checking on parameters, such as ensuring that the zip code or equivalent is valid for the city

- Ensure that additional parameters you pass in when a shopper registers or updates the registration information are correct

# CHECK_INV Process Task

### Calling Commands:

OrderDisplay, OrderItemProcess, OrderItemUpdate

### Expected Behavior:

Determine whether there is enough inventory in stock to cover a request for a given quantity of a given product or item. If not, either set an exception task, return a false value to the calling command, or handle the exception by writing an http response.

### Explicit Input Parameters:

*Table E.59 Explicit input parameters for the CHECK_INV process task.*

| Variable Name | Variable Type | Description |
| --- | --- | --- |
| PRODUCT_REF_NUM | String* | The reference number of the product or item. |
| QUANTITY | String* | The quantity requested. |

### Explicit Output Parameters:

None

### Expected Return Codes:

For exceptions that are handled by setting the CHECK_INV_ERR exception task, the expected return codes are the ones documented as input parameters for that exception task.

**Default Overridable Function:**

CheckInv_1.0 (IBM,NC)

**Usage Examples:**

- With concurrent changes to the UPDATE_INV task, change the way you use the inventory column in the Product table from tracking inventory in stock to simply indicating whether or not there is *any* in stock

- Bypass inventory checking completely

# DO_PAYMENT Process Task

**Calling Commands:**

OrderProcess

**Expected Behavior:**

Process the payment for an order. If unsuccessful, either set an exception task, return a false value to the calling command, or handle the exception by writing an http response.

**Explicit Input Parameters:**

**Table E.60** *Explicit input parameters for the DO_PAYMENT process task.*

| Variable Name | Variable Type | Description |
| --- | --- | --- |
| ORDER_REF_NUM | String* | The reference number of the order. |
| TOTAL_AMOUNT | String* | The total price of the order. |

**Explicit Output Parameters:**

None

**Expected Return Codes:**

For exceptions that are handled by setting the DO_PAYMENT_ERR exception task, the expected return codes are the ones documented as input parameters for that exception task.

**Default Overridable Function:**

DoPayment_1.0 (IBM,NC)

**Usage Examples:**

- Create a log record to be reviewed and processed later

- Use a legacy system to process the payment

# EXT_ORD_PROC Process Task

### Calling Commands:

OrderProcess

### Expected Behavior:

Perform any additional processing required just prior to the completion of the calling command. If unsuccessful, either set an exception task, return a false value to the calling command, or handle the exception by writing an http response.

### Explicit Input Parameters:

**Table E.61** *Explicit input parameters for the EXT_ORD_PROC process task.*

| Variable Name | Variable Type | Description |
| --- | --- | --- |
| ORDER_REF_NUM | String* | The reference number of the order |

### Explicit Output Parameters:

None

### Expected Return Codes:

For exceptions that are handled by setting the EXT_ORD_PROC_ERR exception task, the expected return codes are the ones documented as input parameters for that exception task.

### Default Overridable Function:

DoNothingNoArgs 1.0 (IBM,NC)

### Usage Examples:

- Keep track of the total number of orders placed by each shopper
- Trigger a legacy system to perform further processing

# EXT_SHIPTO_PROC Process Task

### Calling Command:

OrderItemProcess

### Expected Behavior:

Perform any additional processing required for each product or item, just prior to the completion of the calling command. If unsuccessful, either set an exception task, return a false value to the calling command, or handle the exception by writing an http response.

### Explicit Input Parameters:

*Table E.62* *Explicit input parameters for the EXT_SHIPTO_PROC process task.*

| Variable Name | Variable Type | Description |
| --- | --- | --- |
| ORDERITEM_REF_NUM | String* | The reference number of the suborder |

### Explicit Output Parameters:

None

### Expected Return Codes:

For exceptions that are handled by setting the EXT_SHIPTO_PROC_ERR exception task, the expected return codes are the ones documented as input parameters for that exception task.

### Default Overridable Function:

DoNothingNoArgs 1.0 (IBM,NC)

### Usage Examples:

- Keep track of the total number of products and items that the shopper associates with each shipping address and send a catalog to those recipients who exceed a threshold.

- For foreign shipments, determine whether or not there are any restrictions on exporting the product or item. You can also create an exception macro for this task to inform the shopper and request additional information that may be required.

# EXT_SHIPTO_UPD Process Task

### Calling Command:

OrderItemUpdate

### Expected Behavior:

Perform any additional processing required just prior to the completion of the calling command. If unsuccessful, either set an exception task, return a false value to the calling command, or handle the exception by writing an http response.

### Explicit Input Parameters:

*Table E.63* *Explicit input parameters for the EXT_SHIPTO_UPD process task.*

| Variable Name | Variable Type | Description |
| --- | --- | --- |
| ORDERITEM_REF_NUM | String* | The reference number of the suborder |

### Explicit Output Parameters:

None

### Expected Return Codes:

For exceptions that are handled by setting the EXT_SHIPTO_UPD_ERR exception task, the expected return codes are the ones documented as input parameters for that exception task.

### Default Overridable Function:

DoNothingNoArgs 1.0 (IBM,NC)

### Usage Examples:

- Create a log entry to use for compiling statistics
- Trigger a legacy system to perform additional processing

# GET_BASE_SPE_PRC Process Task

### Calling Commands:

OrderDisplay, OrderItemDisplay, OrderItemProcess, OrderItemUpdate

### Expected Behavior:

Determine the price of an item. This price can be different from the price that is returned by the GET_BASE_UNIT_PRC process task, because an item that is associated with a shipping address can have extra features that increase the price. If unsuccessful, either set an exception task, return a false value to the calling command, or handle the exception by writing an http response.

### Explicit Input Parameters:

*Table E.64  Explicit input parameters for the GET_BASE_SPE_PRC process task.*

| Variable Name | Variable Type | Description |
|---|---|---|
| PRODUCT_REF_NUM | String* | The reference number of the item. |
| ORDERITEM_REF_NUM | String* | The reference number of the suborder. |
| CURRENCY | String* | The currency used for the store. |

### Explicit Output Parameters:

*Table E.65  Explicit output parameters for the GET_BASE_SPE_PRC process task.*

| Variable Name | Variable Type | Description |
|---|---|---|
| PRODUCT_PRICE | String* | The price of the item. |

### Expected Return Codes:

For exceptions that are handled by setting the GET_BASE_SPE_PRC_ERR exception task, the expected return codes are the ones documented as input parameters for that exception task.

**Default Overridable Function:**

GetBaseSpePrc_1.0 (IBM,NC)

**Usage Examples:**

- Charge an additional price for each letter to be included in a monogram

- Retrieve the price from a legacy system

# GET_BASE_UNIT_PRC Process Task

**Calling Commands:**

InterestItemAdd, InterestItemDisplay

**Expected Behavior:**

Determine the price of a product or item. If unsuccessful, either set an exception task, return a false value to the calling command, or handle the exception by writing an http response.

**Explicit Input Parameters:**

**Table E.66** *Explicit input parameters for the GET_BASE_UNIT_PRC process task.*

| Variable Name | Variable Type | Description |
| --- | --- | --- |
| PRODUCT_REF_NUM | String* | The reference number of the item. |
| CURRENCY | String* | The currency used for the store. |

**Explicit Output Parameters:**

**Table E.67** *Explicit output parameters for the GET_BASE_UNIT_PRC process task.*

| Variable Name | Variable Type | Description |
| --- | --- | --- |
| PRODUCT_PRICE | String* | The price of the product or item. |

**Expected Return Codes:**

For exceptions that are handled by setting the GET_BASE_UNIT_PRC_ERR exception task, the expected return codes are the ones documented as input parameters for that exception task.

**Default Overridable Function:**

GetBaseUnitPrc_1.0 (IBM,NC)

**Usage Examples:**

- With corresponding changes to the overridable functions that calculate the prices of orders, include taxes in the price that is added or displayed

- Retrieve the price from a legacy system

# GET_ORD_PROD_TAX_TOT Process Task

### Calling Command:

OrderDisplay

### Expected Behavior:

Calculate the total taxes payable on an order. If unsuccessful, either set an exception task, return a false value to the calling command, or handle the exception by writing an http response.

### Explicit Input Parameters:

**Table E.68** *Explicit input parameters for the GET_ORD_PROD_TAX_TOT process task.*

| Variable Name | Variable Type | Description |
| --- | --- | --- |
| ORDER_REF_NUM | String* | The reference number of the order. |
| PRODUCT_PRICE | String* | The total price of the order. |

### Explicit Output Parameters:

**Table E.69** *Explicit output parameters for the GET_ORD_PROD_TAX_TOT process task.*

| Variable Name | Variable Type | Description |
| --- | --- | --- |
| TAX_TOTAL | String* | The total taxes payable. |

### Expected Return Codes:

For exceptions that are handled by setting the GET_ORD_PROD_TAX_TOT_ERR exception task, the expected return codes are the ones documented as input parameters for that exception task.

### Default Overridable Function:

GetOrdProdTaxTot_1.0 (IBM,NC)

### Usage Examples:

- Reduce the taxes payable for shoppers in certain shopper groups
- Retrieve the total taxes payable from a legacy system

# GET_ORD_PROD_TOT Process Task

### Calling Command:

OrderDisplay

### Expected Behavior:

Calculate the total price of the items in an order. If unsuccessful, either set an exception task, return a false value to the calling command, or handle the exception by writing an http response.

### Explicit Input Parameters:

**Table E.70**   *Explicit input parameters for the GET_ORD_PROD_TOT process task.*

| Variable Name | Variable Type | Description |
| --- | --- | --- |
| ORDER_REF_NUM | String* | The reference number of the order. |

### Explicit Output Parameters:

**Table E.71**   *Explicit output parameters for the GET_ORD_PROD_TOT process task.*

| Variable Name | Variable Type | Description |
| --- | --- | --- |
| PRODUCT_PRICE | String* | The total price of the items in the order. |

### Expected Return Codes:

For exceptions that are handled by setting the GET_ORD_PROD_TOT_ERR exception task, the expected return codes are the ones documented as input parameters for that exception task.

### Default Overridable Function:

GetOrdProdTot_1.0 (IBM,NC)

### Usage Examples:

- Offer a discount for orders whose total item cost exceeds a threshold
- Retrieve the total item cost from a legacy system

# GET_ORD_SH_TOT Process Task

### Calling Command:

OrderDisplay

### Expected Behavior:

Calculate the total shipping charges for an order. If unsuccessful, either set an exception task, return a false value to the calling command, or handle the exception by writing an http response.

### Explicit Input Parameters:

*Table E.72  Explicit input parameters for the GET_ORD_SH_TOT process task.*

| Variable Name | Variable Type | Description |
| --- | --- | --- |
| ORDER_REF_NUM | String* | The reference number of the order. |

### Explicit Output Parameters:

*Table E.73  Explicit output parameters for the GET_ORD_SH_TOT process task.*

| Variable Name | Variable Type | Description |
| --- | --- | --- |
| PRODUCT_SHIPPING | String* | The total shipping charges for the order. |

### Expected Return Codes:

For exceptions that are handled by setting the GET_ORD_SH_TOT_ERR exception task, the expected return codes are the ones documented as input parameters for that exception task.

### Default Overridable Function:

GetOrdShTot_1.0 (IBM,NC)

### Usage Examples:

- Offer a discount on shipping charges that exceed a threshold
- Retrieve the shipping charges from a legacy system

# GET_SUB_ORD_PROD_TAX_TOT Process Task

### Calling Command:

OrderDisplay

### Expected Behavior:

Calculate the total taxes payable on a suborder. If unsuccessful, either set an exception task, return a false value to the calling command, or handle the exception by writing an http response.

### Explicit Input Parameters:

*Table E.74  Explicit input parameters for the GET_SUB_ORD_PROD_TAX_TOT process task.*

| Variable Name | Variable Type | Description |
| --- | --- | --- |
| ORDER_REF_NUM | String* | The reference number of the order. |
| ADDRESS_REF_NUM | String* | The reference number of the address book entry associated with the suborder. |
| PRODUCT_PRICE | String* | The total price of all the items in the suborder. |

### Explicit Output Parameters:

*Table E.75  Explicit output parameters for the GET_SUB_ORD_PROD_TAX_TOT process task.*

| Variable Name | Variable Type | Description |
| --- | --- | --- |
| TAX1 | String* | The amount of tax payable for the tax 1 amount. |
| TAX2 | String* | The amount of tax payable for the tax 2 amount. |
| TAX3 | String* | The amount of tax payable for the tax 3 amount. |
| TAX4 | String* | The amount of tax payable for the tax 4 amount. |
| TAX5 | String* | The amount of tax payable for the tax 5 amount. |
| TAX6 | String* | The amount of tax payable for the tax 6 amount. |
| TAX_TOTAL | String* | The total of all tax amounts. |

### Expected Return Codes:

For exceptions that arc handled by setting the GET_SUB_ORD_PROD_TAX_TOT_ERR exception task, the expected return codes are the ones documented as input parameters for that exception task.

### Default Overridable Function:

GetSubOrdProdTaxTot_1.0 (IBM,NC)

### Usage Examples:

- Charge no tax on suborders whose total price exceeds a threshold

- Charge no tax if the recipient is in a different tax jurisdiction

# GET_SUB_ORD_PROD_TOT Process Task

### Calling Command:

OrderDisplay

### Expected Behavior:

Calculate the total price of all items in a suborder. If unsuccessful, either set an exception task, return a false value to the calling command, or handle the exception by writing an http response.

### Explicit Input Parameters:

*Table E.76  Explicit input parameters for the GET_SUB_ORD_PROD_TOT process task.*

| Variable Name | Variable Type | Description |
| --- | --- | --- |
| ORDER_REF_NUM | String* | The reference number of the order. |
| ADDRESS_REF_NUM | String* | The reference number of the address book entry associated with the suborder. |

### Explicit Output Parameters:

**Table E.77** *Explicit output parameters for the GET_SUB_ORD_PROD_TOT process task.*

| Variable Name | Variable Type | Description |
|---|---|---|
| PRODUCT_PRICE | String* | The total price of all items in the suborder. |

### Expected Return Codes:

For exceptions that are handled by setting the GET_SUB_ORD_PROD_TOT_ERR exception task, the expected return codes are the ones documented as input parameters for that exception task.

### Default Overridable Function:

GetSubOrdProdTot_1.0 (IBM,NC)

### Usage Examples:

- Provide a discount for suborders whose total price exceeds a threshold
- Add a surcharge to foreign shipments that is based on the price of the suborder

# GET_SUB_ORD_SH_TOT Process Task

### Calling Command:

OrderDisplay

### Expected Behavior:

Calculate the total shipping charges for all items in a suborder. If unsuccessful, either set an exception task, return a false value to the calling command, or handle the exception by writing an http response.

### Explicit Input Parameters:

**Table E.78** *Explicit input parameters for the GET_SUB_ORD_SH_TOT process task.*

| Variable Name | Variable Type | Description |
|---|---|---|
| ORDER_REF_NUM | String* | The reference number of the order. |
| ADDRESS_REF_NUM | String* | The reference number of the address book entry associated with the suborder. |

### Explicit Output Parameters:

**Table E.79** *Explicit output parameters for the GET_SUB_ORD_SH_TOT process task.*

| Variable Name | Variable Type | Description |
|---|---|---|
| PRODUCT_SHIPPING | String* | The total price of all items in the suborder. |

### Expected Return Codes:

For exceptions that are handled by setting the GET_SUB_ORD_SH_TOT_ERR exception task, the expected return codes are the ones documented as input parameters for that exception task.

### Default Overridable Function:

GetSubOrdShTot_1.0 (IBM,NC)

### Usage Examples:

- Charge no shipping charges on suborders whose total price exceeds a threshold

- Charge no shipping charges if the recipient lives in a city that has a local warehouse

# RESOLVE_SKU Process Task

### Calling Commands:

InterestItemAdd, OrderItemUpdate

### Expected Behavior:

Given a product and a set of attributes, determine the SKU. If unsuccessful, either set an exception task, return a false value to the calling command, or handle the exception by writing an http response.

### Explicit Input Parameters:

*Table E.80* *Explicit input parameters for the RESOLVE_SKU process task.*

| Variable Name | Variable Type | Description |
| --- | --- | --- |
| PRODUCT_REF_NUM | String* | The reference number of the product whose SKU is to be resolved. |

### Explicit Output Parameters:

*Table E.81* *Explicit output parameters for the RESOLVE_SKU process task.*

| Variable Name | Variable Type | Description |
| --- | --- | --- |
| SKU_REF_NUM | String* | The reference number of the item (the product with the given set of attributes) |

### Expected Return Codes:

For exceptions that are handled by setting the BAD_PROD_ATTR or MISSING_PROD_ATTR exception tasks, the expected return codes are the ones documented as input parameters for those exception tasks.

### Default Overridable Function:

ResolveSku_1.0 (IBM,NC)

# REVERSE_INV Process Task

## Calling Command:

OrderProcess

## Expected Behavior:

Reverse a previous reduction in the amount of inventory in stock for a product or item. If unsuccessful, either set an exception task, return a false value to the calling command, or handle the exception by writing an http response.

## Explicit Input Parameters:

*Table E.82* *Explicit input parameters for the REVERSE_INV process task.*

| Variable Name | Variable Type | Description |
|---|---|---|
| PRODUCT_REF_NUM | String* | The reference number of the product or item |
| QUANTITY increased | String* | The quantity by which the inventory is to be |

## Explicit Output Parameters:

None

## Expected Return Codes:

For exceptions that are handled by setting the REVERSE_INV_ERR exception task, the expected return codes are the ones documented as input parameters for that exception task.

## Default Overridable Function:

ReverseInv_1.0 (IBM,NC)

## Usage Examples:

- With concurrent changes to the CHECK_INV task, change the way that you use the inventory column in the Product table from tracking inventory in stock to indicating whether or not there is *any* in stock.

- Update the inventory on a legacy inventory system.

# UPDATE_INV Process Task

### Calling Command:

OrderProcess

### Expected Behavior:

Reduce the amount of inventory in stock for a product or item. If unsuccessful, either set an exception task, return a false value to the calling command, or handle the exception by writing an http response.

### Explicit Input Parameters:

*Table E.83  Explicit input parameters for the UPDATE_INV process task.*

| Variable Name | Variable Type | Description |
|---|---|---|
| PRODUCT_REF_NUM | String* | The reference number of the product or item |
| QUANTITY | String* | The quantity requested |

### Explicit Output Parameters:

None

### Expected Return Codes:

For exceptions that are handled by setting the UPDATE_INV_ERR exception task, the expected return codes are the ones documented as input parameters for that exception task.

### Default Overridable Function:

UpdateInv_1.0 (IBM,NC)

### Usage Examples:

- With concurrent changes to the CHECK_INV task, change the way that you use the inventory column in the Product table from tracking inventory in stock to indicating whether or not there is *any* in stock.

- Update the inventory on a legacy inventory system.

# ADDR_ADD View Task

### Calling Command:

AddressForm, when address_rn is not specified.

### Explicit Input Parameters:

*Table E.84*  *Explicit input parameters for the ADDR_ADD view task.*

| Variable Name | Variable Type | Description |
|---|---|---|
| MACRO_NVP | NVPHash* | A collection of name-value pairs that supercede any equivalent name-value pairs found in the http request. For this task, the collection is empty. |

### Expected Behavior of Overridable Function:

Generate a blank address book page.

### Expected Return Values:

None

### Default Overridable Function:

TaskDisplay_1.0 (IBM,NC)

# ADDR_UPDATE View Task

### Calling Command:

AddressForm, when address_rn is specified.

### Explicit Input Parameters:

*Table E.85*  *Explicit input parameters for the ADDR_UPDATE  view task.*

| Variable Name | Variable Type | Description |
|---|---|---|
| MACRO_NVP | NVPHash* | A collection of name-value pairs that supercede any equivalent name-value pairs found in the http request. For this task, the collection includes the parameters shown below. |

### MACRO_NVP Parameters:

**Table E.86** *MACRO_NVP parameters for the ADDR_UPDATE view task.*

| Variable Name | Variable Type | Description |
|---|---|---|
| ADDRESS_REF_NUM | String* | The updated address reference number. If the address reference number passed into the command refers to a temporary address book entry, and a permanent address book entry exists for the same nickname, this string is set to the reference number of the permanent address book entry. |

### Expected Behavior of Overridable Function:

Generate an existing address book page for updating.

### Expected Return Values:

None

### Default Overridable Function:

TaskDisplay_1.0 (IBM,NC)

# CAT_DSP View Task

### Calling Command:

CategoryDisplay

### Explicit Input Parameters:

**Table E.87** *Explicit input parameters for the CAT_DSP view task.*

| Variable Name | Variable Type | Description |
|---|---|---|
| MACRO_NVP | NVPHash* | A collection of name-value pairs that supercede any equivalent name-value pairs found in the http request. For this task, the collection is empty. |
| HANDLER_NAME | String* | The name of the Net.Data macro that generates the category page on behalf of the overridable function. |

### Expected Behavior of Overridable Function:

Generate a category page.

### Expected Return Values:

None

### Default Overridable Function:

MacroDisplay_1.0 (IBM,NC)

# LOGON_DSP View Task

### Calling Command:

LogonForm

### Explicit Input Parameters:

*Table E.88  Explicit input parameters for the LOGON_DSP view task.*

| Variable Name | Variable Type | Description |
| --- | --- | --- |
| MACRO_NVP | NVPHash* | A collection of name-value pairs that supercede any equivalent name-value pairs found in the http request. For this task, the collection is empty. |

### Expected Behavior of Overridable Function:

Generate a page that allows registered shoppers to log on to the store or mall.

### Expected Return Values:

None

### Default Overridable Function:

TaskDisplay_1.0 (IBM,NC)

# ORD_DSP_COM View Task

### Calling Command:

OrderDisplay, when status is not P or X.

### Explicit Input Parameters:

*Table E.89  Explicit input parameters for the ORD_DSP_COM view task.*

| Variable Name | Variable Type | Description |
| --- | --- | --- |
| MACRO_NVP | NVPHash* | A collection of name-value pairs that supercede any equivalent name-value pairs found in the http request. For this task, the collection is empty. |

### Expected Behavior of Overridable Function:

Generate a page showing the contents of the specified order, which has been already been placed.

### Expected Return Values:
None

### Default Overridable Function:

TaskDisplay_1.0 (IBM,NC)

# ORD_DSP_PEN View Task

### Calling Command:

OrderDisplay, when status is P.

### Explicit Input Parameters:

*Table E.90* *Explicit input parameters for the ORD_DSP_PEN view task.*

| Variable Name | Variable Type | Description |
|---|---|---|
| MACRO_NVP | NVPHash* | A collection of name-value pairs that supercede any equivalent name-value pairs found in the http request. For this task, the collection is empty. |

### Expected Behavior of Overridable Function:

Generate a page showing the contents of the specified order, which has been prepared but not placed.

### Expected Return Values:

None

### Default Overridable Function:

TaskDisplay_1.0 (IBM,NC)

# ORD_LST_COM View Task

### Calling Command:

OrderList, when status is not P or X.

### Explicit Input Parameters:

*Table E.91* *Explicit input parameters for the ORD_LST_COM view task.*

| Variable Name | Variable Type | Description |
|---|---|---|
| MACRO_NVP | NVPHash* | A collection of name-value pairs that supercede any equivalent name-value pairs found in the http request. For this task, the collection is empty. |

### Expected Behavior of Overridable Function:

Generate a page that lists all orders that have been placed.

### Expected Return Values:

None

### Default Overridable Function:

TaskDisplay_1.0 (IBM,NC)

# ORD_LST_PEN View Task

### Calling Command:

OrderList, when status is P.

### Explicit Input Parameters:

*Table E.92* *Explicit input parameters for the ORD_LST_PEN view task.*

| Variable Name | Variable Type | Description |
|---|---|---|
| MACRO_NVP | NVPHash* | A collection of name-value pairs that supercede any equivalent name-value pairs found in the http request. For this task, the collection is empty. |

### Expected Behavior of Overridable Function:

Generate a page that lists all orders that have been prepared but not placed.

### Expected Return Values:

None

### Default Overridable Function:

TaskDisplay_1.0 (IBM,NC)

# ORD_OK View Task

### Calling Command:

OrderProcess

### Explicit Input Parameters:

*Table E.93* *Explicit input parameters for the ORD_OK view task.*

| Variable Name | Variable Type | Description |
|---|---|---|
| MACRO_NVP | NVPHash* | A collection of name-value pairs that supercede any equivalent name-value pairs found in the http request. For this task, the collection is empty. |

### Expected Behavior of Overridable Function:

Generate a page that indicates that the order has been accepted.

### Expected Return Values:

None

### Default Overridable Function:

TaskDisplay_1.0 (IBM,NC)

# PROD_DSP View Task

### Calling Command:

ProductDisplay

### Explicit Input Parameters:

*Table E.94* *Explicit input parameters for the PROD_DSP view task.*

| Variable Name | Variable Type | Description |
|---|---|---|
| MACRO_NVP | NVPHash* | A collection of name-value pairs that supercede any equivalent name-value pairs found in the http request. For this task, the collection is empty. |
| HANDLER_NAME | String* | The name of the Net.Data macro that generates the product page on behalf of the overridable function. |

### Expected Behavior of Overridable Function:

Generate a product page.

### Expected Return Values:

None

### Default Overridable Function:

MacroDisplay_1.0 (IBM,NC)

# REG_NEW View Task

### Calling Command:

RegisterForm, when shopper_rn refers to a shopper who is not registered..

### Explicit Input Parameters:

*Table E.95* *Explicit input parameters for the REG_NEW view task.*

| Variable Name | Variable Type | Description |
|---|---|---|
| MACRO_NVP | NVPHash* | A collection of name-value pairs that supercede any equivalent name-value pairs found in the http request. For this task, the collection is empty. |

### Expected Behavior of Overridable Function:

Generate a blank registration page.

### Expected Return Values:

None

***Default Overridable Function:***

TaskDisplay_1.0 (IBM,NC)

# REG_UPDATE View Task

***Calling Command:***

RegisterForm, when shopper_rn refers to a shopper who is registered.

***Explicit Input Parameters:***

**Table E.96** *Explicit input parameters for the REG_UPDATE view task.*

| Variable Name | Variable Type | Description |
|---|---|---|
| MACRO_NVP | NVPHash* | A collection of name-value pairs that supercede any equivalent name-value pairs found in the http request. For this task, the collection is empty. |

***Expected Behavior of Overridable Function:***

Generate an existing registration page for updating.

***Expected Return Values:***

None

***Default Overridable Function:***

TaskDisplay_1.0 (IBM,NC)

# SHIPTO_ASSOC View Task

***Calling Command:***

OrderItemDisplay, when addr_rn is not specified.

***Explicit Input Parameters:***

**Table E.97** *Explicit input parameters for the SHIPTO_ASSOC view task.*

| Variable Name | Variable Type | Description |
|---|---|---|
| MACRO_NVP | NVPHash* | A collection of name-value pairs that supercede any equivalent name-value pairs found in the http request. For this task, the collection includes the parameters shown below. |

### *MACRO_NVP Parameters:*

*Table E.98 MACRO_NVP parameters for the SHIPTO_ASSOC view task.*

| Variable Name | Variable Type | Description |
|---|---|---|
| ADDRESS_REF_NUM | String | The updated address reference number. If the address reference number passed into the command refers to a temporary address book entry, and a permanent address book entry exists for the same nickname, this string is set to the reference number of the permanent address book entry. |

### *Expected Behavior of Overridable Function:*

Generate a list of products and items in the shopping cart for which the shopper has specified any shipping address.

### *Expected Return Values:*

None

### *Default Overridable Function:*

TaskDisplay_1.0 (IBM,NC)

# SHIPTO_DSP View Task

### *Calling Command:*

OrderItemDisplay, when addr_rn is specified.

### *Explicit Input Parameters:*

*Table E.99 Explicit input parameters for the SHIPTO_DSP view task.*

| Variable Name | Variable Type | Description |
|---|---|---|
| MACRO_NVP | NVPHash* | A collection of name-value pairs that supercede any equivalent name-value pairs found in the http request. For this task, the collection includes the parameters shown below. |

### *MACRO_NVP Parameters:*

*Table E.100 MACRO_NVP parameters for the SHIPTO_DSP view task.*

| Variable Name | Variable Type | Description |
|---|---|---|
| ADDRESS_REF_NUM | String* | The updated address reference number. If the address reference number passed into the command refers to a temporary address book entry, and a permanent address book entry exists for the same nickname, this string is set to the reference number of the permanent address book entry. |

### Expected Behavior of Overridable Function:

Generate a list of products and items in the shopping cart for which the shopper has specified a particular shipping address.

### Expected Return Values:

None

### Default Overridable Function:

TaskDisplay_1.0 (IBM,NC)

# SHIPTO_LST View Task

### Calling Command:

OrderItemList

### Explicit Input Parameters:

**Table E.101** *Explicit input parameters for the SHIPTO_LST view task.*

| Variable Name | Variable Type | Description |
|---|---|---|
| MACRO_NVP | NVPHash* | A collection of name-value pairs that supercede any equivalent name-value pairs found in the http request. For this task, the collection includes the parameters shown below. |

### MACRO_NVP Parameters:

**Table E.102** *MACRO_NVP parameters for the SHIPTO_LST view task.*

| Variable Name | Variable Type | Description |
|---|---|---|
| ADDRESS_REF_NUM | String* | The updated address reference number. If the address reference number passed into the command refers to a temporary address book entry, and a permanent address book entry exists for the same nickname, this string is set to the reference number of the permanent address book entry. |

### Expected Behavior of Overridable Function:

Generate a list of products and items in the shopping cart, which shoppers can select for ordering.

### Expected Return Values:

None

### Default Overridable Function:

TaskDisplay_1.0 (IBM,NC)

# SHOPCART_DSP View Task

*Calling Command:*

InterestItemDisplay

### Explicit Input Parameters:

*Table E.103* *Explicit input parameters for the SHOPCART_DSP view task.*

| Variable Name | Variable Type | Description |
|---|---|---|
| MACRO_NVP | NVPHash* | A collection of name-value pairs that supercede any equivalent name-value pairs found in the http request. For this task, the collection is empty. |

### Expected Behavior of Overridable Function:

Generate the shopper's shopping cart.

### Expected Return Values:

None

### Default Overridable Function:

TaskDisplay_1.0 (IBM,NC)

# Appendix F, Net.Commerce Overridable Functions

This appendix describes all of the overridable functions that are packaged with the Net.Commerce system.

## AuditAddrBook_1.0 (IBM,NC) Overridable Function

***Designed to be called by:***

The AUDIT_ADDR_BOOK process task.

***Behavior:***

1. Determines whether the following columns in table SHADDR were passed in:

    - SALNAME

    - SAADRR1

    - SACITY

    - SASTATE

    - SACNTRY

    - SAZIPC

2. If any column was not passed in, sets the AUDIT_ADDR_BOOK_ERR exception task.

## CheckInv_1.0 (IBM,NC) Overridable Function

***Designed to be called by:***

The CHECK_INV process task.

***Behavior:***

1. Retrieves the quantity of the item that is currently in stock from column PRVENT in table PRODUCT. If the column is null, returns a true value.

2. If the quantity retrieved is less than the quantity requested, sets the CHECK_INV_ERR exception task.

# DoNothingNoArgs_1.0 (IBM,NC) Overridable Function

## *Designed to be called by:*

Any task for which you want to perform no processing.

> **Notes:**
> - If you assign this function to a view task or an exception task, no page is displayed to the shopper.
> - If you assign this function to a process task that expects explicit output parameters, all the output parameters will be empty strings.

## *Behavior:*

Returns without performing any processing.

# DoPayment_1.0 (IBM,NC) Overridable Function

## *Designed to be called by:*

The DO_PAYMENT process task.

## *Behavior:*

1. Determines whether the following columns were passed in implicitly in the HTTP request:

   - CCTYPE, the credit card type

   - CCNUM, the credit card number

   - CCXYEAR, the year in which the credit card expires

   - CCXMONTH, the month in which the credit card expires

2. Ensures that the credit card has a valid number based on the algorithm that credit card issuers use to generate numbers. It does not ensure that the number is assigned to a valid credit card according to the issuer.

3. Ensures that the expiration date has not passed.

4. Creates a new row in table ORDPAYMTHD.

If any column value is invalid, or the row was not created successfully, sets the DO_PAYMENT_ERR exception task.

# GetBaseSpePrc_1.0 (IBM,NC) Overridable Function

### *Designed to be called by:*

The GET_BASE_SPE_PRC process task.

### *Behavior:*

1. Retrieves the product and item prices from column PPPRC in table PRODPRCS for the appropriate shopper group and for the current date and time. If the effective date for a price is null, the effective date is deemed to have passed no matter what the current date is. If the expiry date for a price is null, the expiry date is deemed to be in the future no matter what the current date is.

2. Orders the result by the precedence level that is specified in column PPPRE in table PRODPRCS, and inversely by product reference number. This process places the item before the parent product, because parent products must be defined before their items.

3. Selects the first row that is returned, which is the one with the highest precedence, and returns its price in PRODUCT_PRICE.

4. If the precedence values of an item and its parent product are the same, returns the price of the item in PRODUCT_PRICE.

If any step completes unsuccessfully, sets the GET_BASE_SPE_PRC_ERR exception task.

# GetBaseUnitPrc_1.0 (IBM,NC) Overridable Function

### *Designed to be called by:*

The GET_BASE_UNIT_PRC process task.

### *Behavior:*

1. Retrieves the product and item prices from column PPPRC in table PRODPRCS for the appropriate shopper group and for the current date and time. If the effective date for a price is null, the effective date is deemed to have passed no matter what the current date is. If the expiry date for a price is null, the expiry date is deemed to be in the future no matter what the current date is.

2. Orders the result by the precedence level that is specified in column PPPRE in table PRODPRCS, and inversely by product reference number. This process places the item before the parent product, because parent products must be defined before their items.

3. Selects the first row that is returned, which is the one with the highest precedence, and returns its price in PRODUCT_PRICE.

4. If the precedence values of an item and its parent product are the same, returns the price of the item in PRODUCT_PRICE.

If any step completes unsuccessfully, sets the GET_BASE_UNIT_PRC_ERR exception task.

# GetOrdProdTaxTot_1.0 (IBM,NC) Overridable Function

### Designed to be called by:

The GET_ORD_PROD_TAX_TOT process task.

### Behavior:

Adds the taxes payable on each suborder from column OYTXTOT in table ORDERPAY and saves the result in TAX_TOTAL. If unsuccessful, sets the GET_ORD_PROD_TAX_TOT_ERR exception task.

# GetOrdProdTot_1.0 (IBM,NC) Overridable Function

### Designed to be called by:

The GET_ORD_PROD_TOT process task.

### Behavior:

Adds the item prices for each suborder from column OYPRTOT in table ORDERPAY and saves the result in PRODUCT_PRICE. If unsuccessful, sets the GET_ORD_PROD_TOT_ERR exception task.

# GetOrdShTot_1.0 (IBM,NC) Overridable Function

### Designed to be called by:

The GET_ORD_SH_TOT process task.

### Behavior:

Adds the shipping charges on each suborder from column OYSHTOT in table ORDERPAY and saves the result in PRODUCT_SHIPPING. If unsuccessful, sets the GET_ORD_SH_TOT_ERR exception task.

# GetSubOrdProdTaxTot_1.0 (IBM,NC) Overridable Function

### *Designed to be called by:*

The GET_SUB_ORD_PROD_TAX_TOT process task.

### *Behavior:*

1. Multiplies PRODUCT_PRICE by each tax rate specified in table MALL and saves the result in the corresponding tax amount variable.

2. Adds the value of all the tax amount variables and saves the result in TAX_TOTAL.

If unsuccessful, sets the GET_SUB_ORD_PROD_TAX_TOT_ERR exception task.

# GetSubOrdProdTot_1.0 (IBM,NC) Overridable Function

### *Designed to be called by:*

The GET_SUB_ORD_PROD_TOT process task.

### *Behavior:*

1. For each item in the suborder, retrieves the special unit price from column STPRICE in table SHIPTO and multiplies it by the quantity requested.

2. Adds up all the results and saves the total in PRODUCT_PRICE.

If unsuccessful, sets the GET_SUB_ORD_PROD_TOT_ERR exception task.

# GetSubOrdShTot_1.0 (IBM,NC) Overridable Function

### *Designed to be called by:*

The GET_SUB_ORD_SH_TOT process task.

### *Behavior:*

1. Retrieves the shipping charge calculation method from column PSSPMTHD in table PRSPCODE.

2. Ensures that the shipping mode is valid for the current date and time by checking the effective and expiry dates in tables MSHIPMODE and SHIPPING. If the effective date for a price is null, the effective date is deemed to have passed no matter what the current date is. If the expiry date for a price is null, the expiry date is deemed to be in the future no matter what the current date is.

3.  Calculates the shipping charges based on the shipping method that is specified and stores the result in PRODUCT_SHIPPING.

If unsuccessful, sets the GET_SUB_ORD_SH_TOT_ERR exception task.

# MacroDisplay_1.0 (IBM,NC) Overridable Function

### Designed to be called by:

The CAT_DSP and PROD_DSP view tasks.

### Behavior:

1.  Adds the SESSION_ID variable, the shopper's session ID, to macro_nvp.

2.  Adds the HOST_NAME variable, the site's host name as specified in the Net.Commerce initialization file, to macro_nvp.

3.  Executes the %HTML_REPORT section of the Net.Data macro whose file name is currently stored in the _VAR_HandlerName parameter in the NC_Environment object.

# ResolveSku_1.0 (IBM,NC) Overridable Function

### Designed to be called by:

The RESOLVE_SKU process task.

### Behavior:

1.  For the given product reference number, searches table PRODATR for any required attributes.

2.  If a required product attribute is missing, calls the BAD_PROD_ATTR exception task.

3.  If a product with the specified attributes cannot be found in the database, calls the MISSING_PROD_ATTR exception task.

4.  If the product with the specified attributes exists, sets SKU_REF_NUM to its reference number.

# ReverseInv_1.0 (IBM,NC) Overridable Function

### *Designed to be called by:*

The REVERSE_INV process task.

### *Behavior:*

1.  Adds the quantity requested back to the quantity currently in stock (from column PRVENT in table PRODUCT).

2.  Saves the result back into column PRVENT in table PRODUCT.

3.  If unsuccessful, sets the REVERSE_INV_ERR exception task.

# TaskDisplay_1.0 (IBM,NC) Overridable Function

### *Designed to be called by:*

All view and exception tasks, except CAT_DSP and PROD_DSP.

### *Behavior:*

1.  Retrieves the name of the Net.Data macro to be executed from table MACROS, using the reference number of the calling task and the merchant reference number as the index.

2.  Adds the `SESSION_ID` variable, the shopper's session ID, to `macro_nvp`.

3.  Adds the `HOST_NAME` variable, the site's host name as specified in the Net.Commerce initialization file, to `macro_nvp`.

4.  Executes the macro.

Table F.1 on the next page lists the names of the macros that implement the supplied view and exception tasks, including those that are installed in the database by default, and those that are installed if you install a sample mall or store. All macro names end with the extension `.d2w`. If you have created your own macros, you can obtain their names from the MACROS tables.

***Table F.1*** *The macros that implement the supplied view and exception tasks.*

| View/Exception  Task | Default | Sample1 | Sample2 | Sample3 |
|---|---|---|---|---|
| ADDR_ADD | N/A | N/A | N/A | N/A |
| ADDR_UPDATE | N/A | N/A | N/A | N/A |
| AUDIT_ADDR_BOOK _ERR | N/A | N/A | N/A | err_adrbk |
| AUDIT_REG_ERR | N/A | N/A | N/A | b_err_reg |
| BAD_ADDRESS _BOOK | err_adrbk | err_adrbk | g_err_adrbk | err_adrbk |
| BAD_ADRBK _MODIFY | err_adrbkup1 | err_adrbkup1 | g_err_adrbkup1 | err_adrbk |
| BAD_ORD_DATA | err_han | err_han | g_err_han | err_han |
| BAD_PROD_ATTR | err_shadd | err_shadd | g_err_shadd | N/A |
| BAD_REG | err_reg | err_reg | g_err_reg | b_err_reg |
| BAD_REG_MODIFY | err_regupd | err_regupd | g_err_regupd | N/A |
| BAD_ST_DATA | err_stdata | err_stdata | g_err_stdata | b_err_stdata |
| CHECK_INV_ERR | err_check_inv | err_check_inv | g_err_check_inv | b_err_check_inv |
| DO_PAYMENT_ERR | err_do_payment | err_do_payment | g_err_do_payment | b_err_do_payment |
| EXT_ORD_PROC _ERR | err_ord_proc | err_ord_proc | g_err_ord_proc | err_ord_proc |
| EXT_SHIPTO _PROC_ERR | err_shipto_proc | err_shipto_proc | g_err_shipto_proc | err_shipto_proc |
| EXT_SHIPTO _UPD_ERR | err_shipto _update | err_shipto _update | g_err_shipto _update | err_shipto_update _update |
| GET_BASE_SPE _PRC_ERR | err_spe_prc | err_spe_prc | g_err_spe_prc | err_spe_prc |
| GET_BASE_UNIT _PRC_ERR | err_unit_prc | err_unit_prc | g_err_unit_prc | err_unit_prc |
| GET_ORD_PROD _TAX_TOT_ERR | err_tax_tot | err_tax_tot | g_err_tax_tot | err_tax_tot |
| GET_ORD_PROD _TOT_ERR | err_tot | err_tot | g_err_tot | err_tot |
| GET_ORD_SH _TOT_ERR | err_sh_tot | err_sh_tot | g_err_sh_tot | err_sh_tot |
| GET_SUB_ORD _PROD_TAX_TOT _ERR | err_sub_tax_tot | err_sub_tax_tot | g_err_sub_tax_tot | err_sub_tax_tot |

*Continued on next page*

**Table F.1** *Continued*

| View/Exception Task | Default | Sample1 | Sample2 | Sample3 |
|---|---|---|---|---|
| GET_SUB_ORD_ PROD_TOT_ERR | err_sub_tot | err_sub_tot | g_err_sub_tot | err_sub_tot |
| GET_SUB_ORD _SH_TOT_ERR | err_sub_sh_tot | err_sub_sh_tot | g_err_sub_sh_tot | err_sub_sh_tot |
| LOGON_DSP _SH_TOT_ERR | login | malllogon | g_logon | malllogon |
| LOGON_ERR | login | malllogon | g_logon | malllogon |
| MISSING_PROD _ATTR | err_missattr | err_missattr | g_err_missattr | err_missattr |
| ORD_DSP_COM | orderdspc | orderdspc | orderdspc | b_orderdspc |
| ORD_DSP_PEN | orderdspp | orderdspp | g_orderdspp | b_orderdspp |
| ORD_LST_COM | orderlstc | orderlstc | N/A | orderlstc |
| ORD_LST_PEN | orderlstp | orderlstp | N/A | orderlstp |
| ORD_NONE | ordernone | ordernone | g_ordernone | b_ordernone |
| ORD_OK | orderacpt | orderacpt | g_orderacpt | b_orderacpt |
| ORD_UNLOCKED | err_han | err_han | err_han | err_han |
| PAY_CANCEL | N/A | pay_stat | N/A | N/A |
| REG_NEW | msregform | mallregform | g_msregform | b_msregform |
| REG_UPDATE | msregupd | mallregupd | g_msregupd | b_msregupd |
| RESOLVE_SKU_ERR | N/A | N/A | N/A | N/A |
| SHIPTO_ASSOC | shptodsp | shptodsp | g_shptodsp | N/A |
| SHIPTO_DSP | shptodsp | shptodsp | N/A | N/A |
| SHIPTO_LST | shptolst | shptolst | N/A | N/A |
| SHOPCART_DSP | shopcart | shopcart shopcart1 shopcart2 shopcart3 | g_shopcart | N/A |
| UPDATE_INV_ERR | err_update_inv | err_update_inv | g_err_update_inv | err_update_inv |

**Note:**
The column headings are as follows: Default is the Net.Data macro that is automatically installed in the database when Net.Commerce is first installed; Sample1 is the Net.Data macro for the Metropolitan Mall sample; Sample2 is the Net.Data macro(s) for the East West Food Mart sample; and Sample3 is the Net.Data macros(s) for the Office Window sample.

# UpdateInv_1.0 (IBM,NC) Overridable Function

### *Designed to be called by:*

The UPDATE_INV process task.

### *Behavior:*

1.  Subtracts the quantity ordered from the quantity currently in stock (from column PRVENT in table PRODUCT).  If the column is null, returns true value.

2.  If the result is not less than 0, saves the result back into column PRVENT in table PRODUCT.  If the result is less than 0, sets the UPDATE_INV_ERR exception task.

# Appendix G, The Net.Commerce Object Model

As an alternative to manipulating the database using the ODBC classes and SQL statements, you can use the object model. This model provides an interface between the database schema and your commands and overridable functions. The objects eliminate the need for SQL, thereby freeing you from having to know the current schema, which may change in future versions of Net.Commerce.

> **Note:**
> IBM will not guarantee binary or strict backward compatibility for overridable functions or commands created using the object model. The model is subject to change in future versions of Net.Commerce. If you choose to create your commands or overridable functions using this model, be aware that you may have to modify or recompile them if you migrate to future versions of Net.Commerce.

The object model uses the concepts of entities and homes. They are described below.

## Entities

An entity corresponds to a row in a database table. It is an object that you can create, query, update, and delete. The `SQL_Schema` class is used to implement entities.

### The SQL_Schema Class

The `SQl_Schema` class is built on top of the hash table and uses parameters that are similar to name-value pairs, the only difference being that instead of containing a name, these parameters contain a column. The column contains the type information and the type of key for the column (primary, foreign, or none). This class maintains two states: the actual state, which corresponds to the last known correct state for the object, and the wished state, which represents the values that the user wishes to set but which have not yet been sent to the data store. For example, you might want to retrieve the following object:

```
{ a=1, b=2, c=3 }
```

When you set the column 'a' to 4, your `SQL_Schema` object will have two states for 'a': the actual state will be 1, and the wished state will be 4. The `getValue` functions in this class, by default, return the actual state. The object can save itself and delete itself in the data store. You can also set fields.

The base class for entities uses a relaxed function for concurrency control. When an object is updated, the actual values are used in the WHERE clause. If the object had changed since the last time it was read in, the update will fail.

## Template Entity

The following is a sample `SQL_Schema` derived object. It corresponds to a table 'entity' in the database, and has three columns: refnum, name, and sequence.

### *entity.h*

```
class Entity : public SQL_Schema
{
  public:
    Entity(DataBase& DB);

  public: // Schema column names.
    static const StringWithOwnership _COL_TNAME;
    static const StringWithOwnership _COL_REF_NUM ;
    static const StringWithOwnership _COL_NAME;
    static const StringWithOwnership _COL_SEQUENCE;
};
```

### *entity.cpp*

```
// Schema column names.
const StringWithOwnership Entity::_COL_TNAME("entity");
const StringWithOwnership Entity::_COL_REF_NUM("entity.refnum");
const StringWithOwnership Entity::_COL_NAME("entity.name");
const StringWithOwnership Entity::_COL_DESC("entity.sequence");

// Schema column definitions.
const long EntitySchemaSize = 3L;
static const SQL_Column EntityColumns[EntitySchemaSize] =
{
  SQL_Column(Entity::_COL_REF_NUM , E_SQL_COL_INT,
              E_SQL_COL_PRIMARY_KEY),
  SQL_Column(Entity::_COL_NAME , E_SQL_COL_STRING,),
  SQL_Column(Entity::_COL_SEQUENCE, E_SQL_COL_STRING)
};

// Constructor.
Entity::Entity(DataBase& DB) : SQL_Schema(DB, _COL_TNAME,
                                          _COL_REF_NUM)

{
  ExtendSchema(EntitySchemaSize, Entity Columns);
}
```

The `SQL_Schema` class allows you to set values in other formats; for example, timestamps, NULL values, or 'alternate' values. The following is an example:

```
X->setValue(XXX::_COL_A, SQL_Schema::_STR_NULL_);
X->setValue(XXX::_COL_B, SQL_Schema::_STR_CURRENT_TIMESTAMP_);
X->setAlternateValue(XXX::_COL_C, "UDF_x('Hello')");
```

The constant variable _STR_NULL_ is set to ^~NC_NULL~^. Use this value only to ensure that a string field is not set with ^~NC_NULL~^ as the actual value, as it will be interpreted as a NULL value. The variable _STR_CURRENT_TIMESTAMP_ on an ODBC platform is set to {fn now()}.

The SQL_Schema class will handle it appropriately on other platforms.  At times, you may want to use UDFs or database stored procedures to set values.  The TIMESTAMP acts like an alternate value.

One difference between alternate values and all other data is that the actual value does not get set after a write.  If you update a field with the current time or a UDF, the only way to get the values that were actually set in the database is to look up the object again.

## Interface

```
protected:
    SQL_Schema(DataBase& DB, const String& Table,
               const String& PrimaryKey = _STR_EMPTY_,
               UDWORD HashSize = 53);

protected:
    void ExtendSchema(long SchemaSize, const SQL_Column Columns[]);

public:
    static const StringWithOwnership _STR_CURRENT_TIMESTAMP_;
    static const StringWithOwnership _STR_NULL_ ;

public: // Access functions.
    const String& getValue(const String& ColName, bool Real=true) const;
    bool getValue(const String& ColName, String& Value, bool Real=true)
                                                                  const;
    bool getValue(const String& ColName, char & Value, bool Real=true)
                                                                  const;
    bool getValue(const String& ColName, long & Value, bool Real=true)
                                                                  const;
    bool getValue(const String& ColName, double& Value, bool Real=true)
                                                                  const;

    bool setValue(const String& ColName, const String& ColValue);
    bool setValue(const String& ColName, long ColValue);
    bool setValue(const String& ColName, double ColValue);
    bool setAlternateValue(const String& ColName,
                           const String& ColValue);
    bool setAlternateValue(const String& ColName, long ColValue);
    bool setAlternateValue(const String& ColName, double ColValue);

    bool RemoveValue(const String& ColName);

    const String& getIdentifierString(void);
    long getError(void) const;

public:
    long Count(void);
    int Write(void);
    int Delete(bool KeepCopy );

    int Compare(const SQL_Column* rhs);
    int Compare(const String * rhs);
```

```
bool operator==(const SQL_Column& rhs);
bool operator==(const String& rhs);
```

- The constructor takes a database, a table name, the primary key, and the hash size to hold the name-value pairs.

- The `ExtendSchema` function takes the array of columns to initialize the object.

- The `getValue` functions retrieve fields values. By default, the actual value is returned. If *Real* is false, the wished value, if any, is returned.

- The `setValue` functions set wished values for the named field.

- The `setAlternateValue` functions allow you to set values that are not "simple" (you might want to invoke a certain function in the database). This value will not be interpreted and will be inserted in the SQL statement directly.

- The `RemoveValue` function removes the wished value previously set, if any.

- The `Count` function returns the count of objects in the database that correspond to the wished state of the object (all values are "and-ed").

- The `Write` function attempts to write the object to the database. If the object was initialized with a create, an INSERT statement is generated. If the object was meant to be looked up, an UPDATE statement is generated. The wished values are used to set values, and the actual state is used for the WHERE clause.

- The `Delete` function deletes the object in the database. If `KeepCopy` is true, the actual values are merged into the wished values (old values are overwritten); otherwise, both sets of values are cleaned up.

- The `Compare` and `operator==` functions are here only so that entities can be put into containers. They always return true.

# Homes

A home is a container that is responsible for loading, creating and deleting objects (entities). It reflects tables in the database. Net.Commerces bases homes on the "factory" concept. Homes provide several lookup functions: one with the primary key, and others with fields that represent various unique indexes. They also provide a function to create new entities, which requires fields that are defined as NOT NULL. The `SQL_SchemaMap` class is used to implement homes.

Examine the following entity `E` and its corresponding `Home`:

```
Entity E
   RefNum, primary key
   Name, not null
   Sequence
   unique index (Name, Sequence);

Home E
   Lookup(RefNum);
   Lookup(Name, Sequence);
   Create(Name );
```

# Template Home

To create a home for an entity, you must create your own class, and add the `Lookup` and `Create` functions according to the semantics of your object.

### entity.h

```
class EntityHome : public SQL_SchemaMap<Entity>
{
  public:
    EntityHome(DataBase& DB) : SQL_SchemaMap<Entity>(DB) { }

  public:
    Entity* Create (const String& Name , const String& Sequence,
                    NVPHash& NVPs);

    Entity* Lookup (const String& RefNum, NVPHash& NVPs);
    Entity* Lookup2(const String& Name , const String& Sequence,
                    NVPHash& NVPs);
};
```

### entity.cpp

```
Entity* EntityHome::Create(const String& Name, const String& Sequence,
                           NVPHash& NVP)
{
  Entity* Obj = new Entity(_db);
  Obj->setValue(Entity::_COL_REF_NUM ,
                _DB.getKeyManager()- GetNextKey(_COL_TNAME));
  Obj->setValue(Entity::_COL_NAME, Name);
  Obj->setValue(Entity::_COL_SEQUENCE, Sequence);
  SQL_SchemaMapBase::Create(Obj, NVP);
  if (Obj->getError() != 0)
  {
    delete Obj ;
    return NULL;
  }
  return Obj;
}

Entity* EntityHome::Lookup(const String& RefNum, const NVPHash& NVP)
{
  Entity* Obj = new Entity(_db);
  Obj->setValue(Entity::_COL_REF_NUM, RefNum);
  SQL_SchemaMapBase::Lookup(Obj, NVP);
  if (Obj->getError() != 0)
  {
    delete Obj ;
    return NULL;
  }
  return Obj;
}

Entity* EntityHome::Lookup2(const String& Name,
                            const String& Sequence,
```

```
                              const NVPHash& NVP)
{
  Entity* Obj = new Entity(_db);
  Obj->setValue(Entity::_COL_NAME, Name);
  Obj->setValue(Entity::_COL_SEQUENCE, Sequence);
  SQL_SchemaMapBase::Lookup(Obj, NVP);
  if (Obj->getError() != 0)
  {
    delete Obj ;
    return NULL;
  }
  return Obj;
}
```

# template <class X> SQL_SchemaMap Class

```
SQL_SchemaMap (DataBase& db);
~SQL_SchemaMap(void);

typedef TemplateNC_PList<X, String> SchemaList;
typedef TemplateNC_PList<X, String>::Iterator SchemaListIterator;

SchemaList* Query(const String& WhereClause);
long Count(const NVPHash& NVP);
void Delete(const String& WhereClause);
void Update(const NVPHash& NVP, const String& WhereClause);
void Destroy(X* x);
void Destroy(TemplateNC_PList<X, String>* x);
long getError(void);
```

- The constructor takes a database connection for the home.

- Two typedefs are defined for you to work on lists of objects.

- The Query function takes a where clause (a boolean expression), and returns a list, possibly empty), of objects.

- The Count function counts the number of objects given the name-value pairs specified. These name-value pairs will be "and-ed" together.

- The Delete function takes a where clause, and deletes all objects accordingly.

- The Update function updates a collection of objects according to the where clause, with the given name-value pairs.

- The Destroy functions get rid of objects instantiated by the home. The functions can handle a single object or a list of objects (as returned by the Query function).

- The getError function returns the error code that is returned by the database when the Lookup or Create function fails.

# Using the Object Model

The following example shows how to use the homes and entities in the Net.Commerce object model. It uses the UserGroup entity, which (along with all the other objects) is described later in this Appendix.

```
UserGroupHome Home(_DB);
UserGroup* UG;
NVPHash NVP;

// Create a new user group called "Gold".
NVP.Add(UserGroup::_COL_DESC, "gold");

// An INSERT is performed.
UG = Home.Create("1111", Gold, NVP)

if (Home.getError() != ERR_DB_NO_ERROR)
   // An error occurred.
   return false;

// Set the wished value.
UG.setName("Platinum");

// Perform an UPDATE.
if (UG.Write() != ERR_DB_NO_ERROR)
   // An error occurred.
   return false;

// Change the name of the UserGroup with the reference number
// '1' to 'Silver'.
Home.Destroy(UG);
NVP.Clean(true);

// A SELECT statement.
UG = Home.Lookup("1");

// Equivalent to checking the error code.
if (UG == NULL)
{
   _DB->ReportError();
   return false;
}

// The wished value is "Silver".
UG.setName("Silver");

// Perform an UPDATE.
if (UG.Write() != ERR_DB_NO_ERROR)
   // An error occurred.
   return false;
```

In this example, the home returned a pointer to an object for both the `Create` and `Lookup` functions. If this pointer is NULL, then an error occurred. The error is a database error that can be checked using the `getError` function. If the operation is successful, a pointer to a valid object is returned. This object is created by the home and should also be deleted by the home. The `Destroy` function manages the deletion of the object. The home deletes the pointer.

Homes also have member functions to query, update and delete multiple objects at a time. The Query function returns a list of objects. If the list is empty, no object was retrieved. If it is NULL, an error occurred. The `Query` function, like the `Delete` and `Update` functions, takes a WHERE clause as an argument, which is a String that represents a boolean expression. By using the parameter supplied with the Resource, you can create a boolean expression that will be easily ported when the schema changes, or if your code is used on a data source other than an RDBMS. The `Update` function also takes an `NVPHash` object as an argument, to set the field to the desired values. The `Query` function is more complicated than the other functions, in the same way that the SELECT SQL statement is more complicated than the UPDATE, DELETE, or INSERT statement. Here is an example of an SQL query that is executed using an instance of a home:

```
// Create an instance of the UserHome object called Home, which can
// access the current database.
UserHome Home((DataBase*) Env.Seek(NC_Environment::_VAR_Database));

// Create a pointer to the SchemaList object, to store the results of
// the SQL statement that will be executed.
UserGroupHome::SchemaList* UGList;

// Declare a string to store the WHERE statement.
String WhereClause;

// Resizes the string so that it is large enough for a 1K WHERE
// statement.
WhereClause.Resize(STRLEN_1K);

// Compose a WHERE statement that defines the criteria for the SQL
// statement: the value of merchant reference number in the database
// must equal the value of the previously declared local variable
// MerchantRefNum.
WhereClause << UserGroup::_COL_MERCHANT_REF_NUM << " = "
            << MerchantRefNum;

// Call the Query function to execute the SELECT statement against the
// UserHome object.
UGList = Home.Query(WhereClause);

// If no object is returned (system error), return false.
if (UGList == NULL)
{
   return false;
}
```

```
// Set up an iterator and set it to the beginning.
UserGroupHome::SchemaListIterator I(UGList);
I.Begin();

// If no row is returned, do nothing
if (*I == NULL)
{
   // The current merchant has not defined any user groups
}

// Otherwise, for each row returned, retrieve the name of the shopper
// group in the SHOPGRP table.
else do { String UserGroupName = (*I)->getName();

// Advance the iterator until all rows have been processed.
++I;
} while (*I != NULL);
```

# Entity Classes

The following describes the classes for the entities that are supplied by Net.Commerce.

## User-Related Classes

The user-related classes allow you to retrieve shopper profile and address information.

### User

The User class contains information needed to identify each shopper or user to the Net.Commerce system. It also contains some basic contact and classification information. It maps to the SHOPPER (Shopper Profile) table in the database. Use this class to retrieve this profile information about the current shopper.

```
class User : public Resource
{
   const String& getRefNum(bool Real=true) const;
   const String& getName(bool Real=true) const;
   const String& getPassword(bool Real=true) const;
   const String& getType(bool Real=true) const;
   bool isGuest(bool Real=true) const;
   bool isRegistered(bool Real=true) const;
   bool isAdmin(bool Real=true) const;
   const String& getComm(bool Real=true) const;
   bool isEmail1(bool Real=true) const;
   bool isEmail2(bool Real=true) const;
   bool isPhone1(bool Real=true) const;
   bool isPhone2(bool Real=true) const;

   // Reserved for internal use only.
   const String& getPhList(bool Real=true) const;
```

```
   const String& getLastVisit(bool Real=true) const;
   const String& getLastOrder(bool Real=true) const;
   const String& getTimeRegistered(bool Real=true) const;
   const String& getTimeCanceled(bool Real=true) const;
   const String& getLastChanged(bool Real=true) const;

   // Reserved for internal use only.
   const String& getIBM_Contact(bool Real=true) const;

   const String& getChallengeQuestion(bool Real=true) const;
   const String& getChallengeAnswer(bool Real=true) const;
   const String& getField1(bool Real=true) const;
   const String& getField2(bool Real=true) const;

   int Refresh(void);

   // Transfer all information about the user U (interest items,
   // addresses, order item, orders) to the current user.
   bool TransferAllFrom(User& U);

   // Creates an encrypted session token for the user.  Can be used as a
   // cookie etc....
   String GenerateEncryptedSession(const String& MerchantKey) const;

   // Given an encrypted session, uses authentication to ensure it is
   // the current one for the user.
   bool CheckSession (const String& MerchantKey,
                      const String& EncryptedSession) const;
};

class UserHome : public ResourceHome
{
   User* Create(const String& Name, const String& Type, const
            NVPHash& NameValuePairs);
   User* Lookup(const String& RefNum, const NVPHash& NameValuePairs);
   User* LookupByName(const String& Name,
                      const NVPHash& NameValuePairs);
   User* LookupAndAuthenticate(const String& Name,
                               const String& Password,
                               const String& MerchantKey);
};
```

## Address

The `Address` class contains name and address information for each shopper in the system.  It
maps to the SHADDR (Shopper Address Book) table in the database.  Use this class to retrieve
address information for any shopper.

```
class Address : public Resource
{
   const String& getRefNum(bool Real=true) const;
   const String& getUserRefNum(bool Real=true) const;
   const String& getNickname(bool Real=true) const;
```

```
    const String& getTitle (bool Real=true) const;
    bool isDr(bool Real=true) const;
    bool isMr(bool Real=true) const;
    bool isMrs(bool Real=true) const;
    bool isMs(bool Real=true) const;
    bool isN(bool Real=true) const;
    const String& getFlag(bool Real=true) const;
    bool isOld(bool Real=true) const;
    bool isCurrent(bool Real=true) const;
    const String& getLastName(bool Real=true) const;
    const String& getFirstName(bool Real=true) const;
    const String& getMiddleName(bool Real=true) const;
    const String& getCompany(bool Real=true) const;
    const String& getPhone1(bool Real=true) const;
    const String& getPhone2(bool Real=true) const;
    const String& getFax(bool Real=true) const;
    const String& getAddress1(bool Real=true) const;
    const String& getAddress2(bool Real=true) const;
    const String& getAddress3(bool Real=true) const;
    const String& getCity(bool Real=true) const;
    const String& getState(bool Real=true) const;
    const String& getCountry(bool Real=true) const;
    const String& getZip(bool Real=true) const;
    const String& getEmail1(bool Real=true) const;
    const String& getEmail2(bool Real=true) const;
    const String& getTimeCreated(bool Real=true) const;
    const String& getDayPhoneType(bool Real=true) const;
    const String& getDayPhoneListing(bool Real=true) const;
    bool isDayPhoneListed(bool Real=true) const;
    bool isDayPhoneNotListed(bool Real=true) const;
    const String& getEveningPhoneType(bool Real=true) const;
    const String& getEveningPhoneListing(bool Real=true) const;
    bool isEveningPhoneListed(bool Real=true) const;
    bool isEveningPhoneNotListed(bool Real=true) const;
    const String& getBestPhoneTime(bool Real=true) const;
    bool isBestPhoneTimeDay(bool Real=true) const;
    bool isBestPhoneTimeEvening(bool Real=true) const;
    const String& getPackageInsertion(bool Real=true) const;
    bool isPackageInsertionYes(bool Real=true) const;
    bool isPackageInsertionNo(bool Real=true) const;
    const String& getField1(bool Real=true) const;
    const String& getField2(bool Real=true) const;
};

class AddressHome : public ResourceHome
{
    Address* Create(const String& ShopperRefNum, const String& Nickname,
                    const NVPHash& NameValuePairs);
    Address* Lookup(const String& RefNum,
                    const NVPHash& NameValuePairs);
    Address* LookupCurrentFromRefNum (const String& ShopperRefNum,
                                      const String& RefNum);
```

```
    Address* LookupCurrentFromNickname(const String& ShopperRefNum,
                                       const String& NickName);
    Address* BackupAndCreateCurrent (const String& ShopperRefNum,
                                     const String& Nickname,
                                     const NVPHash& NVP );

};
```

# Merchant-Related Classes

The merchant-related classes allow you to retrieve profile and contact information about merchants, their stores, the shopper groups that the merchants define and the merchants' shoppers.

## Merchant

The `Merchant` class contains information needed to identify each merchant in the system. It contains general profile information about each merchant, including descriptions and merchant reference numbers. It maps to the corresponding columns in the MERCHANT (Merchant Profile) table in the database. Use this class to retrieve profile information about any merchant.

```
class Merchant : public Resource
{
   const String& getRefNum(bool Real=true) const;
   const String& getName(bool Real=true) const;
   const String& getDescription(bool Real=true) const;
   const String& getCategory(bool Real=true) const;
   const String& getImage(bool Real=true) const;
   const String& getHeader(bool Real=true) const;
   const String& getFooter(bool Real=true) const;
   const String& getBase(bool Real=true) const;
   const String& getCurrency(bool Real=true) const;
   const String& getField1(bool Real=true) const;
   const String& getField2(bool Real=true) const;
};

class MerchantHome : public ResourceHome
{
   Merchant* Create(const String& Name, const String& Phone,
                    const String& City, const String& State,
                    const String& Country, const String& Currency,
                    const NVPHash& NameValuePairs);
   Merchant* Lookup(const String& RefNum,
                    const NVPHash& NameValuePairs);
};
```

## MerchantContact

The `MerchantContact` class contains information about the primary contact for each merchant in the system, including names and telephone numbers. It maps to the corresponding columns in the MERCHANT (Merchant Profile) table in the database. Use this class to retrieve the contact information for any merchant.

```
class MerchantContact : public Resource
{
  // Return same as MerchantRefNum.
  const String& getRefNum(bool Real=true) const;

  const String& getMerchantRefNum(bool Real=true) const;
  const String& getLastName(bool Real=true) const;
  const String& getFirstName(bool Real=true) const;
  const String& getMiddleName(bool Real=true) const;
  const String& getTitle(bool Real=true) const;
  const String& getPhone1(bool Real=true) const;
  const String& getPhone2(bool Real=true) const;
  const String& getFax(bool Real=true) const;
  const String& getMail1(bool Real=true) const;
  const String& getMail2(bool Real=true) const;
};

class MerchantContactHome : public ResourceHome
{
  MerchantContact* Create(const String& MerchantRefNum,
                          const String& LastName,
                          const String& FirstName,
                          const String& Phone1,
                          const NVPHash& NameValuePairs);
  MerchantContact* Lookup(const String& RefNum,
                          const NVPHash& NameValuePairs);
};
```

## MerchantAddress

The `MerchantAddress` class contains address information for each merchant in the system, including the company name and the street address. It maps to the corresponding columns in the MERCHANT (Merchant Profile) table in the database. Use this class to retrieve the address information for any merchant.

```
class MerchantAddress : public Resource
{
  // Return same as MerchantRefNum.
  const String& getRefNum(bool Real=true) const;

  const String& getMerchantRefNum(bool Real=true) const;
  const String& getName(bool Real=true) const;
  const String& getPhone(bool Real=true) const;
  const String& getAddress1(bool Real=true) const;
  const String& getAddress2(bool Real=true) const;
  const String& getAddress3(bool Real=true) const;
  const String& getCity(bool Real=true) const;
  const String& getState(bool Real=true) const;
  const String& getCountry(bool Real=true) const;
  const String& getZipCode(bool Real=true) const;
};
```

```
class MerchantAddressHome : public ResourceHome
{
   MerchantAddress* Create(const String& MerchantRefNum,
                           const String& Name, const String& Phone,
                           const String& City, const String& State,
                           const String& Country,
                           const NVPHash& NameValuePairs);
   MerchantAddress* Lookup(const String& RefNum,
                           const NVPHash& NameValuePairs);
};
```

## UserGroup

The UserGroup class contains information about the shopper groups that are defined for each store, including the merchant reference numbers and the names of the shopper groups. It maps to the SHOPGRP (Shopper Group) table in the database. Use this class to retrieve the shopper groups defined for a specific store.

```
class UserGroup : public Resource
{
   const String& getRefNum(bool Real=true) const;
   const String& getMerchantRefNum(bool Real=true) const;
   const String& getName(bool Real=true) const;
   const String& getText(bool Real=true) const;
   const String& getField1(bool Real=true) const;
   const String& getField2(bool Real=true) const;
};

class UserGroupHome : public ResourceHome
{
   UserGroup* Create(const String& MerchantRefNum, const String& Name,
                     const NVPHash& NameValuePairs);
   UserGroup* Lookup(const String& RefNum,
                     const NVPHash& NameValuePairs);
   UserGroup* Lookup(const String& MerchantRefNum, const String& Name,
                     const NVPHash& NameValuePairs);
};
```

## MerchantUserInfo

The MerchantUserInfo class contains information to link shoppers to the shopper group in which they belong and contains additional information about shoppers who have special relationships with the merchant, including the merchant reference number and the shopper group reference number. It maps to the MCUSTINFO (Merchant Customer Information) table in the database. Use this class to retrieve the shopper group information for a specific shopper in a specific store.

```
class MerchantUserInfo : public Resource
{
   const String& getShopperRefNum(bool Real=true) const;
   const String& getMerchantRefNum(bool Real=true) const;
   const String& getShopperGroupRefNum(bool Real=true) const;
   const String& getId(bool Real=true) const;
   const String& getField1(bool Real=true) const;
};

class MerchantUserInfoHome : public ResourceHome
{
   MerchantUserInfo* Create(const String& MerchantRefNum,
                            const String& ShopperRefNum,
                            const String& ShopperGroupRefNum,
                            const NVPHash& NameValuePairs);
   MerchantUserInfo* Lookup(const String& MerchantRefNum,
                            const String& ShopperRefNum,
                            const NVPHash& NameValuePairs);
};
```

# Category-Related Classes

The category-related classes allow you to retrieve information about the product categories that have been defined for a store.

## Category

The `Category` class contains information about all of the product categories and subcategories that have been defined for each store. It maps to the corresponding columns in the CATEGORY table in the database. Use this class to retrieve the name of a category or subcategory based on a merchant reference number.

```
class Category : public Resource
{
   const String& getRefNum(bool Real=true) const;
   const String& getMerchantRefNum(bool Real=true) const;
   const String& getName(bool Real=true) const;
   const String& getField1(bool Real=true) const;
   const String& getField2(bool Real=true) const;
};

class CategoryHome : public ResourceHome
{
   Category* Create(const String& MerchantRefNum, const String& Name,
                    const NVPHash& NameValuePairs);
   Category* Lookup(const String& RefNum,
                    const NVPHash& NameValuePairs);
   Category* Lookup(const String& MerchantRefNum, const String& Name,
                    const NVPHash& NameValuePairs);
};
```

## CategoryDescription

The `CategoryDescription` class contains detailed information about each category or subcategory that has been defined for a store, including brief and detailed descriptions, and images. It maps to the corresponding columns in the CATEGORY table in the database. Use this class to retrieve descriptions of a specific category.

```
class CategoryDescription : public Resource
{
   const String& getRefNum(bool Real=true) const;
   const String& getCategoryRefNum(bool Real=true) const;
   const String& getShortDescription(bool Real=true) const;
   const String& getLongDescription(bool Real=true) const;
   const String& getDisplay(bool Real=true) const;
   const String& getSmallImage(bool Real=true) const;
   const String& getLargeImage(bool Real=true) const;
   const String& getPublish(bool Real=true) const;
   bool isNotPublished(bool Real=true) const;
   bool isPublished(bool Real=true) const;
   bool isMarkedForDelete(bool Real=true) const;
};

class CategoryDescriptionHome : public ResourceHome
{
   CategoryDescription* Create(const String& CategoryRefNum,
                               const String& MerchantRefNum,
                               const String& Name,
                               const NVPHash& NameValuePairs);
   CategoryDescription* Lookup(const String& RefNum,
                               const NVPHash& NameValuePairs);
};
```

## CategoryView

The `CategoryView` class contains information about the Net.Data macros that are used to create the category pages to display to specific shopper groups. It maps to the CATESGP table in the database. Use this class to retrieve the name of the Net.Data macro that displays a category for a specific shopper group belonging to a specific store.

```
class CategoryView : public Resource
{
   const String& getMerchantRefNum(bool Real=true) const;
   const String& getCategoryRefNum(bool Real=true) const;
   const String& getShopperGroupRefNum(bool Real=true) const;
   const String& getDisplay(bool Real=true) const;
   const String& getDescription(bool Real=true) const;
   const String& getField1(bool Real=true) const;
   const String& getField2(bool Real=true) const;
};
```

```
class CategoryViewHome : public ResourceHome
{
   CategoryView* Create(const String& MerchantRefNum,
                        const String& ShopperGroupRefNum,
                        const String& CategoryRefNum,
                        const String& Display,
                        const NVPHash& NameValuePairs);
   CategoryView* Lookup(const String& MerchantRefNum,
                        const String& ShopperGroupRefNum,
                        const String& CategoryRefNum,
                        const NVPHash& NameValuePairs);
};
```

# Product-Related Classes

The product-related classes allow you to retrieve information about the product and items that belong to a specific store.

## Product

The `Product` class contains information about the products and items that have been defined for a store, including the product names, reference numbers, the reference number of the store that sells them, tax codes, and inventory. It maps to the corresponding columns in the PRODUCT table in the database. Use this class to retrieve this information for a specific product that belongs to a specific store.

```
class Product : public Resource
{
   const String& getRefNum(bool Real=true) const;
   const String& getMerchantRefNum(bool Real=true) const;
   const String& getName(bool Real=true) const;
   const String& getKnuTag(bool Real=true) const;
   const String& getShipCode(bool Real=true) const;
   const String& getTaxCode(bool Real=true) const;
   const String& getInventory(bool Real=true) const;
   const String& getAvailability(bool Real=true) const;
   const String& getSpecial(bool Real=true) const;
   bool isOnSale(bool Real=true) const;
   const String& getLastUpdate(bool Real=true) const;
   const String& getField1(bool Real=true) const;
   const String& getField2(bool Real=true) const;
   const String& getField3(bool Real=true) const;
   const String& getField4(bool Real=true) const;
   const String& getField5(bool Real=true) const;
};
```

```
class ProductHome : public ResourceHome
{
   Product* Create(const String& MerchantRefNum, const String& Name,
                                    const NVPHash& NameValuePairs);
   Product* Lookup(const String& RefNum,
                                    const NVPHash& NameValuePairs);
   Product* Lookup(const String& MerchantRefNum, const String& Name,
const NVPHash& NameValuePairs);
};
```

## ProductDescription

The `ProductDescription` class contains detailed information about each product or item being sold in a store, including brief and detailed descriptions, and images. It maps to the corresponding columns in the PRODUCT table in the database. Use this class to retrieve descriptions of a specific product.

```
Class ProductDescription : public Resource
{
   const String& getRefNum(bool Real=true) const;
   const String& getProductRefNum(bool Real=true) const;
   const String& getLink(bool Real=true) const;
   const String& getShortDescription(bool Real=true) const;
   const String& getLongDescription1(bool Real=true) const;
   const String& getLongDescription2(bool Real=true) const;
   const String& getLongDescription3(bool Real=true) const;
   const String& getLargeImage(bool Real=true) const;
   const String& getSmallImage(bool Real=true) const;
   const String& getPublish(bool Real=true) const;
   bool isNotPublished(bool Real=true) const;
   bool isPublished(bool Real=true) const;
   bool isMarkedForDelete(bool Real=true) const;
};

class ProductDescritionHome : public ResourceHome
{
   ProductDescription* Create(const String& ProductRefNum,
                                const NVPHash& NameValuePairs);
   ProductDescription* Lookup(const String& RefNum ,
                                const NVPHash& NameValuePairs);
};
```

## ProductAttribute

The `ProductAttribute` class contains the names of all the attributes that qualify an item as a distinct SKU. It maps to the PRODDSTATR table in the database. Use this class when retrieving a list of the items that belong to the attribute that has a specific name.

```
class ProductAttribute : public Resource
{
   const String& getName(bool Real=true) const;
   const String& getProductRefNum(bool Real=true) const;
```

```
   const String& getDescription1(bool Real=true) const;
   const String& getDescription2(bool Real=true) const;
   const String& getSequence(bool Real=true) const;
};

class ProductAttributeHome : public ResourceHome
{
   ProductAttribute* Create(const String& Name,
                            const String& ProductRefNum,
                            const NVPHash& NameValuePairs);
   ProductAttribute* Lookup(const String& Name,
                            const String& ProductRefNum,
                            const NVPHash& NameValuePairs);
};
```

## SkuAttributeValue

The `SkuAttributeValue` class contains the attribute names and values for each item in a store. It maps to the PRODATR table in the database. Use this class to retrieve the attribute name-value pairs of a specific item.

```
class SkuAttributeValue : public Resource
{
   const String& getSkuRefNum(bool Real=true)
   {
     return SQL_Schema::getValue(_COL_SKU_REF_NUM, Real);
   }
   const String& getName(bool Real=true)
   {
     return SQL_Schema::getValue(_COL_NAME , Real);
   }
   const String& getVal(bool Real=true)
   {
     return SQL_Schema::getValue(_COL_VALUE , Real);
   }
   const String& getField1(bool Real=true)
   {
     return SQL_Schema::getValue(_COL_FIELD1 , Real);
   }
};

class SkuAttributeValueHome : public ResourceHome
{
   SkuAttributeValue* Create(const String& Name, const String& Val,
                             const String& SkuRefNum,
                             const NVPHash& NameValuePairs);
   SkuAttributeValue* Lookup(const String& Name,
                             const String& SkuRefNum,
                             const NVPHash& NameValuePairs);
   String ResolveSku(const String& ParentProductRefNum,
                     const NVPHash& AttributeNameValuePairs);
};
```

## ProductView

The `ProductView` class contains information about the Net.Data macros that are used to create the product pages to display to specific shopper groups. It maps to the PRODSGP table in the database. Use this class to retrieve the name of the Net.Data macro that displays a product for a specific shopper group belonging to a specific store.

```
class ProductView : public Resource
{
   const String& getMerchantRefNum(bool Real=true) const;
   const String& getProductRefNum(bool Real=true) const;
   const String& getShopperGroupRefNum(bool Real=true) const;
   const String& getDisplay(bool Real=true) const;
   const String& getDescription(bool Real=true) const;
   const String& getField1(bool Real=true) const;
   const String& getField2(bool Real=true) const;
};

class ProductViewHome : public ResourceHome
{
   ProductView* Create(const String& MerchantRefNum,
                       const String& ShopperGroupRefNum,
                       const String& ProductRefNum,
                       const String& Display,
                       const NVPHash& NameValuePairs);
   ProductView* Lookup(const String& MerchantRefNum,
                       const String& ShopperGroupRefNum,
                       const String& ProductRefNum,
                       const NVPHash& NameValuePairs);
};
```

## ProductPrice

The class `ProductPrice` contains the prices of all products and items in all stores, including prices that apply to different shopper groups, and those offered for a defined period of time. It maps to the PRODPRC table in the database. Use this class to retrieve the price of a specific product belonging to a specific store.

```
class ProductPrice : public Resource
{
   const String& getRefNum(bool Real=true) const;
   const String& getMerchantRefNum(bool Real=true) const;
   const String& getProductRefNum(bool Real=true) const;
   const String& getShopperGroupRefNum(bool Real=true) const;
   const String& getPrice(bool Real=true) const;
   const String& getCurrency(bool Real=true) const;
   const String& getPrecedence(bool Real=true) const;
   const String& getTimeBegin(bool Real=true) const;
   const String& getTimeEnd(bool Real=true) const;
   const String& getField1(bool Real=true) const;
   const String& getField2(bool Real=true) const;
};
```

```
class ProductPriceHome : public ResourceHome
{
   ProductPrice* Create(const String& MerchantRefNum,
                        const String& ShopperGroupRefNum,
                        const String& ProductRefNum,
                        const String& Price, const String& Currency,
                        const NVPHash& NameValuePairs);
   ProductPrice* Lookup(const String& RefNum,
                        const NVPHash& NameValuePairs); };
```

## InterestItem

The `InterestItem` class contains information about all the products and items that shoppers have added to their Interest List, including prices and currency. It maps to the SHOPPINGS table in the database. Use this class to retrieve all of the products or items that a specific shopper has selected in a specific store.

```
class InterestItem : public Resource
{
   const String& getSkuRefNum(bool Real=true) const;
   const String& getShopperRefNum(bool Real=true) const;
   const String& getMerchantRefNum(bool Real=true) const;
   const String& getPrice(bool Real=true) const;
   const String& getCurrency(bool Real=true) const;
   const String& getLastUpdateTime(bool Real=true) const;
   const String& getField1(bool Real=true) const;
   const String& getField2(bool Real=true) const;
   const String& getField3(bool Real=true) const;
};

class InterestItemHome : public ResourceHome
{
   InterestItem* Create(const String& ShopperRefNum,
                        const String& ProductRefNum,
                        const String& MerchantRefNum,
                        const NVPHash& NameValuePairs );
   InterestItem* Lookup(const String& ShopperRefNum,
                        const String& ProductRefNum,
                        const NVPHash& NameValuePairs );
};
```

# Order-Related Classes

The order-related classes allow you to retrieve information about the orders that are placed by shoppers, the suborders that are destined for different shipping addresses, the payment method, and the links between suborders and entries in the shoppers' address books.

## Order

The `Order` class contains information about orders that are placed by shoppers, including the status of the order, applicable taxes, shipping charges, total charges, timestamps, and the address to which the order will be shipped. It maps to the ORDERS table in the database. Use this class to retrieve information about an order that was placed by a specific shopper in a specific store.

```
class Order : public Resource
{
    const String& getRefNum(bool Real=true) const;
    const String& getShopperRefNum(bool Real=true) const;
    const String& getMerchantRefNum(bool Real=true) const;
    const String& getMerOrderRefNum(bool Real=true) const;
    const String& getBillToRefNum(bool Real=true) const;
    const String& getStatus(bool Real=true) const;
    const String& getLock(bool Real=true) const;
    const String& getLastUpdate(bool Real=true) const;
    const String& getPlacedTime(bool Real=true) const;
    const String& getProductTotal(bool Real=true) const;
    const String& getProductTax(bool Real=true) const;
    const String& getShippingTotal(bool Real=true) const;
    const String& getShippingTax(bool Real=true) const;
    const String& getCurrency(bool Real=true) const;
    const String& getField1(bool Real=true) const;
    const String& getField2(bool Real=true) const;
    const String& getField3(bool Real=true) const;
    const String& getOrderTotal(bool Real=true) const;
};

class OrderHome : public ResourceHome
{

    Order* Create (const String& ShopperRefNum,
                   const String& MerchantRefNum,
                   const NVPHash& NameValuePairs);
    Order* Lookup (const String& RefNum, const NVPHash& NameValuePairs);
    bool UpdateOrderList(String ShopperRefNum);
    Order* FindOrderEntry(const String& ShopperRefNum,
                          const String& Status,
                          const String& MerchantRefNum,
                          const String& OrderRefNum);
};
```

## OrderItem

The `OrderItem` class contains information to link each product and item in a suborder with a shipping address. It contains the price of each product or item, the quantity ordered, and the shipping mode selected. It maps to the SHIPTO table in the database. Use this class to retrieve information about the items or products that are shipped to a specific address for a specific shopper and store.

```
class OrderItem : public Resource
{
  const String& getRefNum(bool Real=true) const;
  const String& getShopperRefNum(bool Real=true) const;
  const String& getProductRefNum(bool Real=true) const;
  const String& getAddressRefNum(bool Real=true) const;
  const String& getMerchantRefNum(bool Real=true) const;
  const String& getShipModeRefNum(bool Real=true) const;
  const String& getComment(bool Real=true) const;
  const String& getCreationTime(bool Real=true) const;
  const String& getField1(bool Real=true) const;
  const String& getField2(bool Real=true) const;
  const String& getLastUpdateTime(bool Real=true) const;
  const String& getOrderRefNum(bool Real=true) const;
  const String& getCurrency(bool Real=true) const;
  const String& getPrice(bool Real=true) const;
  const String& getQuantity(bool Real=true) const;
  const String& getStatus(bool Real=true) const;
};

class OrderItemHome : public ResourceHome
{
  OrderItem* Create(const String& AddrRefNum,
                    const String& ShopperRefNum,
                    const String& MerchantRefNum,
                    const String& ProductRefNum,
                    const String& Quantity, const String& Status,
                    const NVPHash& NameValuePairs );
  OrderItem* Lookup(const String& RefNum,
                    const NVPHash& NameValuePairs);
};
```

## Destination

The Destination class contains information about the charges for each suborder that was placed by a shopper, including taxes payable and shipping charges. (A suborder is a part of an order to be shipped to a single address.) It maps to the ORDERPAY table in the database. Use this class to retrieve order charges information about a specific suborder for a specific shopper.

```
class Destination : public Resource
{
  const String& getOrderRefNum(bool Real=true) const;
  const String& getAddressRefNum(bool Real=true) const;
  const String& getTotalPrdPrice(bool Real=true) const;
  const String& getTotalProdTax(bool Real=true) const;
  const String& getShippingPrice(bool Real=true) const;
  const String& getTax1(bool Real=true) const;
  const String& getTax2(bool Real=true) const;
  const String& getTax3(bool Real=true) const;
  const String& getTax4(bool Real=true) const;
  const String& getTax5(bool Real=true) const;
  const String& getTax6(bool Real=true) const;
```

```
};

class DestinationHome : public ResourceHome
{
   Destination* Create(float ProductTotal, float DiscountTotal,
                       const String& AddressRefNum,
                       const String& OrderRefNum,
                       const NVPHash& NameValuePairs);
   Destination* Lookup(const String& OrderRefNum,
                       const String& AddresRefNum,
                       const NVPHash& NameValuePairs);
};
```

# Index

PTR ▲ PH

**PRENTICE HALL**

**Professional Technical Reference**
*Tomorrow's Solutions for Today's Professionals.*

*Keep Up-to-Date with*
# PH PTR Online!

We strive to stay on the cutting-edge of what's happening in professional computer science and engineering. Here's a bit of what you'll find when you stop by **www.phptr.com**:

**Special interest areas** offering our latest books, book series, software, features of the month, related links and other useful information to help you get the job done.

**Deals, deals, deals!** Come to our promotions section for the latest bargains offered to you exclusively from our retailers.

**Need to find a bookstore?** Chances are, there's a bookseller near you that carries a broad selection of PTR titles. Locate a Magnet bookstore near you at www.phptr.com.

**What's New at PH PTR?** We don't just publish books for the professional community, we're a part of it. Check out our convention schedule, join an author chat, get the latest reviews and press releases on topics of interest to you.

**Subscribe Today!** **Join PH PTR's monthly email newsletter!**

Want to be kept up-to-date on your area of interest? Choose a targeted category on our website, and we'll keep you informed of the latest PH PTR products, author events, reviews and conferences in your interest area.

Visit our mailroom to subscribe today! **http://www.phptr.com/mail_lists**

## IBM International License Agreement for Evaluation of Programs

**Part 1 - General Terms**

**PLEASE READ THIS AGREEMENT CAREFULLY BEFORE USING THE PROGRAM. IBM WILL LICENSE THE PROGRAM TO YOU ONLY IF YOU FIRST ACCEPT THE TERMS OF THIS AGREEMENT. BY USING THE PROGRAM YOU AGREE TO THESE TERMS. IF YOU DO NOT AGREE TO THE TERMS OF THIS AGREEMENT, PROMPTLY RETURN THE UNUSED PROGRAM TO IBM.**

The Program is owned by International Business Machines Corporation or one of its subsidiaries (IBM) or an IBM supplier, and copyrighted and licensed, not sold.

The term "Program" means the original program and all whole or partial copies of it. A Program consists of machine-readable instructions, its components, data, audio-visual content (such as images, text, recordings, or pictures), and related licensed material.

**This Agreement includes Part 1 - General Terms and Part 2 - Country-unique Terms and is the complete agreement regarding the use of this Program, and replaces any prior oral or written communications between you and IBM. The terms of Part 2 may replace or modify those of Part 1.**

### 1. License

**Use of the Program**

IBM grants you a nonexclusive, nontransferable license to use the Program.

You may 1) use the Program only for internal evaluation, testing or demonstration purposes, on a trial or "try-and-buy" basis and make and install a reasonable number of copies of the Program in support of such use, unless IBM identifies a specific number of copies in the documentation accompanying the Program. The terms of this license apply to each copy you make. You will reproduce the copyright notice and any other legends of ownership on each copy, or partial copy, of the Program.

THE PROGRAM MAY CONTAIN A DISABLING DEVICE THAT WILL PREVENT IT FROM BEING USED UPON EXPIRATION OF THIS LICENSE. YOU WILL NOT TAMPER WITH THIS DISABLING DEVICE OR THE PROGRAM. YOU SHOULD TAKE PRECAUTIONS TO AVOID ANY LOSS OF DATA THAT MIGHT RESULT WHEN THE PROGRAM CAN NO LONGER BE USED.

You will 1) maintain a record of all copies of the Program and 2) ensure that anyone who uses the Program does so only for your authorized use and in compliance with the terms of this Agreement.

You may not 1) use, copy, modify or distribute the Program except as provided in this Agreement; 2) reverse assemble, reverse compile, or otherwise translate the Program except as specifically permitted by law without the possibility of contractual waiver; or sublicense, rent, or lease the Program.

This license begins with your first use of the Program and ends 1) as of the duration or date specified in the documentation accompanying the Program or 2) when the Program automatically disables itself. Unless IBM specifies in the documentation accompanying the Program that you may retain the Program (in which case, an additional charge may apply), you will destroy the Program and all copies made of it within ten days of when this license ends.

### 2. No Warranty

SUBJECT TO ANY STATUTORY WARRANTIES WHICH CANNOT BE EXCLUDED, IBM MAKES NO WARRANTIES OR CONDITIONS EITHER EXPRESS OR IMPLIED, INCLUDING WITHOUT LIMITATION, THE WARRANTY OF NON-INFRINGEMENT AND THE IMPLIED WARRANTIES OF MERCHANTABILITY AND FITNESS FOR A PARTICULAR PURPOSE, REGARDING THE PROGRAM OR TECHNICAL SUPPORT, IF ANY. IBM MAKES NO WARRANTY REGARDING THE CAPABILITY OF THE PROGRAM TO CORRECTLY PROCESS, PROVIDE AND/OR RECEIVE DATE DATA WITHIN AND BETWEEN THE 20TH AND 21ST CENTURIES.

This exclusion also applies to any of IBM's subcontractors, suppliers or program developers (collectively called "Suppliers").

Manufacturers, suppliers, or publishers of non-IBM Programs may provide their own warranties.

### 3. Limitation of Liability

NEITHER IBM NOR ITS SUPPLIERS ARE LIABLE FOR ANY DIRECT OR INDIRECT DAMAGES, INCLUDING WITHOUT LIMITATION, LOST PROFITS, LOST SAVINGS, OR ANY INCIDENTAL, SPECIAL, OR OTHER ECONOMIC CONSEQUENTIAL DAMAGES, EVEN IF IBM IS INFORMED OF THEIR POSSIBILITY. SOME JURISDICTIONS DO NOT ALLOW THE EXCLUSION OR LIMITATION OF INCIDENTAL OR CONSEQUENTIAL DAMAGES, SO THE ABOVE EXCLUSION OR LIMITATION MAY NOT APPLY TO YOU.

### 4. General

Nothing in this Agreement affects any statutory rights of consumers that cannot be waived or limited by contract.

IBM may terminate your license if you fail to comply with the terms of this Agreement. If IBM does so, you must immediately destroy the Program and all copies you made of it.

You may not export the Program.

Neither you nor IBM will bring a legal action under this Agreement more than two years after the cause of action arose unless otherwise

wise provided by local law without the possibility of contractual waiver or limitation.

either you nor IBM is responsible for failure to fulfill any obligations due to causes beyond its control.

here is no additional charge for use of the Program for the duration of this license.

BM does not provide program services or technical support, unless IBM specifies otherwise.

he laws of the country in which you acquire the Program govern this Agreement, except 1) in Australia, the laws of the State or territory in which the transaction is performed govern this Agreement; 2) in Albania, Armenia, Belarus, Bosnia/Herzegovina, Bulgaria, Croatia, Czech Republic, Georgia, Hungary, Kazakhstan, Kirghizia, Former Yugoslav Republic of Macedonia (FYROM), Moldova, Poland, Romania, Russia, Slovak Republic, Slovenia, Ukraine, and Federal Republic of Yugoslavia, the laws of Austria govern this Agreement; 3) in the United Kingdom, all disputes relating to this Agreement will be governed by English Law and will be submitted to the exclusive jurisdiction of the English courts; 4) in Canada, the laws in the Province of Ontario govern this Agreement; and 5) in the United States and Puerto Rico, and People's Republic of China, the laws of the State of New York govern this Agreement.

## Part 2 - Country-unique Terms

### AUSTRALIA:

**No Warranty (Section 2):** The following paragraph is added to this Section: Although IBM specifies that there are no warranties, you may have certain rights under the Trade Practices Act 1974 or other legislation and are only limited to the extent permitted by the applicable legislation.

**Limitation of Liability (Section 3):** The following paragraph is added to this Section: Where IBM is in breach of a condition or warranty implied by the Trade Practices Act 1974, IBM's liability is limited to the repair or replacement of the goods, or the supply of equivalent goods. Where that condition or warranty relates to right to sell, quiet possession or clear title, or the goods are of a kind ordinarily acquired for personal, domestic or household use or consumption, then none of the limitations in this paragraph apply.

### GERMANY:

**No Warranty (Section 2):** The following paragraphs are added to this Section: The minimum warranty period for Programs is six months.

In case a Program is delivered without Specifications, we will only warrant that the Program information correctly describes the Program and that the Program can be used according to the Program information. You have to check the usability according to the Program information within the "money-back guaranty" period.

**Limitation of Liability (Section 3):** The following paragraph is added to this Section: The limitations and exclusions specified in the Agreement will not apply to damages caused by IBM with fraud or gross negligence, and for express warranty.

### INDIA:

**General (Section 4):** The following replaces the fourth paragraph of this Section: If no suit or other legal action is brought, within two years after the cause of action arose, in respect of any claim that either party may have against the other, the rights of the concerned party in respect of such claim will be forfeited and the other party will stand released from its obligations in respect of such claim.

### IRELAND:

**No Warranty (Section 2):** The following paragraph is added to this Section: Except as expressly provided in these terms and conditions, all statutory conditions, including all warranties implied, but without prejudice to the generality of the foregoing, all warranties implied by the Sale of Goods Act 1893 or the Sale of Goods and Supply of Services Act 1980 are hereby excluded.

### ITALY:

**Limitation of Liability (Section 3):** This Section is replaced by the following: Unless otherwise provided by mandatory law, IBM is not liable for any damages which might arise.

### NEW ZEALAND:

**No Warranty (Section 2):** The following paragraph is added to this Section: Although IBM specifies that there are no warranties, you may have certain rights under the Consumer Guarantees Act 1993 or other legislation which cannot be excluded or limited. The Consumer Guarantees Act 1993 will not apply in respect of any goods or services which IBM provides, if you require the goods and services for the purposes of a business as defined in that Act.

**Limitation of Liability (Section 3):** The following paragraph is added to this Section: Where Programs are not acquired for the purposes of a business as defined in the Consumer Guarantees Act 1993, the limitations in this Section are subject to the limitations in that Act.

### UNITED KINGDOM:

**Limitation of Liability (Section 3):** The following paragraph is added to this Section at the end of the first paragraph: The limitation of liability will not apply to any breach of IBM's obligations implied by Section 12 of the Sales of Goods Act 1979 or Section 2 of the Supply of Goods and Services Act 1982.

# ABOUT THE CD

The CD enclosed contains the 60-day evaluation copy of Net.Commerce PRO version 3.1.1 for Windows NT. It also contains all the sample code presented in the chapters stored in the `\samples` directory under the root, and the templates and graphics needed for the workshops, stored in the `\workshops` directory under the root.

See page xxvii of the Preface for more detailed instructions.

## Technical Support

Prentice Hall does not offer technical support for this software. However, if there is a problem with the media, you may obtain a replacement copy by e-mailing us with your problem at: disc_exchange@prenhall.com